'You have to die in Piedmont!' An old folk song, still played in the western Alps, tells of the French regiments that were coming from the Mongeneve Pass in order to attack a combined Austro-Sardinian force entrenched on the Assietta Plateau, 2,500 metres up in the Cottian Alps. This crucial position controlled two main roads from France to the Kingdom of Sardinia's capital, Turin. The battle occurred on 19 June 1747, and was the bloodiest single day action not only of the War of Austrian Succession (1740-1748) in Italy, but in the whole military history of the Alps.

The strategic goal of the French offensive was the siege and the capture of the Fort of Exilles, in the Susa Valley on the road from Briançon to Turin. An army of about 20,000 soldiers under the command of the Chevalier de Belle-Isle was divided into two corps: one went down the Moncenisio towards Exilles, while the other advanced towards the Val Chisone to attack the Assietta ridge from the south. Having predicted that the French would move through the area, Carlo Emanuele III of Savoy had fortified the area with an entrenched camp garrisoned with 7,000 men. French intelligence discovered that the allied forces were fortifying the pass, while the main Austrian army had left the siege of Genoa to reach the Alps. So, the decision was taken to attack immediately. The forces involved amounted to 32 French battalions against nine Sardinian and four Austrian battalions. Despite the desperate effort of the soldiers and the personal valour of the French officers, all the attacks were repulsed with heavy losses. In a matter of three hours of murderous combat, some 5,000 soldiers, out of 27,000 men engaged, became casualties: even the French commander, Belle-Isle, was killed in the struggle. From that day, the Battle of Assietta became a sort of military legend for the Sardinian forces, and subsequently for the Italian Army, but no serious attempt to reconstruct the event was ever made. Only at the end of the nineteenth century did the French try to develop a more detailed study of the struggle by publishing the manuscript written by *Lieutenant-Général* de Vault in the second half of eighteenth century. This is therefore the first full work to address the history of this battle, based firmly on extensive archival and printed sources, and fully supported by maps, illustrations and tabular data as well as a comprehensive index.

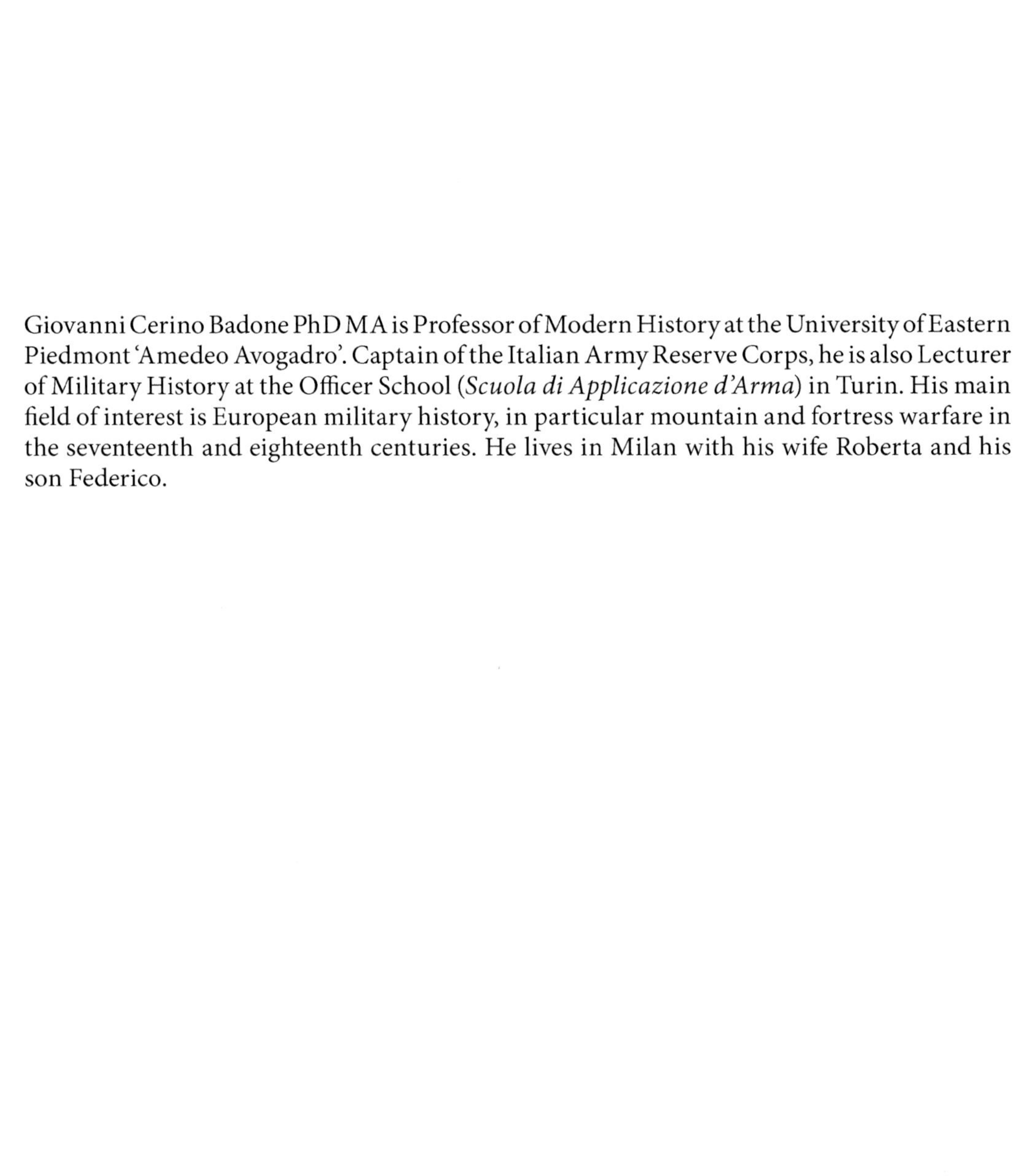

Giovanni Cerino Badone PhD MA is Professor of Modern History at the University of Eastern Piedmont 'Amedeo Avogadro'. Captain of the Italian Army Reserve Corps, he is also Lecturer of Military History at the Officer School (*Scuola di Applicazione d'Arma*) in Turin. His main field of interest is European military history, in particular mountain and fortress warfare in the seventeenth and eighteenth centuries. He lives in Milan with his wife Roberta and his son Federico.

'You Have to Die in Piedmont!'

The Battle of Assietta, 19 July 1747. The War of the
Austrian Succession in the Alps

Giovanni Cerino Badone

Helion & Company

Helion & Company Limited
Unit 8 Amherst Business Centre
Budbrooke Road
Warwick
CV34 5WE
England
Tel. 01926 499619
Email: info@helion.co.uk
Website: www.helion.co.uk
X (formerly Twitter): @Helionbooks
Facebook: @HelionBooks
Visit our blog at https://helionbooks.wordpress.com/

Published by Helion & Company 2023. This paperback edition 2026
Designed and typeset by Mach 3 Solutions (www.mach3solutions.co.uk)
Cover designed by Paul Hewitt, Battlefield Design (www.battlefield-design.co.uk)

Text © Giovanni Cerino Badone 2023
Illustrations © as individually credited
Maps drawn by George Anderson © Helion & Company 2023

Cover: The last charge of the Chevalier de Belle-Isle. Original artwork by Giorgio Albertini © Helion & Company 2023

ISBN 978-1-806723-69-0

British Library Cataloguing-in-Publication Data.
A catalogue record for this book is available from the British Library.

For details of other military history titles published by Helion & Company Limited, contact the above address, or visit our website: http://www.helion.co.uk

We always welcome receiving book proposals from prospective authors.

Contents

List of Plates

List of Maps

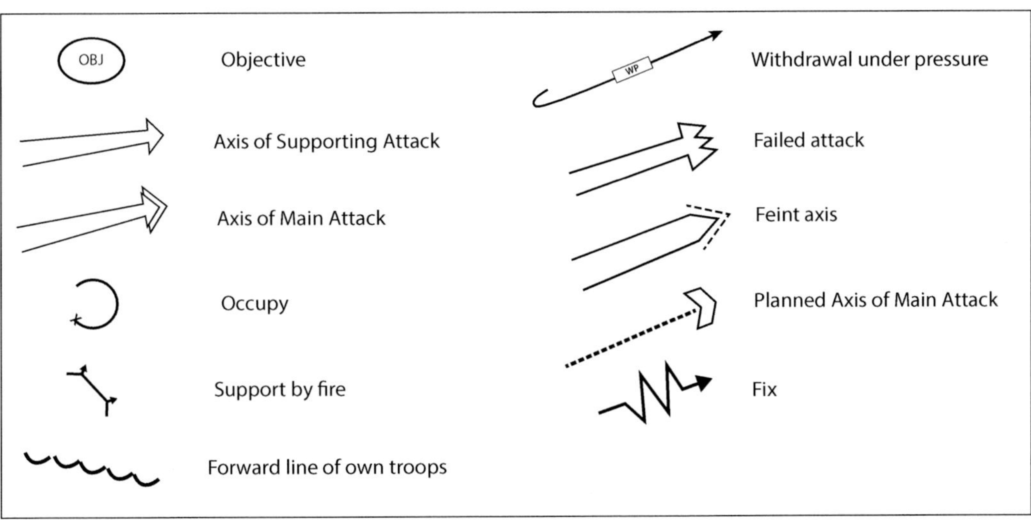

OBJ
Objective

Axis of Supporting Attack

Axis of Main Attack

Occupy

Support by fire

Forward line of own troops

WP
Withdrawal under pressure

Failed attack

Feint axis

Planned Axis of Main Attack

Fix

Introduction: Six Days in July

Armies have a purpose: to win wars. Today we like to think that they can also serve another purpose, but that is not how this Great Game works. Wars are won by winning battles, and in this book we will talk about a battle. On the watershed between Val Chisone and Val di Susa, on the plateau called Assietta – flat – on the afternoon of 19 July 1747 a combined Austro-Sardinian force of 6,000 soldiers, under the orders of *Luogotenente Generale* Cacherano di Bricherasio, faced a French army of about 16,000 men commanded by the Chevalier de Belle-Isle. At nine o'clock in the evening, the French were in retreat after losing a quarter of their troops. The military history of Piedmont, and later that of Italy, is all wrapped up in the unfolding of this battle, in both its positive and negative aspects. The victory was mythologized, emphasized, became dogma. However, no serious analysis was attempted, and even today the operational aspect remains in the background. We know little about the wars fought by the House of Savoy in the eighteenth century and even less about how their armed forces went into battle, their operational and tactical doctrines, their logistic system, in short what the Sardinian way of warfare was.

Italy had been one of the main and decisive theatres of the War of the Spanish Succession (1701-1714). However, the double expulsion of the Habsburg dynasty from Spain and of the Spanish Crown from Italy (1707), as well as the subjection of the entire peninsula to the Anglo-Austrian condominium recognized by France, severed the geopolitical connection between Italy and Germany, and more generally between the Mediterranean and northern Europe.

With the allied victory at Turin (1706) and the Bourbon surrender of Milan (1707) the epicentre of European conflict shifted from Italy to Germany. The isolation and defeat of Spanish revanchism (1717-1720) proved that Italy was not worth a European war. Instead, Germany was the real stake in the three other great European wars of the eighteenth century; the War of the Polish Succession (1733-1738), the War of the Austrian Succession (1740-1748) and the Seven Years War (1757-1763). The first two were also fought in Italy. However, the military campaigns of 1733-1735 and, above all, 1742-1748 were rather two regional Austro-Spanish wars, the second of which combined with the Anglo-Spanish naval war, imposed by the dynastic obsession of Queen Elisabeth Farnese. In 1748 Spain's exit from the scene finally ensured Italy's neutrality, something that had not happened since the fifteenth century, but not the strength to decide its own destiny.

Until 1746, the stake in the particular Italian game was the Crown of Lombardy, an ephemeral chimera that in seven years of war devoured more than a hundred thousand lives and all that remained of Spanish power. The only crown gained by the Spanish sword, but on behalf of an all-Italian dynasty, was that of the Two Sicilies. The national character of this new state was consecrated in 1744 by repelling the imperial offensive. It later broke Spanish vassalage (1746) and dynastic unity with the accession of Charles of Bourbon to the Spanish throne. The more numerous and cosmopolitan Bourbon army of the Two Sicilies did not, however, deprive the Sardinian army of its regional military supremacy. Guided in the field by its sovereign, Carlo Emanuele III of Savoy, paid for by the British and half made up of foreign contingents, the Sardinian army was the decisive factor in both the War of Polish Succession and the War of the Austrian Succession, on a par with the British Mediterranean Fleet. In the campaigns of 1733-1735 it was the contribution of the Sardinian army and the neutrality of the British squadron that ensured the success, not decisive, of the Bourbon armies. In 1742-1748 it was these two military instruments that determined the definitive expulsion of the Bourbons of France and Spain from the Italian peninsula, keeping it under Austrian-British domination until the War of the Alps (1792-1796).

Four of the 10 battles fought in Italy during the War of Austrian Succession took place in 1744, and three of them, Villefranche, Pietralunga and Madonna dell'Olmo, on the Piedmont front. For Carlo Emanuele III's army, that year marked the definitive end of any independent offensive initiative and the idea of a 'parallel war' without the help of the imperial troops, whose intervention was from then on often hoped for, requested and implored. Having started the war with a lightning advance along the Via Emilia, the conflict for the House of Savoy became a mere question of survival. The army, its tactics, the entire doctrine of employment and the overall strategy, were reconverted and conceived with a single purpose; defence to the bitter end and saving the country army, becoming in fact an 'army in being' to be safeguarded almost at any cost. If in 1745 Maillebois had almost brought the Kingdom of Sardinia to its knees with a daring outflanking manoeuvre from the Riviera, separating Carlo Emanuele III from the Empire and isolating him from the English naval squadron without large-scale combat – with the exception of the battle of Bassignana on 27 September 1745, which cost the Sardinians 2,500 losses – in 1744 Conti and La Mina inflicted unprecedented losses on the Sardinian army, which experienced a record of three consecutive pitched battles, on 20-21 April at Villefranche, 17-19 July at Pietralunga and 30 September at Madonna dell'Olmo, with a net total of 8,000 men lost in action, approximately one-sixth of the balanced force. On the evening of the battle of Madonna dell'Olmo, Carlo Emanuele III exclaimed in despair 'my poor soldiers, my poor soldiers!'.[1] It is not surprising, therefore, that after 1745 the Sardinian army was always very reluctant to accept battle, and the first major field engagement after Bassignana was Assietta, fought almost two years later.

All this, however, was later forgotten. Savoyard hagiography deliberately erased or flattened the defeats, raised monuments to the (few) victorious battlefields, and threw everything else into the mists of legend. With the exception of a few specific studies that we will now list, the narration of the war campaigns in which the Sardinian army played a leading role had long since become little more than a hagiographic exercise in favour of the House of Savoy. During the nineteenth century, after the disasters of the War of the Alps, an attempt was made to recover the memory of the military splendour of what was becoming known as 'old Piedmont'. In 1816 a veteran of the War of the Alps, the Marquis Joseph Henri Costa de Beauregard, who had lost his son Louis Marie Eugène in the conflict, published the *Mémoires Historiques sur la Maison Royale de Savoie*, with the third volume dedicated to

---

1   D. Carutti, *Storia del Regno di Carlo Emanuele III* (Torino: Gianini e Fiore, 1859), Vol.I, p.271.

the great wars fought in the seventeenth and eighteenth centuries.[2] In 1818 the five volumes of the *Histoire Militaire di Piémont* by Alessandro Saluzzo were printed,[3] in the two-year period 1845-1846 followed the trilogy by P. de Choulot and Gabriele Ferrero dedicated to the regimental stories of the Sardinian army.[4] It was necessary to refresh and revive the splendour of an army that in 1796 had been overwhelmed by the forces of Republican France, but which in 1792 had already suffered a serious military setback that had caused the presumed rather than real status of Italy's leading military power to crumble like a house of cards.[5] An effective analytical approach of the eighteenth century campaigns, and then also the following ones, always remained a chimera. In Piedmont we do not find texts with complex statistical tables and tactical analyses, such as the volumes edited by Gottlob Naumann in 1782 concerning Prussia,[6] but at most the polemical arrows of General Pinelli in the *Storia Militare del Piemonte in continuazione di quella del Saluzzo cioè della Pace di Acquisgrana fino ai dì nostri* [*Military History of Piedmont in continuation of that of Saluzzo that is from the Peace of Aachen up to our days*],[7] a work that insofar as the eighteenth century and the War of the Alps are concerned is a collection of inaccuracies and inventions.

In the late nineteenth century the need became clear to engage in less hagiographic and technical studies on the wars of the Kingdom of Sardinia, and in particular to the Alpine countryside of the Austrian Succession War and that of the Alps, because the risk of a war against France was again a real danger. One of the first studies was that of 1887 carried out by an infantry colonel, Carlo Buffa di Perrero, who published a volume entitled *Carlo Emanuele III di Savoia a difesa delle Alpi nella campagna del 1744* [*Carlo Emanuele III of Savoy in defence of the Alps in the campaign of 1744*]. The subject was topical as it dealt with and described war events that took place on the same theatre of operations where the Kingdom of Italy would eventually have to confront France, now a republica. Buffa di Perrero carried out a real historical-archaeological operation, searching for unpublished documents at the State Archives of Turin and the Royal Library, reasoning and analysing the events also through a reconnaissance of the battlefields, which the intelligent officer covered and studied for six years. However, he was not interested in academic or monetary awards. For Buffa di Perrero, this was a work intended to better prepare the Italian army for the future war against France, a conflict that was anything but improbable for triplicist Italy:

> [T]he nature of my work, while leading me to narrate the facts from the historical point of view, also required me to make considerations of various kinds, particularly

---

2 J.H. Costa de Beauregard, *Mémoires Historiques sur la Maison Royale de Savoie* (Turin: Pierre Joseph Pic, 1816).

3 A. de Saluces, *Histoire Militaire du Piémont* (Torino: Pierre Joseph Pic, 1818).

4 P.de Choulot, G. Ferrero, *Histoire de l'Armée Sarde* (Torino: Bocca, 1845-1846).

5 On 30 September 1792, after the loss of Savoy, the Russian ambassador in Turin, Prince Alexander Bélosselsky de Bélozersk, wrote that 'the Sardinian army has lost all the consideration it enjoyed'. L. Troubetzkoi (ed), *Un Ambassadeur Russe à Turin (1792-1793). Dépêches e S.E. le Prince Alexandre Bélosselsky de Bélozersk* (Paris: E. Leroux, 1901), pp.103-104.

6 G. Naumann, *Sammlung ungedruckter Nachrichten, so die Geschichte der Feldzüge der Preußen von 1740 bis 1779* (Dresden: Waltherischen Hofbuchhandlung, 1782).

7 F. Pinelli, *Storia Militare del Piemonte in continuazione di quella del Saluzzo cioè della Pace di Acquisgrana fino ai dì nostri* (Torino: Degiorgis, 1854).

military ones. While with regard to the former I dare to hope that I have attained my purpose, which was to trace the truth, I have done my utmost, with regard to the latter, to make them of practical use. It is true that nothing is absolute, especially in judgments concerning military operations, which may be considered from many points of view, and the result of which depends on a number of causes which are not always known. However, having taken into account, as far as possible, in my analytical examination, the reason of things, and having always brought the utmost impartiality and serenity to my deductions, I want to believe that I have, if nothing else, opened the way for the scholar[8].

In addition to the 1744 campaign, the other great *exemplum* par excellence remained the Battle of Assietta. *Tenente Colonnello* Vittorio Amedeo Dabormida, professor of Military History at the War School of Turin, in 1891 also wrote a military historical study, *La battaglia dell'Assietta. Studio storico (The Battle of Assietta. Historical Study).*[9] Vittorio Amedeo, son of the Minister of War Vittorio Dabormida, went on to be one of the most brilliant minds in the Italian army of the nineteenth century. His work dedicated to the Assietta was more of a naïve book commemorating the Sardinian army than a historical-military treatise intended to prepare a campaign in the Western Alps. No one dared criticize him directly, not even one who knew Sardinian history like Baron Antonio Manno, but at least his book led to the search for new documents and sources on the battle.[10] On 1 March 1896 Dabormida was amongst those massacred by the Abyssinians at the Battle of Adowa, together with the whole brigade under his command; his book went straight to the 'kill zone' of the man who remains, to this day, the best Italian military historian ever: Adriano Alberti.[11] The latter, then, in his excellent *La battaglia dell'Assietta (19 di luglio del 1747). Note e documenti (The Battle of Assietta (19 July 1747). Notes and documents)* printed in 1902 aimed at refuting piece by piece the narrative presented by Dabormida and his main source, Count Roberto Malines di Bruino,[12] missing out on a precious opportunity to describe the planning process and management of the confrontation by a modern-era army. Alberti's writing triggered a short but fortunate period of research of unpublished documents, which led to the discovery of one of the most important sources on the Battle of Assietta, the first draft of the Priocca Report,[13] substantially different from the one now preserved in the Turin State Archives; here it is immediately clear that San Sebastiano disobeyed an order from

---

8   C. Buffa di Perrero, *Carlo Emanuele III di Savoia a difesa delle Alpi nella campagna del 1744* (Torino: Fratelli Bocca, 1887), pp.vii-viii.

9   V.E. Dabormida, *La Battaglia dell'Assietta. Studio Storico* (Torino: Carlo Voghera, 1877).

10   E, Rocchi, *Guerra di Montagna. La campagna del 1747 sulle Alpi* (Roma: Carlo Voghera, 1893); A. Manno, 'Breve nota sulla Battaglia dell'Assietta a proposito di una pubblicazione del Commendatore Carlo Negroni', *Atti della R. Accademia delle Scienze di Torino*, Volume 17, 1881, pp.799-811.

11   A. Alberti, *La battaglia dell'Assietta (19 di luglio del 1747). Note e documenti* (Torino: Enrico Voghera, 1902).

12   This study used the edition of P. Robbone (ed.), 'Le "Memorie" del Conte Roberto Malines', *Annali dell'Istituto Superiore di Magistero del Piemonte*, Vol.VI, 1932.

13   F. Gabotto, 'La Verità sulla Battaglia dell'Assietta secondo la minuta della Relazione Priocca', in *Bollettino Storico-Bibliografico Subalpino*, Anno XI, N. III, 1906, pp.227-234. This report is henceforth cited as Priocca Report I, to distinguish it from the final draft, which we will quote as Priocca Report II, kept in the State Archives of Turin: AST, Corte, Museo Storico, *Rélation de l'affaire de l'Assiette faite par Mr le Compte de Priouque, 19 Juillet 1747.*

his superior, Alciati, due to a wrong tactical evaluation. Alciati, in turn, had not understood the intent of his commander, but all these important details were omitted from the final report.[14]

At the same time the French were also devoting themselves attentively to the study of the North Italian operational theatre. The dances were opened in 1888 with an edition of the writings by Pierre-Joseph de Bourcet, *Principes de la Guerre de Montagne*, based mainly on the war events of the years 1743-1747.[15] The French General Staff invested resources in the study of Italian theatre, and the events of the War of the Austrian Succession were also subjected to study and analysis. On the basis of the *Relation des Campagnes faites par S.M. et par ses Généraux avec des Corps Séparés dans les années 1742 et 1748*, made by the veteran of the war itself, a former infantry captain of the Sardinian Army and then Abbot Daniel Minutoli, Henri Moris in 1896 realized his *Opérations militaires dans les Alpes et les Apennins pendant la guerre de succession d'Autriche (1742-1748)*.[16] Six years later *Colonel* Paul Arvers, the founder of military mountaineering in France,[17] took up a collection of documents collected by *Lieutenant Général* de Vault, and compiled the fundamental text of the War of the Succession of Austria in Northern Italy: the *Guerre de la Succession d'Autriche (1742-1748)*, published in Paris and Nancy in two volumes in 1892.[18]

At the Battle of Assietta, alongside the Sardinian-Piedmontese, Austrian contingents also fought, and their presence was also remembered. In 1842 the *Österreichische Militärische Zeitschrift* published the narration by *Feldmarschall-Leutnant* L. von Rothkirch of the 1747 campaign of the War of Succession of Austria, in an article entitled 'Der Feldzug 1747 in Italien'.[19] The first properly military-historical study of the campaign, conducted with modern scientific criteria, was carried out at the beginning of the twentieth century by *Major* Maximilian Ritter von Hoen, director of the Kriegsarchiv in Vienna. The work was entitled *Kriege unter der Regierung der Kaiserin-Königin Maria Theresia* in 1896, with the intention of covering all wars undertaken by the Habsburg Empire during the reign of Empress Maria Theresia.[20] Having started with the *Österreichischer Erbfolge-Krieg 1740-1748*, unfortunately for us the publication was interrupted in 1905 with Volume VIII dedicated to the Italian campaign of 1744; the First World War forced a break in this and other studies that the Kriegsarchiv was carrying out.

After the First World War the study of Assietta became, in Italy as in France, of less and less interest to the general staff. However, others became increasingly interested in the study of the

---

14 On the whole affair see the enlightening and well-documented G. Mola di Nomaglio, 'La Marchesa di Spigno, l'Assietta, le società segrete. I Novarina, tra enigmi e intrighi, nella Storia del Piemonte', in *Studi Piemontesi*, Dec. 2002, Vol.XXXI, pp.407-427.

15 P.J. de Bourcet, *Principes de la Guerre de Montagne* (Paris: Imprimerie National, 1888).

16 H. Moris, *Opérations militaires dans les Alpes et les Apennins pendant la guerre de succession d'Autriche (1742-1748)* (Paris-Turin: L. Baudoin et Cie, Fratelli Bocca, 1886).

17 On this important figure, see the recent excellent biography by C. Becker, *Aux origines de l'Alpinisme Militaire. Fondation des Chasseurs Alpins et rôle du Général Arvers* (Villers-sur-Mer: Editions Pierre de Taillac, 2018).

18 F.-E. de Vault, P. Arvers, *Guerre de la Succession d'Autriche (1742-1748)* (Paris-Nancy: Librairie Militaire Berger-Levrault et Cie., 1892).

19 L. von Rothkirch, 'Der Feldzug 1747 in Italien', in *Österreichische militärische Zeitschrift*, XI, 1842, pp.120-135.

20 M. von Hoen, *Kriege unter der Regierung der Kaiserin-Königin Maria Theresia. Österreichischer Erbfolge-Krieg 1740-1748* (Wien: L.W. Seidel & Sohn, 1896-1905).

War of Austrian Succession and the battle in the Alps. Oxford University Professor of Military History, Spenser Wilkinson, published in 1927 *The Defense of Piedmont 1742-1748. A Prelude to the Study of Napoleon.*[21] Famous for his *The Brain of an Army*, printed in 1890,[22] one of the first studies devoted specifically to the function of a general staff, Wilkinson argued, and rightly so, that the Napoleonic campaigns in Italy of 1796-1797 could not be understood without a careful study of the Italian countryside, and the Piedmontese countryside specifically, of the War of Succession of Austria. He was then among the first historians to consider the reconnaissance of the battlefields an integrated part of his research: 'During the last twenty years I have often spent my holidays examining the passes of the Western Alps, many of which are fortified'.[23] In 1924 the English historian visited the Colle delle Finestre and the Assietta, accompanied by *Major* Dacomo of the 3° Reggimento Alpini. However, the visits of Anglo-Saxon historians did not end here. From the United States at the end of the 1940s came Robert T. Pell, a member of the Pell family who, in 1908, decided to begin the restoration work of Fort Carillon, later renamed Fort Ticonderoga and subsequently fallen into disrepair. Pell claimed that in 1758 Major General Louis-Joseph Marquis de Montcalm, at the head of a tiny French army, had defeated a superior British army of forces thanks to the experience gained during the Battle of Assietta.[24] To do this he went to Italy and he wanted to visit the battleground; as a Foreign Service Reserve Officer in Milan, he was able to get in touch with Italian officers of the Alpine troops. Thanks to *Major* Louis della Longa he was introduced to *Colonnello* Di Rovere, who had translated into English the text by Adriano Alberti, and he accompanied him to the Assietta Ridge. Di Rovere 'with untiring care, planned the visit and, with generous courage mounted to the height and, with military maps spread out in the winds, relived the battle step by step'.[25] Pell, probably thanks to his guide, was able to meet *Tenente Generale* Celestino Bes in Turin, who before the Second War World had been Inspector of the Alpine Troops and who in 1934 was the founder of the Central Military School of Mountaineering of Aosta. He was also able to shake hands, one would imagine to his great joy and amazement, with the elderly but always active Adriano Alberti who was born in Milan in 1870. Thus the circle closed here.

Some 15 years later, in 1969, *Settecento riformatore* by Franco Venturi traced an insurmountable barrier between what the professional historian would study, that is, ideas and concepts, and what the local scholar would study, that is events.[26] The battles and armies, then,

---

21   S. Wilkinson, *The Defence of Piedmont 1742-1748. A Prelude to the Study of Napoleon* (Oxford: Clarendon Press, 1927).
22   S. Wilkinson, *The Brain of the Army. A Popular Account of the German General Staff* (Westminster: Archibald Constable & Co, 1895).
23   Wilkinson, *The Defence of Piedmont*, p.viii.
24   R.T. Pell, 'The Cradle of Carillon: Assietta', *The Bulletin of the Fort Ticonderoga Museum*, Volume VIII, Number 7, 1951, pp.269-299.
25   Pell, 'The Cradle of Carillon', p.272.
26   F. Venturi, *Settecento riformatore. Da Muratori e Beccaria 1730-1764* (Torino: Einaudi, 1969), Vol.I. The only book quoted was Bartolomeo Giuliano, *La campagna militare del 1744 nelle Alpi Occidentali e l'assedio di Cuneo* (Cuneo: Società per gli studi storici, archeologici ed artistici della Provincia de Cuneo, 1967), specifically about the role of the peasant militias in the 1744 campaign; Venturi, *settecento riformatore*, pp.189-198. Giuliano produced the best volume ever written in the Italian language on a war campaign of the War of the Austrian Succession, but his thesis is exactly opposite to that presented in the volumes quoting Venturi's judgment. The village militias adopted a territorial

were relegated to the few enthusiasts, collectors, or the few scholars in uniform,[27] who still had the time and the desire to try their hand on the military history of the modern era.[28] The reasons for this are very simple: historians dealing with war and the military world in general avoid visiting the battlefields. This is a real short-circuit, since military history was born precisely as an internal and reserved function of the ministries of war and navy, which originated, as chance would have it, in the second half of the seventeenth century, as an auxiliary activity of the great strategic and operational planning. Military history was born as a central element of intelligence activities, such as systematic and statistical research and processing of any kind of information useful for strategic, tactical and operational planning in relation to possible theatres and environments of war. Military technical history declined when, in the second half of the nineteenth century, the wrong answer was given to the problem of the growing complexity of military operations, namely specialization, by clearly separating the cartographic, information and historical services. In the Italian Army, the historical military services gradually moved from the Operations Department to the Propaganda Department – or V Department – after the Second World War, where they are still located today amidst a thousand budgetary difficulties. The disappearance of this historical dimension of strategic intelligence seemed to be compensated for by the simultaneous flourishing of a new model of military history, accepted and assimilated also by the academic world. Now a mere specialization of 'general' history was privileged. Since this was subdivided into major epochs, it was finally possible to create an 'ancient', 'medieval', 'modern' and 'contemporary' military history, all independent of each other. What is more, in terms of method and interest, they are actually political, social and economic histories of war and military institutions, and not military history. Complicating the situation was the British approach of the War and Society School, led by Michael Howard, Geoffrey Best and Brian Bond. The British were joined by other scholars such as Peter Paret in the United States, Wilhelm Deist in West Germany, and more recently Hew Strachan, John Gooch, Michael Geyer and Robert Tombs. At the heart of the War and Society School's new approach to the subject is the idea that every element related to society, economy and even culture gives each conflict a definite character. Thus, there are no eternal principles governing warfare, which on the contrary the *Kriegsgeschichtliche Abteilung* of Wilhelminian Germany continued to seek,[29] but a great variety of developments based on

---

defence of their own community and its goods, and they were far from implementing a widespread, planned and, above all, unconditionally loyal resistance to the Crown.

27   For example, G. Amoretti, 'Celebrazione di un anniversario', in G. Amoretti, M.F. Roggero, M. Viglino (eds), *I Trinceramenti dell'Assietta 1747-1997* (Torino: Omega, 1997).

28   This kind of historiography, although weak, often naive, and almost always biased, has nevertheless the undeniable merit of keeping alive the memory, and very often resurrecting it, of wartime events destined to remain almost forgotten. We should note, among others, G. Gariglio, *Battaglie alpine del Piemonte sabaudo. Tre secoli di guerre sulle Alpi Occidentali*, (Collegno; Chiaramonte Editore, 1999).

29   The German *Kriegsgeschichtliche Abteilung* (military historical office) produced, indeed, works of considerable historical value that can still be appreciated today. In particular, considerable efforts were made in the 1902 edition of the 13-volume *Die Kriege Friedrichs des Grossen*, which was never completed due to the outbreak of the First World War (although the manuscript of a final volume was finally published in 2007). The volume of documents consulted and the topographical research carried out remain unsurpassed. The negative aspect of this, and similar research carried out by other historical offices of the period, is the tacit comparison with the armies of the time of the authors of the series, who could not understand how much difference there was between an army of the eighteenth century and one of the

multiple factors. This methodology was not limited only to the analysis of campaigns and battles, but also incorporated political, social, economic and cultural history.

Since then, the greatest energy in the field of research has been spent on aspects inherent to relations between civilians and the military and the role of the development of the armed forces in peacetime, to the point that military historians are now more capable of developing texts dedicated to the situations of civilian populations in war and in peace than to soldiers and battles. This imbalance has raised numerous questions on the meaning and usefulness of military history and on the meaning of carrying out research dedicated to this topic.[30] At the same time, the analysis of war events was revised from below, focusing more on the events of individual soldiers, both in their life in the barracks and on the battlefield. Recently in Italy some historians stressed a return to the study of battles as significant events in history.[31] Speaking personally, I do not see a return to the study of battle and armed conflict in modern times. On the contrary, I can dramatically see an impoverishment of our knowledge, now reduced to a dim light if not completely extinguished.

The historians associated with the New Military History, that is, the new historiographic current generated by the War and Society School, have dealt with everything except the battlefield and the reality of combat, considered 'old, unhappy, distant things'.[32] Despite reading really important works such as these by Jeremy Black,[33] John Lynn,[34] John Keegan,[35] and by Christopher Duffy,[36] Parker's idea prevailed, according to which for the New Military Historian 'it is relatively easier to write the history of battles, a campaign, even a war; it is extremely difficult to write the history of the men, the regiments, and the weapons that fought'.[37] Thus, military historians at the beginning of the millennium know little about the

---

early twentieth century, not only in terms of combat performance, but also in logistics, speed of march and control of field operations. The German disaster of 1914 is proof of this basic misunderstanding.

30   T. Kühne, B. Ziemann (eds), *Was ist Militärgeschichte?* (Paderborn: Ferdinand Schöningh Verlag, 2000); J. Nowosadtko, *Krieg, Gewalt und Ordnung. Einführung in die Militärgeschichte* (Tübingen: Kimmerle, 2002); S. Förster, *The Battlefield: Towards a Modern History of War* (London: German Historical Institute London, 2008).

31   A. Buono, G. Civale (eds), *Battaglie. L'evento, l'individuo, la memoria* (Palermo: Mediterranea, 2014), pp.7-16.

32   T.L. Knutsen, 'Old, Unhappy, Far-Off Things: The New Military History of Europe', in *Journal of Peace Research*, Vol.24, n.1, pp.87-98.

33   J. Black, *European Warfare, 1660-1815* (London: Routledge & Kegan Paul, 1994).

34   J.A. Lynn, *The Bayonets of the Republic. Motivation and Tactics in the Army of Revolutionary France* (Chicago: University of Illinois Press, 1984) and *Giant of the Grand Siècle. The French Army 1610-1715* (Cambridge: Cambridge University Press, 1997).

35   Above all the masterpiece J. Keegan, *The Face of Battle* (London: Jonathan Cape, 1976). The book, published in 1976, has had more influence on classical, Roman and medieval military history than on modern history. Keegan displaces Delbrück's thesis that in military-historical studies the numbers of forces in the field are of fundamental value, and this fact has finally made the investigation of classical warfare a less laborious and arid exercise than it was before, now aimed at reconstructing the reality of battle for those who fought and died.

36   In particular C. Duffy, *The Military Experience in the Age of Reason*, London 1998 and the two monographs devoted to the Austrian army during the Seven Years' War: *Instrument of War* (Rosemont: Emperor's Press, 2000) and *By Force of Arms* (Chicago: Emperor's Press, 2000).

37   H. Parker, 'Review of *Servants of the Sword: French Intendants of the Army, 1630-70* by Douglas Clark Baxter; *The Army of Charles II* by John Childs; *Les Francais et l'armee sous Louis XIV: D'apres les*

weapons adopted by the armies they study, their effectiveness, not to mention the operational theatres – that is, the fields where war is fought – which are only imagined, almost never studied, explored or understood. This historiographical vacuum makes it very difficult to reconstruct modern-day combat. Robert M. Citino has therefore noted that military history must necessarily return to the battlefield; an army, a military institution has on the battlefield the verification of the strength of its units, the effectiveness of its training, the slenderness and efficiency of its logistics, its organization.[38] It is therefore at the tactical and operational level that military history proper finds a new dimension: the analysis of weapon systems, their effectiveness on the battlefield, the study of the topography of the places of war, be they camps, cities or strongholds, as well as the road network or ports (river or sea) used for logistics. This logic also inspires the *Nouvelle Histoire Bataille* proposed by the *Institut de Stratégie et des Conflits-Commission Française d'Histoire Militaire* (Institute of Conflicts Strategy – French Military History Commission), the works by Paddy Griffith,[39] Mark Adkin,[40] and Scott Bowden,[41] which have in fact overturned the stereotyped image we had of certain campaigns. Among the most recent publications, the volume that most caught my attention is certainly that of Gregory Hanlon, *Italy 1636. Cemetery of Armies*.[42] The Canadian historian's ability to investigate sources related to tactics, logistics, and the psychology of the soldiers, using also sources not usually considered, such as material and archaeological sources, was the model to which I resorted several times during the writing of this volume.

This volume tells the story of the Battle of Assietta, the most important battle fought by a pre-unification Italian army in modern times. This was a battle which, as we shall see, has left traces and marks both in history and in today's Italian institutions. Following Gregory Hanlon's suggestion, and also looking for new ways forward given the absence of a real school of Italian military historians, like a late nineteenth-century mountaineer-explorer I have tried to open a new route on that impervious wall that is military history. The main sources used, the basic pegs to be precise, come mainly from the State archives and the Royal Library of Turin, the *Service Historique de la Defense* (SHD) in Paris-Vincennes and the *Kriegsarchiv* in Vienna, and consist of orders of operations, reports, memoirs, instructions, journal entries and cartographic apparatus. These archival repositories, in particular Paris and Vienna, have shown that research into the campaign and the Battle of Assietta may still hold important discoveries.

---

mémoires des intendants, 1697-1698 by Andre Corvisier', *The Journal of Modern History*, Vol.50, No. 1 (Mar. 1978), p.148.

38   R.M. Citino, *The German Way of War. From the Thirty Years' War to the Third Reich* (Lawrence: Kansas University Press, 2005), pp.xv-xviii; Förster, *The Battlefield*, pp.22-23. Also Bernhard R. Kroener, former director *Militärgeschichte/Kulturgeschichte der Gewalt* at the University of Potsdam, has also pointed out the need for a return to 'a history of war that does not overlook the action of killing': B.R. Kroener, 'Stato, società, «militare». Prospettive di una rinnovata storia militare della prima età moderna', C. Donati, B.R. Kroener (eds), *Militari e società civile dell'età moderna (secoli XVI-XVIII)* (Bologna: Il Mulino, 2007), p.21.

39   P. Griffith, *Battle Tactics of the American Civil War* (Ramsbury: The Crowood Press, 1987).

40   M. Adkin, *The Waterloo Companion. The Complete Guide to History's Most Famous Land Battle* (Mechanicsburg: Aurum, 2001) and *The Gettysburg Companion. A Guide to the Most Famous Battle of the Civil War* (Mechanicsburg: Aurum, 2008).

41   S. Bowden, *Glory Years. Napoleon at Austerlitz 1805-1807* (Chicago: Emperor's Press, 1997).

42   G. Hanlon, *Italy 1636. Cemetery of Armies* (Oxford: Oxford University Press, 2018).

The study of the operational reality of the Sardinian/Piedmontese army in the 18th century is therefore a field of research in military history that has yet to be explored. To succeed in this endeavour, it is necessary to come up against three strong points of historiographic resistance:

- the absence of a background of recent and valid studies on Savoyard military history.[43]
- the absence of works dedicated to the operational history of the Sardinian army.[44]
- the distorted perception we usually have of the eighteenth-century war.

A few considerations must be made on this last point. The eighteenth century has long been regarded as a period of war limited in objectives and means, in contrast to the seventeenth century, the 'century of iron' *par excellence*. It is argued that the eighteenth century was an era of manoeuvres, that battles were fought half-heartedly and only when both sides wished. Combat was conceived as the result of a mathematical formula, in which it was necessary to identify 'whether the advantages of winning proportionately outweigh the damage to be suffered in the event of defeat'.[45] Still others have argued that even the best generals avoided battle because of the uncertainty of certain victory.[46] There were certainly reasons for these prejudices against battle. Soldiers were simply too expensive to be sacrificed lightly. Each man in uniform meant on average three years of training, valuable equipment and a large sum of money, a figure that increased for specialized corps and cavalry. The system of taxation and voluntary enlistment was still so underdeveloped that it was difficult to recoup losses. The relatively small size of armies in the countryside imposed a number of limitations on their actual operational capabilities. Hans Delbrück wrote that at that time in history, it was impossible for armies to 'annihilate the enemy's forces, occupy his capital or his best provinces, even after a great victory'.[47] Overthrowing the opponent in a single day of battle was, in other words, only a fantasy. Therefore, an age of limited resources could only sustain a limited war. Defeating the enemy did not so much mean destroying him completely as

---

43   The three main texts that today form the starting bibliography for anyone wishing to approach Piedmontese military history are the volumes presented here. Walter Barberis has helped to sweep away a whole series of commonplaces, historiographic even before descriptive, linked to the supposed 'military traditions' of Piedmont; W. Barberis, *Le armi del Principe. La tradizione militare sabauda* (Torino: Einaudi, 1988). Paola Bianchi is the author of one of the most important texts on the relations between the army and society in *Ancien Régime* Piedmont; P. Bianchi, *Onore e Mestiere. Le riforme militari nel Piemonte del Settecento* (Torino: Zamorani, 2002). Sabina Loriga, on the other hand, has pointed out the importance of the regimental rolls to tell, through a statistical study, who the Sardinian soldier in the eighteenth century was; S. Loriga, *Soldati. L'istituzione militare nel Piemonte del Settecento* (Venezia: Marsilio, 1992).

44   This remains one of the most serious gaps in Italian military history. The most recent works with a valid scientific structure are those by Virgilio Ilari, *Tra i Borbone e gli Asburgo* (Ancona: Nuove Ricerche, 1996), and *La Corona di Lombardia* (Ancona: Nuove Eidizioni, 1997), produced in collaboration with Ciro Paoletti and Giancarlo Boeri. There is therefore no alternative but to rely on the old studies, some of which are still valid, by Arvers and de Vault, Moris, Buffa di Perrero and Alberti.

45   Turpin de Crissé, *Essai sur l'art de la guerre* (Paris: Prault, Jombert, 1754), Vol.I, p.382.

46   M. Jähns, *Geschichte der Kriegswissenschaften vornehmlich in Deutschland* (Leipzig: K. Oldenbourg, 1890), Vol.III.

47   H. Delbrück, 'Über die Verschiedenheit der Strategie Friedrichs und Napoleons', in *Historische und politische Aufsätze* (Berlin: G. Stilke, 1907), pp.241-242.

exhausting him. Delbrück again argued that although this was theoretically possible through battle, it was certainly much more possible through manoeuvre warfare. A general could seek a position from which he would be able to threaten the enemy's stores and communications while protecting his own. This scheme of ideas also presents macroscopic problems. With the introduction of the flintlock, the firearm became identified with the very concept of infantry. The European military system of the eighteenth century produced its fair share of battles, the list of which fills a book. Although living in an age of 'limits', armies did their best to achieve the destruction and annihilation of the enemy. It is difficult to read the reports of an eighteenth-century battle, with the two adversaries standing within a few dozen metres of each other and inflicting losses of 30-40 percent of their number, and if we could interview the surviving French soldiers at the end of the battle of Assietta, they would be surprised to discover that they had just participated in an episode of 'limited warfare'.

The battlefield of 19 July 1747 is virtually intact. The emerging discipline of conflict archaeology is proving capable of placing in the hands of military historians a remarkable and previously unthinkable study tool for reconstructing and understanding the battlefield.[48] Already a great pioneer of military historiography, Hans Delbrück (1848-1929), had demonstrated that many traditional accounts of military operations are pure nonsense by a simple, intelligent inspection of the terrain. An English follower of his, Alfred Higgins Burne (1886-1959), proposed to extend to all major battlefields a principle he had proved to be valid, consisting of Inherent Military Probability and which, used with circumspection, constitutes an interesting field of investigation.[49] Reconnaissance in the field, carried out under various weather conditions, has proved to be as important as documentary sources,[50] provided one is familiar with the tactics and weaponry of the period. War has its own grammar, which must be known well in order to describe its climax, the battle. I have therefore placed particular emphasis on researching the Sardinian, French and Austrian tactical treatises of the period, how they were applied on the battlefield and with what effect.[51] This in turn informed an investigation about the armaments, individual firearms and artillery, what was the actual effects of these weapons on the human body, the ranges, the maintenance.[52] Finally, it is necessary to consider a fundamental, but usually overlooked, aspect of modern warfare: logistics.[53]

---

48   R.A. Fox, *Archaeology, History, and Custer's last Battle* (Norman: University of Oklahoma Press, 2003); P. Harrington, *English Civil War Archaeology* (London: Batsford, 2004); by D. Scott, L. Babits and C. Haecker (eds), *Fields of Conflict. Battlefield Archaeology from the Roman Empire to the Korean War* (Westport: Praeger, 2007).

49   The principle of Inherent Military Probability consists in solving a tactical problem on the basis of what an experienced soldier would have done under the same circumstances.

50   For the timing of troop column movements, their composition, marching times and the calculation of logistical supplies, old military manuals that were used by company commanders in the late-nineteenth and early-twentieth century as field *vademecums* and notebooks are always useful. This study employs a field notebook of the Italian Royal Army R. Lambert, *Ricordi Logistici e Tattici* (Firenze: Barbera, 1930).

51   Black, *European Warfare*; D. Chandler, *The Art of Warfare in the Age of Marlborough* (Staplehurst: Spellmount, 1990); B. Nosworthy, *The Anatomy of Victory. Battle Tactics 1689-1763* (New York: Hippocrene Books, 1992); C. Telp, *The Evolution of Operational Art, 1740-1813* (Abingdon: Routledge, 2003).

52   B.P. Hughes, *Firepower. Weapons Effectiveness on the Battlefield, 1630- 1850* (London: Da Capo Press, 1974).

53   M. Van Creveld, *Supplying War. Logistic from Wallenstein to Patton* (Cambridge: Cambridge University Press, 2004).

The other major, relatively recent tool that opens up entirely new scenarios for understanding past combat is the so-called Killology. Invented by Lieutenant-Colonel Dave Grossman, this branch of psychology investigates the psyche and physiology of the soldier during combat; the results of its investigations have helped us to understand what French, Austrian and Sardinian soldiers experienced, felt and perceived during combat, how they reacted, how the training they received affected them, how they killed, and what effect this had on their psyche.[54]

Military historians, as Keegan already pointed out, should spend as much time as possible in the company of military personnel. I had the good fortune to serve in the Italian Army for four consecutive years, and I have to say that the observation that 'armies remain essentially the same' is less trivial than it might seem. Inside a barracks, during a march or an exercise, the casual observation of trivial events can serve to illuminate the understanding of many problems of the past that would otherwise almost certainly remain obscured.

In the rucksack we have everything we need. We start our climb, into the smoke of the gunfire. Straight into the heat of battle, whistling that ancient bellicose ballad that suggested to me the title of this book, *You Have to Die in Piedmont!*:

> *In the Pragelato Valley*
> *the French have arrived.*
> *The well-prepared Piedmontese*
> *served him a salty salad.*
> *The dish was hot*
> *and it burned his heart.*
> *Mr Belle-Isle you have to die!*
> *But what did you think?*
> *But what were you doing?*
> *Mr Belle-Isle you have to die,*
> *you have to die in Piedmont!*[55]

---

54   On the psychology of the soldier in combat see D. Grossman, *On Killing. The Psychological Cost of Learning to Kill in War and Society* (New York: Back Bay Books, 1996) and *On Combat. Psychology and Physiology of Deadly Conflict in War and in Peace* (New York: PPCT Research Publications, 1999), and the always valid, despite the historiographical offensive that sees it at the centre of important criticism, S.L.A. Marshall, *Men Against Fire. The Problem of Battle Command* (New York: Infantry Journal, 1947).

55   This song, not exactly friendly towards the French, is one of the two known variants of the *Chanson dell'Assiette* written in the eighteenth century. The version presented here was collected and harmonized by Federico Ghisi in 1958. F. Ghisi, 'Complaites e canzoni storiche (XII-XIX sec.)', in *BSSV*, No.134, 1973, pp.122-134. In 1967, in Varaita Valley, the scholar of alpine culture Sergio Ottonelli had the good fortune to hear, and transcribe, from an old lady born in the nineteenth century, the verses reproduced here. See on the history of the composition A. Genre, D.E. Tron, 'Una canzona dell'Assietta in patois?', in *La Beidana. Cultura e storia nelle valli valdesi*, No.30, July 1990, pp.71-78. For those who would like to hear the piece played, see the version proposed by the Piedmontese folk group *Lou Dalfin* in their 1984 album, *L'aze d'Alegre*: <https://www.youtube.com/watch?v=F7TuKdylpGk> accessed 12 August 2021.

1

Tired Warriors

The War of the Austrian Succession had broken out in 1740, and in Italy French, Spanish, Austrian and Sardinian armies had been fighting since 1742. For four years the Spanish and French armies had had only one goal: to cross the Alps and occupy the Duchy of Milan. For four years the lily armies tried to reach Lombardy, opening their way by fighting against the allied armies of the King of Sardinia, Carlo Emanuele III of Savoy, and the Empress of Austria, Maria Theresia. In 1745 Paris and Madrid, thanks to the alliance with Genoa, had bypassed the Alpine bastion from the south and they had almost succeeded in the enterprise; they had separated the two enemy armies defeating the Sardinian army at Bassignana and dismantling the network of fortresses in eastern Piedmont. At the end the city of Milan was occupied, even if a small Austrian garrison inside was still present. Carlo Emanuele III, with his army on the brink, was ready for a separate peace. However, disagreements and strategic differences between the Spaniards and the French transformed an announced triumph into a disaster. In 1746 the offensive return of the Austrian army had led to the reconquest of Milan, preventing the defection of an increasingly tired Carlo Emanuele III and inflicting a decisive defeat to the Franco-Spanish army at Piacenza. The victory had been of such proportions that the Austrians, although they could not destroy the remains of the opposing forces, were able to conquer Genoa: on 6 September 1746 the city, abandoned by its allies, surrendered to the Austrian armies. In November, with the capture of Tortona, the Sardinians had completely liberated Piedmont; they were also able to conquer Savona and, thanks to the presence of the Austrian army, to block any French offensive coming from the Dauphiné and Provence. The game was now over, and the contenders, especially the Sardinians and the French, were sufficiently exhausted to close the hostilities. Yet facts intervened to reshuffle the deck, and the players returned to the table for one last game; some lost their treasure, others their reputation and others their life.[1]

---

1   On the War of Succession of Austria and its general events: M.S. Anderson, *The War of the Austrian Succession 1740-1748* (New York: Routledge, 2013); R. Browning, *The War of the Austrian Succession* (Stroud: Sutton Publishing, 1995); F. El Hage, *La guerre de la Succession d'Autriche (1741-1748). Louis XV et le déclin de la France* (Paris: Economica, 2017); J. Weil, *La guerre de succession d'Autriche* (Paris: L. Baudoin, 1897); Wilkinson, *The Defence of Piedmont*. For a more navalist approach, R. Harding, *The Emergence of Britain's Global Naval Supremacy. The War of 1739-1748* (Woodbridge: Boydell, 2010). For the Italian front the fundamental text remains Arvers and de Vault, *Guerre de la Succession d'Autriche*. Also important is Moris, *Opérations militaires dans les Alps et les Apennins*. Quite old, but still interesting, is Vol.V of Saluzzo, *Histoire Militaire du Piémont*. In Italian the reference text remains

The Italian peninsula in 1747. The map suggests the strategic importance of the Kingdom of Sardinia for the control of the Western Alps. For the French and Spanish side the main strategic goal of the 1747 campaign was to have the Republic of Genoa in safe hands and remove the Kingdom of Sardinia from the struggle in Italy.

War Economy

In 1747 every European chancellery felt the need for peace. The Wars of the *Ancien Régime* absorbed an impressive amount of money; the armies had to be recruited, the soldiers had to receive their pay regularly, and in addition the state would bear the costs of dressing, arming and training them for war. Among the main contenders we find in the Alpine countryside of 1747, there were those who were short of breath, those who were panting and those who were about to collapse due to the war effort.[2]

In Turin the war expenses had risen beyond all expectations.[3] The liabilities of the kingdom's finances in 1747 were 11,599,764 lire, practically the budget of a whole year. To finance the campaign it was necessary to scratch the bottom of the barrel. Direct taxes managed to rake in 5,354,291 lire, to which 2,424,346 lire could be added in May recovered with the extraordinary amount on immune ecclesiastical assets, authorized by Pope Benedict XIV.[4] The interest rates of the Monti di Pietà, a sort of war bonds, and specifically that of San Giovanni Battista, brought to the Turin coffers another 2,000,000 lire, together with the important British subsidy, which rose to 3,775,000 lire, for a total of 13,553,637 lire. Other revenues, guaranteed by extraordinary taxes and the opening of mortgages, guaranteed a total income of 29,720,678 lire which, against a total expenditure of 23,400,000 lire, would have allowed the financing of the Sardinian war effort and the payment of the rates on the loans taken out.[5] This effort could not yet be sustained for long; the annual debt was on average 8,070,000 lire, while the extraordinary taxes to support the war effort rose to 2,306,000 lire a year.[6]

On the matter of British subsidies, by the Provisional Convention, ratified on 10 February 1742, England had paid £200,000 to Turin on the condition that, if the Austro-Sardinian alliance were confirmed, this sum would be considered an advance of future British subsidies. Otherwise, it should have reverted to Britain. The Treaty of Worms of 13 September 1743 made definitive the Austro-Sardinian alliance under these auspices and the English participation. In this treaty, and specifically in Article 8, it was clarified that the English subsidy of £200,000 per year was payable quarterly in advance starting from 1 February 1742. With the Hague Convention of 26 January 1748, the British subsidy to the House of Savoy, for the military campaign of that year, had increased to £300,000, under certain

---

    Ilari, Boeri, Paoletti, *La Corona di Lombardia*. For the diplomatic struggle M. Cesa, *Alleati ma rivali. Teoria delle alleanze e politica estera settecentesca* (Bologna: Il Mulino, 2007).

2   On the financial aspects of the wars of the eighteenth century, see C Storrs (ed.), *The Fiscal-Military State in Eighteenth-Century Europe. Essays in honour of P.G.M. Dickson* (Farnham: Ashgate, 2009).

3   For a study of the economy of the Savoy states see the chapter by C. Storrs, 'The Savoyard Fiscal-Military State in the Long Eighteenth Century', in Storrs (ed.), *The Fiscal-Military State*, pp.201-236. Still useful G. Prato, *La Vita economica in Piemonte a mezzo il Secolo XVIII* (Torino: Officine Grafiche della Società Tipografico-Editrice Nazionale, 1908), but the fundamental and almost unknown work is that by Paolo Norsa, *La Finanza Sabauda dal 1700 all'Unità d'Italia* (Unpublished Manuscript, 1957). These are 11 volumes of typewritten notes, prepare for a never published volume. The revenues of the Kingdom of Sardinia during War of Succession are in Vol.II., pp.326-393.

4   Norsa, *La Finanza Sabauda*, Vol.II, p.338; Carutti, *Storia del Regno di Carlo Emanuele III*, p.67.

5   Norsa, *La Finanza Sabauda*, Vol.II, p.338; Table VI.

6   Norsa, *La Finanza Sabauda*, Vol.II, p.376.

conditions. That said, the amount of British subsidies received by Turin was six shares of £200,000 each, and one of £300,000, for a total of £1,500,000 which, with the exchange rate at the time, corresponded to 28,312,500 lire.[7]

Like the Kingdom of Sardinia, the Austrian Empire needed to enter into peace negotiations as soon as possible. Although the Germanic territories and Bohemia were now far from the roar of the battlefield, especially after the 1745 Treaty of Dresden with Prussia, the periphery of the Habsburg dominions was suffering all the hardships of the war. The commander of the French troops in the Austrian Netherlands, the famous Maurice de Saxe, was sucking up all the resources of those territories like a veritable vampire. The Duchy of Lombardy, one of the most precious gems of the imperial crown of Maria Theresia, was so saturated with debts that half of the tax revenues were immediately paid to pay off debts or pay interest on mortgages activated to cover extraordinary war expenses, plunging Milan into the cyclone of galloping inflation.[8] The war until then weighed on the imperial coffers for an amount of 185.85 million florins, and a part of the richest lands, on which it was expected to recover part of the expenses, had been ceded to Friedrich II's Prussia.[9]

If Athens wept, Sparta certainly did not laugh. France was in a paradoxical situation: in 1747 it was by far the nation that, with Prussia, had achieved the most successes ever on the battlefields. Under the leadership of Maurice de Saxe, the French army had achieved triumphs such as had not been seen since the times of Turenne and the Prince de Condé. The victory of Fontenoy of 11 May 1745, for example, had been one of the highlights of the campaign to conquer the Austrian Netherlands, an operation that could be considered almost complete. Yet few states like France were suffering the economic costs of the ongoing conflict. It had been necessary to activate several additional taxation systems, such as the *Capitation*, which affected all people, including nobles and clergy, and the *Dixième*, decreed to support military expenses, which was based on actual income and property value. Meanwhile an ever-increasing number of recruits were being incorporated into the *Armée Royale*, with the result that manufacturing centres and farms were deprived of the necessary manpower. The confrontation on the seas with England had not been positive, and foreign trade had dried up, leaving merchants without products to sell, consumers without goods, and the kingdom without its regular commercial income. The climatic conditions completed the work: the continuous rains ruined the crops, causing a ferocious famine. In 1747 France was a land plunged into misery. Some, like the *Maréchal* de Belle-Isle and Maurice de Saxe, hoped and claimed to continue the conflict; if not to achieve total victory, then at least to continue fighting another campaign by gaining decisive or important victories on all major war fronts to negotiate a final peace from a point of strength.[10]

---

7   Norsa, *La Finanza Sabauda*, p.338.

8   M. Hochedlinger, 'The Fiscal-Military State and International Rivalry during the Long Eighteenth Century', in Storrs (ed.), *The Fiscal-Military State* pp.55-94.

9   P.G.M. Dickson, *Finance and Government under Maria Theresia 1740-1780* (Oxford: Oxford University Press, 1987), Vol.II, pp.318, 388, tables 4.1, 4.2; W. Wess Mitchell, *The Grand Strategy of the Habsburg Empire* (Princeton: Princeton University Press, 2018), p.67.

10   J. Félix, F. Tallett, 'The French Experience 1661-1815', in Storrs (ed.), *The Fiscal-Military State*, pp.167-199. The chapters presented in the volume edited by Christopher Storrs are excellent for a general and bibliographic introduction. For France in particular, please also refer to the vast and well-curated bibliographic review present in the work by Joël Fèlix, *Économie et finances sous*

The Italian Strategic Situation

The fall of Genoa in September 1746 had opened the doors of the Riviera di Ponente to the Austro-Sardinian allies. In a short time, the capture of Savona followed – but not yet the fort of Priamar which would not surrender until 18 December – and the conquest of Finale.[11] Such successes put the allies in a dilemma: what next?

Vienna and Turin had different goals. Maria Theresia, after having reconquered Lombardy, intended to move her armies south and retry the conquest of Naples, an undertaking which she had not succeeded in 1744. Carlo Emanuele III instead wanted to deal with the dismemberment of the Genoese Republic and the reconquest of Savoy. On the contrary London demanded and obtained a resumption of hostilities in a grand style since Britain was still the main sponsor of the conflict in Italy, and the main financier of the army of Carlo Emanuele III. At the end of September 1746, a council of war was held in Savona during which the British ambassador snatched from the allies, albeit with difficulty, the general commitment to continue the offensive beyond the Varo, with the logistical and tactical support of the naval squadron under Captain the Hon. George Townsend.

It was a repeat of the operations of 1707, but again the Austrians participated reluctantly. Their goal remained Naples, which appeared to be completely unguarded. For this purpose, once the operations near Piacenza and eastern Piedmont were concluded, they were transferring the cavalry units to Cremona, Mantua and Modena, where the new units arriving from Tyrol were also concentrated. Preparations were underway to the point that the depots needed to guarantee logistical support for the imperial armies headed south were already being set up in the occupied territories of the Papal States. These preparations did not escape the notice of the Spaniards, who sent 12 battalions in Naples to reinforce the king, Charles VII of Bourbon, who immediately began to garrison strongholds and coastal defences. The French were doing the same for the defence of Toulon; the lack of strategic surprise and the British pressure convinced Empress Maria Theresia to definitively abandon the idea of conquering Naples and concentrate her efforts on Provence.

The Austrian command estimated it needed at least 30,000 men to reach Toulon and invest the place, so after capturing Nice on 17 October 1746, they stopped their advance waiting to receive the necessary reinforcements sent by the British fleet. Opposite there were just 17,000 Franco-Spaniards, all that remained of the army of *Maréchal* Maillebois. Carlo Emanuele III, although he wanted to devote himself mainly to the capture of Savoy and to the defensive arrangement of Finale, saw in this offensive an opportunity to revive his reputation as a military commander, somewhat tarnished after the defeats of Madonna dell'Olmo and Bassignana. Smallpox struck him on 20 November, and *Feldzeugmeister* Browne promptly replaced him at the head of the combined Austro-Sardinian army; on

---

l'Ancien Régime. Guide du chercheur 1523-1789 (Vincennes: Comité pour l'histoire économique et financière de la France, 1994), pp.17-46. Also useful is M.A. Bailly, *Histoire Financiere de la France, depuis l'origine de la monarchie jusq'a la fin de 1786* (Paris: Moutardier, 1830), Vol.II, pp.120-128; M. Marion, *Histoire Financière de la France depuis 1715* (Paris: Librairie Armand Colin, 1914-1931) Vol.I; Deon de Beaumont, *Mémoire pour servir a l'Histoire Generale des Finances* (Amsterdam: Compagnie Néerlandaise des Indes Orientales, 1760), Vol.II, pp.117-120.

11 P. Calcagno, 'Occupare una città in Antico Regime', in *Mediterranea*, N. 24, Anno IX, 2012, pp.81-110.

30 November 1746, 20,000 Austrians and 10,000 Sardinians crossed the 250 metres of the stony banks of the River Varo and entered the kingdom of France.

Disaster in Genoa

Meanwhile, the imperial generals had succeeded in ruining the fruits of an entire campaign. Hoping to assert its neutrality towards Austrian Empire, the Republic of Genoa had surrendered to the Austrian general Botta d'Adorno, the son of a Genoese nobleman sentenced to death and banished for political reasons; this was really a bad choice. Genoa was the capital of one of the many small city-states, not governed by a monarchy, which coexisted alongside the great European dynastic states. Although it had just 50,000 inhabitants residing within the city walls in 1746, Genoa 'the Superb' was a regional power not to be underestimated. The Dukes of Savoy knew this well, and during the seventeenth century they had tried, in vain, to steal coastal and inland areas from it. Headquarters of one of the main European financial centres of seventeenth and eighteenth centuries, it also directly controlled the Novi Ligure stock market, where the main Western European stock transactions took place during four trade fairs in February, May, August and November, involving and dictating the fluctuations of the Spanish, French, Italian, Dutch and German business centres between Hamburg, Frankfurt am Main and Nuremberg, and even Vienna. It was really a bank with a city around it, and the elites who owed great trade and commerce companies dictated the timing of foreign policy.

Feldzeugmeister Maximilian Ulysses Graf von Browne (1705-1757). In early 1747 he was appointed field commander of all imperial forces in Italy. In the course of the 1747 campaign he was forced to withdraw his forces from the siege of Genoa and redeploy them in Piedmont to block the French offensive in the Alps. He died on 26 June 1757 from wounds sustained during the Battle of Prague fought against the Prussians on 6 May 1757. (Plate from *Œuvres de Frédérick le Grand*, Vol.III, Tome I)

Determined to remain neutral during the campaign of 1744, at the end the Genoese saw in the possibility of a transfer of the Marquisate of Finale to the Kingdom of Sardinia, as foreseen by the Treaty of Worms of 13 September 1743, a mortal danger for the republic. It was thus decided to go to war alongside France and Spain. During the triumphant campaign of 1745, Genoa had provided its allies with men and artillery, lent money at discounted rates to the courts of Paris and Madrid and gained a well-deserved military prestige for the conduct of its troops during the siege of Tortona. However, the offensive return of the adversaries in 1746 had dampened any enthusiasm and any belligerent ambitions, and on 6 September 1746 the city had surrendered without fighting the Austrian forces. The *Feldzeugmeister* Antoniotto Botta d'Adorno, commander of the Austrian troops, in a little diplomatic way decided to ask the city for an indemnity of 3 million genoine, equal to 22.8 million lire, to be paid in three instalments with deadlines of two, eight and 15 days. The figure corresponded to all the cash existing in the Republic and the first million meant paying the entire proceeds of 30 years of customs revenue. A similar tribute, with which Botta intended to punish Genoa for the help given to the Franco-Spanish armies, pay the wages and goods necessary for his troops and avenge the exile of his family, could not do other than exasperate the feelings of the population.

The Austrian management of the city was nothing more than a rapid accumulation of explosive mixture which, by the end of 1746, was triggered by the famous Revolt of Portoria on 5 December. The presence of a boy, a certain Giovanni Battista Perasso, known as 'Balilla', who threw a stone in front of the Austrian officer who forcibly asked the citizens of the Portoria district to free a mortar sunk in a hole, is not confirmed by any documentary evidence. The municipal commission set up in Genoa in 1881, intended to shed light on the issue, found the grandchildren of some witnesses to the facts; they claimed to have

Jean Baptiste François des Marets, Marquis de Maillebois (1682-1762). One of the most capable French commanders of the War of Austrian Succession, he devised the circumvention of the Alpine bastion by manoeuvring along the Ligurian coast in 1745, succeeding in bringing the Bourbon flags back to Milan and forcing the King of Sardinia to consider a separate peace. The Austrian offensive in 1746 and the defeat at Piacenza caused his plans to fail, but they were successfully resumed by Napoleon in 1796. (Engraving by Vincenzo Vangelisti, author's collection)

known the 'Balilla', a certain Giambattista Perasso, son of Antonio Maria, born on 26 October 1735. Except that the documents found showed that Perasso was not known as much as 'Balilla', but rather as 'Mangiamerda', literally 'shit eating'.[12] Certainly the episode seems to have been only the pretext for a revolt already planned for the previous weeks.[13]

On 11 December the Austrians, unable to control the city centre, left Genoa. In Turin they immediately understood that this revolution was in fact a 'fatal catastrophe' for the cause of the allies of Worms, and for the offensive recently launched against Provence.[14] Versailles and Madrid would have dealt with the fate of Genoa, to take advantage of the unexpected opportunity to keep the Italian front open, and control any revolutionary contagion.

---

12   D. Pizzorno, 'Perasso, Giambattista detto il Balilla', in DBI, <http://www.treccani.it/enciclopedia/giambattista-detto-il-balilla-perasso_(Dizionario-Biografico)> accessed 10 August 2021.
13   Ilari, Boeri, Paoletti, *La Corona di Lombardia*, p.216.
14   Browning, *The War of the Austrian Succession*, p.293.

A Small Offensive

The insurrection of Genoa had dealt a severe blow to the Austrian strategy. In an instant it sank the planned expedition to Naples and torpedoed the one just started on Toulon. Communications along the coast suddenly became much less secure. The Franco-Spanish army had split into two sections. A body of 12,000 French had remained in Cagnes to cover Provence, while the Spaniards had moved in Savoy. However, the alliance ties between Versailles and Madrid had been reaffirmed with a new treaty, signed the 22 November; the Spanish soldiers retraced their steps, while other troops arrived from the Rhine and Flanders fronts. To command the new army was chosen *Maréchal* Belle-Isle, whose star was rising again after the German disasters of 1742. As a *sine qua non* condition, Belle-Isle required the arrival of important reinforcements destined to obtain a decisive numerical superiority against the enemy. In addition to this, he was joined by his beloved brother, the Chevalier de Belle-Isle. On November 30, the Austro-Sardinians crossed the Varo and continued along the coast. To stop them, *Maréchal* Belle-Isle intended to move his forces into the middle valley of the Varo, and threaten the left flank of the Brown's army, while the first reinforcements were arriving at the main camp located in Puget.

The Austro-Sardinian allies continued to advance slowly, arriving on December 10 at the gates of Antibes. The stronghold seemed to be an easy prey, but on the very same day the revolt in Genoa deprived the expeditionary force of the necessary siege artillery. While the allies were painstakingly trying to recover other guns, the French port was surrounded and put under blockade. Browne was able to secure sufficient logistical supplies by agreeing with the local communities, and he was able to convert money imposed as a war tribute into contributions of food, fodder, fagots, wood and *corvèe*. The coffers of the invading army managed to get a decent income, and the system also yielded an unexpected gain for the Provençal peasants, discouraging the usual habit of hiding goods and people in front of the head of the marching columns. The timing of the operations around Antibes was dictated by the arrival of the siege park. On 3 and 4 January the siege batteries were set up waiting to be armed with the 18 pieces taken from Savona by the British Royal Navy. The rough seas, and the presence of

Charles-Louis-Auguste Fouquet, Duc de Belle-Isle (1684-1761). *Maréchal de France* from 1741, the Duc de Belle-Isle was one of the main protagonists of the War of the Austrian Succession. In 1747 he authorised the Alpine campaign against Piedmont. (Engraving by Carlo Domenico Melini after a portrait by Maurice Quentin de la Tour from 1748, author's collection)

Belle-isle's army, compelled the allies to leave the siege guns on the British ships; it was better to have them aboard rather to disembark and give them directly to the enemy.

The 'Genoa Express' and the Necessity of a Second Front

Paris was preparing to launch a diplomatic and military counter-offensive, and the revolt in Genoa meant that the main effort would be concentrated on the Italian front. The success of the Genoa revolt had to be contained, as the strategic implications of such an episode could be disruptive. It was necessary to directly support the city government, because by doing so the popular movement would be defused from within by the bourgeois and noble families. The presence of Franco-Spanish allied troops could only accelerate this fact. The French help to Genoa did not offend anyone in Europe, as they had already supported the Jacobite rebellion in Scotland in 1745. Starting from February 1747, French money began to arrive in the Ligurian capital, soon followed by French and Spanish soldiers who landed in the port after having evaded the British blockade. The French intervention was decisive; it saved Genoa from the Austrian counter-offensive and France from a revolution that could have spread 42 years before that of 1789.

On 21 January 1747, Belle-Isle launched his counter-offensive against the Austro-Sardinians in Provence; 44,000 infantry and 6,000 horsemen moved against the right flank of the opposing army, and at that point Browne had to order a general retreat. He had originally hoped to be able to defend a front line on the Siagne River, but realized that this position could be outflanked. He then renounced any attempt to preserve a portion of French territory and he ordered to his forces to abandon the siege of Antibes and to retreat east of the Varo. By 3 February 1747 France was free of enemy troops.

Maria Theresia, meanwhile, was furious. She had had to abandon her beloved project to conquer the Kingdom of Naples, yet the offensive in Provence ended even more disastrously than that of 1707. The epicentre of the struggle inevitably shifted to Genoa. While his army was locked in the mountains between the Turchino and Bocchetta passes and the sea, Botta Adorno was replaced in January 1747 by Ferdinand Ludwig Oeynhausen, also known as Graf von Schulenburg-Oeynhausen. In February, Browne became commander-in-chief of all the Austrian forces of the Mediterranean Theatre; he also held an imperial appointment to negotiate directly with the minister of war of the kingdom of Sardinia, Conte Bogino, for the cooperation of the kingdom of Sardinia for the second siege of Genoa. On 4 May 1747, Vienna, Turin and London completed the planning for the conquest of the republic's capital, signing a treaty that provided for British assistance to a land army of 90,000 men, two-thirds of whom were Austrians and a third Sardinian; a part had to cover the Riviera di Ponente, while another 12 battalions had to approach the city under the command of *Luogotenente Generale* Della Rocca. The allies were ready for the investment of Genoa, even if the strategic differences of the three countries began to appear more and more evident. Vienna wanted revenge, London the ruin of France, and Turin to defend the Alpine bastion.

On the other hand, the Franco-Spanish approach appeared to be more solid. In 1746 Maillebois's army, in full retreat, had not been able, or it did not want, to help its Ligurian ally, who had had to surrender to the advancing Austrian armies. Now the situation had changed, and immediately the first attempts were made to introduce reinforcements into

Genoa. With the Austro-Sardinian armies able to control every approach by land, the only way of access was by sea. Yet the sea was the undisputed domain of the British Royal Navy, owner of the Gulf of Genoa and of the whole Ligurian Sea. *Maréchal* Belle-Isle began organizing convoys made up of small boats, mainly tartanes, with the task of introducing a body of 6,000 men to the city under the orders of *Brigadier* Mauriac. Thus began a risky and dangerous game of cat and mice, something similar to the 'Tokyo Express' saga in the Pacific War during the Second World War, when a delivery service organized by the Japanese Navy between August 1942 and February 1943 transported supplies and personnel to the disputed island of Guadalcanal.[15] The 'Genoa Express' organized by Belle-Isle was a risky operation; the first convoy, made up of 70 tartanes which sailed from Toulon and Marseille between 16 and 17 March, lost no less than 15 units and 900 embarked men.

By mid-April 3,000 Franco-Spaniards had landed in Genoa; some had arrived from the east through the port of Portofino, Sestri and La Spezia, others, sailing from the Provence, managed to evade the British naval blockade by calling in Corsica. Belle-Isle had also succeeded in the enterprise of introducing 200,000 livres into the city to pay troops and war materials, as a guarantee of the commitment of the crowns of France and Spain towards Genoa. The city Senate perfectly understood the opportunity that was presenting itself and offered Mauriac, commander of the Franco-Spanish forces, the direction of the city defences. On 30 April the 'Genoa Express' landed from a felucca the *Lieutenant Général*, and Peer of France, Joseph-Marie, Duc de Boufflers. The duc had been chosen by Louis XV himself to testify to the whole world that the king of France would not allow the city to fall back into the hands of the Austrians. Boufflers then enlivened the defenders with a thunderous speech from the Genoa Senate, closing with this solemn promise: 'Show me the danger, my job is to recognize it, my glory will be in protecting you from it'.[16]

It was now up to *Maréchal* Belle-Isle to find a way to free Genoa from a siege that was known to be imminent. A second front had to be opened, but the choice of how and what to do had to be discussed and planned with the Spanish ally who had geostrategic priorities different from the French ones. The Marqués de La Mina, commander of the Spanish troops attached to the French army in Provence, proposed the most obvious of plans; to launch an offensive along the coastal road and reach Genoa from the Riviera di Ponente. Such a manoeuvre would have forced the Austro-Sardinians to fight with their backs threatened by a relief army, and it would have allowed the Spaniards to gain the most direct route to Piacenza, where the Court of Madrid hoped to place one of its own members of the royal house. Belle-Isle, on the other hand, was now becoming convinced that the strategic objectives of France, namely the defence of Genoa, could be achieved with the opening of a second front not on the Mediterranean coast, but on the Alps. By now, the period of a policy of conciliation vis-à-vis Carlo Emanuele III had definitely faded: it was necessary to attack

---

15   The Japanese used fast military ships, such as destroyers, and later submarines, to transport men and supplies between the islands of Rabaul and Guadalcanal. J.D. Coombe, *Derailing the Tokyo Express. The Naval Battles for the Solomon Islands that Sealed Japan's Fate* (Harrisburg: Stackpole Books, 1991).

16   A. von Arneth, *Maria Theresia's erste Regierungsjahre* (Wien: Wilhelm Braumüller, 1863-1865), Vol. III, p.291. To celebrate the importance of the speech of the Duc de Boufflers, it was also transcribed and printed in a pamphlet; *Discours du Duc de Bouffles au Senat de Genes* (Couret de Villeneuve 1747).

Piedmont thoroughly, force it to sue for peace, and at that point in the Italian theatre Maria Theresia would have found herself completely isolated. The long struggle for supremacy in Italy could have ended with a Franco-Spanish victory.

After a mild, and unconvinced, assent by the Spanish counterpart to an offensive in two directions, *Maréchal* Belle-Isle and his staff began planning the attack from the Alps, the direction from which promised better results. The *maréchal* did not know the Italian theatre at all when he was placed at the head of the French forces stationed in Provence. But he was lucky enough to have in his staff an officer who knew the territory deeply; *Colonel* Pierre-Joseph Bourcet. Together they began planning the invasion of Piedmont from the Alps. Immediately they choose the Susa valley as the area of their offensive.

The Operational Area

The Western Alps were, and they still are, a rather difficult area of operations for any army. The frontier between the kingdoms of Sardinia and France ran mainly on the watershed, a high and rugged land, even if it was crossed by many mule tracks and some important roads. It had an independent course in Nice and Savoy, but the war operations had in fact forced the contenders to line up on the watershed itself, the so called "military frontier". The western side of the Alps, the Italian side, is short and steep, and it is characterized by radial, transversal, very narrow valleys with few and difficult entrances. In addition, and this was a further problem for the Sardinian commands, the main Piedmontese plain, the western part of the Po Plain, is relatively close to it. The French side, on the other hand, is three times wider, with few and large valleys, first longitudinal, then transverse, then longitudinal again, with at least three assembly areas for an army with both an offensive and defensive posture. From a planimetric point of view, the French territory surrounds the Piedmontese one, which narrows due to the presence of the Ligurian Gulf. The Austro-Sardinian lines of operations had necessarily to diverge to cover the entire front, while the French ones converged having the capital of the Kingdom of Sardinia, Turin, as the final objective.

By the end of the seventeenth century, three areas of operations had been identified: southern, central and northern ones, separated from each other by the groups of the Monviso Peak and the Levanne Massive. The French offensive against the Susa Valley, the most important route of invasion, was facilitated by a complete convergence of passages from the Briançon and Modane basins to that of Bardonecchia, by the greater ease of access on the French side and by the clearly offensive attitude that the Briançon stronghold guaranteed. It was, in fact, an excellent logistical base served by very good roads and covered by a series of massive fortifications. The attack against Montgenèvre would have affected the Cesana basin, the Colle del Sestriere, and the whole sector of the upper Val di Susa and Chisone. The easy passages of the Gimont, Bousson and Chabaud gaps converged on Cesana; from the Guil those of the valleys of Thures and Ripa. The various enemy lines of penetration, deriving from the abundance of easy passages through the alpine ridge, highlight the importance of some positions that in this area allowing them to counter and to manoeuvre effectively against an invasion force.

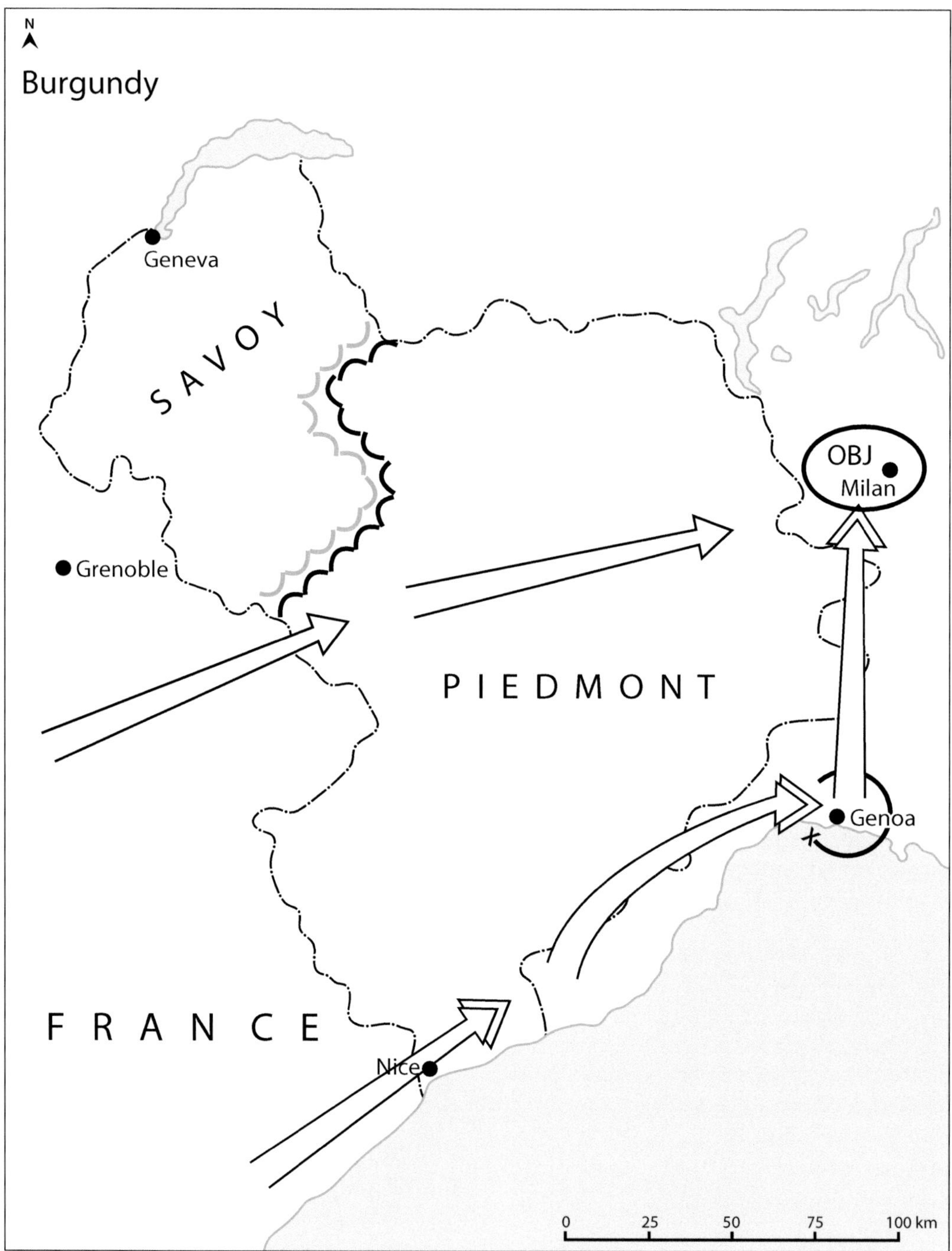

The French plan for the Italian 1747 campaign. The main objective was, as usual, the conquest of the Duchy of Milan. In order to enable this, the besieged allied city of Genoa had to be seized, while a secondary thrust was planned across the Alps in order to compel the King of Sardinia to abandon the Austrian alliance.

One of these key pieces of terrain was the Assietta plateau, or Colle dell'Assietta. It is a plateau located on the ridge that separates the Dora and Chisone valleys and served by many of roads that run along the ridge line. The plateau is characterized by rounded and passable peaks, although the average height is about 2,500 metres above sea level, up to the impenetrable Orsiera group. Various military roads, mule tracks and paths covered the area, in particular the major Susa-Fenestrelle road. The importance of the Assietta Plateau derived not only by its practicability and possibility to concentrate large forces, but also due to its position in correspondence of a very penetrable area near two critical lines of invasion, which it separates and dominates. This characteristic in 1747 was perfectly understood by both contenders.[17]

Maps and Climate

In the eighteenth century, planning a military operation, such as the 1747 Alpine Offensive, was a complex operation. For at least two centuries, and we can fix this change starting from the middle of the sixteenth century, maps and charts, printed or in manuscript form, became an increasingly present tool in the development phase of a military plan. Conflicts of the magnitude of the War of the Austrian Succession convinced the military leaders to change the perspective of elaboration of the plans. The war was becoming an increasingly complex challenge and the planning process began to move faster and faster from a level of personal knowledge of the terrain, which explains why Bourcet's personal experience was so valuable to Maréchal Belle-Isle, at a level that we can define as 'bird's eye'. This remained closely linked to a strategic and operational level. More detailed information, useful for planning tactical action, was collected in real time on the battlefield rather than on maps.

The French command knew that they had a limited amount of time to secure Assietta, surround Exilles and take the fort. Usually, the French had just over five months, from June to October, to start their operations over the Alpine ridge. The other months of the year were characterized by heavy snowfall, with the result of making any military activities impractical. Thus, in April 1741 the battlefield of Mollwitz, in Silesia, was still covered with snow, while in October 1743 in Val Varaita the Franco-Spanish army had risked remaining in Piedmont, cut off from its starting points, due to the first, intense, snowfalls.

This condition was typical of the Little Ice Age that had been ravaging Europe from the second decade of the fourteenth century. After the climatic optimum of the Late Middle Ages there were several centuries characterized by cold waves, which each time led to an advance of the glaciers. The 1740s were among the coldest years of the eighteenth century, a fact that caused a new subsistence crisis across the European continent, with death rates in some cases very high. The pastor of Mühlstadt, Johann Rudolph Marcus, described

---

17   Up to the Second War World the Assietta Plateau, for the Italian Royal Army was still a very important strategic area for the defense of the Western Alps. BSMT, *Geografia Militare. Considerazioni militari sui Teatri d'Operazioni Terrestri, Aerei, Marittimi e Coloniali*, 1925, pp.13-19); E. Bobbio, *La Valle Chisone*; N. Brancaccio, *Appunti su alcune operazioni militari nelle Alpi* Cozie, 1913; U. Stefanini, *Monografia della Valle della Dora Riparia*, 1913; *Il Piemonte. Saggio e descrizione in scala topografica di una regione naturale*,1922; *Teatro d'Operazioni Italo-Francese*, 1930)

the situation in Saxony and the rest of Europe in his *Nachricht von dem im ietzigen 1740ten Jahre eingefallen ausserordentlichen strengen und langen Winter*: thermometers burst due to the intense cold, bridges shattered, wine froze in cellars and ink in inkwells. Even in Russia it was colder than usual, so much that frozen animals were found in the woods. In Persia people were dying of cold, and in Scandinavia all the lakes and rivers were frozen. The water mills could no longer function, so industrial production had stopped. Those who had to leave the house were having a hard time: in Amsterdam the postillion from South Holland was frozen together with his horse, while the one from Hamburg arrived dead, stiff in the saddle. The same fate had happened to the diligence for Berlin, on which the driver and all the passengers were found frozen dead. Flu epidemics with lethal consequences broke out in France and England. In Paris and the surrounding provinces there were many cases of illness, and a good number of those infected died 'of colds and flu. It is estimated that from the beginning of the year [1740] until

Pierre Joseph de Bourcet (1700-1780). *Colonel* Bourcet was the main architect of the 1747 Alpine campaign. Originally from Val Chisone, he had a deep knowledge of the operational theatre of the Western Alps, and he strongly believed that an offensive action against the Sardinian defences in the Susa Valley was possible. (Engraving after an oil portrait by L.-F. Lecamus, author's collection)

May more than 40,000 people were buried and that, in April alone, more than 4,000 died in hospitals. It is believed that these diseases, epidemics, sudden deaths were caused by this too cold winter, or by what it left in the bodies, although usually the cold puts a stop to plagues'.[18]

Added to this was the rinderpest that flared up in Northern Italy between 1745 and 1749:[19] 40,000 animals died in Piedmont alone, 180,000 in Lombardy[20]. Everyone, some more and

---

18   J.R. Marcus, *Nachricht von dem im ietzigen 1740ten Jahre eingefallen ausserordentlichen strengen und langen Winter* (Leipzig: Johann Christoph Coernern, 1741), pp.15-16.

19   J. Broad, 'Cattle Plague in Eighteen-Century England', in *The Agricultural History Review*, Vol.31, No. 2 (1983), pp.104-115; D. Gasperini, 'Mortalità de' bovini seguita nel territorio trivigiano nell'anno MDCCXI', in D. Perco (ed.), *Malgari e pascoli. L'alpeggio nella provincia di Belluno* (Feltre: Pilotto, 1991), pp.171-204. To understand how this plague was faced see T. Bottani, *Delle Epizoozie, ossia delle epidemie contagiose e non contagiose che influirono negli animali domestici, utili principalmente all'agricoltura del veneto dominio in Italia* (Venezia: Tipografia Picotti, 1819), Vol.VII.

20   S. Cadet, 'Proposta dell'Etiope minerale o Solfuro nero di Mercurio contro le Epizoozie di morbi acuti, ossia di corso rapido degli animali domestici', in *Atti della Reale Accademia dei Lincei*, Tomo

some less, ran for cover. England began buying cereals in Russian regions on the Baltic Sea, in Egypt and in its own colonies in North America, not only wheat and rye, but also rice. Prussia had such a quantity of cereals in its stores that Friedrich II, after having started the War of the Austrian Succession by invading Silesia, an integral part of the Hapsburg Empire, was in a position to bestow seeds on his new farmers, so as to conquer their fidelity. Prices skyrocketed, and family economies, having to spend more on bread, were put to the test; as a result, thousands of recruits showed up for the recruiting teams looking for new cannon fodder.[21]

The Invasion Plan

Bourcet and Belle-Isle had two objectives. The first was to free Genoa from the siege, the second to deliver a sufficiently serious blow to the Sardinian forces to force Carlo Emanuele III to sign a separate peace. The fort of Exilles seemed to be a target within the reach of the forces available in that spring of 1747. Two years earlier, in 1745, during what became known as the 'Diversion of Exilles', *Maréchal* Maillebois had planned a secondary operation with the aim of attracting as many enemy forces as possible to the western Alpine front. The offensive, led by *Lieutenant Général* Comte de Lautrec, began on 28 August 1745, and it had as its objective the conquest of the Fort of Exilles.[22] Built on the bottom of the Susa Valley, the fort was located in a tactically unsustainable position and the Duke of Savoy Victor Amadeus II conquered it quite easily in 1708 during the War of the Spanish Succession. Unfortunately for its garrison, evaluations of mere economic convenience forced the Turin court to update the old French fortification. The works, designed by the engineer Ignazio Bertola, had led to an improvement of the structures, but the fort remained what it was; a splendid artillery target.[23]

Lautrec's corps had a total strength of 17 Franco-Spanish battalions, with a siege park. The encirclement of the fort was completed on 11 September; on 14 September the siege park could leave Briançon to reach the Susa Valley. On 24 September the artillery opened fire on the walls of Exilles. The day before, the French had managed to contain and repel

XXIV – Anno XXIV, Roma 1870, p.189.

21   The most important work on this topic is W. Behringer, *Kulturgeschichte des Klimas. Von der Eiszeit bis zur globalen Erwärmung* (München: Beck C.H., 2010). The notes of Henri Louis Duhamel de Monceau are important for the reconstruction of the climate during the 1747 campaign. The famous French scientist, botanist and agronomist, member and three times president of the Royal Academy of Sciences of France, from 1740 had begun to record meteorological variations; M. De Hamel, 'Observations botanico-météorologiques. Faites au château de Denainvilliers près Pliviers en Gâtinois, pour l'année 1747', in *Histoire de l'Academie Royale des Sciences*, Paris 1747, pp.500-530.

22   E. De Rossi, *La diversione di Exilles. Episodio della Guerra della Prammatica Sanzione* (Roma: Rivista Militare Italiana, 1897), p.5.

23   Regarding the Fort of Exilles, see C. Duffy, *The Fortress in the Age of Vauban and Frederick the Great, 1660-1789* (London: Routledge & Kegan Paul, 1989), pp.101-105; G. Amoretti, P. Petitti (eds), *Dal forte di Exilles alle Alpi. Storia e architettura delle fortificazioni di montagna* (Torino: Omega, 2003); F. Barrera, *I sette forti di Exilles. Metamorfosi architettonica di un complesso fortificato* (Torino: Museo Nazionale della Montagna, 2002); G. Amoretti, P. Petitti (eds), *Il Forte di Exilles di Ignazio Bertola 1729-1745* (Torino: Omega, 2003).

the attempt to break the encirclement of the fort, but the advanced season convinced the French commander to suspend the siege operations and bring the siege artillery park back to the west of the Alps. Maillebois however wanted to keep Lautrec's contingent camped in the upper Val di Susa. At the same time in eastern Piedmont on 27 September the decisive Battle of Bassignana was fought: it was a clear French-Spanish victory and one after another the Sardinian strongholds on the border with Lombardy fell under French control; Tortona, Alessandria (but not its important citadel), Valenza and Asti.

In the Alps, at the end of September the Sardinian forces were encamped near the village of Josseaud in Val Chisone. It consisted of three battalions in all – Meyer, Nizza, 2/Saluzzo – for a total of 2,803 men, under the command of *Maggior Generale* Giovanni Giacomo de Rossi, who was making himself noticed for his total static posture. Deaf to the calls of mountain warfare experts, including *Capitano* Rouzier at the head of the Vaudois militia, he preferred to remain in his positions, which could be enveloped from all sides. On 11 October the French took advantage of the unfortunate tactical situation of the enemy and attacked de Rossi's men: the three Sardinian battalions were routed, losing 416 confirmed casualties, two flags, and a brigade of 50 mules. The Piedmontese commander himself was taken prisoner during the battle.[24] Bourcet, and the entirety of Belle-Isle's general staff, evaluating the experiences of the 1744 and 1745 campaigns, were strictly convinced that the soldiers of the Sardinian army 'were not good for the mountains, the plain is more favourable for them to fight, so I think they will not return to wait for the enemy in these ridges, since they always have been defeated'.[25]

The 1745 diversion had fully fulfilled its function: to attract precious enemy units from the decisive front to a decentralized and secondary sector. In 1747 the operational concept was partially modified. The attack should have taken place as much as possible by surprise, in order to surround the Fort of Exilles and force it to surrender. This conquest would presumably have drawn a significant part of the Sardinian army to the Alps. In a subsequent campaign it would have been possible to isolate, or block, the Forte della Brunetta and proceed to the siege of the Fenestrelle forts. Between March and April 1747, while the army of *Maréchal* Belle-Isle was resting in its winter quarters, Bourcet took the opportunity to prepare two written memoirs that he presented to the *maréchal* regarding plans for the relief to Genoa. In the first memorial, entitled *Mémoire sur le moyens d'entrer en Italie par le Comté de Nice,*[26] it was pointed out that the enemy was now master of all the fortresses and strongholds scattered along the coast between the Var and Genoa: for this reason it was completely impractical for the Franco-Spanish armies to move along the coast to reach Genoa. On the contrary, an attack across the Alps would have forced Carlo Emanuele III to withdraw his men from Genoa to face the enemy offensive, while he had also to ask for the

---

24   AST, Corte, Materie Militari, Imprese, Mazzo 6 d'Addizione, *Relation de la Bataille donné à Josseaud le 11me 8bre 1745 par les Troupes de France sous les ordres de Monsieur de Lautrec, à celle de Sardaigne commandée par Monsieur le General de Rossÿ.*

25   The judgment is by Don Bernard Tholosan, curate of Chianale and Pont in Val Varaita from 1734 to 1783. E. Garellis (ed.), *L'alta valle Varaita a età Settecento. Don Bernard Tholosan e le sue 'Memorie storiche sui fatti d'arme occorsi nella valle di Vraita nella guerra del 1742'* (Cuneo: Società per gli studi storici, archeologici ed artistici della Provincia di Cuneo, 2001), p.208.

26   This memorial is dated 5 April 1747. Bourcet, *Principes de la Guerre de Montagne,* pp.274-277.

help of his imperial ally. The Austrian forces would not be numerous enough to continue the siege operations and conquer Genoa, as the garrison was continuously reinforced by regular Franco-Spanish troops through the 'Genoa Express' convoys. The operations along the coast, as they had been carried out in 1745, were no longer practicable in 1747 as there were two new difficulties.

First of all, the army could only use a single road on the coast, moving corps of 4,000 or 5,000 men, each separated by one- or two-days' march, and also because the route often allowed only two men to march side by side. It was not possible to assemble large corps of troops except in Albenga, Oneglia or Finale: from these places, moreover, the assembled troops could only set off again for one division at a time. The King of Sardinia, on the contrary, could move his army to Ormea, certain of the enemy's line of advance. He could concentrate his forces at any of the meeting points or close their access, separating the divisions from each other or simply interrupting the advance west.

The second difficulty lay in the length of the communications to be protected. The Franco-Spaniards would have been forced to leave troops in the county of Nice to resist an attack from the Col di Tenda. It would also have been necessary to invest the fortresses of Finale and Savona, and possibly Ceva, with all the intrinsic difficulties to transport the artillery necessary for a siege. Everything would have to happen by land transport, as the British fleet dominated the Mediterranean Sea. Furthermore, at that time there was a shortage of draft horses and mules for the transport of tows and supplies. There had also been problems in logistics in 1745, when the Genoese had helped to solve the shortcomings that were found along the way. However, at that moment everything had to be transported from Provence, the starting point of the offensive.

For all these reasons, Bourcet thought it was impractical to replicate the plan of 1745. The right way was presented in the *Projet d'opération concernat les vallées de Suze et de Pragelat.*[27] Originally from Usseaux in the Pragelato Valley, alias Val Chisone, Bourcet knew every inch of that area of operations. The purpose of the manoeuvre was the siege and capture of the Fort of Exilles, after which it was necessary to blockade the Fort of Brunetta and to besiege the Forts of Fenestrelle. The army destined for this operation should have been concentrated in Briançon, and therefore it would have moved beyond the Alps, deploying close to the Colle del Sestriere and the village of Cesana. From here the advance had to continue along the wide ridge that separates the Val Chisone from the Val di Susa until it reached the Assietta plateau. From this point a detached body would have descended towards the bottom of the Val di Susa to destroy the bridge over the Dora between Exilles and Chiomonte, thus interrupting the communication between the fort and the main Piedmontese plain. Exilles would have been invested from the left bank of the Dora by the troops sent through Salbertrand. The fort was to be hit and destroyed by siege artillery, an operation which the campaign of 1745 had shown to be possible.

Meanwhile the main body would have pushed along the ridge from Assietta to Colle delle Finestre and there it would have secured the conquests made while waiting to prepare the siege of Fenestrelle for the 1748 campaign. With the fort of Exilles conquered, the road to Turin was virtually open, on the condition of having a detached body capable of putting the

---

27   This Memorial is dated 23 March 1747. Bourcet, *Principes de la Guerre de Montagne*, pp.278-279.

Brunetta fortress under blockade. However, having Fenestrelle as main objective, it became irrelevant for the French to march on Turin.[28] Carlo Emanuele III would have tried to defend the great stronghold of Val Chisone to the extreme since if it were to be taken by the French Piedmont would really have been at their mercy. Convinced of the solidity of Bourcet's ideas, Belle-Isle returned to his headquarters in May. On the way, at Bagnols, he met the commander of the Spanish army, the Marqués de La Mina;[29] the two generals decided that the main body of both armies would invade the county of Nice, while a detached force would be deployed in the Dauphiné for the attack on Exilles.[30]

So the armies began to prepare for the great Alpine campaign of 1747.

28   The expected exploitation of the success by the French was later confused with the objective of the campaign, the fort of Exilles. For example, here is what the Marquis de Sade wrote during a trip to Piedmont in 1775: 'The entrenched camp of Assietta can be seen very clearly on the mountain chains that enclose you on the right. It is located on the crest of a mountain that seems inaccessible. You know, Madame Countess, the story of the stubborn persistence (effect, it is said, due to a bottle of Spanish wine) which caused the death – in the attack launched against these fortifications – of the Chevalier de Belle-Isle and of seven thousand of our best French troops. The fortifications were defended by the Piedmontese Guards regiment. Everyone, and especially the locals, agree that this attack was useless, and therefore all the more reckless. There are roads in the mountains (and the Chevalier de Belle-Isle must have known them) which allowed an enemy to penetrate as far as the fort of Exilles without worrying about the Assietta. On the contrary, these ensured that a shrewd general would safely arrive at the gates of Turin, leaving behind the Assietta, Exilles and Susa, and all the fortifications of the king of Sardinia. Would not the Chevalier de Belle-Isle have been better off risking the lives of his soldiers in such an attempt than having him slaughtered in homage to a stubborn idea of courage? Just look at the mountains to see the possibility of this manoeuvre, and in the area there are those who offer to be your guide to prove it. These walks, however, are prohibited, and displease the King [of Sardinia]'. D.-A.-F. de Sade (ed. Maurice Lever), *Viaggio in Italia* (Torino: Bollati Boringhieri, 1996), p.9. Yet Belle-Isle's tactical problem was not to infiltrate light troops and reach Susa or the plain of Turin, but rather to secure the Assietta plateau to proceed with the siege of Exilles.
29   Jaime Miguel de Guzmán-Davalos y Spinola, Marqués de la Mina (1690-1767). A veteran of the Italian campaigns, from 1746 he had been appointed commander in chief of all the Spanish forces present in Italy. For his biography see E. Barea Amorena, *Jaime de Guzmán y Spinola, Capitán General de Cataluña, II Marqués de la Mina* (San Vincente – Alicante: Editorial ECU, 2016).
30   An effective summary of Bourcet's planning activity is presented in Wilkinson, *The Defence of Piedmont*, pp.294-297.

2

The Shield of Piedmont

In the mountains of western Piedmont in July 1747 four opposing armies were fighting: the Sardinian army, the Austrian imperial army, the French *Armée Royale* and the Spanish army. The units involved were mainly infantry although, especially on the Franco-Spanish side, the artillery and cavalry units played a not-insignificant role during this campaign.

The combined Austro-Sardinian army that fought at Assietta in 1747 had been assembled in haste, from units not needed at that time at the siege of Genoa or along the front of the Riviera di Ponente.[1] For the Sardinian army, the following units were available:

- Ten infantry battalions on the central Alpine front. 1/Guardie, 2/Savoia; 1/Monfort; 2/ and 3/Kalbermatten; 1/Sicilia; Meyer (one battalion); 3/Roi; Casale (one battalion); Chiablese (one battalion, in garrison in Turin).
- Four infantry battalions in reserve; two of the garrison in Cuneo, one in Fenestrelle and the fourth in Susa. 2/Schulemburg and one battalion of Nizza were stationed in Cuneo. The garrison of the Fenestrelle forts was provided by 1/Keller. 1/ and 2/Salis, one battalion of Corsica and the reserve company of the Torino provided the garrison of the Fort of Brunetta and the Fort of Exilles.
- Ten battalions used for the operations in Liguria: after the end of the siege of Genoa they were placed to control the outlet of the Stura di Demonte Valley at Borgo San Dalmazzo. 2/Guardie; 1/Savoia; 1/Monferrato; Vercelli (1 battalion); Pinerolo (1 battalion); 2/Monfort; 1/Schulembourg; 1/ and 2/ Roi; 2/Piedmont.
- 16 infantry battalions, the bulk of the forces, deployed between Oneglia and Saorgio. 1/Piemonte; 2/Monferrato; 2/Saluzzo; 1/Fucilieri; La Marina (1 battalion); La Regina (1 battalion); Tarantasia (1 battalion); Aosta (1 battalion); Torino (1 battalion); Asti (1 battalion); 1/ and 4/Kalbermatten; 2/Burgsdorff; 2/Baaden; 1/ and 2/Outtiger.

---

1   The whole theatre situation, on the Sardinian and Austrian side, is effectively described in *État des Troupes de S.M. le Roy de Sardaigne destinées en Campagne en 1747; État des Troupes de S.M. Imperiale et Royale destinées en Campagne en 1747*. AST, Corte, Materie Politiche per Rapporto all'Interno, Storie della Real Casa, Mazzo 24; Minutoli, Atlante, Vol.II, *Disegno e Piani de Campamenti, Ordini di Battaglia, Trinceramenti, e Tabelle per l'Istoria Militare nelle Campagne degli Anni 1745, 1746, 1747*, Plate 99.

In addition, 2/Fucilieri, 1/Burgsdorff, 1/Saluzzo and 1/Lombardia were concentrated in Savona, and the single-battalion Reggimento Mondovì was placed in Finale.

The Imperialists had a total of 80 infantry battalions and 38 cavalry squadrons. After the failure of their *Strafexpedition* against Genoa, the *Italien Armee* had split into three large fighting groups:[2]

- The first group, under the orders of the *Feldzeugmeister* Maximilian Ulysses Browne, had 48 infantry battalions and was destined for the defence of Piedmont. The regiments, with their respective battalions, were the following: Traun (1), Hildburgehausen (2), Wallis (2), Alt-Daun (3),Schulemburg (3), Pallavicini (3), Königsegg (2), Mercy (2), Grüne (3), Bärnklau (2), Piccolomini (3), Roth (2), Gyulai (1), Palffy (1), Starhemberg (2), Andlau (3), Colloredo (1), Andrassy (3), Sprecher (3), Forgách (1), Deutschmeister (3), 2,000 Warasdiners.
- The second group, under the orders of *Feldmarschall-Leutnant* Nádasdy, with 15 infantry battalions and 17 cavalry squadrons, was encamped near Ovada, with the task of covering any offensive enemy returning from Genoa. Seven battalions of line infantry: Jung-Daun (2), Esterházy (3), Vettes (2); two corps of Croatian and Slavonian light infantry, about 3,900 effectives, comparable to a force of eight battalions; cavalry squadrons of DR Hessen-Darmstadt (7), HR Splényi (5), HR Trips (5).
- The third group, 13 infantry battalions under the orders of *Feldmarschall-Leutnant* Novati, were sent to the west and they were grouped with the Sardinian forces under Leutrum, with the task of defending the Ligurian West. Jung-Daun (1), Starhemberg (1), Mercy (1), Palffy (2), Forgách (1), Alt-Wallis (1), Bärnklau (1), Hagenbach (1), Gyulai (1), Königsegg (1), a detached corps of Warasdiners.

In addition there were two other detached corps:

- 21 cavalry squadrons, which were quartered near Savigliano in Piedmont: CR Portugal (7), CR Lobkowitz (7), CR Berlichingen (7).
- Four infantry battalions in garrison in Lombardy, intended to be aggregated to the Sardinian reserve in the Chisone and Susa valley. One battalion Traun, 3/Forgách, 3/Colloredo, one battalion Hagenbach.

As can be seen, the combined Austro-Sardinian armies in the summer of 1747 were totally unbalanced towards the south/southwest along the front of the western Riviera. Covering a second front was possible, but it would have required a speed of planning and decision that, in 1745 and 1746, the Sardinian general staff had been totally lacking. Furthermore, the 10 Sardinian battalions would have had to fix an opponent which, according to the latest experiences gained on the Alpine front, in the best of cases could end in a disastrous defeat. The expectations of success, therefore, were by no means taken for granted and, indeed,

---

2   Minutoli, *Atlante*, Vol.II, Plate 99. The distribution of the Austrian regiments is taken from documents in the Kriegsarchiv in Wien, KA, Alten Feldakten I-VI, Krieg in Italien, 1747: *Ständ und Dienst Tabella*, 18 Juni 1747, 581, and the *Diensdtbarer Stand der östreichischen Streitmacht im Genuesischen für Juni 1747*, by Rothkirch, 'Der Feldzug 1747 in Italien', p.31.

the need for a retreat behind the Exilles-Colle delle Finestre-Fenestrelle defensive line was almost certain.

Chain of Command

Operations in the Alps were under Sardinian control. The supreme command of the army was in the hands of Carlo Emanuele III, king of Sardinia; in reality the king had not fought at the head of his troops since the Battle of Bassignana in September 1745,[3] and the real thinking brain was now the Minister of War Giovanni Battista Lorenzo Bogino, who concentrated in his hands both the diplomatic and military powers. He was in fact acting simultaneously as plenipotentiary minister and the army chief of staff.[4]

There were about 60 governors directly under the control of the Ministry of War who directly managed the fortresses, garrisons and territorial militias intended to defend the territories of the kingdom and to support field operations.[5] In times of war they could mobilize all the resources existing in the areas they managed, in such a way as to perform a valid blocking action against any enemy threat. For the 1747 campaign in the Western Alps, and the Assietta campaign specifically, the Minister of War directly activated four governorates: Susa, Pragelato, Fenestrelle and Pinerolo. This involved the call of a certain number of militia units, the census of all human and material resources available and, if necessary, their removal to prevent them from being used by the enemy. The governors were ordered to raise a precise number of militia units, a levy which had to be agreed with the local communities based on the quantity of men available to serve. They also had to provide the quantity of weapons that could be supplied to them by the royal armouries present in the area or, if necessary, directly from the great Turin Arsenal. The availability of these armaments in 1747 was by no means taken for granted, given the shortage that was occurring in central depots. The ability of these gentlemen to create an important relational network at the local level able to provide first-hand information on the enemy forces present in the area was also fundamental; civil traffic and the movement of convoys had not been blocked by the belligerents, and it could easily happen that a merchant from Susa had the possibility, upon agreement between the parties, to go to the Dauphiné or in Savoy and carry out his business.

---

3   There are some who see in Carlo Emanuele III a leader of exceptional quality; C. Paoletti, *Capitani di Casa Savoia* (Roma: USSME, 2007) and *Dal Ducato all'Unità, Tre secoli e mezzo di storia militare piemontese* (Roma: USSME, 2011). For a more traditional interpretation, see Carutti, *Storia del Regno di Carlo Emanuele III*; G.B. Semeria, *Storia del Re di Sardegna Carlo Emanuele il Grande* (Torino: Reale Tipografia, 1831); G. Quazza, *Le riforme in Piemonte nella prima metà del Settecento* (Modena: Società editrice modenese, 1957). The figure of a military commander is barely sketched in G. Ricuperati, 'Il Settecento', in P.Merlin, C. Rosso, G. Symcox, G. Ricuperati (eds), *Il Piemonte Sabaudo. Stato e Territori in Età Moderna* (Torino: UTET, 1994), pp.471-514.
4   This overlapping of tasks can be seen in particular from the reading of the transmission of orders to field commanders and governors. AST, Sezioni Riunite, Ministero della Guerra, Regia Segreteria di Guerra, Lettere ai Governatori, Mazzo 42, Mazzo 43.
5   P. Bianchi, 'I documenti sui governatori nel Piemonte del Settecento', in L. Antonielli and C. Donati (eds), *Al di là della storia militare: una ricognizione sulle fonti* (Soveria Mannelli: Rubbettino, 2004), pp.77-98.

His Majesty the King of Sardinia, Carlo Emanuele III (1701-1773), in the uniform of a general commanding the Sardinian troops. During the War of the Austrian Succession he was present in no less than four battles, three of which were defeats. From 1744 onwards, the strategic and operational management of the conflict fell increasingly into the hands of the Minister of War, Bogino. (Painting by Giovanni Duprà, courtesy of the Centro Studi e Ricerche storiche sull'Architettura Militare del Piemonte CeSRAMP)

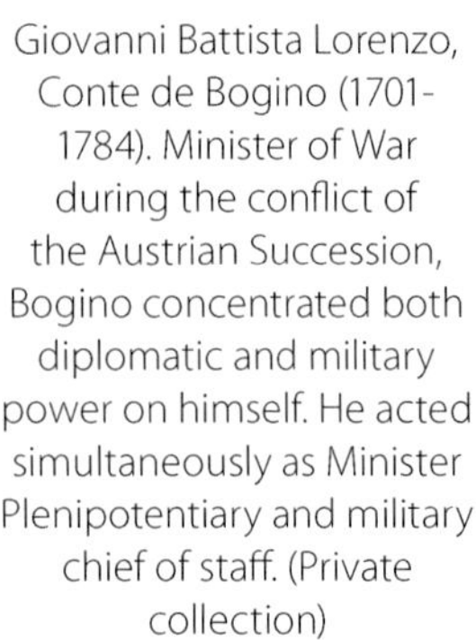

Giovanni Battista Lorenzo, Conte de Bogino (1701-1784). Minister of War during the conflict of the Austrian Succession, Bogino concentrated both diplomatic and military power on himself. He acted simultaneously as Minister Plenipotentiary and military chief of staff. (Private collection)

These were valuable human intelligence sources, which the governors handled themselves. This, of course, could also happen on the opponent's side.[6]

The pawns of the armies ran on this administrative-military chessboard. The commanders in chief of the armies involved received direct orders from Turin regarding the area of operations; the governors in turn received detailed provisions regarding logistical support and which of their troops, if any, were to be attached to the army in the field. The territorial appurtenances were well marked, and the move from a sector to another had to be planned in Turin, and finally authorized by written order. The king and the minister, assisted by the first engineer, Count Ignazio Bertola d'Exilles, during the planning at the strategic and operational level, chose and appointed the officers who were to command the armies in the campaign. For the defence of the Alps in 1747 the choice fell on Giovanni Battista Cacherano, Conte di Bricherasio, promptly promoted to *Luogotenente Generale*, the highest operational rank in the Sardinian army; thus he was guaranteed independent command, without any interference from the Governors. He would have had *Maggior Generale* Francesco Alciati and *Brigadiere Generale* Federico Martinengo, Conte da Barco, under his command. Later, only after the diplomatic intervention of Minister Bogino, four battalions of imperial infantry under the command of *General-Feldwachtmeister* Colloredo, were placed under the orders of Bricherasio. As had happened previously, the Imperialists tended not to recognize the corresponding Sardinian ranks as their equivalent, as noted in a contemporary account:

> The Germans, after their supreme rank of field marshal [*Feldmarschall*], have that of general of artillery [*Feldzeugmeister*], and then that of general of cavalry [*General der Kavallerie*], and after this the rank of general marshal lieutenant [*Feldmarschall-Leutnant*], and finally that of major general [*General-Feldwachtmeister*]. We used the custom of the French, who, after their supreme rank of marshal [*maréchal*], have the rank of lieutenant general [*lieutenant général*], which is succeeded by the rank of field marshal [*maréchal de camp*], and after this the rank of brigadier. Now due to this difference in the denomination, it happened that general marshal lieutenants claimed to have the same rank as our lieutenant general [*luogotenente generale*], and the major generals with our field marshals [*marescialli di campo = maggior generale*], and they did not want to recognize brigadiers as generals; our lieutenant generals, being only one degree from the supreme marshal, claimed to have the same rank as the artillery and cavalry generals, and likewise the field marshals with

---

6   The whole section of the Materie Militari of the National Archive of Torino, Corte, is a great intelligence database, where dispatches and reports destined for operational and tactical planning are collected. Collections of information from 'Humint' sources are rarer to trace. Concerning the 1747 campaign, see AST: Corte, Materie Militari, Imprese, Mazzo 7 da inventariare; Sezioni Riunite, Ministero della Guerra, Regia Segreteria di Guerra, Lettere ai Governatori, Mazzo 42, Mazzo 43. Other traces relating to the collection of information are also kept at Kriegsarchiv, Wien: KA, Alten Feldacten, Krieg in Italien, 16. The French also had built their own data collection network, as confirmed in Arvers and de Vault, *Guerre de la Succession d'Autriche*, Vol.II, pp.729-731. The local clergy were often suspected by Sardinian authorities, with some basis, of being a source of information for adversaries. See in this sense Garellis (ed.), *L'alta valle Varaita a età Settecento*.

the lieutenant marshals, because they were no longer separated from their supreme rank; and for the same reason our brigadiers were equal to the major generals.[7]

Even allowing for some mangling of the Austrian ranks, this makes it clear that the situation was rather a mess.

The presence of Alciati and, above all, of Bricherasio would have eliminated any doubts regarding the hierarchical scale on the battlefield. Since there were no brigades with a previously established task organization, but ad hoc units based on the available forces and the missions that the commander received from the top, the chain of command for the 1747 campaign can be summarized as follows:

- *Luogotenente Generale* Conte di Bricherasio, commander-in-chief of the Austro-Sardinian forces deployed in the Alta Val di Susa–Val Chisone sector, including the Forts of Exilles and Fenestrelle.
- *Maggior Generale* Francesco Alciati. He functioned as the deputy commander of the Austro-Sardinian forces in the sector of the central Alps in July 1747. He replaced Bricherasio in the latter's absence, as he did in the western sector of the battlefield on 19 July.
- *Brigadiere Generale* Martinengo and *General-Feldwachtmeister* Colloredo. They would be responsible for the tactical command of the forces present in the theatre. In all there were 10 Sardinian and four Austrian battalions, for a total of 14 battalions. Each officer had the possibility of commanding a rather heavy brigade of 7 infantry battalions. These were never gathered in one place; only 10 of these were present at the Assietta camp, divided into two distinct brigades of five battalions.
- Territorial militias. *Maggiore* Perrone, Pragelato militia; *Capitano* Rouzier, Waldensian militia; *Cavalier* Tana, Val di Susa militia. These officers each commanded a group of 500 militiamen, whose main function was to screen the units present in the sector and to provide the fundamental collection of information directly on behalf of the supreme commander.

Command and Control, Leadership and Command Style

Sardinian land operations were almost always planned in Turin. The king, the Minister of War Bogino and some of his senior officers who enjoyed sovereign trust usually gathered around a table to evaluate what to do. One of these was Ignazio, Conte Bertola, commander of the corps of engineers. War plans were transformed into written operations orders, which rarely exceeded four or eight handwritten pages. Once an operations order was received by the sector commander, usually a *luogotenente generale*, he summoned the brigade commanders under him and, if possible, the regimental commanders, to verbally inform them of the orders received. Together they formulated a battle plan which, through military

---

7   G. Galleani d'Agliano, *Memorie Storiche sulla Guerra del Piemonte dal 1741 al 1747* (Torino: Stamperia Reale, 1840), pp.105-106.

messengers, had to be communicated to the commanders of the basic tactical units, the battalions; although, in some cases, and almost always in operations in the mountains, particular assignments could also be detailed for company commanders. On the battle-field orders were transmitted verbally or through musical instruments, especially drums; a precise sequence indicated the advance or retreat, the opening of fire, and so on. Three languages were spoken in the Sardinian army: Italian, French and German. The regiments were formed with linguistically homogeneous companies where the same language was used by soldiers as by the officers. This was to make sure that the orders given were correctly understood and executed.[8]

The human and material resources of the Sardinian army were always scarce. This made the loss of any single battalion a difficult one to replace, if not in the medium/long term. Therefore, the doctrine of command and combat of the Piedmontese armies was always characterized by a strong ability to plan and conduct defensive operations, while the offensive ones were always characterized by a confused and, in essence, not very effective conduct. Having chosen this approach there was no need to develop a command style based on the 'Mission Tactics', the *Auftragstaktik* of German thinking, whereby the field commander was given considerable freedom to accomplish his mission. In those years in Prussia the approach was as follows:

> [T]he officer must be considered more than a machine that works only when acti-vated. He must often act without orders. There are occasions when an officer has to command or move a single platoon, or give it special instructions. Sometimes the orders he is given are inadequate, or he finds himself in new and unprecedented circumstances. In all these cases the officer will be able to help himself more easily if he has an understanding of the manoeuvre in its entirety, of its goal and of its part to achieve the goal.[9]

In Piedmont, on the other hand, the operations orders, drawn up on the desks of the Minister of War, were delivered directly into the hands of the commanders in the field. They had the obligation to transmit every single detail to their subordinates. The most capable and intelligent officers fully grasped the danger of this approach, since usually they had to face enemy forces with better manoeuvring skills and greater independence of command. In 1746, the engineer Vedani, who with Bricherasio would plann the defences of the Assietta plateau in 1747, received an operations order where he had to organize the siege of Valenza, occupied by the Franco-Spanish forces; it was a very detailed instruction, written and signed in Turin by the commander of the engineers, Bertola. Unfortunately, 90 kilometres away, the tactical

---

8   Field regulations and tactical exercises were also printed in French-German bilingual volumes to allow the Swiss troops to better integrate into the Sardinian army. These books, distributed among officers and non-commissioned officers, are today extremely rare and interesting documents. *Recuil de ce qui se pratique dans le Régiment Suisse de Saconay, au service de Sa Majesté Britanique persentement dan les Armées de Son Altesse Roiale de Savoie, sous les Ordres de Mylord Galloway, à l'égard de la Justice & Police du Régiment: avec l'exercice Militaire, mis en François & en Allemand, pour l'intelligence des Officiers qui n'entendent que l'une de ces deus Langues*, (Ivreé: Unknown Publisher, 1694).

9   F.M. Rohr, *Des Herrn Grafen Turpin von Crissé. Versuche über die Kriegskunst* (Potsdam: Johann George Bauer, 1756) Vol.I, p.xvi.

situation was different from how the Secretary of War and the First Engineer remembered or simply imagined it.

> [Vedani] complained that his bread had been cut too minutely, while he had been given a plan of the whole attack made by Commendatore Bertola, on which everything that had to be done had been outlined in detail, and Baron von Leutron and Signor Vedani had to conform completely to him.[10]

This command approach led to the affirmation of the combination of general officer-engineer officer. This was the peculiar feature of the Sardinian army during the conflict. The campaign of 1744 formed the efficient tandem composed of Baron Leutrum and the captain of engineers Lorenzo Bernardino Pinto, Conte di Barri. The two had fought together for the first time at the siege of Cuneo. Since then, Leutrum wanted Barri to be under his command. The general and the engineer were the material executors of the 1746 offensive and their collaboration continued until the end of the conflict. The tactical and operational skills of the German general and the technical skills of Pinto worked very well due to the 'trench warfare' characteristics of the years of the 1746-1748 campaigns in the Ligurian Riviera. Another less known duet, but no less effective from a tactical point of view, was precisely the one formed in the summer of 1747 by Giovanni Battista Cacherano, Conte di Bricherasio, and by the captain of engineers Giuseppe Vedani. Bricherasio, an unimaginative commander, who survived the rout of his regiment, La Regina, at the battle of Madonna dell'Olmo, was however a tenacious officer, the ideal man to oversee the defence of the entrenched 'blocking' camps placed to defend Piedmont's borders. He fully understood the value of Vedani with whom 'he had been commissioned, at the end of June, to carefully visit the mountain ridges and the places we have talked about and to choose, with engineer Vedani, the places that could be entrenched in order to make them stronger and thus remedy as far as possible the disproportion in numbers'.[11]

Although all of them received their ranks by the king himself, the officers were recruited by the individual regiments, on the proposal of the colonel, and of the military and civil authorities to whom they responded. Generally, each regiment had a list of aspirants, often used for years as alternates during the licenses and absences of the holders, from whom they drew, not always respecting their seniority, those necessary to cover the vacancies. Of course, there was an ample space for children, brothers and relatives, so each regiment was monopolized by a small number of families in the province of its recruitment and garrison. As in all armies of the period, the fracture between noble officers and those not titled, otherwise known as *roturiers*, was very present, with its aftermath of resentment and envy. A well-known and well-studied phenomenon,[12] in campaign it produced situations like this one, described effectively by *Leutnant* Gorani at the camp of the imperial army of Zittau in 1757:

---

10   Galleani D'Agliano, *Memorie Storiche*, p.298.
11   AST, Corte, Memorie politiche per rapporto all'interno, Storie della Real Casa Mazzo 24; Minutoli, *Relation des Campagnes*, Vol.V, p.193.
12   Loriga, Soldati, pp.40-70; L. Tuetey, *Les Officiers sous l'ancien régime. Nobles roturiers* (Paris: Plon-Nourrit, 1908).

The new colonel treated me with kindness, but not as much as the one who had enlisted me. The captain, to whom I had been assigned, forgave me nothing and he spoke to me with extreme harshness. He was a man of fortune [that is, he was not a nobleman and he had gained his ranks over the years], who detested nobility: he could not be persuaded that a nobleman could have common sense. The senior lieutenant of the company was also a man of fortune, very rude, and the second lieutenant, who was the son of a blacksmith, no less brutal. The other officers in the regiment, except four, were nothing but old men, addicted to wine and girls, who gave me no edifying examples at all. Of those four, of which I could offer a flattering eulogy, three were in the grenadiers, who formed a separate body, detached from the regiment. The fourth was Lieutenant Colonel Baron Terzi, a man of true merit, and who gave me a lot of instructions.[13]

So not all that glittered was gold, and even the officers of the 'fighting' regiments, the Swiss ones, were viewed with suspicion and annoyance. Within an army with few resources at its disposal, they seemed to absorb a large part of the funds allocated by the Crown. The accusations, then, came not only from Piedmontese colleagues, but also from other foreign infantry officers, who did not fail to bring their recriminations to the attention of the king.[14]

The Commanders

There were four officers who carried key responsibilities for command duties; three Piedmontese and one Austrian. They were Giovanni Battista Cacherano, Conte di Bricherasio, Francesco Alciati, Federico Martinengo and Antonio Colloredo.

As soon as it was realized in Turin that the French could launch an offensive on the Alps, it became necessary to choose who would command the troops in that sector which, moreover, was not even the most important, nor the most threatened. On the Ligurian front gravitated the main effort of the Franco-Spanish armies, and for this reasons the best commanders and the most efficient units were sent to western Liguria. The more capable and younger generals who had emerged during the conflict, such as Leutrum, Alfieri, Chiesa di Cinzano and Monfort, were all sent in Liguria. The only one at that time could be used in a rear service was Giovanni Battista Cacherano, Conte di Bricherasio, at that time governor of Savona.

Born on 14 November 1706 in the little Piedmontese town of Bricherasio, he was known for having raised in 1734 at his own expense a regiment of infantry of national ordinance, called La Regina – The Queen – in honour of Queen Polissena d'Assia, wife of Carlo Emanuele III, becoming the first colonel. The opportunities for fighting at the head of his own unit came during the War of the Austrian Succession, when in 1742 he participated at the capture of Modena, and then he fought in 1743 in Val Varaita. Promoted *brigadiere generale* on

---

13   G. Gorani (ed. A. Casati), *Memorie di giovinezza e di Guerra* (Milano: Mondadori, 1936), p.75.
14   AST, Corte, Materie Militari, Levata Truppe Straniere, Mazzo I d'addizione, *Promemoria del Principe di Baden contenente alcune rimostranze dal medesimo fatte all'occasione della riforma del suo Reggimento, Colle determinazioni date da S.M. in proposito.*

22 January 1744, during the hard campaign of 1744 he was present, but not directly involved, at the battle of Pietralunga in July. When the front moved to the plains, and the siege of Cuneo started, Bricherasio took part in the Battle of Madonna dell'Olmo. The action was badly planned by the Sardinans and conducted even worse, and the fight ended in a harsh Sardinian defeat. The Reggimento La Regina, deployed on the left flank of the first line, was the unit that suffered the highest losses; at the end of the day it counted 58 dead, 75 wounded and 206 missing or prisoners and at least one of its battalions was broken, losing a flag.[15]

Wounded in action, Bricherasio recovered quickly, also comforted by the promotion to *maggior generale* that he received on 9 May 1745. Transferred to Savona and Finale, he remained in command of these strongholds until his appointment as *luogotenente generale* and commander of the Sardinian forces in the Upper Val di Susa and Chisone and the fortifications of Exilles

Giovanni Battista Cacherano di Bricherasio (1706-1782). One of the generals who emerged during the conflict, he was a perfect product of Sardinian combat doctrine: methodical, fussy, obedient to orders, prudent and strictly static at a tactical level. (Private collection)

and Fenestrelle. On 22 June 1747 he received the transfer order for Piedmont. The choice of appointing Bricherasio did not depend, of course, only on the fact that he was the first available commander. The tragedy of 1745, when the brigade commanded by *Maggior Generale* de Rossi was surprised by the expeditionary force of the Comte de Lautrec in the upper Val Chisone, should not have been repeated. Bricherasio was one of the 'newcomers', one of those senior officers that the war had brought up in the hierarchy; he was a very meticulous man, attentive observer and always concentrated in his work. His main defects were to leave little freedom of action to his subordinates, hypercritical towards their work, and always ready to intervene personally in actions that did not foresee his presence. However, he was

---

15   BRT, Manoscritto Militare 154, *État que le Roy de Sardaigne a eu de Tuez, Blessés, Perdus ou Prisonnier de Guerre à l'Affaire de N.D, de l'Orme le 20 7bre 1744.*

able to immediately identify dangers and strengths in a particular situation. All these qualities and defects put together made him a perfect product of the Sardinian fighting doctrine: methodical, fussy, loyal to orders, prudent and rigorously static on a tactical level.[16]

Another officer was awaiting Bricherasio in Val Chisone, a person who owed his career to what he demonstrated on the field; *Maggior Generale* Francesco Alciati. Born in Vercelli on 19 July 1694, he enlisted in the army of the Duke of Savoy as an ensign in the Reggimento Maffei. Later he was transferred to the Reggimento Vercelli, in which on 5 September 1713 he obtained the rank of *luogotenente*. On 6 April 1714 he was *capitano, maggiore* on 4 February 1734, and then *luogotenente colonnello* on 13 March 1735. Commander of Reggimento Vercelli since 5 January 1742 with the rank of *colonnello,* he valiantly led the unit at the siege of Cuneo in 1744. Promoted *brigadiere generale* 11 May 1745 he was destined to command a body made up of four battalions and militia units with the task of blocking the upper Val Tanaro during the 1745 campaign. The same year, on 27 February, he was transferred to the National Ordinance infantry to the command of the Reggimento Monferrato. He took part in the campaign of 1746 against the Republic of Genoa, during which he managed to escape the annihilation of his forces by the Genoese militia during the battle of Zuccarello. Alciati was promoted *maggior generale* on 18 January 1747, and he was later transferred to the Alpine front. Tenacious and always ready to react effectively to emergencies, he had, unlike Bricherasio, the bad habit of dealing with his subordinates in an often intimidating and contemptuous way. The events of the battle of 19 July, and the clash with the Conte di San Sebastiano, were typical aspects of his character.[17]

Federico Martinengo, Conde da Barco was directly under Alciati. He was a subject of the Republic of Venice who had been in the service of the House of Savoy since 14 January 1726, when he had obtained the rank of *capitano* in the Reggimento Sicilia. *Maggiore* in 1735, *luogotenente colonnello* in 1739, Martinengo had finally been promoted *colonnello* on 2 March 1744, but only in February of the following year did he obtain the command of the Reggimento Sicilia. Placed at the command of the Modena garrison in 1745, on 29 March of the following year, by his own initiative, he decided to attack the head bridge over the Enza stream, garrisoned by the Spanish infantry:

> [T]he [Spanish] marquis Castellar tried to pass the Lenza as soon as possible, and burnt the bridge so that the Nadasti could not follow him closely; but Count Martinengo, having left Modena at the same time, went to the other bridge that the Spaniards had over the Lenza on the Romera road, which Castellar had fortified with a strong redoubt on the Modenese side and always there were held about three hundred men on guard. In spite of this, Martinengo, having with him about five hundred soldiers from his garrison, all people very well animated for every enterprise, attacked the redoubt with such force and vigour that, despite the intrepid defence, he became master of the redoubt and the bridge after having killed half

---

16   For a brief biography of Giovanni Battista Cacherano di Bricherasio, see the entry in the DBI, edited by Valerio Castronovo: <http://www.treccani.it/enciclopedia/giovanni-battista-cacherano-conte-di-bricherasio_(Dizionario-Biografico)>, accessed 20 January 2022.

17   The bibliographic data of Francesco Alciati are collected, in a fragmentary way, in Alberti, *La Battaglia dell'Assietta,* pp.73-79.

of the Spaniards who defended it and made the survivors prisoners of war, losing about a hundred of his own and sustaining a serious wound himself, from which he then found it hard to recover.[18]

For this action he was promoted to the rank of *brigadiere generale* on 17 January 1747 and assigned to the Alpine front.

The imperial contingent in Piedmont was commanded by Graf Antonio Colloredo-Melz und Wallsee (14 November 1707–17 March 1785). He was the son of Graf Gerolamo (1674–1726), a leading figure in the Austrian imperial administration, who had been the first governor of Moravia between 1714 and 1717 and, subsequently, governor of Milan. Antonio was his second son, and he was destined for a military career. In 1728 he was enlisted into the imperial army; he soon proved to be a capable and skilled officer, and the War of the Polish Succession was his stepping stone to the higher ranks. In 1737 he became *Oberst* of the prestigious IR Hoch-und-Deutschmeister. The outbreak of the War of the Austrian Succession was for Antonio Colloredo the most important war trial in which he took part. In 1742, in fact, he received the rank of *General-Feldwachtmeister* and in 1744 he raised an infantry regiment with his own name, the IR Colloredo. Destined for the Italian front in 1747, by decision of the commander of the imperial troops in Italy *Feldzeugmeister* Browne, he was placed in command of the imperial brigade destined to fight in the Cottian Alps. A methodical officer, attentive and loyal to orders, during the 1747 campaign he demonstrated a strong sense of adaptation to the tactical situations of fighting at high altitude, a completely new reality for him and for his men.[19]

The Army of the King of Sardinia

The infantry was always the main element of the Sardinian army. The defence of the kingdom relied of eight regiments of infantry of national ordinance, 10 regiments of infantry of provincial ordinance, two regiments of German infantry, three regiments of Swiss infantry, two regiments of Italian infantry and one regiment of foreign infantry (mixed), divided as follows:

- Infantry of National Ordinance: Reggimento Guardie, 2 bns: Reggimento Savoia, 2 bn.; Reggimento Monferrato, 2 bns.; Reggimento Piemonte, 2 bns.; Reggimento Saluzzo, 2 bns.; Reggimento Fucilieri, 2 bns.; Reggimento La Marina, 1 bn.; Reggimento La Regina, 1 bn.
- Infantry of Provincial Ordinance: Reggimento Chiablese, 1 bn.; Reggimento Tarantasia, 1 bn.; Reggimento Aosta, 1 bn.; Reggimento Nizza, 1 bn.; Reggimento Torino 1 bn.;

---

18   Galleani D'Agliano, *Memorie Storiche*, pp.292-293.
19   C. von Wurzbach, *Biographisches Lexicon des Kaiserthums Oesterreich* (Wien: L.C. Zamarski, 1856-1891), Vol.II, pp.419-420; G.B. di Crollalanza, *Memorie Storico-genealogiche della Stirpe Waldsee-Mels, e più particolarmente dei Conti di Colloredo. Con documenti* (Pisa: Direzione del Giornale Araldico, 1875), pp.234-235; L. von Leitnertreu, *Geschichte der Wiener-Neustädter Militärakademie* (Hermannstadt: Theodor Steinhaussen, 1852), p.90.

Reggimento Mondovì, 1 bn.; Reggimento Vercelli, 1 bn.; Reggimento Asti, 1 bn.; Reggimento Pinerolo, 1 bn.; Reggimento Casale, 1 bn.
- German Infantry: Reggimento Schoulembourg, 2 bns.; Reggimento Rehbinder, 2 bns.
- Swiss Infantry: Reggimento Rietmann/Kalbermatten, 3 bns.; Reggimento Guibert, 2 bns.; Reggimento Diesbach, 2 bns.
- Italian Infantry: Reggimento Sicilia, 1 bn.; Reggimento Lombardia, 1 bn.
- Foreign Infantry: Reggimento Audibert, 2 bns.

In 1742-1743, another 11 foreign battalions were raised:

- Seven Swiss infantry battalions; one Bernese (3/Diesbach; 3/Roguin in 1744 and then 3/Roi), one from Luzern (3/Guibert), three from the Grisons (Reggimento Reydt, which became Salis in 1746), two from Luzern (Reggimento Keller).
- Two battalions of German infantry; Reggimento Baaden-Dourlac.
- Two battalions of Italian infantry; 2/Sicilia, 2/Lombardia.

In 1744 another four foreign battalions were raised, three of which created new regiments:

- Two Swiss infantry battalions; Reggimento Meyer (Glaris-Appenzell), 1 bn.; 4/Rietman (from Valais; became 4/Kalbermatten 24 May 1744).
- Two battalions of Italian infantry; Reggimento Sardegna, 1 bn.; Reggimento Corsica, 1 bn.

The regiments of the infantry of national ordinance, made up of subjects from the mainland states who presented themselves as volunteers, were generally organized into two battalions, and the battalion was the basic tactical unit, whose peacetime strength was about 600 men. Each had nine companies of fusiliers and one of grenadiers, in addition to the regimental staff.

During the War of the Austrian Succession, more precisely in 1744, the battalion strength rose to 700 men. In 1747 the battalions were further strengthened, reaching 800 men, although there were often variations based on the type of regiment.[20] The composition of the companies included a captain, a lieutenant, a standard bearer, four quartermasters, two sergeants, four corporals, a drummer and a variable number of soldiers, usually 70.[21]

The men were all volunteers, even if the very concept of 'volunteer' must be contextualised. The soldiers of the eighteenth century were young, and 62.6 percent of the total were under 22. Far from dreaming of a life in the service of their homeland, these men enlisted

---

20   BRT, Manoscritto Militare 155; Memorie politiche per rapporto all'interno, Storie della Real Casa, Mazzo 21, 22; Minutoli, *Relation des Campagnes*. The increase in the strength of the battalions, which should be investigated with greater precision, seems to have already been decided with the Royal Decree (*Regio Viglietto*) on 10 June 1744. Probably the war events made an effective increase possible only between 1747 and 1748. *Raccolta per ordine di Materie delle Leggi cioè Editti, Patenti, manifesti, Ecc. emanate negli stati di terraferma sino all'8 dicembre 1798 dai Sovrani della Real Casa di Savoia dai loro Ministri, Magistrati, Ecc. compilata dagli Avvocati Felice Amato e Camillo Duboin proseguita dall'Avvocato Alessandro Muzio colla direzione dell'intendente Giacinto Cottin* (Torino: Davico e Picco, 1863), Book 26, Vol.28, pp.221-224.
21   *Raccolta per ordine di Materie delle Leggi cioè Editti, Patenti, manifesti, Ecc.*, Book 26, Vol.28, p.196.

because they had no work, due to problems with the law, disagreements with their families or lack of credible means of support. The recruiting officers were chosen by their regimental commanders for their storytelling skills, and they managed to 'get into families and meddle in all the affairs of the village'. It was important

> [T]o go to all the country fairs, to not propose anything for the first two or three days and to wait for the money to start running out, that's when the peasants are ready to enlist. With a little wit and precision you can take advantage of quarrels. There are always riots on these occasions and, rather than dealing with justice, young people enlist.[22]

The human material was of this quality, and it was then a duty of the battalion commanders to transform a hodgepodge of riotous and ill-disposed people into real soldiers through effective training. In some regiments, such as in Guardie and Savoia, this process was fully successful, elsewhere, especially where the officers were more attentive to the social climb than to the efficiency of their units, much less.[23]

The regiments of infantry of provincial ordinance were composed of conscripts enrolled in each of the provinces of the kingdom. These conscripts served for a limited period of time during the year. In the regiments it was expected that three percent of those suitable were recruited, chosen or drawn from among men aged between 18 and 40, possibly belonging to large families that would therefore able to replace them in case of need. The provisions of 1714 provided for the 'assembly', that is the meeting for the purpose of review and training, three times a year for the companies and once for six consecutive days in May for the complete battalion/regiment. Company assemblies were abolished two years later, replaced by two battalion-level training cycles of 10 days each, in keeping with agricultural work in May and October.[24]

Usually recruitment was a choice, coordinated by the community and by officers of the so-called *Prima Ispezione* (Primary Inspection), the War Ministry office responsible for recruit selections; that choice often fell on a crowd of miserable, crippled, homeless people without the ability to afford the price of a replacement. The colonels, in front of such a mass of individuals, could not help but complain by force to the officers of the *Prima Ispezione*, who chose the soldiers, or resign themselves to the command of a shoddy regiment.[25] Unlike fellow commanders of Infantry of National Ordinance, they did not have enough time to turn an awkward recruit into a trained soldier. This was also well known to the supreme command; for this reason, these units were used as much as possible only for garrison duties. The number of troops in the provincial regiments was increased with the *Regio Viglietto* on 5 May 1742, and the total strength of the units, each of a single battalion, went from 600 to

---

22   Please refer to the unsurpassed text: Loriga, *Soldati*, pp.117-119.
23   On drill see C. Duffy, *The Military Experience in the Age of Reason* (London: Routledge & Kegan Paul, 1998), pp.71-76.
24   Bianchi, *Onore e Mestiere*, p.95.
25   Loriga, *Soldati*, p.132.

Uniform of the Reggimento Guardie in 1744. The print depicts a private soldier in the official uniform used in 1744; in the campaign he would also have worn a pair of white gaiters to protect his stockings and shoes. (AST, Corte, Biblioteca antica, jb III 16)

700 men.[26] In 1747 the provincial infantry regiments saw their battalions expanded to reach the strength of 800 men each. Only the Reggimento Chiablese and Reggimento Tarantasia remained with a battalion of 700 men; as also happened for the Reggimento Savoia, the Spanish occupation of transalpine provinces did not guarantee a constant flow of new recruits.[27] From 1735 a reserve company was created in each provincial regiment, which served as a depot to replace the gaps in the regiment of national ordinance.[28] In reality, the term 'company' disguised something more akin to a weak second battalion, generally used as a garrison in the various strongholds. The composition of these reserve companies,

---

26 *Raccolta per ordine di Materie delle Leggi cioè Editti, Patenti, manifesti, Ecc.*, Book 26, Vol.28, pp.556, 572.

27 On the recruiting in Savoy, see J. Nicolas, R. Nicolas, *La vie quotidienne en Savoie aux XVIIe et XVIIIe siècles* (Montmélian: Cedex, 2005), pp.55-59.

28 *Raccolta per ordine di Materie delle Leggi cioè Editti, Patenti, manifesti, Ecc.*, Book 26, Vol.28, p.572.

again according to the *Regio Viglietto* of 5 May 1742, was the following: one captain, two lieutenants, two standard bearers, six quartermasters, eight sergeants, 14 corporals, four drummers, 40 soldiers, and 200 new conscripts, for a total of 271 men. The actual strength of the reserve companies could vary considerably. In 1747 they stood as follows: Reggimento Chiablese 230, Reggimento Tarantasia 230, Reggimento Aosta 700, Reggimento Torino 900, Reggimento Nizza 300, Reggimento Mondovì 750, Reggimento Vercelli 900, Reggimento Asti 800, Reggimento Pinerolo 800, Reggimento Casale 800. The assembly area of the reserve companies took place in the following locations: Susa, Reggimento s Chiablese, Tarantasia; Ivrea, Reggimento Aosta; Cuneo, Reggimento Nizza; Torino, Reggimento Torino; Vercelli, Reggimento Vercelli; Asti, Reggimento Asti; Mondovì, Reggimento Mondovì; Pinerolo, Reggimento Pinerolo; Casale, Reggimento Casale.[29]

The regiments of foreign infantry Audibert/Monfort, German infantry Rehbinder/Bourgsdorff, Schoulembourg, Baaden-Dourlac, and Italian infantry Sicilia, Lombardia and Corsica had a particular organization that depended on their respective capitulations, although generally they were organized in two battalions and the number total number of soldiers was similar to that of the National Ordinance.

The Swiss infantry regiments (Rietman/Kalbermatten, Guibert/Utiger, Roguin/Roi, Keller, Reydt/Salis, Meyer) divided their battalions into four large companies of 175 men each, as was also the case in Louis XV's *Armée Royale*. Each company had its own share of grenadiers who, grouped together at battalion level, formed a company, of about one third of the strength of a fusilier company. In 1747 all the Swiss battalions engaged in the Assietta campaign had a grenadier company. The Swiss infantry units became, during the conflict, effectively brigades in their own right. The Regiment Kalbermatten in 1744 had four battalions, for a total strength of 2,800 men, and the regiments Reydt/Salis, Diesbach/Roguin/Roi, Guibert/Utiger three battalions each. However, it was quite rare for these formations to operate with all their battalions together. The Sardinian combat doctrine provided at least two battalions of a single regiment under the same command. This was to avoid a colonel finding himself commanding an excessive number of men in combat and obliged to act as a superior officer.

In case of necessity, especially on occasions of enemy invasions, the Militia could be raised, to which all those capable of bearing arms were ascribed. Established on a territorial basis, it was organized into companies with commanders already recognized by the militiamen themselves, officers whom the men trusted. For the campaign of 1747, 1,500 men belonging to the Pragelato, Pinerolo and Waldensian militia were raised by order of the Secretariat of War.

The backbone of the Sardinian infantry was made up of the Swiss and German units. The nineteenth-century military historiography always saw them in a bad light. See, for example, some hilarious passages contained in Pinelli's military history of Piedmont:

> These foreign regiments were a really big disgrace: [...] and it is truly surprising
> that the royals of Savoy, who at all times, but especially at this time, could always

---

29   ASTO, Corte, Memorie politiche per rapporto all'interno, Storie della Real Casa Mazzo 24; Minutoli, *Relation des Campagnes*, Atlante, Vol.2; *Stato Generale delle Truppe di S.M. esistenti in Terraferma, ed in Sardegna, e della loro rispettiva Forza, 1747.*

Waldensian and City of Mondovi militiamen in 1747. The militia usually wore civilian clothes, while their armament was provided by the state arsenals. (Source, AST, Corte, Biblioteca Antica, H-VIII-53)

count on the love of peoples and their subjects, lords of a warrior nation, trusted to these mercenary bands: but Naples had Swiss, Spain had Swiss, France had Swiss, therefore Savoy also had to have Swiss: such was the urge to imitate the Bourbons in our lords! It should be added that the Swiss enjoyed at that time, and I really don't know too much why, an extraordinary reputation of value, to which I do not see they were more entitled than the national troops, which they certainly had never demonstrated themselves.[30]

This poor impression was due to some episodes such as the surrender of the castle of Bard on 7 October 1704 and the capture of the Piccolo San Bernardo pass in April 1794 during the War of the Alps. On 7 October 1704, after three days of blockade, the castle of Bard, defended by a battalion of the Swiss Reggimento Reding, commanded by the colonel himself, *Maggior Generale* Jean François Reding de Biberegg, surrendered to the French forces under Vendôme and La Feuillade. The ancient medieval fortress could not withstand the siege of the two French armies, and Reding felt it was more prudent to reach a discretionary surrender. Released on parole he went to Turin to justify his behaviour, but he found Duke

---

30   Pinelli, *Storia Militare del Piemonte*, Vol.I, pp.15, 42.

Uniform of the Reggimento Kalbermatten in 1744. (AST, Corte, Biblioteca antica, jb III 16)

Uniform of the Reggimento Roi still called by its former name of Diesbach, in 1744. (AST, Corte, Biblioteca antica, jb III 16)

Victor Amadeus II strongly ill-disposed towards him, and he never forgave him for that surrender. He therefore abandoned service under the House of Savoy and at the end of the year he joined the French army, as *brigadier*. On 3 March 1705 he raised a Régiment Reding for the King of France. He died in Madrid in 1706, with the rank of *maréchal de camp*. In the unified Italy of the second half of the nineteenth century, his name became synonymous with traitor. Commenting on his change of flag after the Bard affair, Prato wrote that 'unfortunately no Piedmontese ball reached him in the French service'.[31] Much more serious was the behaviour of Capitano Bégoz of the Bernese Reggimento Roch-Mondet who, according to his contemporaries, gave up his entrenched positions at the Little St Bernard Pass on 23 April 1794. His shortcomings, voluntary or not, were however a convenient expedient to cover the disastrous moral and material situation of the Sardinian army, whose units disbanded during the battle in the face of enemy. With regard to the fighting spirit of the Swiss units, little account was subsequently taken of episodes such as the action of the 2nd grenadier company of the Reggimento Christ, commanded by the *Capitano* Paolo Schreiber and *Luogotenente* Ippolito Schreiber, in San Michele di Mondovì on 19 April 1796.[32]

However, this historiography has masked the value of these units during the 1740s. Raised thanks to the important financial subsidies of London, which in fact managed to set up its own proxy army on Italian soil, these Swiss regiments fought in the course of the conflict much better and with greater determination than other far more prestigious Sardinian units, proving to be the best forces at the disposal of Carlo Emanuele III. This was due to the skills and passion that the regimental and battalion commanding officers had for combat. Characters such as Bruno Kalbermatten, Augustin Gabriel Roguin, Pierre Antoine Louis Roi and Alexandre Guibert de Syssac had credible military skills, and put a lot of emphasis on drill and training their men.[33] In 1744 out of 57 infantry battalions (47,681 men in total), 24 (16,400 men) were Swiss or German infantrymen. The ratio of foreign troop (34.5 percent) was higher than both that of the Infantry of National Ordinance (23.5 percent) and that of the Infantry of Provincial Ordinance (32 percent). The war operations greatly depleted the regional character of some Swiss units, which compensated for the lack of recruits from the original cantons by accepting soldiers of other nationalities, provided that they spoke – depending on the nature of the regiment – German or French. Therefore, towards the end of the War of the Austrian Succession the colonels had only one fifth of their regiments made up of troops of Swiss nationality: 'the others are almost all Germans, but there are also French and even Savoyards, who deny their homeland and they declare themselves Swiss'.[34] The recruits reached the Sardinian army from all over Europe: those men marching from northern Europe crossed the Alps to the Gran San Bernardo and they were concentrated in the districts of Aosta, Ivrea and Turin and, depending on the position

---

31   G. Prato, *Il costo della Guerra di Successione Spagnola e le spese pubbliche del Piemonte dal 1700 al 1713* (Torino: Bocca, 1907), p.281.
32   V. Ilari, P. Crociani, C. Paoletti, *La Guerra delle Alpi* (Roma: USSME, 2000), pp.161-163, 295-296.
33   For the biographies of the Swiss officers in the Savoy service in the eighteenth century see May de Romainmoitier, *Histoire militaire de la Suisse et celle des Suisses dans les différent services de l'Europe, composée et rédogée sur des ouvrages et pièces authentiques* (Lausanne: Heubach et Comp., 1788), Vol. VII.
34   Loriga, *Soldati*, p.8.

of the regiment, in Novara or Cuneo. Here the men were dressed, summarily trained, and sent to the unit where they would complete the training process.

The Sardinian Army in 1747

The studies dedicated to the Battle of Assietta focus their attention on the performances of the 1st Battalion of the Reggimento Guardie, forgetting practically all the others. Obviously, every reference is linked to the stubborn resistance against the repeated French attacks upon the redoubt on Testa dell'Assietta.[35] This view immediately appears partial and it does not consider the general situation of the units that marched up to the mountains to take part in the combat. Each battalion commander had a clear vision of the combat capacity of his own unit, a situation that certainly did not fail to be communicated to the Conte di Bricherasio during the planning phase. The historian's perspective, however, must be different and we must ask ourselves: what were the real operating conditions of the Sardinian units? To obtain a general view of the situation requires analysis of both the general conditions of the king's army in the campaign of 1747, and the conditions of each single unit deployed on the battlefield on 19 July 1747.

The army of Carlo Emanuele III fought seven major battles during the War of the Austrian Succession: Camposanto, 8 February 1743; Casteldelfino, 7-10 October 1743; Villefranche, 21 April 1744; Pietralunga, 19 July 1744; Madonna dell'Olmo, 30 September 1744; Bassignana, 27 September 1745; Assietta, 19 July 1747. Only at Camposanto were there more imperial troops present than the Sardinian ones.[36] Three of these battles (Camposanto, Casteldelfino and Villefranche) were non-decisive tactical victories. In Villefranche, then, the Sardinians were forced to abandon both the battlefield and the bay in the days following the battle, evacuating the entrenchments embarking on the vessels of the English fleet under Admiral Mathews. Only Assietta can be considered a clear victory, even if strategically useless. Genoa had already been rescued by the Bourbons and the imperial siege was still broken regardless of the Sardinian success. At Camposanto it was the imperial *Feldmarschall* Otto Ferdinand Graf von Abensberg und Traun who decided to attack, while the only offensive action planned by the Sardinian command, Madonna dell'Olmo, ended with a serious defeat and the loss of one sixth of the forces engaged. After 1744, Carlo Emanuele III carefully avoided engaging the enemy in battles with an uncertain outcome. Thereafter, the Bourbons were able to force the Sardinians to fight only in two occasions, Bassignana in 1745 and Assietta in 1747.

---

35   Amoretti, 'Celebrazione di un anniversario', pp.11-47.

36   At Camposanto there were 15 imperial battalions and nine Sardinian. The cavalry was made up of 21 imperial and six Sardinians squadrons, 12 imperial guns and 10 Sardinian. The troops of Carlo Emanuele III, commanded by François Louis Emmanuel d'Alinges, Conte di Apremont, had the following order of battle; Schulemburg 2 bns.; 1/ and 2/Diesbach; 1/Rehbinder; Piemonte 2 bns.; Savoia 2 bns; Savoia Cavalleria 3 sqns.; Dragoni della Regina 3 sqns.: ten 4-pounder guns. HstAM, Karten, WHK 21/50, *Plan de la Bataille de Campo Santo, donné le 8eme fevrier 1743*; AST, Corte, Memorie politiche per rapporto all'interno, Storie della Real Casa Mazzo 24; Minutoli, *Relation des Campagnes*, Atlante, Vol.I, *Ordine di Battaglia Esercito Austro-piemontese, Battaglia di Camposanto 8 febbraio 1743*.

Four of these fights took place in mountainous terrain. However, the army of Carlo Emanuele III was not a force drilled for mountain warfare. Despite the important successes achieved in the western Alps, the presence of an almost uninterrupted chain of permanent and field fortifications from Mont Blanc to the Mediterranean Sea and the strategic need to defend a mostly mountainous front, the Sardinian army fought in the Alps reluctantly, proving itself to be clumsy, predictable, passive, slow, and unable to anticipate the opponent's actions with the necessary countermeasures or carry out energetic offensive manoeuvres.

The most spectacular and successful actions, both on a tactical and strategic level, were not, as one might think, those of Casteldelfino in 1743 or Assietta in 1747, where in the end the demerits of the opponent counted more than the merits of the defenders, but the Po Valley campaign of 1742 and, above all, the Piedmontese campaign of 1746, planned by the engineer Ignazio Bertola and the Minister of War Giovanni Battista Bogino. Very well directed by the German-born *Generale di Fanteria* Karl Sigismond Friedrick Wilhelm Leutrum, 'Baron Litron', the Sardinian offensive saw no less than 20 separate columns converge simultaneously on Asti, recaptured on 7 March, with the capture of nine battalions French (about 5,000 men), 27 flags and eight cannon. On 10 March also the Citadel of Alexandria was freed from the blockade and on 17 April the stronghold of Valenza was invested; it was reconquered on 4 May 1746.

In the Alps the situation was very different. The second campaign in Savoy in December 1742 was a rude awakening for the Savoy command. It was entered into with optimism thanks to the happy outcome of the operations on the eastern front between March and August, which ended with the destruction of the House of Este's small army in Modena. On 1 September 1742 the Spanish army of Provence invaded Savoy, and in a few days the province was completely occupied and subdued. Carlo Emanuele III therefore abandoned the Romagna front and he had gone to the Alps, attacking the enemy on 30 September. This manoeuvre, successful and well carried out, allowed the Sardinians to recover the lost province by 16 October. On 18 December the Spanish army, reinforced by new units and now under the command of the Marqués de la Mina, invaded Savoyard territory again. Considering the Spanish attack a simple demonstration, Carlo Emanuele III failed to correctly assess the danger. The Spaniards, exploiting their bases in French territory, spread everywhere notwithstanding that the forces in the field, 18,000 Sardinians and 20,000 Spaniards, were almost equivalent. Deceived at the operational level, without any credible tactical grip to stop the enemy advance, the King of Sardinia was forced to order a general retreat on the Alpine watershed. It was a hard-fought retreat, signalled by rather hard-fought clashes on 1 January in Aigueblanche and Rocheleplus, and again on 5 January in Saint-André. The last Sardinian unit returned to Piedmont on 10 January 1743. On 4 January, King Charles Emanuel III arrived in the capital from the Savoy at the head of a tired army. One hundred days of fighting beyond the Alps at the cost of 9,000 casualties including dead, wounded and prisoners, the huge expense of nine million lire and the abandonment of all the transalpine territories.

The Alpine campaigns of 1744 and 1745 were even worse. In the first case a secondary French column, with 10 battalions, was able to defeat the bulk of the Sardinian army at the end of the Battle of Pietralunga, which began on 16 July 1744. The clash lasted for three days, with high losses on both sides. The action was characterized by numerous local clashes, the bloodiest of which occurred at the Monte Passet redoubt, along the ridge that separates the Valle Varaita di Bellino from that of Castello. At the end of the fighting, on 19 July 1744, the Piedmontese lines were shattered, enabling the Prince de Conti to force the Piedmontese barriers of the Stura di Demonte valley and permitting the investment of the Fort of Demonte and, subsequently, the siege of Cuneo. Carlo Emanuele III, convinced that he was facing the main body of the combined armies of France and Spain, ordered the retreat on Sampeyre which took place 'with the greatest disorder'. Here he was joined the following day by seven battalions under Baron Leutrum, who was rebuked for the delay accumulated. Calming the sovereign, the German general managed to convince him of the uselessness of such a hasty retreat.[37] On 12 October 1745, *Maggior Generale* Giovanni Giacomo de Rossi was surprised with three battalions (Meyer, Nizza, 2/Saluzzo) at the camp of Joussaud at the entrance of Val Troncea. Deaf to the calls of mountain warfare experts, captains Rouziers, Bernardi and Garessio, he preferred to remain firm in his positions, which could be bypassed on all sides. The French took advantage of this tactical situation and attacked de Rossi's men, routing the three Sardinian battalions inflicting 416 losses on them, capturing two flags and 50 mules out of a total of about 2,500 men engaged in combat. De Rossi himself was taken prisoner. The witty Don Bernard Tholosan, curate of Chianale and Pont from 1734 to 1783 and accused of connivance with the enemy, grasped the essential: 'our troops [he wrote in 1744] are not good for the mountains, the plain is most propitious for them to fight, so I think they won't come back to wait for the enemy in these straits, since they always have the worst of it'.[38]

Unable to counter the enemy's moves, the Sardinian army was forced to conceive of mountain warfare only as the static defence of field fortifications. When this element was lacking, the commanders would find themselves in deadly traps such as that of Joussaud, while the troops, deprived of the solid parapets of the entrenchments, soon lost courage. On 7 October 1743, in the initial phase of the Battle of Casteldelfino, the Franco-Spaniards had taken possession of the fortifications of Castello:

> [This] in part lowered the spirits of some of our soldiers, who were at first over-confident because of the strong situation in which they found themselves, and because of the abundance of provisions which reached the camp and the great difficulties which they knew the enemy to have to overcome. Knowing that they [i.e. the enemy] lacked any means of subsistence, then seeing what advantage those same enemies had gained, our soldiers recalled in their minds the successes of the preceding period, and the great difficulties they knew the enemy had to overcome, they recalled in their minds the successes of the preceding Savoy campaign, in which, believing ourselves already sure of preventing the enemies from entering that province, we had then been forced to evacuate it.[39]

It could not have happened otherwise. The soldiers were recruited and trained to sustain a close firefight and there was no specific request for personnel suitable for combat at high altitude. Nor there was any particular necessity to organize regular units for mountain warfare or to develop particular combat tactics for the Alpine theatre. The province that provided the highest number of recruits was Asti, followed by Pinerolo, Turin, Cuneo, Vercelli and Casale. Thirty percent of the recruits were of urban extraction, due to the strong incentive to

---

37   Garellis (ed.), *L'alta valle Varaita a età Settecento*, p.207.
38   Garellis (ed.), *L'alta valle Varaita a età Settecento*, p.208.
39   Galleani d'Agliano, *Memorie storiche*, pp.91-92.

recruit given by the presence of permanent garrisons. About a third of the troops, therefore, had never seen any mountains before enlisting and, once they were in uniform, their only experiences in peacetime were limited to transfer marches from one garrison to another along the valley bottom and the main communication routes.

However, troops suitable for operating in mountainous terrain did exist. The Waldensian militias were able to manoeuvre effectively, whether in offensive, reconnaissance or covering operations. In the Alps, a body of about 2,000 Waldensian militiamen, commanded by *Capitano* Jean Baptiste Rouzier, was distinguished for a series of raids deep into the enemy territory. This skilled officer and his men provided excellent light troops for the Sardinian army, especially during the Alpine campaigns of 1743, 1744, 1745 and 1747.

The losses suffered by the Sardinian army in combat during the War of the Austrian Succession were much more serious than we are led to believe. In the first three years of the war, about 18,000 men were lost on the battlefields.

Table 1. French and Sardinian Losses on the Italian Front, 1742-1747

Year	Sardinian Losses	French Losses	Percentage of Sardinian losses compared to the total available forces
1742	9,000	-	30.3%
1743	1,000	3,900	2.3%
1744	8,000	8,000	18.9%
1745	3,500	2,600	7.0%
1746	1,500	6,000	3.0%
1747	1,000	6,000	1.8%

Source: Ilari, Boeri, Paoletti, *La Corona di Lombardia*.

All armies have a breaking point. It can be reached when the men of the combat units are led to calculate that the chances of survival have crossed the dividing line between possibility and probability, between the random death that can occur and its apparent statistical recurrence. This line is usually felt when the casualties suffered during a conflict equal the structural number of soldiers in each unit. The primary Sardinian field army, on which all the weight of the war of maneuverer was laid, was made up of a fixed group of regiments. The average size of the corps was of about 20,000 men. By the spring of 1745 the soldier must have known that his army could still withstand only a battle of great proportions, after which the chances of survival would turn against him; 'my number is up', to put it in British Tommy parlance. In 1745, after the Battle of Bassignana (27 September 1745), the overall losses reached 21,500. Thus, in the difficult winter of 1745-1746 the Sardinian armies reached the point of collapse. Defeated militarily and with the Franco-Spanish forces now a day's march from Turin, Carlo Emanuele III gave way to peace negotiations and he hypothesized a change of alliances.[40] Yet, contrary to what happened in 1796 during the war against the French Republic, nothing

---

40   The Franco-Spanish advance-guard stormed the castle of Gabiano on 12 November 1745, reaching 40 kilometres from Turin. P. Savio, *Asti occupata e liberata (1745-1746)* (Asti: Michele Varesio, 1927), p.81.

similar to the surrender signed with the Armistice of Cherasco and the Peace of Paris materialized. In March 1746, just seven months after Bassignana, the Sardinian army launched an all-out offensive on the eastern Piedmont front, and it was stopped only eight months later on the banks of the Varo River on the southern border of France.

There were two main elements that avoided the defeat and allowed a prodigious recovery of strength.

Firstly, the defensive cordon set up in the War of the Austrian Succession was much more flexible than that set up in the 1792-1796 War of the Alps. The Sardinian corps moved, changed positions and operational theatres, and they were redeployed according to the situations and strategic needs of the moment. The observation corps stationed in Val Varaita had the precise purpose of controling the sector where the greatest enemy effort was recognized. In 1744 the army moved to Cuneo, in 1745 it headed to Bassignana in order to protect the eastern borders of Piedmont. In July 1747, having abandoned the siege of Genoa and fearing an invasion in the Val di Susa, over 9,000 Sardinians, not counting the imperial forces, were ready to reach Bricherasio's corps at Assietta.

Secondly, the Treaty of Worms of 13 September 1743 made Carlo Emanuele III the proconsul of Britain in Italy. This allowed the British Mediterranean fleet, 31 sail of the line, three frigates and 13 minor units, to operate in the Upper Tyrrhenian Sea, adding to the bases of Menorca and Gibraltar also the bay of Villefranche. Strategically, the kingdom of Sardinia was never left alone; the British continued to provide financial aid, to which they added a bonus of £ 60,000 for the year 1743 intended for the raising of 10,000 men. With these sums, the Sardinian army would have had to maintain a force of 45,000 men. This army allowed Vienna to plan and to attempt the conquest of the kingdom of Naples. Although the relations were by no means idyllic and often marked by mutual distrust, Vienna and Turin remained allies, the British pounds were never lacking, and the Sardinian army, thanks to the presence of a powerful imperial aid, avoided surrender, resuming the following year the strategic initiative. In 1792, by contrast, the kingdom of Sardinia was in the unfortunate situation of having to fight against an ex-ally, France, alongside the main ex-enemy, the Empire. Without any diplomatic weight or margin of negotiation, every national strategic design of the kingdom of Sardinia was subordinated to the support of imperial interests. In 1745, protecting Turin had cost Vienna the invasion of Parma, Modena and the occupation of Milan. Nevertheless, the dependence on British money and the overall strategic plan had forced the Empress Maria Theresia to cooperate with Carlo Emanuele III. In the War of the Alps, however, Vienna was confident that France would be satisfied with control of the border on the Alps and the fate of the Sardinian army and that of the hated kingdom of Sardinia left the imperial strategists completely indifferent.

If until 1744 the court of Turin considered a 'parallel war' against the crowns of France and Spain to be possible, after Bassignana it understood how decisive the imperial contribution was for the keeping of the Alpine line. Although the army increased its strength to 55,641 men, of which 51,471 were infantry, the length of the front – which stretched from the eastern Ligurian Riviera up to the Little St Bernard Pass – as well as the strategy adopted for its defence, effectively nullified the numerical superiority, forcing the Sardinian commands to insistently request, if not implore, the presence of an imperial contingent. From the end of the summer of 1745, with the army of Carlo Emanuele III reaching its breaking point, the imperial units aggregated to the Savoyard forces were increasing. From the campaign of 1746 the army of Carlo Emanuele III limited itself to siege operations or, in the case of pitched clashes, avoided fighting in the open field and instead scrupulously waited for the enemy behind solid entrenchments previously set up on battlegrounds already carefully selected, studied, mapped and adapted to a static defence. The Franco-Spaniards, failing to engage the enemy in a manoeuvre battle of great proportions, had no other option but to attack complex entrenched camps head-on or to attempt costly enveloping manoeuvres, wasting a lot of time, men and materials. Indeed, at Bassignana on 27 September 1745 Carlo Emanuele III tried to retire as soon as the enemy's offensive intentions were clear. Only the Brigade Piemonte, attacked in the central sector of the front, did not have time to disengage. At Piacenza, despite being able to reach the field in time for the great battle of 16 June 1746, the Savoyard army marched with such a slow pace to suggest that the intention of Carlo Emanuele III was to spare his forces and witness the battle from an acceptable safety distance.[41]

This policy allowed the Sardinian command in the two-year period 1746-1747 to limit the losses on the battlefield to 2,500 casualties while inflicting more than 12,000 on the enemy, even if this made the army a sort of 'army in being'. In naval warfare, the 'fleet in being' is a naval force that extends strategic influence without ever leaving its port; the enemy is forced to continuously deploy forces to monitor it. In 1745, despite the military defeat, the army was still virtually intact; at least it was still a credible force to deal with. It would take a long and laborious campaign, if not two, and a bloody and uncertain battle against fortified positions, before it might be possible to finally annihilate the Sardinian army, deployed behind a screen of powerful fortresses and complex entrenched camps. Unable to destroy it, both the Franco-Spaniards and the Anglo-Imperialists needed to have the Sardinian army allied or, at least, neutral, to guarantee themselves a decisive advantage in the Italian campaign. Thus, the army of the king of Sardinia always remained an important card to play in diplomatic negotiations, with Vienna, London, Madrid and Paris.

The Fighting Power of Bricherasio's Army

The units that took part in the defence of the Assietta Plateau were deployed on the battlefield on the basis of their fighting power.[42] Bricherasio and his staff certainly had in mind the state of every single unit available; it was no coincidence that on 18 July he was already able to place every single battalion in a specific area of the battlefield. To calculate the fighting power of each single unit requires that we evaluate the following criteria: numerical strength, training and morale, state of equipment, experience, and losses suffered. The language spoken by soldiers is also explained; the battalions were grouped together, also seeking linguistic homogeneity.

---

41   Browning, *War of Austrian Succession*, pp.273-276; Ilari, Boeri, Paoletti, *La Corona di Lombardia*, pp.179-181, 200-201.

42   Fighting Power is the set of material and non-material elements capable of generating a destructive or disruptive force that a military unit can use against an opponent at a given moment. It consists of three elements: physical, cognitive and moral. In NATO armies Fighting Power represents potential capability, while Combat Power represents actual capability. These concepts are present in the NATO doctrine: AJP 1(E), Ed. 2017; AJP 3.2 (A), Ed. 2016; ATP 3.2.1 (RD1, Ed.B V1), Ed. 2018. See also K-J.H. Brathwaite, 'Effective in battle: conceptualizing soldiers' combat effectiveness', in *Defence Studies*, Vol.18, no.1, (2018), pp.1–18.

Table 2. The Infantry Units of the Army of the Kingdom of Sardinia Present at the Battle of Assietta

Unit	Effective force 19 July 1747	Denomination	Battle Roll	Losses 1742–1746	Losses as % of established strength	Officer losses (%)
1/Guardie	745/845	Infantry of National Ordinance	A, C, F, I	252	30%	43%
2/Savoia	551/700	Infantry of National Ordinance	B, C, E, F, I	700	100%	53%
1/Sicilia	622/700	Italian Infantry	D	997	142%	10%
Casale	316/800	Infantry of Provincial Ordinance	F, H	–	–	–
Chiablese	672/700	Infantry of Provincial Ordinance	A, G, L	–	–	–
1/Monfort	623/700	Foreingn Infantry	A, C, F, I,	1,185	169%	56%
2/Kalbermatten	595/700	Swiss Infantry	A, C, G, I	–	–	–
3/Kalbermatten	699/700	Swiss Infantry	F, I	–	–	–
3/Roi	708/700	Swiss Infantry	F, L	680	97%	20%
Meyer	721/700	Swiss Infantry	M	654	93%	35%
Total of line infantry	6,252/ 7,245					
Pragelato militia	500	Militia				
Val di Susa militia and reinforcements	500	Militia				
Waldensian militia	500	Militia				
Total	7,250					

In the column 'Effective force 19 July 1747', the effective force is compared with the theoretical force of each battalion. In the columns 'Battle Roll' the following code is employed: **A**, Savoia 1742; **B**, Camposanto 1743; **C**, Casteldelfino 1743; **D**, Villefranche 1744; **E**, Pietralunga 1744; **F**, Madonna dell'Olmo 1744; **G**, Siege of Cuneo 1744; **H**, Siege of Tortona 1745; **I**, Bassignana 1745; **L**, Blockade of Alessandria 1745-1746; **M**, Susa-Chisone 1745.

Sources: AST, Sezioni Riunite, Ministero della Guerra: Ufficio Generale del Soldo; Ruolini di Rivista; Reggimento Guardie, Vol.79-89, 1742-1747; Reggimento Savoia, Vol.72-82, 1742-1747; Reggimento Sicilia, Vol.37-56, 1742-1747; Reggimento Casale, Vol. 33, 1747; Reggimento Chiablese, Vol. 20, 1747; Reggimento Audibert/Monfort, Vol.72-84, 1742-1747; Reggimento Kalbermatten, Vol. 58, 1747; Reggimento Diesbach/Roguin/Roi, Vol.20-30, 1746-1747; Reggimento Meyer, Vol.1-8, 1747: Ordini Generali e Misti, 1747, Mazzo 48, *Stato de Battaglioni trovatisi presenti agli attacchi ed interventi alla difesa de Trinceramenti dell'Assietta li 19 scorso Luglio*; N. Brancaccio, *L'Esercito del Vecchio Piemonte (1560-1859) – Sunto dei principali Corpi* (Roma: Stabilimento Poligrafico per l'amministrazione della Guerra 1922).

1/Reggimento Guardie

At Assietta the battalion counted 745 soldiers, against a theoretical strength of 800 men (93.1 percent).[43] On 19 July 1747 it was commanded by *Luogotenente Colonnello* Paolo Novarina di San Sebastiano.[44] In the ranks the Italian language was spoken.[45]

The first in terms of seniority among the infantry of the national ordinance regiments, Reggimento Guardie was considered the elite of the Sardinian Army, even if it was trained exactly like the other infantry regiments. The peculiarity was mainly in the differences of uniform, in the higher pay and in a superior *esprit de corps*, which was also reflected in a reduced rate of desertion, just 23 percent of all losses suffered in the course of the conflict.[46] Nevertheless, the morale of this unity was quite high and only seven men deserted in the first half of 1747. The unit consisted of trained, well-equipped soldiers, hardened by five years of war, while inexperienced or yet to be trained recruits were a minority.

Uniforms and equipment of 1/Guardie were all in perfect condition. Even the gauntlets of grenadiers and sappers were all new, since the officers, 'having found them in bad condition… had new pairs made'.[47] The tents, on the other hand, were not in perfect condition. In a review in the spring of 1747, the tents of the battalion were reported as 'very worn out, and even if the king permitted the distributions of new items, there are still sixty-two out

---

43   Note that the overall battalion's strength had recently been increased, rising from 700 to 800 men. Therefore, we can assume that the 745 troops were actually the beginning of the planned expansion. AST, Sezioni Riunite, Ministero della Guerra, Ufficio Generale del Soldo, Ruolini di Rivista, Reggimento Guardie, Vol.89, 1747.

44   The command functions of the Conte di San Sebastiano, who played a prominent role during the Battle of Assietta, were those of a major in command of a battalion. It is no coincidence that he was titular commander of the Compagnia Maggiora [Major's Company], and due to his seniority he was 'decorated with the rank and seniority of lieutenant colonel in the Infantry' since 28 March 1747. The Reggimento Guardie at that time counted in the ranks a colonel commandeant, Conte Giuseppe Ottavio Cacherano Osasco della Rocca, a second colonel, Conte Filippo Andrea Faletti di Montaldo, and a lieutenant colonel, Giuseppe Ignazio Scaglia di Verrua. BRT, Manoscritto Militare 36, *Personale degli Ufficiali dell'esercito del Re di Sardegna dal 1745 a tutto il 1747*; AST, Sezioni Riunite, Ministero della Guerra, Ufficio Generale del Soldo, Ruolini di Rivista, Reggimento Guardie, Vol.89, 1747.

45   About the Reggimento Guardie, see D. Guerrini, *La Brigata dei Granatieri di Sardegna* (Torino: Roux e Viarengo, 1902); P.de Choulot, G. Ferrero, *Historie de l'Armée Sarde. Essai sur le Brigades des Gardes et de Savoie* (Turin: Bocca, 1845), pp.21-85.

46   The losses suffered between 1742 and 1747, including dead, wounded, prisoners, deserters, discharged for incapacity of service, or other causes, were of 16 officers and 1,037 privates in all. AST, Sezioni Riunite, Ministero della Guerra, Ufficio Generale del Soldo, Ruolini di Rivista, Reggimento Guardie, vol.79-89, 1742-1747.

47   *Determinazioni di S.M. Relazione della Revista d'Ispezione datasi alle infrascritte Truppe in Aprile, e Maggio 1747. 1.mo Batt.ne di Guardia.* AST, Sezioni Riunite, Ministero della Guerra, Ufficio Generale del Soldo, Ordini Generali e Misti, 1747, Mazzo 48. Studying the desertion rate of a military unit is important to observe its solidity. The percentage of deserters varied from unit to unit, it was higher at the start of the war – many soldiers simply 'changed sides' – and in the weeks following a large-scale battle. The desertion rate was about 1.9 percent in peacetime and 25 percent in wartime. About this problem, see A. Corvisier, 'La mort du soldat depuis la fin du Moyen Age', in *Revue Historique*, 254, Fasc.1 (515) (Jul.-Sept. 1975), pp.3-30; W. Fann, 'Peacetime Attrition in the Army of Frederick William I 1713-1740', in *Central European History*, XI (1978), pp.323-334; D.E. Showalter, *The Wars of Frederick the Great* (London: Longman, 1996), pp.23-24.

of service'.[48] Since a single battalion had a total of 211 tents,[49] this was a reduction of 29.4 percent.

The battalion had been lucky; although it had been present in battles of great proportions, it had always found itself very far from the epicentre of the struggle and suffered only marginal losses. Nevertheless it participated in all the main campaigns of the conflict, passing from theatres such as the Po Valley, the Ligurian Riviera, the hills of eastern Piedmont to the Savoy Alps.

By 1747 the battalion lamented the loss of 252 men, 31.5 percent of its theoretical strength[50]. These losses resulted from the 'normal' strain of military operations. The officer corps, the fundamental element of leadership and control of the troops in battle, had suffered relatively more serious losses, 43% of the total, but they maintained a certain continuity among the company commanders.

1/Guardie was an elite unit that, in fact, had not yet sustained a real fight, and it kept its combat efficiency intact. Bricherasio therefore decided to place it in one of the most exposed places in the field, the communication between the redoubts of the Assietta Plateau and the Peak of Assietta, reinforcing it with a company of grenadiers from Reggimento Casale.

2/Reggimento Savoia

The battalion on 19 July 1747 had a total of 551 men, just over 78 percent of the theoretical total.[51] The battalion was commanded by *Luogotenente Colonnello* Gaspard de Guige,[52] and the French language was spoken in the ranks.[53]

One of the oldest regiments of army of the Kingdom of Sardinia, Savoia enjoyed a solid reputation, perfectly perceived by the troops. In 1747, however, the unit had seen its combat efficiency plummet due to the heavy casualties it suffered during the 1744 campaign, after which it had had to add massive numbers of unreliable recruits into the ranks. No longer being able to look for new soldiers in Savoy, a favourite area for the recruitment of this regiment, increasing numbers of men were accepted from the Aosta Valley and from the valleys of the Western Alps such as the Val di Susa and Chisone. French or Piedmontese deserters able to understand French, the language of the unit, were also incorporated.[54] Losses due to

---

48   *Determinazioni di S.M. Relazione della Revista d'Ispezione datasi alle infrascritte Truppe in Aprile, e Maggio 1747. 1.mo Batt.ne di Guardia.* AST, Sezioni Riunite, Ministero della Guerra, Ufficio Generale del Soldo, Ordini Generali e Misti, 1747, Mazzo 48.

49   Guerrini, *La Brigata dei Granatieri di Sardegna*, pp.86-87.

50   AST, Sezioni Riunite, Ministero della Guerra, Ufficio Generale del Soldo, Ruolini di Rivista, Reggimento Guardie, vol.79-89, 1747. For 1/Guardie, as for the other units, the total of the losses is the sum of dead, wounded, prisoners, and deserters.

51   AST, Sezioni Riunite, Ministero della Guerra, Ufficio Generale del Soldo, Ruolini di Rivista, Reggimento Savoia, Vol.72-82, 1742-1747.

52   BRT, Manoscritto Militare 36, *Personale degli Ufficiali dell'esercito del Re di Sardegna dal 1745 a tutto il 1747.*

53   On the Reggimento Savoia the only published materials of importance are the old studies by Choulot, Ferrero, *Historie de l'Armée Sarde*, pp.111-159.

54   As foreseen in various internal regulations, such as that of 4 September 1744, or Specific Royal Decree, such as that of 16 April 1745. *Raccolta per ordine di Materie delle Leggi cioè Editti, Patenti, manifesti, Ecc.*, Book 26, Vol.28, pp.230-231, 235-236.

desertion, despite the unreliability of the recruits, were low, and the battalion complained of the flight of only 19 men between January and June 1747.

Perfectly armed, this unit had benefited from the distribution of new uniforms and materials, 'for having the old ones totally worn out'. The soldiers' gaiters were also particularly battered after long marches, and some were completely unusable. The battalion tents had likewise seen better days, and 56, 26 percent of the total, were totally unusable.[55]

2/Savoia was one of the units that had been most engaged in the conflict, and it could boast particularly intense combat experiences; it had fought in Camposanto in 1743, in the bloody days of Pietralunga in 1744, and the same year it was again in the epicentre of the fight at Madonna dell'Olmo. Undoubtedly it could be considered a veteran regiment, even if the very serious losses suffered made it after 1745 a regiment no longer as reliable as before.

By the beginning of 1747 it had suffered 700 losses, exactly 100 percent of its theoretical strength. This meant that the battalion had been destroyed and rebuilt at least once. The officer corps also had a 56 percent casualty rate, a sign that the veteran officers were beginning to be a minority.

2/Savoia was a veteran unit but, like many eighteenth century infantry regiments, after a series of glorious but bloody battles, it was no longer reliable in combat due to veteran soldiers suffering from what would now be termed post-traumatic stress disorder and young recruits still to be trained. On the day of the battle, Bricherasio assigned it to the garrison of Colle delle Finestre, an important position for communications between Val Chisone and Val di Susa, but in fact in the rear.

1/Reggimento Sicilia

For the campaign of 1747 1/Sicilia had 622 soldiers, 88.8% of the theoretical force.[56] The battalion was commanded by *Luogotenente Colonnello* Nicolao Giulio Rambosio; the commanding colonel was *Brigadiere Generale* Federico Martinengo, Conte da Barco, who had another command post on the day of the battle.[57] The soldiers spoke in Italian.

A regiment of Italian infantry, this unit was organized in two battalions; the second was garrisoned in Sardinia, while the first was employed on the continent. The campaign of 1744 had seen the destruction of this battalion, which had been painstakingly rebuilt over the course of the year. That of 1747, after long periods of garrison, saw the battalion return to the front but with a still shaky morale. Between January and June 1/Sicilia lost 104 men by desertion, 14.8 percent of the total force.[58]

The first great battle in which the battalion took part it was also the last; during the Battle of Villefranche in 1744 it was surrounded and forced to surrender. The regimental colour remained on display as a trophy in Madrid's Armeria Real for over a century, until a fire in

---

55   *Determinazioni di S.M. Relazione della Revista d'Ispezione datasi alle infrascritte Truppe in Aprile, e Maggio 1747. 2.do Batt.ne di Savoia.* AST, Sezioni Riunite, Ministero della Guerra, Ufficio Generale del Soldo, Ordini Generali e Misti, 1747, Mazzo 48.

56   AST, Sezioni Riunite, Ministero della Guerra, Ufficio Generale del Soldo, Ruolini di Rivista, Reggimento Sicilia, vol.37-56, 1742-1747.

57   BRT, Manoscritto Militare 36, *Personale degli Ufficiali dell'esercito del Re di Sardegna dal 1745 a tutto il 1747.*

58   AST, Sezioni Riunite, Ministero della Guerra, Ufficio Generale del Soldo, Ruolini di Rivista, Reggimento Sicilia, vol.37-56, 1742-1747.

1884 destroyed it. The disastrous debut of Villefranche and the increasing rate of desertion caused the loss of 997 men, 142.4 percent of the total established strength. However, only 10 percent of the officers had been lost, so this unit could still fight in static positions, at least to defend itself with some effectiveness. Unsuitable for high-intensity combat against the French, it was sent to garrison in the rear, at Colle delle Vallette.

Reggimento Casale

A single-battalion regiment of the infantry of provincial ordinance. On 19 July about 316 men from the Reggimento Casale were present at Assietta,[59] 42.4% of a total strength of 745.[60] This battalion was also undergoing expansion, and its personnel would have to grow to 800 men. By 1747, however, 93 percent of that number had been reached; recruitment, always very complicated for provincial infantry regiments, was still continuing. The soldiers spoke in Italian.

Casale was a provincial infantry regiment, which meant that the soldiers of this regiment were men recruited with an embryonic conscript system. They wore uniforms only for a limited number of days a year during the peacetime. It was anything but a fair system of selection, as the choice was made by the communities, who tried at the first opportunity to get rid of those 'unwelcome' elements. After all, being selected to be part of a provincial regiment could lead to official enlistment for one of the national infantry regiments, a practice often used especially in those years of war when recruits were scarce.[61] So the unit was anything but ready to sustain a high intensity combat. The exceptions were the Granatieri of *Capitano* Giorgio Scozia and the Colonnella company of the Cavaliere Sobrino, which could be equated with normal companies of a regiment of national ordinance.

The unit was fully equipped, although, most likely, the individual armament of the men was not of the highest quality, or it had not been recently replaced. During the review of spring 1747 it was noted how much all private soldiers' items were 'in need of various repairs, and orders have incessantly been given to have them performed'.[62] In other words, the weapons broke continuously, since they were old, worn or simply defective, and they had to be repaired all the time.

Casale had fought at Madonna dell'Olmo, where it was lucky to find himself on the left wing of the Sardinian Army, in the second line. The battalion's casualties there were limited

---

59 AST, Sezioni Riunite, Ministero della Guerra, Ufficio Generale del Soldo, Ordini Generali e Misti, 1747, Mazzo 48, *Stato de Battaglioni trovatisi presenti agli attacchi ed interventi alla difesa de Trinceramenti dell'Assietta li 19 scorso Luglio*. The figure declared in the document is 350 but this is the theoretical strength of one grenadier and three fusilier companies of a battalion already brought to the full strength of 800 men. The most valid document is undoubtedly the volume of rolls, cited in the following note, which reports the figure of 316 effectives.

60 AST, Sezioni Riunite, Ministero della Guerra, Ufficio Generale del Soldo, Ruolini di Rivista, Reggimento Casale, Vol.33, 1747.

61 It was a de facto practice institutionalized through some Royal Decrees, including those of 11 June 1743 and 7 June 1744, to the detriment of the amazement of the subjects involved. *Raccolta per ordine di Materie delle Leggi cioè Editti, Patenti, manifesti, Ecc.*, Book 26, Vol.28, pp.215-217, 219-220.

62 *Determinazioni di S.M. Relazione della Revista d'Ispezione datasi alle infrascritte Truppe in Aprile, e Maggio 1747. Regg.to di Casale.* AST, Sezioni Riunite, Ministero della Guerra, Ufficio Generale del Soldo, Ordini Generali e Misti, 1747, Mazzo 48.

to 99 men, 13.34 percent of the total, of whom 58 were taken prisoner. However, it did not go so well in Tortona in 1745; it was one of the five battalions in charge of the defence of the fort, which was forced to surrender by the Franco-Spanish army of Maillebois. The regiment was made prisoner; rebuilt, the unit was used for garrison duty until the campaign of 1747.

Casale did not give sufficient guarantees of combat effectiveness. The unit was dismembered and the more solid companies, the Granatiera, Colonnella, Maggiora and Ottiglio, were used for the construction of the entrenched camp in the first half of July, and they remained to defend the fortifications, alongside more solid units. The grenadiers, after the commander had evaluated their training and preparation, were joined to those of 1/Guardie for the defence of the Testa dell'Assietta.

Reggimento Chiablese

A single-battalion regiment of the infantry of provincial ordinance, Chiablese had 672 effectives, 96 percent of the theoretical strength.[63] The regiment was commanded by *Colonnello* Francesco Giuseppe Sallier de la Tour.[64] The French language was spoken in the ranks.

The Reggimento Chiablese had all the known congenital defects of the regiments of infantry of provincial ordinance, with the aggravating circumstance that, together with the Reggimento Tarentaise, it was one of the regiments recruited in Savoy, at that time occupied by the Spaniards. Therefore it remained with an established strength of only 700 men, like the Tarentaise and Savoia regiments, as the Spanish occupation did not guarantee a constant flow of new recruits from the transalpine provinces. For the Savoyard soldiers to know that the enemy was occupying their homes was certainly not pleasant and, instead of raising the fighting spirit of the troops, it knocked them down.

The general appearance of the regiment was disastrous: 'the clothing is in poor condition, due to the long and disastrous campaign, [there are a] maximum [of] about sixty coats, which need to be refurbished, to be able to serve until next winter, when replacements will arrive'. Likewise, all the leather parts of the equipment, shoes, belts, cartridge belts, were damaged, and even the flags 'are completely useless'.[65]

Apart from the difficult campaign of 1742/1743 in Savoy, Chiablese was almost always assigned to garrison roles, and with these duties it faced his main war experiences: the siege of Cuneo in 1744 and the blockade of Alessandria in 1745/1746. It was a unit unsuitable for high-intensity combat. Nonetheless, in July it was forced to leave Turin to arrive by forced marches to the Argueil, where it replaced 3/Reggimento Roi, which was immediately sent up to the Gran Serin.

---

63   AST, Sezioni Riunite, Ministero della Guerra, Ufficio Generale del Soldo, Ruolini di Rivista, Reggimento Chiablese, Vol.20, 1747.

64   BRT, Manoscritto Militare 36, *Personale degli Ufficiali dell'esercito del Re di Sardegna dal 1745 a tutto il 1747.*

65   *Determinazioni di S.M. Relazione della Revista d'Ispezione datasi alle infrascritte Truppe in Aprile, e Maggio 1747. Regg.to del Ciablese.* AST, Sezioni Riunite, Ministero della Guerra, Ufficio Generale del Soldo, Ordini Generali e Misti, 1747, Mazzo 48.

1/Reggimento Monfort

On 19 July 1747 1/Monfort had 623 men, 89 percent of its establishment.[66] The battalion was commanded by *Luogotenente Colonnello* Daniele de Crousaz.[67] The French language was spoken in the ranks.[68]

Formed as a regiment of foreign infantry from soldiers of various nationalities, Monfort was a regiment that counted in its ranks soldiers recruited primarily from deserters from other armies who were able to speak French, the language of the unit. The real problem always remained the losses due to desertion, which were very high. Between 1742 and 1746 only, the battalion reported the loss of 841 deserters. Nevertheless, the regiment always showed a remarkable combativeness; at Madonna dell'Olmo in 1744 it had 160 dead and 184 wounded, for a total of 344 losses, 24.5 percent of its strength, without any act of desertion reported.

As for the individual equipment, the battalion had nothing to report. Only 'the flags are out of service, but the Colonel has assured that the new ones are ready, and that he is awaiting the meeting of the two Battalions, to distribute them'. The main deficiency concerned the tents, since 'the long and disastrous campaigns have completely destroyed the tents of the Regiment'.[69]

1/Monfort was engaged intensively until the Battle of Madonna dell'Olmo in 1744. The losses suffered in that occasion made it a no longer reliable unit, and it was replaced by less tried battalions. The intense operational life of the battalion and the foreign origin of the soldiers, meant that the losses reached 1,185 men in June 1747, 169.3 percent of the strength, of which 841, 71 percent of the total, were deserters. Destroyed and rebuilt at least once, in July 1747 the battalion was certainly not a solid unit. Exhausted by the losses suffered, 1/Monfort was not judged suitable for the defence of the entrenched camp, but it was equally placed as a garrison at the Colle del Gran Lago, in the immediate vicinity of the key point of the Gran Serin peak.

2/ and 3 Reggimento Kalbermatten

A regiment of Valais Swiss infantry; the German language was spoken within the two battalions.[70]

---

66   AST, Sezioni Riunite, Ministero della Guerra, Ufficio Generale del Soldo, Ruolini di Rivista, Reggimento Audibert/Monfort, Vol.72-84, 1742-1747.

67   BRT, Manoscritto Militare 36, *Personale degli Ufficiali dell'esercito del Re di Sardegna dal 1745 a tutto il 1747.*

68   For the foreign regiments in the Sardinian Service, see P. Bianchi, *Sotto diverse bandiere. L'internazionale militare nello Stato sabaudo d'antico regime* (Milano: Franco Angeli, 2012).

69   *Determinazioni di S.M. Relazione della Revista d'Ispezione datasi alle infrascritte Truppe in Aprile, e Maggio 1747. P.mo di Monfort.* AST, Sezioni Riunite, Ministero della Guerra, Ufficio Generale del Soldo, Ordini Generali e Misti, 1747, Mazzo 48.

70   Concerning Swiss regiments under the Sardinian flag; Bianchi, *Sotto diverse bandiere*; Giovanni Cerino-Badone, "'An Army inside the Army'. The Swiss regiments of the Sabaudian army 1741-1750', R. Jaun, P. Streit, H.D. Weck (eds), *Schweizer Solddienst. Neue Arbeiten – Neue Aspekte. Service étranger Suisse. Nouvelles études – nouveaux aspects* (Porrentruy: Schweizerische Vereinigung für Militärgeschichte und Militärwissenschaft, 2010), pp.171-198.

The second battalion had a total force of 595 men, 85 percent of the expected strength, while the third battalion, with 699 soldiers present in the ranks, was in fact at full strength.[71] The two battalions were commanded by *Luogotenente Colonnello* Marc-Antoine de Courten. More specifically, the second battalion was commanded by de Courten himself, while the third was under the orders of *Maggiore* Benoit des Vignes.[72]

Led by trained officers, scholars of tactics and fully dedicated to their profession of soldiers, the Reggimento Kalbermatten became one of the two best combat units of the Sardinian army, together with the Reggimento Roi. The battalion commanding officers, aware of the impoverishment that the war would have imposed on the regional character of the units, did everything to keep it intact at the level of non-commissioned officers. The result was that, despite the arrival of ever-increasing numbers of deserters from the imperial army and quickly enlisted as green recruits, the *esprit de corps* and the peculiarity of the 'Swiss' element never failed. However, the recruits never quite managed to meld with the original section, and in the first half of 1747 the second and third battalions lost 108 and 84 deserters respectively, 74 and 63 percent of the total losses suffered.

The two battalions had undoubtedly lost some of their equipment, given the very intense operational life to which they were subjected. We have a report of a review carried out of the second battalion which certifies how 'the soldiers' clothing was partially worn out, and the necessary repairs are made by the soldiers: the same is practiced with regard to the armament'. They were worn out materials, but they were still repaired and maintained in efficiency. On the other hand, it was pointed out that 'about the flags only the poles remain'.[73]

The combat experience of these two units, in particular that of the second battalion, was truly remarkable. 2/Kalbermatten had participated in all the campaigns of 1742, it was present at Casteldelfino in 1743, at the battle of Villefranche and at the defence of Cuneo in 1744, and again at Bassignana in 1745. The third battalion had been less busy in action, fighting at Madonna dell'Olmo in 1744 and at Bassignana in 1745. These very intense operational cycles had allowed the officers to store a considerable combat experience; on 19 July 1747, on the top of the Gran Serin, they knew which was the best tactical formation to adopt to face the opposing columns. However, the two battalions had suffered heavy losses, forcing the recruiting teams to beat the Piedmontese and Swiss countryside in search of suitable recruits. Concerning the second battalion, 'the captains represent the serious losses suffered pending the Provence Campaign, being unable to remit [in force] their Companies,

<hr>

71   AST, Sezioni Riunite, Ministero della Guerra, Ufficio Generale del Soldo, Ruolini di Rivista, Reggimento Kalbermatten, Vol.58, 1747. Unfortunately, the rolls of this regiment, although still existing, are no longer available for the years 1742-1746 due to the damage suffered during the Second World War.

72   BRT, Manoscritto Militare 36, *Personale degli Ufficiali dell'esercito del Re di Sardegna dal 1745 a tutto il 1747*; AST, Sezioni Riunite, Ministero della Guerra, Ufficio Generale del Soldo, Ruolini di Rivista, Reggimento Kalbermatten, Vol.58, 1747.

73   *Determinazioni di S.M. Relazione della Revista d'Ispezione datasi alle infrascritte Truppe in Aprile, e Maggio 1747. 2.o di Kalbermatten.* AST, Sezioni Riunite, Ministero della Guerra, Ufficio Generale del Soldo, Ordini Generali e Misti, 1747, Mazzo 48.

without the effects of the Royal graces they implore',[74] which meant the disbursement of more money for the prizes of engagement.

The two battalion were of proven efficiency, commanded by experienced officers and hardened by five years of intense fighting. Bricherasio decided to have them to defend the key point of the entire entrenched camp: the high ground of the Gran Serin.

3/Reggimento Roi

The third battalion of a regiment of Bernese Swiss Infantry, the battalion spoke entirely in German.

The battalion was at full strength,[75] and under the orders of *Maggiore* Georges Augustin Roguin.[76]

The Reggimento Roi, with the Reggimento Kalbermatten, represented the best combat units of the Sardinian army in the year 1747. Commanded by capable officers, these the units were continuously employed in action. The Swiss element, however, was severely depleted, and it was kept alive by the officer corps, who had lost only had 20 percent of their original number, and, above all, by the non-commissioned officers, of whom the majority (67.1 percent) remained of Swiss origin. The battalion in the spring of 1747 was 'in excellent condition, except for the flags, which are completely ruined'.[77]

Raised in 1743, 3/Roi. had had a less intense operational life than that of the first two battalions of the regiment. It participated in the Battle of Madonna dell'Olmo in 1744 and it had been part of the garrison of the Citadel of Alessandria during the blockade of 1745/46. After that date it had been employed in the offensive in eastern Piedmont and in Emilia. Between 1743 and 1746 battalion lost a total of 680 men, 97.1 percent of its strength. The losses due to desertion, always relatively low, had increased during the blockade of the Citadel of Alexandria and in subsequent operations; between July 1745 and December 1746, 347 men had fled from the ranks. Nevertheless, through massive recruitment campaigns, the effective strength always remained within the expected numbers.

This battalion was one of those with the greatest combat power in the entire Sardinian army. It is no coincidence that Bricherasio requested its presence at the Assietta field; once it arrived, it was assigned to defend the Gran Serin redoubt, one of the key points of the battlefield.

Reggimento Meyer

A single-battalion regiment of Swiss Infantry of Glaris and Appenzell; within the regiment, orders and communications were in German. With 721 men present, the regiment not only

---

74   *Determinazioni di S.M. Relazione della Revista d'Ispezione datasi alle infrascritte Truppe in Aprile, e Maggio 1747. 2.o di Kalbermatten.* AST, Sezioni Riunite, Ministero della Guerra, Ufficio Generale del Soldo, Ordini Generali e Misti, 1747, Mazzo 48.

75   AST, Sezioni Riunite, Ministero della Guerra, Ufficio Generale del Soldo, Ruolini di Rivista, Reggimento Diesbach/Roguin/Roi, Vol.20-30, 1746-1747.

76   BRT, Manoscritto Militare 36, *Personale degli Ufficiali dell'esercito del Re di Sardegna dal 1745 a tutto il 1747.*

77   *Determinazioni di S.M. Relazione della Revista d'Ispezione datasi alle infrascritte Truppe in Aprile, e Maggio 1747. 3.o di Roy.* AST, Sezioni Riunite, Ministero della Guerra, Ufficio Generale del Soldo, Ordini Generali e Misti, 1747, Mazzo 48.

was completed, but had in fact reached 103 percent of the expected total.[78] On 19 July 1747, the colonel-commandant, Adrien Meyer, was present.[79]

The regiment was raised in 1743, and it became operational during the first months of 1744. Created as a garrison unit, it was intended to serve the sole purpose of rendering other Sardinian units free from garrison activities. With the whole Army under stress, it was necessary to use the Reggimento Meyer in the first line. In 1745 it participated in the Alpine campaign, operating against the forces of the French general Lautrec. On 12 October 1745 it was involved at the Battle of Joussaud, losing 151 men, 27.5 percent of the total. The regiment was hit hard, and it had to be rebuilt with recruits of dubious, if not poor, reliability. In addition, the backlash in terms of morale was such that the desertion rate, of about five men per month between January 1744 and June 1745, doubled, rising to an rate of 11 desertions per month. Officers worked hard to keep the unit together, with mixed results. By 1747 Meyer seemed to have returned to the standards of the first half of 1744. In the spring magazine of 1747 'the Battalion found itself without tents, which must have been lost in the Jossaud affair'.[80]

By June 1747 Meyer had lost 654 men, 93 percent of its establishment. Officers also suffered relatively large losses, 35 percent of their strength. However, despite the losses suffered in 1745 in Val Chisone and the subsequent crescendo of desertions, the battalion in 1747 had been rebuilt, re-equipped and it was ready to fight. The regiment knew the battleground of Assietta well since it had already operated in the area in 1745. Bricherasio placed it on the western edge of the Assietta plateau, alongside the imperial battalions.

Militias of Pragelato, Val di Susa, and Waldensians

For the campaign of 1745, three militia corps were raised, from Pragelato, Val di Susa and inside the Waldensian Valleys (Gemanasca and Pellice), each with a strength of 500 men, for a total of 1,500 militiamen.[81] The three contingents were under the orders, respectively, of *Maggiore* Perrone, the Cavaliere Tana, and *Capitano* Rouzier of the Reggimento Monfort.[82]

The militia was essentially a defensive organization, and, given its nature, it was unthinkable to train men according to regulations and schemes suitable for regular troops. Many of the militiamen possessed their own weapons, with which they were engaged in hunting, target shooting and, very often, for illegal activities. The value of these units, in addition to

---

78   AST, Sezioni Riunite, Ministero della Guerra, Ufficio Generale del Soldo, Ruolini di Rivista, Reggimento Meyer, Vols.1-8, 1747.

79   BRT, Manoscritto Militare 36, *Personale degli Ufficiali dell'esercito del Re di Sardegna dal 1745 a tutto il 1747.*

80   *Determinazioni di S.M. Relazione della Revista d'Ispezione datasi alle infrascritte Truppe in Aprile, e Maggio 1747. Meyer.* AST, Sezioni Riunite, Ministero della Guerra, Ufficio Generale del Soldo, Ordini Generali e Misti, 1747, Mazzo 48.

81   The task-organization and the overall strength of the Piedmontese militias employed in the Alpine Campaign of 1747 are described in the documents collected in in AST, Sezioni Riuniti, Ministero della Guerra, Regia Segreteria di Guerra, Lettere ai Governatori, Mazzo 43. This is an important collection in which the methods of raising militia units, rally points, the chain of command and tactical missions are described.

82   AST, Sezioni Riunite, Ministero della Guerra, Regia Segreteria di Guerra, Lettere ai Governatori, Mazzo 43, Lettera del 23 giugno 1747 della Segreteria al Vassallo di Morgenex, Governatore di Pinerolo.

the perfect knowledge of the territory, as happened in July 1747, lay in the fact that men and officers belonged to the same community, knew each other perfectly, and they were linked together by ties that disregarded the oath made to the Crown. The Waldensian militia, commanded by one of the most skilled officers of the entire Sardinian army, Jean-Baptiste Rouzier, was probably the most feared unit of the entire Sardinian army from the end of the seventeenth century. The deep knowledge of the alpine terrain, their ability with weapons, their capable officers and a good dose of religious fanaticism made this unit a fundamental tool for conducting the war in the Western Alps.[83]

The militia could be supplied with weapons coming from the Arsenal of Turin or it presented itself to the call of its commanders with the weapons it had at its disposal. The militia units present at the Battle of Assietta were all equipped with firearms.

The militias of the Val di Susa and Pragelato had already been activated during the Campaigns of 1745 and 1746. The same had happened for the Waldensian Militia which, due to its undoubted ability to manoeuvre in mountainous territory, was often used at some distance from its usual area of operations, such as the Maritime Alps. The three militia groups were the only real mountain troops available to Bricherasio. Fast, motivated, well armed and equipped, commanded by skilled officers, perfectly at ease on a terrain they knew perfectly, these were by far the best units that Bricherasio could have. The commander rightly decided to use them as light infantry to monitor the enemy's moves in real time, from the border to the vicinity of the Assietta entrenched camp.

Colloredo's Brigade

Maria Theresia's imperial army in 1747 was no longer that weak and disorganized band of 1740, when the War of the Austrian Succession broke out and the Empire was attacked by its enemies. Seven years later it had:

- Faced Friedrich II's kingdom of Prussia in two separate conflicts. In the end the Empress was defeated but the experience gained in the field had forged a new army.

---

83 Regarding the Waldensian Militia, see E.A. Rivoire, *Appunti cronologici sulle Milizie Valdesi* (Teramo: B. Cioschi, 1932); E. Tron, 'Alcune precisazioni sul "Reggimento Valdese"', in *Bollettino della Società di Studi Valdesi*, Vol.72 (1951, n. 92), 75 (1954, n. 95), pp.41-65, 37-68. The most recent work, which breaks down many clichés relating to the use and equipment of these units, is an article by E. Garoglio, 'I Valdesi in armi, da banditi religionari e miliziani del Re di Sardegna', in S. Tourn Boncoeur, E. Garoglio (eds) *Le collezioni di armi del Museo valdese di Torre Pellice* (Torre Pellice: Museo valdese, 2015), pp.41-52. On Jean Baptiste Rouzier, see G. Cerino Badone, 'Gli eserciti sabaudo e francese durante la Guerra di Successione Austriaca. L'impiego in campo', in R. Sconfienza (ed.) *La campagna gallispana del 1744. Storia e Archeologia Militare in un anno di guerra fra Piemonte e Delfinato* (Oxford: Archaeopress, 2012), pp.187-225. Concerning other militia units, see N. Brancaccio, *L'esercito del Vecchio Piemonte. Gli Ordinamenti, Parte I – Da 1560 al 1814* (Roma: Stabilimento Poligrafico per l'amministrazione della Guerra, 1923), pp.269-271. Regarding low-intensity operations, the fundamental work is that by S. Picaud-Monnerat, *La petite guerre au XVIIIe siècle* (Paris: Economica, 2010) and specifically S. Picaud-Monnerat, 'De la petite guerre «à la hongroise» a la petite guerre «à la française»: le rôle moteur de la guerre de succession d'Autriche (1740-1748)', in H. Gábor (ed.), *Az értelem bátorsága tanulmányok perjés géza emlékére* (Budapest: Argumentum 2005), pp.519-538.

- Demonstrated its operational and tactical superiority over the Bavarians and the French.
- Effectively employed it light infantry, which it had become famous throughout Europe for its ferocity and efficiency.
- Fought and won the biggest battle of the conflict on the Italian front in 1746 at Piacenza.

The Austrian forces in Italy always had a fluctuating presence, at least until 1746. In the winter of 1741, facing the Prussian aggression in Silesia and relying on the dissuasive effect of the English Fleet in the Mediterranean, Vienna halved the garrison of Lombardy, transferring 14 infantry battalions and one hussar regiment to Austria, for a total of 8,000 men, leaving just 10 battalions in the Duchy of Milan. In the meantime, the empress was forced to reopen negotiations with the Turin court, which she had interrupted until then. Maria Theresia had initially remained convinced that the English blockade of the Spanish coasts would be enough to avert the Bourbon expedition without having to resort to a Sardinian alliance, which certainly would have entailed a high political price; lands in exchange for closing the Alpine passes. The landing and the subsequent advance of the Spanish army under the orders of the Duque de Montemar towards the Po Valley pushed Turin and Vienna to set aside their mutual differences and demands to make a common front against the new threat. In the following winter, after the Spanish landing in Tuscany, the Lombardy garrison was reinforced; in 1742 there were 18 understrength battalions, while the skeletal cavalry units numbered 12 squadrons of cuirassiers and three of hussars. In all there were 9,500 infantry and just 3,000 horsemen.

The situation did not change much during 1743. In 1744 the Imperialists, thanks also to the fact that their right flank was protected by the Sardinian army, did very little to contain the Franco-Spanish offensive on Cuneo, but they launched an offensive against Naples. The advance was quite easy until it reached Velletri near Rome, where it was blocked by a joint Spanish-Neapolitan army. A body of 5,500 men, one third being irregular light infantry and the remainder infantry from the regiments of Pallavicini and Clerici, participated in the operations in southern Piedmont. Again drained of men in 1745 due to the resumption of hostilities against Friedrich II's Prussia, the *Lombardei-Armee* was split in two by the Franco-Spanish offensive. In the winter of 1745-1746, *Feldzeugmeister* Maximilian Ulysses Graf von Browne finally came to Italy with a veteran army of 30,000 men. During 1747 the flow of troops along the Brenner-Mantua-Milan route did not seem to decrease, and in the autumn the Austrian army had about 70,000 men, equal to 86 battalions and 15 cavalry regiments, all completed and at full strength.[84]

---

84   K.k. Generalstab, *Oesterreichischer Erbfolge*-krieg, Vol.8. Unfortunately, the outbreak of the First World War interrupted the publication of this important series, which ends with the year 1744. For the 1747 Campaign, please refer to the following articles, based on original sources from Kriegsarchiv Vienna, published in *Österreichische militärische Zeitschrift*: Rothkirch, 'Der Feldzug 1747 in Italien', Vol.X, (1842), pp.3-31, Vol.XI, (1842), pp.121-135. Other important considerations on the Austrian imperial army, alongside geopolitical considerations on the War of the Austrian Succession, are in V. Ilari, C. Paoletti, P. Crociani, *Bella Italia Militar. Eserciti e Marine nell'Italia pre-napoleonica (1748-1792)* (Roma: USSME, 2000), pp.337-427.

Table 3. The Austrian Forces on the Piedmontese Front, 1744-1747

Year	Numerical strength of the imperial forces on the Piedmontese front
1744	5,500
1745	10,000
1746	45,000
1747	25,000

Sources: AST, Corte, Materie Militari, Imprese, Mazzi 2-8 d'addizione; Memorie politiche per rapporto all'interno, Storie della Real Casa, Mazzo 22, 23, 24; Minutoli, *Relation des Campagnes faites par S.M.*

While the siege of Genoa drew to a close, with the defeat of the imperial army unable to recapture the city, the King of Sardinia managed to get a skeletal Austrian infantry brigade, made up of four battalions, sent to fight in the Alps. Commanded by Graf Antonio Colloredo-Melz und Wallsee, this was made up of the following battalions, stationed in the Duchy of Lombardy waiting to receive reinforcements from Austria: 3/IR Colloredo, 3/IR Forgách, and a battalion each of IR Hagenbach and IR Traun.

It was really a very weak formation, 1,076 men at all. The campaign of 1746 in Provence and that of 1747 against Genoa had been very expensive in terms of men and equipment, and the campaign had left all the Austrian battalions heavily understrength. An imperial battalion in 1747 should have had 700 men, which meant

Antonio, Graf Colloredo-Melz und Wallsee (1707-1785). Colloredo had received in 1742 the rank of *Generalfeldwachtmeister*. In 1747 he was placed in command of the small Austrian brigade present in Lombardy and destined to reinforce the Alpine front. (Collection of the Military Academy of Wiener-Neustadt)

that theoretically 2,800 men were expected at Assietta. Less than half of them were in fact available, but their morale was excellent. The Sardinian cavalry lieutenant Gaspare Galleani d'Agliano recalled how the Austrians 'showed themselves very proud by making pomp of their forces greater than ours, and at every step they celebrated their military actions, remembering their victory in Piacenza, and finally appointing themselves as the liberators of Italy'.[85]

As for the Sardinian units, we will try to calculate the fighting power of the imperial units, evaluating the following criteria: recruiting area, numerical strength, combat experience and losses suffered.[86]

3/Infanterie Regiment Colloredo

The regiment recruited in the *Österreichische Vorlande*, the western territories of the Austrian Empire. On 19 July 1747 it had 218 men in all, 31.1 percent of its establishment. The regiment was undoubtedly very tried from the beginning of the campaign. In April 1747 the two battalions employed on the Ligurian front had a total force of 448 men.[87]

At the outbreak of hostilities, the regiment was stationed in Piacenza. Subsequently it participated at the Battle of Camposanto in 1743, and in the operations of 1744 for the reconquest of Naples. It then returned to Northern Italy, and it fought in the Po Valley in 1746, participating in the battle of Piacenza. It was then amongst the units to occupy Genoa in 1746 and it took part to the expedition to Provence. The battalion that fought at Assietta, the third, was in Lombardy waiting to replenish its forces with the arrival of new recruits from Austria.[88]

IR Colloredo was a solid unit with a good reputation. In July 1747 during the Alpine campaign the third battalion had the honour to come under the command of its *Inhaber*, Graf Colloredo.[89] Despite its limited numerical strength, comparable to that of a company of a Swiss regiment of the Sardinian Army, the battalion was placed along the main line of the Assietta entrenchments, to the left of the IR Forgách.

3/Infanterie Regiment Forgách

IR Forgách was one of the first Hungarian regiments raised at the request of Empress Maria Theresia. The third battalion, commanded by the *Obristwachtmeister* [Major] Josip Graf von Drašković, was sent to complete its armament in Bratislava. The weapons, however, were late in arriving and they were delivered to the battalion only in late January.[90] In 1741, while

---

85   Galleani d'Agliano, *Memorie storiche*, pp.362-363.

86   The strengths of the imperial battalions are deduced from *Ständ und Dienst Tabella* of 18 June 1747. KA, Alten Feldakten I-VI, Krieg in Italien, 1747.

87   Rothkirch, 'Der Feldzug 1747 in Italien', Vol.X, p.31; G. Amon von Treuenfest, *Geschichte des k.k. Infanterie-Regiments Nr. 20 Friedrich Wilhelm, Kronprinz des Deutschen Reiches und Kronprinz von Preussen* (Wien: Verlag des Regiments, 1878), p.141.

88   The information that the battalion sent to Assietta was the third is present in A. Wrede, *Geschichte der k.u.k. Wehrmacht. Die Regimenter, Corps, Branchen und Anstalten von 1618 bis Ende des XIX Jahrhunderts. Hrsg. von der Direktion des k.u.k. Kriegsarchivs* (Wien: L.W. Seidel & Sohn, 1898-1905), Vol.I, pp.256-263.

89   The Austrian regiments each had a commander-owner, *Chef* or *Inhaber*, who gave his name to the regiment. Very often these were generals or senior officers, unable to command the unit directly. For this reason there was a colonel-commander, who exercised the effective command. Graf Colloredo was the *Inhaber* of the regiment, but not its actual commander.

90   E. Seeliger, *Geschichte des kaiserlichen und königlichen Infanterie-Regiments N° 32* (Budapest: Pester Buchdruckerei-Actien-Gesellschaft, 1900). p.14.

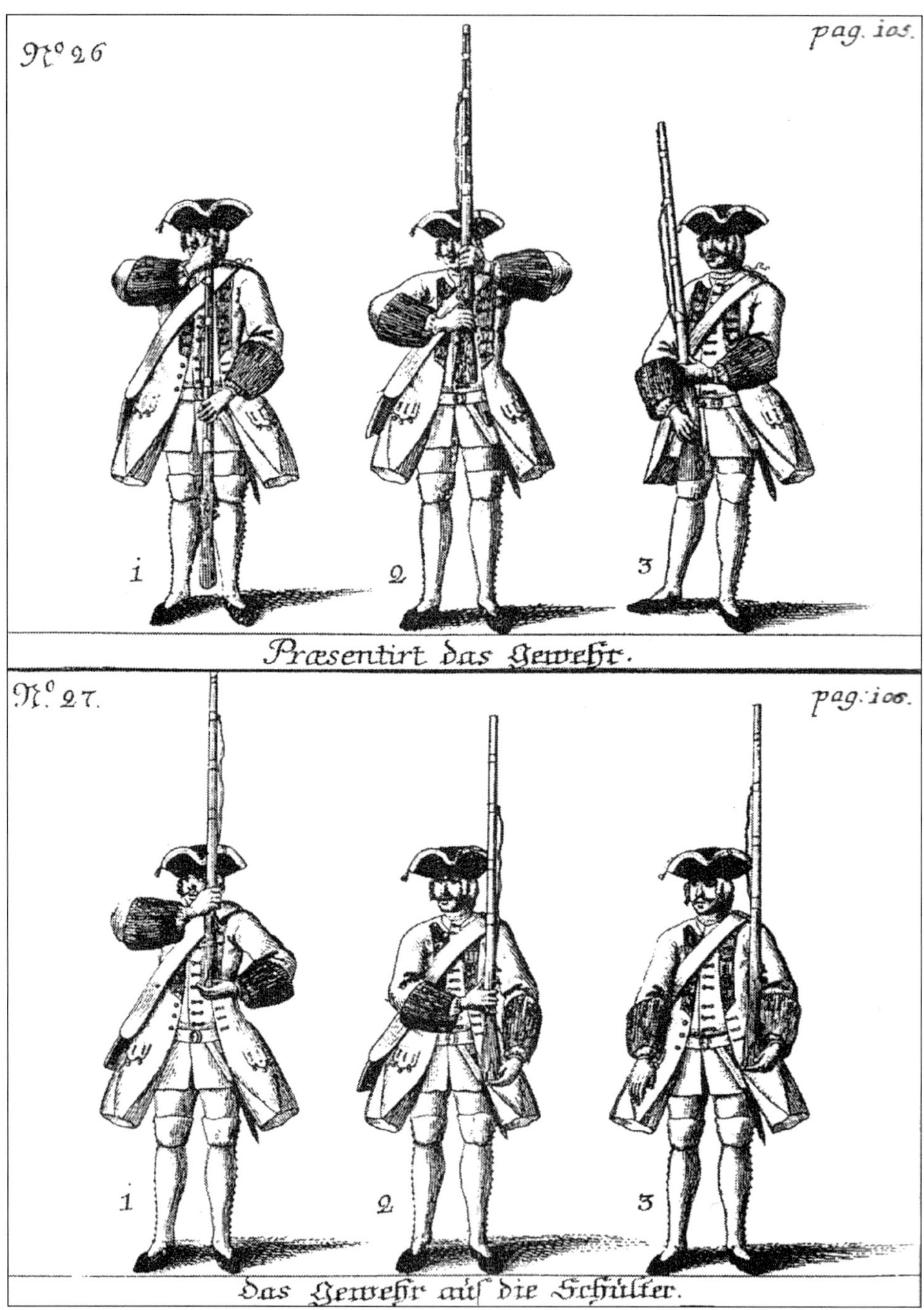

An Austrian infantryman is practising the handling of weapons, as presented by the *Regulament und Ordnung des Gesammten Kaiserlich-Königlichen Fuß-Volks of 1749*, which formalised the experiences gained during the War of the Austrian Succession. (*Regulament und Ordnung des Gesammten Kaiserlich-Königlichen Fuß-Volks*, tables 26 and 27)

garrisoned in Brno in Bohemia, the battalion had a total of 530 men.[91] In July 1747 it had a company of 68 grenadiers and 190 men in four companies of fusiliers, for a total of 258 men, 48 percent of the original force[92].

3/IR Forgách, after having carried out garrison service in Vienna, in 1744 was sent to fight on the Rhine front, and later in South Bohemia, where it was heavily engaged in combat. In August 1744, Drašković was promoted to *oberstleutnant* for distinguished service. After having fought in 1745 against the Prussians in Moravia, the following year the battalion was transferred with the whole regiment to Italy, where it fought at Piacenza and at the capture of Genoa.[93]

The battalion, although understaffed, was commanded by one of the most aggressive and skilled officers in the Imperial Army, already promoted for distinguished service.[94] Bricherasio decided to place it along the main line of defence, with the battalion of IR Traun on the left and the Sardinian Swiss Reggimento Meyer on the right.

Infanterie Regiment Hagenbach

The regiment recruited in Silesia. In July 1747 the battalion of IR Hagenbach serving with Colloredo's brigade had 297 men in its ranks, 42.4 percent of the theoretical force.[95]

Heir to the old IR Alt-Wallis that fought in Piedmont during the War of the Spanish Succession, IR Hagenbach had fought in 1743 in Camposanto. It did not participate in any major action between 1744 and 1745, and only in 1746 it took part at the conquest of Genoa and at the expedition to Provence. In 1747 one of his three battalions, probably the third, was detached on the Alpine front.[96] It was a unit with limited combat experience. Bricherasio preferred to have it in reserve, in the entrenchments built across the road that went up from Val Chisone.

Infanterie Regiment Traun

The unit recruited in the German-speaking territories of the Empire. In July 1747 the battalion at Assietta, probably the third, had 303 men, 43.3 percent of the planned force.[97]

---

91   Seeliger, *Geschichte des kaiserlichen und königlichen Infanterie-Regiments N° 32*, p.15.
92   KA, Alten Feldakten I-VI, Krieg in Italien, 1747, *Ständ und Dienst Tabella* of 18 June 1747.
93   Wrede, *Geschichte der k.u.k. Wehrmacht*, Vol.I, p.347; Seeliger, *Geschichte des kaiserlichen und königlichen Infanterie-Regiments N° 32*, pp.15-20; A. Thürheim, *Gedenkblätter aus der Kriegsgeschichte der K.K. oesterreichischen Armee* (Wien und Teschen: Buchhandlung für Militär-Literatur, 1880), Vol.I, p.212.
94   The presence of Drašković is confirmed by Colloredo Report, KA, Alten Feldakten, Krieg in Italien, VII, 1.
95   KA, Alten Feldakten I-VI, Krieg in Italien, 1747, *Ständ und Dienst Tabella* of 18 June 1747. The regiment suffered heavy losses and it was never able to replace them with the arrival of new recruits. After the Assietta campaign, the battalion and its companies, decimated by losses and illnesses, were transferred to Parma in the spring of 1748 for the necessary rest. G. Hubka von Czernczitz, *Geschichte des k. und k. Infanterie-Regiments Graf von Lacy Nr. 22, von seiner Errichtung bis zur Gegenwart* (Zara: Verlag des Regiments, 1902), p.531. This work describes the events related to the history of IR Roth, which at the end of the War of the Austrian Succession absorbed the IR Hagenbach, disbanded because its recruitment area, Silesia, had been annexed to the Kingdom of Prussia.
96   Wrede, *Geschichte der k.u.k. Wehrmacht*, Vol.II, pp.214-216. Information about this regiment is rather sparse as it was disbanded in 1748, as soon as the conflict was over.
97   KA, Alten Feldakten I-VI, Krieg in Italien, 1747, *Ständ und Dienst Tabella* of 18 June 1747.

The regiment fought at Camposanto in 1743 and at the capture of Genoa in 1746.[98] Even though it was a unit with little combat experience, it was placed in a very delicate sector, at the point where the communication with the Testa dell'Assietta joined the main defence of the camp.

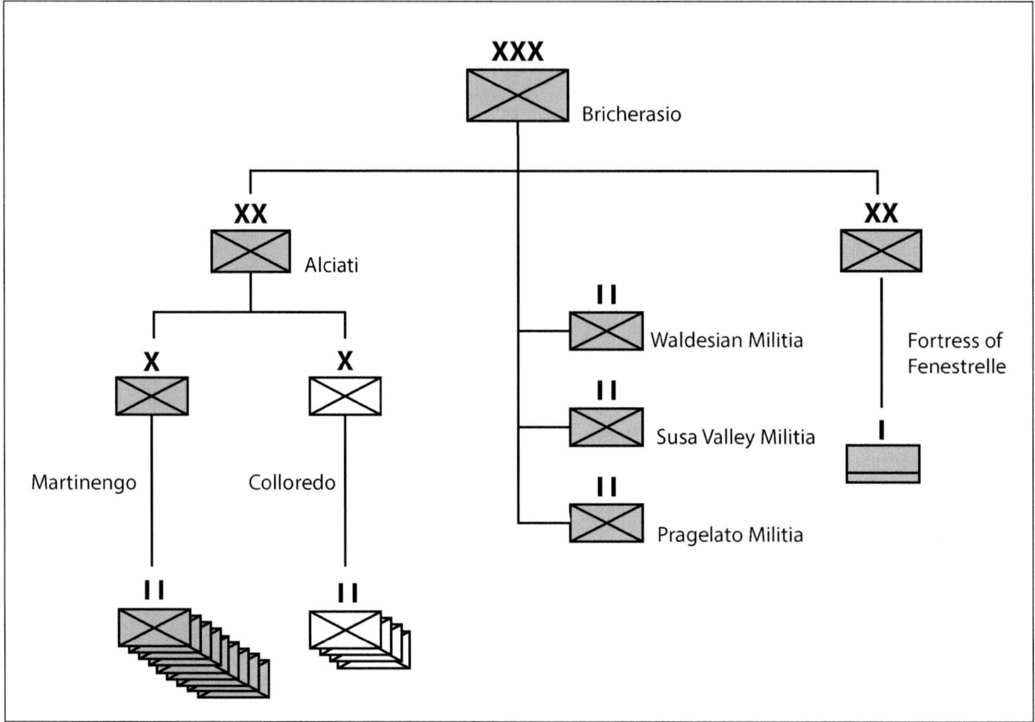

The task organisation of the forces available to the Conte di Bricherasio for the 1747 Alpine campaign. Note how the militia units, essential for gathering information in the field, reported directly to the commander in chief, while the logistic support depended on the governor of the fortress of Fenestrelle. (Diagram by George Anderson © Helion and Company 2022)

---

98   Wrede, *Geschichte der k.u.k. Wehrmacht*, Vol.II, pp.217-218. Information about IR Traun is rather sparse as it was disbanded, like IR Hagenbach, in 1748.

3

The Army of His Most Christian Majesty

The Peace of Vienna of 18 November 1738 ended the War of the Polish Succession, burying the House of Savoy's ephemeral dream of a Kingdom of Lombardy and truncating the plan to create a great Italian Confederation under the protection of Paris. Moreover, it cut the peninsula into two distinct areas of influence, one under the Austrian Habsburgs, now extended to all of northern Italy, and one under the Bourbon dynasty, limited to the south. This arrangement Spain tried to question in 1742-1748, with the result of extending the Austro-English protectorate also to the Kingdom of Two Sicilies. This system remained in equilibrium, despite underground aftershocks and the threat of Napoleon Bonaparte, until the mid-nineteenth century when the main antagonist of the House of Austria, the kingdom of Sardinia, found in the France of Napoleon III an ally determined to change the whole situation and overthrow the Habsburg hegemony in Italy.

The France of Louis XV had espoused the strategy of Charles Fouquet, Duc de Belle Isle, who had conceived a vast plan to subject the Empire and the whole Europe to French influence. Despite the constitution of an *Armée d'Italie* since 1741 France did not intend to repeat any action against Milan. Co-belligerence with Prussia had shifted the entire strategic axis to the German-Bohemian front, threatening Vienna itself, and it made no sense to divert forces to a secondary and impervious front like the Italian one, where France's Spanish allies could be left to engage additional imperial forces.

The Court of Versailles had little interest in changing the structure of Italy accepted with the peace of 1738, even if it could not deny its direct support for the parallel war that Spain intended to wage in the peninsula. Strengthened by numerous sympathizers in all Italian states, the Spanish intended to reconquer Parma, Piacenza, Milan and Mantua, with the plan to make the infante Don Filippo, younger brother of the King of the Two Sicilies, sovereign of these lands. Having gained the secret alliance of the Duke of Modena, the Bourbon forces began the attack on the Italian front. The Madrid initiative led Carlo Emanuele III to sign a 'provisional agreement' on 1 February 1742 with Maria Theresia. His strategic choice was relatively forced. Having come out of the War of the Polish Succession with reduced expectations, he could not trust the proposals that Cardinal Fleury, chief minister of Louis XV, had advanced in 1741; he would receive the whole Lombard territory up to the Adda river, in exchange for Savoy and Parma, Piacenza, Mantua and eastern Lombardy to Don Filippo. Despite the destruction of the Este forces of Modena and the blows suffered by the troops of the Duque de Montemar, in 1742 the army of the Marqués de la Mina was able to occupy Savoy and inflict a serious defeat on Carlo Emanuele III.

The failure of diplomatic negotiations with the kingdom of Sardinia, the ratification of the Treaty of Worms, the defeat of Casteldelfino in 1743 and the naval domination of British fleet clearly gave evidence to France how complex it would be to break through the Alpine front. Nonetheless, the kingdoms of France and Spain could field an impressive number of men, almost 400,000 from the French *Armée Royale* alone, and simultaneously engage multiple fronts. As in the War of the Spanish Succession, France and Spain fought in Flanders, on the Rhine, in Italy and in the colonies, not counting the Navy.

Table 4: State of the Land Forces of His Most Christian Majesty in May 1748

Infantry	Battalions	Soldiers
National infantry	356	261,455
Foreign infantry	84	59,183
Irregular infantry	13	9,569
Cavalry	**Squadrons**	**Troopers**
Cavalry regiments	301	47,531
Dragoon regiments	85	13,824
Irregular mounted forces	25	3,120

Source. J. Campbell, *The Present State of Europe; Explaining the Interests, Connections, Political and Commercial Views of its Several Powers, Comprehending also, A clear and Concise History of each Country, so far as to show the Nature of their Present Constitutions*, (London: Thomas Longman and Charles Hitch, 1753), pp.300-302.

Table 5. The Strength of the Franco-Spanish Forces on the Piedmontese Front

Year	Campaign	Total forces
1742	Second Savoy Campaign	20,000
1743	Casteldelfino	30,000
1744	Villefranche	30,000
1744	Western Alps	55,000
1745	Maillebois Army	65,000
1745	Lautrec Observation Corps	13,000
1746	Gage/Maillebois Army	40,000
1747	Franco-Spanish Army of Provence	50,000
1747	Armée d'Italie under Chevalier de Belle-Isle	22,000

Source. Arvers and de Vault, *Guerre de la Succession d'Autriche*.

Thanks to the strength of these numbers, the military forces of the Bourbon allies on the Italian front were very powerful.

Various solutions were attempted to pierce the Alpine bastion. Only in 1745 was the most convenient was found; bypassing the Alps to the south, taking advantage of the Ligurian coast and the passes of the Apennines. The Franco-Spanish offensives always had a very specific objective: to occupy a stronghold 'beyond' the Alps, to then be able to resume the offensive in the following spring, in order to detach the kingdom of Sardinia from its alliance with the Empire and Britain. The fortresses of Demonte, Cuneo, and Exilles were the main objectives of these operations. Only Demonte, however, fell into Bourbon hands during the campaign of 1744. The course of the campaigns can be summarised as follows:

- 1742-1743, the Swiss option. With the occupation of Savoy, the Spanish could organize an offensive against Milan by taking advantage of the Simplon pass after having crossed the Valais and the Grisons.
- 1743, the breach of the Val Varaita. Taking advantage of the absence of permanent fortifications in Val Varaita, the Bourbon offensive of October 1743 was launched along this valley. The Sardinian defence and, above all, the bad season, caused the failure of the whole operation.
- 1744, assault on the Alpine bastion on several columns. With nine detached columns, the Prince de Conti managed to overcome the Alpine front. The limited forces at his disposal and the guerrillas that raged in the rear finally forced him to retreat while besieging Cuneo, the strategic object of the entire campaign.
- 1745, strategic bypass to the south. Taking advantage of the alliance of the republic of Genoa, *Maréchal* Maillebois went around the alpine bastion to the south, penetrating between Lombardy and Piedmont, overcoming the Apennines at the Bocchetta pass above Genoa, hitting the Sardinian main forces from behind. In 1745 the Franco-Spaniards had occupied Casale and they arrived at the castle of Gabiano about 40 kilometres from Turin. As in 1704-1706, this great manoeuvre enabled them to advantageously engage the Sardinian forces over the course of the Po and make it possible to transport supplies for the siege of Turin.
- 1746-1747, the defence of Genoa. Maillebois' coup was not accompanied by a credible diplomatic initiative intended to separate Turin from Vienna. The Spanish ambitions slowed the French race on Turin along the Po. This made a recovery possible, the arrival of a powerful imperial rescue force and the launch of an all-out offensive in the spring of 1746, which culminated in the terrifying battle of Piacenza (16 June 1746), one of the bloodiest of the eighteenth century, narrowly won by the army of Maria Theresia. The Franco-Spaniards in subsequent campaigns still attempted an advance along the west coast, but by now the game had been discovered and the Austro-Sardinian forces had become particularly efficient in slowing and halting the opposing offensive thrust along the Ceva-Savona line. The strategic objective for northern Italy remained the defence of Genoa, which was achieved despite the British naval domination.

Bourbon strategic plans were often appropriate and bold. In particular that of *Maréchal* Maillebois for the campaign of 1745, which envisaged the attack from the Ligurian Apennines, the breaking of the Savoy-Imperial line at the junction between the two enemy armies and the search for the decisive battle, was extensively analysed and successfully applied by Napoleon Bonaparte in the 1796 campaign, the first phase of which ended with the armistice of Cherasco and the surrender of the Kingdom of Sardina. However, the French already in 1794 had been able to demonstrate their total tactical superiority over Victor Amadeus III's army, attacking the Alpine bastion from the front. On 25 July, after taking possession of the main Alpine passes (Little St Bernard, Monginevro, Moncenisio, Colle dell'Agnello, Colle della Maddalena, Colle di Tenda) they launched their offensive against

Cuneo, descending from the Stura, Maira and Varaita valleys. The operation, which it had already begun under good auspices and had seen the French forces go as far as Borgo San Dalmazzo, was suspended on 9 August due to the coup d'état of Thermidor and the death of Robespierre. Fearing civil war, the troops were recalled to their homeland and all actions in this operational theatre were suspended. The French revolutionary army, forged in the last third of the eighteenth century, fully demonstrated all the improvements and progress made since the sad days of the Seven Years War. For the Sardinian army, abandoned by the allies and poorly conducted on the battlefield, there could not have been a more demanding opponent; if in 1744 it could hold the comparison with the French one, in 1794, despite the logistical shortcomings of the Republicans, the Sardinian army was outclassed from every point of view; tactical, technological and moral.

Chain of Command

On 10 June 1747 *Lieutenant Général* Louis Charles Armand Fouquet, Chevalier de Belle-Isle, arrived in Guillestre to take command of the *Armée du Dauphiné*. The Chevalier depended directly on the commander-in-chief of the French troops operating on the Alpine-Northwest Italy theatre, *Maréchal* Charles Louis Auguste Fouquet, Duc de Belle-Isle, his elder brother. The forces he was going to command were quite impressive; 29 infantry battalions, about 20,000 men, tasked with the conquest of a limited and rather weak target, the Fort of Exilles. Two years earlier, the Comte de Lautrec had almost succeeded with much weaker forces, 17 infantry battalions for a total of about 12,000 men, half of them Spanish.[1] Now the situation was very different.

The French army of the first half of the eighteenth century did not have a rigid organization, although it clearly needed to divide its forces into columns, which would later be known as divisions, and brigades, the latter made up of four or five battalions.[2] Each of these brigades was named after the oldest battalion or regiment. In 1747 the *Armée du Dauphiné* was divided into three distinct sections:

- A strong vanguard, under the command of a *maréchal de camp*, usually the Comte d'Arnaud.
- The central body, under the direct command of the Chevalier de Belle-Isle.
- A detached body, destined to march parallel to the main group, under the command of *Lieutenant Général* de Villemur.

---

1   The order of battle of the Franco-Spanish forces, which operated during what became known as the 'Diversion of Exilles', are present in Vault, Arvers, *Guerre de la Succession* d'Autriche, Vol.II, p.354.
2   P. Griffith, *The Art of War of Revolutionary France 1789-1802* (London: Greenhill Books, 1998), pp.156-157. On the creation of divisions in the French army, see S.T. Ross, 'The Development of the Combat Division in Eighteenth-Century French Armies', in *French Historical Studies*, Vol.IV, no.1, pp.84-94. L.H. Bacquet, *l'Infanterie au XVIIIe siècle. L'Organisation* (Paris-Nancy: Berger-Lavrault, 1907) is always useful on the evolution of the organization of the French army during the eighteenth century.

The Régiment Royal Roussillon is preparing to leave for the Alpine front. The officer portrayed, probably the deputy commander of the regiment, *Lieutenant Colonel* de Bourdeville, is giving the necessary instructions to his men, who are about to leave the camp; within a few days he will be engaged against the Sardinian positions on the Gran Serin, where he will lose 30 percent of his men among the dead, wounded and missing. (Courtesy of the director of the Fort Ticonderoga Museum, Dr Matt Keagle)

The organization of the forces of the *Armée du Dauphiné* continued at least until 14 July, the day of the invasion of Piedmont. At that date the command structure was as follows:

- *Lieutenant Général* the Chevalier de Belle-Isle was the commander-in-chief of the French forces destined for the invasion of Piedmont, with the mission of conquering the Fort of Exilles. Each variant of the plan had to be authorized by the French theatre commander, the Duc de Belle-Isle, who in turn had three interlocutors: the commander of the Spanish forces operating in the Southern France/North Western Italy theatre, the Marqués de la Mina, and the Secretary of State and Minister War, Comte Voyer de Paulmy d'Argenson.
- *Lieutenant Général* de Villemur. Second-in-command in seniority, he was placed in command of a column that had to march parallel to that of the main body, with three brigades under his orders.

- *Marechaux de Camp* Larnage de Brunier, Mailly d'Hautcourt, d'Arnaud and d'Andlau. Each of these commanders, with duties similar to those of a major general, was placed on the head of a group of brigades, usually two, on the base of each tactical task.
- *Brigadiers.* Some regimental colonels also had this rank of general, but only when they received specific orders could they be placed in command of a brigade: that is, a group of battalions, usually four or five in total, which were activated to carry out a specific mission at operational or tactical level. Once the mission was completed, these units could be assigned to other tasks, some battalions detached to other mission, or the brigade simply disbanded. In the culminating phase of the campaign, seven brigades were activated; Brigade Bourbonnais, under the command of *Brigadier* Louis de Biran d'Armagnac, Comte de Goas; Brigade La Reine, under the command of *Brigadier* Henri-Bernard de Thimbrune, Marquis de Valence; Brigade Artois under *Brigadier* de Montcalm; Brigade Mailly under *Brigadier* François-Joseph de Demas, Marquis de Ruffey; Brigade Royal Roussillon under *Brigadier* Charles de Cleron, Comte d'Haussonville; Brigade Condé under *Brigadier* Charles Claude Marquis de Langeron; a provisional brigade under *Brigadier* François-Marie de Pérusse, Marquis d'Escars.

While his operations in New France are well known, the command action of Louis Joseph de Montcalm (1712-1759) on 19 July 1747 has yet to be investigated. Montcalm was colonel commander of the Régiment d'Auxerrois with the rank of *brigadier*, and during the 1747 campaign he also held the command of the Brigade Artois, delegating the management of his regiment to *Lieutenant Colonel* Damour. He was wounded during the second assault on the Testa dell'Assietta by a shot that left him senseless on the ground. (P. Blin, *Portraits des grands hommes, femmes illustres et sujets mémorables de France* (Paris: Chez Blin, 1786, p.145))

Staff, Leadership and Leadership Style

Among the officers who planned the 1747 operations was *Colonel* Pierre-Joseph de Bourcet, with the role of chief of staff. The principle of the general staff in the first half of eighteenth century was quite simple: it was a group of officers with the task to assist the commander in planning, to turn his intentions into operational orders, to help manage combat and to oversee the logistics of the army. With the increasing complexity of military operations, the organization of the general staff became more and more complex. In 1747 this organization was still in its embryonic state and Bourcet could basically manage a first section of the general staff, directly subordinate to him, which handled the movements of the troops and the transmission of orders. In particular, on every occasion that an important decision had to be taken, Bourcet wrote a memorandum in which he analysed the situation in detail, presenting to the commander his reccomended solution to adopt. Then there was a second section, entrusted to a *Maréchal de Logis*, which would take care of the logistics: supplies, hospitals, camps. Since there was no codified structure at the institutional level, this general staff did not have a stable task organization. In any case, in the course of 1747 the general staff of Duc de Belle Isle was able, in a reasonably short time, to plan, draw up, issue orders and set in movement two armies in a particularly difficult operational theatre like that of the Western Alps.[3]

Compared to its Sardinian counterpart, the French leadership style left more freedom to the commanders in the field. This also depended on the simple fact that the Alps are much further from Paris than they are from Turin. The French Secretary of State for War could not interfere directly in operational and tactical planning, therefore he was forced to limit his control directly to the commander of the *Armée de Provence*, the Duc de Belle-Isle. He, on the contrary, seems to have wanted to maintain a much more stringent control over his brother; between 9 and 19 July the two brothers exchanged no less than 13 letters, with an average of at least one letter or a detailed report a day.[4] Six are from the Duc, the other seven from the Chevalier, and they are all letters that contain not only confidential information, but real operations orders. It is clear that the Chevalier de Belle-Isle was not entirely at his ease as a commander of an army, and he continually sought approval, or advice, informing his elder brother every day about the current events.

To his subordinate commanders, the Chevalier de Belle-Isle undoubtedly left a lot of initiative. However, in order to be sure that his general officers carried out his orders perfectly, he always carried with him a copy of the operation orders he had issued, a copy of the task organization of his troops and the same correspondence concerning the transmission of the orders; this was a weakness determined by his inability to keep his large units under control and, after he was killed in action, all this sensitive material fell into the hands of

---

3   On the French General Staff J.D. Hittle, *The Military Staff. Its History and Development* (Harrisburg: Military Service Division, The Stackpole Company, 1961). For the planning activities of Bourcet, later promoted to the rank of *lieutenant général* and founder of the French General Staff, see Bourcet, *Principes de la Guerre de Montagnes*, pp.184-191. A modern critique of his work can be found in A. Alberti, 'Bourcet', in *Memorie Storico Militari*, Fascicolo III, December 1909, pp.263-279; C. Becker, *Relire Principes de la Guerre de montagnes du lieutenant général Pierre-Joseph de Bourcet* (Paris: Economica, 2008).

4   The letters of the Belle-Isle brothers have been transcribed and published in Arvers and de Vault, *Guerre de la Succession d'Autriche*, Vol.II, pp.717-740. These letters were placed in the SHD archives around 1800 by Abbot Jean- Baptiste Massieu, the archivist librarian of the Ministry of War, according to what is reported by Arvers and de Vault, *Guerre de la Succession d'Autriche*, Vol.I, p.598, note 1. Massieu succeeded in placing the papers of the Belle-Isle family, Maurice de Saxe and the de Broglie family into the army archives. E. Welvert, 'Jean-Baptiste Massieu', in *Revue d'Histoire de l'Eglise de France*, 1921, 36, pp.241-251.

Louis-Charles-Armand, Chevalier de Belle Isle (1693-1747). Younger brother of Charles Louis Auguste, he was appointed field commander of the army destined to invade Piedmont. This was his first truly independent command, the last stage of a brilliant military career but due more to his brother's influence than to his leadership or true qualities as a commanding officer. This is to date his only known portrait, a detail from a German-language poster entitled *Gesprach des marshalls von Bell'Isle und seines Bruders des Chevalier Bell'Isle in ihrem einsamen Aufenthalt zu Osterode*, published following their capture on 13 November 1744. (Author's collection)

the Sardinians who found it of extreme interest. This was an unforgivable levity, just as unforgivable was the choice to throw oneself into the heart of the fighting. This was a sign that the Chevalier still thought as a brigade or division commander, and not a true army commander.

The subordinate general officers of the *Armée du Dauphiné* were not unprepared: some of them had fought on the European battlefields for decades, and they had fought both in the Wars of Spanish and Polish Succession. Their worst deficiency lay in the supine acceptance of the attack doctrines *à la Folard*, which during the battle of 19 July cost them dearly, while at the operational level they proved to be officers with much more ability to manoeuvre than their opposite numbers. What they lacked in understanding the effects of firepower, they compensated for with their ability to manoeuvre. Enemy entrenchments, bad weather conditions and an excessive confidence in their attack tactics – which until then had given satisfactory results – were among the causes of their failure.

On the day of the battle these gentlemen marched at the head of the attack columns. We can definitely see a certain utility tactical choice in this exposed position; the *maréchaux de camp* wanted to be sure that the attack followed a precise direction and hit a precise point on the opposing front, and delegating this task to a less experienced officer could lead to unpleasant misunderstandings. The Sardinians were not considered particularly difficult adversaries, and on at least two occasions the French had managed to break through the main defensive line of a Sardinian entrenched camp, at Villefranche and Pietralunga during the 1744 campaign. This aspect was also grasped by Voltaire: 'They became much more daring about this enterprise because of the memory of the days of Montalbano and Casteldelfino, which seemed to justify so much audacity'.[5]

However, we should also not underestimate the cult of honour among the officers, a fact that forced them to place themselves in particularly exposed and dangerous areas of the battlefield. This attitude has been described as a 'prolonged and endless initiation rite',[6] and the emphasis on physical courage helps us today to understand at least in part what the term honour meant for a 18th-century officer. A man of honour refused to remove the symbols of his rank while under fire by sharpshooters, or with an air of self-satisfaction he threw down his protective armour, in fact a bulletproof vest of the time, when he was ordered to undertake a dangerous assault. Those who felt unable to command a fight from the front were advised to resign and to stay at home, rather than risk the wrath of their peers. It was not a virtual danger: in 1748 the captains and lieutenants of a company of the Régiment de Médoc faced an officer who for the whole duration of the war had always avoided the dangers of battle. They dragged him in front of the regiment, took off his uniform and tore it to pieces, broke his sword, beat him and drove him from the ranks.[7] We speak about courage and not about recklessness:

> Courage seems to be more suited to the general and to all those who command; recklessness is necessary for the soldier and for all those who receive orders. Recklessness is in the blood, courage is in the soul, the first is a kind of instinct, the second is a virtue, one is an almost mechanical movement, the other is a noble and sublime feeling.[8]

These ideals were contaminated with the violence and indiscipline typical of the period, an era which, it should be remembered, had an orderly, clean and geometric facade, but violence, grudges and struggles below the surface. Resentful and touchy, many eighteenth-century officers lived in a perennial state of war against humanity; if they were not at war, they were often in conflict with anyone who was seen as disrespectful of their rank and honour. Waiters, privates, shopkeepers were beaten up at the first opportunity, while an encounter with another noble often provoked a duel. Honour was continuously tried and reiterated, at every opportunity and the columns *à la Folard*, with the officers lined up in the first ranks to indicate 'to the soldiers the paths of victory, or death',[9] seemed to provide the perfect context for them to celebrate and refresh their honour. Some who escaped the carnage of battle then complained of their fate: 'I unlucky! I would rather have been shot down by a bullet, since my greatest wish is to die on the field of honor! My father, my grandfather and my great grandfather were all killed in the war, while I can still carry my white

---

5   Voltaire, *Le siècle de Louis XV. Par l'Auteur du siècle de Louis XIV* (Unknown Publisher, 1769), p.192.
6   M. Dixon, *The Psychology of Military Incompetence* (London: Basic Books, 1976), pp.199-200.
7   Duffy, *Military Experience in the Age of Reason*, p.57.
8   Turpin de Crissé, *Essai sur l'Art de la Guerre*, Vol.I, p.6.
9   Priocca I.

head over the threshold of my home'.[10] It is no coincidence that registers and dictionaries dedicated to the nobility, both French and other states, multiplied during the eighteenth century and many families had their point of honour in being able to boast a certain number of relatives in uniform who died in combat.

Obviously, for the rank and file, being under the orders of similar commanders could be as intense as it was brief experience. The young – he was 27 years old in 1747 – *Colonel* Innocent-Marie de Vassinhac, Marquis d'Imécourt, commander of the Régiment de Périgord, was one of those officers who put glory and honour above a more careful tactical planning. At Piacenza his regiment, deployed in column for an attack *à la Folard*, had to withstand the Austrian fire that decimated the unit. The regimental history of 81eme Régiment d'Infanterie, heir to the Périgord traditions, proudly recounted this anecdote:

> It was at that moment that a corporal from Périgord gathered around him about twenty men of the regiment still standing, grouped them around the flag he held in hand and he gave this answer to *Lieutenant Général* [sic – then a *Brigadier*] de Mailly who asked him: "What are you doing there, corporal?" – "I hold the position of the Regiment with what remains of it".[11]

Indeed, the unit had lost 177 men killed, including 6 officers, and 146 wounded, including *Colonel* d'Imécourt and 21 other officers; 60 percent of their total strength.

It was not just a French peculiarity, and on the other side of the barricade the Austrian *Leutnant* Giuseppe Gorani confided that:

> Since my arrival at the camp I have heard all the officers, from the Colonel to the last of the Ensigns, pronounce the word *Honour*; my ears were constantly bombarded with it, since this word was, by the way, used for every occasion. But what certainty in the definition of honour could I expect from these people, some attached to the most sordid earnings, who profit from their fellow officers, soldiers and the sick people. Others, knowing only how to handle the cards and the dice, cheating and defrauding. Others take advantage of all the free time that the service has left them to request and obtain the favours of plagued nymphs, who infect them and knock them out unable to continue the campaign. And finally, what about the others, three quarters of every night and every day drunk? What false definitions of the word *value* have almost all these officers given me, they, who shamefully drew their swords for courtesans of the dirtiest kind, or to defend the most notorious and criminal gamblers! It was fortunate that I had a positive disposition by nature, so that after spending the first few years of my youth in such bad company, I was able to maintain such precise ideas about honour that I would never allow no action to hurt it.[12]

---

10   A.E. Schertel von Burtenbach, *Betrachtungen und Erfahrungen über Verschiedene Militärische Gegenstände* (Nuremberg: Felsecker, 1779), p.66.

11   P. Grémillet, *Un Régiment pendant deux siècles (1684-1899). Historique du 81e de Ligne, ancien 6e Léger "l'Intrépide", cy-devant Périgord, La Marche, Conti, l'un des régimentes des princes* (Paris: Unknown Publisher, 1899), pp.85-86.

12   Gorani (ed. Casati), *Memorie di giovinezza e di guerra*, pp.77-78; italics as original.

The Commanders

The offensive to conquer the Fort of Exilles seemed to be a relatively simple operation. The fortification to be conquered was little more than a medieval castle integrated with new fortifications, a typical example of the 'Bertola Class' works, which in 1744 in Demonte and in 1745 in Exilles and Tortona, had shown all their structural limits.[13] In addition, the bulk of the Sardinian army was engaged in the south, along the Riviera, and it would hardly abandon its positions to reach the Susa Valley. It could have been a good opportunity to occupy an enemy fortress, albeit a small one but still an important card to be presented at the peace table which, as it seemed, was now imminent. There were all the prerequisites for fame and glory, and the Duc Belle-Isle placed his ambitious brother in command of the expeditionary force destined or to the siege of Exilles.

Nephew of the famous Nicolas Fouquet, superintendent of finance of Louis XIV who later fell in disgrace, Louis Charles was born on 19 September 1693 in Agde, and he had begun his military career in 1707 as a Mousquetaire du Roi, participating in the Flanders campaign. Belonging to the great nobility of France, he rose swiftly; in 1715, at the age of 22, he was made Chavalier of the Order of St Louis. He received the rank of *brigadier* on 20 February 1734, participating in his first real battle on 8 April 1734 in Trarbach. He took part in sieges and minor clashes and on 1 March 1738 he became *maréchal de camp*. The rising star of his brother allowed him to advance his own career. While Charles-Louis-Auguste de Belle-Isle became *maréchal de France* in February 1741, Louis Charles, on 27 February of the following year, was promoted *lieutenant général*, joining the French army in Bohemia alongside his brother. He took part in the action at Suffelsheim on 23 August 1744, subsequently being captured with his brother in Hanoverian territory on 13 November 1744 during a diplomatic mission.[14] At the end of a long negotiation he was freed and destined for the *Armée de Flandres*, where on 11 October 1746 he fought at the Battle of Rocoux. In November of the same year he obtained the title of comte, although in all official correspondence he was always referred to as Chevalier of Belle-Isle, and he was assigned to the army in Provence again serving alongside his brother. Thanks to his brother's interest, in the summer of 1747 he received the command of the army destined for the invasion of Piedmont, in fact the most important event of a career hitherto characterized more by diplomatic duties than combat ones. The Chevalier de Belle-Isle at that juncture proved to be a methodical officer, imbued with fortitude and sense of duty, which led him to expose his life in the first person, but also by excessive fussiness and a certain lack of trust in his subordinates, which would lead him to flood his chain of command, both up and down, with written orders. Voltaire described him thus:

---

13   Regarding the 'Bertola Class' fortresses, see Giovanni Cerino Badone, *Sulla Strada di Fiandra. Storia della Cittadella di Alessandria 1559-1859* (Alessandria: FAI, 2014); E. Garoglio, 'Fortezze Piemonte. Geopolitica, tecnologia e uso tattico-strategico delle fortezze del Regno di Sardegna tra Antico Regime e Restaurazione, 1713-1831', in Chiara Devoti (ed.), 'Gli Spazi dei militari e l'urbanistica della città. L'Italia del Nord-Ovest (1815-1918)', in *Storia dell'Urbanistica*, October 2018, pp.30-101.

14   On the diplomatic case caused by the arrest of the Belle-Isle brothers, see J.C.D. de Flassan, *Histoire Générale et raisonnée de la Diplomatie Française, opi de la politique de la France depuis la fondation de la Monarchie, jusqu'à la fin du règne de Louis XVI* (Paris: Treuttel et Würtz, 1811), Vol.V, pp.246-249.

> The Chevalier de Belle-Isle had the same ambition [as his brother], the same views, but even more thorough, because a more robust health allowed him a more tireless work. His darker appearance was less attractive, but he subdued when his brother insinuated. His eloquence matched his courage; one could guess, behind a cold and attentive facade, something violent; he was able to imagine, to arrange and to make everything.[15]

With his brother he had failed to defend Prague; with him he had repelled the Austro-Sardinians from Provence, now he had to conquer Exilles alone.[16]

Lieutenant Général Jean-Baptiste-François de Villemur-Riotor was his second in command. Born on 30 July 1698, he began his career in 1716 as a *maréchal des logis* in a company of the Grenadiers à Cheval. Equipped with the necessary noble lineage, he managed rather quickly to become *colonel*: on 5 October 1730 he took command of the former Régiment de Bassigny when this became the Régiment de Villemur.[17] While officers like Belle-Isle advanced their careers in the salons of the palace and thanks to their diplomatic activities, de Villemur had to make his way directly on the battlefields. In 1734 he fought both in Parma and in Guastalla, where he received a shot in the thigh. While recovering from this dangerous wound he obtained the rank of *brigadier* in October of the same year, and he fought again in Italy during the 1735 campaign. Returning to France he immediately obtained another operational assignment: on 2 December 1737 he set sail for Corsica, where he was employed in intense counter-guerrilla operations until April 1741. His leadership skills had earned him, in January 1740, the rank of *maréchal de camp*; the same year he abandoned the command of his regiment. Ordered to the continent at the outbreak of hostilities in August 1741 he was ordered to reach the *Maréchal* Maillebois on the front of the Lower Rhine. Before he could proceed to the front, on 16 September 1741 he received an important appointment as *Inspector général d'infanterie*. This made him a kind of supervisor in charge of developing the tactical doctrine of the army and checking that the various royal *Ordonnances* were applied by the regimental commanders. He did not stay long in this position, and on 11 February 1742 he was transferred to the front, in Bohemia, where he fought with the remnants of the retreating French army from Prague. The following year he was added to the *Armée du Rhin*, fighting under the orders of *Maréchal* de Noailles during the unfortunate battle of Dettingen. In 1744 he was transferred to Italy, under the orders of the Prince de Conti. During the intense campaign he fought on April 19 at the Battle of Villefranche. On 2 May 1744 he was promoted to *lieutenant general*: he was then assigned to command the third attack column during the French general offensive against the Alpine front and he took part in the Battle of Madonna dell'Olmo. He followed the Prince de Conti the following year to the Lower Rhine front, but he did not participate in any battle. In 1746 he was present at the sieges of Mons, Charleroy, Namur, and he fought at Rocoux. In January 1747 he was transferred back to the Italian front, and in the first days of July he was in Tournoux, under the orders of the Chevalier de Belle-Isle; aware of the fact that his

---

15   Voltaire, *Le siècle de Louis XV*, p.51.
16   A biography of the Chevalier de Belle-Isle can be reconstructed in detail by reading M. Pinard, *Chronologie Historique-Militaire* (Paris: Claude Herissant, 1760-1778), Vol.V, pp.248-251.
17   G. Susane, *Histoire de l'Infanterie Française* (Paris: Terana, 1985), Vol.V, pp.320-321.

rank had been conquered piece by piece at the cost of great sacrifices and dangers, he tried whenever possible to claim his independence of command. It is no coincidence that Belle-Isle, who could claim more powerful friendships but a less prestigious military pedigree, entrusted him with a semi-independent command during the Assietta campaign with only the obligation to coordinate the movements with those of the main body.

At the disposal of the two lieutenant generals were four *maréchaux de camp*. They were the men who were supposed to carry out the plans of their superiors. The first of these was Pierre de Brunier de Larnage; born in 1683, he was a veteran of the Spanish War of Succession and the Piedmontese front. Company commander of the Régiment de Sauzay, *Capitaine* de Larnage had fought in 1704 under the orders of the Duc de La Feuillade in Savoy, Val di Susa, had participated in some counter-guerrilla operations in Val Germanasca and subsequently took part in the occupation of the Valley of Aosta. He had survived the siege and blockade of the fortress of Verrua sul Po between 1704 and 1705, and the following year he had fought the siege of Turin, during which he was wounded. After the campaign of 1707 in Provence, he always remained to fight in the Alps with the *Armée du Dauphiné*, participating in the campaigns of 1708 – during which he took part in the Battle of Cesana – 1709, 1710, 1711 and 1712. In the meantime, he became *lieutenant colonel*, in 1732 he took part in the War of the Polish Succession, fighting on the Rhine front. On 1 March 1738 he reached the rank of *brigadier*, without obtaining the effective command of his old regiment. This could have happened because promotion to regimental colonel was in effect a royal nomination, and it seems that Larnage, who did not belong to the great nobility of France, did not have enough weight, or support, to obtain the necessary nomination licenses.

Larnage subsequently took part in counter-guerrilla operations in Corsica between 1739 and 1741 and, at the outbreak of the War of the Austrian Succession, he was sent to fight in Bohemia during the 1742 campaign. After having participated to the defence of Prague and the following retreat, in 1743 he remained for some time in France, obtaining the appointment on 20 February as *maréchal de camp*. He left his service in his old regiment, which in the meantime had become Fleury, and he was sent to the Rhine front where he fought at Dettingen. In 1744 he was transferred to the army of the Prince de Conti destined for the invasion of Piedmont; he took part in the campaign in the Alps, fighting in Villefranche, in the Stura di Demonte valley, at the sieges of Demone and Cuneo and at the Battle of Madonna dell'Olmo. In 1745 he was in the ranks of Maillebois' army destined to operate in Piedmont; we find de Larnage at the sieges of Tortona, Alessandria, Valenza, Asti, Casale and at the Battle of Bassignana. The following year he participated in the Battle of Piacenza and managed to return to Provence where he was placed under the orders of the Duc de Belle Isle. In 1747 he was destined to fight under the orders of the Chevalier de Belle-Isle, and he was regarded as the veteran par excellence of the Alpine countryside. He joined the other old warhorse of the Italian front, Villemur.[18]

The second *maréchal de camp* was Léonard, Comte d'Andlau. Born in 1710, he had always served in the cavalry, participating in the War of the Polish Succession. Commander of the Régiment d'Andlau Cavalerie since 16 April 1738, in 1741 he was assigned to the *Armée d'Allemagne*, participating in the capture of Prague during the same year and remaining

---

18   Pinard, *Chronologie Historique-Militaire*, Vol.V, pp.383-385.

in Bohemia until the surrender of the city. In February 1743 he returned to France, where his promotion to *brigadier* and the campaign on the River Rhine against the British awaited him, culminating in the battle of Dettingen. He remained on the same front throughout 1744, and the following year with his regiment he joined the French army in Flanders; promoted to *maréchal de camp* in November, he abandoned the command of the regiment and joined the army of the Prince de Conti first, and that of Maurice de Saxe with whom he later fought in Rocoux. In 1747 he was assigned to Provence and subsequently sent to the *Armée d'Italie*. The campaign of 1747 would be his first in Italy and in a mountain theatre.[19]

The third officer was Augustin-Joseph, Comte de Mailly d'Haucourt. Born on 5 April 1707, he had had a much smoother career than de Larnage's troubled one. Mousquetaire du Roi in 1726, standard bearer in the Régiment de Mailly in 1728, standard bearer in the Compagnie des Gendarmes de

Augustin-Joseph, Comte de Mailly (1708-1794). De Mailly had already fought in Italy in 1746. The following year he was placed under the orders of the Chevalier de Belle-Isle, and put in command of one of the three main columns. (Private collection)

la Reine in 1733, he found himself in the middle of the War of the Polish Succession with the rank of *lieutenant colonel* of cavalry at only 21 years of age. He participated in a series of minor clashes that led to his promotion to *mestre de camp de cavalerie* in 1734. In 1738 he became *capitaine-lieutenant* of the Compagnie des Gendarmes de Berry in April 1738, and then he moved on to the prestigious Compagne des Gendarmes Ecossois in January of 1742. This unit, part of *Maison militaire du Roi*, guaranteed him important entrances at the court of Louis XV. During the War of the Austrian Succession, his main war experience was the fight at Wissembourg in 1744, where he had a horse killed, while at Fontenoy the following year he had spent the entire day protecting the Dauphin. 1746 was decidedly a more animated year; he was transferred to Maillebois' *Armée d'Italie*, participated in the Battle of Piacenza and followed the events of the French army in Italy until their retreat to

---

19   For a biography of d'Andlau, see the usual fundamental Pinard, *Chronologie Historique-Militaire*, Vol.V, pp.530-531.

the coasts of Liguria. Returning to France he took part in the defence of Provence and, in 1747, he was assigned to the *Armée du Dauphiné* under the Chevalier de Belle-Isle.[20]

The fourth and last *maréchal de camp*, in order of seniority of service, was Gabriel d'Arnaud; born in Paris in 1684, he was a veteran of the War of the Spanish and Polish Succession. In September 1741, with the rank of *lieutenant colonel*, he had been transferred with his unit, the Régiment de Montboissier, to the Rhine front. He managed to return to France in February 1743, obtaining promotion to *brigadier* on the 20th of the same month. Sent to the Flanders front in 1744, he participated in the sieges of Menin, Ypres and Firnes. In July he was sent to Alsace, and later to the Rhine. In November 1745 he obtained promotion to *maréchal de camp*, remaining in garrison at Landau throughout 1746. His great moment came in April 1747, when he was sent to the Dauphiné front and, finally, he obtained the command of an attack column of the *Armée du Dauphiné* under the Chevalier de Belle-Isle.[21]

The Fighting Power of the *Armée du Dauphiné* of 1747

In 1747 the magnificence of the armies of Louis XIV was now only a memory. Controversial, very quick in changing moods, and with a persistent tendency to insubordination; these were the main characteristics of the French soldier in the mid-eighteenth century. Many criminals and unemployed were among the 'volunteers' who made up most of the line infantry, just like in the Sardinian forces. Many chose the army because it offered them a job at a time when civilian life did not guarantee it. These were often people who had sought their fortune in the city after leaving their native country village, others who could not or did not want to pursue their father's profession. Still others had been kicked out of work due to the economic downturn, or their crops had been devastated by nature or human action. For all of them, the enlistment bounty paid in cash, the new clothing and, in addition, the promise for the future of pay and looting, could seem an attractive alternative to a life as a civilian in which it was often difficult to obtain work and wages, with, in addition, the real risk of being looted by passing troops or being ruined by heavy taxes. A second large group of volunteers included those who wanted to 'change the air'. Those forced by a momentary domestic crisis such as a debt (which could be liquidated using the enlistment bounty), the threats of a family member or the prospect of having to appear before an ecclesiastical or secular court.

---

20   *Maréchal de France* in 1783, Mailly was the commander of the troops responsible for defending the royal family during the riots of the Tuileries, and was guillotined in 1794 at the age of 86 years. As such, he is much better known than his colleagues of the *Armée d'Italie* of 1747. During the Restoration, he had a hagiographic eulogy: J. Lacorix, *Eloge de le M. le Maréchal de Mailly, précédé d'un coup d'oeil historique sur le principaux évenemens militaires du régne de Louis XV* (Perpignan: P. Tastu, 1819). For a complete biography: A. Ledieu, *Le Maréchal de Mailly. Dernier Commandant pour le Roi à Abbeville* (Paris: Alphonse Picard et Fils, 1895); Pinard, *Chronologie Historique-Militaire*, Vol.V, pp.527-530; for completeness one should also mention: A. Lendru, *Histoire de la Maison de Mailly* (Paris: Emilie Lechevalier, 1893), Vol.I, pp.509-519; J.Y. Duval, *Le prix du sang bleu. Joseph-Augustin de Mailly 1708-1794* (Paris: Editions Le Sémaphore, 2000); S. Surreaux, *Les Maréchaux de France des Lumières, Histoire et Dictionnaire d'une élite militaire dans la société d'Ancien Régime* (Paris: SPM, 2013), pp.952-955.

21   Pinard, *Chronologie Historique-Militaire*, Vol.VII, pp.247-248.

Contrary to current standards, the quintessential professional soldier was a middle-aged man who had a long period of service and was potentially on his second or third military engagement. A robust man of 30 or 40 could withstand much better the fatigues of war than adolescent or barely 20-year-old boys, as well as possessing the stability and experience necessary to guarantee him a distinct superiority over recruits in the tight combat formations of the period. The French army, for its part, enthusiastically welcomed entire regiments of foreign troops, formed by Walloons, Germans, Irish and Italians, organized in units like the French line infantry, or by Swiss with their particular large regiments with two-three battalions of four companies of 200 men each. In practice, about 20 percent of the French troops were recruited abroad.

What made the French army battalions distinctive was the large number, almost out of proportion, of the recruits gathered from urban centres. At least a third of them came from medium or large cities, which made these soldiers rowdy, opportunistic and totally insensitive to the calls of their superiors. The pay was poor and the supplies, which depended on civilian contractors, were often completely absent. Hence the natural need to devote oneself to looting, an activity that was not only tolerated, but even encouraged.

The lower officer corps was definitely unsatisfactory:

> The old convictions of our fathers, their enthusiasm for the service of God, of the king and of the ladies, which had accompanied their warrior heroism for so long, faded from day to day. Army officers were no longer those rude and fanatical fighters of the sixteenth century; those enthusiastic and devoted gentlemen of the great king: they were a generation of doormats, libertines, frivolous, superficial, buffoons, more assiduous to brothels than to their companies, always brave, eager for a beautiful death, but on condition not to suffer with the soldiers.[22]

At Dettingen in 1743 the Comte de Stainville, later to become the Duc de Choiseul, three times heard *Maréchal* Noailles shout to the troops to take up a position, but 'all his efforts were thwarted by ignorance, panic, the noise of battle and the lack of silence on the part of our troops. A single shot from the cannon, which the enemy rarely fired, was enough to instil the hope of retreat to spread throughout the army'.[23]

Maurice de Saxe tolerated and even encouraged the licentiousness and vices of his men, but in battle he demanded the utmost efforts on the part of all to achieve victory. Only with energetic commanders did the French soldiers seem to emerge from their habitual riotous state of indiscipline. In the War of the Austrian Succession there were truly capable senior officers, but when men of the quality of Maurice de Saxe and the Prince de Conti, brilliant strategists like Maillebois, or aggressive tactical leaders such as François Chevert were lacking, painful and humiliating defeats came quickly, first of all that of Rossbach, on 5 November 1757.

Discipline, combat quality, and desertions varied in every battalion. The regiments, in fact, continued to distinguish themselves according to seniority of service. The structure of

---

22   Susane, *Histoire de l'Infanterie Française*, Vol.I, p.232.
23   H. Choiseul, *Mémoires du duc de Choiseul* (Paris: F. Calmettes, 1904), pp.9-10.

a regiment was variable, and ranged from two-four battalions for the older units, down to the recently raised single-battalion regiments. According to the *Ordonnance* of 15 May 1741 each battalion had a theoretical strength of 40 officers and 650 non-commissioned officers, musicians and private soldiers divided into 15 companies, 14 of 40-man fusiliers and one of 45-man grenadiers. Each company had a captain, a lieutenant, a second lieutenant, two sergeants, a drummer, three corporals and three lance corporals and 28 simple soldiers.

The French army was a huge war machine. In 1742, the year of the outbreak of hostilities against the Kingdom of Sardinia, it numbered 182,957 infantrymen; in 1743 these had risen to 240,803, in 1744 there were 249,368 enlisted men and the following year, 1745, 256,648. But the increase did not stop there; in 1746 the numbers reached 277,549, and by the end of the 1747, 308,341 officers, NCOs and private men were mobilized; they increased to 333,802 in 1748, 182 percent of the initial figure.[24]

Just as it was the case with his predecessor, the continuous necessity of soldiers persuaded Louis XV to introduce a compulsory military service. The recruits initially served in ad hoc small units dedicated to escort the artillery trains, the logistic convoys and to serve as the garrison. The first *Ordonnance de la Milice* of 1688 in fact obliged one unmarried man from each parish to serve in the militia. Subsequently the candidates were drawn by lot, with the possibility of redeeming themselves and being replaced, at the expense of finding volunteers for the ordinary troops. The huge numbers of troops needed meant that over the years even married people were included in the militia roles. After seven years of service, return to civilian life was rewarded with tax exemption for one year, raised to nine years for a soldier with a family. The *Ordonnances de Levée* were repeated every year from 1742 onwards, and crumbled all records; in 1741, with the war in theatres far from the borders of the kingdom, 30,000 militiamen were recruited, rising the following year to 78,600. In the following years, between 1744 and 1748, 365,368 men were called to arms, with an average influx of 73,000 men per year. The combat efficiency of the militias should not be underestimated. As with the Waldensian militias or the local Piedmontese militias, soldiers specialized in mountain warfare were found precisely by these units, whose cadres and enlisted personnel often had an intimate knowledge of the mountains in which they operated. It is no coincidence that the Chevalier de Belle-Isle had at his disposal at least two companies of the Milice de Briançon.

From the militia also came the elite troops of the Grenadiers Royaux. All those soldiers, who seemed to have the necessary physical and psychological characteristics like grenadiers of the line regiments, were selected from within the militia battalions and collected together in special units. On 15 September 1744 a Royal Ordinance sanctioned the rise of the Grenadiers Royaux, and on 10 April 1745 the creation of the Grenadiers Royaux regiments was finally decided. One of these regiments, initially organized with one and then with two battalions (the latter the so called *Grenadiers postiches*), was placed under the command of Pierre de Raymond de Villeneuve, Chevalier de Modène. Despite the initial

---

24   On the increase in the strength of French infantry during the reign of Louis XV: V.L.J.F. Belhomme, *Histoire de l'Infanterie en France* (Paris-Limoges: Henri Charles-Lavauzelle, 1893-1902), Vol.III, pp.131-132, 142, 151, 156, 164, 170, 173-174.

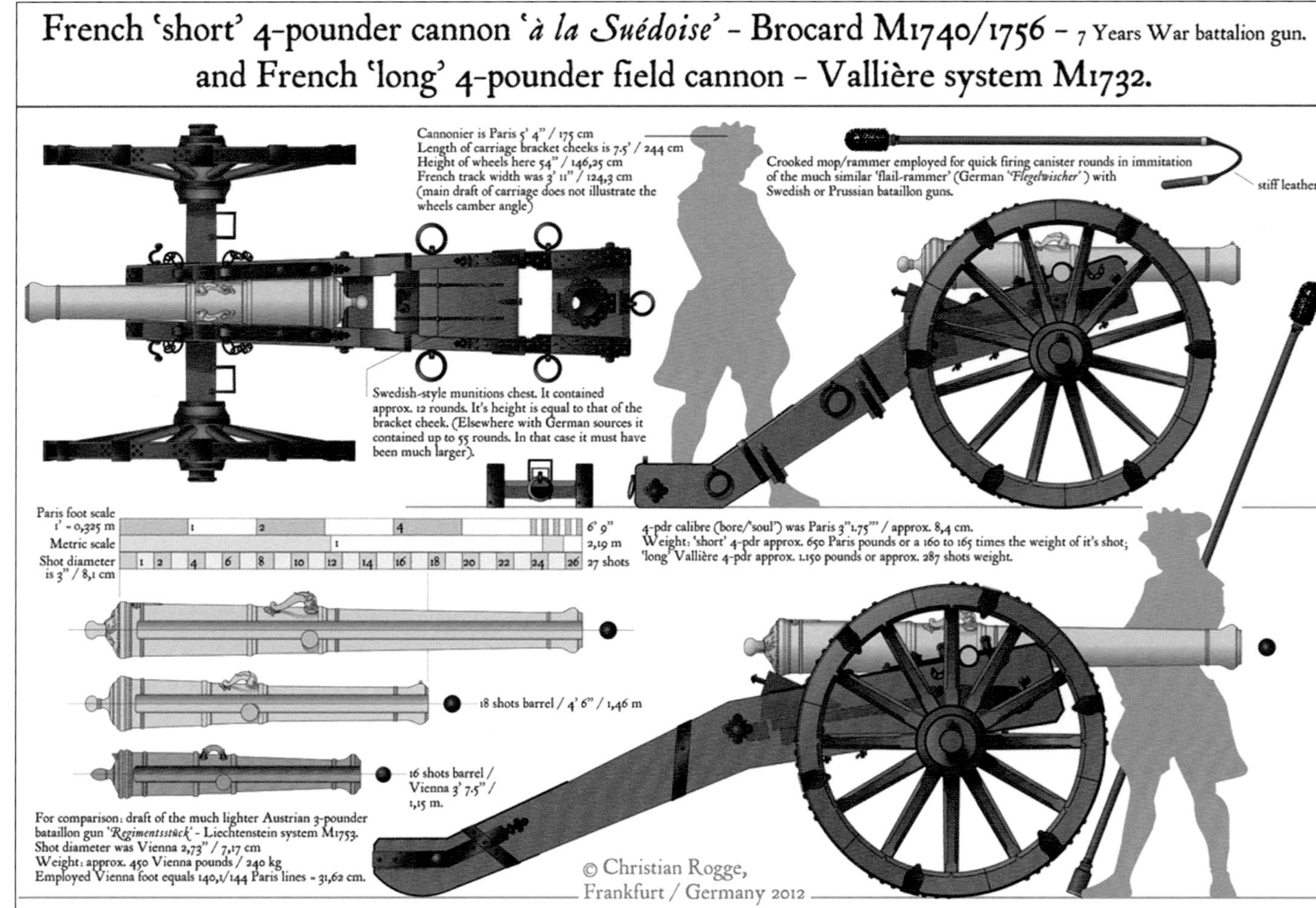

The specifications of the 4-pound field piece, Vallière System. The availability of these pieces on the battlefield had the potential to ensure victory for the French forces. The problem was moving these heavy ordinances through difficult mountain terrain. (Courtesy of Christian Rogge)

scepticism – 'the militia it's just a mockery'[25] – these units became one of the most important tactical tools among those available to the French commanders during the War of the Austrian Succession.[26]

In addition, during the War of the Austrian Succession, specialized light infantry units began to be raised, including the Volontaires de Gantes, who had tasks of exploration and protection of the rear during the 1747 campaign.

In the 1747 invasion of Piedmont the following units were employed:

Table 6: French Regiments Employed in 1747 in the Western Alps

Brigade	Regiment	Battalions deployed	Seniority	Campaigns in Italy	Rating
	Bourbonnais	1er, 2e, 3e	1584	-	Elite unit, it was one of the five Petit Vieux Corps.
Brigade Bourbonnais	Soissonais	Single	1684	-	Regiment never used in battle.
	Des Landes	Single	1693	1743, 1744, 1745, 1746	Veteran of the Italian front. Remarkable experience in mountain warfare.
	La Reine	1er, 2e	1634	1744, 1745, 1746	Veteran of the Italian front.
Brigade La Reine	Béarn	1er	1684	-	Regiment with a strong reputation.
	Guise	Single	1688	-	Regiment with little combat experience.
	Dragons du Roi	1 Sq.	1744	1744, 1745, 1746	Cavalry unit raised to operate in Italy.
	Artois	1er, 2e	1610	-	Regiment with little combat experience.
	Aunis	Single	1684	-	Regiment with little combat experience.
Brigade Artois	Auxerrois	Single	1692	1744, 1745, 1746	Veteran of the Italian front.
	Santerre	1er	1692	1744, 1745, 1746	Veteran of the Italian front, in 1746 it was captured at Casale. Limited combat ability.

---

25   L. Hennet, *Les Milices et les Troupes Provinciales* (Paris: Librairie Militaire de L. Baudoin et Cie., 1834), p.106.

26   On the provincial militias: Chevalier Des Pommelles, *Tableau de la population de toutes les provinces de France, Mémoire sur les Milices* (Paris: Unknown Publisher, 1789); J. Gebelin, *Histoire des Milices Provinciales (1688-1791)* (Paris: Librairie Hachette et Cie., 1882).

Brigade	Regiment	Battalions deployed	Seniority	Campaigns in Italy	Rating
Brigade Mailly	Mailly	1er, 2e, 3e	1693	1744, 1745, 1746	Veteran of the Italian front.
	Boulonnais	1er	1684	-	Veteran of the Flanders front.
	Agenois	Single	1692	1744, 1745, 1746	Veteran of the Italian front.
Brigade Royal-Roussillon	Royal Roussillon	1er	1657	-	Regiment never used in battle.
	Guyenne	Single	1684	1744, 1745, 1746	Veteran of the Italian front.
	Périgord	Single	1684	1744, 1745, 1746	Veteran of the Italian front, it was one of the most combative battalions.
	Beaujolais	Single	1685	-	Veteran of the German and Flanders fronts.
Brigade Condé	Condé	1er, 2e	1644	-	Veteran of the German and Flanders fronts.
	Saintonge	Single	1684	-	Regiment with little combat experience.
	Beauce	Single	1684	1743, 1744, 1745, 1746	Veteran of the Italian front. Heavily engaged in all major actions.
Special units	Grenadiers Royaux de Modène	1er, 2e	1745	1745, 1746	Veteran of the Italian front.

Sources. Susane, *Histoire de l'Infanterie Française*; L. Susane, *Histoire de la Cavalerie Française* (Paris: J. Hetzel 1874); Arvers and de Vault, *Guerre de la Succession d'Autriche (1742-1748)*.

The combat efficiency of the French units under the command of the Chevalier de Belle-Isle can be evaluated through their use in combat and their presence on the Italian theatre. Obviously, discipline, combat quality and desertions varied from unit to unit. The regiments, in fact, continued to distinguish themselves according to seniority of service. In addition to the *Maison du Roi*, whose units were never present on the Italian front, the most prestigious units were divided into *Vieux Corps* (Picardie, Champagne, Navarre, Piémont, Normandie, La Marine) and in *Petit Vieux Corps* (Auvergne, Leuville, Bourbonnais, Tallard, Boufflers, Le Roi). In 1747 the Chevalier de Belle-Isle had at his disposal one of the *Petit Vieux*, the Bourbonnais Regiment; three battalions strong, it formed the main part of the Brigade Bourbonnais attached to de Mailly's column.

Combat experience could improve a unit's combat skills, turn young recruits into veteran experts and officers into skilled tacticians, but it could also impoverish the unit's human potential. The Régiment de Santerre was destroyed during the 1746 campaign, while the Régiment de Périgord had paid a very high price in terms of human life for the thirst for glory of its colonel. Out of 28 infantry battalions and one cavalry squadron, only five battalions (17 percent) had little or no combat experience. The majority of the units assigned to the *Armée du Dauphiné*, 17 battalions and the only regular cavalry squadron present (60 percent), were veterans of the Italian campaigns. Some regiments, such as the Des Landes and Beauce, had been fighting on the Alpine and Piedmontese battlefields for four campaigns and they could be considered expert in mountain warfare. The campaign of 1747 would have been for many of them yet another combat test in the Western Alps.

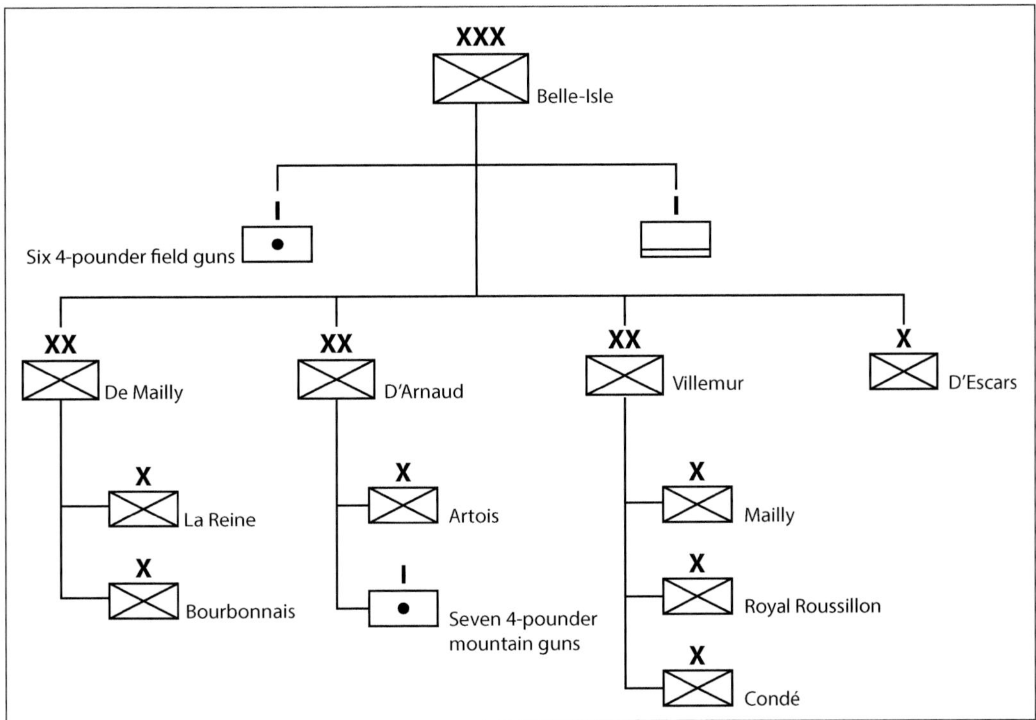

The task organization of the forces of the *Armée de Dauphiné* under the command of the Chevalier de Belle-Isle. Note how the Chevalier placed the 4-pounder field artillery battery under his direct orders, a clear sign of the tactical importance attached to these weapons. (Diagram by George Anderson © Helion and Company 2022)

4

Tactics, Weapons and Psychology

The 1747 campaign and the Battle of Assietta were fought almost entirely by infantry units. By 1740s, the European armies were universally convinced of the effectiveness of the muzzle-loading flintlock.[1] During the War of the Spanish Succession (1700-1713) the firepower developed by an infantry battalion equipped with such weapons was the winning element on the battlefield. At Cassano d'Adda (16 August 1705) and Turin (7 September 1706), just to mention two battles that took place in the Italian theatre, the struggle between opposing foot soldiers was now based solely on the ability of the infantry to develop a continuous and devastating fire. The best shooting discipline was crucial during the fight between the allied and French infantry under the walls of Turin during the battle of the 7 September 1706.[2] It was the Prussian battalions that broke through the French line; these units emphasized discipline and speed of loading and firing, to the point that Leopold, Fürst von Anhalt-Dessau, commander of the Prussian corps attached to the forces of Prince Eugene, had adopted iron ramrods in his regiment instead of wooden ones. Obviously not everybody drew the same conclusions from those events, and the armies that fought in the Piedmontese mountains in the summer of 1747 fought with significantly different tactics from each other.

The Tactics of the Sardinian Army: Fire and Defence

'Experience made us learn…' thus begins the *Reglement d'Exercice et de Manouvres* of 15 May 1709.[3] The experience to which the *Reglement* referred was that of the War of the Spanish Succession, and specifically the battle of Turin in 1706. Struck by the firepower

---

1   For a general view of these weapons, their use and impact on the battlefield G. Cerino Badone, *Potenza di Fuoco. Eserciti, tattica e tecnologia nella guerre europee (1500-1800)* (Milano: Edizioni Libreria Militare, 2013); Chandler, *Art of Warfare in the Age of Marlborough*; Nosworthy, *Anatomy of Victory. Battle Tactics 1689-1763*; A. Starkey, *War in the Age of Enlightenment 1700-1789* (Westport: Praeger, 2003); Telp, *Evolution of Operational Art 1740-1813*.

2   G.C. Boeri, G. Cerino Badone, 'Quattro Armate in Piemonte', in G. Cerino Badone (ed.), *Le Aquile e i Gigli. Una Storia mai scritta* (Torino: Omega, 2007), pp.57-61.

3   AST, Corte, Materie Militari, Ordini e Regolamenti, Mazzo 4, *Regolamento militare per il servizio di Campagna*; BRT, Saluzzo 488. *Reglement d'Exercice et de Manouvres. A' Coni le 20 Mai 1749. Maniere de tirer de pied ferme contre l'Infanterie, donnée le 15e Mai 1709.* The organization of the work suggests that, united in a single manuscript, there are actually two distinct works, the regulation for movement

developed by the Prussian and imperial infantry, in May 1709 the Duke of Savoy Victor Amadeus II established a *Reglement* for his infantry which, with some modifications, remained the tactical regulation of the Sardinian infantry until the 1750s. The Sardinian army borrowed its tactical doctrine from that of the Anglo-Dutch allies, abandoning the French tactics hitherto in vogue in the Duchy of Savoy. Having fully understood that the main purpose of the infantry was to destroy the adversary with firepower, it was therefore necessary to deploy the greatest number of flintlocks on the battalion front. Exactly as in the Dutch and English armies, the Sardinian battalions usually deployed in four ranks, with the group of flags gathered in the centre of the unit a few steps from the first line. When a battalion, whose strength was 700 men, had to face a firefight, it was arranged in three ranks, dividing into 13 platoons (12 of fusiliers and one of grenadiers), one of which was placed behind the central colour platoon. This divided the remainder of the battalion into two wings of six platoons each, lined up on a front of 156 metres. This fire tactic allowed the battalions to improve their firepower. In an infantry firefight, the platoon leaders were placed on the outer sides, on the right in the right platoons, on the left in the left ones. The roll of the drums commanded the fire. First, two platoons on the right opened fire, then the two on the left. Then, from the wings towards the centre, two platoons began to shoot. The result was to maintain continuous fire throughout the battalion front. Fire was delivered from the three ranks at the same time, with the first one kneeling. However, the platoon fire was not a fixed rule; fire by rank had not only not been abolished, but it was considered still effective and included in the *Reglement*. The old tactical doctrines were still used in combat and in 1755 regularly practiced in drills.[4]

The *Reglement* of 1709 appeared to be one of the most advanced of the period when it was adopted, but by the 1740s it was already becoming outdated. Its main features can be summarized in the following points:

- Emphasis on firepower. In this the *Reglement* was nothing short of futuristic. While the Imperialists and the French maintained their heavy four- or five-rank formations, the Sardinians on the battlefield could employ either four- or three-rank formations depending on tactical needs. For firing, three-rank firing with platoon fire was always recommended. The aim was to saturate a front of about 150 metres wide by 75 metres deep with 2,000 balls per minute. A barrage of fire that, if kept unaltered, would have swept anything in front of a battalion deployed in line. To achieve this, each soldier had among his equipment a large leather cartridge box containing no less than 30 cartridges.[5]

---

and for the delivery of fire. It still remains to be understood the extent to which this *Maniere de tirer de pied* was really employed by the Sardinian army.

4   BRT, Manoscritto Militare 234, *Recoeuil de plusieurs plans des differentes manouvres que la troupe de Sa Maiesté le Roy de Sardaigne doit faire, tel qu'il l'ordonne d'exeuter dans le reglement qu'il donné l'an 1755.*

5   F. Sterrantino, *Le armi da fuoco del Vecchio Piemonte 1683-1799* (Torino: Accademia di San Marciano, 2002)), Vol.I., p.134. The 30 rounds deposited in the cartridge box of the Piedmontese soldiers were not large numbers, especially when compared with the 80 cartridges available to the Prussian soldier of the period; C. Duffy, *Prussia's Glory. Rossbach and Leuthen 1757* (Chicago: Emperor's Press, 2003), p.15. It is probable that each soldier had about fifty cartridges in 1747. In the same period, in fact, according to the *Code Militaire à l'usage du corps des Volontaire Royaux*, published on 15 August

- Poor effectiveness in attack. The biggest shortcoming was the almost total lack of credible attack tactics. The advance in line was too slow to exploit advantageous tactical situations.
- The disengagement manoeuvre, due to the necessity to break the main linear formation into small platoons moving to the rear, again put every Sardinian unit in a difficult situation facing an enemy counterattack. During the Battle of Madonna dell'Olmo the French columns really put the Sardinian brigades in great difficulty, both in the offensive and defensive phases. Fortunately for the Sardinians, cavalry was not used, which could have exploited the gaps between the platoons and overwhelmed the isolated units.
- Good defence effectiveness. In defensive operations the firepower developed was able, if well used, to beat any frontal assault. It was very difficult to drive out a Sardinian infantry battalion from its fortified positions through direct attacks.

The *Reglement*, unlike today's tactical regulations, appeared to be more a sort of general indication to the regimental commanders, than the mandatory tactical model for troop training. As it was also the case in the French *Armée Royale*, each regimental commander interpreted and adapted them to the needs of the moment. It is no coincidence that after the war, Carlo Emanuele III ordered the drafting of a new tactical regulation to be adopted uniformly for the entire army.[6] In the course of the conflict some tactical regulations were issued, such as the one present in the Operations Order of 6 October 1743, issued by *Generale* Seissel d'Aix on the eve of the Battle of Casteldelfino. It codified a new defensive tactic based on an unprecedented formation of two ranks.[7] This emphasised greater firepower:

> The soldiers will arrange themselves in two ranks behind the entrenchments, without mixing the ranks or letting the numbers 2 approach the parapets before the numbers 1 have fired. You have to be sure to have for the numbers 2 the space for a reverse march per rank; [...] All the battalions will have with them a reserve of ammunition, [...] since there is no doubt that in some points the fire will be more lively than in the others, and perhaps in other places it will not be at all; [...] all the officers who have muskets, and who know how to use them well, will leave their

---

1745 on behalf of the King of France, authorised 'a cartridge box containing fifty cartridges'. Most likely this is the institutionalization of the increasing use of ammunition on the battlefield. M. Petard, *Equipements Militaires de 1600 à 1870* (Olonne sur Mer: Sitol-Guibert, 1984), Vol.I, pp.103-104.

6   BRT; Manoscritto Militare 233, *Nouvel Exercice Militaire pour les Troupes d'Infanterie de SA Maiestè le Roi de Sardaigne adapté dans le Congrès tenus à la presence de S.A.R. le Duc de Savoie avec l'explication de chàque tems en figure, 1751*; Saluzzo 256, *Etude de l'infanterie au recherche des regles propres au service de SMS, composée de Troupes Nationales & Etrangerés, à Alexandrie MDCCLII*. This last document is particularly interesting, since it depicts tactical evolutions of several battalions. The album appears to be the result of a training camp held in the city of Alessandria immediately following the conclusion of the War of the Austrian Succession. The Swiss Reggimento Kalbermatten can be recognized among the depicted units.

7   AST, Corte, Materie Militari, Imprese, Mazzo 4 d'addizione; *Relazione giornaliera dell'operatosi dall'Armata accampata nella Valle di Casteldelfino, comandata dal Marchese d'Aix, compilata dal colonnello Monfort che vi fece le funzioni di Magg. Generale.*

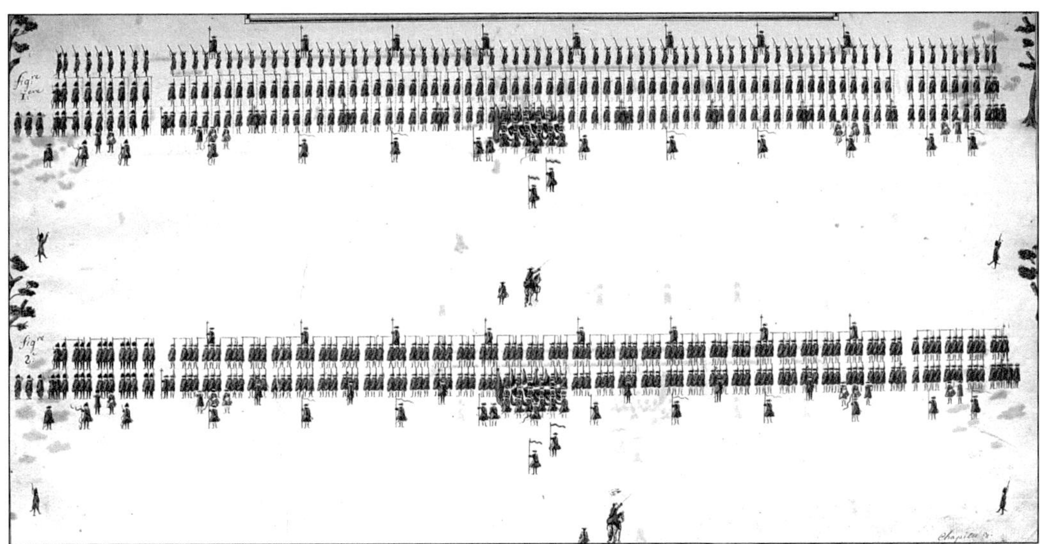

A battalion of the Swiss Reggimento Salis exercising. Sardinian infantry battalions deployed three ranks in an open field or two for the defence under the cover of field fortifications, as depicted in this drawing. (Private collection, c.1750)

Field fortifications manned and troops ready to open fire. In this context, the works are manned by no less than four battalions, identifiable by their flags, deployed in two ranks. This tactical arrangement ensured the coverage of as large a front as possible and the exploitation of all available firepower. On the left a battalion is placed in the second line, as a reserve. In case of need it would go to support the unit on the front line. (Detail from the Battle of Casteldelfino by J.P. Verdussen, private collection)

partizans [polearms] in the camp and they will take their firearms with them; the sergeants will leave all halberds and instead use their muskets.

This two-ranks tactical arrangement proved crucial for the defence of the Alpine field fortifications during the campaign of 1747. A single 700-strong infantry battalion alone could cover a 119-metre front when deployed in four ranks, 156 in three and 238 metres when arranged in only two ranks. To facilitate the counter-marches between the two ranks, the battalion could extend its front up to 476 metres. The latter option allowed for a very important choice if, as often happened to the Sardinian Army during the conflict, the available units were few, the operations were specifically defensive, and one could count on strong field fortifications built on the battlefield.[8]

The tactical instructions by *Generale* Seissel d'Aix were perfect to stop an enemy attack through the use of firepower and field fortifications. The increasing losses that the Sardinian army suffered on the battlefields, and consequently the collapse of the fighting qualities of its own units, made it necessary to evolve its tactics in this direction. In addition, after 1743 it became clear to the Sardinian command that the war should be fought inside Piedmont and it could be a conflict of friction around the central nucleus of the kingdom. By 1747 defensive tactics had reached a high degree of efficiency, making them arguably among the best in Europe. The Sardinian defensive tactical doctrine underwent continuous improvements, in part suggested by the officers who had effective command on the battlefield, in part by the military engineers who had to plan and to build the entrenchments. It is possible to identify three distinct moments in the evolution of such tactics:

- 1743-1744; defensive cordon. The units were deployed in an entrenched line, reinforced by artillery. This arrangement had no depth, since it was without advanced or rear works. The main element of defence relied on firepower that could be developed frontally. The lack of depth of the defences allowed the attacker, once the entrenchment line was forced, to undermine the entire defensive perimeter, due to the lack of rear positions from which to continue the defence. Only reserve forces deployed in the immediate vicinity had a chance of closing the breach, but if this was unsuccessful the entire line was effectively pierced and the battle lost. This tactical organization was employed in 1743 and 1744 during the battles in Val Varaita and in the Battle of Villefranche. In the first case the Franco-Spaniards were not able to punch through the Sardinian entrenched line. At Villefranche, however, the line of entrenchments was pierced in at least two sectors. The infantry reserves, mostly composed of German and Swiss infantry battalions, among the best of the Sardinian army, fought hard to close the breaches. The Sardinians eventually remained masters of the battlefield, but the losses suffered, 2,500 men, did not allow them to maintain control of the harbour, which was abandoned the following day. The Battle of Pietralunga, fought from 16 to 19 July 1744, marked the

---

8   For the reconstruction of the tactics of a Sardinian battalion training the most important document is the *Regolamento militare per il servizio di Campagna*, Corte, Materie Militari, Ordini e Regolamenti, Mazzo 4; BRT, Manoscritto Militare 234, *Recoeuil de plusieurs plans des differentes maneuvres que la troupe de Sa Maiesté le Roy de Sardaigne doit faire, tel que'il l'ordonne d'executer dans le reglement de l'ecercice qu'il a donné l'an 1755.*

decline of this tactic. The entrenched line was pierced at its central point, without any possibility of remedy.

- 1745-1747; line of defence with detached redoubt. It became evident, after the tragic days of Val Varaita, that the entrenched lines had to increase the depth of their defences. The first attempts in this direction took place along the 'Leutrum Line' in the western Ligurian Riviera. Baron von Leutrum, a general of German origin in the service of the King of Sardinia, had to block with relatively weak forces opposing masses of infantry much greater in number than his own. He decided to supplement his entrenched line with a series of detached works, capable of slowing down and exhausting the enemy's initial offensive momentum, forcing him to a complex and slow approach. The entrenchments of Val Roja were supplemented by three to five successive line of redoubts and strongholds. Located mostly on mountain or hilly ridges, these chains of fortifications appeared to be real fortified corridors. Arranged on the side of an alpine valley, despite the depth of the system the redoubts cooperated only partially with each other. The French, however, always preferred elaborate flanking operations, rather than bloody frontal attacks. This allowed Leutrum to successfully defend the front of the western coast until the end of the war.

- 1747-1748; circular entrenched camp. Starting from 1747, the detached works were connected to each other by extensive entrenched systems. The field works, when they were carried out, turned out to be rather complex, but allowed a small force to have an all-around defence rather than just a frontal one. This solution appeared advantageous above all on the front of the Western Alps, along mountains ridges. Having to face an enemy capable of enveloping their positions and attempting to attack their works from the rear, as occurred in Pietralunga in 1744, this was the best possible solution. The entrenched camp of Assietta, the most famous of those built by the Sardinian army in the eighteenth century, falls into this category. The latest generation of the Sardinian entrenched camps appeared to French observers to be quite bizarre. The entrenchment of Assietta was thus described three days before the battle by the Chevalier de Belle-Isle: 'Their entrenchments are extremely unusual; they have, they told me, a chain of redoubts connected to each other by an entrenchment'.[9]

The army of Carlo Emanuele III was the first among those of the House of Savoy to be equipped with a regular flintlock musket; the 28 June 1730 Royal Decree sanctioned the birth of this pattern, defined Model 1730. Before that date the weapons, although they all had the same calibre – one ounce, equating to 17.3mm – they still differed from each other in shape, weight and details. At the outbreak of the War of the Austrian Succession, the Sardinian infantry was equipped with either the Model 1730 musket with barrels and flint lock from Brescia, Suhl, St Etienne and the Arsenal of Turin, or the French Model 1728 musket with a calibre of 17.5mm.

The French Model 1728 muskets had been purchased in 1736. During the War of the Polish Succession, France, with the approval of Turin, had created storage depots in Piedmont for

---

9   Chevalier de Belle-Isle to Duc Belle-Isle, quoted in Arvers and de Vault, *Guerre de la Succession d'Autriche (1742-1748)*, Vol.II, p.731.

the supply of the army operating on the Lombard front. At the end of the war, the weapons stored in the depots were offered to Carlo Emanuele III, who promptly proceeded with the purchase; 10,004 Model 1728 muskets were delivered to the Turin Arsenal, while 3,848 were acquired in Pavia and another 4,100 in Cremona. Simple and functional, the French design fastened the barrel to the stock with metallic bands rather than with pins. This detail greatly facilitated the disassembly and maintenance of the weapon. The first phases of the War of the Austrian Succession immediately made evident the superiority of the French Model 1728 over its opponents. The lightness, a weight of 4.1 kilograms compared to 4.6 kilograms of the Sardinian model, the great ease of maintenance, and its simple construction meant that the troops and commands appreciated the French musket more than the Sardinian one. It was therefore decided to create a new variant of the Model 1730, called Model 1730/45, which introduced many features similar to the French gun. The most evident modification was the abolition of the pins and the adoption of iron bands.

Therefore, the army now found itself with three different 'regular' flintlock musket models. Individual armament soon became quite heterogeneous, as other models of weapons were distributed to the troops:

- Spanish muskets captured or bought by deserters.
- Captured French Model 1728 muskets.
- Austrian muskets.
- Muskets of the Duchy of Modena.
- Hunting guns of various sizes.

Table 7: Infantry Muskets Available to the Piedmontese Army 1730-1751

French Model 1728	17,952
Model 1730	67,575
Model 1730/45	12,961
Total	98,488

Source. AST, Sezioni Riunite; Regi Viglietti e Dispacci, Vol. IV; Carte antiche di artiglieria, Vol. XVI.

The gunpowder contained in the cartridges reached a weight of half an ounce (15.37 grams). The recoil was violent; the soldiers worried about the excessive recoil of the weapon and they usually paid less attention to aiming. In 1744, after the adoption of the firing tactics proposed by *Generale* Seyssel d'Aix in October 1743, a new cartridge was adopted with a charge reduced to three eighths of an ounce (11.5 grams). Experience on the battlefield confirmed the improved accuracy of the new ammunition.[10]

After a failed attempt in 1735 to build iron ramrods for the Model 1730, on 9 February 1742 the Intendency was ordered to distribute weapons equipped with an iron ramrod.[11] The first to benefit from this item was the Reggimento Fucilieri. The delivery to the regiments

---

10   AST, Sezioni Riunite, Regi Viglietti e Dispacci, Vol.IV, 1742-1747.
11   AST, Sezioni Riunite, Carte Antiche d'Artiglieria, Vol.XVI.

of this new equipment was accelerated during 1743. In February, after the review of the troops returning from Savoy, it was decided to distribute new weapons, already equipped with the iron ramrod.[12] The lack of homogeneity in the armament created many problems for the Savoy Intendency; spare parts, ammunition, and supplies varied from one regiment to another.[13] The consumption of the individual weapons was so intensive – for example, the grenadier company of 1/Guardie had 30 percent of its individual weapons put out of service during the Battle of Assietta[14] – that it was necessary to hire a large number of master gunsmiths in order to be able to maintain a sufficient production rate. The galloping demand for weapons caused many problems; during the war it was noted that in a certain number of barrels produced the breech plug was too long by a few millimetres, blocking the touchhole.[15]

In 1747 the Sardinian army seriously risked not being able to fight on, due to lack of weapons. The losses exceeded the productive capacities of the Sardinian state, and even the supplies from abroad were insufficient to make up the shortfall. In 1742 the Armory of the Royal Arsenal stocked 35,000 muskets of various models, and between 1743 and 1747 the workers of the Arsenal had assembled 21,500 new muskets, with an average of over 350 pieces per month. Yet by 1747, just over 8,000 infantry muskets were available. In five years of war, as many as 50,000 weapons had been lost, and at that time alarming signs of failure began to appear in the production, storage and distribution systems. Every private firearm was requisitioned, in particular no fewer than 6,000 muskets were collected in order to equip the militia. Despite these measures, on 22 June 1747 the governor of the city of Saluzzo was forced to dismiss four militia companies due to lack of armament.[16]

The Austro-Sardinian army on 19 July 1747 did not have any artillery pieces at its disposal. This, however, does not mean that the presence of guns was totally excluded in the planning phase. Indeed, the presence of the artillery was a constant inside the Sardinians entrenchments, even if their effectiveness was often lower than expected. The Sardinian army was equipped between 1743 and 1744 with two particularly interesting models of artillery, the 1-pounder Janner rifled breech-loading iron gun, and the 4-pounder Bertola mountain gun. The second model had been used during the 1744 Campaign, when two guns fired during the Battle of Pietralunga, and at the end of the day they were captured by the enemy.[17] In 1747 an artillery brigade was assembled with four Bertola guns and five Jenner rifled guns; they were destined to defend the entrenched camp of Assietta. The brigade took several days to be set up, due to the difficulties in transporting these particular ordinances by mule. The

---

12   AST, Sezioni Riunite, Ufficio Generale del Soldo, Raccolta sovrane Det n° 1; Febbraio 1743, Rivista Ispezione Rg.to Guardia, Vestiario perso nella campagna in Savoia; *Tutti i soldati sono provvisti di ghette e abersacchi: si propone di far distribuire al Rgto un nuovo armamento di fucili colla bacchetta di ferro, atteso che le piastre sono nella maggior parte di poco buon uso.*

13   AST, Sezioni Riunite, Carte Antiche d'Artiglieria, Vol.XVI.

14   *État des Pertes faites par le Premier Bataillon du Regiment des Gardes à l'Affaire du 19.e Juillet 1747 au Col de l'Assiette.* AST, Sezioni Riunite, Ministero della Guerra, Ufficio Generale del Soldo, Ordini Generali Misti, Mazzo 81, 1747-1748.

15   Sterrantino, *Le armi da fuoco*, Vol.I, p.134.

16   AST, Sezioni Riunite, Regi Viglietti e Dispacci, Vol.IV, 1742-1747.

17   G. Cerino Badone, 'Il Cannone Disgiunto di Ignazio Bertola', in *Armi Antiche* 2003, pp.35-83.

group passed through Fenestrelle on 22 July to go up to the entrenchments. Their presence would certainly have been more useful three days previously.[18]

Tactics of the French Army: Bayonets and Folard's Fury

In the years that followed the War of the Spanish Succession, the European military questioned for a long time what lesson to draw from the conflict just ended. The liveliest debates, which opened a dispute that would drag on until the end of the century, took place within the French army; the armed force that had suffered the greatest military defeats. In France progress was made to achieve speed in tactical movements and rate of fire, but no specific regulations were developed. Instead, each regiment followed its own tradition about combat tactics and organization of the chain of command. Only the four-ranks arrangement became a common element throughout the army.

The biggest shortcomings concerned firepower. Despite attempts to improve battle effectiveness, the habit of employing and training infantry as an element of choreography for celebrations and parties remained a common use in the French army. One of the most representative soldiers of the eighteenth century, François Chevert, recalled with amusement the success he had obtained, when he was still *aide-major* in the Régiment de Beauce, during the final phase of a revue in having the men of his battalion deployed to form the phrase *Vive le Roy* before giving a salvo.[19]

The cadence of fire, the movements on the battlefield, practically all the tactical arrangements for combat, were left to the inspiration of the colonels. The exercise of arms was still regulated by the old *Ordonnance* of 2 March 1703, which remained unchanged throughout the War of the Polish Succession (1733-1738) and replaced by a new instruction only on 1 March 1746.[20] The result of these shortcomings was that throughout the War of the Austrian Succession there were not two units in the French army capable of fighting in the same way. On 6 February 1750 on the esplanade of the Hôtel des Invalides, in the presence of the Minister of War d'Argenson, some infantry units carried out a fire exercise. Each of them seemed to employ individual drills and tactical movements according to their own patterns. The minister decided on a further investigation and on February 15 he ordered the Régiments de Picardie, Piémont, Champagne, La Marine, Flandre, Cambrésis, La Roche Aymon, La Sarre and Soissonais to move to the Invalides in Paris or to send detailed written reports to examine the manoeuvres adopted by each unit. Although all were now arranged in four ranks, no two regiments used the same fire and movement instructions. Only five of them trained the men to shoot and were able to carry out a fire action. In addition to platoon fire two of them also utilised the obsolete fire by ranks. The commander of the Régiment La

---

18   AST, Sezioni Riunite, Azienda Generale d'Artiglieria, Carte Antiche d'Artiglieria, Vol.II, p.278.

19   J. Colin, *l'Infanterie au XVIIIe siècle. La Tactique*, (Paris-Nancy: Berger-Levrault & Cie., 1907), p.32.

20   *Ordonnance du Roy, sur le Maniement des armes de l'Infanterie. Du premier Mars 1746*, Paris 1746. On the War of the Polish Succession and its operational history, especially for the Italian front, see Ilari, Boeri, Paoletti, *La Corona di Lombardia*, pp.11-56; F.F. d'Espié, *Mémoires de la Guerre d'Italie, depuis l'Année 1733, jusqu'en 1736, par un ancien Militaire qui s'est trouvé à toutes les Actions de ces trois fameuses Campagnes* (Paris: Duchesne, 1777).

Sarre had his men make a counter march to clear the shooting range at the back rank, causing the indignant astonishment of the Ministry's inspector, Victor Maurice de Broglie, future *Maréchal de France*. Yet these were not second-rate units: Picardie, Piemont, Champagne and La Marine were four of the six *Vieux Corps*. In the *Armée Royale*, fire discipline was simply less important than cold steel. Only with the *Ordonnance* of 7 May 1750 was a regulation for the exercise for the infantry introduced, while the officers still complained of an absolute lack of training in shooting.[21] In 1740 an officer noted that 'in France, there is no attention for giving the troops a good drill. They are usually content with teaching them how to handle weapons and making soldiers march well. This is good, but it is not enough'. Still others complained that

> [T]he recruit still has to be dressed, who is already on guard duty and he is left to the attention of a sergeant or corporal. The officers don't care at all; the new soldier barely knows how to hold his musket, and he is put directly in the ranks, which has no other purpose than to prevent others from doing their exercise well.[22]

At this point it becomes interesting to observe how the French and Sardinian regiments fought side by side.

> At the battle of Parma [in 1734] the Piedmontese infantry was in three ranks, and this is what they were trained to do; then a battalion was about to open fire, when the lord of Coigny [François de Franquetot de Coigny, who with *Maréchal* de Broglie the elder was the field commander of the combined Franco-Sardinian forces] had it deployed in four ranks, with the order for the first and second ranks to fix the bayonet and not to fire, and to get on their knees when the other two ranks behind had to open fire. After that they would stand up again, with the musket on their left arm. This is a good way to complicate your life; to put soldiers into combat in a way they have never trained for. [...] The result was that, in a general confusion, the front ranks fired, those behind did not, contrary to what Coigny had ordered. Eventually it happened that, except for two German regiments in the service of the king of Sardinia, all the army started firing without any order *à la Croate*, as light infantry, and all four ranks knelt down to take cover, without any will to get up and shoot.[23]

During the War of the Spanish Succession the opinion had spread, far from supported by the facts, that the typical character of the French soldiers was ideal only for *coups de main* and cold steel attacks. The French tactical doctrine began to favour bayonet attacks to the detriment of shooting. It was observed that the enemy infantry:

---

21   *Ordonnance du Roy, sur le Maniement des armes de l'Infanterie françoise & étrangère. Du 7 Mai 1750*, Paris 1750.
22   Colin, *l'Infanterie au XVIIIe*, p.33.
23   C.E. von Warnery, *Anecdotes et Pensées historiques et militaire, ecrites vers l'année 1774* (Halle: Jean Jacques Court, 1781), p.83.

[H[as long been accustomed to firing in platoons; their three ranks are closed to the tip of the sword; the first puts one knee on the ground, the second curves the back, and the third holds himself straight; in this way, they maintain a continuous fire and never disperse, when the French know only the use of the bayonet, and fight with an infinite disadvantage when the ground does not allow them to reach the enemy.[24]

However, during the War of the Austrian Succession, at least on the Italian front, the French army remained faithful to the concept of 'French Fury' and to its main prophet, the Chevalier Jean-Charles de Folard. The adoption of a linear formation made firepower the only viable option. It was convenient to deploy a battalion in as lengthy a formation as possible, in order to allow the greatest number of muskets to open fire. However, the line had some drawbacks. The units so deployed were slow, vulnerable to cavalry and more suited to defensive combat than attacking action. The alternative was an assault with the battalions arranged in a column, as Folard preached throughout the first half of the eighteenth century.

Jean-Charles de Folard, otherwise known as the 'French Vegetius', was born in Avignon on 13 February 1669. Member of a noble family of lesser rank, exalted by reading Julius Caesar's *Commentaries*, he decided to enlist at a young age as an infantry cadet in the Régiment de Berry. In 1688, at the outbreak of the War of the Grand Alliance, he was placed in command of a company of pro-French partisans on the Flanders front. Returning to his regiment, in 1702 he was assigned to the Italian front during the War of the Spanish Succession. He planned an assault, never carried out, on the imperial depots of Mesola, thus signalling himself to the Duc de Vendôme, who appointed him his aide-de-camp. On 1 June 1705 he participated in the Battle of the Bolina and on 16 August he was present at the Battle of Cassano. His actions of command, in particular at Bolina, earned him the Cross of St Louis, the title of Chevalier and a pension of 400 Livres, even if he never obtained a battalion command. Bolina was a hard infantry close combat during which the Austrian soldiers had used the cover of farmhouses and canals to get closer to the French strongholds that defended the few passages over the Chiese river. With about 200 men – a company apiece from the Régiments La Marine, Leuville, Bretagne, and Esgrigny – Folard kept control of a bridge and the nearby fords, hinging on the Bolina farmhouse, a solid rural building near Muscoline. Assaulted by 1,500 Austrian infantrymen and about a thousand cavalry commanded by the Prince of Württemberg, he fought fiercely; the perimeter of the farmhouse was forced several times but the well-directed defence repelled all attacks. 'The enemies, desiring the glory of being the first to enter, pushed on one another, and they entered two by two. We rejected them with bayonets, and all those who entered were slaughtered without being able to resist'.[25] After the Austrians managed to seize the courtyard, Folard was able to reorganize the defences and to continue the resistance in the chapel, in the dovecote, in the barns, in the house itself and even in the chicken coop. A clash, therefore, that took place in very small spaces that forced the contenders to use their sidearms. During one of these close-quarters combats Folard was wounded by a sword blow to the

---

24   Colin, *l'Infanterie au XVIIIe*, p.34.
25   Chevalier de Folard, *Mémoires pour servir à l'Histoire de Monsieur le Chevalier de Folard* (Ratisbonne: Unknown Publisher, 1753), pp.25-26.

belly, luckily for him not badly. In spite of everything, the defence held: when the Grand Prieur de Vendôme, brother of the duke, finally came to his rescue he had only lost the position of the chicken coop. That was the main war action in which Folard took part as an independent commander. It was a fierce battle, prolonged and broken up into various episodes, in which courage, determination and predisposition to fencing and brawling counted more, rather than the ability to dispose considerable firepower or elaborate manoeuvres. The walls of the farmhouse represented a mortal threat to any enemy cavalry unit that ventured nearby, not to mention that they constituted an impenetrable defence for the regimental pieces available to the imperial infantry.[26]

Thereafter, Folard fought in Lombardy in 1706, he took part in the defence of Modena and in 1707 he was posted in Val di Susa. Once again employed by Vendôme, he participated in the Battle of Malplaquet, suffering a serious wound in the thigh. In 1711 his services were rewarded with the governorship of Bourbourg. At the end of the War of the Spanish Succession, after a short period spent in Malta, he fought under Charles XII of Sweden and with the Duc de Berwick during the short War of the Quadruple Alliance of 1718-19. On his return to France, he was promoted *Mestre de Camp*: determined to go to Sweden, in a shipwreck he lost all the notes of his commentaries on Polybius which were rewritten and printed in 1724 in Stockholm with the title of *Nouvelles Decouvertes sur la guerre dans une dissertation de Polybe*. Between 1727 and 1730 the seven volumes of the *Histoire de Polybe* followed the previous edition, at the opening of which he placed a treatise on columns and deep-order. Folard spent the rest of his life, which ended in Avignon on 23 March 1752, fighting all the criticisms directed against his theories.[27]

Folard never commanded a battalion deployed in line in a battle and he saw 'from behind' all the great clashes in which he took part, serving as an officer on the general staff. The reverses of the War of the Spanish Succession convinced him that the French infantry gave their best in hand-to-hand combat and that they were not well suited for a defensive battle. This view, which was actually an oversimplification, had too strong an appeal for a generation of military theorists and writers. In the eighteenth century tactics were the domain of the majors and colonels, commanders of regiments and battalions. Only they could judge, facing the enemy, how their own battalion and regiment fought, fired, resisted and attacked. Folard, in fact, did not have a sufficient background to suggest the correct changes to the tactics of the French army. He was not present at Turin, where the French infantry was defeated at the end of three close firefights that lasted for over an hour. Allied attacks and lack of ammunition had routed the French Brigade La

---

26   The Battle of the Bolina has been reconstructed in detail in M. Zane, *Notte di Pentecoste. La battaglia di Bolina. 1 giugno 1705* (Brescia: Liberedizioni, 2008). Other interesting information can be found in Folard's own writings: *Mémoires pour servir a l'Histoire de Monsieur le Chevalier de Folard; Histoire de Polybe, nouvellement traduite du grec par Dom Vincent de Thuillier, Bénédictin de la Congregation de Saint Maur. Avec un commentaire ou un corps de science militaire enrichi de notes critiques et historiques, ou toutes les grandes parties de la Guerre, soit pour l'Offensive, soit pour la Défensive, sont expliquées, demontrées, & représentées en Figures. Ouvrage très-utile non seulement aux Officiers Généraus, mais méme à tous ceux qui suivent le parti des armes. Par M. de Folard, Chevalier de l'Ordre de St Louis, Meistre de Camp d'Infanterie* (Paris: Pierre Ganduin, Julien-Michel Gandouin, Pierre-François Giffart, Nicolas-Pierre Armand, 1753-1754), Vol.III, pp.228-247; Vol.V, pp.352-360.

27   J. Chagniot, *Le chevalier de Folard: la stratégie de l'incertitude* (Paris and Monaco: Du Rocher, 1997).

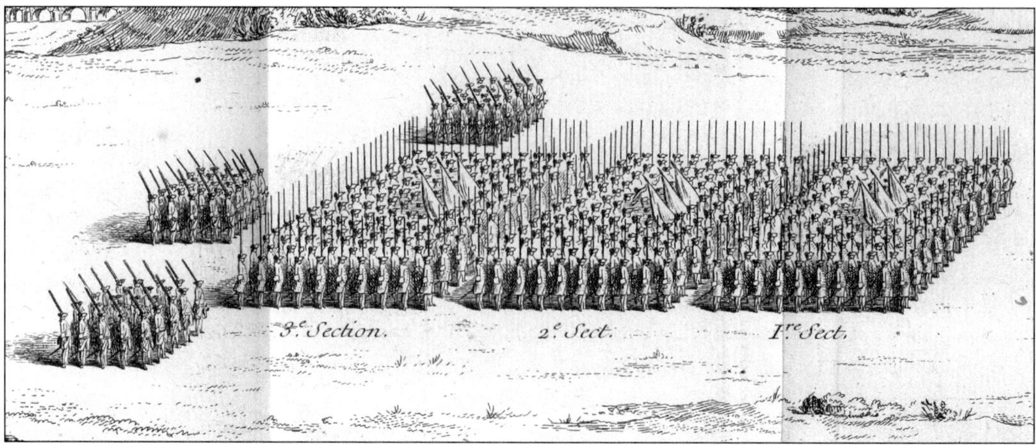

Two French battalions lined up for an attack *à la Folard*. The troops are actually massed in a heavy column, only partially supported by grenadier companies on the sides of the formation. During the War of Austrian Succession it was quite common to see grenadiers deployed at the front of the column. (G. Le Blonde, *Élémens de Tactique* (Paris: C.A. Jombert, 1758), Table XVIII)

Marine. Events like this were caused, according to Folard, by the fact that the battalions deployed in line were particularly vulnerable. According to him battles such as Marsaglia (1693), Speyerbach (1703) and Denain (1712) had been won with bayonet assaults carried out by infantry columns that had not opened in line to develop their own musket fire. On the contrary, he harshly criticized the conduct of *Maréchal* Villars in Malplaquet (11 September 1709) for having maintained an exclusively defensive attitude, betraying the typical character of the people of France, more suited to attacking with cold steel than to maintaining the position and delivering well-timed musket salvoes. It mattered little to him that the *Enfants de la Gloire* had inflicted on the enemy 24,000 casualties – a quarter of the total strength – against their own 12,000 (3,000 of which were prisoners), thus causing the end of the Duke of Marlborough's career.[28]

Folard proposed a series of columns, from a single battalion up to massive formations of six battalions, lined up side-by-side and preceded by formations of light infantry. The largest columns had to have a front of 24 or 30 files, and a depth of 40 or 50 ranks. One in five men was to be equipped with a pike, to be placed on the flanks and in front for impact and for defence from cavalry. The smaller columns, of two battalions, were 16 files and 30-36 ranks. The tactical doctrine proposed by Folard was quite simple: to close as quickly as possible against the centre of the enemy line, to break-in, and to split the attack column into two sections which in turn would annihilate respectively the enemy right and left wing. It was in fact a return to the tactics of the late fifteenth century. Despite the continuous and bloody denials that came from the battlefields, Folard's fame and fortune, especially in France, remained in vogue until the mid-eighteenth century. This was not ensured by his

---

28   A. Corvisier, *La Bataille de Malplaquet 1709. L'effondrement de la France évité* (Paris: Economica, 1997).

works, vast and dispersive, nor by the summary extracted by Friedrich II of Prussia and the reflections of his admirer and correspondent Maurice de Saxe, with whom he always remained in contact;[29] rather, Folard's tactics cost little in terms of time, materials, and effort. Establishing all their tactical doctrine on a direct collision with the enemy's forces allowed the regimental commanders a considerable saving in terms of gunpowder and time dedicated to drill men. A battalion deployed in column was easier to manoeuvre, to train and to manage in combat and, in the opinion of many, it was perfectly in line with the basic characteristics of the French army, which was thought to be unsuitable for any defensive or fire action, while it gave its best in hand-to-hand combat with cold steel.

Folardian columns, as originally conceived, were completely inapplicable on the modern battlefield. This was a fact that was understood even by the most ardent supporters of the use of columns (*ordre profond*). During the War of the Austrian Succession it became common practice to deploy the basic tactical unit, the battalion, in columns of various depths.[30] There were usually three choices:

- Battalion column. This was usually formed by 16 fusilier companies and one grenadier company for a total of 720 men, with a front of four men.[31] It was 274 metres in length, suitable for marches and along sufficiently wide roads and paths.
- Battalion column with a front of eight men. The front in this case was that of a company, which was deployed in a massive formation of five ranks. The length of the column was about 160 metres.
- Battalion column with front of 16 men. It was a front of two companies, always of five ranks, with a length of approximately 91 metres. This formation was the one that best since it enabled the use of fire for close defence, trying to combine fire and movement.[32]

In January 1747, due to the proliferation of enemy field fortifications, a special Royal *Ordonnance* prescribed that in each company of grenadiers 10 men should be equipped

---

29   Some of their letters, in particular those relating the capture of Prague on 26 November 1741, were published in the *Mémoires pour servir a l'Histoire de Monsieur le Chevalier de Folard*, pp.114-148. After Folard's death, the king of Prussia had the synopsis of Folardian tactical principles published, with his own anonymous preface, already composed by his order in 1740 by *Oberst* von Seers, suggesting that he himself was the author; *L'Esprit du Chevalier Folard tiré de ses commentaires sur l'Histoire de Polybe pour l'usage d'un officier* (Leipzig: Unknown Publisher, 1761). Folard had meanwhile been scientifically analysed and contested by de Sarvonin in 1732 in his *Sentiment d'un Homme de Guerre sur le nouveau système du chevalier de Folard* where a series of simulations, in different tactical contexts, invariably ended with the defeat of the Folardian columns, destroyed by enemy firepower: Savornin, *Sentimens d'un homme de guerre sur le nouveau système du chevalier de Folard, par rapport à la colonne et au mélange des différentes armes d'une armée* (La Haye: Jean van Duren, 1732).

30   Although nothing was ever made to put these principles into doctrine through a *Ordonnance Royal*, the use of battalion columns as a basic tactical formation is effectively described in *Mémoires techniques sur infanterie 1740-1749*, SHD, 1M 1703. In 1753 this tactic inspired the *Instruction sur l'Exercice de l'Infanterie, du 29 Juin 1753*, pp.2-5.

31   For the internal organization of a French infantry regiment of the period C. Bacquet, *l'Infanterie au XVIIIe siècle*, pp.1-72.

32   About this problem, see S. Reid, *British Redcoat vs French Fusilier* (Oxford: Osprey, 2016, pp.26-27).

with a large axe, while the fusilier companies should always have at least 10 digging tools with them.[33]

The French example did not fail to influence the Spanish doctrine of the period as well. The Spanish infantry regiments also fought in the French style, and it maintained this approach throughout the reign of Felipe V (1700-1748) and that of Fernando VI (1748-1759). Only in 1768, with the volume reforms by Carlos III through his *Ordenanza Militar,* was there a shift.[34]

The Franco-Spanish columns, although vulnerable to enemy fire, on the Alpine front functioned quite well when used against the static and often isolated Sardinian battalions. During the Battle of Villefranche in 1744, they broke through the enemy defence lines, bypassing and forcing the surrender of surrounded enemy units that had been unable to fall back in time. Even more successful, albeit bloody, was the use of the Folardian columns at the Battle of Pietralunga of 16-19 July 1744. This operation actually masked the main offensive thrust made by the Prince de Conti, who in the meantime managed to force the Piedmontese defences in the Valle Stura di Demonte and he was able to start the investment of the Fort of Demonte and the fortress-city of Cuneo.[35] In the same way, the Sardinian battalions, slow in countering the opposing action and excessively diluted on a too-long battle front, held a static line in the face of a numerical enemy superiority and against the speed of the Franco-Spanish columns at the Battle of Bassignana in 1745. If well conducted, these columns could put even cavalry units at a disadvantage. At Bassignana, on the left wing of the Sardinian front, the cavalry of Della Manta was forced to retreat in front of the continuous pressure of the Spanish units that were fording the Tanaro River. *Luogotenente Colonnello* Della Villa was sent to protect the retreat with a force of 300 mounted sharp-shooters. On this occasion, manoeuvring rather skilfully, and leaning on the valleys that interrupt the Bassignana plain, Della Villa managed to delay the enemy's advance as much as possible, until, on the Cascina Grossa ridge, his detachment, attacked from the side and the front by something like 20,000 Spaniards, was annihilated and he himself taken prisoner. After this action, the attackers were able to surprise the rear squadron of the retreating Sardinian columns, and one squadron of the Reggimento Dragoni di Piemonte was literally cut to pieces with the loss of 160 men and two standards.[36]

Only starting from the campaign of 1746, with an increasingly massive field fortification use by the Sardinians, did the column assault become increasingly risky, and the tactical triumphs of 1744 and 1745 became a happy memory for the French commanders. The columns ceased to be truly effective when the adversaries were no longer the static

---

33   Belhomme, *Histoire de l'Infanterie en France,* Vol.II, p.169.

34   I am indebted to David Alberto Abián Cubillo for all the information presented in this volume regarding the Spanish infantry. On the Spanish infantry in general see also E. Martínez Ruiz, *El ejército del Rey los soldados de la Ilustración* (Madrid: Editorial Actas, 2018); for the Swiss regiments J. Bragado Echavarrìa's doctoral thesis, *Los regimientos suizos al servicio de España en el siglo XVIII. Diplomacia, guerra y sociedad militar (1700-1755)* (Madrid 2018); ibid., 'Los regimientos suizos al servicio de España en las guerras de Italia (1717-1748)', in *Cuadernos de Historia Moderna* 41 (2), 2016, pp.295-312.

35   Garellis (ed.), *L'alta valle Varaita a età Settecento,* p.207.

36   Browning, *War of Austrian Succession,* pp.273-276; Ilari, Boeri, Paoletti, *La Corona di Lombardia,* pp.179-181, 200-201.

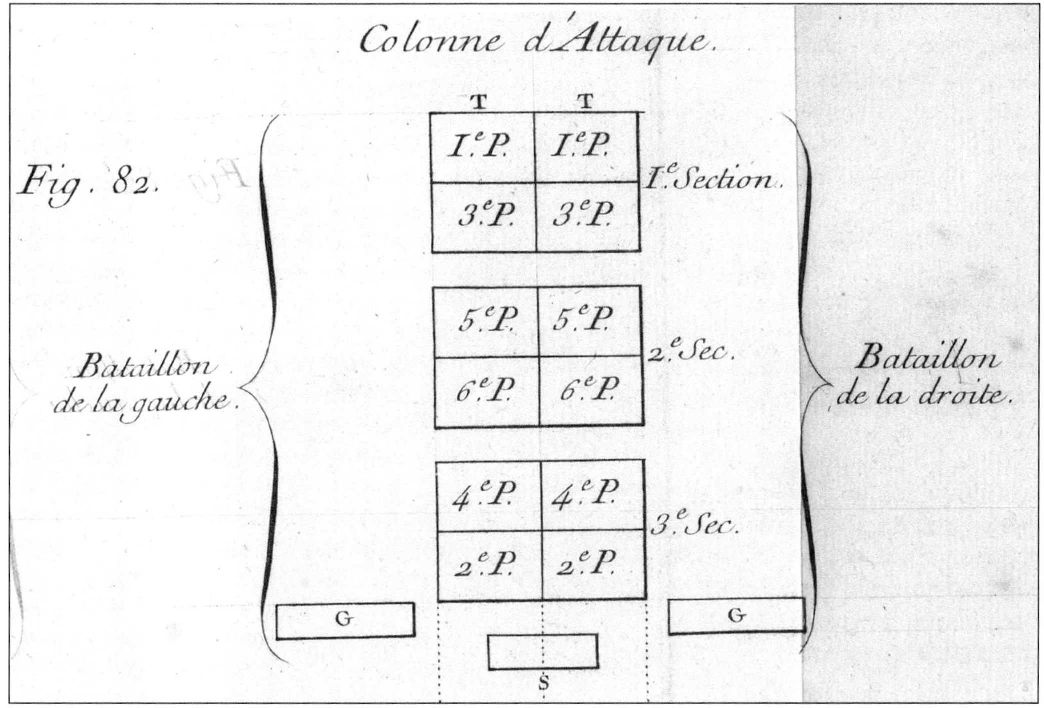

Scheme of manoeuvre of an attack *à la Folard* carried out with two infantry battalions. It is clear that impact was considered the winning element to the detriment of firepower. (Le Blonde, *Élémens de Tactique*, Table XVIII)

Sardinian battalions, but veteran Austrian imperial battalions hardened by the battles on the Silesian front against the Prussian army. The Battle of Piacenza, fought in June 1746, should have been a wake-up call for many supporters of the Chevalier de Folard.[37] However, in 1747 the lesson had not yet been fully learned, and the French commanders planned the attack against the Assietta entrenched camp with these principles and examples well present in mind.

Concerning armament, the French soldier was equipped with the Model 1728 musket, one of the best of the time. It was a superb weapon, whose technical characteristics marked the construction of firearms until the end of the nineteenth century. The soldiers immediately appreciated the new ordinance, which gained curious nicknames; *La Tendresse, Va de bon Coeur, Sans Chagrin, Brin d'Amour*. In 1728 28,000 pieces were ordered and in 1745 450,000 muskets had been produced, of which 10,000 were the heavy sniper variant. The French manufacturers were also able to satisfy the foreign market, one customer being the kingdom of Sardinia as already noted. In 1741 an iron ramrod was introduced, replacing the wooden one. The replacement of the old equipment was, however, very slow, and in 1757

---

37   Browning, *The War of Austrian Succession*, pp.274-276.

wooden ramrods were still distributed to the line regiments. In 1746 a new model of musket was produced, the Model 1746; between 1746 and 1748 211,500 pieces were produced. In 1750, 341,500 Model 1746 muskets were ready to be distributed to infantry units.[38]

In 1747 the French army transported in Piedmont its field and mountain artillery. They, however, had to face a difficult operational theatre, the Western Alps, unsuited for the heavy carriages of an ordinance that had been designed for everything except its mobility on rough terrain. The materials of the French army, in fact, had been conceived and made for the wars of the first half of the eighteenth century; the Vallière System was introduced on 7 October 1732. Its namesake, Jean-Florent de Vallière (1667-1759), began his career in the miners' company in 1690. Fresh from the siege of Turin he was promoted to colonel-inspector of the artillery in 1720 and finally he obtained general rank in 1732. As director general of the artillery he had created a system in which he had restricted the calibres used in the French army to five (4-, 8,- 12-, 16- and 24-pounders) and the mortar models to two (8- and 12-inch).[39]

The Vallière system had the advantage of standardizing the calibres in the French army, even if there were no difference in field, fortress or siege carriages. These were very heavy pieces whose movement on the battlefield was limited. In the War of the Austrian Succession the best way to use the Vallière pieces was to entrench them in tactically strong positions and from those batteries hit any opponents who entered the killing zone. However, more and more pressing requests came from the front for the pieces to accompany the battalions in their attack manoeuvres. The typical piece of campaign was the 4-pounder cannon, of which a battery would take part in the Battle of Assietta. It had a barrel weighing 562.35 kilograms with an overall length of 219 centimetres, and it was able to throw a 1.956 kilogram cannonball. This ordinance remained blocked on the slopes of Piedmontese mountains during the decisive day of 19 July 1747, forcing the French to fall back on the smallest, and ineffective, little 4-pounder mountain gun. Amicably nicknamed 'mule cocks', these pieces were used with anti-personnel rather than anti-structure functions. Analysing their tactical use, the Sardinian gunners came to the following conclusions:

> If the theatre of the war is in the mountains or in other very difficult places, the infantry alone will be enough to form the army, to which some 4-pound sakers will be allocated to be placed well before the action in fortified places, and every time military operations are defensive, they will require similar points of support. But if the army has to act offensively in the Alpine mountains, it will completely dispense with its artillery.[40]

---

38   J. Boudriot, *Armes a feu francaises. Modeles reglementaires 1717-1836* (La Tour du Pin: Cédex, 1997) Vol.I; H. Vuillemin, *Du silex au piston. La grande aventure des fusils réglementaires français 1717-1865* (Paris: Tradition, 1997).

39   A.L. Dawson, P.L. Dawson, S. Summerfield, *Napoleonic Artillery* (Ramsbury: Crowood Press, 2007), pp.56-57; F. Naulet, *L'Artillerie Française (1665-1765). Naissance d'une Arme* (Paris: Economica, 2002).

40   V. Papacino d'Antonj, *Dell'Artiglieria pratica per le Regie Scuole d'artiglieria e fortificazione* (Torino: Stamperia Reale, 1775), Vol.II, p.265

The Imperial Army's Tactics: Adam Bauer's *Stellungskrieg*

The harsh experience of the two Silesian Wars had left their mark. The empress was not satisfied with the way her army had fought, especially the infantry, and in 1749 she had proclaimed to whole imperial army that 'We received the news that Our Imperial infantry does not possess common training, nor a uniform regulation on military practices. These two shortcomings not only create various disorders, but also promote dangerous, noxious and harmful situations both in the campaign and in the garrison'.[41] As with the armies of the kings of France and Sardinia, even that of the empress Maria Theresia at the outbreak of the conflict in 1740 did not have a uniformed and assimilated regulation in use by all regiments. Although a *Regulament und Ordnung* had already been printed in 1737,[42] no one used or demonstrated knowledge of that text. Rather internal regulations were issued and employed in the individual regiments; the best known and most interesting were those of IR Wallis (1705), IR Browne (1717), IR Regal (1728). Other tactical texts were also popular, but the result was equally daunting. Not a single battalion fought like any other. An attempt to remedy was made immediately:

- In 1741 *Feldmarschall* Neipperg prepared a first tactical text for infantry and cavalry, which was completed in July of the same year.
- In 1744 a general regulation was promoted by *Feldmarschall* Ludwig Andreas Khevenhüller.
- In 1746 *Feldzeugmeister* Maximilian Browne drew up a list of tactical principles. These principles he had circulated among the armies he commanded, in particular in the units destined to operate in Italy.
- In 1747 *General-Feldwachtmeister* Joseph Esterhàzy wrote and published a *Regulament*, the first authentic tactical printed regulation of the imperial army.[43]

Thanks to these intense intellectual and training activities, in 1747 the imperial army was well on its way towards its complete metamorphosis; from a decayed institution linked to the Prince Eugene's glories, it was transformed into a war machine designed to fight against the Prussians of Friedrich II. On that occasion it failed to reach the level of the opposing foe; however when in 1746 the imperial army launched its counter-offensive on the Lombard front it was superior to any opposing and allied counterpart. Remarkable combat efficiency, marching speed, versatility and the tactical intuition of their officers were all qualities that were fully demonstrated during the Alpine campaign of July 1747, and the four imperial battalions were certainly one of the decisive factors that contributed to the Austro-Sardinian victory. The basic tactical unit was the battalion – each regiment had three – organized with

---

41   *Regulament und Ordnung des Gesammten Kaiserlich-Königlichen Fuß-Volks* (Wien: Johann Peter van Gehlen, 1749), p.2; C. Duffy, *The Army of Maria Theresa. The Armed Forces of Imperial Austria, 1740-1780* (London: David & Charles, 1977), p.76.

42   *Regulament und Ordnung, nach welchem sich gesambte unmittelbare Kayserliche Infanterie* (Wien: Johann Paul Krauß, 1737).

43   Duffy, *The Army of Maria Theresia*, p.76; C. Duffy, *Instrument of War* (Rosemont: Emperor's Press, 2000), pp.378-379.

five fusilier companies and one of grenadiers, for a total of 700 men.[44] The unit was deployed in four ranks, with an overall front of about 110 metres.

On a tactical level, Maria Theresia's army knew how to fight with remarkable effectiveness; the Austrian commanding officer, however, often lacked initiative, usually limiting himself to choosing good terrain and tenaciously defending it; the passive *Stellungskrieg*, the war of position, seemed to remain the main feature of 'Adam Bauer', as the imperial soldier was often nicknamed.[45] It is therefore not surprising that the Austrian army also codified its own combat tactics in defence of a field fortification, known as *Retranchement-Feuer*. The text of the regulation, which was also deemed suitable for the *Regulament un Ordnung* of 1749, deserves to be transcribed in full:

> [T]he battalion is formed with ranks and files open in two ways. One must understand that, when the battalion or regiment is deployed in battle order and eight to ten paces [about six metres] away from the parapet, all four ranks of the fusiliers and the four of the grenadiers fix bayonets. The major orders all the troops to get ready and to approach the shooting position, bringing their weapons up and to the right in front of them; as soon as the enemy is within musket range, the first rank climbs onto the firestep, and the other three approach, so that the second comes to the distance of the first, the third to that of the second, and the fourth to that of the third. After the first rank has advanced to the parapet, and it is necessary to open fire, the major commands: *Schlacht an; Feuer*. After the first rank man has made his shot, he bring his weapon up and straight in front of him, takes a half turn on his heel, and marches fast, each man passing through the gap between the file he is in. When the reverse is done by ranks, the first rank occupies the space that the fourth had previously.[46]

Once they reached the rear, the men had to load their weapon and prepare to advance. The other solution, recommended in night fights and in the defence of the fortress, was to keep the ranks fixed, passing forward the weapons that were loaded by the fourth rank men through an uninterrupted passage of muskets from the first to the fourth rank.[47]

It appears clear, however, that either the Sardinian regulations influenced the Austrian tactical doctrine – the fire management in defence of the entrenchment is almost identical – or that both armies arrived at the same solution through parallel ways. In any case, they were ready to defend in the best possible way, using almost identical tactics, the entrenchments of the Assietta.

The Austrian army entered the campaign of 1747 with the *Ordinäre Flinte* Model 1722, which was essentially a copy of the French Model 1717 musket. With a bore of 18.3 millimetres, it was loaded using a beechwood ramrod, which had an unwelcome tendency to

44 Wrede, *Geschichte der k.u.k. Wehrmacht*, Vol.I, p.34, Tav.1; *Uebersicht über die Standes-Verhältnisse eines kaiserlichen Infanterie-Regiments (Regiments zu Fuss) in den wichtigsten Perioden*.

45 'Adam Bauer' appears in an enlistment paper in the *Instruction für die Kriegs-Commissariatische Beamten* of 1749; analogous to the later British 'Thomas Atkins'. Duffy, *Instrument of* War, p.192.

46 *Regulament und Ordnung*, pp.194-196.

47 *Regulament und Ordnung*, p.197.

crack in the middle of the action. On 8 December 1744 it was decided to introduce an iron ramrod, borrowed from the Prussian *Infanteriegewehr* Model 1740. Only in 1748, when the war ended, did all the Austrian infantry began to be rearmed with new models, not always successfully, up to the introduction of the excellent *Commiss-Flinte* Model 1754.[48]

Grenadiers and Psychology

The grenadier companies, Sardinian, Austrian and French, had a very intense employment during the Alpine campaign of 1747, and during the battle of 19 July they played a decisive part. Today we associate the figure of the grenadier with that of men of great stature who, with large fur caps, stand guard in front of the presidential or royal palaces. In the eighteenth century the importance of these men on the battlefield was determined by the particular characteristics of these soldiers.

To understand their true tactical value we must go back to November 1741. The previous year, in 1740, the king of Prussia, Friedrich II, had invaded Silesia. The conquest had been so easy and rapid that it led to the creation of a coalition of states, formed by the kingdom of France and the electorates of Bavaria and Saxony, determined to conquer as many territories as possible from the young sovereign and to definitively overthrow the Habsburg monarchy. After Silesia, the next gem to snatch from Vienna's crown was Prague and the kingdom of Bohemia. Formerly the seat of the imperial court, the city was the second most important after Vienna. By early November 1741, an invasion force of 13,000 Franco-Bavarians and 20,000 Saxons had advanced under the walls of Prague. Now it was necessary to decide what to do. The governor of the city, *Feldzeugmeister* Hermann Carl von Ogilvy, was preparing to face the siege; he had just 2,500 men at his disposal, all that had been left behind as a garrison due to the constant requests for troops from the empress to face other emergencies on other war fronts. In addition, the city was divided into two parts by the Vltava River, connected to each other by the Charles Bridge allowing direct communications between the two banks of the river. Many in the city expected not so much a siege conducted 'according to the rules' but a real deliberate assault by the allied forces.

In the afternoon of 25 November 1741, Friedrich August, Graf Rutowski, commander of the Saxon contingent, in fact the largest among those present under the walls of Prague, made the decision to storm the city that same night. A traditional siege would have taken too long, and the autumn season was too late to wait any longer. The walls were between 10 and 11 metres high, too much to be climbed with excessive ease.[49] Nevertheless, a diversionary attack and the darkness of the night would have allowed a select group of assailants equipped with sufficiently long ladders to penetrate the city and lower the drawbridge of one of the gates. At that point the bulk of the forces would break in and occupy Prague. In all three columns were designated to capture the city. Two of

---

48   E. Gabriel, *Die Hand-Faustfeuerwaffen der habsburgischen Heere* (Wien: ÖBV, 1990), pp.30-34, 204-205; H. Müller, *Das Heerwesen in Brandeburg und Preussen von 1640 bis 1860. Die Bewaffnung* (Berlin: Brandenburgisches Verl.-Haus, 1991), pp.88-91.

49   Folard *Mémoires pour servir à l'Histoire*, pp.133-134.

these columns were commanded by French generals and should have been simple feints: one, under the orders of the Comte de Polastron, would attack the *Reichs-Thor* [Imperial Gate] to the west along the hilly salient at 1:00 a.m. on 26 November. A second column, commanded by Comte Maurice de Saxe, would launch an attack at 2:30 a.m. against *Neu-Thor* [New Gate] to the west. Still to the west, a little further south, at 4:30 a.m. the Saxons would launch the main attack on *Carls-Thor* [Charles's Gate]. The illumination was also guaranteed by the fact that that night was just the third since the full moon of 22 November.[50]

To many French senior officers this plan seemed rather unrealistic, but nevertheless they gladly accepted this mission: it was up to them to plan and conduct the diversionary attack. The famous Maurice de Saxe was placed at the head of the column that would have had as its objective the *Neu-Thor*.[51] He had at his disposal 1,000 infantry and 2,000 cavalrymen of chosen forces. Altogether there were four companies of grenadiers, 192 in all between officers, NCOs and grenadiers. Covering fire would be provided by 700 chosen infantry of the Brigade Roi (Régiment du Roi, four battalions, and Régiment Royal-Bavière, two battalions),[52] 400 Carabiniers, and elements of three regiments of dismounted dragoons. Once the gates were opened, a mixed cavalry regiment of 1,200 troopers would have rushed into Prague.[53] Maurice de Saxe had at his disposal at that time one of the most aggressive and capable officers then in service with the army of the king of France, *Lieutenant Colonel* François Chevert of the Régiment de Beauce. This officer was placed in charge of the assault group and they would scale the walls on the left flank of the bastion that covered the gate. Meanwhile, Chevert and his men would take care of eliminating the sentries and cut down the drawbridge, Maurice de Saxe and the bulk of the forces would deliberately draw the fire of the defenders. Chevert received the only two scaling ladders available which were distributed to the grenadiers:

> I ordered the senior sergeant to go up with eight grenadiers and not to shoot once he reached the top; I told him to cut the throats of the sentries, if they could catch them by surprise, and not to defend himself except with the bayonet, if there was resistance on the ramparts. Later four companies of grenadiers would arrive, followed by the detachments of the Dragoons, and these in turn followed by the four infantry picquets, and so it happened.[54]

Chevert must have noticed at this point the indecision in the eyes of the sergeant, Jacob Pascal.[55] He approached Pascal and, looking him straight in the face, he said:

---

50   A. Cappelli, *Cronologia, Cronografia e Calendario Perpetuo* (Milano: Hoepli, 1988), pp.58-59.
51   Browning, *War of Austrian Succession*, p.78.
52   *Ordre de bataille der Mitte November 1741 vor Prag befindlichen französischen Truppen*, in Kriegsgeschichtlichen Abteilung des k. und k. Kriegs-Archivs, *Oesterreichischer Erbfolge-Krieg 1740-1748*, Vol.V, p.603.
53   Pajol, *Les Guerres*, Vol.II, pp.120-121.
54   Folard, *Mémoires pour servir à l'Histoire*, pp.134-135.
55   Pajol, *Les Guerres*, Vol.II, p.121.

You will go up there [...] and, crossing the parapet, they will shout at you: *Who is there?* You will not answer. They will ask you the same thing a second time; you will not answer, and you will still remain silent at the third call. They will shoot you, they will miss you and you will slaughter the sentry, and we will come to that point to help you.[56]

Pascal and his men did exactly what Chevert had ordered them to do, and so did the enemy sentries, who missed their target and they were shot down one after another. The French managed to quickly secure control of *Neu-Thor*, just as the Saxon attack to the south, which started at 4:00 a.m., did not register the expected progression. Maurice de Saxe was beginning to worry about the fate of his grenadiers when the drawbridge came down on the bridge; like a bolt of lightning the French cavalry galloped along the streets of the *Neu-Stadt* in the direction of the Charles Bridge and the *Reichs-Thor* to in turn open the gates to the Saxon allies. The governor Ogilvy, as soon as he saw the French commander before him, offered the surrender of the city without too many ceremonies. Prague had fallen.

The speech that François Chevert made to *Sergent* Pascal soon became very famous. However, the curious, almost divinatory aspect of those words was always emphasized, but the reasons that led him to speak in such way were never investigated. Today we can reasonably assume that Chevert knew very well that the Austrian sentinel would have missed his target. He had worn the uniform of the French army from 1706, and by 1741 he had been in service for 35 years. He therefore knew very well the soldier's psychology, his behaviour in combat, his weaknesses, his fears and his strengths. Although he may not have had deep knowledge in the field of psychology, Chevert certainly understood what a soldier's greatest fear was: that of killing.

This theory was first formally recorded by Brigadier General Samuel Lyman Atwood Marshall, a US Army officer in the Pacific theatre during World War II and later US historian of the European theatre.[57] Until then it was believed that the soldier would kill the enemy in combat simply because he was ordered or because this was essential to defend his own life and those of his fellow soldiers. The alternative was panic and flight. During the Second World War, Marshall interviewed soldiers who had just come out of the battlefield and asked them what they had really done in combat. He employed a team of historians who carried out individual or group interviews with thousands of soldiers belonging to more than 400 infantry companies sent to the fronts in Europe and the Pacific. The talks generally took place shortly after the end of close combat against German or Japanese troops. The results were always the same: only 15 to 20 percent of American infantry soldiers opened fire on the enemy. The others, on the contrary, voluntarily took great risks in rescuing comrades in arms, carrying ammunition, or carrying messages. They simply did not take up their

---

56   This instruction, probably one of the most famous military commands of the eighteenth century, swiftly became known as an interesting and hilarious anecdote in the years following the War of the Austrian Succession. The oldest quotation currently known is that reported in *Dictionnarie des Portraits Historiques, Anecdotes, et traits remarquables des Hommes Illustres* (Paris: Lacombe, 1758), Vol.II, pp.517-518.

57   For a brief biography, see the introduction by R.W. Glenn to the 2000 edition of Marshall, *Men Against* Fire, pp.1-8.

weapon and did not try to kill the enemy, a situation that remained constant regardless of the duration of the action.[58]

Marshall came to the conclusion that thousands of soldiers would never have shot against the enemy: 'The sane man has such an innate and spontaneous repulsion to kill that he will never kill of his own accord if he can avoid doing so. At the decisive moment the soldier becomes a conscientious objector'.[59] Men kill if they are obligated to do so, and in a combat unit are subjected to a strong social pressure to do this, but most of them are not natural born killers. The fact that the common man does not kill has been largely ignored by those trying to understand what happens on the battlefield. Looking another human in the eye, consciously making the decision to shoot him down, and watching him die due to one's own choice, are moments that combine to form the fundamental, and traumatic, action of war. One of the elements that has contributed to misinterpreting the psychology of the soldier on the battlefield is the misapplication of the fight-or-flight model. This model is based on the fact that, in the face of a danger, a series of psychological and physiological processes prepare and support a wild animal in the choice of fighting or fleeing. When we examine this animal's reaction to aggression from its own species, the choices are greater and also include attitude or surrender. The application of these response models present in the animal kingdom – to fight, to flee, to assume posture, surrender – to the world of human warfare was first explained by Grossman in the volume *On Killing*.[60] The combat between animals of the same species does not provide for an instant kill, but it passes through a series of postures that are almost always bloodless. These actions have the purpose of convincing the opponent that the enemy is dangerous and frightening. When a posturing beast fails to dissuade an opponent from attacking it, the options left are to fight, flee, or surrender, but the opponent is rarely expected to die either. The pose, the mock battle, and the submission

---

58   There has been considerable debate over the research of Marshall and the subsequent work of D. Grossman, *On Combat*; ibid, *On Killing*. Some studies like R.J. Spiller, 'S.L.A. Marshall and the Ratio of Fire', in *The RUSI Journal*, Winter 1988, pp.63-71, suggest that the volume of fire in the Second World War was much higher than Marshall assumed, openly criticizing his way of collecting data in the field. However, Ardant du Picq's nineteenth-century work seems to indicate Marshall's interpretation is correct. Other studies that seem to confirm Marshall's thesis are: R.A. Gabriel, *Military Psychiatry: A Comparative Perspective* (New York: Praeger, 1986); ibid., *No More Heroes: Madness and Psychiatry in War* (New York: Hill & Wang, 1987); R. Holmes, *Acts of War*, (London: Weidenfeld & Nicolson, 2003); B. Shalit, *The Psychology of Conflict and Combat* (New York: Praeger, 1988); H.X. Spiegel, 'Psychiatry with an Infantry Battalion in North Africa', in W.S. Mullens, A. J. Glass (eds.), *Neuropsychiatry in World War II, Vol.2, Overseas Theaters*, Washington, D.C. 1973, pp.111-126. Recently, the chorus of criticism has also been added to by R.C. Engen, with the very interesting *Canadians under Fire: Infantry Effectiveness in The Second World War* (Montreal and Quebec: McGill-Queen's University Press, 2009). The approach by Engen is really important, because he brings the experience and post-combat interviews of 150 Canadian officers describing how their units had behaved in combat through a questionnaire. The problem is that officers in battle command rather than fight. If they use their own weapons instead of managing the fight they are bad officers, or the tactical situation is really serious and the cohesion of the unit is compromised. The author's experience as a military lecturer at the Italian Army Officer School in Turin has allowed him to come into contact with over 600 captains attending the General Staff Course, some of whom could boast considerable combat experience in Iraq and Afghanistan. All, without exception, confirmed the truthfulness of Grossman's words.
59   Marshall, *Men Against Fire*, p.79
60   Grossman, *On Combat*, pp.39-44.

process are vital to the survival of the species. These behaviours avoid unnecessary deaths and ensure the survival of a young male in the first fights, during which his opponents are usually larger and better prepared. We certainly speak of aggression and competitiveness, but only at an extremely low level of real violence.

The pose and the standard fight-or-flight model help explain many of the actions that take place on a battlefield. When a man is frightened, he literally stops thinking with his forebrain, the mind of the human being, and begins to think with the midbrain, the portion of the brain that is essentially indistinguishable from that of an animal, and in the mind of an animal the one who makes the most noise and looks bigger wins. One method of posturing can be found in richly decorated armour, like that of the Greeks and Romans, or like the shiny surfaces of fifteenth-century armour which made knights who were equipped with them seem brighter and brighter. This performance saw its apex in modern history with the voluminous fur caps used by the units of Sardinian and Austrian grenadiers: they had no other function than to show and make the person wearing them feel a taller and more dangerous creature. A corps of grenadiers was an imposing force, and not only in the aspect of their person. Comparable to the presence on the battlefield of a battery of heavy field guns, their moral effect on the opponent should not be underestimated. Their appearance in combat restored confidence to their comrades and inspired terror to their enemies:

> We have learned through experience that a grenadier, simply because he is called grenadier, is considered a better soldier, he is less prone to desertion and fights better. I have often noticed that when soldiers are assigned by other companies to that of the grenadiers, they take something of the spirit of the grenadiers at the same time they put on the fur cap. Appearance and conduct are transformed.[61]

Psychological implications also existed in the maintenance of the weapon. Well-maintained equipment was a symbol of the unit's discipline, efficiency and solidity. The Prussians of the Fürst von Anhalt-Dessau in the Battle of Turin in 1706 had 'every part of their equipment as shiny as a mirror – the musket, the sword, and the brass shield on the flap of the cartridge box. [...] Only headless people will condemn this splendour as useless. It increases the soldier's courage and confidence, and increases the dignity of the whole army'.[62] After all, it was certainly an impressive sight to watch thousands of shiny gun barrels sparkle in the first light of the sun; war played, and still plays today, on these psychological aspects.

Similarly, the roars of two ferocious animals that are posing are also replicated by men in combat. For centuries cries of war have rang out on the battlefields, the cry of the Greek phalanx, the *hurra!* of the Russian infantry, the lament of the Scottish bagpipes or the *Avanti Savoia!* of the Royal Italian Army. Soldiers have always instinctively tried to impress the enemy through non-violent means before coming to physical confrontation, and they have always tried to encourage one another and impress themselves with ferocious cries

---

61   J. Cogniazzo, *Freymüthige Beytrag zur Geschichte des östreichischen Militairdienstes* (Frankfurt: Unknown Publisher, 1779), p.106.

62   J.W. Archenholtz, *Gemälde der preussischen Armee von und in dem siebenjährigen Kriege* (Osnabrück: Biblio Verlag, 1974), pp.16-18.

while simultaneously employing a particularly effective means of covering the unpleasant scream of the enemy.[63] The greater noise of gunpowder, its ability to guarantee an aggressive attitude, allowed the rise of firearms on the battlefield. The bow would still have been used in eighteenth century wars if the crude mathematics of killing efficiency had been all that mattered, since both the firepower and accuracy of the bow were greater than that of a muzzle-loading smoothbore flintlock. Yet a frightened man, who is thinking with his midbrain and does a mere 'ploink, ploink, ploink' with his bow, has no chance of defeating an equally frightened opponent who makes 'BANG! BANG!' with his own gun.[64] Firing a musket clearly satisfies the deeply ingrained need to posture, and with it the requirement to be relatively harmless to the enemy.

Ardant du Picq, an infantry colonel in Napoleon III's army, was one of the first to document the common tendency among soldiers to shoot in the air simply for the sake of shooting. Du Picq carried out the first careful investigation into the nature of combat by interviewing many French officers army during the 1860s. A common answer during these interviews was that 'many soldiers shoot in the air to long distances', while another noted that 'a number of our soldiers fired in the air, no aim, ostensibly for desire to be stunned, to get drunk with rifle fire during this contingent crisis'.[65] Infantry fire during the eighteenth century wars was incredibly ineffective. This ineffectiveness did not depend solely on the quality of the weapons used; in a fire exercise in 1755, *Generalmajor* Hans Karl von Winterfeldt had a target six metres wide and three metres high set up for firing two grenadier platoons. At 180 metres only 13 percent of the shots hit, at 120 metres the percentage rose to 16.6 percent, while at 90 metres the shots that hit the target amounted 46 percent. Better known is the experiment conducted in 1810 by Gerhard von Scharnhorst, who used a target 30 metres wide and two metres high, firing 200 shots at five different distances. The result was as follows:

Table 8. Results of the 1810 Prussian Firing Experiment With Muzzle-loading Smooth-bore Flintlock Muskets

Distance	60	120	180	240	300
Scores	92	64	64	42	26

Source: G.J. Scharnhorst, *Über die Wirkung des Feuergewehrs* (Berlin: Nauck, 1813), pp.80-83.

---

63   In the eighteenth century the most used cry by the Germanic nations was *Victoria!*, while the Imperialists also shouted *Römisch Reich!* The German units of the Roman Catholic faith invoked *Unser Frauen!* (Our Lady!). The French used the well known *Vive le Roi!* Each regiment, then, seems to have its own motto or cry to be used in battle. In the excitement of combat it was common to hear soldiers screaming *Tuer! Tuer!* Since the Middle Ages, the Savoy army opened battle to the war cry *Savoye! Bonnes Nouvelles! Saint-Maurice!* and then limited to *Savoye!* O. de Watteville, *Le Cri de Guerre chez les différerents Peuples* (Paris: É. Lechevalier, 1889).

64   Grossman, *On Combat*, pp.86-90, 198-199.

65   Ardant du Picq, *Études sur le Combat* (Paris: Hachette-Dumaine, 1880), pp.363, 373. The text came out posthumously since Colonel du Picq died on 18 August 1870 at the military hospital of Metz following wounds sustained three days earlier in combat at Longeville-lès-Metz, during the Franco-Prussian War of 1870. Subsequently translated into English as *Battle Studies. Ancient and Modern Battle*, (New York: Macmillan, 1921).

Experiments like this confirmed the basic idea that poor shooting quality had to be compensated for with an increased rate of fire, but the consumption of ammunition during a fire fight became enormous at that point. The revelations of Mauvillon about the Battle of Chotusitz in 1742, when the Prussians fired some 650,000 cartridges, causing just 5,000 deaths and wounds to the enemy, not all hit by a musket ball, emphasise this point.[66]

Cannon fire, like that of the machine gun of World War II, is a completely different matter, and on particular occasions it was able to inflict more than 50 percent of the overall losses. The muzzle-loading flintlock muskets, such as those used by soldiers of the armies that fought at Assietta, could shoot from one to three shots per minute, depending on the skill of the soldier and the weapon's condition. Within their usual range, these weapons had more than a 50 percent chance of hitting someone or something, and the average kills per minute would have been hundreds of soldiers killed in matter of minutes, instead of just one or two. The weak link between the potential and actual killing capacity of these units was the soldier. For the simple fact that he was dealing with a living, thinking opponent instead of an inanimate target, the soldiers posed to try to look as lethal as possible, but ultimately most of them fired over the heads of the enemies.

However, they stopped missing the target as soon as the opponent fled. Once the course of the action forced the soldiers of one of the two armies to turn their backs and to escape, then the killings began in earnest. Almost six years after the events at Prague, French grenadiers and soldiers, pressed against the stony walls of the Sardinian entrenched camp, refused to retire until almost the end of the battle. There are two factors at play that determine this increase in kills against a fleeing enemy, and this fear of turning one's back on the enemy. The first factor is the concept of the hunter's instinct, which is present in most animals; in the course of a chase, a hunter, both human and animal, chases and cuts down anything that runs. As long as one's back is turned, one is in danger. The second factor that comes into play is the distance from the victim's face; the killer may, or may not, see the face of the enemy and soldiers intuitively understand that when they turned their backs on the opponent they ran a greater risk of being killed. Not having to look at the victim's face provides a form of psychological distance that assists the soldier in rationalizing and accepting the killing of another human being. The wide eyes that pop out of the exploded sockets, the puffs of blood mixed with saliva and vomit, are not seen. The price men have to pay for a close-range kill is the perennial reminder of the agonizing, suffering, or devastated face of the slain enemy.

Psychological studies developed at the end of the Second World War revealed the existence of two percent of soldiers defined as 'aggressive psychopaths, devoid of the normal reluctance to kill. The negative connotations associated with the term 'psychopath', or its modern equivalent 'sociopath', are inadequate, since this behaviour is what is generally desirable for the soldiers in combat, to kill the enemy. In practice, there is two percent of the male population who, if pushed to do so or given a legitimate reason, will kill without remorse or regret. Not surprising at all, at this point, is the data showing that only two percent of the fighter pilots of the US Army Air Corps were responsible for 40 percent of all the enemy aircraft downed carried out by the US side during the Second World War.

---

66   E. Mauvillon, *Histoire de la dernière Guerre de Bohême* (Amsterdam: David Mortier, 1756), Vol.I, pp.100-101.

In the eighteenth century this two percent of men naturally predisposed to combat obviously did not end up as pilots of a fighter plane, but by the more or less rational choice of their commanders were put in the grenadier units. Today we are led to believe that the selection criterion was mainly due to height. In the eighteenth century this was not the main characteristic that a grenadier must have. Certainly, sturdy and handsome men were always in demand, since 'a big man can better bear the weight of his weapons, his backpack, his rations of bread and the rest of his equipment. He is better able to load and aim with his musket, and to strike with the bayonet. He has an advantage in jumping over a moat, climbing a field fortification or dealing with other similar situations'.[67] The French regulations of the period required infantry recruits to have a minimum height of 154 centimetres; by the mid-eighteenth century over a third of the civilian population of the kingdom of France was shorter than this size, and tall grenadiers were rarely seen. In this regard, in the second half of the century some veterans admired the exploits of a certain 'captain of the grenadiers of a foreign regiment in the service of the king of Sardinia, named *Lucadou* … a fearless man, … only five feet tall', about 150 centimetres. The 'foreign regiment' was the Reggimento Audibert, and the officer in question was Benoit Lucadou (1683-1772); a Frenchmen originally from Languedoc: exiled for his religious faith, he enlisted in the Sardinian Army. He won the admiration of his contemporaries as he decided to face an officer of the imperial grenadiers during the Battle of Parma in 1734. 'Lucadou, an intrepid man, no taller than five feet attacked the enemy and he gave him a bayonet thrust in the belly, and at the same time he shot, knocking him down. The fall of the German struck his soldiers so much that they no longer thought of crossing the moat to recover their officer, in whose belly Lucadou found his bayonet'.[68] Benoit Lucadou in December 1746 was still in service in the Reggimento Monfort with the rank of *colonnello*. He died in Geneva on 17 February 1772.[69]

This was certainly not a giant, even in the Sardinian army, where the men recruited had to be between 159 and 172 centimetres in height.[70] The selection criteria were then others, including one which stipulated that 'men had not to be too tall, should be strong, active, non-fat'.[71] Even armies very attentive to physical appearance, such as the Prussians, selected their grenadiers not on the basis of height, but on their 'reliability, their robustness, and on the fact that they were mature men and good marchers'.[72] In addition to this, the officers identified those individuals they considered the best fighters:

> [E]verywhere, grenadiers are regarded as the elite of the infantry, and are selected from the fusiliers. In many armies they have high pay, and they are always the

---

67   Duffy, *Military Experience in the Age of Reasons*, p.70.

68   Warnery, *Anecdotes et Pensées historiques et militaire*, p.17. The author of the volume, Carl Emanuel von Warnery auf Langerdorf, an officer in the imperial service, and later in the Prussian one, probably saw the episode in person.

69   AST, Sezioni Riunite, Ministero della Guerra, Ufficio Generale del Soldo, Ruolini di Rivista, Reggimento Audibert/Monfort, Vol.81, 1746.

70   *Raccolta per ordine di Materie delle Leggi cioè Editti, Patenti, manifesti, Ecc.*, Book 27, Vol.29, p.117.

71   P. Sumner, 'General Hawley's Chaos', in *Journal of the Society for Army Historical Research*, XXVI, No.111 (Autumn 1949), p.91.

72   Toulongeon and Hullin, *Une mission militaire en Prusse, en 1786* (Paris: Firmin Didot, 1881), p.216.

ones who have to carry out the most difficult missions. In some countries the largest men are chosen for grenadiers, in others those of medium size, robust and with large moustaches, and in others, especially in France, there the grenadiers themselves who choose their comrades; it is enough that the candidate has shown himself courageous, he is a good marcher, he renounces his engagement award and he swears never to ask for leave. This means that it is not only the size that a soldier makes, and this also applies to grenadiers, who are always, and in every army, the best troops.[73]

Grenadiers were veteran soldiers, experienced, well trained and belonging to that minimal percentage of born fighters. Unlike the Austrian sentries, who fought but did not kill anyone on the walls of Prague, these men really fought to kill. At Assietta assigned their grenadiers to their key points of defence, whilst the French gave their grenadiers the most dangerous tactical tasks of the day.

---

73   Warnery, *Anecdotes et Pensées historques et militaire*, p.26.

5

Last Moves – First Moves

The great Franco-Spanish counter-offensive in Provence, which ended on 3 February with the reaching of the right bank of the Var, a little river that signified the border with the kingdom of Sardinia, was followed by the allied investment of the city of Genoa. Now, everyone was expecting the opening of a second front along the Alps. The French wanted this second front, the Spaniards did everything to sabotage the plan, the Sardinians feared it more than anything else, the Austrians were concentrating only on their *Strafexpedition* against Genoa.

3 June. Western Ligurian Front, City of Nice

The court of Turin was particularly anxious. The operations in Liguria were seen as a useless waste of energy as the enemy advanced along the west coast and was about to attack the Alpine bastion. On 31 May, instructions were issued by the Secretariat of War to verify the state of the works and depots of the forts of Exilles and Brunetta in Susa. However, the minister of war himself had to admit that 'up to now it does not seem that they combine to put us in such apprehension of these frontiers, [...] while they have only five Battalions in Briançon, whereby HM reserves to give major orders about this matter'.[1]

The king decided to send reinforcements to the Alps,[2] even if on 3 June the war resumed on the Ligurian front. The Duc de Belle-Isle pushed 40 battalions of infantry beyond the Var, to gain the city Nice. As he was about to attack the enemy he had already to duel with the commander of the Spanish forces, the Marqués de la Mina. After long and exhausting negotiations, Belle-Isle finally succeeded in persuading the Spanish commander that the attack on the Italian front should take place not along one route but two. The offensive to the south would be developed along the coastal road, and during its progression towards the west it would invest the various centres and strongholds in the hands of the Austro-Sardinians. The advance should progress to Genoa, where these forces would attack from behind the enemy army

---

1   AST, Sezioni Riunite, Ministero della Guerra, Regia Segreteria di Guerra, Lettere ai Governatori, Mazzo 43. Letter to the Governor of Susa, 31 May 1747.

2   On 3 June 1747 3/Roi was assigned to the sector of the Susa Valley. AST, Sezioni Riunite, Ministero della Guerra, Regia Segreteria di Guerra, Lettere ai Governatori, Mazzo 43. Letter to the Governor of Susa, 3 June 1747.

engaged in the siege of the city. While the offensive was being launched along the Ligurian front, a second army would be gathered in the Dauphiné, and it would attack the Alps and Piedmont, the heart of the kingdom of Sardinia. The operational objective was the same as in 1745, the weak Fort of Exilles, while the strategic one that Belle-Isle proposed in La Mina was to force the Piedmontese forces to abandon the siege operations against Genoa itself. So, the units of the newly formed *Armée du Dauphiné*, no less than 30 infantry battalions, marched on Tournoux while 48 others were investing the enemy's defences along the coast.

The double Franco-Spanish advance forced Baron Leutrum to immediately abandon the Var defensive line, and to withdraw his 27 battalions up to the mountains of Oneglia, covering Piedmont, leaving only small garrisons on the coast in Villefranche and Ventimiglia, with the purpose of holding back the enemy advance and gaining time.

7 June. Ministry of War, Turin

The political and military leaders in Turin were experiencing serious moments of concern. The staff of the Minister of War Bogino wanted to avoid the disasters of the 1745 campaign, when eastern Piedmont was invaded and occupied, and the Alpine front threatened. To face the threat in the east, the minister would have negotiated with the Imperialists the presence of an army powerful enough to block any enemy progression from the coast. Another sufficiently large army corps had to be set up in the Alps to slow down the enemy advance, giving time for the bulk of the army to reach the threatened sector. The Sardinian sector commanders, specifically the military governors, began to plan the defence of the Susa and Chisone valleys against an enemy invasion. In particular, the upper Val di Susa was considered the most vulnerable area:

- Compared to the Val Varaita, it entered directly into territories considered crucial for the Crown of Turin, in particular the middle and lower Val di Susa.
- The Fort of Exilles was an extremely vulnerable fortification.
- The experience of 1745 had taught that the French knew how to manoeuvre effectively in this sector of the Alps and they were able to transport a siege artillery park to the western side of the Alps.

The French would certainly try again to break through the Alpine front; moreover, two years earlier they had almost succeeded in the enterprise of conquering the Fort of Exilles. Everyone was convinced of this, in particular the court of Turin and the Governor of Susa, Cesare Alberico Balbiano, Marchese di Viale. At the beginning of June, reflecting on the combat experiences of 1745, the governor had informed the Secretariat of War that he had prepared a project, or rather a war plan, on how to deal with the invasion force. On 7 June Bogino transmitted the details of 'his Project, to bring the Troops to the aforementioned object'.[3] As proof of the desire to reinforce this sector, the departure of 2/Salis from Susa was

---

3   AST, Sezioni Riunite, Ministero della Guerra, Regia Segreteria di Guerra, Lettere ai Governatori, Mazzo 43. Letter to the Governor of Susa, 7 June 1747.

suspended,[4] and the procedures for raising the militia units of the Val di Susa were decided and their chain of command organized. On 10 June the War Secretariat ordered the raising of the militias from Val di Susa and those from Pragelato. The governor of Susa would be responsible for the units organized in the area of his responsibility, while the command on the ground would belong to a veteran of the campaign of 1745, *Maggiore* Perrone. The Pragelato militia was instead under the direct orders of the Governor of Pinerolo de Morgenex.[5] Two days later, he received another order: the king ordered the raising of 500 Waldensians under command of a specialist in mountain warfare and special operations, *Capitano* Rouzier of the Reggimento Monfort. The company would take up a position at the Sestriere Pass, along French entrenchments erected in 1745 and now put back into operational condition.[6]

In Turin, Carlo Emanuele III, his Minister of War and the engineer Ignazio Bertola had analysed the project of the Governor of Susa for the defence of the Chisone and Susa valleys. The new defensive plan suggested concentrating forces not so much to protect Colle delle Finestre, which had always been considered a fundamental point as it put the Susa and Chisone valleys in direct communication along a north-south road axis, but to advance the defence to the west and anchor it on the Assietta plateau. Although circumventable, Assietta's position had the following advantages:

- It was proportionate to the available force.
- It was flat and traversed by several mule tracks.
- It also constituted an excellent flank position against any direction of movement or attack
- It prevented the enemy from completing the encirclement of the fort of Exilles.

As they understood in Turin:

> [Assietta] was actually subject to fewer dangers and offered greater advantages than the others: we would have covered Exilles and Fenestrelle at the same time, without fear of being bypassed. The locations we are talking about were strong by their nature and if despite this we had been unfortunately forced to abandon them, we

---

4   AST, Sezioni Riunite, Ministero della Guerra, Ufficio Generale del Soldo: Ordini Generali Misti, 1747-1748, Mazzo 81, *Nota delle Tappe assegnate per la marcia deg'infrascritti Battaglioni, nel Cambiamento delle loro Destinazioni. Giugno 1747*; Ruolini di Rivista, Reggimento Reydt-Salis, Vol.13, 1747. Secondo quanto riportato nell'*État des Troupes de S.M. le Roy de Sardaigne destinées en Campagne en 1747*, in AST, Corte, Materie Politiche per Rapporto dall'Interno, Storie della Real Casa, Categoria III, Storie Particolari, Mazzo 24, D. Minutoli, *Report des campagnes faites par S.M. et par ses generaux avec des corps sèpares pendant les années 1747 et 1748, c'est à dire jusq'a la fin de la guerre*, Vol.II, Tavola 99.
5   AST, Sezioni Riunite, Ministero della Guerra, Regia Segreteria di Guerra, Lettere ai Governatori, Mazzo 43. Letter to the Governor of Susa. 10 June 1747.
6   AST, Sezioni Riunite, Ministero della Guerra, Regia Segreteria di Guerra, Lettere ai Governatori, Mazzo 43. Letter to the Governor of Pinerolo, 12 June 1747. For the entrenchments of Colle del Sestriere E. Garoglio, F. Zannoni, *La difesa nascosta del Piemonte sabaudo. I sistemi fortificati alpini (secoli XVI-XVIII)* (Torino: Centro Studi e Ricerche storiche sull'Architettura Militare del Piemonte, 2011), pp.208-211.

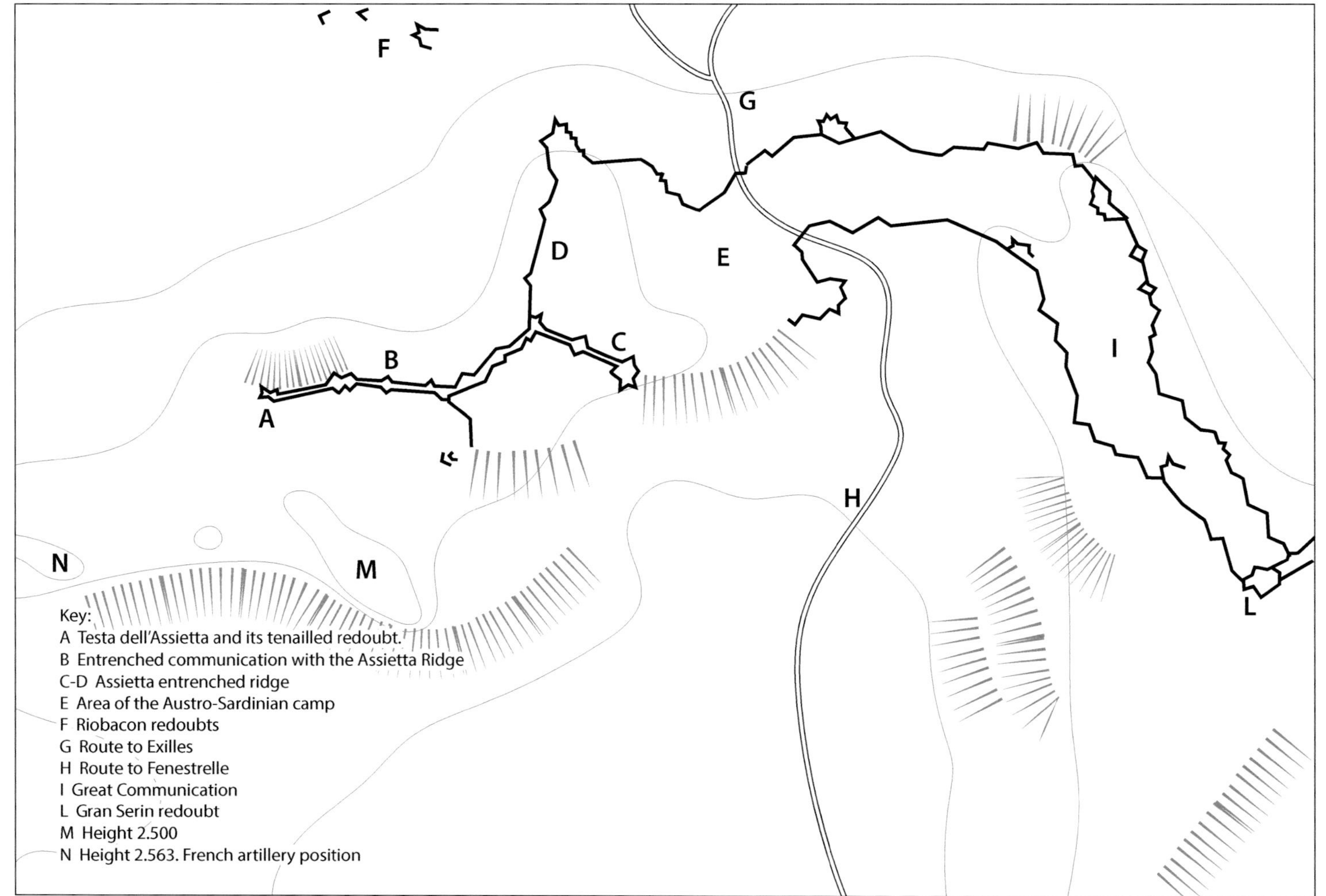

The Assietta battlefield. The north is on the upper side of the map.

could have retreated by putting the troops inside the forts of Fenestrelle and of Brunetta, and we could have reached the famous Catinat's Camp if we had judged it useful. In truth the enemies could have made the siege of Exilles from the heights of San Colombano, but they could not have cut off the communication with this fort, so that they would not have easily conquered it.[7]

On June 14, the king approved the plan and Minister Bogino was able to communicate to the Marchese di Balbiano that:

HM agrees your project for the disposition of troops destined for the defence of these borders, finding it the most proper to oppose the enemies, protecting the forts, and at the same time he reserves his orders for the execution of the same, when he feels that a body of enemy troops is nearby such as to make this providence necessary. He therefore wishes that, the infantry will continue for now to maintain their positions, and the Militia units to occupy the most convenient places to close the first entrance of the enemies, and to always be warned in time of their movements in order to be able to suitably rush there in some instantaneous occurrence. To the same also [to inform you that] *Capitano* Rouzier has been sent to the Valleys for the purpose of taking care of the establishment of such places. He has orders to formulate his project, and to communicate it to you. Messers Vassallo, Rasino and De Morgenex are responsible for having the militias from the Pragelato and the Pianura di Pinerolo, and by a detachment of troops to occupy those other posts that concern them. Mr Commendator Vedani, Engineer Captain, will leave somewhat earlier to visit the places, and to assist You in the recognition of what remains to be seen.[8]

13 June. Gulf of Genoa

While a French attack was expected in the Alps and the defence of the front was planned, in Liguria the Bourbon offensive coincided with the arrival in Sestri of the Austrian siege park destined for the siege of Genoa. Struggling against time Schulenburg, with the help of the British Royal Navy, in early June had the siege guns put aboard ships to transport them to the coast east of the city, where the attack front was scheduled to be opened. The castle of Sturla was occupied on 13 June, the siege artillery was laboriously disembarked and the siege of Genoa could actually begin. In reality, the operations were directed more against the system of field works outside the city, rather than against the main walls; a long and costly series of battles, which did nothing but increasingly thin out the scarce human resources of the imperial army.[9]

---

7   AST, Corte, Materie Politiche per Rapporto dall'Interno, Storie della Real Casa, Categoria III, Storie Particolari, Mazzo 24, Minutoli, *Report des campagnes faites par S.M*, Vol.V, pp.193-201.

8   AST, Sezioni Riunite, Ministero della Guerra, Regia Segreteria di Guerra, Lettere ai Governatori, Mazzo 43. Letter to the Governor of Susa, 10 June 1747.

9   On the situation of the imperial units committed against Genoa *Diensdtbarer Stand der östreichischen Streitmacht im Genuesischen für Juni 1747*, in Rothkirch, 'Der Feldzug 1747 in Italien', Vol.X, p.31

The Franco-Spanish-Ligurian resistance became more and more rigid, and casualties could not be replaced. At the same time, a massive relieving force of the enemy was marching along the western coast. It was necessary to hurry, but the Bourbon advance unleashed the latent conflict between Vienna and Turin. On paper, the Austro-Sardinians were almost double the enemy: 80,000 men, with 111 battalions and 103 squadrons, of which 45 and 30 were Sardinians. However, these forces were spread over an enormous front, from Susa to Oneglia, and from Genoa to Mantua. Above all, the strategic objectives of the two allies were now quite different, no longer reconcilable: the Austrians were interested in the siege of Genoa, the Sardinians interested in the defence of Piedmont. Vienna granted only few units, mostly in the process of being reconstituted; on 10 June Turin had confirmation that a skeletal Austrian brigade, formed by the remains of four infantry battalions, for a total of 1,076 men, would be detached from the Duchy of Milan, where it was in garrison waiting to receive new recruits to be trained, to the alpine front of Val Chisone.[10]

Although the Sardinian intelligence service had reported an ever-increasing concentration of troops at Guillestre in Dauphiné since 13 May, the bulk of the Sardinian forces had remained in defence of the Ligurian coast. In June the French had launched raids along the Valle Stura di Demonte, and the false news artfully circulated by the Duc de Belle-Isle led Carlo Emanuele III to order the reinforcement of the Fort of Demonte, concentrating reserve forces to Saluzzo and southern Piedmont in order to rush into the threatened sector. Often presented efficiently and on time,[11] the Sardinian information service was completely groping in the dark and they had no idea what the French were planning, who were trying with every means attract as many enemy forces to the south. A corps of 12 battalions was deployed to restore the roads that led from Col d'Argentière to Valle Stura di Demonte, and those that from Col de Vars led to Briançon and Mont-Dauphin.[12]

Meanwhile the *Armée du Dauphiné* was moving slowly north, waiting to deploy along the starting line of the offensive: it was a mass of 50 battalions which could not but attract the attention of the enemy intelligence, and in fact on 9 June the Barone di Breglio, governor of Mondovì, was informed of a possible enemy attack along the Valle Stura di Demonte. The information was deemed credible to the point that the governor himself, who required a period of care at the thermal baths in Sant'Anna di Valdieri, was ordered not to travel in the valley or at best to appoint a substitute in case of absolute necessity. Also the Conte di Asinari, governor of Nice, confirmed the presence of grenadier companies in the Argentera area in the Maritime Alps sector and close to the Valle Stura di Demonte, and he received the order to reinforce the garrison of Demonte.[13] News concerning the sighting of French troops continued to come in: on 13 and 17 June French troops were reported in Barcellonette, Tornoux and in the neighbouring valleys; on 19 June the arrival of a contingent of eight battalions and artillery ammunition in Briançon was confirmed for the first time. However, the following day the governor of

---

10   AST, Sezioni Riunite, Ministero della Guerra, Regia Segreteria di Guerra, Lettere ai Governatori, Mazzo 43. Letter to the Governor of Novara, 10 June 1747.

11   Alberti, *La battaglia dell'Assietta*, p.3.

12   Arvers and de Vault, *Guerre de la Succession d'Autriche (1742-1748)*, Vol.I, p.572.

13   AST, Sezioni Riunite, Ministero della Guerra, Regia Segreteria di Guerra, Lettere ai Governatori, Mazzo 43. Letter to the Governor of Mondovì, 9 June 1747; Letter to the Governor of Nizza, 9 June 1747.

the Demonte Fort reported that enemy forces had been spotted at Colle della Maddalena in Valle Stura.[14]

It seemed that the enemy wanted to replicate, on an even greater scale, the offensive of 1744. However, in Turin there were those who did not overlook the possibility that the real objective of the Bourbon army of the Alps was not the Fort of Demonte but that of Exilles. So on June 16, while intelligence reports informed of the arrival of new enemy contingents to the west side of the Alpine bastion but nothing more, it was decided not to neglect the defensive organization of the Chisone and Dora valleys. On 14 June the defence plan for these valleys was definitively approved, and the first measures began to be implemented.

The militias of Pragelato, Val di Susa and the Waldensians were put on alert. On 16 June, the Ministry of War decided that Fenestrelle would be the logistics hub of the valley, and the main support area for an observation corps in the Chisone-Dora area that was constituted in those days. The Minister of War informed the Governor of Fenestrelle that:

> H.M. sends to you the 2nd Battalion of the Regiment Savoia, which will arrive there tomorrow and when some unexpected movement of enemies put you in a justified concern to have more troop reinforcements, H.M. allows you to ask to Vassallo Sr. of Morgenex one of two battalions of Kalbermatten, which are garrisoned in Pinerolo or both, even the Monfort one, which also will come in that city the 18th of this month. For now, you will not move any of these battalions, except in the case of a specific necessity, the enemy shows himself determined to cross borders and this provisionally until a General Officer will arrive there, whom H.M. thinks to send you in a few days. the Cavaliere Vedani captain of engineers, who is presently in Susa, has the incumbency to also visit the Valleys of this Department, to recognize the defences, and project and realize all the field works, which he deems necessary.[15]

The initial nucleus of the new Observation Corps was therefore made up of 2/Reggimento Savoia, 2/ and 3/Reggimento Kalbermatten and 1/Reggimento Monfort, for a total of about 2,500 men to be added to 1,500 militiamen. It was now necessary to find a commander who would plan the defence on a tactical level.

11 June. Western Ligurian Front

While an enemy offensive was expected in the Alps and the defence of the front was planned, in Liguria the Franco-Spanish offensive was in full swing. For them, things seemed to be going well; on 11 June Villefranche and its fortifications were conquered, two weeks later, on 1 July, Ventimiglia also fell and the Franco-Spanish armies pushed their advance guard

---

14   AST, Sezioni Riunite, Ministero della Guerra, Regia Segreteria di Guerra, Lettere ai Governatori, Mazzo 43. Letter to the Governor of Valenza, 13 June 1747; Letter to the Governor of Susa del 17 June 1747; Letter to the Governor of Susa, 19 June 1747; Letter to the Governor of Demonte, 20 June 1747.

15   AST, Sezioni Riunite, Ministero della Guerra, Regia Segreteria di Guerra, Lettere ai Governatori, Mazzo 43. Letter to the Governor of Fenestrelle del 16 June 1747.

as far as San Remo, slowed only by the bad condition of the roads. The offensive seemed promising, and the month of July, if things proceeded in this way, would have put a strain on the alliance between Vienna and Turin, the real obstacle to Bourbon strategic objectives in Italy.[16]

The enemy advance had forced Baron Leutrum to withdraw his 27 Austro-Sardinian battalions as far as the mountains of Oneglia, to cover the passes towards Piedmont. The little strongholds he had left along the road along the coast, Villefranche and Ventimiglia, had been overcome and now only the Priamar Fortress in Savona remained to stop the enemy advance. Leutrum was now rightly concerned about the situation in his sector, and he had asked for the return of the Austro-Sardinian troops previously placed under his command and sent east to support the Imperial operations against Genoa. The imperial commander, Schulenburg, on 21 June denied any support, but he could not prevent at least the Sardinian units, under the command of *Luogotenente Generale* Della Rocca, from starting preparations for departure. The siege had now failed, and the Austrians were left with no choice but to re-embark the siege artillery, finding that the Austrian troops alone were too few and too fatigued to be able to invest alone the Ligurian capital. The Genoese forces correctly interpreted the movements they could observe inside the Ponente and Levante camps, and on 25 June they carried out a sortie which, however, was unsuccessful. Inside the city, the commander of the Franco-Spanish forces, Boufflers, fell ill with smallpox, a disease that took him to his grave on 2 July.

In Turin, Carlo Emanuele III and his minister Bogino believed that, after the siege of Genoa was abandoned, the defence of Piedmont should remain the only strategic paying objective, despite what the imperial commanders present in the theatre might think. So, on 2 July the king ordered Della Rocca to leave the siege of Genoa, informing the Imperialists of the decisions taken. Schulenburg was not surprised and, on the contrary, the Sardinian decision probably provided him with the necessary pretext to carry out that operation which, now necessary under a military profile and already prepared, could not be immediately implemented as it was contrary to the precise political mandate received from his sovereign: to punish Genoa.

So, while two Sardinian battalions moved east to Savona and 10 others marched into Piedmont, the imperial army completed the evacuation of all its materials, partly by sea and partly by land routes, and on the night of 6 July decamped, setting fire to what it could not carry. Having crossed the Bocchetta pass and sacked the village of Voltaggio, the imperial army stopped under the walls of the Fort of Gavi, already conquered the previous year. Here the forces destined to reinforce the Alpine front in Piedmont were detached; Schulenburg gave the command to Browne and left for Vienna to report to the empress.[17] The *Strafexpedition* against Genoa was over.

---

16   For a general account of the Ligurian campaign see Browning, *War of the Austrian Succession*, p.310; R. Capaccio, B. Durante, *Marciando per le Alpi. Il ponente italiano durante la guerra di successione austriaca (1742-1748)* (Marene Marene: Gribaudo, 1993), pp.115-123; Ilari, Boeri, Paoletti, *La Corona di Lombardia*, pp.236-240; Wilkinson, *Defence of Piedmont*, pp.297-300.

17   Ferdinand Ludwig, Graf Oeynhausen, sometimes rendered Schulenburg-Oeynhausen even though he had never been part of the Schulenburg family, faced the disappointment of Maria Theresia for failing to punish the Genoese rioters. He retired to Graz, where he died on 16 February 1754 due to

22 June. Ministry of War, Turin

The Austro-Sardinian armies were now divided into three separate groups. The first group was the army of Baron Leutrum committed to block the Franco-Spanish advance along the coast. The second group, the main one, was represented by the two armies returning from the failed siege of Genoa that were repositioning themselves north of the Apennines. In fact, they formed a strategic reserve ready to rush to where the offensive on the Alps would appear. The third group, the smallest, was the observation corps deployed between the Chisone and Susa valleys. At this point it was necessary to find a commander for those latter forces; the Conte di Bricherasio, former governor of the city of Savona, was chosen. On 22 June, Minister Bogino informed the count of his promotion to *luogotenente generale*.[18] The next day and on 24 June, the necessary instructions were given to the governors of Pinerolo, Fenestrelle and Susa regarding the new chain of command that was being created and the subsequent planning phases for the defence of the valleys.[19]

Bricherasio took command of the Sardinian troops stationed in the Chisone and Susa valleys, with *Maggior Generale* Alciati as his deputy. His mission was to 'act in the countryside for the defence of the Valleys of Pragelato, and Exilles, and of the Forts of Exilles and Fenestrelle, particularly in the event that the Enemies actually attempted to address themselves against them'.[20] To carry out this mission, he had at his disposal all the troops present in the area, 2/Reggimento Savoia, Reggimento Meyer and Reggimento Chiablese; all the units of the Waldensian militias, of Pragelato and those of the upper Val di Susa were also placed under the command of Bricherasio and the governors of Susa, Fenestrelle and Pinerolo had to communicate all intelligence information to him. The logistic base to support the troops of the observation corps was the Fenestrelle Fortress, where from 23 June materials, food and ammunition began to be stored for the troops operating at high altitude between the hill of Finestre and the Assietta plateau. The governor of Fenestrelle was charged to accompany the new commander 'to recognize all the Posts and Heights of these Frontiers'.[21] The new commander arrived at his new command post in Fenestrelle on 24 June, while Alciati, who should have preceded him, had not yet been sighted in Val Chisone on 25 June.

Meanwhile in Turin, Minister Bogino lived hours of intense anguish and indecision. The information that came to him from all over the Alpine front indicated the certain presence of a second Franco-Spanish army to the west of the Alpine ridge, but there were no clear signs where the threat would appear. Confirmations were beginning to arrive on the arrival

---

a fall from a horse. B. von Potem, 'Ferdinand Ludwig Graf von Oeynhausen', in *Allgemeine deutsche Biographie*, (Leipzig: Duncker & Humblot, 1887), Vol.XXV, pp.28-30.

18   AST, Sezioni Riunite, Ministero della Guerra, Regia Segreteria di Guerra, Lettere ai Governatori, Mazzo 43. Letter to the Conte di Bricherasio, 22 June 1747.

19   AST, Sezioni Riunite, Ministero della Guerra, Regia Segreteria di Guerra, Lettere ai Governatori, Mazzo 43. Lettera al Governatore di Fenestrelle, 23 June 1747; Letter to the Governor of Pinerolo, 23 June 1747; Letter to the Governor of Susa, 24 June1747.

20   AST, Sezioni Riunite, Ministero della Guerra, Regia Segreteria di Guerra, Lettere ai Governatori, Mazzo 43. Letter to the Governor of Fenestrelle, 23 June 1747.

21   AST, Sezioni Riunite, Ministero della Guerra, Regia Segreteria di Guerra, Lettere ai Governatori, Mazzo 43. Letter to the Governor of Fenestrelle, 23 June 1747.

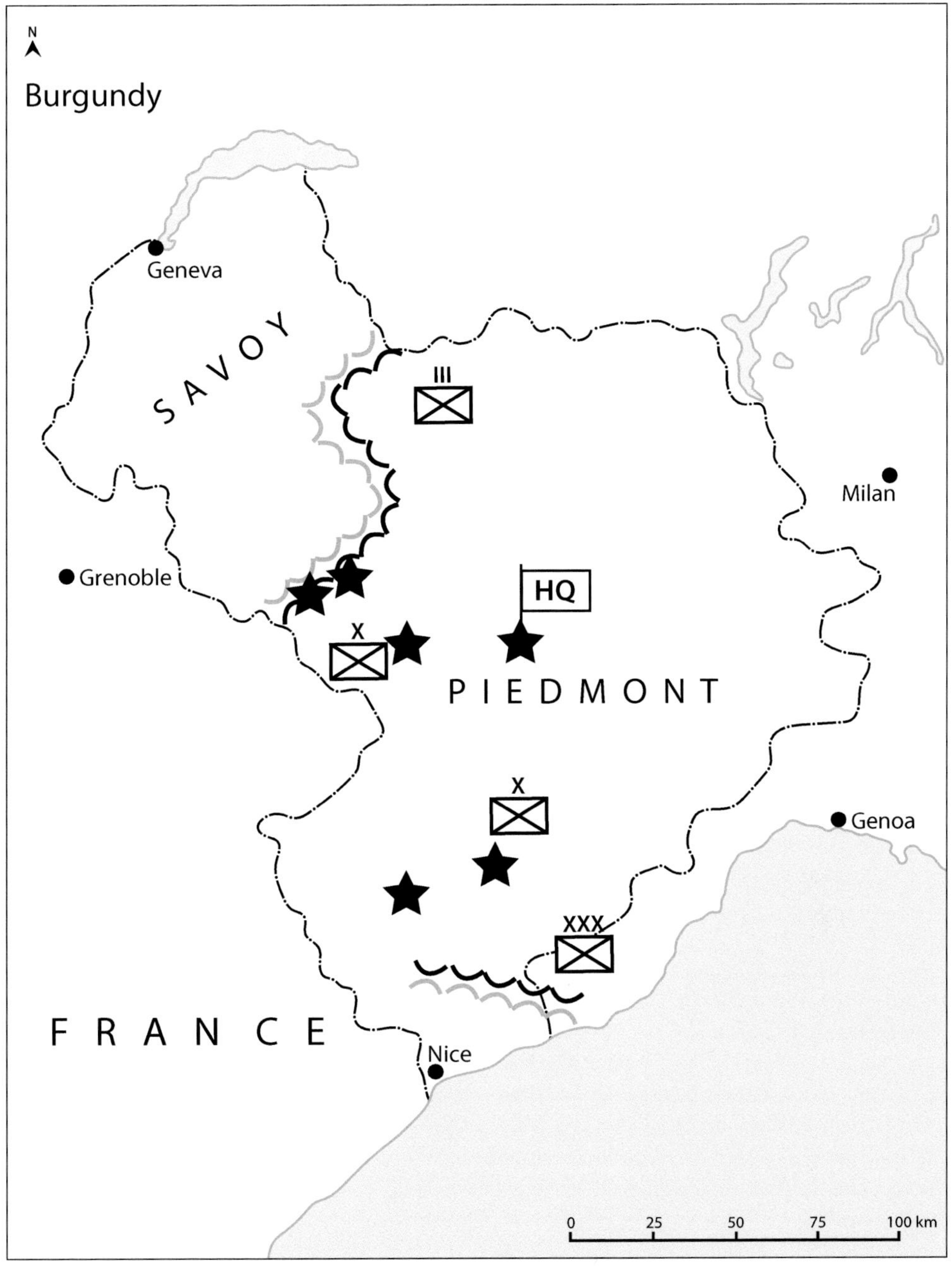

The operational disposition of the Sardinian forces on the western front in 1747. The main body of the Sardinian forces were deployed in the south, along the Ligurian eastern front under the orders of Baron Leutrum. Two smaller corps, of the size of a brigade, were in the Alps. The force in the south had to cover the fortresses of Cuneo and Demonte, while the other had to cover the fortresses of Fenestrelle in Chisone Valley, and Exilles and Brunetta in the Susa Valley. A smaller force, of the size of a regiment, was deployed in the Aosta Valley.

of French contingents in Briançon, while raids on the passes in Valle Stura di Demonte took place daily. From Val Chisone they awaited his orders to start the fortification works on the Assietta ridge; if he authorized these works, all the resources of the sector would remain tied up in that place. It might have been the right choice if the enemies would attack from Montgenèvre, but if the attack had occurred further south it would have unnecessarily wasted resources and worn out the troops in fieldwork operations at high altitude. During the day he also discussed it with the engineer Bertola, a confrontation that increased his doubts rather than clarified them. Carlo Emanuele III, then, decided that the time was over and that for now he did not expect to leave troops at Assietta and in other places at high altitude.[22] Bogino in his heart should not have been too convinced of the king's choices, and in any case he ordered the Marchese di Balbiano to set up a system of signals to warn the troops of an enemy offensive and to carefully plan the demolition of the necessary roads and bridges along the Susa Valley:

> In cases where it is necessary to occupy advantageous places in the mountains, it is customary to place signals from mile to mile away made of wood piled with straw and hay, and guarded by militias equipped with fire to light them one after another, whenever the enemy advances with superior forces; similar signals could also be prepared for the frontiers from the Sestrieres Valley to the vicinity of the Assietta Camp, and in those other places where they are to be useful. It will finally be of paramount importance that you instruct the governor of Exilles to have the right time to break the roads and bridges where the French and the Spaniards had already planned two years ago for their artillery to pass.[23]

Another source of concern for the minister was the lack of coordination and communication between the governors and the field commander: the Marchese di Balbiano on 26 June went up to Assietta alone to carry out reconnaissance on the ground. Despite the orders received, he had not given any news to Bricherasio:

> Since you went to visit Col de Sietta alone, for the future you could agree with the Conte di Bricherasio on the time and place where you and he could meet. On the same occasion it will be good for you to speak to him about all the plans and logistic facilities just realized.[24]

Meanwhile, the Austrians were organizing the arrival in Piedmont of Colloredo's brigade. Coming from Milan, on 27 June it would enter the territory of the King of Sardinia at Trecate, directed to Vercelli; the battalions marched separated, Hagenbach was the first on 27 June, on 1 July Traun, followed on 3 July by the 3/Forgách and the following day by 3/

---

22   AST, Sezioni Riunite, Ministero della Guerra, Regia Segreteria di Guerra, Lettere ai Governatori, Mazzo 43. Letter to the Governor of Susa, 24 June 1747.

23   AST, Sezioni Riunite, Ministero della Guerra, Regia Segreteria di Guerra, Lettere ai Governatori, Mazzo 43. Letter to the Governor of Susa, 24 June 1747, first letter.

24   AST, Sezioni Riunite, Ministero della Guerra, Regia Segreteria di Guerra, Lettere ai Governatori, Mazzo 43. Letter to the Governor of Susa, 24 June 1747, first letter.

Colloredo. Between 11 and 13 July the Austrian brigade concentrated in Pinerolo waiting to move to the area threatened by the expected French offensive.[25]

The day of 24 June passed with a thousand doubts and uncertainties. At nine o'clock in the evening a letter arrived from the governor of Susa indicating the arrival of enemy units in the surroundings of Briançon, at least eight battalions. This was the strength of two infantry brigades, a really important signal but the minister remained sceptical, as this news

> [C]ontradicts those that have recently occurred on that side, which exclude greater movements and preparations than the others already made before. What is certain is that it will be done equally in other parts and that naturally we will want to take over from someone, so it is not possible so far to form a just judgment of the enemy's aims.[26]

What did the enemy have in mind? They could hit the Susa Valley or the Chisone Valley, with the goal of besieging and conquering the Fort of Exilles as they had tried to do in 1745, or they could cross the Val Varaita and Valle Stura di Demonte again, as had happened in the campaigns of 1743 and 1744. In any case, the minister was not at all comfortable with the defensive system of the Chisone-Dora valleys, and the next day he would talk to the king about it again, and 'to take his orders, regarding the encampment of the troops to use them for the field fortifications and how to build them on the Assietta Plateau'.[27]

The following day further information arrived in Turin: 15 battalions, an entire army corps, had arrived in Guillestre while in Briançon other troops arriving in the city were sighted: the news had been confirmed by the governor of Pinerolo. The War Ministry immediately notified Bricherasio and the Governor of Susa of the operational situation and the two men, who, until then, had acted in total autonomy from each other, were ordered to coordinate, to communicate directly with each other. Bogino met the King and informed him about the situation. Regarding the possibility of sending troops up to the Assietta, Carlo Emanuele III revoked the prohibition of the previous day and required the governor 'to have some Battalions in the camp for the prompt execution of the works'.[28]

On Monday 26 June Bricherasio, the captain of engineers Vedani, and the governor of Susa, went up to the Assietta plateau to carry out a joint survey of the place. Vedani on that occasion for the first time on the ground demonstrated his fortification plans to the commander of the Sardinian forces; his request was for 6,000 personnel to be deployed in the entrenched camp, whose construction had begun on the same day, anchoring itself to the entrenchments previously made during the 1745 campaign.

---

25   AST, Sezioni Riunite, Ministero della Guerra, Ufficio Generale del Soldo, Ordini Generali Misti, 1747-1748, Mazzo 81.

26   AST, Sezioni Riunite, Ministero della Guerra, Regia Segreteria di Guerra, Lettere ai Governatori, Mazzo 43. Letter to the Governor of Susa, 24 June 1747, second letter.

27   AST, Sezioni Riunite, Ministero della Guerra, Regia Segreteria di Guerra, Lettere ai Governatori, Mazzo 43. Letter to the Governor of Susa, 24 June 1747, second letter.

28   AST, Sezioni Riunite, Ministero della Guerra, Regia Segreteria di Guerra, Lettere ai Governatori, Mazzo 43. Letter to the Governor of Susa, 24 June 1747, second letter.

In the meantime, the French continued to plan their action. They restored the roads to facilitate the transit of the siege artillery against the Fort of Exilles and they continued to maintain the centre of gravity of their forces anchored to the Tournoux camp. In doing so, they made the Sardinians believe they were about to attack the Stura Valley. The French plan seemed to give the desired results: to the alarmed governor of the Fortress of Fenestrelle, who signalled the arrival of new French forces in Briançon and requested urgent reinforcements, Bogino replied confidently that the defence plans were now the responsibility of Bricherasio alone, and he could also say to him that 'I know that the major preparations should rather be made towards the Barcellonette Valley'.[29] The deception concocted by the Duc de Belle-Isle was working: the Sardinian reserves remained for the moment far from the Susa Valley. On June 28, the Ministry of War informed the governor of Susa that all intelligence sources in his possession indicated 'that the greatest efforts of the enemy are directed against Stura Valley from Barcellonette, and up to now there is less to fear for these [the Val di Susa] borders'.[30]

In the meantime, Carlo Emanuele III denied further reinforcements to the Bricherasio; the Assietta entrenched camp would be defended only by the forces he had at his disposal, and with the three units of militia, Susa, Pragelato and Waldensian, of 500 men each and not 1000 as required. The assembly area for these units, their weapons and ammunitions' depot were established inside the Fenestrelle Fortress.[31] The only concession was made with the creation of four squads of 'hunters', or volunteers, to be recruited locally.[32] By now everyone in Turin was convinced that the Valle Stura di Demonte hypothesis was the most credible scenario, supported by continuous feedback and sightings in the field. On the 29th the governor of Cuneo began planning all the demolition works to the detriment of the road infrastructures along the Valle Stura di Demonte;[33] on the 30th, with the Minister Bogino mourning the death of his wife[34], Carlo Emanuele III confirmed to the governors that 'the clues are always growing, that the aims of the Enemy are directed against the Valle di Stura, according to the other notices, which also exist on that side, what will clarify the departure of the troops from Briançon, carried out as rumoured'.[35] In addition, the king asked Bricherasio not to bring other battalions up to the mountains, in addition to those already present, so as not to subject them to the wear and tear of tented life in the high altitudes, as 'the enemy battalions coming from Briançon are about to throw themselves in the

29   AST, Sezioni Riunite, Ministero della Guerra, Regia Segreteria di Guerra, Lettere ai Governatori, Mazzo 43. Letter to the Governor of Fenestrelle, 27 June 1747.
30   AST, Sezioni Riunite, Ministero della Guerra, Regia Segreteria di Guerra, Lettere ai Governatori, Mazzo 43. Letter to the Governor of Susa, 25 June 1747.
31   AST, Sezioni Riunite, Ministero della Guerra, Regia Segreteria di Guerra, Lettere ai Governatori, Mazzo 43. Letter to the Governor of Pinerolo, 30 June 1747.
32   AST, Sezioni Riunite, Ministero della Guerra, Regia Segreteria di Guerra, Lettere ai Governatori, Mazzo 43. Letter to the Governor of Susa, 28 June 1747.
33   AST, Sezioni Riunite, Ministero della Guerra, Regia Segreteria di Guerra, Lettere ai Governatori, Mazzo 43. Letter to the Governor of Susa, 29 June 1747.
34   AST, Sezioni Riunite, Ministero della Guerra, Regia Segreteria di Guerra, Lettere ai Governatori, Mazzo 43. Letter to the Governor of Susa, 1 July 1747.
35   AST, Sezioni Riunite, Ministero della Guerra, Regia Segreteria di Guerra, Lettere ai Governatori, Mazzo 43. Letter to the Governor of Susa, 1 July 1747.

Barcellonette Valley; H.M. would then be in the event of consequently recalling and also addressing those who had intended to serve under your orders from these parts'.[36]

22 June. French Headquarters, Menton

The Duc de Belle-Isle had come up with a brilliant plan. The problem now was putting it into practice. Despite the initial consensus, now the Spanish command absolutely did not want to open a new front and it was doing its best to make the invasion plan fail. In an interview with *Brigadier* de Montcalm at his Menton command post on 22 June, Belle-Isle informed the officer that he would be moving his troops north anyway, as he knew the Spaniards would do anything to make fail his plan, and addressing Versailles for help should mean, 'as experience had taught him, addressing Madrid'.[37] On 23 June he sent three infantry brigades north towards Briançon, and he decided to face La Mina in a frontal attack to force him to stick to the agreed plan. The Duc de Belle-Isle wanted to be able to count on the reinforcements that the Spaniards were then receiving at the port of Toulon, to put them on the road directly to the logistics hub of Briançon without concentrating them in Nice as La Mina wanted. The Spanish commander, after two days of waiting, informed Belle-Isle that he intended to acclimatise the troops and complete the training of the recruits in Nice, so he did not intend to detach any units. On 24 June the Spaniards were marching west, but along the coast. At this point the Duc de Belle-Isle decided to ask for the support of the Court of Versailles; pending the king's decisions, Ventimiglia capitulated on 1 July. It seemed that there were no more obstacles to the immediate implementation of the attack against the Alpine front, but the Spaniards did not want to invest the Fort of Exilles, but to free Genoa. In the meantime, a storm coming from the south hit the coasts from 3 July onwards;[38] three days later the siege of Genoa was finally broken, also thanks to the movements along the western Ligurian coast and the presence of massive forces deployed immediately to the west of the alpine ridge. At this point the Duc de Belle-Isle expected the sovereign's authorization to begin his offensive in the Alps; sure of his business and of having the unconditional support of Louis XV, he gave the command for the *Armée du Dauphiné* under his brother to move forwards. The Chevalier de Belle-Isle reached his command post in Barcellonette on 7 July. He had received specific orders to attack Exilles no later than 14 July and to immediately put in place a series of feints to disorient the enemy on the real main direction of the attack.

The Duc de Belle-Isle and La Mina met again face to face at Cagnes to discuss how to carry out the ongoing campaign and coordinate the actions already underway. The meeting between the two ended without agreement on anything and both parties left the final choice to their respective sovereigns. Belle-Isle and his staff burned down their supplies of candles to complete their memorial in a single night's work before La Mina and his staff were able to

---

36   AST, Sezioni Riunite, Ministero della Guerra, Regia Segreteria di Guerra, Lettere ai Governatori, Mazzo 43. Letter to the Governor of Susa, 1 July 1747.

37   Pell, 'The Cradle of Carillon', p.274.

38   M. du Hamel, 'Observations botanico-météorologiques. Faites au château de Denainvilliers près Pliviers en Gâtinois, pour l'année 1747', in *Histoire de l'Academie Royale des Sciences*, Paris 1747, p.510.

complete theirs and ship it to Madrid. The *maréchal* informed Louis XV that the Spaniards had already pledged to support him militarily for the offensive against Exilles; he also wrote that the end of the siege of Genoa had allowed the enemy to dispose of large quantities of men and materials that would be sent either west along the coast or to garrison the Alps, so it was necessary to speed up timings; finally that it was useless to concentrate troops in Nice as it was important to concentrate more and more forces in Briançon and Barcellonette. Even in the Spanish command, few officers were able to rest. At dawn, a courier was already galloping towards Madrid with a memorial similar to the French one, but diametrically opposed in its intended objectives. Belle-Isle did not have to wait long to know its contents; a copy was graciously delivered to his command. La Mina wrote that Spain's main enemy was Austria, and not the kingdom of Sardinia. Therefore, the main theatre had to be the Riviera di Ponente, and therefore the attack on Exilles was a gamble that La Mina did not intend to take.

Belle-Isle felt sure of his own business: he was sure of Versailles' support and the arguments presented by the Spanish commander were entirely inconsistent for him. Whose were the bullets that had hit the Spanish regiments in Madonna dell'Olmo in 1744? Was it Austrian or Piedmontese lead? While he was carving the tip of the pen to write his reply, a messenger from the king of France rushed into Menton with a letter from Louis XV. Its contents destroyed the *maréchal*'s expectations; yielding to pressure from Madrid, the king ordered him to suspend the attack from Montgenèvre and to continue with all the forces at his disposal the advance in Liguria to free Genoa.

Having recovered from the initial shock, the Duc de Belle-isle returned to duel with La Mina. While the Spanish commander ordered the French to bring back the 20 battalions that he knew had been routed to the Dauphiné in the previous days, Belle-Isle wrote to his brother who was waiting on what to do in Tournoux; he had no intention of complying with the order received. The suspension of the siege provided the *maréchal* with the opportunity to consider the order of Louis XV as outdated and to return to the original plan, moving the main attack from the Ligurian Riviera to the Piedmontese Alps, assigning the main role to the *Armée du Dauphiné* in command of the Chevalier de Belle-Isle. Consequently, the French forces still present in Liguria, instead of advancing on Oneglia, retreated to Nice and Ventimiglia, and a part of these forces was sent to Barcellonette to lure the enemy towards Cuneo and Demonte.

The Sardinians seemed to have taken the bait: Carlo Emanuele III and Bogino were convinced that the French would attack in Val Stura di Demonte. French intelligence confirmed that 'the King of Sardinia fears more for Demonte and Cuneo than for Exilles'.[39] The Chevalier de Belle-Isle had concentrated his forces between Tournoux and Guillestre, his command post was precisely in those places. All these clues could only indicate an offensive arriving along the Colle della Maddalena or, at most, from the Colle dell'Agnello. However, large forces had also been sighted in Briançon; probably the French intended to protect their left flank. The Conte di Bricherasio would face the attack with the forces he had at his disposal, and the Assietta field fortifications. He could count, in case of need, on

---

39 BRT, Manoscritto Militare 73, *Copie de quelques papiers trouvés sur M.r de Belleisle et d'Arnault tués à l'attaque de l'Assiette le 19 juillet 1747*. Letter from Duc de Belle-Isle to the Chevalier de Belle-Isle, Menton, evening of 13 July 1747.

five battalions in reserve: Chiablese quartered in Turin and the four Austrian battalions in Pinerolo. If the threat should manifest itself further south, these five battalions, and all the forces under the Bricherasio's command, would have to reach the Maritime Alps to join the 10 battalions placed under the command of *Maggior Generale* Guillaume de Budé de Monfort.

11 July. Camp of the *Armée du Dauphiné*, Tournoux, Ubaye Valley

On 11 July the Duc de Belle-Isle ordered his brother to cross Montgenèvre; the *Armée du Dauphiné* in the pouring rain left its camp at Tournoux in the Ubaye valley on the same day and, after a stage of 20 kilometres, crossed the Col de Vars and reached Vars. On the 13th the invasion army proceeded north for another 19 kilometres, arriving at Guillestre. False information was artfully disseminated and the Chevalier de Belle-Isle had already set up his headquarters in Tournoux on 12 July, in order to 'give the enemies uncertainty about the intentions on the Stura Valley'.[40]

The Chevalier took from his pocket the order of operations that *Colonel* Bourcet had prepared for him on 1 July:

> Remarks for M. Chevalier de Belle-Isle
> In Barcelonnette
> 1. Arriving at Barcelonnette, he will give orders to the brigades of La Roche-Aymon and Poitou to go to the camp of Tournoux, as well as to the brigades of Bourbonnais and Condé, whether they remained in Lubac and Jausiers, or whether they remained in Larche.
> 2. The Bourbonnais and Condé brigades must be at the Tournoux camp on 10 July. The brigades of La Roche-Aymon and Poitou must have arrived on the 12th.
> 3. He will advance, on the 12th, the mountain artillery following the brigade of La Roche-Aymon, and that following Poitou, up to Guillestre, so that they can follow the body of M. de Villemur who will march to the right.
> 4. He will give orders to the brigade of Poitou and to a Spanish battalion[41] to go on the 13th from Tournoux to Guillestre, from where they will leave on the 14th with the Grenadiers Royaux [the 2nd Battalion], who will be present here, for Arvieux where they will remain until ordered.
> 5. He will order the La Roche-Aymon brigade and the Bourgogne brigade, as well as the second Spanish Battalion, to remain at the Tournoux camp until further notice.
> 6. He will order that the brigades of Bourbonnais, La Reine, Condé and Royal-Roussillon be provided on day 10 with four days of bread, i.e. for days 11, 12, 13

---

40   Arvers and de Vault, Vol.I, p.573.
41   The two Spanish battalions were actually one squadron of the Dragones de Merida and one battalion of the Regimiento de Aragón.

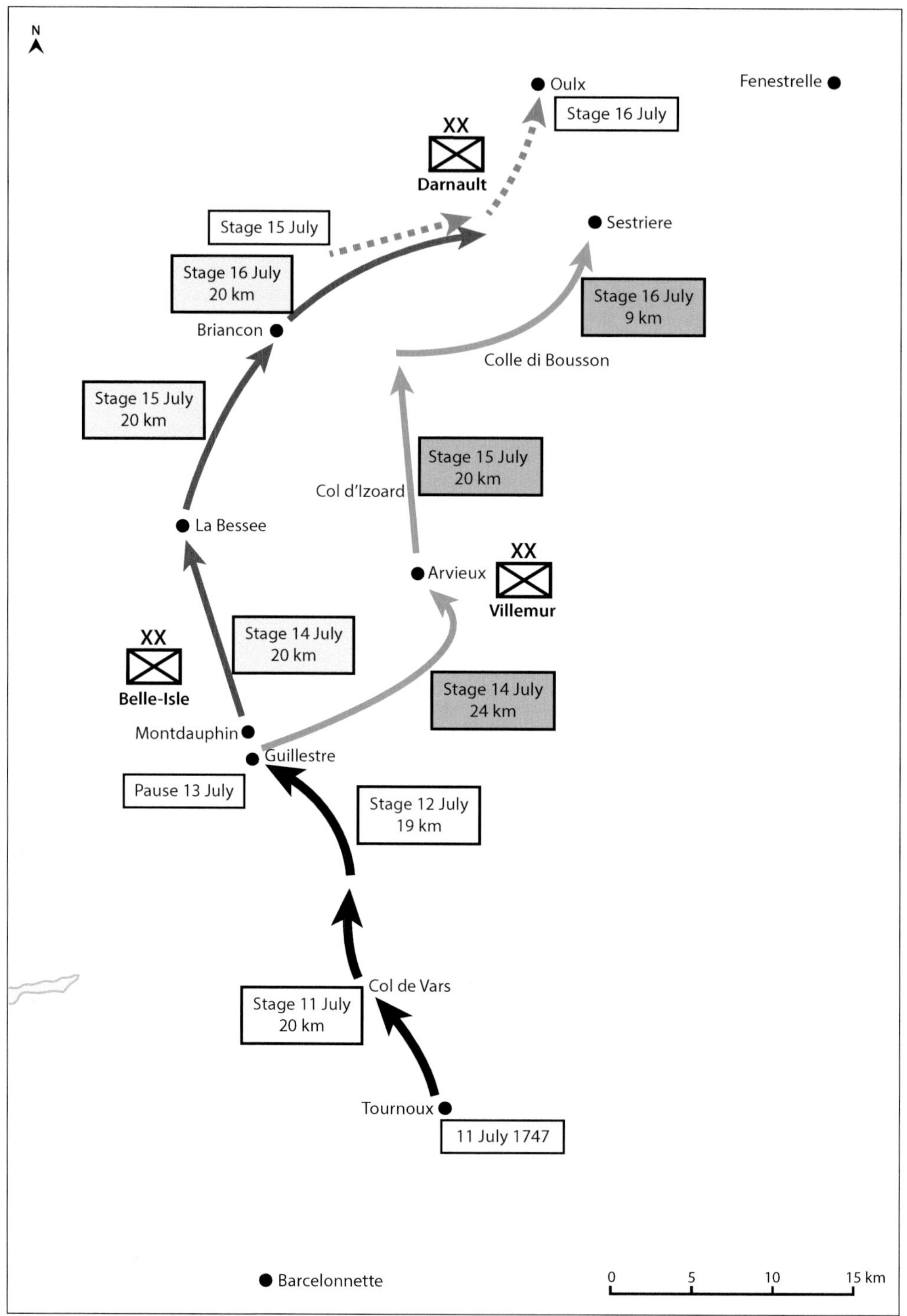

The French advance towards Piedmont from 11 to 15 July 1747.

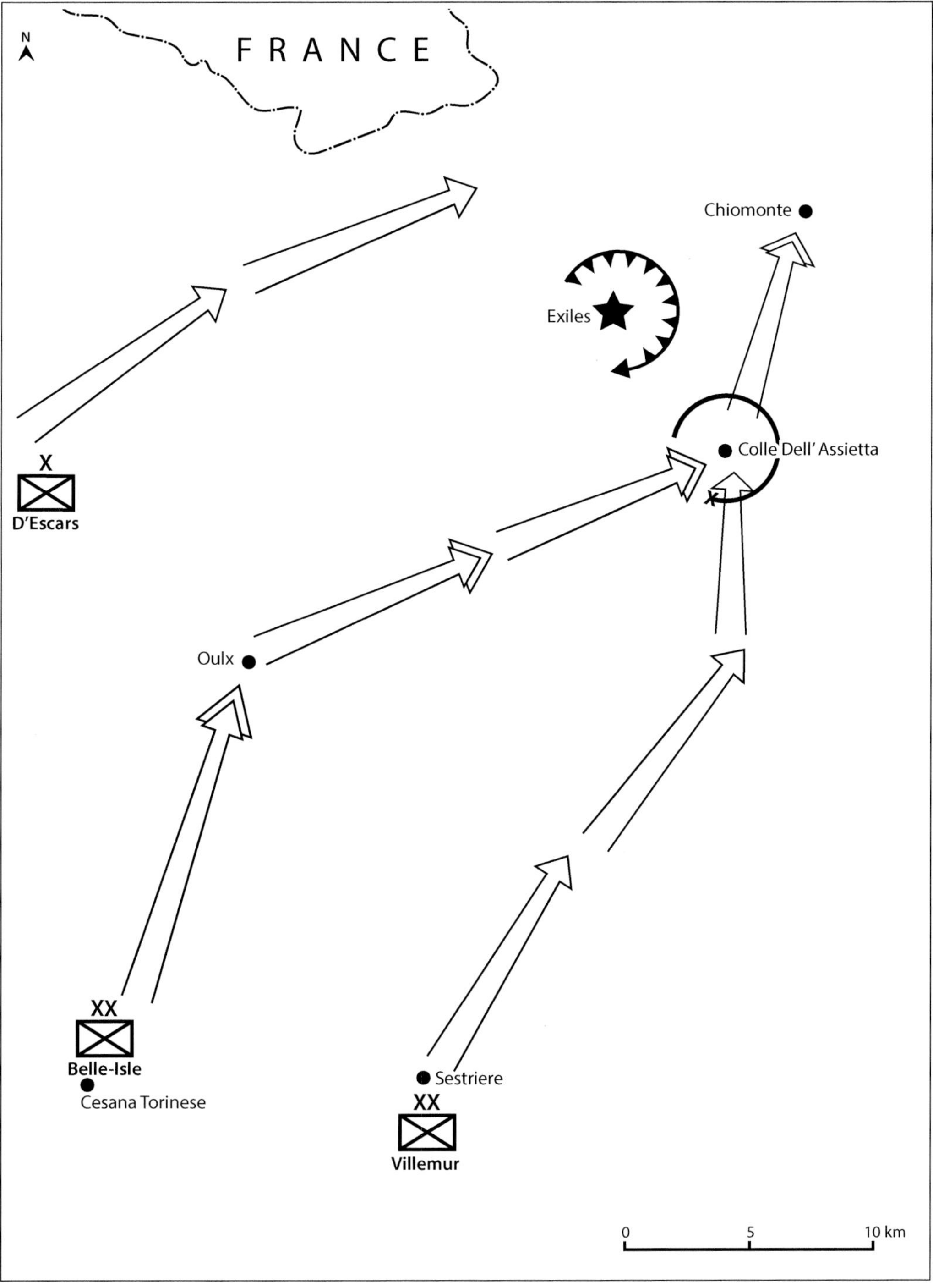

The French plan to isolate the Fort of Exilles. The conquest of the Assietta Plateau was a vital component of the whole plan.

and 14, and that they be chased by a convoy for another four days, which will be days 14, 16, 17 and 18.

In Guillestre and Mont-Dauphin
1. He will give order to the Mailly brigade, those of Condé and Royal-Roussillon, as well as the mountain artillery to leave on the 12th from Guillestre to go to Arvieux the same day, bringing hay and wheat for one day, the 13th in Cervieres where they will stay on the 14th, pushing the grenadiers and the pickets of their vanguard up to Bourget on the 14th in the morning.
2. He will march the Bourbonnais and La Reine brigades on day 12 from Guillestre to La Bessée, and on day 13 to Briançon, where they will stay on day 14 and join the Artois brigade. This same day, they will advance their grenadier companies and their pickets to Montgenèvre.
3. He will leave in Guillestre or Montdauphin on the 12th orders to advance the Engineers and the artillery officers, who will arrive there only on the 13th, and to the Vareix battalion of the Royal Artillerie Regiment, which will arrive there only on the 19th July.
4. He will order that fifty or sixty thousand rations of biscuit bread be made in Guillestre and Montdauphin for the 14th day, to be transported to Briançon on the 15th to be served at the distribution on the 18th, which will leave Briançon on the 17th, whose convoy will divide in Cesana, to start one half in Sestrieres and the other half in Oulx, what it will provide for the days 19, 20, 21, and 22, and will give time to create a collection centre in Cesana in view of the distribution of the day 22.

In Briançon
1. The provisions for the artillery march, which will be able to climb Montgenèvre on the 17th, and which will go up to La Vachette on the 16th.
2. The provisions of the subsistence for the distribution of the 18th day, which will start from Briançon on the 17th, and for the establishment to be set up in Cesana, which can be started from the 15th day in the evening.
3. The distribution of the Briançon [militia] companies, two or three of which will go to Bourget, and likewise to Montgenèvre.
4. The instruction to Mr. de Villemur for the organization of the marches and the body that will be under his orders.

In Cesana
1. The restoration of the road in the descent of Montgenèvre. That of Cesana in Oulx, and that of Cesana in Rollieres, and Champlas-del-colle, as well as the verification of the solidity of the bridge.
2. The location of the artillery park, which will need to be placed on the left bank of the Torrente Dora.
3. The restoration of the road that communicates from Cesana to the Coche hill, and from the Coche hill to Montgenèvre.

4. The construction of some redoubts to the right of the town of Cesana to defend this place.[42]

The Chevalier finished reading, folded the sheets in four and put them in his pocket. The dance could begin.

---

42 BRT, Manoscritto Militare 73, *Copie de quelques papiers trouvés sur M.r de Belleisle et d'Arnault tués à l'attaque de l'Assiette le 19 juillet 1747. Observations pour Mons.r le Chev.r de Belleisle.* It should be noted that this is a much less complete document, and moreover concerning the operations of the previous days, compared to *Mémoire et Observation pour le Chevalier de Belle-Isle*, in Bourcet, *Principes de la Guerre de Montagne*, pp.280-283. Either the order of operations never reached the Chevalier de Belle-Isle, or this document was written ex-post by *Colonel* Bourcet. It was certainly not in the French commander's pocket at the time he was killed in action.

6

The Assietta Entrenched Camp

On Monday 26 June the Conte di Bricherasio, the engineer captain Vedani and the governor of Susa, the Marchese di Balbiano, went up to the Assietta plateau to carry out a joint reconnaissance of the place and to plan the defence. The entrenched camp of Assietta, like that of Bunzelwitz in Silesia built by Friedrich II of Prussia in 1761,[1] and that of Valley Forge, built by the American Continental Army in the winter of 1777,[2] was surely one of the most famous and celebrated of its time. Analysing the planning process that led to its construction is an important step in understanding how an eighteenth-century commander set about building, supplying and defending an entrenched camp.

The Assietta Plateau

The Colle dell'Assietta (Assietta Pass, or Col), at an altitude of 2,472 metres, is located on the ridge that separates the Chisone and Susa valleys. A large flat area – *Assiette* in French means flat – is closed by two spurs. The first, located to the west, is the Testa dell'Assietta (Head of the Assietta), altitude 2,556 metres; the second, which dominates the area from the east, is the Gran Serin, altitude 2,589 metres. The plateau of the Assietta is connected to the Gran Serin by a wider ridge, crossed by a slight groove, called Piano di Grammi (Plain of Grammi). The Gran Serin is connected to the south, on the side of the Val Chisone, with the peak of Cèrogne, 2,387 metres, which dominates the village of Pourrieres.

To the south of the plateau, the side of the mountain rises slightly to fall back with a rocky wall and form a ravine that extends from north-east to south-west, opening in a larger area, the valley of Assietta, where it meets the Vallone dei Morti (Valley of the Dead). Going up from the Assietta valley to the Gran Serin, the path is steep but becomes easier and easier, unlike the approaches of the Vallone dei Morti, whose slopes always remain steep. The northern side of the watershed line, in the section near the Assietta plateau, is very steep and covered with larch and coniferous forests. A group of huts located in this area takes the name of Riobacon.

---

1   Duffy, *By Force of Arms*, pp.319-323.
2   W.H. Burk, *Historical and Topographical Guide to Valley Forge* (Philadelphia: John C. Winston 1912).

The approaches to the plateau from the southern side are difficult and almost inaccessible, while the path becomes very easy from the eastern side, where the ridge is crossed by the Val Chisone-Valle Susa mule track. In 1747 the hill was a crossroads of roads. The main one went up from Exilles, reached the entrenched camp of Argueil, and went up to the Assietta pass before descending to Pragelato. The second artery began near Exilles, but moved further west to reach the grange 'delle Ruine' (of the Ruins) and then climbed the ridge line and it intersected with the previous road. The path continued, always on the ridge, eastwards to the top of the Gran Serin and the Cima delle Vallette. From there one could only go down to the north, on the slopes of the Susa Valley, to get around the Cima delle Vallette, or to the south descending towards the village of Balboutet. Except for the one that went up to the Gran Serin, the roads were all deemed practicable with carts, so they could also be used by small one-axle wagons and, consequently, also by artillery trains. The other communications were instead for pedestrians only.

The position has two weaknesses, one tactical and one logistical; the site could be bypassed, especially from the north side, and the water sources were not numerous. In addition, in the cold summers of the 1740s, in the midst of the Little Ice Age of the eighteenth century, too many soldiers could not be left to garrison in that position due to adverse weather conditions.

The Tactical Arrangement

Walking among the heights of Assietta, Bricherasio and Vedani were already clear that the entrenched camp should have very specific characteristics. Five years of war had shown that only a camp completely surrounded by field works would have a chance to repel a direct attack. The defensive perimeter should also have had a certain depth to contain and absorb any opponent's breakthroughs.

The Assietta ridge and plateau had already been fortified in 1745, and this position was equipped with a defensive system with detached redoubt which was in vogue between 1745 and 1746. The main ridge that dominated the pass was covered by an entrenchment, as was the Gran Serin which was already fortified and defended by a tenailled redoubt.[3] However, the two positions were 1,200 metres apart, so they were unable to cooperate with each other. An enemy force could bypass them, isolate from each from the other and conquer them with a direct assault.

Bricherasio and Vedani decided that the redoubts of Assietta and those of the Gran Serin should be connected to each other and transformed into a single entrenched camp, capable of being defended at 360 degrees, rather than just 180 degrees. This solution was especially advantageous along the watershed lines. Anticipating attack by an enemy capable of circumventing their positions and attempting an attack on the throat of their works, as had happened in Pietralunga in 1744, this seemed the best possible solution. The two officers understood that the keystone of the entire fortified device was the summit of the Gran

---

3   Archive *Hadtörténeti Intézet és Múzeum*, Budapest, H III e 965, *Carte topographique des environs de Suse et d'Exilles*.

Serin, which was integrated into a series of field fortifications anchored to the crest that dominated the Assietta hill, giving to the defence the greatest depth possible. This area was called the Great Communication, due to the presence of the main military road that put in communication the Gran Serin with the Assietta pass. It was therefore decided to integrate the Testa dell'Assietta into the defensive perimeter, a relief of 2,566 metres located along the rocky crest that stretched towards the west. Defending that position would have required an entire battalion, but in return a good depth was guaranteed in one of the most delicate sectors of the entrenched camp.

Construction

Having decided on the tactical organization, it was now up to *Capitano* Vedani to create a sufficiently strong entrenchment to withstand prolonged artillery fire and the assault of opposing infantry. The plant of the works was that typical of military engineering of the eighteenth century; a series of redans and tenailles would allow the defenders to saturate the killing zones in front of the field fortifications with the fire of their individual weapons.

Part of the works had already been built in 1745. It was now a question of restoring the existing structures and connecting them. At the end of June there remained to be built:

- About 800 metres of entrenchment between the Assietta Plateau and the Testa dell'Assietta. Here the fortifications would have been carried out with dry stone walls, with particular attention to the Assietta Tenaille on the Testa, with a height between one-and-a-half to two metres.[4]
- Approximately 1,400 metres of entrenchment to connect the works carried out near Colle dell'Assietta to the Gran Serin on the northern slope towards Exilles.
- 1,300 metres of entrenchment between the Colle dell'Assietta and the Gran Serin on the southern side, towards the Val Chisone. These works were made not only with dry stone, but in earth. On 19 July 1747 they were still incomplete.

In total, about 3,500 metres of field works had yet to be built. Although at first sight it may seem like a titanic work, these field fortifications were built almost entirely in earth on the side of the Val Chisone and Susa, while the segment to be built on the Testa dell'Assietta was made with dry stone walls. Construction times can be calculated as follows:

- To move and compact one cubic metre of very strong earth, or soft rocks, required at least four hours.
- To create drywall masonry, a team of two men – a stonemason and a labourer – could prepare one cubic metre in eight hours of work.[5]

---

4   G. Amoretti, R. Sconfienza, F. Zannoni, 'Le vicende costruttive della "Butta" dei granatieri', Amoretti, Roggero, Viglino (eds), *I Trinceramenti* dell'Assietta, p.204.

5   Ministero della Guerra. Ispettorato dell'Arma del Genio, *Istruzione sui lavori da zappatore* (Roma: SMRE, 1937), pp.86-87, 118.

Vedani, with the forces at his disposal, 1,061 men from 1/Guardie and the Reggimento Casale, began to organize the work. First, he organized his workforce into teams, to which he would later also aggregate some civilian workers recruited locally who would climb to Assietta from 26 July. Vedani knew well that the performance of men depended on the nature of the soil to be excavated, but also on the training and the moral and physical state of the workers, the length of work shifts and their frequency, and the workers' ability to dig and to endure fatigue. The animating action of the platoon and company commanders and their continuous surveillance would have had a decisive influence on the performance of the workers themselves.

No less than 1,000 soldiers and 350 civil workers were put to work. The daily average, between soldiers and workers, was about 1,200 men. Despite the difficulties, the works went on with sufficient rapidity, and by 14 July the main perimeter had been completed. The profiles of the entrenchments remained to be completed; they were still too low, especially in the sector towards the Val Chisone in the segment that connected the Assietta pass with the Gran Serin. However, starting from 3 July a storm from the Mediterranean hit the western Alps, and the works were severely slowed down. On 19 July the entrenched camp could be said to be complete in its general lines, but not entirely completed.

Table 9. Military and Civilian Personel Present at the Assietta Entrenched Camp, 25 June- 14 July

Date	Battalions and civilian workers	Total Men	Weather conditions
25 June-1 July	1/Guardie, Casale	1,061	Variable
2 July	1/Guardie, Casale, workers	c.1,400	Covered deteriorating
3-13 July	1/Guardie, Casale, workers	c.1,400	Overcast with rain
14 July	1/Guardie, Casale	1,061	Overcast with rain

20 days in total; Average personal per day 1,247. Eight days in good weather. From 3 July, weather is disturbed. On July 14, military operations began and workers are evacuated.

Sources: AST, Sezioni Riunite, Ministero della Guerra, Ufficio Generale del Soldo, Ruolini di Rivista; Reggimento Guardie, Vol. 89, 1747; Reggimento Casale, Vol. 33, 1747; G. Amoretti, R. Sconfienza, F. Zannoni, 'Le vicende costruttive della "Butta" dei granatieri', in Amoretti, Roggero, Vigliono (eds), *I Trinceramenti dell'Assietta*, pp.199-241; Hamel, 'Observations botanico-météorologiques', pp.500-530.

Logistical Organization of the Sardinian Army

Although located in a rather inaccessible mountainous area, the Assietta Plateau had the undeniable advantage of being reachable on foot in two or three days from Turin, capital of the kingdom of Sardinia and fulcrum of the Sardinian Army's logistic system. Two other major logistic nodes, Susa and Pinerolo, were nearby, and two large fortresses, Brunetta and Fenestrelle, could guarantee the necessary services support the troops deployed in that area of operations.

Built to defend the fort of Exilles in Val di Susa, the entrenched camp of Assietta was mainly managed by exploiting the logistics network of Val Chisone. Using the current terminology, we can reconstruct what the logistic nodes of the valley were and how the material distribution took place. The stronghold of Fenestrelle became the brigade support area of the Austro-Sardinian forces in the operational theatre, with the Assietta entrenched camp able to function as logistic release point for the deployed units. Inside the camp, a casualty collection point was created with an adjoining field hospital, and a storage centre, from which food and ammunition could be distributed to the units deployed on the main combat position. The approach road was that of the Gran Vallone, definitely not the most comfortable as regards the slopes, but it had the undeniable advantage of being controlled from the Balboutet guard post and of being, for the most part, hidden from the view of any enemy sentry positions on the Sestriere Pass.

Arrival, Movement and Support

The Sardinian command had to accurately calculate the dispatch of the units to high altitude. The difficulties of managing a military unit at these elevations made the presence of a large contingent particularly onerous. The first troops began to climb the Assietta hill on 25 June 1747, after receiving orders directly from the War Ministry.[6] Two battalions, 1/Guardie (745 men) and the battalion of the Reggimento Casale (a grenadier company and three fusiliers companies, for a total of 316 men), were chosen to reach the Assietta plateau, garrison the position and start the necessary work. There were 1,061 men at all, who had to be guaranteed shelter, food and water and enabled to fight.

A first camp was built on the plateau; the tents were enough for all the men, even if during the previous campaigns some of the materials had been lost. For example, 1/Guardie had lost 29 percent of the field materials at its disposal. Barracks, prefabricated single-storey wooden buildings, were built to store the most perishable materials, such as food or gunpowder, or to house the tactical command post for senior officers. When the camp was laid out, the need to create a latrine was recognized. This measure may be of little importance to scholars who focus only on tactics and armaments, but it was a question of disposing of one to two thousand defecations a day, counting only the men in uniform. We have no archaeological and documentary evidence that testifies to the presence and location of septic ditches for the use and benefit of the military population on the Assietta plateau. The *Istruzione sui lavori da zappatore* informs us that the field latrines 'are quickly set up by digging a ditch as wide as the shovel allows, that is, about thirty centimetres wide, about a metre deep and proportionally long to the section that must use it'. Furthermore:

> [T]o avoid exhalations and possible causes of infections it will be necessary to exercise assiduous supervision, often covering the ditches with earth, after spreading quick-lime milk on the materials to be covered. The latrines are always built downstream of the housings and in the wind, masking them with earth banks, gratings, hedges.[7]

The outer front of the entrenchments could have served this purpose perfectly. According to some treatises of the time, a pit was dug about 100 metres away from the defensive perimeter

---

6   AST, Sezioni Riunite, Ministero della Guerra, Regia Segreteria di Guerra, Lettere ai Governatori, Mazzo 43, Letter to the Governor of Susa, 24 June 1747.
7   Ministero della Guerra. Ispettorato dell'Arma del Genio, *Istruzione sui lavori da zappatore*, pp.141, 143

of the field,[8] even if this work could be completely neglected by the commanders. After all, the men of the eighteenth century had the habit of defecating and urinating wherever they had the necessity to do so, without particular attention to the place.[9] The presence of the field, the smell of burnt wood and of the humanity that inhabited it, could be felt even hundreds of metres away, assuming one had a nose not accustomed to such situations.

Regarding ammunition, the Sardinian soldiers had a personal supply of 30 cartridges, for a total of 0.36 kilograms of gunpowder each.[10] The two battalions on the mountains in the days preceding the battle had 31,830 rounds at their disposal, a total of 388 kilograms of black powder, useful for a day of battle, excluding the existing stocks. The force at the disposal of the Conte di Bricherasio on 19 July, 10 infantry battalions, could have had no less than 184,000 rounds in their cartridge boxes, for a total of 2,255 kilograms of powder. Given the dynamism of the campaign, and the sudden arrival of eight infantry battalions and other militia units, it seems that the creation of a gunpowder magazine inside the camp was not planned. This explains Bricherasio's constant concerns about the consumption of ammunition during the fight and the urgency of getting a convoy with a load of gunpowder up from Fenestrelle as soon as possible.

For the Alpine campaign of 1747 the Ministry of War, in June of the same year, established that the ration establishment for an infantry battalion of 410 men should be a total of: 6,200 rations of biscuit (3,100 kilograms); 4,435 litres of wine; 590 kilograms of rice; 461 kilograms of lard; 50.6 kilograms of oil; 359.58 kilograms of cheese; 55.32 kilograms of salt. The individual supply therefore consisted of 15 rations of biscuit (7.5 kilograms), 10.81 litres of wine, 1.4 kilograms of rice, 1.12 kilograms of lard, 0.87 kilograms of cheese, 0.13 kilograms of salt.[11] In total, each soldier had at his disposal 11.02 kilograms of food and just little less than one litre of wine, the latter used as a food substitute even before a drink. Every day each *pistapauta* – 'mud pest', the nickname with which the infantry Sardinian soldiers were indicated by Piedmont's population – could consume half a kilo of biscuit, and 0.226 kilograms of cheese and rice, to be washed down with 0.72 litres of wine. It was certainly not a generous lunch, especially for men who had to work on the construction of field fortifications at high altitude. We can assume that a good part of the pay went into the pockets of local suppliers who guaranteed the troops the necessary food additions. The

---

8   L.A. Porzio, *The Soldier's Vade Mecum* (London: R. Dodsley, 1747), p.128.

9   The problem of latrines and the lack of attention by soldiers and officers about this problem is beautifully described in Hanlon, *Italy 1636. Cemetery of Armies*, pp.172-174. Also very useful is P. Lenihan, *Fluxes, Fevers, and Fighting Men. War and Disease in Ancien Régime Europe 1648-1789* (Warwick: Helion, 2019).

10   Sterrantino, *Le armi da* fuoco, Vol.I., p.134.

11   AST, Sezioni Riunite, Ministero della Guerra, Ufficio generale del soldo, Ordini Generali e misti, 1747, mazzo 48: *Stato della provisione de Viveri, che si propone a farsi a beneficio de Trinceramenti de Colli di Fenestre, e Fattieres, regolata col Presidio d'Uomini Quattro Cento e Dieci, compresi gli Uffiziali, Forrieri, e Sovrastante qual potrà servire di Guardamagazeno. Detti Viveri da distribuirsi nel corso di giorni quindici tale essendo la R.a Intenzione.* Detailed studies on individual equipment, such as food and ammunition, related to the Sardinian army are currently not available. The data presented here is taken from Ilari, Boeri, Paoletti, *La Corona di Lombardia*, p.96. Their data is extracted from Brancaccio, *L'esercito del Vecchio Piemonte.*

Turin command had also established that 15,000 pieces of wood were distributed for 410 men, necessary to light the fires necessary for the kitchens and to warm up.[12]

The ammunition, food and everything necessary to make the troops operate on the Assietta plateau had to be carried either on the shoulders of a bearer on foot, or on the saddle of a mule.[13] The table below summarizes the logistical needs and transport necessary from 25 June to 19 July inclusive, indicating the number of mules and porters needed to allow the troops to operate at Colle dell'Assietta. The calculation also includes the workers who worked for the construction of the camp between 26 June and 13 July.

Table 10. Logistical Requirements 25 June–19 July

Date	Units	Battalions	Total men	Necessary rations	Number of porters/ mules for food	Ammunition for a day of combat	Number of porters/ mules for ammunition
25 June–2 July	1/Guardie, Casale	2	1,061	1,549 kg	62 porters or 20 mules	31,830 cartridges / 388 kg	16 porters or 5 mules
3–13 July	1/Guardie, Casale, workers	2	c.1,500	2,190 kg	88 porters or 28 mules		
14–17 July	1/Guardie, Casale	2	1,061				
18 July	1/Guardie, Casale, Hagenbach, Traun, Meyer, 2/ & 3/ Kalbermatten	7	3.676	5,367 kg	215 porters or 67 mules	110,280 cartridges 1,345 kg	54 porters or 17 mules
19 July	1/Guardie, Casale, Hagenbach, Traun, Meyer, 2/ & 3/Kalber-matten, 3/Roi, 3/Forgách, 3/Colloredo, militia, volunteers	10	6,160	8.994 kg	360 porters or 113 mules	184,800 cartridges / 2.255 kg	90 porters or 29 mules

Sources: Lambert, *Ricordi Logistici e Tattici*. AST, Sezioni Riunite, Ministero della Guerra: Ufficio Generale del Soldo; Ruolini di Rivista; Reggimento Guardie, Vol.89, 1747; Reggimento Kalbermatten,

---

12 AST, Sezioni Riunite, Ministero della Guerra, Ufficio generale del soldo, Ordini Generali e misti, 1747, mazzo 48: *Stato della provisione de Viveri, che si propone a farsi a beneficio de Trinceramenti de Colli di Fenestre, e Fattieres, regolata col Presidio d'Uomini Quattro Cento e Dieci, compresi gli Uffiziali, Forrieri, e Sovrastante qual potrà servire di Guardamagazeno. Detti Viveri da distribuirsi nel corso di giorni quindici tale essendo la R.a Intenzione.*

13 According to the tables presented in R. Lambert, *Ricordi Logistici e Tattici* (Firenze: Barbera, 1930), pp.504-505, a porter could carry a weight of 25 kilograms on his shoulders, while a mule could carry 80 kilograms of various material.

Vol.58, 1747; Reggimento Roi, Vol 30, 1747; Reggimento Meyer, Vol.8, 1747; Reggimento Casale, Vol.33, 1747: Ordini Generali e Misti, 1747, Mazzo 48; KA, Alten Feldakten I-VI, Krieg in Italien, 1747: Ständ und Dienst Tabella, 18 June 1747, Cartone 581.

To support the corps of the Conte di Bricherasio, a brigade of 142 mules or 450 porters was therefore needed. During the 1747 campaign, 142 mules were mobilized in the upper Susa Valley;[14] more than enough to set in motion 2,000 kilograms of powder, the quantity necessary to guarantee a day of fire for the 10 battalions at Assietta, excluding the militia, or to carry 1,369 individual rations of food, a day's worth of provisions for the two battalions during the days preceding the battle but sufficient for just under one quarter of the force present on the day of the battle itself.

---

14   L.F. Peracca, *La Valle di Oulx e le Guerre di Successione d'Austria (1740-1750)* (Torino: Tipografia M. Massaro, 1909), p.326; E. Patria, 'Due ricerche storiche sull'Assietta', in *Armi antiche. Bollettino dell'Accademia di San Marciano*, Torino 1973, p.322.

7

14–18 July 1747. Snow, Rain and Light Infantry

Weather Conditions 1–18 July 1747

The weather conditions in July 1747 could not have been worse. The winds from the south had pushed northward a disturbance from the Mediterranean and, from 3 July, the sky was covered with clouds. Every day was noted for the continuous rainfall: 'water fell every day, often very little, but not a day was without rain'. In the Alps, above 2,000 metres of altitude, this precipitation took on a snowy character: 'the fog degenerated into rain, snow and frozen rain. It fell in abundance, and you could not see 20 paces away'.[1] Until 18 July there were no significant variations in the weather conditions.[2]

14 July 1747

On rain-flooded mountain roads the French offensive began on 14 July 1747, as outlined in the Chevalier de Belle-Isle's Plan of Operations. The soldiers, about 20,000 men, set out along the routes assigned to them. The Brigades Bourbonnais and La Reine left Guillestre and, marching along the Montgenevre road, went up the Durance Valley towards Briançon. Fifteen battalions of infantry, five squadrons of dragoons, six 4-pounder field guns and three mountain pieces camped at l'Argentière-la-Bessée. The Chevalier de Belle-Isle decided not to stop there and he continued, with nine companies of grenadiers, a body of sappers and three mountain pieces, towards Briançon to reunite with the Brigade d'Artois, under *Maréchal de Camp* d'Arnaud, to form the vanguard of the army. They had to march for a further 20 kilometres, added to the other 20 they had already travelled during the day. We can imagine the toasts that were raised to the Chevalier's health.

Lieutenant Général Villemur's column, with the brigades of Mailly, Conde, and Royal Roussillon, left Guillestre to move northwest along the Combe du Queyras to reach Château-Queyras and Arvieux, where they set up a camp; they had covered 25 kilometres, facing a positive vertical drop of 800 metres. In all, there were 14 infantry battalions, accompanied by militia and four pieces of mountain artillery.

---

1   Arvers and de Vault, *Guerre de la Succession* d'Autriche, Vol.II, p.732.
2   Du Hamel, 'Observations botanico-météorologiques', p.510.

On the Austro-Sardinian side, no noteworthy moves were reported, except for the fact that on the Assietta Plateau the field fortifications were still being perfected by the garrison troops. All the listening instruments were pointed towards the west, but for the moment there was no news about the enemy's attack.

15 July 1747

On 15 July the French army had set in motion its vanguards towards the upper Susa Valley. The first to reach the Piedmontese area were six grenadier companies and six picquets from the Brigade d'Artois, already part of the column under the command of *Brigadier* d'Escars. After passing the Colle della Scala, d'Escars descended on Bardonecchia where he reunited with two battalions of the Regimiento de Schwaller, Swiss in Spanish service. These units came from Savoy, to be precise from Modane, and they had passed the Colle de la Roue. D'Escars had the task of securing Rochemolles and reaching the Colle del Séguret above San Colombano, a ridge on the north side of Exilles. These forces had to occupy the area north of the fort, while the two Swiss battalions provided a screen in the area of the Great and Little Mont Cenis Gaps.[3]

In the meantime, the first fight took place. The vanguard led by *Maréchal de Camp* d'Arnaud had crossed Montgenèvre and it had taken possession of Cesana. When the advanced patrols reached San Sicario, a small village on the western slopes of Monte Fraiteve, they were welcomed by Sardinian militia. A detachment of 200 men of the Pragelato militia, under the command of *Maggiore* Perrone, had been already in place for days.[4] Their tactical task was to provide a screen;[5] once understood that they were facing a real offensive on a large scale instead of a limited raid, the militiamen retreating towards Sestriere. The French subsequently advanced to Fenils, where they stopped by the destruction of the road bridges.

The bulk of the forces left the camp of Argentière-la-Bessée and advanced beyond Briançon, stopping at La Vachette, where they were joined by the Chevalier de Belle-Isle.

De Villemur's column had faced a long day's march; this force had climbed the Izoard pass and from Arvieux the column had reached Cervières, after a march of about 20 kilometres. The French now had an entire brigade, that of Artois, west of the Alpine ridge, well inside Piedmont.

The rest of the brigades were instead grouped in Briançon – Brigades Bourbonnais and La Reine – and in Cervières, 11 kilometres to the west, where the Brigades Mailly, Condé, Royal-Roussillon and Poitou were concentrated.

---

3   For an identification of each unit and their tactical mission, Arvers and de Vault, *Guerre de la Succession d'Autriche*, Vol.I, p.684; Vol.II, p.701.

4   According to French reports there were 200 Waldensians. Arvers and de Vault, *Guerre de la Succession d'Autriche*, Vol.II, p.701. The French usually identified the Sardinian light infantry units as 'Waldensian', signifying the prestige that the real Waldensians enjoyed in the enemy side.

5   AST, Sezioni Riuniti, Ministero della Guerra, Regia Segreteria di Guerra, Lettere ai Governatori, Mazzo 43.

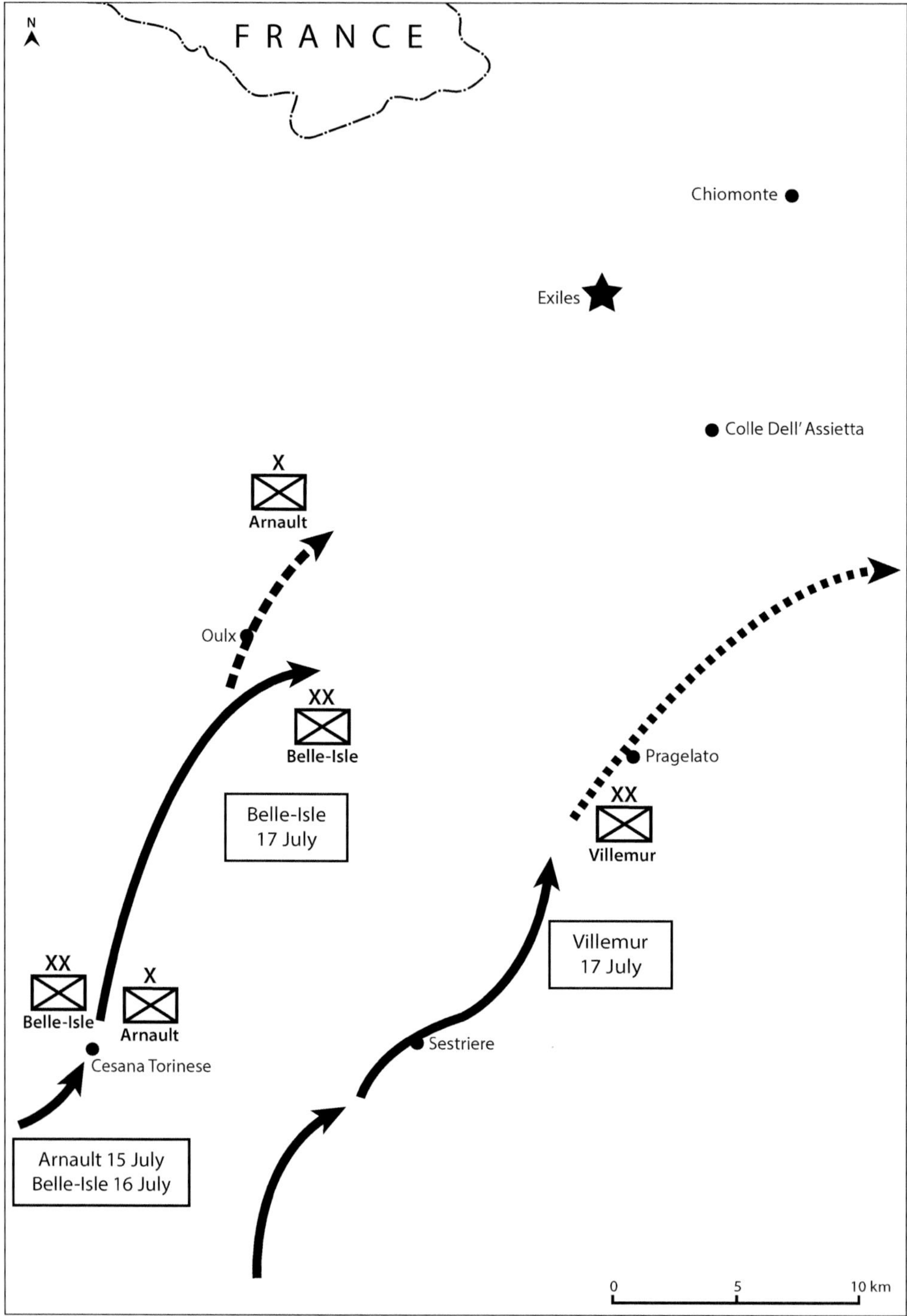

The French invasion of Piedmont. The advance of Villemur's column was blocked by the presence of the Fortress of Fenestrelle, that controlled the Chisone Valley.

The Sardinian command, at that time located inside the Fortress of Fenestrelle where it remained until 18 July,[6] was now on full alert. While the French attack had not yet fully manifested, the commander in chief of the Sardinian troops had certainly not gone to isolate himself on the high plateau, in the midst of a disturbance. All the logistics were planned along the Val Chisone along the Pinerolo-Fenestrelle road, so the Bricherasio command post was placed inside the Fenestrelle Fort. The French were launching not a limited raid behind the border against little villages, but a full-scale offensive. Their goal was easily understood; the Fort of Exilles. The Conte di Bricherasio began to evaluate the forces at his disposal; to face this threat the first Sardinian troops in the valley were lined up on the heights of Giaglione, an advanced detachment of the garrison of Susa. Forward, isolated, only the Fort of Exilles remained in Sardinian hands, garrisoned by a composite battalion with men drawn from 2/ and 3/Reggimento Salis, the battalion of the Reggimento Corsica and the reserve company of the provincial Reggimento Torino, units that were already part of the garrison of Susa. In Chisone Valley the situation was more complex. The Fortress of Fenestrelle was in reality a composition of three major fortifications, Fort Mutin, Fort St Charles and the Fort of the Valleys, connected to each other by a long wall interrupted by a series of small redoubts. It was a sort of improved retrenchment that cut completely the Chisone Valley. Even if it was – and it still is – a majestic collection of fortified buildings, it had many serious tactical disadvantages, for example, it had no bomb-proof gun batteries. The garrison of the Fortress of Fenestrelle was composed of 1/ Reggimento Keller and the reserve company of the Reggimento Pinerolo,[7] while 2/and 3/ Reggimento Kalbermatten and 1/Reggimento Monfort were concentrated in the villages located near the fortifications. In the village of Puy, not far from Fenestrelle under the shadows of the ramparts of the Fort of the Valleys, 2/Savoia was stationed,[8] while 1/Sicilia had been destined to garrison the fundamental Finestre Gap.[9] The Reggimento Meyer was added to these units;[10] originally it was quartered in the village of Mentoulles, on

<hr>

6   Report by Graf Colloredo, KA, Alten Feldakten, Krieg in Italien, VII, 1.

7   AST, Corte, Materie Politiche per Rapporto dall'Interno, Storie della Real Casa, Categoria III, Storie Particolari, Mazzo 24, Minutoli, *Relation des campagnes faites par S.M. et par ses generaux avec des corps sèpares pendant les années 1747 et 1748, c'est à dire jusq'a la fin de la guerre*, Atlante, Vol.II, tavola 95, *Repartition des Troupes de S.M. le Roi de Sardaigne pour sa Campagne prochaine le 6 April 1747*; Sezioni Riunite, Ministero della Guerra, Ufficio Generale del Soldo; Ruolini di Rivista, Reggimento Keller, Vol.13, 1747. It should be noted that this battalion, according to the dispositions known to date of the Ministry of War, was placed under the Governor of Fenestrelle, and at disposal of the Conte di Bricherasio. In fact, it was never calculated among the forces available for the defence of the field works on the mountains.

8   AST, Sezioni Riunite, Ministero della Guerra, Ufficio Generale del Soldo, Ruolini di Rivista, Reggimento Savoia, 1747, Vol.84.

9   1/Sicilia was already in position at Finestre Gap, a fundamental step for the defence of the Chisone and Susa Valleys. On 16 July 1747, soldier Gerolamo Mollinar, of Corbini's company, fell into the void during a patrol, being killed by the fall. AST, Sezioni Riunite, Ministero della Guerra, Ufficio Generale del Soldo, Ruolini di Rivista, Reggimento Sicilia, 1747, Vol.55.

10   AST, Sezioni Riuniti, Ministero della Guerra, Regia Segreteria di Guerra, Lettere ai Governatori, Mazzo 43.

the road between Fenestrelle and Pinerolo.[11] The Swiss Reggimento Roi, for the moment, was placed in defines of the field fortifications at Argueil huts on the slopes of the Susa Valley north to the Assietta Camp.[12] All these units had a total strength of 5,600 men: not an insignificant number but certainly not enough to stop or block the enemy advance. According to the tactical planning decided in Turin, at least 6,000 men had to concentrate inside the entrenched camp of Assietta or in its vicinity to have sufficient guarantees of resistance. Bricherasio had to play in advance and immediately to ask for reinforcements; he sent a relay to the capital with a report on the tactical situation in the valleys and an urgent request for reinforcements. Once in Turin his messages were delivered directly to the Minister of War Bogino. He immediately gave the order to the Reggimento Chiablese, the first infantry unit he had at his disposal, to move to Susa. Initially destined for Susa, on 17 July the regiment received the order to reach the Argueil camp. It covered 70 kilometres, and a climb of 1,913 metres, with a march of two days. The battalion, with an average of about 30 kilometres per day, managed to reach its destination in the afternoon of 19 July. The four Austrian battalions quartered in Pinerolo were required to reach Bricherasio's command post in Fenestrelle as soon as possible.[13]

Militia units were reorganizing after the first clashes. The militia of Pragelato and the Waldenses went to line up respectively between the villages of Chezal-Duc and Jousseaud in Chisone Valley, while Susa's nilitia companies under the Cavaliere Tana were reinforced by a contingent composed of about a hundred volunteers. The volunteers, present in numerous reports from Sardinian side, were not soldiers who presented themselves for specific missions, nor were they civilians who volunteered to defend their country. The figure of the volunteer had been defined by the Royal Decree of 22 June 1744, which prescribed 'the recruiting of volunteers to be carried out with bandits', that is, with outlaws destined to guarantee themselves a reduction of the sentence or royal pardon for the future. Each company, with a minimum strength of 50 and a maximum of 100 men, was to be commanded by officers from regular units, three in all – a captain, a lieutenant and a second lieutenant – who also had a drummer for the transmission of orders. The combat quality of these units was not high; their armament, entrusted to the good will of the individuals, was extremely inhomogeneous, while the discipline had to be somewhat relaxed as the same Decree pointed out that 'we are not going to establish any NCO from the volunteers to avoid any fights that would arise if a bandit had to depend from the other'. The three officers in charge of commanding the volunteers in the days preceding the Battle of Assietta were *Luogotenente* Gattinara of the Reggimento Guardie, *Luogotenente* Thomasset, of 3/Kalbermatten, and *Alfiere* Pattono of the Reggimento Casale. On 19 July, Thomasset remained in command of the company.[14] The militia were also reinforced by regular soldiers taken from the regiments of Casale and

---

11   AST, Sezioni Riunite, Ministero della Guerra, Ufficio Generale del Soldo, Ruolini di Rivista, Reggimento Kalbermatten, 1747, Vol.58; Reggimento Monfort, 1747, Vol.84.

12   Minutoli, *Relation des campagnes faites par S.M*, Vol.V, pp.224-225.

13   The order to move was given by the Minister of War in person. AST, Sezioni Riunite, Ministero della Guerra, Ufficio Generale del Soldo Ordini Generali Misti, Mazzo 81; Report by Graf Colloredo, KA, Alten Feldakten, Krieg in Italien, VII, 1.

14   *Relation des campagnes faites au service de S.M. le Roy de Sardaigne pendant la guerre en Italie (1742-1747)*, BRT, Manoscritto Militare 5; see also Relations Priocca I, Priocca II.

Kalbermatten. Placed between Serre Gountard and the Seu inside the Gran Bosco forest, they awaited the enemy, with the following orders: observe the opponent's movements and, where possible, delay his advance with the use of demolitions along the approaching roads to the Assieta Plateau, while the bridges along the Dora were destroyed as planned.[15]

Sardinian intelligence now had to retrieve as much information on the enemy as possible. The reports from the Piedmontese side inform us that the Conte di Bricherasio was 'exactly informed of all those [enemy] movements, by trusted emissaries, and by some advanced patrol'[16]. It is clear that the Sardinian command retrieved information on the enemy through the following channels:

- Direct observations made by advanced detachments of militia and infantry.
- Civilian officers and clergymen loyal to the crown.
- Local nobles or families hostile to the French.

Other local informants could be merchants or men of commerce in transit – such activities and the movements connected with them were not forbidden – or occasional spies moved by the possibility of an easy gain through reward, such as prostitutes.[17] A lot of useful information could be collected through these channels. It was then up to the commander in chief to interpret them correctly.

16 July 1747

On 16 July the main French column, at the head of which rode the Chevalier de Belle-Isle, left the La Vachette field and reached Cesana beyond the Montgenèvre pass. This is the description that De Sade made of during his trip to Italy in July 1775. 'The road, although very steep, is beautiful and very well maintained for the whole part that depends on France', while on the Piedmont side:

[T]he path is so steep that a man on foot can hardly keep himself upright. The precipice is terrifying, and whoever unfortunately slips would fall into the abyss forever… On the other hand, it is a policy of the King of Sardinia to let this passage go badly. Yet it would be very useful for all communications from the southern French provinces, and also from Spain. In this way the King forces whoever wants to enter his states to pass through the Mont Cenis, and therefore cross the territory of his good friends the Savoyards, who otherwise would die of hunger.[18]

---

15   AST, Sezioni Riuniti, Ministero della Guerra, Regia Segreteria di Guerra, Lettere ai Governatori, Mazzo 43; Brunet de l'Argentière, *Mémoire de la Guerre sur le frontières du Dauphiné et de Savoie de 1742 à 1747* (Paris: A la Direction du Spectateur Militaire, 1887), p.71; Arvers and de Vault, *Guerre de la Succession d'Autriche*, Vol.II, p.685, 729.
16   Priocca I.
17   For intelligence operations during the eighteenth century, see Duffy, *Military Experience in the Age of Reason*, pp.135-138.
18   The policy of the King of Sardinia was to keep the Alpine roads impassable to vehicles on wheels and, essentially, to the artillery trains of an invading army: de Sade (ed. Lever), *Viaggio in Italia*, pp.7-8.

Teams of pioneers were thus diverted to repair the road that would have had to withstand the passage of thousands of men, mules and vehicles.

D'Arnaud's force was pushed forward as far as Oulx, with the task of taking over the ruins of Pont Ventoux to re-establish the passages on the Dora River and permanently occupying Sauze-d'Oulx and Jouvenceaux to form a start line for subsequent operations in the direction of Monte Costapiana.

De Villemur and his men faced another day of alpine marching, and they climbed their third pass in two days, the Col Bousson at an altitude of 2,154 metres. The journey was not particularly long if compared with that of the previous days, but the weather was always bad; furthermore, the French were now operating in enemy territory, and a series of tactical measures had to be implemented. The main body of the column made a stop between Sauze di Cesana and Bousson, and it was able to cover the right flank of the Belle-Isle column from any surprise. De Villemur sent forward patrols to observe the practicability of the roads and, above all, to obtain information on the position and consistency of the enemy forces. The French patrols went to Champlas du Col and a detachment of Pragelato militia placed to control the village withdrew without resistance. In fact, the Sestriére Gap, that put in connection the Susa Valley with that of Chisone, was by now in French hands and de Villemur immediately took advantage of sending two Briançon militia companies on the ridge above the Sestriére village: if one wanted to conquer Assietta, one had to take some key passages, first of all Col Bourget at an altitude of 2,297 metres.[19] Then he sent other patrols in the direction of Fenestrelle to check where the Piedmontese units had ended up.

Towards the north, d'Escars' column began the ascent of the Valfredda; they found the necessary guides in Bardonecchia, but the march was immediately extremely difficult. The rain showed no sign of ending; reached the village of Rochemolles – 1,619 metres – bad weather conditions began to scourge the Franco-Spanish soldiers. Low clouds minimized visibility, while on the trails a thick blanket of snow covered the path. The Franco-Spaniards still had a vertical drop of over 1,500 metres in front of them before reaching the Galambra pass at 3,050 metres. D'Escars began to question the validity of the entire plan of operations later in the day.[20]

The Chevalier de Belle-Isle had successfully completed the first phase of the offensive. All the brigades had been brought without too much trouble beyond the Alpine watershed. Now it was necessary to begin the second phase of the offensive, the conquest of the Assietta pass and the Quattro Denti Ridge, which was a necessary condition for proceeding to the third phase of the operation, the investment of the fort of Exilles. 'But it turns out that, in order to take Exilles, all these plateaus have to be occupied [Costapiana, Assietta, Arguel, Faitieres, Finestre Gap and Quattro Denti], so there is nothing left to decide on this matter'.[21] By 18 July, the Chevalier wanted his columns to engage the enemy in combat along the Assietta ridge, following the occupation of the Costa Piana gap, at 2,320 metres. To do this he needed to know exactly if Assietta was clear of enemy forces, and, if not, where they were deployed

---

19   The conquest of the Bourget Gap on July 16 is confirmed in de Villemur's letter to the Chevalier de Belle-Isle at 5 am on July 17. BRT, Manoscritto Militare 73.

20   The events of d'Escars brigade are deduced from Arvers and de Vault, *Guerre de la Succession d'Autriche*, Vol.II, pp.684, 687, 701.

21   Arvers and de Vault, *Guerre de la Succession d'Autriche*, Vol.II, p.685.

and how many there were in total. At Cesana, where he set up his tactical command, he had a meeting with *Maréchal de Camp* d'Arnaud, whose units were suffering delays due to the destroyed bridges over the Dora and its tributaries. The Sardinians, who apparently had long been expecting an attack in the Val di Susa, had taken care to evacuate all the cattle, grain, wine and forage from the Upper Susa and Chisone Valleys. Everything that could be useful for the support of the troops of the king of France in the west of Exilles and Fenestrelle fortifications had been removed or destroyed. The Chevalier wrote to his brother from his camp in Cesana on the morning of July 16; according to the information gathered by d'Arnaud, the enemy in Assietta 'currently has 8 battalions; those [spies] of Brunet [de l'Argentière, an officer on the Chevalier's staff] say the same thing, and he adds that the enemy has 10 more battalions ready to arrive... In all these field works there are 18 battalions, which I verified to be different from those on the list of 14 you sent me, which are located on the Riviera of Genoa'. That same day, in the evening, he repeated to his brother that the enemy had '8 battalions in the entrenchments, and 10 in the Fenestrelle valley, of each I have the name'. The French information service had found its sources, shepherds, workers, deserters, all willing to tell the state of the works of the field fortifications at Assietta. The Sardinian army lost 25 men by desertion between 16 and 18 July 1747, divided as follows: 1/Guardie one; Meyer three; 3/Roi four; 2/Savoia seven; 2/Kalbermatten five; 3/Kalbermatten five. To these were added another five who fled from the four Austrian battalions. For the French intelligence these were very important sources for understanding the state of the field fortifications, and verifying the arrival of reinforcement contingents.[22]

> For what concerns the entrenchments they are extremely singular; it is, they say, a chain of redoubts connected to each other by an entrenchment; they occupy the top of Monte Costapiana. There are similar redoubts and a similar arrangement in front of the Argüel and the so-called Col de l'Assiette. This line of redoubts is joined to that of Costapiana by a communication similar to what I have described, and the path is covered with lunettes. Similar redoubts, and a very similar communication, can be found in the mountains of the Fattiere and Finestre, and in all these works there are 18 battalions.[23]

Accordingly, it became necessary to transport the field artillery up to the mountains; orders about the guns' movement were immediately given.[24] It remained to be seen how many defenders there actually were. The intelligence seemed to suggest the presence of a strong contingent of infantry, which was far from true. Belle-Isle wrote to de Villemur to find out what information he had been able to discover in this regard.

---

22   AST, Sezioni Riunite, Ministero della Guerra: Ufficio Generale del Soldo; Ruolini di Rivista; Reggimento Guardie, Vol.89, 1747; Reggimento Kalbermatten, Vol.58, 1747; Reggimento Roi, Vol 30, 1747; Reggimento Meyer, Vol.8, 1747; Reggimento Casale, Vol.33, 1747; Reggimento Savoia, 1747, Vol.84: Ordini Generali e Misti, 1747, Mazzo 48, *Stato de Battaglioni trovatisi presenti agli attacchi ed interventi alla difesa de Trinceramenti dell'Assietta li 19 scorso Luglio*; KA, Alten Feldakten, Krieg in Italien, VII, 1747: Ständ und Dienst Tabella, 18 June 1747; Report by Colloredo.
23   Arvers and de Vault, *Guerre de la Succession d'Autriche*, Vol.II, pp.729-731.
24   Arvers and de Vault, *Guerre de la Succession d'Autriche*, Vol.II, p.686.

Bricherasio, on the other hand, was counting every single man he could deploy behind the Assietta entrenchments. He needed to concentrate all the forces under his command within the camp, to reach a sufficiently large number of men to be able to defend it effectively. At that moment, however, as far as he knew, the French could have got around the camp from the north side, occupying the vital Finestre Gap. For this reason, he decided to keep the garrison at the Alpe dell'Argueil. As foreseen by the Sardinian tactical doctrine, Bricherasio had the primary objective of deploying his troops behind robust field fortifications, saving his forces as much as possible. If the enemy had attacked them in force there would have been no escape. After all, he had both to save his small army from annihilation and to protect the fort of Exilles. More troops were needed and quickly; he sent couriers to solicit the march of the Austrian units headquartered in Pinerolo. The four battalions had actually received the order of departure on 16 July, and *General-Feldwachtmeister* Graf Colloredo had his weak infantry brigade on the march, with the intention of dividing the route between Fenestrelle and Pinerolo in two stages; that day they would have covered the 17 kilometres that separated Pinerolo from Perosa, and here they would have stopped to resume the march the following day up to Fenestrelle, which was 16.5 kilometres away.

The Austrian contingent had left Pinerolo with the appreciation of the local population. The regiments of Maria Teresa from the battle of Piacenza, fought on 16 June 1746, considered themselves the true liberators of Italy from the Franco-Spanish forces. They had already fought in the past alongside the Sardinian forces, although 'they have not a very great account of [the Piedmontese] troops, and they show themselves very proud, showing off their number greater than ours, at every step reminiscing their military facts, remembering their victory in Piacenza, and finally appointing himself liberators of Italy...'[25] The population considered them just as such, and they had greeted the arrival of the Austrian troops in a rather warm way, to the point that Colloredo 'was delighted with the way he was welcomed here'.[26]

But the day of departure came. We usually think about the marches of eighteenth century soldiers as colourful parades of gaudy uniforms, since we are accustomed to imagine the soldier of the period filtered by films and historical re-enactments. The soldiers lived experience was rather different:

> [T]o the end came the so long awaited moment, preceded by the order *Allons, ins Feld!* [Let's go, to the camp!]… Each soldier was loaded like a mule: first the belt with the sabre, then the cartridge box with a five-inch strap; on the other shoulder the knapsack full of linen, and then that of the bread sack full of bread and other things to eat and in addition everybody had to carry some of the common tools: flasks, a kettle, digging tools and so on, all always over the shoulder. Finally, the muskets. So we had five straps crossed over our chest, so much that at first everyone believed we were suffocating under the weight. As if this were not enough, we were

---

25   Galleani d'Agliano, *Memorie Storiche*), p.362.

26   Letter from the intendant Baldoino from Santa Margherita written in Pinerolo 17 July 1747, AST, Corte, Materie Militari, Imprese, Mazzo 7 da inventariare. It must be said that the respect paid to the Austrian contingent, given the difficult situation, was probably particularly calculated to flatter an ally in a very precious moment.

squeezed by our tight uniforms, in a hellish heat that it seemed to us walking on hot coals. As soon as I unbuttoned myself a little to cool my chest, steam was released like from a boiler. Soon I no longer had a dry thread on my body, and I was parched with thirst.[27]

When the troops were marching the fresh air could hardly pass through the ranks and files close together. The men were crowded, sweating profusely, wetting and soaking clothes and luggage. Their sense of smell no longer caught the stench they emanated, but this struck and impressed the civilians and senior officers who watched the passage of a marching unit. During the hot season the strong and penetrating smell of the marching troops remained in the air for hours after the regiments had passed.[28]

Before arriving in Perosa, the Austrian commander received a message sent by the Conte di Bricherasio: 'I immediately set off on the march but, even before I reached Perusa, the commander of Fenestrelle, Signor Briqueras [sic], very eagerly warned me that the enemy was approaching, urging me to bring the soldiers on the same day as far as Fenestrelle. This was done with no little inconvenience to the troops'.[29] The discomfort was understandable, as the Austrians that day covered a total of 34 kilometres. As had happened two days earlier to the Chevalier de Belle-Isle, also on this occasion we can only imagine the raising of the chalice and the toasts that were made to the health of the Conte di Bricherasio.

17 July 1747

On 17 July, the Chevalier de Belle-Isle had decided to carry out a reconnaissance in person to check the access roads to the ridge. He wanted his field guns at the Costapiana Pass whatever it cost. 'I'll go up on horseback tomorrow before dawn, and I'll go to gather information to find a road that can get the six 4-pounder guns to Monte Costapiana; these guns are to be considered decisive against entrenchments'.[30] The orders issued in this sense were very clear: 'The army will move the same day to Oulx, and the six long 4-pounder pieces will be sent to M. d'Arnaud'.[31]

The weather, however, did not bode well. Low clouds covered the mountain slopes and in the course of the morning the rain began to fall again. At high altitudes the rain turned into snow and ice, with visibility reduced to just 10-20 metres. The French offensive movements were practically blocked for the duration of the day.

The French forces in Susa Valley on the Sauze-d'Oulx-Jouvenceaux start-line were reorganized into two main bodies; the Chevalier de Belle-Isle placed himself at the head of d'Arnaud's command with the intention of moving along the road that led to Col Bourget

---

27   U. Bräker, *Lebensgeschichte und Natürliche Ebentheuer des Armen Mann im Tockenburg* (Zürich: Orell, Gessner, Füssli, 1789), pp.140-142.

28   Duffy, *The Military Experience*, p.169.

29   Report by Colloredo, KA, Alten Feldakten, Krieg in Italien, VII, 1.

30   Arvers and de Vault, *Guerre de la Succession d'Autriche*, Vol.II, p.686.

31   BRT, Miscellanea Militare 73. *Copie de quelques papiers trouvés sur M.rs de Belleisle et d'Arnault tués à l'attaque de l'Assiette le 19. juillet 1747*, orders of 17 July.

and, from there, reaching Costapiana Gap. Continuing along the ridge line, the French commander wanted to reconnoitre those positions facing the Assietta Plateau. The other column, under the command of *Maréchal de Camp* de Mailly, would have followed the path towards Monfol-Seu to approach from the northwest to Lauson Gap and the road near the Assietta. For the moment, however, venturing into a wood – specifically the Gran Bosco (literally 'Great Wood') – in conditions of poor visibility and with the weather clearly deteriorating and without coordination with de Villemur's column, seemed a gamble for the French command. All the French battalions present in Susa Valley, both from de Mailly's and d'Arnaud's columns, remained in their quarters. Only the special forces units remained on the ground; two companies of the Briançon militia and one of grenadiers were deployed with the task of carrying out a reconnaissance to Col Bourget and occupying it. Belle-Isle and d'Arnaud, both on horseback, accompanied this detachment, but bitterly noticed that the fog covered everything:

> [W]e went up with the necessary precautions, both in a bad mood to see that the fog prevented us from taking advantage of our efficiency. In some moments we had some brightening; we could see [enemy] sentinels,[32] and after a while about twenty muskets shots were fired. Later they abandoned a particularly badly constructed redoubt[33] which they built on Col Bourget to defend the passage.[34]

Belle-Isle and d'Arnaud, leaving the two militia companies in that position, advanced with the grenadiers towards Monte Costapiana, 'which is very close to the Assietta entrenchments',[35] where they were stopped not by the enemy firepower – not even an enemy infantryman or militiaman was detected – but by the poor visibility conditions and by the abundant snow that fell. It did not seem prudent to advance, as the risk of activating an enemy unit was considerable, and the French commander 'did not want to bring 5 or 6 companies of grenadiers with him' for his protection.[36] The Chevalier de Belle-Isle, with all his staff, remained at high altitude until 1:00 p.m., after which, having lost all hope of seeing the weather conditions improve, he went down to Oulx, where he arrived before 11:00 p.m.[37] He began to deem an attack in force necessary against the Assietta positions on 18 July. He had received de Villemur's report on the state of the enemy forces, which confirmed the presence of seven infantry battalions,[38] but by now a fixed scenario was outlined in his head that would never abandon him. The opposing forces were numerous, at least eight battalions according to his sources, to which another 10 battalions were to be

---

32   It was a detachment of the Susa Militia.
33   This redoubt is still visible at Colle Bourget at 2,299 metres above sea level. For a description see Garoglio, Zannoni, *La difesa nascosta del Piemonte sabaudo*, pp.163-164.
34   Arvers and de Vault, *Guerre de la Succession d'Autriche*, Vol.II, p.732.
35   Arvers and de Vault, *Guerre de la Succession d'Autriche*, Vol.II, p.732.
36   Arvers and de Vault, *Guerre de la Succession d'Autriche*, Vol.II, p.732.
37   As can be deduced from de Villemur's 5:00 p.m. letter. BRT, Manoscritto Militare 73.
38   French patrols identified one battalion of Guardie, and two each of Savoia, Sicilia and Kalbermatten. In reality at that time there were only six battalions in Fenestrelle, in addition to the two located to Assietta. There were in total five battalions arriving from Piedmont; the four Austrian battalions under the command of Colloredo and the Reggimento Chiablese directed to Susa.

added in the area of operations. These units would stand behind field fortifications awaiting the French attack. In addition, once the siege of Genoa was broken, the entire Austro-Sardinian army would have headed in force towards the Cottian Alps. Thus, he began to abandon all activities of careful planning and began to reason with a single imperative; hurry up. He asked de Villemur to bring his forces to the crest line in the face of Assietta by the morning of the 18th. Orders were issued for the advance guards of the columns of d'Arnaud and de Villemur to meet at 2:00 a.m. on 18 July. These combined forces, placed under the orders of d'Arnaud, would occupy Monte Costapiana and reach the Assietta Plateau, which would be attacked in concert with the left column (de Mailly), which would attack from the north side from the Susa Valley, and the right column (de Villemur) would attack from the south side from the Chisone Valley.[39]

Belle-Isle did not forget the cannon, whose firepower would have been useful for demolishing the entrenchments, and the need to take care of the supply for the troops, given the scorched earth policy implemented by the Sardinians. His logistical staff officer, Brunet de l'Argentière, immediately understood that he would have very intense days:

> The Chevalier de Belle-Isle arrived on the 17th in Oulx with the rest of the infantry and four 4-pounder guns. I was charged with a miners' officer to rebuild Pont Ventoux, and I was busy giving the necessary orders to the pioneers to carry four guns to Costapiana through Saint-Marc [San Marco], Jouvenceauz [Jouvenceaux] and Sauze [Sauze d'Oulx]. I was ordered to build ovens, since the bread took too long a journey to be brought from Briançon without tiring the mules too much.[40]

In Val Chisone, de Villemur could only notice that 'the roads are so bad on this side, that if the rain continues, I do not know how the troops will walk at night'.[41] Nevertheless, the French column had moved and advanced along the upper Val Chisone, colliding with two militia companies; that of Pragelato under *Maggiore* Perrone deployed at Chezal-Duc and the Waldensian one commanded by *Capitano* Rouzier assigned to Joussaud. The militiamen, more than 500 strong, only had the task of observing the enemy's moves, and, after a brief firefight, they retreated, quickly disappearing along the slopes that led to the Assietta Plateau. The French avant-gardes stopped their advance at the villages of Traverses and Plan. The French general quickly arranged his command post at the little village of Duc and he received the first reports from the advanced patrols. His men reported that in all the Sardinians had seven infantry battalions, 'which have long been scattered there at Balboutet, Assietta and the Arguel pass, with an advanced post on the Monte Costapiana'.[42] These indications did not coincide with the number of 18 battalions that Belle-Isle had reported to him. Who was right? He immediately sent his report to the commander in chief. He and his staff probably had a clearer view of the situation at the operational level.

---

39   Arvers and de Vault, *Guerre de la Succession d'Autriche*, Vol.II, p.688.
40   Brunet de l'Argentière, *Mémoire de la Guerre*, p.71.
41   BRT, Manoscritto Militare 73; Letter from de Villemur to the Chevalier de Belle-Isle at 5:00 a.m. 17 July.
42   BRT, Manoscritto Militare 73; Letter from de Villemur to the Chevalier de Belle-Isle at 5:00 a.m. 17 July.

Meanwhile, de Villemur's column was supposed to reach the ridge line and advance to the west. The Chevalier de Belle-Isle had already sent the two companies of Briançon militia, supported by units of grenadiers, to occupy Col Bourget, where on the morning of 18 July it could facilitate the linkup between this avant-garde and that of d'Arnaud's column. De Villemur had immediately given the order to carry out a detailed survey of the roads towards Monte Costapiana, believing that he had more time at his disposal to be able to advance his men safely. At five in the evening he received a new letter from the Chevalier de Belle-Isle; de Villemur did not believe his eyes. The reunion with d'Arnaud the following morning was confirmed, but only for the forces of the vanguard. The orders for the 18th now were to advance the bulk of the column towards Pragelato, climb to the village of Grand Puy, and from there climb the mountainside to reach Col Lauson – 2,497 metres – and hit the right flank of the entrenchments of the Assietta Camp, the real state of which was still unknown, in a general assault. All this by marching in hostile territory in the middle of a snowfall. Rather annoyed, he could only answer in this way: 'If you gentlemen want the manoeuvre to be done in its entirety, it is necessary to resolve to operate on the 19th'.[43] Nevertheless, he confirmed the movements for the next day. During the early hours of the day, his vanguard would realize the link-up at Col Bourget with d'Arnaud' column, after which de Villemur would manage the march of his brigades towards the village of Puy, and then towards the crest of the mountains. Moving only during the daytime, de Villemur's column would only arrive in sight of Assietta during the morning of the 19th. 'I will not take any kind of field equipment, I believe we will be even more effective after we get rid of it, and I will leave 400 men here to keep them together with the Volontaires de Gantés'.[44] The Volontaires de Gantés was a light corps with a total strength of 500 men, organized into four companies of fusiliers, one of dragoons and two of hussars. The presence of this combined-arms unit explains why we find in Piedmontese sources the presence of *miquelets*, that is light mountain troops, and of hussars.[45] Meanwhile, the Brigade Poitou advanced, with three battalions of the Régiment de Poitou, to garrison the Sestriere Gap and protect the important position from enemy attacks. Two Spanish units would also be detached to garrison this position; a battalion of the Regimiento de Aragón and one squadron of the Dragones de Merida.

D'Escars column, despite the presence of local guides, was almost blindly groping in the fog. The snowfall made the advance along the Valfredda slow and painful and during the day the progression towards the head of the valley was minimal.[46] Informed of the situation, the Chevalier de Belle-Isle ordered d'Escars to stop at the grange of Rochemolles to rest the troops.[47]

Fenestrelle and adjacent villages on the morning of 17 July 1747 were very crowded places. Bricherasio's small army was concentrated here, for a total of nine battalions: 2/ and 3/ Kalbermatten, 1/Monfort, 2/Savoia, 1/Meyer and the Austrians of 3/Colloredo, 3/Forgách,

43   BRT, Manoscritto Militare 73; Letter from de Villemur to the Chevalier de Belle-Isle at 5 am on July 17th.
44   BRT, Manoscritto Militare 73; Letter from de Villemur to the Chevalier de Belle-Isle at 5:00 a.m. on 17 July.
45   *Ordonnance du Roy, concernant le Corps des Volontaires de Gantés du 22 avril 1747*, Paris 1747.
46   Arvers and de Vault, *Guerre de la Succession d'Autriche*, Vol.II, p.686.
47   Arvers and de Vault, *Guerre de la Succession d'Autriche*, Vol.II, p.730.

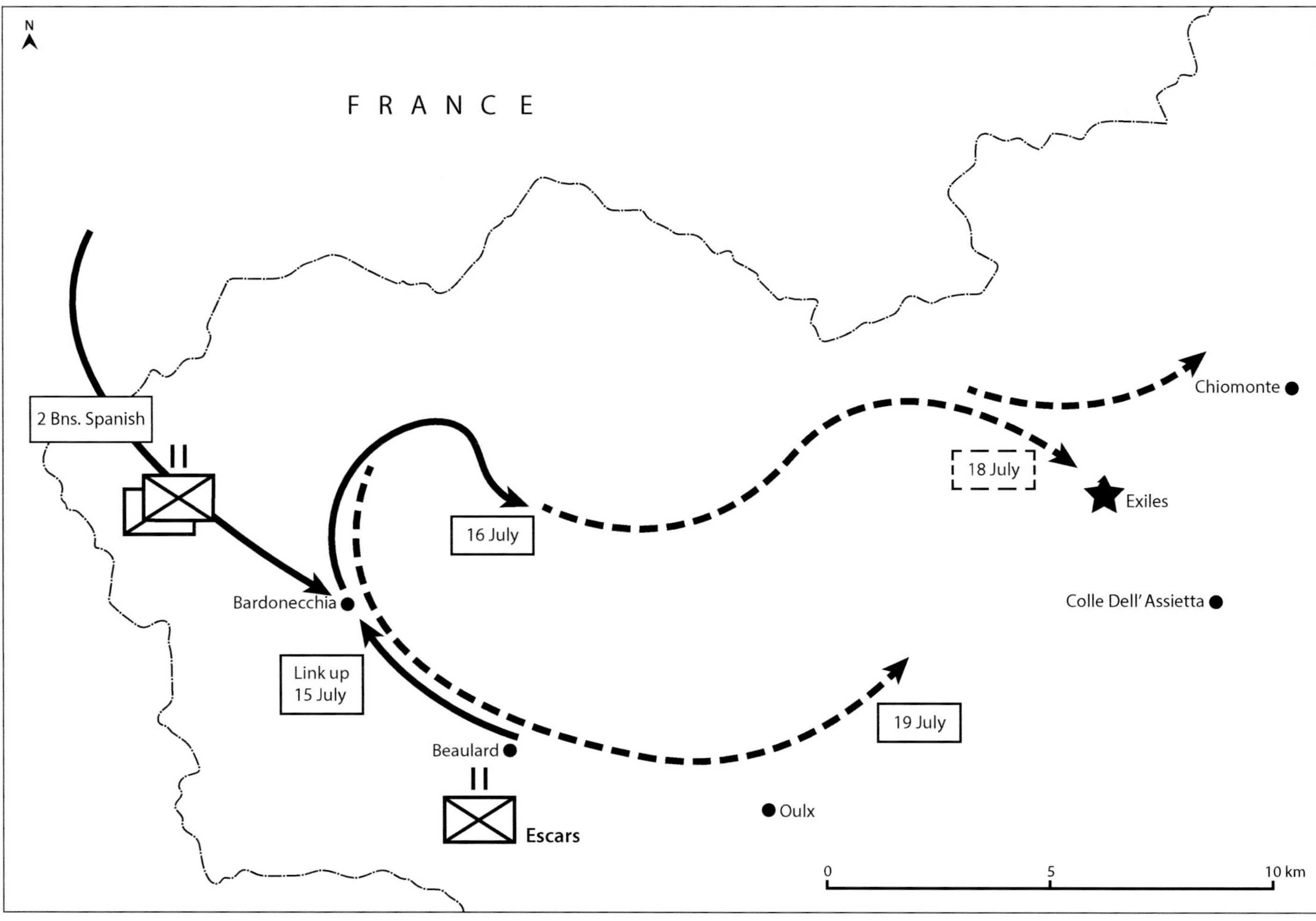

The first failure, the march of d'Escars' column. This formation had to secure the ridge north of the Fort of Exilles, but the bad weather and the snow on the mountains compelled the combined French-Spanish force to withdraw.

and the battalions of Hagenbach and Traun. The total force was now of 4,625 men, and if one also counts the two battalions already present at the Assietta camp, 1/Guardie and Casale, together with the 1/Sicilia deployed at the Finestre Gap, the total strength reached 5,948 men; the entrenchments would be defended as planned. During the morning the French had advanced to the west of the Colle del Sestiere and had pushed back the militia companies deployed to control the road. Bricherasio at this point estimated that the enemy could:

- Attack Assietta on 18 July.
- Cut the communications between Assietta and the fortress of Fenestrelle.
- Carry out a bombardment and a strike against Fenestrelle.

The last hypothesis seemed the least probable; at the moment the militiamen did not report the presence of siege artillery trains, and the fortifications of Fenestrelle were too large and well equipped to be conquered with an escalade. The other two hypotheses, on the other hand, had to be considered carefully. At Assietta there were only two infantry battalions, which at that moment held their position in the middle of a snowfall. The camp, with a march towards the village of Balboutet, could be isolated from the fortress of Fenestrelle. It was necessary to act immediately:

- Colloredo and *Brigadiere Generale* Martinengo with 2/Savoia, 3/Colloredo and 3/Forgách were sent to garrison the village of Balboutet. A picquet of two companies, de Cerisier and de Viry of 2/Savoia, 109 men at all, were posted in the village of Gran Puy to guard the roads approaching Assietta.[48]
- The battalions of Hagenbach and Traun were assigned to the Assietta camp to reinforce the garrison at high altitude.
- The Reggimento Chiablese, marching towards Susa, would have headed for the entrenched camp of Argueil.

Meanwhile, the militia units had not moved far away, and the Pragelato's militia company under Perrone was deployed at Villardamont, about 1,500 metres from the opposing camp, while Rouzier sent part of his men to guard the Pis and Albergian positions.

The weather conditions, for the entire duration of July 17, were very bad, and that limited the movements of the French as well as those of the Austro-Sardinians. The two Austrian battalions were unable to reach the Assietta plateau during the day. It was thus decided that they would go up to the entrenched camp the following day in the morning.[49] Nonetheless, at least towards the valley floor, visibility seemed good. Colloredo went up with his men to the small plateau of Balboutet. Placed at an altitude of 1,557 metres, a direct observation

---

48   AST, Sezioni Riunite, Ministero della Guerra, Ufficio Generale del Soldo, Ruolini di Rivista, Reggimento Savoia, 1747, Vol.84.

49   Report by Colloredo, KA, Alten Feldakten, Krieg in Italien, VII, 1. The two battalions, however, never reached the entrenched camp during the day of the 17 July, but only on the morning of the 18th, as written in the Priocca I and Priocca II reports: 'On the 18th in the morning we were reinforced by two Austrian battalions of Traun and Hagenbach'. The bad weather conditions not only affected the French, but also limited the maneuvers of the Austro-Sardinians, as in this case.

inside the French camp of Duc/Traverses/Plan was possible. The French had set up their tents and Colloredo was able to judge the opposing detachment '12 or 15 battalions strong'.[50] The Austrian general's observation and judgment capabilities proved to be excellent; de Villemur had 13 infantry battalions at his disposal.

18 July 1747

On 18 July 1747 the weather was still bad, but at for the moment the rain had stopped falling and it was no longer snowing at high altitude. According to the French order of operations this was to be the day of the advance at high altitude towards the Assietta Plateau; and the French moved on.

The first to move, but not forwards, were the soldiers of d'Escars' column, who had been fighting for two days against the snows of the Val Fredda, and began to retreat towards the bottom of Susa valley. Despite the attempts made it was not possible to advance and keep the expected progression times. On the evening of the 18th d'Escars and his tired troops entered Oulx to look for at least a shelter to spend the night.[51]

The Chevalier de Belle-Isle had no time, at the moment, to worry about the fate of d'Escars' column. de Villemur had communicated to him the impossibility of advancing and reaching their positions. It was necessary to postpone the planned attack. The French commander still wanted a rapid advance along the ridge, and he went in person to oversee the movements. According to reports from the front the enemy had from seven (according to de Villemur) to eight (according to d'Arnaud) battalions deployed in the entrenchments. If he wanted to take the Assietta against an enemy still small in number, then he had to move as fast as possible and surprise the enemy forces with the speed of his manoeuvre. Belle-isle now intended to bring his manoeuvring mass close to the Assietta ridge in order to have on 19 July his troops in position to attack the entrenched camp on 19 July. He began issuing the necessary orders:[52]

- Vanguard. The Vanguard was a mixed unit made up of detached forces from de Villemur's column – for a total of 10 grenadier companies and 10 infantry companies – to which the vanguard of d'Arnaud's column was supposed to join. Departing from their departure bases around midnight, they would have made the link-up to Bourget Pass at 2:00 a.m. This assembled force would advance towards Monte Costapiana to open the passage to the Central Column coming from Sauze d'Oulx.
- Central Column (d'Arnaud). Composed by the Brigade d'Artois, plus attached forces, it would leave Sauze d'Oulx at 2:00 a.m. with destination of Monte Costapiana, where it would make the link-up with the Vanguard. The assembled forces would advance

---

50   Report by Colloredo, KA, Alten Feldakten, Krieg in Italien, VII, 1.
51   Arvers and de Vault, *Guerre de la Succession d'Autriche*, Vol.II, p.701.
52   BRT, Miscellanea Militare 73. *Copie de quelques papiers trouvés sur M.rs de Belleisle et d'Arnault tués à l'attaque de l'Assiette le 19. juillet 1747*, orders of 17 July; Arvers and de Vault, *Guerre de la Succession d'Autriche*, Vol.II, p.689.

along the ridge with the task of occupying Mount Gran Costa and advancing towards Assietta. The six 4-pounder field artillery pieces would follow this unit.

- Left Column (de Mailly). Composed of the Brigades Bourbonnais and La Reine, it would take the path of Sauze d'Oulx around 2:00 a.m. and through the mule tracks that crossed the Gran Bosco. It would reach and attack the Assietta ridge from the northern side.
- Right Column (De Villemur). The column, which started the march from the camp lying between Traverses, Plan and Duc around 4:00 a.m., was composed of the Brigades Mailly, Royal Roussillon and Condé. Its orders were to reach Lauson Pass from the side of the Chisone Valley, following the path that was supposed to go up from the village of Grand Puy and continue towards Mount Gran Costa. Once it reached the ridge line it would attack the southern flank of the Colle dell'Assietta.

The columns, between midnight and 2:00 a.m. on 18 July, set out along the paths that had been designated for them. In spite of the fog and the certain presence of enemy units placed nearby, the columns started moving in the dark:

> [T]he night, among all, is the most suitable time to march towards the designated place; care will be taken to leave early enough to be on hand for the attack an hour or two before the day. Care must be taken that there is no moonlight at this time, or at least that it is hidden when we intend to start the attack: the soldiers will be ordered to march two by two, lightly equipped, making as little noise as possible, especially when you have to pass near enemy sentries. They will also be advised not to speak, not to spit and not to smoke.[53]

Guides recruited locally guaranteed the correctness of the itineraries; the clouds still enveloped the mountains, and it was necessary to make use of people who knew the route well. The choice of reliable guides was not an operation to be carried out lightly, and the commanders had to have very clear ideas on how to use and manage them:

> If you have to lead an attack against an enemy position by means of spies or guides; before using them, it is necessary that all the details we believe we need and the path through which they propose to accompany us are discussed with them. The reason for this is that we have often seen simple people who, whether motivated by profit motives or not, believe they can easily lead a troop and yet have only a lot of good will. But if we recognize in those who offer themselves the qualities necessary for this, we must first make sure of them, as far as possible, and make them fear the destruction of their home and the plundering of their possessions, if they lead the troop into some traps. We can also ask them to hold their wives or children hostage as a token of their loyalty; and at the time of the march, we will position our guides between the two corporals placed in the first ranks, tied with a chain or a rope; this

---

53   J.L. Le Cointe, *Le Science des Postes Militaire, ou Traité des Fortifications de Campagne, à l'usage des Officiers particuliers d'Infanterie qui sont détachés à la Guerre* (Paris: Desaint & Saillant, 1759), pp.191-192.

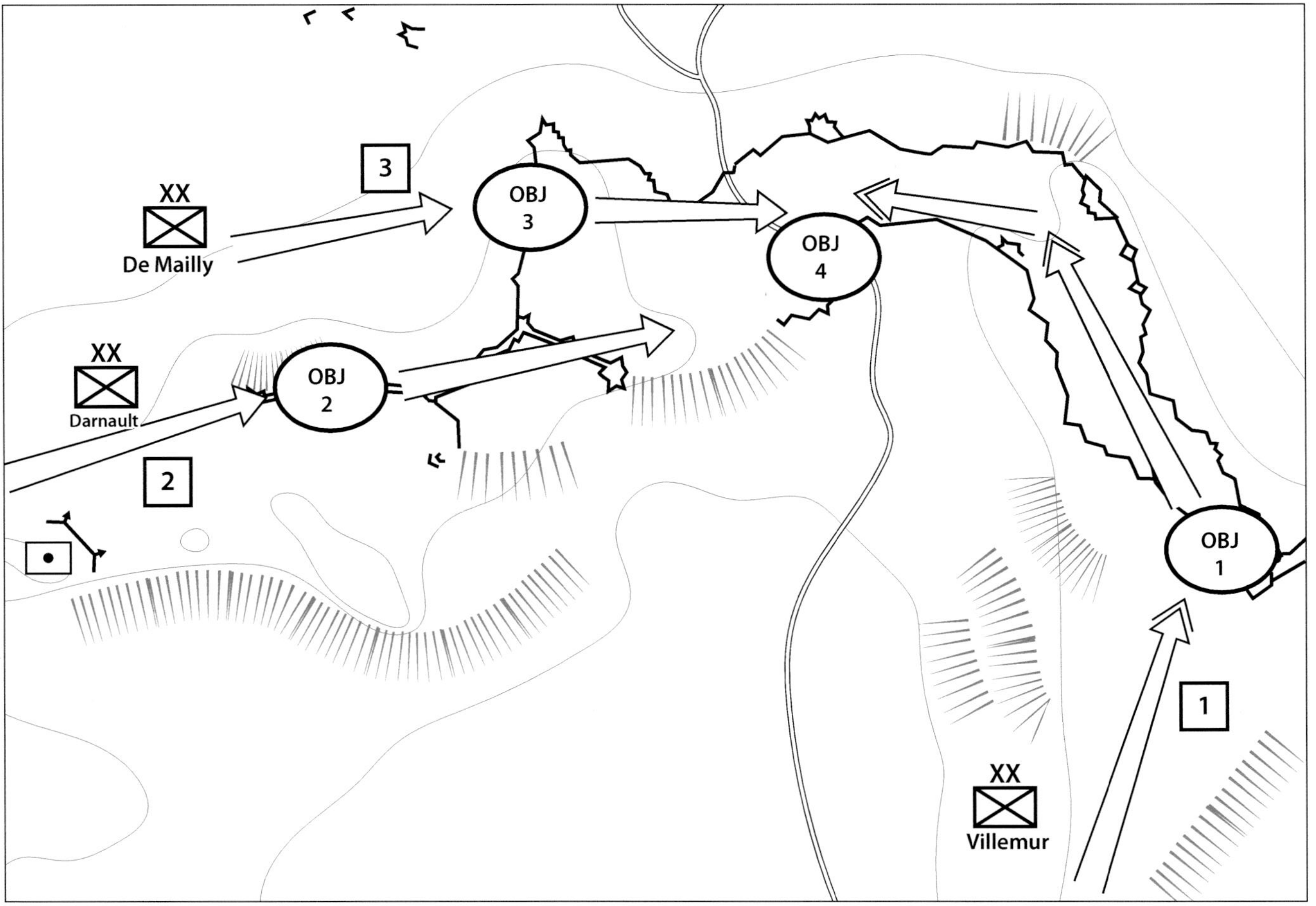

The French tactical plan to size the Assietta plateau. The main effort was on the shoulders of Villemur's column (No.1), which had the task to conquer the Gran Serin hill (Obj 1), the key position of the whole battlefield. Two secondary attacks had to size the Testa dell'Assietta (Obj 2) and to breach the enemy main line of defense (Obj 3). All the three columns had to exploit their success by clearing their pass and conquering the Assietta plateau (Obj 4). At the end of the action the route for Exilles and the Susa Valley would be open.

last precaution is all the more essential since we have often seen traitors, who under the pretext of being used to reaching a certain place, led detachments in an ambush in the middle of the night and disappeared at the moment of execution. Therefore, if on the one hand it is hoped that these guides can obtain a reward proportional to the service they can offer, in the event that they behave well, on the other hand, we must make them fear the most cruel pain, if they behave badly.[54]

The contingents that formed the vanguard made the link-up at 2:00 a.m. at the Bourget Pass, and they began to push west along the ridge to reach Monte Costapiana and secure this position quickly as possible. At least 3,400 infantrymen from the Central Column, the field artillery train and all the logistics dedicated to them were expected in this place during the morning. It was a substantial mass of men and beasts of burden that must have taken up a lot of space. For the infantry alone, the column was about three kilometres long, with a parade time of over one-and-a-half hours. Over all, the French, marching without any precaution and on perfectly equipped roads, would have covered the journey to Colle Lauson from Sauze d'Oulx in about three-and-a-half to four hours, completing the assembly in about six hours. But this was not a transfer march, but a real leap forward intended to engage the enemy in combat. Therefore all sorts of precautions were taken, not to mention the logistical difficulties. In addition, the mountain was immersed in a misty blanket: the low clouds covered the view and the weather was always interspersed with rain.

Behind the vanguard advanced, with difficulty, the Central Column of *Maréchal de Camp* d'Arnaud, which had left Saulze d'Oulx during the night. Belle-Isle and d'Arnaud managed to reach the Lauson Pass and the slopes of the Mount Gran Costa only around 7:00 p.m. The chosen itinerary was about 12 kilometres long with an ascent of just over 1,000 metres; all paths had to be widened and put in the conditions to be able to withstand the transit of thousands of men and a battery of field artillery without collapsing under their weight. The logistics chief, the weary Brunet de l'Argentière, was busy 'working on the roads to move the guns; there were not enough pioneers and I was forced to command workers even among the troops to replace them'.[55] The difficult weather conditions and the poor visibility given by the low-altitude clouds that covered the mountains, and the need to have advanced patrols to avoid ambushes or surprise attacks by the enemy, greatly delayed the advance.

The left column under de Mailly had the most difficult tactical task, namely that of crossing the Gran Bosco near Oulx and arriving on the left flank of the entrenchments. De Mailly had about 5,100 men under his orders, if one counts the infantry alone, excluding personnel dedicated to other services and baggage impedimenta. His column therefore had an estimated length of about 4,300 metres, with a parade time of about two-and-a-quarter hours. On a normal mountain roads with no blocks or preventive reconnaissance, de Mailly would reach the link-up area in about three hours and 40 minutes, and in six hours would have his entire column gathered on the ridge.[56] The crossing of the thick wood certainly did

---

54   Le Cointe, *Le Science des Postes Militaire*, pp.189-190.
55   Brunet de l'Argentière, *Mémoire de la Guerre*, pp.71-72.
56   La *Mémoire sur l'attaque des retranchements de l'Assiette* by de Mailly is published in Arvers and de Vault, *Guerre de la Succession d'Autriche*, Vol.II, pp.742- 752 and in Bourcet, *Principes de la Guerre de Montagnes*, pp.284-292, after which one can find an *Extrait des États de service de M. Le Compte*

not promise an easy game: the vegetation was dense, although crossed by mule tracks and paths, and the militia of Upper Susa Valley, assisted by the volunteers, in all about 600 men, had contributed to create a lot of troubles: 'Obstacles of every type were found during the march, at the entrance and in the passages inside the forest of Oulx, due to the abatis that the enemies had made', wrote de Mailly.[57] A cluster of tree trunks arranged along a mountain path is a particularly challenging obstacle. The difficulty of overcoming such a barrier increases if there are armed men nearby who intend to hit anyone who stops in front of the abatis. In fact:

> [T]he most formidable obstacle that can be opposed to the enemy is to stop his advance, interrupt the paths, and surround the enemy forces with fallen trees... The trees, which are used to make these abatis, must have many large branches from which the tips are sharpened and from which all the leaves are removed; these trees are arranged as close as possible to each other, so that the branches are well intertwined, making sure that these are slightly inclined towards the enemy.[58]

In practice, these were barriers that had the same tactical function as barbed wire, that is, to delay the progression of the infantry. In addition, the opposing light infantry had the bad habit of putting a small aggressive platoon near the road interruptions. De Mailly had no intention of stopping his march in front of the abatis and getting dragged into a gruelling firefight. Once identified, the enemy position was fixed with fire from a platoon of infantry, the maximum that the width of the paths allowed to deploy, while units of grenadiers tried outflank on the right and on the left, depending on the nature of the terrain, the enemy force. The enemy, in order not to be isolated, withdrew without excessively prolonging his defensive action; after all, their mission had remained to observe and report. Piedmontese losses were decidedly light, only a dozen soldiers took advantage of the confusion of the fight to desert.[59]

The sound of gunfire began to echo along all the slopes of the valleys, to the point that the Chevalier de Belle-Isle began to think that de Mailly had attacked the entrenched camp alone: 'as the fire was very sustained, M. le Chevalier de Belle-Isle ordered [de Mailly] not to attack until his column was in position'.[60] Once the area had been cleared it was necessary to open the passage, cutting the logs and pushing them away, but the French were fast enough and at 10:00 a.m. on 18 July the vanguards of de Mailly's column were established on the plateau below the flat summit of Mount Gran Costa. The march times had been

---

de Mailly, pp.293-294. The version used for this study is the one presented by Arvers and de Vault, hereinafter presented as De Mailly, *Mémoire sur l'attaque.*

57   De Mailly, *Mémoire sur l'attaque.* The fighting in the woods was certainly less intense than was presented by de Mailly himself in his report; otherwise the advance would have been much slower and more tiring.

58   Le Cointe, *Le Science des Postes Militair*, p.53.

59   They were 11 soldiers from the Reggimento Kalbermatten – six from the second and five from the third battalion – and probably three other soldiers from the Reggimento Casale, all from the Ottiglio Company. AST, Sezioni Riunite, Ministero della Guerra: Ufficio Generale del Soldo; Ruolini di Rivista; Reggimento Kalbermatten, Vol.58, 1747; Reggimento Casale, Vol.33, 1747.

60   De Mailly, *Mémoire sur l'attaque.*

respected and the French column stopped on the southern edge of the Gran Bosco, at an altitude of about 2,380 metres, building in turn an abatis to cover its front of attack.[61] The abattis erected in this case by the French were, probably, different, and they were tree trunks used as real parapets to cover the troops from enemy fire. This tactical function was already contemplated in the treatises of the time:

> Sometimes we take refuge even in a simple abattis, when we are not in design or when we do not have time to cover ourselves with a trench of the earth, but we must therefore be careful to put the tree trunks superimposed as much as possible on each other, in order to make these trunks a real fortification; since otherwise the enemy would advance in force against the same abattis, and therefore having the advantage of seeing from foot to head those who would be behind, he could have killed them one after the other.[62]

At 7:00 p.m. the link-up with the centre column was made. That on the right, on the other hand, seemed to have disappeared into thin air. Only sporadic couriers were able to 'give information' on the progression of de Villemur's forces.[63]

The Column of the Right, under the orders of *Lieutenant Général* de Villemur, had advanced during the morning along the slopes of the Chisone Valley towards Pragelato, and then reached the village of Gran Puy. The left column had a total of 6,900 infantrymen. In marching order they formed a column about 5,900 metres long. The parade times were about three hours, plus the four hours of walking from the valley floor to Colle Lauson, for a total of no less than seven hours before reaching the crest line. The fog, the certainty of the presence of enemy units, and the large amount of men to manage meant that, firstly, de Villemur decided at a certain point to stop the advance towards the ridge to rest the men and carry out the necessary reconnaissance; secondly, only the improvement of the meteorological conditions starting from 5:00 a.m. on the following day allowed the column to continue the advance even in the early hours of 19 July.

The Pragelato and Waldensian militia retreated at the same pace as the French advanced. They had no intention of stopping the enemy, but they kept retreating and watching his movements. In all there were about 800 men who moved like ghosts in the mist that enveloped the sides of the mountain. The French were well aware of the danger to which they were exposed in such a tactical situation, and took all necessary precautions. Patrols were sent in advance to recognize the paths and observe if the path was actually clear of any pitfalls. Besides the danger of not seeing a Waldensian militia company a few metres from them only to notice the same at the first fusillade, the march in the mist exposed the French to other dangers, such as loosing orientation. The soldiers were warned not to stray from the column, to follow the path and not to lose distance from the companions in front of them:

> [W]hether they go on foot or on horseback, they [the officers] and their sergeants must pay great attention to making the soldiers hurry who slow down, that they

---

61   De Mailly, *Mémoire sur l'attaque*.
62   Le Cointe, *Le Science des Postes Militaire*, p.54.
63   De Mailly, *Mémoire sur l'attaque*.

walk in close ranks and on all the lines that the path will allow: that they do not stop when they want and that they observe the deepest silence in order to hear the different orders you will want to give them.[64]

Given the need to implement these precautions column de Villemur advanced very slowly, and almost certainly he decided at some point to stop the advance and make a long stop. Only at 08:00 in the morning of 19 July, after a night spent marching, the French contingent was able to reach the Lauson pass and make the link-up with de Mailly's and d'Arnaud's columns.

In Fenestrelle, the Conte di Bricherasio was beginning to receive increasingly worrying reports from his intelligence sources. By 18 July the French were on the move, and it was necessary to have precise information on what they intended to do and how many battalions were present. Reports that came from militia units or from informants behind the lines had to be carefully compared and analysed. The commanders of the light units confirmed the presence of at least two, if not three, columns marching towards the Assietta plateau. In the evening, or by the morning at the latest, they would be close to the entrenched camp. The informers behind the enemy lines had the challenge of needing to to obtain valid data on the opposing forces and to send them in a short time to the Sardinian command. French dragoons and light infantry patrols were able to effectively isolate marching troops from overly curious civilians. The spies saw large units moving, but they could not help but report desolately that 'we still ignore the number of [enemy] troops, even though two deserters who passed through here last night claim that there are about twenty thousand men between cavalry and infantry, including those arriving from Savoy'.[65] At a time when it was necessary to have immediately fresh news, at most a few hours old, that available to Bricherasio dated back to 16 July.[66]

Only in the course of the 18th was Bricherasio able to receive a more detailed report from an agent in Oulx. This described the movement of the opposing forces, which were moving along at least two directions, from Sauze d'Oulx and along the Val Chisone. Their target was the Assietta entrenched camp, and it was certainly not a feint or an outflanking manoeuvre. The French came to fight:

> It is estimated that the enemy force marching to Assietta has a strength of between 20 and 25 battalions, and that a corps of a similar strength is in Bousson, and it has gone up to Sestrieres and it is marching on the heights on the side of Pragelato. They sent six pieces of artillery up to Sauze d'Oulx yesterday evening... the Corps that passed through Col de la Roue, through that of Scala, and that marched through the Rochemolles to the Vallone is made up of 6 battalions.[67]

64   Le Cointe, *Le Science des Postes Militaire*, p.81.
65   Letter from the superintendent Baldoino of Santa Margheruta written in Pinerolo on 18 July 1747. AST, Corte, Materie Militari, Imprese, Mazzo 7 da inventariare.
66   Letter from the superintendent Baldoino of Santa Margherita written in Pinerolo on 18 July 1747. AST, Corte, Materie Militari, Imprese, Mazzo 7 da inventariare.
67   *Relation venenat d'Oulx du 18 juillet* 1747, KA, Alten Feldakten, Krieg in Italien, 16.

A more precise description was not possible, but it was reported that:

> [T]he roads have been entirely repaired for the passage of artillery from Brançon to Cesana, and there is a large number of peasants from the valleys [of Susa] and the Briançon area who are actively working on the road from Cesana to Oulx. [...] They are building two large bread ovens in Oulx. The road from Mount Dauphin to Briançon is full of wagons [crammed with] bombs, cannonballs, and other war ammunition and I cannot quantify the number of wagons with grain, and flour, that are advancing along the two roads that arrive from Grenoble.

The design of the manoeuvre could not have been more explicit; occupy Assietta in order to besiege Exilles.

On the morning of 18 July, the Conte di Bricherasio was now certain that there would be a battle with the enemy within the next 48 hours. The reports that came to him from the outposts located along the slopes of the Assietta ridge left no room for doubt: the French were advancing in strength towards his positions. The elements he had to evaluate were the following:

- On 15 July the French had passed the Monginevro Pass and had gone to camp in Cesana.
- On 16 July the enemy had advanced both along the Val di Susa and in the Val Chisone. The French columns had reached Oulx and Jovenceaux.
- On 17 July, large concentrations of troops were underway around Sauze d'Oulx. Other hostile movements had been monitored by militia units arranged along the Val Chisone. French troops had seized the Colle del Sestriere and had made a reconnaissance as far as the gates of Fenestrelle.
- In the night between 17 and 18 July, despite the bad weather conditions, at 2:00 a.m. the French had appeared on Col Bourget at 2,297 metres above sea level and now two, if not three, columns pointed west towards the Assietta Plateau from Oulx and Pragelato. A total of 50 battalions, 20,000 men, were preparing to attack the Piedmontese defences.

The Chevalier de Belle-Isle wanted to invest the Fort of Exilles, but to do so he had to occupy Assietta and the nearby hills. Bricherasio decided to defend the entrenched camp, or at least delay its occupation by the enemy as much as possible while awaiting the Austro-Sardinian army arriving from Genoa. Defending the entrenched camp, repelling the enemy's assault or delaying his advance as much as possible: this was his tactical objective since 18 July. He began to issue the necessary orders:

- By morning the Hagenbach and Traun battalions had to reach the entrenched camp of Assietta.
- The single-battalion Reggimento Meyer had to reach the entrenched camp of Assietta and coordinate with the battalions of Guardie, Casale, Hagenbach and Traun.
- 2/ and 3/ Reggimento Kalbermatten had to reach Colle dell'Assietta and stand in defence of the Gran Serin.
- 1/ Reggimento Monfort had to reach the Gran Lago Pass and the head of the Vallone dei Morti.

- 1/ Reggimento Sicilia was to garrison the Colle delle Vallette.
- The militias of Pragelato, Susa Valley and the Waldensians, with the volunteers, would settle on the line of Monte Gran Costa-Testa del Mottas.
- The companies de Cerisier and de Viry of 2/Reggimento Savoia would join their battalion in the village of Balboutet.
- The order for the Reggimento Chiablese to reach the entrenched camp at the Arguel remained unchanged. On 18 July the unit had arrived in Susa.[68]

Bricherasio at this point informed the Minister of War of the situation and began to move his command directly into the perimeter of the entrenched camp at high altitude. In the event of a battle, he would command his troops himself; before doing this, he made the necessary arrangements to be traceable by his chain of command, by the governors and the Minister of War. He organized the logistic network to supply of the camp which, by the hour, was becoming increasingly crowded. During the day, units began to flock to the Assietta camp and to be sent to the sectors assigned to them. On the morning of the 18th the two Austrian battalions Hagenbach and Traun arrived, followed by the other units. During the day, Bricherasio himself also arrived and from there he began planning the defence of the camp. In the afternoon, with *Maggior Generale* Alciati present, he summoned all the battalion commanders and gave the necessary orders for the defence of Assietta;

- The Austro-Sardinian forces would resist the enemy attack by deploying the infantry battalions to the fortifications of the entrenched camp.
- The defenders would delay the conquest of Colle dell'Assietta as much as possible.
- In case of need, the retreat was to be made towards the Gran Serin.

The battalions were divided into two combat groups; the first had to directly defend the Assietta pass by forming a barrier perpendicular to the expected arrival of the enemy along the ridge line. To this group was assigned the 1/Guardie, which was to defend the communication between the main defensive line of the Assietta and the hill known as 'Butta dell'Assietta', fortified with a tenailled work, manned the grenadier companies of 1/Guardie and of Casale. The Austrian battalions were placed with one, Traun, within the Assietta Redoubt, together with the Colonnella, Maggiora, Ottiglio and Scozia companies of the Reggimento Casale. The other Austrian battalion, Hagenbach, was placed astride the road that led from Val Chisone to Colle dell'Assietta itself. The Swiss Reggimento Meyer in Sardinian service was deployed along the entrenchment which descended from the Assietta Redoubt. In reserve, between the communication and a secondary entrenchment, later known as the 'Redoubt of the Waldensians', the Colonnella Company of the Reggimento Casale was placed in reserve. The second combat group, stationed on the Gran Serin, had to defend communications with the passes of Vallette and delle Finistra and prevent the first group from being cut off by an enemy attack carried out on the southern flank. They were lined up, from east to west 3/Kalbermatten to defend the reduced fortifications on the

---

68   Alberti, *La Battaglia dell'Assietta*, p.3.

summit of Gran Serin, and just below 2/Kalbermatten. On the left the Swiss should have connected with the men of 1/Monfort.

Despite every good will, the battalion commanders could not help but evaluate what was the best distance within which to engage the enemy, define the most appropriate killing zones, but they could plan little else.[69] The picture for Bricherasio was disheartening: to defend Assietta he had seven battalions at his disposal, a total of 3,676 men. Too few, and the defences were excessively wide, especially along the western front. The Swiss of Reggimento Meyer and the Austrians of Traun, alone, had no hope to block a frontal attack in force. The Piedmontese commander accordingly gave the order to both reserve units still available to reach the field; *Brigadiere Generale* Martinengo and Graf Colloredo would leave the field of Balboutet and go up to Assietta as soon as possible. At that point, with the militia, the total number of men at Bricherasio's disposal would rise to nearly 5,500.

In no document known today is it specified which was the exact location of the command post of the Conte di Bricherasio. Surely he was not at the Butta dell'Assietta, as Minister Bogino recalled in 1778: 'Bricherasio was in command of the troops, who were in the Assietta Plateau, when the famous affair followed; but he was not in person in the defence of those entrenchments which were attacked, supported by the subordinate officers, who were there to command the various posts'.[70] The most suitable place to place a command post was at the Gran Serin. This place allows one to observe the whole fighting area. The fact that, practically, the Piedmontese commander never appeared in person in any of the clashes of 19 July on the western edge of the plateau suggests the Gran Serin hypothesis as the right one.

At the Balboutet camp, Colloredo continued to monitor the activity of the opposing troops. At six in the afternoon he could see that 'the enemy tents were still visible early, but most of the troops had disappeared'.[71] In the late afternoon Bricherasio ordered him to reach the Assietta field. The itinerary, which, given the presence of strong opposing infantry contingents, provided for the ascent to Colle delle Vallette was not an easy path. In all there were two battalions, the 3/Forgách with 258 soldiers, 3/Colloredo with 218, for a total of 476 men. The length of the column was 400 metres, with an extension time of about 15 minutes. The path followed was: Camp of Balbouté 1,557 metres; Chalvets 1,874 metres; Vallone delle Vallette and Colle delle Vallette 2,551 metres. A climb of 994 metres over a total distance of 4 kilometres. Departure around 7:00 p.m.; four hours of marching plus 15 minutes of parade therefore equates to arrival in Vallette at midnight. Allowing for a break of half an hour and recommencement of the march at 0:30 a.m., indicated arrival at the Assietta field at about 2:00 a.m., after having marched about 3,800 metres from the Vallette pass. At about 2.30 a.m. the two battalions were well inside the main camp.[72] The imperial troops suffered a lot in that nocturnal excursion at high altitudes, and as Colloredo reported 'in the night along

---

69   The representation of a Bricherasio who, on the strength of his knowledge about the enemy's moves, on the evening of 18 July gave clear and clear orders to all the commanders of the department as reported in Minutoli, *Relation des campagnes faites par S.M.*, Vol.V, pp.224-226, is far from reality. He had not yet received three battalions; two of them (3/Colloredo and 3/Forgách) had not received any orders.

70   C. Negroni, Lettere di Gian Lorenzo Bogino di Prospero Balbo e del conte di Perrone, in *Miscellanea di Storia Italiana, edita per cura della Regia Deputazione di Storia Patria*, Tomo XXI, 1883, pp.86-87

71   Report by Colloredo, KA, Alten Feldakten, Krieg in Italien, VII, 1.

72   KA, Alten Feldakten I-VI, Krieg in Italien, 1747: Ständ und Dienst Tabella, 18 June 1747.

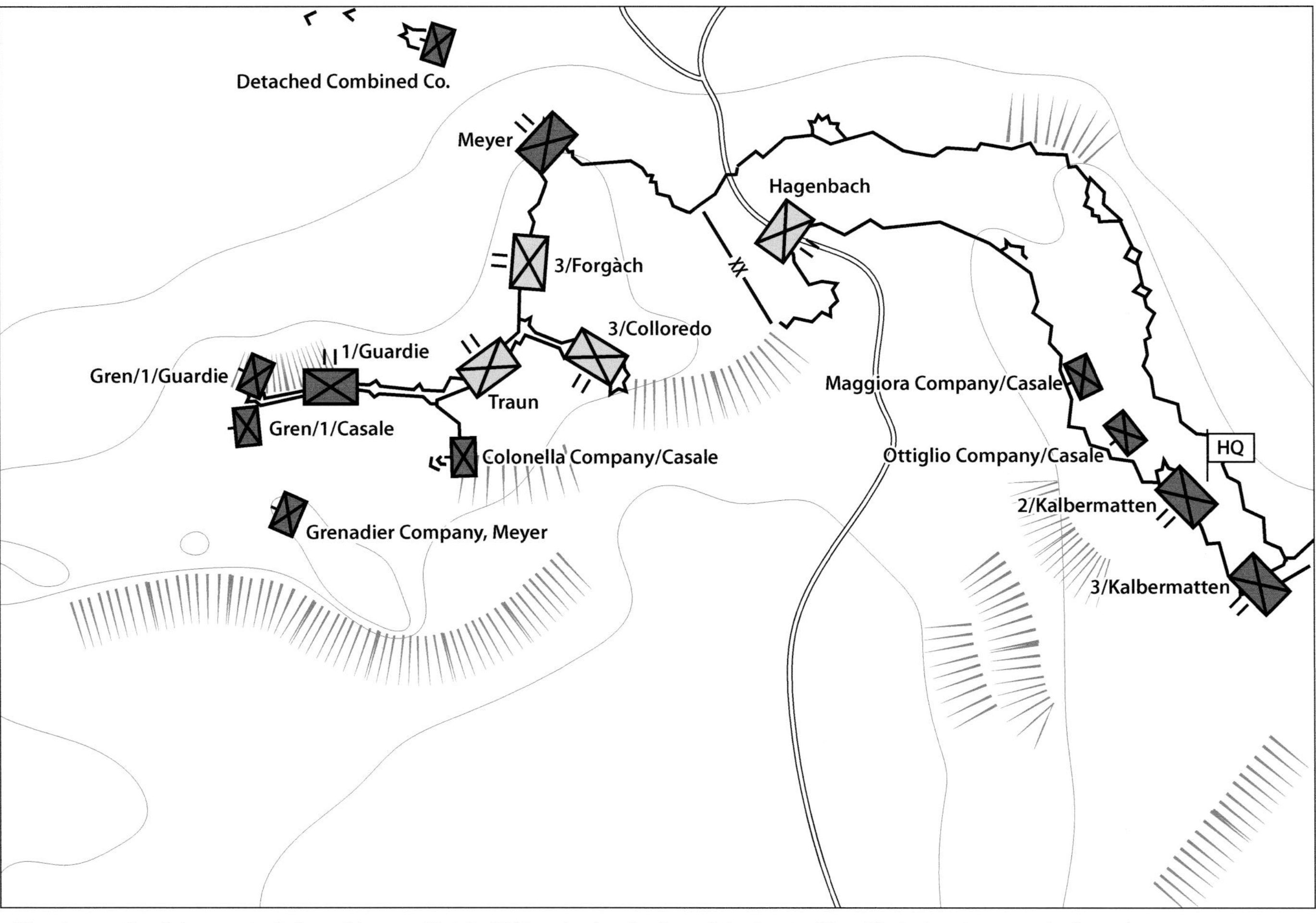

The Austro-Sardinian tactical disposition on 19 July 1747, at the beginning of the battle. The allied planning was dedicated to stop an enemy thrust from the western ridge, and to prevent the conquest of the Gran Serin, the key position of the whole camp. Quite obviously the Austro-Sardinian headquarters was sited here.

almost impassable roads, crossing the high mountains with unprecedented effort, I reached Vallette and even before the day I entered the trenches of the Coll della Sieta'.[73]

Bricherasio, in his command post, continued to receive reports from intelligence: 'Another report on the same day [the 18th] at 10 o'clock in the evening. All the sides of the mountains of Puy, de Bourget, up to Costapiana, and further on to the Blegier pass are covered with troops, marching towards Assietta'.[74] He would try to defend himself as long as possible, after which he would retire.

Reports from the Alps threw the court circles into panic. Despite the years of war, and the crises faced and overcome, Carlo Emanuele III immediately summoned the Minister of War, Bogino. The news that a corps of 50 battalions were preparing to attack the Austro-Sardinian forces present in the area, 14 battalions in all, led them to believe that the breakthrough of the Alpine front was imminent. Without too many ceremonies the king 'sent Count Bogino his first secretary of war to Milan, to Count Brown[e], in order to solicit the march to Piedmont, as soon as possible, of the imperial troops who were still near Genoa, although the siege had been abandoned for more than 15 days'.[75] Expectations were not very promising during the night of 18-19 July.

73   Report by Graf Colloredo, KA, Alten Feldakten, Krieg in Italien, VII, 1.
74   *Relation venenat d'Oulx du 18 juillet 1747*, KA, Alten Feldakten, Krieg in Italien, VII, 16.
75   Minutoli, *Relation des campagnes faites par S.M.*, Vol.V, pp.227-228.

8

19 July 1747. The Day of Battle

During the night of 18-19 July, the weather was not, at least initially, kind. The French noted that during the late afternoon of 18 July 'there was fog and some snow was falling'.[1] The wind, blowing from the south, moved the storm front to the west of the Alps and the sky became completely clear of clouds.[2] By early morning, the storm front had definitely left the Alps and visibility was excellent: from the top of the mountains, the entire valley floor of both the Susa and Chisone valleys could be seen. Temperatures, however, were far from mild.

1:00 a.m. Monte Gran Costa, French columns' link-up area

The rain had stopped, but low clouds moving northwards covered the pasture area below the Gran Costa Mountain with a thick fog. Visibility was greatly reduced and, happy to have gathered two columns there, the Chevalier of Belle-Isle awaited the arrival of Villemur's column. In all, there were 14 battalions with a total of about 8,400 men. He wanted to attack the enemy camp, but he wanted to have all his forces together. The right-hand column occasionally made contact via relays, but communications were sporadic; a fairly typical situation for fighting in mountainous areas.

In the meantime, other deserters had arrived, this time Austrians,[3] a detail that alarmed the French command: 'it was learned from some deserters that several Austrian battalions were arriving from the camp in front of Genoa, followed the next morning by a few others and, according to the report of other deserters who arrived during the night, the following day there would be twenty-eight battalions in the trenches'.[4] The information reported by deserters always had to be evaluated carefully: 'If you rely only on what others have reported, you must be careful not to easily believe people who have only the desire to betray you or to receive some reward. On the contrary, you must question them separately, write down what

---

1   *Relation de l'attaque des retranchements de l'Asiette du 19 Juillet 1747*, SHD, Serie A1, Volume 3240-34.

2   Du Hamel, 'Observations botanico-météorologiques', p.510.

3   The Austrians lost a total of five deserters. Colloredo Report, KA, Alten Feldakten, Krieg in Italien, VII, 1.

4   De Mailly, *Mémoire sur l'attaque*.

they say, compare their testimonies and then judge what may be true or false'.[5] As early as the evening of 18 July, this information was reported to the Chevalier de Belle-Isle; news that only further alarmed the commander about the arrival of large reinforcement forces at the camp.

1:30 a.m. Summit of Monte Gran Costa, Piedmontese militias' combat position

From the start of the attack, the Piedmontese militia fought divided into three distinct groups, of which only two tried to coordinate their actions. At that moment, due to the French advance, the three contingents, the Pragelato contingent under Perrone, the Susa Valley contingent under Tana, and the Waldensian militia under Rouzier had been pushed towards each other and found themselves on the Mottas–Gran Costa line. This amounted to a total force of 1,300 militiamen, who had been monitoring the adversary's activities since the previous evening, which could be distinctly heard at a distance of 6-700 metres. No fires had been lit, so it was not clear how many French had arrived. The most recent reports gave the presence of only one column as certain, the one that had come up the Gran Bosco path. The weather, however, was clearly improving and the first light broke through the fog, revealing to the Piedmontese commanders present on the Gran Costa that the French were massing less than two kilometres from the entrenched camp defences. A relay race set off immediately towards the Assietta Pass.

2:00 a.m. Col dell'Assietta, Bricherasio's tactical command post

The French were half an hour's march from the entrenchments. Bricherasio gave the order to put the camp on alert: the battalions would reach the agreed positions, lined up for battle and ready for combat. Fortunately for the defenders, the link-up between the three enemy columns had not yet taken place, and not a single French battalion appeared on the summit of the Gran Costa or the Mottas. The defenders gained valuable time to reshape their defence plan which, as it had been set up the previous day, would not have withstood an attack in force. Bricherasio now had at his disposal two more Austrian battalions, 3/Colloredo and 3/Forgách, which had arrived at the Assietta camp at that very moment, and another 1,300 men between militiamen and volunteers. He immediately issued his orders:

- The militia forces, except for 100 men of a unit of volunteers under the command of *Luogotenente* Thomasset, of 3/Kalbermatten,[6] would withdraw inside the camp and be distributed as follows: the Waldensian and Pragelato militias, in all about 800 men, would go to reinforce the left flank of the principal communication between the Assietta Redoubt and the Testa dell'Assietta's tenailled redoubt, flanking the Colonnello company of the Reggimento Casale; the Susa Valley militias would provide the links

---

5   Cointe, *Le Science des Postes Militaire*, p.185.

6   AST, Sezioni Riunite, Ministero della Guerra, Ufficio Generale del Soldo, Ruolini, Reggimento Kalbermatten, Vol.58, 1747.

between 3/Kalbermatten and the 1/Monfort and temporarily garrison the Gran Serin redoubt;

- 3/Roi, once reached by the Reggimento Chiablese approaching from Susa to the Argueil camp, would immediately climb to Assietta, take over the militia of the Val di Susa and deploy in the Gran Serin redoubt making contact on its left with 1/Monfort and on its right with 3/Kalbermatten.
- 2/Savoia would immediately leave the Balboutet camp to go to the Colle delle Finestre along the Pian dell'Alpe gap.

With the two new Austrian battalions and the militia units, the balance of power with the enemy had improved slightly; in all, there were 5,486 men in the camp, to which the 708 personnel of 3/Roi were to be added. The defence plan was thus reshaped:

- Outside the entrenched camp, on Monte Gran Costa, 100 volunteers would monitor the enemy's movements.
- The advanced defence, consisting of the Testa dell'Assietta's tenaille, would be defended by the grenadier companies of 1/Guardie and Casale.
- The communication between the Testa and the Assietta redoubts would be manned by 1/Guardie.
- The main line of defence, formed by the three Assietta redoubts, was to be defended from north to south by the regiments of Meyer, Forgách, Traun and Colloredo. To the south, closing off the crest of the Assietta, 800 Waldensian and Pragelato militiamen, under the orders of *Maggiore* Perrone, and the Colonnello company of Casale would be positioned.
- The entrenchment known as the *Grande Comunicazione* (Great Communication) between the Assietta pass and the Gran Serin would be garrisoned and defended by 2/ and 3/Kalbermatten and the Maggiore and Ottiglio companies of Casale.
- The Gran Serin redoubt was allegedly garrisoned by 500 militiamen from the Susa Valley under the orders of the Cavaliere Tana.
- In reserve was the battalion of the Regiment Hagenbach, deployed astride the road up to the Assietta pass from the Val Chisone.

The objectives set by Bricherasio were as follows:

- To resist the enemy attack by supporting the infantry battalions on the entrenched field fortifications. The main attack would probably develop either along the ridge line or against the communication held by the Reggimento Meyer.
- Delay the conquest of the Assietta Pass as long as possible. In the event of a break-through, it was necessary to try to contain the exploitation of the success by the enemy.
- Retreat when necessary to the Gran Serin. Given the force ratios of 1:4 in favour of the enemy, it appeared very likely that the battle would turn into a hard-fought retreat towards the summit of Gran Serin. For this reason, it was necessary to maintain posses-sion of the *Grande Comunicazione* and the passes to the west of the Gran Serin, the Colle delle Vallette and, above all, the Finestre Gap. For this reason, on 19 July Bricherasio preferred to leave three infantry battalions to guard the passes on the crest rather than engage them in combat.

The battalions reached the parapets of the entrenchments, deployed in the places that had been indicated to them, and assumed the combat formation envisaged for each of the two armies: in two ranks for the Sardinian army, in four for the imperial army. Given the particularly cold and wet night, the officers made their men take certain precautions: 'the commander [...] will place the [loaded] weapons on the parapet and you will have the soldiers place their rucksack over the lock of their musket, so that the dirt or mud does not make them unusable, or that the dew of the night does not wet the gunpowder'.[7] Precise instructions were also given as to the firing to be carried out: 'the parapet is to be manned by all available soldiers; and the bayonets are to be fixed to the first and second rank. These will have to shoot only when the enemy is on the rampart'.[8]

The Austro-Sardinian army was ready for battle.

3:30 a.m. Monte Gran Costa, French columns' link-up area

At 3:27 a.m., dawn began to break; the weather was getting better and better, and the surrounding landscape, which only a few hours before had been completely covered by a thick fog, could be seen through wide openings. The sun would rise at around four o'clock in the morning,[9] and it seemed the best time to check the state of the enemy's defences. The Chevalier de Belle-Isle ordered a reconnaissance of the Assietta entrenched camp, for which he commissioned de Mailly; the *maréchal de camp* sent some officers from his staff to check the state of the Assietta defences. Such an operation had to be carefully prepared; light-coloured horses and those with a tendency to neigh were discarded, and watchwords were shared. A whole series of tricks were adopted that only long experience in the field could guarantee:

> [To] carefully examine the places through which you will pass to approach the place to be attacked, sounding out the ground with long sticks, to check that there are no traps or covered pits into which we can fall; you will leave branches of trees with their leaves on the path, to indicate the way at the moment of the attack; you will have to observe exactly where the sentries are positioned, how many there are and whether they are far apart... In the end, we will try to find out how many men are in the garrison's guardhouse, what elements it is overlooking, whether it is being replaced or reinforced, whether it has cannons, etc.[10]

---

7   The quotation is taken from Le Cointe, *Le Science des Postes Militaire*, p.105. This treatise was based on the author's experience during the War of the Austrian Succession; therefore it is likely that these measures were also used by the units present at the Assietta Campaign.

8   The officers ordered their men to open fire at close range, no further than 100 metres. Le Cointe, *Le Science des Postes Militaire*, p.147.

9   On 19 July 1747 it began to get light at 3:27 a.m., while the sun rose at 4:02 a.m. For the exact calculation of the solar and lunar phases, a good number of online sites are now available. For this work the following have been consulted: <http://www.agopax.it/Archaeoastronomy%20Program/Effemeridi_Vsop87_Light/Effemeridi.html>; <http://www.spectralcalc.com/solar_calculator/solar_position.php>, both accessed 1 August 2022.

10   Le Cointe, *Le Science des Postes Militaire*, pp.183-184.

In the course of the reconnaissance, a small sketch of the left flank of the enemy's entrenched camp was drawn up and attached to a first report.[11]

De Mailly also requested the opportunity to attack the heights overlooking the Gran Costa pastures; the enemy light infantry had established themselves on the Gran Costa and the Testa del Mottas, and effectively dominated the link-up area. Belle-Isle, on the other hand, wanted to have all the forces at his disposal concentrated before taking any action. For the moment, however, no action was authorized and the front remained silent.

5:00 a.m. Monte Gran Costa, French columns' link-up area

'At five o'clock in the morning the sky became beautiful again';[12] the sun, which had risen at four in the morning, was illuminating the mountains for the first time in weeks. The Chevalier de Belle-Isle went to consult de Mailly: while waiting for de Villemur's arrival he wanted to check the results of the first reconnaissance and start preparing for the attack planned for the day. After hearing his subordinate's report, the French commander wanted to see the camp and the enemy's positions for himself, and Monte Gran Costa seemed perfect for this purpose. At 2,615 metres above sea level, it had a completely flat summit about 350 metres long with a west-east orientation, from which there was an exceptional view over the entire Colle dell'Assietta and the Val Chisone as far as the Fort of Fenestrelle. This was the ideal place to set up his command post, but *Luogotenente* Thomasset of the volunteers did not share this view, 'and it was not possible to get close because of the continuous fire from the enemies occupying the high ground'.[13] In spite of himself, the Chevalier de Belle-Isle was forced to recognize the error of not having allowed de Mailly to occupy the high ground during the night; the order to attack was authorized at around 6:00 a.m., and in less than an hour both the Gran Costa and the Testa de Mottas were occupied by the French. In fact, as soon as they sighted the grenadier units that were deploying for the assault, the volunteers withdrew to occupy a rocky rise that was in an advanced position to the left of the Testa dell'Assietta.

From the heights of Monte Gran Costa de Mailly saw de Villemur's column approaching Colle Lauson; at 8:00 a.m. the first battalions of the left column set foot on the ridge line. By 11:00 a.m. the entire column would reach the assembly area.

7:00 a.m. Col dell'Assietta, Bricherasio's tactical command post

The general alarm was sounded at 2:00 a.m., and the rolling of drums accompanied the frantic movement of the battalions to the trenches. Five hours had passed, and no enemy attack had appeared. The cold and lack of sleep were tormenting the soldiers; no one appeared on the horizon, and Bricherasio gave orders for the units to retire to their quarters.

---

11   It is possible that the drawing is attached to the *Relation de l'attaque des retranchements de l'Asiette du 19 Juillet 1747*, SHD, Serie A1, Volume 3240-34.

12   *Relation de l'attaque des retranchements de l'Asiette du 19 Juillet 1747*, SHD, Serie A1, Volume 3240-34.

13   De Mailly, *Mémoire sur l'attaque*.

Soldiers began to cook their own breakfast, others tried to get a little sleep. The enemy was near, and everyone was aware that combat was imminent.

9:45 a.m. Monte Gran Costa, Belle-Isle's tactical command post

After de Mailly's men had cleared the heights, the Chevalier de Belle-Isle moved his tactical command to Monte Gran Costa, at an altitude of 2,615 metres. This new observation point was about 1,800 metres from the nearest enemy positions as the crow flies, but at this time the clear morning air – the disturbance that had been plaguing the Western Alps had finally moved eastwards – ensured a complete overview of the Assietta Pass and the enemy positions.

He had managed to concentrate an imposing force, some 16,000 men, close to the enemy forces and at that point he had to start planning the attack on the enemy entrenched camp. He was not alone: with him and his aide-de-camp, *Capitaine* Blondel d'Azincourt, were eight staff officers, specially seconded from the army of the Chevalier's brother, the Duc de Belle-Isle. The full staff consisted of *Maréchaux de Camp* de Larnage and d'Andlau, who were in charge of operations; there were also *Adjudant Maréchaux Général de Logis* de Corsac, de Domgerman and de Landivisiau, who planned the logistical support of the manoeuvre. To these were added the infantry *Adjutants Major* d'Agieu, de Grille and de La Taille, who were in charge of transmitting orders.

These officers would plan the attack together with the Chevalier; unlike modern armies, the commander's staff did not follow a standard procedure for analysing the known elements and drawing up an order of operation, but merely transcribed the commander's orders and suggested, and sometimes moderated, actions, corrections and criticisms from subordinate officers. On 19 July 1747, exactly the same thing happened, with the difference that all the assumptions that had been made about the enemy positions and the forces of the adversaries were dropped, thanks also to the splendid position that Belle-Isle and his staff had chosen to observe the battlefield.

The French commander at this point had to:

- Carefully verify the tactical situation, reconsider his mission and understand what his intent was to fulfil it.
- Analyse the information he had at that time about the terrain, the time available to carry out the attack and the enemy forces.
- Formulate a plan.
- Transmit orders.
- Wait for feedback from its subordinates and evaluate possible variants.

Belle-Isle's intent was to occupy the Assietta plateau, in order to have the heights free from hostile forces to start the siege of the Fort of Exilles, his main mission. Since the position was manned by enemy units, which had also fortified themselves, it had to be occupied by force in order to control it for the continuation of the campaign. At the end of the action, the French units had to be able to use the important road junction represented by the Assietta Pass in order to envelop the Fort of Exilles from the south, in dominion of altitude, and prevent it from being rescued from the lower Susa Valley or from the Finestre Gap.

The field of Assietta seen from the Gran Costa summit. This was the view that the Chevalier de Belle-Isle and his staff had of the enemy camp at 9:45 a.m. on 19 July 1747. The field works observed were already known to French intelligence, while the enemy force was estimated at no less than nine battalions; it was estimated that another 10 battalions would reach the camp the following day. (Author's photo, annotation by George Anderson)

Intelligence was first to shed light on the nature and characteristics of the battlefield, with particular interest in the fortifications the Sardinians had erected in the preceding weeks, and the forces at their disposal for the defence of the entrenched camp. The French began by first assessing the characteristics of the battlefield, taking into account:

- A general assessment of the field
- The approach routes to the enemy positions
- The key and decisive points whose possession would guarantee tactical success
- The analysis of obstacles and field fortifications set up by the enemy.

The focus of the French action was the Assietta Pass, a pass linking the Chisone Valley with the Susa Valley. In reality, the pass, known as Colle dell'Assietta, was a vast plateau – in French *assiette* means flat – where roads reaching the valley floor crossed from north to south and a road ran along the vast summit ridge from west to east. The area was, and still is, completely free of tall vegetation and is characterized by the presence of vast meadows used as pastureland.

Belle-Isle and his staff were able to observe that the Col de l'Assietta could be attacked from at least five different lines of approach:

1. From the north, following the mule track that climbs from the Susa Valley, one could reach the Col directly.
2. From the west, coming from the Testa del Mottas, one passed the Testa dell'Assietta to the north and overtook the 2,555-metre hill that dominated the pass.
3. From the ridge line that led from Testa dell'Assietta (2,566 metres) to the 2,555-metre hill.
4. From the south-west up the mule track from Fenestrelle.
5. From the line of crest that broke away from the summit of Gran Serin and that opened up into a vast meadow area unoccupied by fortifications or adversary troops.

The key and decisive point for dominating the battlefield was the summit of Gran Serin at an altitude of 2,629 metres. As the adversaries themselves had already understood, the control of that peak was decisive because 'this place, dominating in full that of Assietta, all the resistance, which we had made in this last place, became useless, if the first was forced'.[14]

The reconnaissance carried out to identify enemy positions and to verify the state of his field fortifications had so far proved to be either too optimistic or fragmentary and incomplete. In reality, the Sardinians had already been established on the Assietta plateau for some time and their entrenched camp appeared to be a much more substantial obstacle than had been expected. On the morning of 19 July, the Chevalier de Belle-Isle was finally able to have a complete and direct view of the enemy's defensive device, which until then he had only been able to appreciate indirectly through the reports of his subordinates. The French commander now realized that the entrenchments erected by the Sardinians:

---

14   Priocca Report I.

[E]xtended from the heights in the direction of Fenestrelle, where the left of the enemy was leaning, to the river Dora [Riparia] which closed their right, and which ended more or less straight at Exilles. The length could be about five or six leagues [from 22.24 to 26.69 kilometres], taking into account the sinuous nature of the perimeter; and the whole front [of the entrenchment] generally had its centre and left flank placed on a steep escarpment, and was built as a dry stone wall, from five to six feet high, depending on the position. In the extension that [from the main front of the hill reached the Testa dell'Assietta] there were in some places redoubts, some built with dry stone walls, others from fascines, and others were also equipped with battlements and loopholes, and were fifteen to eighteen feet high depending on the front, particularly the one that was the objective of the central column… Finally, the right of the entrenchment, which was to be attacked from our left, presented a receding corner of more than eight hundred tense [1,559.2 metres], the segments of which were covered by an entrenchment formed by a dry wall above a very sloping wall, from which a branch of the entrenchment detached itself, which went straight through the woods until it almost touched the river Dora; this sector of the front was only four feet, built of earth or grass, depending on the soil… This was the state of the trenches, very different from those described by Monsieur d'Arnaud, who believed that they were nothing more than earth and at most three to six feet high.[15]

'These entrenchments were without ditches or palisades and with a parapet that was very easy to climb over, but this was not recognized exactly'.[16] In reality, what the French perceived was the existence not of a 360-degree enclosed entrenched camp, as was the case at Assietta, but a continuous fortified line, quite similar to those they had encountered up until then along the Alps and in the Ligurian theatre of operations.

After taking note of the nature of the battlefield, the only remaining doubts concerned the numerical strength of the opponent. After days of uncertainty and general information that had to be verified, now the enemy battalions were there, perfectly visible, arranged in battle order and lined up side by side. There were not eight battalions lined up in the trenches, as expected, but nine. A tenth, 3/Roi, had been ordered to reach the fortified camp but had not yet moved from the Argueil fortifications.[17] On the contrary, the Chevalier de Belle-Isle and

---

15   De Mailly, *Mémoire sur l'attaque*.
16   Bourcet, *Principes de la Guerre de Montagnes*, p.190.
17   The Chevalier of Belle-Isle was convinced that in the area of operations there were 8 entrenched battalions at Assietta and another 10 attested in Val Chisone, 'of which I have the name of each'. Letter of July 16; Arvers and de Vault, *Guerre de la Succession d'Autriche*, Vol.II, p.731. In reality, the forces present in Valle Chisone and Val di Susa were in all 16 battalions. AST, Corte, Materie Politiche per Rapporto dall'Interno, Storie della Real Casa, Categoria III, Storie Particolari, Mazzo 24, Minutoli, *Relation des campagnes faites par S.M. et par ses generaux avec des corps sèpares pendant les années 1747 et 1748, c'est à dire jusq'a la fin de la guerre*, Atlante, Vol.II. Plate 99, *État des Troupes de S.M. le Roy de Sardaigne destinées en Campagne en 1747*. To these must be added 1/Keller, garrisoning the Fortress of Fenestrelle (Ruolini; Ufficio Generale del Soldo, Ordini Generali Misti, Mazzo 81, *31 Maggio 1747. Nota delle Tappe assegnate per marcia degl'infrascritti Battaglioni, nel Cambiamento delle loro Destinazioni. Giugno 1747*) and the four imperial battalions, which arrived in groups in Piedmont starting from 1 July 1747 (Ordini Generali Misti, Mazzo 81, *31 Maggio 1747. Nota delle Tappe*

his staff were convinced that no less than 10 Sardinian battalions were now a few hours' march from the entrenched camp and about to appear on the battlefield.[18] In reality, the reinforcements immediately available were a total of two battalions, 2/Schulembourg and Reggimento Nice. Initially deployed in southern Piedmont, 'they were transferred from Cuneo to Pinerolo where they arrived on July 22'.[19] Another 10 Sardinian battalions were actually on the march from the moment the siege of Genoa was lifted; on 12 July, these units were camped along the western Ligurian Riviera, near the towns of Borghetto, Alassio and Diano, waiting to move, depending on operational developments, along the coast towards the west or to cross the Apennine chain and enter Piedmont.[20]

Belle-Isle and his staff were optimistic about the outcome of the attack. This was not the first time the French had attacked an entrenched camp defended by Sardinian troops. After the debacle of 1743 in Val Varaita,[21] the French had learned how to attack their opponents' defences effectively. In April 1744, they forced the entrenched camp built to defend the road-stead of Villefranche.[22] In July of the same year, a French column responsible for securing the bulk of the Sardinian troops in Val Varaita had fought for three days in a row, from 17 to 19 July, against overwhelming enemy forces. The commander of the column, the Bailli de Givry, assisted by tactically very aggressive commanders, never gave up the initiative and while the bulk of the army, under the command of the Prince de Conti, broke through the front in the Stura di Demonte valley without encountering too much resistance, the Val Varaita column attacked the Sardinian entrenched camp and irredeemably pierced it in its central sector, forcing the enemy to retreat about 15 kilometres to the east.

The 'King of Sardinia's Patrol', as the Sardinian Army was called, was not considered a formidable opponent on the battlefield; on at least two occasions the French had managed to break through the defences of a Sardinian entrenched camp, at Villefranche and Pietralunga, both battles fought during the 1744 campaign. That the forcing of Sardinian entrenchments was considered by the command of the Chevalier of Belle-Isle as a not particularly difficult task, a judgment based on previous combat experiences, especially in 1744, is also confirmed in the narration of Voltaire: 'They were much more daring with this attack because of the

assegnate per marcia degl'infrascritti Battaglioni, nel Cambiamento delle loro Destinazioni. Giugno 1747).

18   Arvers and de Vault, *Guerre de la Succession* d'Autriche, Vol.II, pp.729, 731, 777.

19   Minutoli, *Relation des campagnes faites par S.M.*, Atlante, Vol.II. Plate 99, *État des Troupes de S.M. le Roy de Sardaigne destinées en Campagne en 1747.*

20   Moris, *Opérations militaires dans les Alpes et les Apennins*, p.272, Minutoli, *Relation des campagnes faites par S.M.*, Vol.V, pp.185-186. The reported approaching units, initially commanded by the Conte della Rocca and from 7 July by *Maggior Generale* de Monfort, were the following: 2/Guardie, 1/Savoia, 1/Monferrato, Vercelli, Pinerolo, 2/Monfort, 1/Schulembourg, 1/ and 2/Roi, 2/Piedmont. Minutoli, *Relation des campagnes faites par S.M.*, Vol II, Plate 99. On 23 July these units were still on their way to Pinerolo when they came to stop and camp in southern Piedmont near Costigliole Saluzzo (CN) and Verzuolo (CN), over 80 kilometres away from the Assietta plateau. They resumed their march towards the Chisone Valley on the 27th. Ordini Generali Misti, Mazzo 81, lettera del Ministro Bogino del 23 e del 27 luglio 1747.

21   On the Battle of Casteldelfino, fought from 7 to 10 October 1743, see P. Chomon Ruiz, 'Battaglie in Val Varaita', in *Armi Antiche. Bollettino dell'Accademia di san Marciano Torino*, 1968, pp.73-112.

22   On the Battle of Villefranche, fought on 20 April 1744, see Giuliano, *La Campagna militare del 1744*, pp.40-56.

memory of the days of Mountalban and Chateaudauphin, which seemed to justify such audacity'.[23] The situation with regard to the imperial troops was different. The Austrian infantry proved to be tenacious opponents with a combat power far superior to that of the Sardinians, as they had demonstrated during the 1746 Campaign and the Battle of Piacenza. The four battalions that had appeared behind the entrenchments of Assietta were, in the eyes of the French command, the most insidious obstacle on the battlefield.

In terms of planning, Belle-Isle decided to concentrate the main effort against the Gran Serin, while two secondary attacks were to be launched simultaneously against the Testa dell'Assietta redoubt and against the left flank of the entrenched field. The enemy forces were not numerous: a large portion of the Austro-Sardinian battalions would have been fixed by the frontal action of the first two columns, while the main attack would have occupied the Gran Serin making any further attack by the adversary useless. To sum up, the concept of operations of the Chevalier of Belle-Isle developed as follows:

- Main attack against enemy positions on the Gran Serin at an altitude of 2,629 metres.
- Secondary attack against the left flank of the enemy entrenchment, along the enemy entrenched front between elevations 2,555 and 2,551, simultaneously with the main attack.
- Secondary attack against the redoubt built at Testa dell'Assietta at an altitude of 2,566 metres.

Given the strength of the field fortifications, the fire support offered by the 4-pounder field artillery became a decisive element at this point. Belle-Isle had already decided to take these cannon with him for the attack on the Assietta. Now, having seen for himself how imposing the Sardinians' entrenchments were, he decided that he could not do without the six 4-pounder pieces. The seven pieces of the smaller mountain version, also of four-pound calibre, would certainly have arrived on the battlefield and increased the firepower of the infantry battalions, but now the heavier pieces were needed to open wide breaches in the massive dry walls of the entrenched camp. Orders designed to speed up the march of the guns were sent out and the Chevalier began to await with increasing impatience the arrival of what he believed to be the decisive weapon.

Overall, this was the general outline of the Chevalier of Belle-Isle's plan to conquer the Assietta entrenched camp.

---

23   Voltaire, *Le siècle de Louis XV*, p.192.

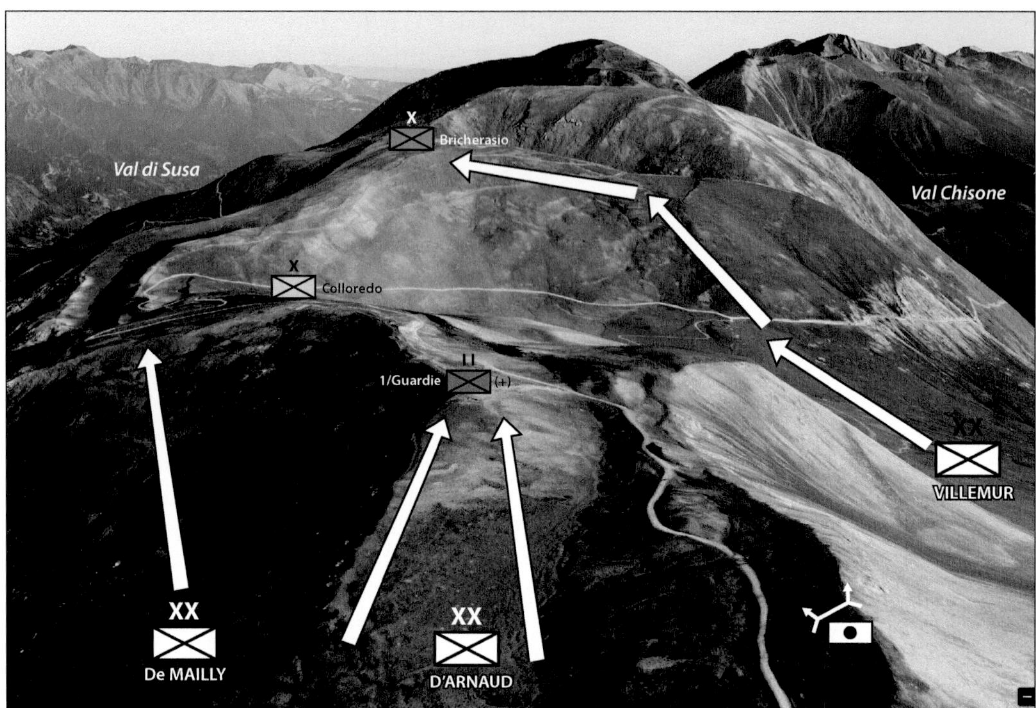

General view of the three attacks planned by the French on the morning of 19 July 1747 with the progression of their columns seen from the west. In the foreground on the right the battery of 4-pounder mountain guns was deployed in support of Arnaud's column. (Author's photo, annotation by George Anderson)

Table 11: Synchronization Matrix of the French Plan Against the Austro-Sardinian Entrenched Camp at the Colle dell'Assietta

Time	c.11:00 a.m.	c. 4:00 p.m.	Exploitation	End State
Artillery	Marching from Oulx to the Testa del Mottas.	Battery deployed at Hill 2,563 opens fire against the Testa dell'Assietta and the communication behind it.	Fire against retreating or moving enemy units along the great communication between the Assietta Pass and the Gran Serin. Mountain artillery follows the progress of Arnaud's column.	Suspension of artillery fire.
Mailly's Column	Deployed on the start line for the attack.	Attack on the left flank positions.	Opening of a breach in the trenches and advance towards the Assietta Pass.	Link-up of forces on the Assietta Pass.
Arnaud's Column	Deployed on the start line for the attack.	Attack on the Testa dell'Assietta.	Opening of a breach in the trenches and advance towards the Assietta Pass.	
Villemur's Column	Marching towards the start line for the attack on the Gran Serin.	Attack on Gran Serin.	Conquest of the Ridotte del Gran Serin and descent towards the Colle dell'Assietta.	

Logistics support	Movement of artillery ammunition to Hill 2,563.	At the end of the attack columns.	Support and supply of ammunition to units engaged in combat.	Casualty collection.

Sources: Mailly, *Mémoire sur l'attaque des retranchements de l'Assiette*, in Arvers and de Vault, *Guerre de la Succession* d'Autriche, Vol.II, pp.742-752; Bourcet, *Principes de la Guerre de Montagnes*, pp.284-292.

Once the planning phase was completed, the actual orders were issued. In this case, no actual written order of operations was drawn up, but we can try to reconstruct it, thanks to the memoirs of *Maréchal de Camp* de Mailly.

The manoeuvre scheme that the staff of the Chevalier de Belle-Isle drew up consisted of three distinct columns of attack, referred to as the left column (Mailly), the central column (d'Arnaud) and the right column (Villemur). The orders that were given to the commanders were as follows[24]:

- 'The right-hand column, under the orders of Messrs de Villemur and de Larnage, was ordered to move to the left of the entrenchments [placed] at Fenestrelle, with the order to mask [the main attack towards the summit of Gran Serin] on its right flank, the approaches coming up from Fenestrelle.'
- 'The centre column, commanded by Monsieur Chevalier de Belle-Isle, with the *Maréchaux de Camp* Messrs d'Arnaud, de Monteynard and d'Andlau under his command, was to form the centre attack and move to the redoubt [defending the Testa dell'Assietta].'
- 'The left column, commanded by Monsieur de Mailly, was to enter and advance in the receding corner and attack the deepest point of the entrenchments': that is, to strike the communication between the Testa dell'Assietta and the main line of defence at its base.

Once his concept of operations had been expressed, the Chevalier of Belle-Isle waited for feedback from his senior officers. Most of them had no doubt: the attack would result in a decisive victory. 'Monsieur d'Arnaud had assured the success of his central column and was so sure that he immediately ordered the mountain artillery to march towards the redoubt [of the Testa dell'Assietta]'. The commander of the central column was so sure that he would be able to break through the enemy defences that he had already, in the planning stage, ordered the battery of 4-pounders to follow his units as soon as the clearing of the sector under siege was completed. *Lieutenant Général* de Villemur was also optimistic. Already on 17 July, when questioned by courier by his commanding officer, he had replied, 'since you order me to inform you of my opinions, I can only say that I am convinced that the enemy, seeing themselves outflanked from left and right, will leave nothing but places in the trenches, which will not be difficult to conquer, marching as quickly as you are doing'.[25]

Less sure of an easy victory was *Maréchal de Camp* de Mailly. The Chevalier de Belle-Isle had instructed him to attack the left flank of the entrenched communication between the Col and the Testa dell'Assietta. It was now clear that the sector in question was partly

---

24   De Mailly, *Mémoire sur l'attaque*.
25   BRT, Manoscritto Militare 73; Letter de Villemur to the Chevalier of Belle-Isle of 17 July.

garrisoned by Sardinian troops and partly by imperial troops. In addition, the sector he was to attack formed a recessed right angle, where the fire of two opposing battalions would hit the same engagement area. It was now clear to him that the plan drawn up by the commander could not work and he went to the command post of the Chevalier de Belle-Isle: in a direct confrontation de Mailly said that the decision to attack the receding corner was madness and that his column 'would be annihilated before it even reached the base of the entrenchment'. He therefore proposed two things:

- That the attack assigned to him was to be regarded as a feigned attack intended to pin at least four enemy units to his own lines at that time.
- That the real attack on the left should not involve the great communication, but rather the entrenchments that descended towards the Susa Valley; that is, towards the Rio Bacon entrenchments.

De Mailly pointed out that he himself had carried out reconnaissance in that sector of the front and that he expected satisfactory results from an attack conducted as he proposed. The Chevalier de Belle-Isle, in spite of the advice and protests of the commander of the left column, was adamant; he could, if he thought it necessary, detach forces to take the entrenchments that descended along the Susa Valley, but the main attack had to be along the great entrenched communication, and specifically against the re-entrant identified by de Mailly.

De Mailly took the commander's negative response and returned to the head of his column, where he began issuing orders and making the necessary arrangements for the forthcoming attack.

10:45 a.m. Mount Mottas, French forces' link-up area

The plateau at an altitude of 2,522 metres just west of the Testa del Mottas was at that time very busy. The battalions of the various columns were moving to their respective bases for the attack and the commanders of the attacking columns met to discuss among themselves which tactical set-up would be the best to approach and breach the enemy entrenched camp.[26] The three generals had received their orders and now had to plan the attack, and they all agreed that an attack *à la Folard* was the best solution to force the Austro-Sardinian defences, each with some variations determined by the characteristics of the front they had to attack.[27] They all agreed on one thing:

---

26 We do not have a document that tells of the existence of this meeting, but that this actually took place we can deduce from de Mailly's report, which describes the tactical structure adopted by the individual columns. De Mailly, *Mémoire sur l'attaque.*

27 The choice to attack *à la Folard* is also confirmed by the story that two deserters of Villemur's column, one of the Régiment de Périgord and one of the Régiment de Mailly, made to the Intendant Baldoino of Santa Margherita al Forte di Fenestrelle, an *ante litteram* officer of Sardinian military intelligence and in charge of collecting information on the movements and composition of the enemy forces: '[they] were ordered to advance with bayonets on the musket without firing'. AST, Corte, Materie Militari, Imprese, Mazzo 7 da inventariare.

[I]t will be necessary... to provide the first two ranks of each column with shovels and picks, and to have the soldiers carry their muskets in bandoliers. When all preparations are completed, and as soon as the commanders see or hear the signal [of attack], all these columns will stand at attention and on command march forward quickly... The first two ranks, [having arrived at the base of the entrenchment] will immediately begin to demolish the corners and parapet of the Redoubt, to facilitate the climb for the rest of the troops. The commanders of each column will take care that the soldiers armed with muskets who have arrived in the vicinity do not remain there as obstacles but, on the contrary, will protect those who are intent on demolishing the escarpment of the redoubt, firing left and right and always remaining ready to repel any enemies who may arrive. As soon as the parapet has been demolished, pierced, torn to shreds by axe blows, and opened so that it is possible to pass through, and when the breach is completed, the pioneers will abandon their tools and, taking their weapons which they have carried in their bandoliers, they will mount the bayonet assault together and hurl themselves at the enemy shouting, *tué, tué* [kill! kill!]. The commanding officer must always be ready to order the attack of the communication through which the enemy can reach other equally important places, in order to be able to completely interrupt this communication: the people who see themselves attacked with force, and who have no hope of being able to retreat or obtain help, will soon demand the surrender of those who attack them.[28]

After this exchange of views, the commanders saluted each other and reached their respective columns. It was now 11:00 a.m. and at least for de Mailly's and d'Arnaud's forces it was necessary to come up against some advanced forces of the adversaries.

Around 11:00 am from the link-up area the French columns began to move towards their respective lines of departure for the attack on the entrenched camp. The Austro-Sardinian forces in the entrenched camp, now definitely on the alert and formed up in the line of battle, could observe that 'around eleven o'clock a large number of troops descended from the [Gran Costa]'.[29]

De Mailly's column, moving to the left of the ridge that rises up to the Testa dell'Assietta, came to a halt on the vast pastures to the north of the main watershed ridge, without crossing the 2,563 level on its right. At this time, it was not yet clear whether the enemy had any artillery pieces, and it was necessary to begin deploying their forces at a relatively safe distance.

D'Arnaud's forces were also tasked with securing the rocky ridge at Height 2,563, on which the 4-pounder batteries were to be placed. From the tactical perspective of the Chevalier de Belle-Isle, the ridge in question seemed to guarantee an immediate approach to the enemy camp. In reality, there was a wide valley, 380 metres wide, from which rose the crest of the Testa dell'Assietta, the tactical objective of d'Arnaud's column. In order to take up a position in complete safety, it was necessary to seize Height 2,563, an operation for which *Maréchal de Camp* d'Arnaud promptly issued the necessary orders. Four companies

---

28   Le Cointe, *Le Science des Postes Militaire*, pp.193-195. according to the *Ordonance du Roy* of 19 January, 1747, each company of grenadiers had 10 men equipped with a large axe, while the fusiliers companies had at least 10 digging tools.

29   Priocca Report I.

of grenadiers attacked the position, attempting to circumvent the summit from the north.[30] The attack, carried out with two lines of penetration, forced the defenders, the 100 volunteers of Thomasset, to retreat rather quickly. The actual fighting was rather brief; the Sardinians fired a few shots at the French column that was bypassing their position, killed or wounded four soldiers, and disengaged almost immediately. In fact, Thomasset, having recognized the risk of being outflanked and cut off from the entrenched camp, hastily retreated eastwards, risking moving along a ridge perpendicular to the communication with the Testa dell'Assietta, at an altitude of 2,500 metres. At least one of the volunteers remained behind and was captured by the enemy.[31]

By 11:30 a.m. the French had mastered the high ground; in the course of the brief action they realized that the enemy had no artillery. The manoeuvre of the grenadiers had exposed their left flank to the enemy entrenchments, but not a single cannon shot had been fired, although they were well within range of a medium-calibre field artillery. The Austro-Sardinians had the opportunity to hit the enemy column in the flank, but 'we had no artillery',[32] and the enemy was able to 'understand from the silence of our artillery that we had none, and they did everything at their leisure'.[33] That is, once it was clear that no one was going to fire a single cannon shot, the French began to distribute supplies to their troops. By this time, the staff of the Chevalier de Belle-Isle had left the command post on Monte Gran Costa to take up position on Hill 2,563. From this position he would be able to observe and manage the action of the three attacking columns simultaneously. Once on the summit, the Chevalier and all his staff had 'a very good lunch'.[34]

---

30   Barthélémy Augustin Blondel d'Azincourt, *Du champ de bataille vis-à-vis des retranchements d'Exilles, le 19 juillet 1747 à minuit*, in *Mémoires du duc de Luynes sur la cour de Louis XV (1735-1758), publiés sous le patronage de M. de duc de Luynes par MM. L. Dussieux et E. Soulié. Tome 8 – 1746-1748* (Paris: Firmon Didot Frères, Fils et Cie., 1860-1865), p.411. The writer of the letter, *Capitaine* Blondel d'Azincourt, was an officer of the Régiment de Normandie and in 1747 aide-de-camp to the Chevalier of Belle-Isle. In 1745 he had earned the Chevalier's Cross of St Louis for his fighting action in Ghent, when at the head of 40 men he had captured 288 enemies; see Susane, *Histoire de l'Infanterie Française*, Vol.II, p.440. For a brief military biography – Blondel d'Azincourt was also a friend and correspondent of Rousseau – see A. Mazas, *Histoire de l'Ordre Royal et Militaire de Saint-Louis* (Paris: Firmin Didot Frères, Fils et Cie., E Dentu, 1851) Vol.III, pp.537-538. The original letter addressed to his father, the famous art collector Augustin Blondel de Gagny, is kept at SHD, A1, Vol.3240, pièce 33. According to another report, *Relation de l'attaque des retranchements de l'Asiette du 19 juillet 1747*, SHD, A1, Vol.3240, pièce 34, only two companies were employed.

31   *Relation de l'attaque des retranchements de l'Asiette du 19 juillet 1747*, SHD, A1, Vol.3240, pièce 34. It is no coincidence that one of the three Sardinian soldiers taken prisoner, *Caporale* Martin Beckisch, a Saxon from Transylvania, belonged to the Maggiora company, the same as Thomasset. This fight was probably the occasion that led to the capture of Beckisch. AST, Sezioni Riunite, Ministero della Guerra, Ufficio Generale del Soldo, Vol.58, 1747. Other regular soldiers certainly came from the Reggimento Casale, as specified in the *Stato de Battaglioni trovatisi presenti agli attacchi ed interventi alla difesa de Trinceramenti dell'Assietta li 19 scorso Luglio*, AST, Sezioni Riunite, Ministero della Guerra, Ufficio Generale del Soldo, Ordini Generali e Misti, 1747, Mazzo 48. On the same occasion, Carlo Giuseppe Graziano, of Verrua, and Antonio Francesco Mossi, of Grazzano, both of the Colonnello company were taken prisoner.

32   Priocca Report I.

33   Priocca Report I.

34   Blondel d'Azincourt, *Du champ de bataille vis-à-vis des retranchements d'Exilles*, p.411.

12:00 Noon. Start line for de Mailly's and d'Arnaud's columns

Just below the crest of the ridge that led to the Testa dell'Assietta, d'Arnaud began to make the necessary arrangements for the attack, deploying in divisions that would attack the enemy positions.

The terrain magnificently supported the attack manoeuvre: at the base of the ridge there is a vast plateau, about one kilometre long and 500 metres wide, on which it was possible to organize the battalions according to the most congenial set-up for the approach to the adversary's fortifications. The ridge leading to the redoubt of Testa dell'Assietta is about 300 metres long as the crow flies, with a drop of 50 metres. A good 180 metres of this route is completely deflected by the slope of the terrain, which here has a gradient of 23.5 percent. The remaining 120 metres have a gradient that drops to 7.8 percent, which allowed the defenders to have visual contact with the opposing units already within their own engagement area. The reaction time for the Austro-Sardinian troops after the French emerged from the dead ground would therefore have been minimal.

According to de Mailly, d'Arnaud's attack group 'was simply deployed in columns'.[35] The French general, who would have had artillery support, decided to deploy his column with a classic attack front of two battalions. Each battalion presented a column front of 16 men lined up; that is, two companies side by side in a massive formation of five ranks each. Altogether in this sector the French deployed eight battalions – a total of 3,460 men – all part of the Brigade d'Artois, staggered as follows:

- First line: one battalion of converged infantry picquets, one battalion of converged grenadiers.
- Second line: 2/Régiment d'Artois; 1/Régiment d'Artois.
- Third line: one battalion Régiment d'Auxerrois; one battalion Régiment d'Aunis.
- Fourth line: one battalion Régiment Santerre.

Taking advantage of the ridge rising to the Testa dell'Assietta, the column would be divided into two parts, one right and one left, both about 20 metres wide and 430 metres long. Both columns, headed by two selected infantry and grenadier units, were to advance towards the trenches without opening fire, force them, and continue the advance inside the entrenched camp. D'Arnaud did not think it necessary to detach units on the flanks of the columns to support the advance with their fire. Four-pounder field pieces would provide the necessary firepower. Finally, at the rear of the column followed the columns of mules carrying seven mountain pieces.

De Mailly was to attack the best fortified sector of the perimeter of the entrenched camp. The ridge that comes off to the north from Hill 2,555, roughly at the point where communication with Testa dell'Assietta begins, had been identified as the line of maximum resistance by *Capitano* Vedani who had planned these defences. Basically, it was an entrenched redan line dominating from an altitude of 250 metres above the ground that the French would use to approach. Before arriving at the entrenchments and engaging in close quarters

---

35   De Mailly, *Mémoire sur l'attaque.*

combat with the enemy, the French would have had to face an ascent with a gradient of 36 percent, a third of which would have been under fire from the defenders. Furthermore, de Mailly seemed to want to attach too much importance to the small enemy advance works built on the left – the Riobacon Ruins redoubts – while he was completely pessimistic about his men's ability to force the entrenchment. He would not have had artillery fire at his disposal, so he was forced to deploy his attacking column with special precautions. The brigades under his command, Bourbonnais and La Reine, totalling some 5,142 men, were arranged as follows:

- Vanguard: one battalion of converged grenadiers – at the rear of this battalion there was a company of pioneers,[36] which, having reached the entrenchments, would begin to demolish the enemy field works; one battalion of 12 converged picquets – in the front line but shifted to the left, destined to attack the Riobacon Ruins redoubts
- First line, Brigade Bourbonnais: 1/Régiment Bourbonnais.
- Second line, Brigade Bourbonnais: 3/Régiment Bourbonnais; 2/Régiment Bourbonnais; on each side of this column two companies – 'half picquets' – were deployed in line to provide the necessary fire support in case of need.
- Third line, Brigade Bourbonnais: one battalion Régiment Soissonais; one battalion Régiment Des Landes.
- Fourth line, Brigade La Reine. 2/Régiment La Reine; 1/Régiment La Reine. On each side of the column two companies were deployed in line for necessary fire support.
- Fifth line: Brigade La Reine: one battalion Régiment Guise; one battalion Régiment Béarn.
- Rearguard: detachment Dragons du Roi. These closed the column with the task of catching any deserters who were fleeing after abandoning their position, or preventing straggling soldiers from stopping along the way.[37]

De Mailly would attack the enemy *à la Folard*, but unlike the centre column he would not have the support of field artillery firepower. He would have tried to give a minimum of infantry support by keeping four companies lined up on either side of his main column.

The final deployment saw each of the two brigades occupy a rectangular area on the ground with a 60-metre front and a length of 205 metres. The two leading battalions had a 20-metre front and a depth of 205 metres. In total, therefore, de Mailly's column stretched across the battlefield for a length of approximately 650 metres.

---

36   This company of 'pioneers' was none other than a part of soldiers equipped with axes and hollow tools, 10 per company, present in the vanguard battalion; see Belhomme, *Histoire de l'Infanterie en France*, Vol.II, p.169; *Ordonnance du Roy, portant règlement pour l'habillemente de l'Infanterie françoise. Du 19 Janvier 1747.*

37   Arvers and de Vault, *Guerre de la Succession d'Autriche*, Vol.II, p.733.

12:00 Noon. Assembly area for de Villemur's column

From the assembly area near the Testa del Mottas, *Lieutenant Général* de Villemur still had a long way to go. He had to cover about five kilometres before he could attack the enemy entrenchments on the Gran Serin, bypassing the entire Assietta range from the south. To do this he had to first reach the Alpe Assietta facilities and from there organize the ascent along the south-west ridge of Gran Serin. The first part of the march, a distance of about 3,200 metres, was the easiest, all slightly downhill with a negative height difference of 300 metres. The main problem lay in the presence of the enemy, who from the southern outlet of the Assietta Pass could have attacked the flank or the head of his column, which was 7,342 strong and the most numerous of those destined to attack the Assietta camp. Therefore precautions had to be taken.

Each battalion was to march in four ranks, thus ready to face any possible threat, which at that moment would most probably take the form of an attack on the left flank of the marching column. The three brigades under the command of de Villemur moved out no earlier than 11:30 a.m. The composition of the column was as follows: Brigade Mailly, Brigade Royal Roussillon and finally Brigade Condé.

The column began to wind its way towards the southern slopes of the mountain in an easterly direction. Given the formation in four ranks, the French units stretched one after the other for a length of about 3,150 metres towards a flat area at the base of the Colle dell'Assietta, today known as Alpe dell'Assietta. The route, all downhill, did not present any particular risks, but, as mentioned, the march was in fact in front of enemy positions and advance patrols were certainly sent out to spot enemy units that could come either from the Assietta camp or from the Fenestrelle stronghold. With the necessary precautions the journey times were rather long, despite the relative proximity of the area to be occupied. The head of the column reached the plateau at the base of the Gran Serin at around 12:30 p.m., and here it took at least an hour and a quarter for all the troops to regroup. Immediately some units – at company level – were sent along the western slopes of the Gran Serin to reconnoitre the route up to the summit ridge. De Villemur waited until 1:40 p.m. for the column to march out, and finally had all his brigade and regimental commanders close to him.

According to orders, de Villemur was to conquer the summit of the Gran Serin. The location of his improvised command post meant that he had no view of the adversary's positions and the field fortifications that he had to force. With difficulty, he could see the entrenchments that closed the Assietta pass just above him. He quickly made decisions, disbanded the brigades he had and reorganized them into three different attack columns:[38]

---

38   The attack scheme of Villemur's column is reconstructed keeping in mind mainly the report by de Mailly and the *Carte Topographique en mesure d'une partie des Vallès d'Oulx et Pragelas, avec le Rétranchèmens de L'Assiette, les Campemens et mouvemens des François et les postes qu'ils attaquerent le 19 Juillet 1747*, AST, Corte, Carte Topografiche e Disegni, Carte Topografiche per A e B, Pragelato 1. Another important element is the seniority of the regiment and the percentage of losses sustained in combat. Susane, *Histoire de l'Infanterie Française*; SHD A1: 3227, 198, 199; 3240: 35, 36.

- Column 1, under de Larnage. This column was to be the force in charge of making the main breakthrough on the Gran Serin and, immediately, opening the way for the Villemur column. At the head of the column were two composite battalions, composed of an amalgamation of companies, 13 in all, from battalions at de Villemur's disposal and six companies detached from the Grenadiers Royaux du Modène. Two other battalions followed, 1/ and 2/Condé.
- Column 2, under de Villemur in person. This was the main nucleus of the forces that would attack the Gran Serin. It was composed of 1/, 2/, and 3/Mailly; 1/Boulonnais; 1/ Royal Roussillon, Guyenne, Périgord, and Saintonge.
- Column 3, under de Laval. This column, the smallest of the three, was made up of the units that were most tired from the approach march and would have had a simple covering role. It was composed of one battalion each from the regiments Agenois, Beaujolais, and Beauce.

De Laval's column would climb the road leading up to the Assietta Pass, in order to secure the largest number of enemy troops along the defences of the communication route from the Gran Serin down to the Pass. The other two columns, made up of the less tired troops and those who seemed to exhibit a greater fighting spirit, would climb to the Gran Serin. In addition, by leaving the third column stationary at the Grange dell'Assietta, the French commander guaranteed that his back was covered against an eventual Austro-Sardinian attack that could come either from Assietta or from the bottom of the valley.

After receiving the first reports from the reconnaissance party and making the final arrangements necessary for the perfect execution of the manoeuvre, the march towards the summit resumed. By then it was 2.30 p.m.

12:30 p.m. Testa dell'Assietta Redoubt

Since 10:00 a.m. the Austro-Piedmontese had been watching the French troops' progress and a full-scale assault on the entrenched camp was now certain. Once again, the drums sounded the alarm and battalions lined up for battle along the entrenchments. Bricherasio abandoned his tactical command on the summit of the Gran Serin and went to observe the manoeuvres of the French along the western edge of the camp, probably also reaching the advanced tenaille on the Testa dell'Assietta. He summoned the three generals present, Alciati, Colloredo, and Martinengo, along with the battalion commanders to analyse the situation together. The dominance of altitude with respect to the starting line of the French attack made it immediately clear that the adversary had no less than 29 infantry battalions at his disposal, not counting artillery and special units.[39] Bricherasio confirmed the tactical planning of the morning, which included the following objectives:

---

39   In reality, the French forces were initially estimated to be between 50 and 48 battalions, as reported in Minutoli, *Relation des campagnes faites par S.M.*, Vol.V, pp.221-234; and in the very first report presented by Cavalier Panissera to the king on the morning of 20 July; BRT, Manoscritto Militare 154. Subsequently the opposing units were valued at 40, a figure that was also accepted by Carlo Emanuele III. *Relazioni della vittoria riportata sui francesi dalle Truppe di S.M., ed Imperiali sotto il comando del*

- Resist the enemy attack by supporting infantry battalions at the entrenched camp fortifications.
- Delay the conquest of the Assietta Pass as long as possible.
- Retreat when necessary to the Gran Serin.

The movements of Villemur's column made it clear that the main target of the enemy maneuver was the Gran Serin, but the proximity of a large enemy force to the Testa dell'Assietta and the Col itself meant that no other forces could be immediately detached. Moreover, the column heading for the Gran Serin would take several hours to reach the starting point of the attack. Bricherasio sent relays to solicit the departure of another battalion, 3/Roi, stationed at the field fortifications of the Alpe dell'Argueil, with which he would reinforce the defences. It was now necessary to remain in position and await the enemy's moves, defending the Gran Serin at all costs, 'on the preservation of which all the King's troops depended, and our only [route of] retreat'.[40]

> There is no doubt that the Serrant post is the most delicate of all those that form the defensive line of the Assietta pass. Not enough precautions will ever be taken to protect it from being forced; since such an event could have the most disastrous consequences, since the square of Exilles would be absolutely uncovered on that side, communication with Susa via the Argueil road would be lost, as would that of Fenestrelle; I cannot believe that the victorious enemies would give us the time to escape from the communication route called "delle Ruine", which leads to Exilles and is the only road that can be taken in this sad circumstance.[41]

However, no one was confident about the outcome of the battle. Bricherasio himself, before abandoning the western edge of the field and returning to his command post on the Gran Serin, ordered that 'all the flags of the battalions be sent to the Vallette pass with an escort'.[42] It was better to remove the standards from the battlefield before they were sure to fall into enemy hands. At that point it was immediately clear to everyone, from the senior officers to the last infantryman, how dangerous the situation was.

After the commander had left, the officers began to exchange their impressions of what was about to happen, and the air at *Maggior Generale* Alciati's command post immediately became very tense. *Luogotenente Colonnello* Priocca tells us that he and the other

---

conte di Bricherasio al Colle dell'Assietta presso Exilles. Con copia di lettere dei generali francesi relative ai feriti, AST, Corte, Materie Militari, Imprese, Mazzo 8 addizione.

40 Priocca Report I.

41 *Osservazioni sulla difesa delle valli Stura, Mayra, Varaita, di San Martino, di Pragelato, & di Exilles*, in AST, Carte Topografiche e Disegni, Carte Topografiche Segrete, 7 FII rosso.

42 The episode of the flags removed from the battlefield is confirmed in BRT, Manoscritto Militare n. 5, *Relation des campagne faites au service de S.M.* Some of the Sardinian battalions were in fact devoid of flags. For example, in the course of a review carried out on 4 June 1747, it was recorded of 2/Kalbermatten that 'about the flags there is only the pole'. 3/Roi was in the same situation, whose flags 'are completely destroyed'. AST, Sezioni Riunite, Ufficio Generale del Soldo, Ordini Generali e misti, 1747, Mazzo 48; *Determinazioni di S.M. Relazione della Rivista d'Ispezione datasi alle infrascritte truppe in Aprile, e Maggio 1747.*

officers present spent at least four hours 'playing war with telescopes and regretting the field cannons, mountain artillery and carbines that we lacked to prevent the enemy from standing in front of us with such a threatening attitude'.[43] However, unlike the previous day, they were no longer in any doubt as to where the French intended to attack and planned their defence in detail. Alciati, who was responsible for the defence of the western sector of the camp, began to discuss with Martinengo and Colloredo how to deal with the central column, which appeared to be the closest to the battlefield. The tenaille's front alone did not seem large enough to deploy a sufficient number of guns to stop the enemy's advance. The rocky ridge on the left could accommodate a sufficiently large number of men, at least one reinforced company, to hit the flank and the rear of the enemy units launched to assault the Testa dell'Assietta. Moreover, no one on the enemy side had yet occupied that position. When the time came, he would send an elite company to occupy the high ground.

It was midday. In the meantime, those who had the cannon were deciding to use them for real.

12:30 p.m. Height 2,563, Belle-Isle Tactical Command Post

The Chevalier de Belle-Isle had lost patience. From his forward command post at Height 2,563 he could observe and manage the action of the three attacking columns simultaneously. In addition, he had an excellent view of the Sardinian entrenchment line, which appeared at close range to be much stronger than he and his staff had anticipated. Indeed, he had expected a similar situation, and had already ordered on 17 July that the field artillery at his disposal, a total of six 4-pounder pieces, be attached to Arnaud's column[44]. By now it was clear that the ridges had been fortified and these cannon were for the Chevalier 'decisive against palisaded entrenchments',[45] so he had personally followed their movements and the choice of roads to take.[46] Placed at the rear of the columns, so as not to penalize the movements of the infantry units, the heavy artillery had suffered the delays in the marching column that now afflicted all French marching columns. Thus, on 17 July, it was not until 2:00 p.m. that the guns finally reached Sauze d'Oulx, slowly continuing their ascent towards the Assietta ridge. Still on the 18th, the Chevalier had transmitted his order of operations to Count de Mailly, informing him that 'the two brigades [Bourbonnais and La Reine] will be followed by the 6 pieces of cannon whose ammunition will be carried by mules; there will be no stopping during the march to wait for the artillery'.[47]

Yet at that moment, around 12.30 p.m., while three of the two columns were already lined up on the starting line and the third was on its way, the guns were not there. For the French, the day of 18 July had been plagued by delays, mishaps and bad weather, the tail end of the disturbance that had been affecting the western Alps for the past few days. The fog that shrouded the sides of the mountains, which at times seemed about to open up, had instead turned into

---

43   Priocca Report I.
44   Arvers and de Vault, *Guerre de la Succession d'Autriche*, Vol.II, p.724.
45   Arvers and de Vault, *Guerre de la Succession d'Autriche*, Vol.II, p.731.
46   Arvers and de Vault, *Guerre de la Succession d'Autriche*, Vol.II, pp.730-731.
47   Arvers and de Vault, *Guerre de la Succession d'Autriche*, Vol.II, p.742.

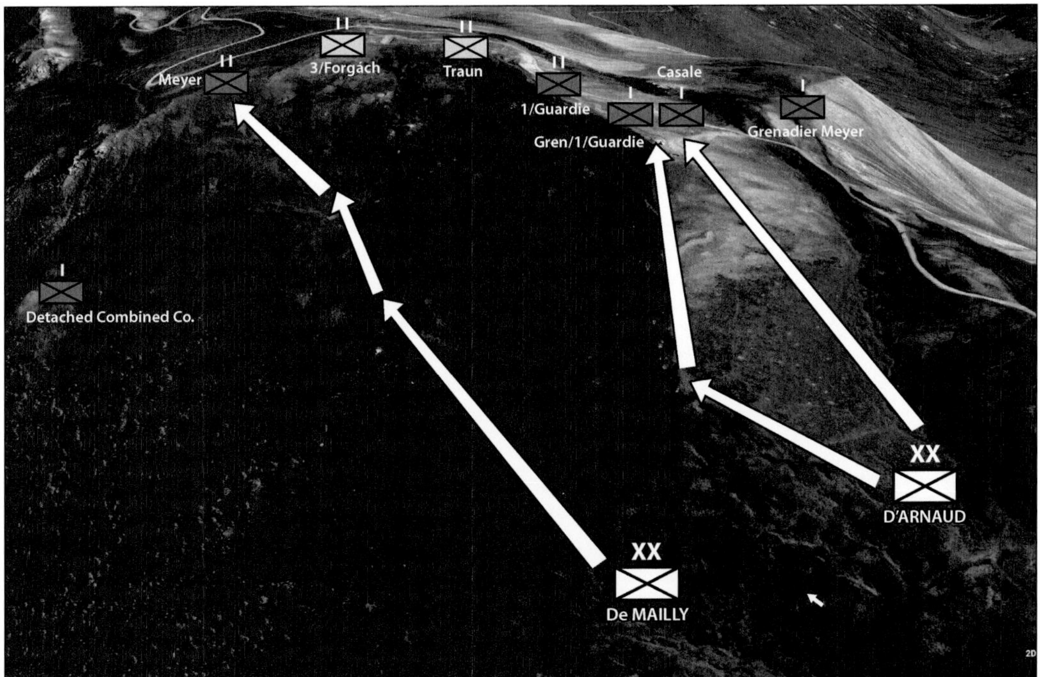

The progression of de Mailly and d'Arnaud's columns in the course of the battle. This illustration highlights the tactical choice of *Maggior Generale* Alciati to place a line of selected infantry companies in front of the main line of defence. This deployment worked very well along the southern flank on the Val Chisone side, but almost cost the Reggimento Meyer's mixed elite company. (Author's photo, annotation by George Anderson)

heavy rain, interspersed with sleet. The Chevalier described to his brother the meteorological conditions of the day in these terms: 'the fog descended, and the weather degenerated into rain, snow and very abundant ice, to the point that visibility reduced to no more than 20 paces in front of us'.[48] In addition, it was necessary to find arms quickly to drag the cannons, each of which had a bronze barrel 2.19 metres long and weighed 522 kilograms. Men were needed to transport the 6-pounders and personnel were needed to prepare the roads to the Assietta Pass, with a positive height difference of over 1,000 metres to be overcome – Sauze d'Oulx is at 1,510 metres above sea level. Recruitment problems among the local population had already been encountered on 16 July at the Cesana camp. The French were unable to find sufficient local manpower to be able to make the logistical network of their forces in action work as well as possible. Belle-Isle himself had to note that there were 'few resources among the villagers, not because of [their] ill will, but because there is no one left in the villages; they have followed the cattle, or are commandeered for Piedmontese work'.[49] The *Commissaire de*

---

48   Arvers and de Vault, *Guerre de la Succession d'Autriche*, Vol.II, p.732. The bad weather conditions – 'during the day there was fog and some snow fell' – are also confirmed in the *Relation de l'attaque des retranchements de l'Assiette du 19 juillet 1747*, SHD, A1-3240-34.
49   Arvers and de Vault, *Guerre de la Succession d'Autriche*, Vol.II, p.730.

guerre, Brunet de l'Argentière, had continued throughout 18 July 'to work on the roads for the cannon; I did not have enough pioneers and had to command workers from among the troops to make up for their lack'.[50] The cannon, despite the small number of personnel dedicated to them, finally reached Col Blegier, at an altitude of 2,381 metres.[51] The artillery trains were now less than 3,000 metres from the starting line of de Mailly and d'Arnaud's columns. Yet at that moment the ridges of Mont Blegier must have seemed too steep for the French pioneers. Or, more simply, they had run out of time to reach the battlefield.

Part of the Italian military historiography misinterprets the words of the Chevalier of Belle-Isle and those of de Mailly.[52] The Chevalier of Belle-Isle did not order the abandonment of the field artillery along the way; on the contrary, he wrote a brief detailed report to his brother on the situation of the artillery trains, where he pointed out their actual location in the afternoon of the 17th, but did not give the order to stop their ascent to Assietta. The orders of 18 July, written at 7:00 a.m. from the Col du Bourget, are very clear. They only say 'we will not stop in the march to wait for the artillery', that is, the infantry and artillery columns will advance at different speeds.[53] Belle-Isle ordered the *Commissaire des guerres* Brunet de l'Argentière to reactivate the bridge at Ventoux for the transit of artillery. De l'Argentière was also charged 'with a miners officer to restore the Ventoux bridge, and to draw up the orders to command pioneers to bring the four pieces from Costa Piana to Saint-Marc, Jovenceaux and Sauze'.[54] The official biographer of the Duc de Belle-Isle, François Antoine de Chevrier, confirms that 'the only error that can be attributed to the Chevalier of Bell'Isle lies in the fact that he did not wait for the road through which the cannons could pass to be completed; but the reports of the spies, which were true, had announced that the following day a reinforcement of eight battalions would reach the enemy commander, the Conte di Bricherasio'.[55] De Mailly's complaints about the absence of artillery on the battlefield refer not to the fact that Belle-Isle ordered to stop their march towards Sauze d'Oulx, but to the fact that these guns did not reach the battlefield on time; 'The impassable paths forced [the Chevalier of Belle-Isle] to abandon them'.[56]

As he continued to wait with increasing anxiety for the arrival of the guns, the Chevalier de Belle-Isle was obsessed with the Sardinian reinforcements that, according to his information, were about to arrive at Assietta. After waiting for about an hour, he finally got impatient and ordered the 4-pounder mountain pieces to be put into battery. According to the orders he had given, they were to follow d'Arnaud's column after the breakthrough at the

---

50   Brunet de l'Argentière, *Mémoire de la Guerre*, pp.71-72.
51   Fundamental in this sense, for the reconstruction of the movements of the French field artillery trains and the impact they had on the final phases of the Assietta campaign was the discovery, made by Dr Eugenio Garoglio, of the *Carte Topographique en mesure d'une partie des Vallès d'Oulx et Pragelas, avec le Rétranchèmens de L'Assiette, les Campemens et mouvemens des François et les postes qu'ils attaquerent le 19 Juillet 1747*, AST, Corte, Carte Topografiche e Disegni, Carte Topografiche per A e B, Pragelato 1; Garoglio, Zannoni, *La Difesa nascosta del Piemonte sabaudo*, pp.168-169.
52   In particular G. Amoretti, 'Celebrazione di un anniversario', in Amoretti, Roggero, Viglino (eds), *I Trinceramenti* dell'Assietta, p.25 and M. Minola, *Assietta. Tutta la storia dal XVI secolo ad oggi* (Sant'Ambrogio di Torino: Susalibri, 2006), p.105.
53   Arvers and de Vault, *Guerre de la Succession d'Autriche* cit, Vol.II, p.742.
54   Brunet de l'Argentière, *Mémoire de la Guerre*, p.71.
55   Chevrier, *Vie politique et militaire de M. le Maréchal Duc de Bell'Isle* (La Haye: Unknown Publisher 1762), p.223.
56   De Mailly, *Mémoire sur l'attaque*.

Testa dell'Assietta. The Chevalier decided that the firepower of this artillery was sufficient to open a breach in the enemy's defence. At 12:30 he ordered the battery of 4-pounders mountain guns attached to Arnaud's column to move to Height 2,563 and to open fire against the redoubt at Testa dell'Assietta.

The soldiers on both sides, with the exception of those of Villemur's column who were on the move, spent about four hours waiting for the combat to begin. The sources available to us concentrate on what the officers and commanders did, and little is said about the soldiers, particularly in the quiet hours before the attack.

On the French side, once the units were deployed at their bases for the offensive action, the soldiers were given the opportunity to cook their own food and wait for the order to attack.[57] Refreshed, they could also sit, smoke, pray and keep themselves somewhat occupied. But most of the men slept on the spot, or at least tried to do so. It can be said with good reason that the soldiers of most armies, at least before the development of mechanical transport, went into battle already tired, if only because they had to march to the battle site under the weight of their weapons and equipment. The French who fought at Assietta had been marching in the operations area since 15 July. Their adversaries were less fortunate; the Austro-Sardinians were already awake before dawn, and except for three hours in the morning between 7:00 and 10:00 a.m., they were constantly on their feet in tactical combat formation near the trenches. Everyone was hungry, however, and they were about to face combat on an empty stomach. Only in the Austro-Sardinian camp was anything cooked the night before, between the 18th and 19th, but not all the battalions present had had a chance to get something to eat. Certainly not the Austrian units, for whom the afternoon and evening of the 18th were dedicated to the march towards the battlefield.

Hungry, cold, sleepy, exhausted from marching and guard duty: this was the condition of the Assietta fighters at the start of the battle. Those who spent the night in the alpine pastures, 'lying down in a bivouac, in the coldest weather of the season',[58] faced the short summer night in the worst conditions, or did not sleep at all. Few Sardinian battalions, and only part of those present within the perimeter of the main camp, had the luxury of the shelter of a tent. All of them, however, 'suffered greatly from the cold'.[59]

Before combat, all weapons were checked; cartridge boxes filled with 30 to 60 rounds depending on units, and the muskets' flints were replaced.[60] On average, each flint allowed

---

57   Blondel d'Azincourt, *Du champ de bataille vis-à-vis des retranchements d'Exilles*, p.411.

58   Brunet de l'Argentière, *Mémoire de la Guerre*, p.72.

59   Report of 20 July 1747, AST, Corte, Materie Militari, Mazzo 8 d'addizione.

60   Surirey de Saint Remy, *Mémoires d'Artillerie* (Paris: Rollin, 1697), p.290. It was pointed out that a soldier had to carry at least one pound of powder and two pounds of lead, for a total of 40 cartridges. Puységur, *Art de la guerre*, p.108. The cartridge boxes of both sides had neither a shape nor a standard capacity. According to the *Code Militaire à l'usage du corps des Volontaire Royaux*, printed the 15 August 1745, 'the quartermasters, corporals, graded and soldiers will be armed with a cartridge box with fifty shots. [...] The grenadiers will have sixty shots at their disposal in their cartridges. The soldiers involved in the battle will have a cartridge box with fifteen shots'. This was a considerable reserve of fire, even if an *Ordonnance* of 1747 prescribed the use of cartridge boxes capable of carrying 20 cartridges, already increased to 30 in 1750. Most likely these two ordinances did nothing but institutionalize the growing use of ammunition by soldiers. On this topic see the important Petard, *Equipements Militaires de 1600 à 1870*, Vol.I, pp.103-104. Given the influence that the French army had upon the Sardinian one, we can reasonably assume that the individual endowment was

28 shots, after which it had to be replaced. Spare flints were therefore already prepared in the cartridge box, wrapped in lead foil to facilitate gripping by the jaw of the hammer. In combat, the flint was thus already ready for use, without wasting time shaping the lead. The firearm was carefully checked and cleaned; the soldier's life depended on it. Good maintenance of the firearm meant that the flint could be changed every 30 shots, with a likelihood of one misfire out of 10 shots – for which the pan had to be re-primed – and one partial misfire out of 20 shots, when it was sufficient to re-cock the hammer and shoot again. With good maintenance, especially before a battle, the weapon's effectiveness in combat improved considerably. This was of extreme importance, particularly in the Austro-Sardinian army where the firepower would block the advance of the enemy columns. There were psychological implications to the maintenance of the weapon. After all, it was certainly an impressive sight to watch thousands of shiny muskets barrels sparkling in the summer sunlight: war played, and still plays today, on these psychological aspects as well.[61]

It does not appear that the armies present at Assietta were better prepared spiritually and mentally for battle than they were physically. There were no religious ceremonies, for 19 July 1747 was a Wednesday and there was no need. What was not lacking was the use of personal amulets and charms. Medals, cards with good luck phrases and prayers with sacred images circulated in every unit of both armies. The most famous, especially among the Sardinian troops, was the image of the Madonna of the Consolata, which after the siege of Turin in 1706 became a real good luck charm for the soldiers, who did not disdain to wear a card with the image of the Madonna on their hats. The French made wide use of such paper amulets, where magic phrases, prayers, exhortations were written in manuscript or printed on small squares of paper. Another element necessary for the cohesion of the units and to raise the fighting spirit was the distribution of alcohol and tobacco. Smoking and snuff were two typical companions of the soldier's life: 'Tobacco is mainly smoked in special clay pipes. Experience shows that it is a wonderful cure for discomfort and illness'.[62]

At 12:30 p.m. the French opened fire with their mountain artillery. The small guns were only 441 metres away from the forward tenaille built on the Testa dell'Assietta. The French artillerymen had at their disposal seven 4-pounder mountain guns, with which they immediately tried to hit the enemy infantry lined up along the advanced trench and the large redan communication linking it to the rest of the camp. The pieces at the disposal of the Chevalier de Belle-Isle were affectionately known among the lily troops as *Vit de mulet,* or 'Mule cocks'. Their function was anti-personnel, rather than anti-structure; however, the impact of the 4-pounder balls produced 'a kind of breach [...] at the recessed corner of the tenaille'.[63] Their small barrels, unable to withstand powerful charges, did not allow the projectile to reach velocities sufficient to be used effectively to open a larger breach[64]. While

---

30 cartridges, as suggested in Sterrantino, *Le armi da* fuoco, Vol.I., p.134. For the Austrians the minimum supply was 36 rounds; see Duffy, *Instrument of War*, p.246.

61   Grossman, *On Killing.*

62   H.F. Fleming, *Der Vollkommene Teutsche Soldat* (Unknown Publisher), p.356.

63   AST, Corte, Materie politiche per il rapporto all'interno, Storie della Real Casa, Categoria III, Mazzo 23; Minutoli, *Relation des campagnes faites par S.M.*, Vol.III, p.241.

64   Blondel d'Azincourt reports that these small pieces of mountain artillery 'could be carried by a single mule with their carriage. You can judge by this detail their size'. Blondel d'Azincourt, *Du champ de bataille vis-à-vis des retranchements d'Exilles*, p.411.

waiting for the 4-pounder campaign pieces, it was hoped that the small mountain guns would force the defenders to partially evacuate the exposed butte position.

For this purpose, the French artillerymen used solid ball ammunition. The heavy cast iron balls were the most versatile ammunition available to artillerymen. It is clear that great reliance was placed on this ordinance rather than on other types of projectile. A French 4-pounder cannon fired a ball weighing 1,956 kilograms, to destroy men, animals and materials. In this latter role, even these light pieces had a devastating effect against any kind of obstacle, animate or not, that was in their trajectory and range. They were capable of causing numerous casualties even with a single shot, on first impact and during the following bounces of the ball, and could not be considered harmless until they had finally stopped. They could cause irreparable damage to even the strongest artillery shaft, and thus to a transport wagon, as well as splitting a man or a horse in two. The closed infantry formations, necessary to maximize the firepower of muzzle-loading flintlock musket, made men vulnerable to spherical projectiles, and evasive manoeuvres virtually impossible. On average, each shot, fired at the correct range and angle of elevation, could kill three or four men on impact, and maim or seriously wound four or five others, for a total of about eight men knocked out.

Nevertheless, the French artillery fire was far less effective than might have been expected. Losses were negligible on the Austro-Sardinian side mainly because the pieces were operating at the limit of their capacity. The larger guns, such as the 24-pounder, could fire a projectile over 600 metres, but the 4- and 6-pounder guns were ineffective beyond 500 metres. The shots came slowly, many rolling, or at the limit of the power of the launching charge. Nevertheless, there were casualties, mainly between the two companies of grenadiers, of the regiments Guardie and Casale: 'a cannon shot severed the head of a Guardie grenadier, and Signor Conte Martinengo, who was standing next to him, had his whole face splattered with the dead man's brains. Other similar incidents have occurred',[65] but far less serious and numerous than can be supposed after more than three continuous hours of cannonades. The high profile of the Testa's Redoubt was able to intercept most of the artillery fire. The Sardinian units emerged almost completely unscathed from the bombardment, convinced in their hearts, like many soldiers of the first half of the eighteenth century, that 'cannon fire does not cause serious damage in war, and there is a proverb among our men that you have to be particularly unlucky to be killed by a cannon shot in combat'.[66]

3:00 p.m. Fort San Carlo, Fenestrelle

Cannon shots were heard in both the upper Susa and Chisone valleys. This was nothing new, as the sound of fighting had already been heard for days, and even on the morning of 19 July the crackling of guns was heard. Now, after a long period of calm, the voice of the cannon could be heard. The governor of the Fenestrelle forts, Giuseppe Antonio Bonaventura, Conte di Rasino, urgently summoned Signor Giovanni Battista Guigas, a trader from Fenestrelle with some duties relating to provisions and logistics, and ordered him to go up

---

65   Priocca Report I.
66   Mauvillon, *Histoire de la dernière Guerre de Bohême*, Vol.II, p.101. Probably most, if not all, of the casualties suffered by the two grenadier companies – 16 killed in action – were hit by cannonballs.

to the Assietta camp to meet the Conte di Bricherasio and learn 'what was happening'. At 4:00 p.m. Guigas came out of the secondary gate of Fort San Carlo[67].

4:00 p.m. Height 2,563, Belle-Isle's Tactical Command Post

At the same time, the Chevalier de Belle-Isle was rapidly losing his overall view of events to focus on three elements that seemed to be magnetizing all his attention:

- Ten to 14 Austro-Sardinian battalions were about to make their appearance on the battlefield. The information, as we have seen, was correct in terms of the numbers of forces arriving, but the threat would manifest itself in a few days, not a few hours. Belle-Isle's staff were unable, at that time, to analyse the information and facts and help the commander to get a clear view of the situation.
- The 4-pounder field pieces were blocked at Col Blegier and could not progress with the necessary speed because of the work on widening the road to Assietta. They would probably be available for the following day, the 20th.
- The head of Villemur's column had finally set foot on the southern ridge of the Gran Serin at 3:30 p.m. In a couple of hours at the most he would be fully on the starting line for his attack.

The options at this point were two: to halt the operation in progress and wait for the guns, or to continue the attack. The Chevalier had no doubts; the enemy was reinforcing and he had to exploit his numerical advantage to the full. Moreover, the advance of de Villemur's column was now too far advanced to be called off any time soon. He then remembered that in the morning his commanders had said they were confident of success. He therefore decided to continue the offensive action against the enemy camp.

Bricherasio continued to monitor the situation at the Gran Serin, the key terrain of the battlefield. By now, numerous enemy battalions were beginning to mass in front of him. Other relays were immediately sent to the Argueil Redoubt to urge the arrival of the Reggimento Roi. On the western front, *Maggior Generale* Francesco Alciati had decided to maintain the garrison at the Ridotte delle Ruine di Riobacon in force. This consisted of a total of one composite company of the Swiss Reggimento Meyer, 120 fusiliers strong. At the same time, he decided to deploy the Meyer grenadier company, 58 men in all, to the south on a 'ridge parallel to the redoubt [the tenaille of the Testa dell'Assietta]',[68] where *Luogotenente* Thomasset's 100 volunteers had also gathered.

---

67   F. Gabotto, 'La verità sulla battaglia dell'Assietta secondo la minuta della relazione Priocca Report', in *Bollettino Storico-Bibliografico Subalpino*, Anno XI, N. I-II, Torino 1906, p.232n; E. Peyronel, B. Usseglio, *Di qui non si passa!... forse. Forti, fortificazioni minori e fatti d'arme nella valli Pragelato, Perosa, Pellice e San Martino fra XVI e XVIII secolo* (Pinerolo: Alzani, 2015), p.383; *Lettre écrit par M. Perron major des Milices et châtelain Royal de Val Cluson a Guigas Sécretaire de Guerre de S.M. de Fenestrelles le 19 Juin 1769*, BRT, Miscellanea 102.
68   Priocca Report I.

The advance of de Villemur's column as seen from the south. (Author's photo, annotation by George Anderson)

4:30 p.m. Testa dell'Assietta

French: five infantry battalions, two mixed infantry battalions, 3,460 men. Austro-Sardinians: one infantry battalion, two companies of grenadiers, one company of volunteers, 955 men.

At 4:15 p.m. Belle-Isle communicated, from his command post in the vicinity of the battery, the attack order to the de Mailly and d'Arnaud columns, which moved towards their objectives.[69]

Inside the camp the units, already on the alert since 10:00 a.m., were preparing to withstand the enemy's impact. Bricherasio probably did not consider his forces sufficient to withstand the adversary's impact and was in fact preparing to manage a retreat, in as organized

---

69   The attack occurred at 4:15 p.m. according to de Mailly, while according to the Priocca Report it happened at 4:30 p.m. The difference is probably explained by the fact that the Piedmontese report does not indicate the start of the advance, but the first contact with the enemy, which took place in front of the Testa dell'Assietta at 4:30 p.m. We do not know what the conventional signal adopted on that occasion was. For example, for the Battle of Bassignana on 27 September 1745, the Franco-Spaniards launched three rockets in succession. A. de Pezay, *Histoire des Campagnes de M. le M.al de Maillebois en Italie, pendant les annés 1745 & 1746* (Paris: Imprimerie Royale, 1775), Vol.II, Tome I, p.151, Vol.II, Tome II, p.74.

The path used as an attack axis by d'Arnaud's column. On the left in parallel was de Mailly's column heading towards the Assietta ridge, visible in the background on the left. (Author's photo, annotation by George Anderson)

a manner as possible, towards Gran Serin, where he was at the time, or towards Fenestrelle. On the western edge of the field the Austrian and Sardinian commanders went to stand between the battalion of Traun and 1/Guardie. From that position they could handle both the fighting at Testa dell'Assietta and on the right flank.

D'Arnaud had recognized the approach road to the Testa dell'Assietta, and with the officers of his staff would take part in the assault. He placed himself at the head of the first battalion on the right, the grenadiers, and began to incite his men with the classic war cry 'Vive le Roy!'[70] Just as the guns ceased their fire, he gave the order to advance. A small breach had formed in the receding corner of the tenaille, which could not be repaired for the moment.[71] The column had its base for the attack to the right of de Mailly's column. While that column was 780 metres from the attack front, d'Arnaud and his men had to cover a distance of just under 500 metres before they found themselves facing the tenaille front of the redoubt of the Testa dell'Assietta. The first part of the route, about 200 metres, was essentially flat, while the remaining 300 metres were uphill. The terrain, initially very steep with a gradient of 23.5 percent, allowed the column to approach about 120 metres from the Testa dell'Assietta redoubt. Here the terrain suddenly dropped to a gradient of 7.8 percent and the French took advantage of the more permissive terrain to overrun the enemy

---

70   Blondel d'Azincourt speaks of 'numerous [cries of] Vive le Roy!'. Blondel d'Azincourt, *Du champ de bataille vis-à-vis des retranchements d'Exilles*, p.411.

71   Minutoli, *Relation des campagnes faites par S.M.*, Vol.V, p.241.

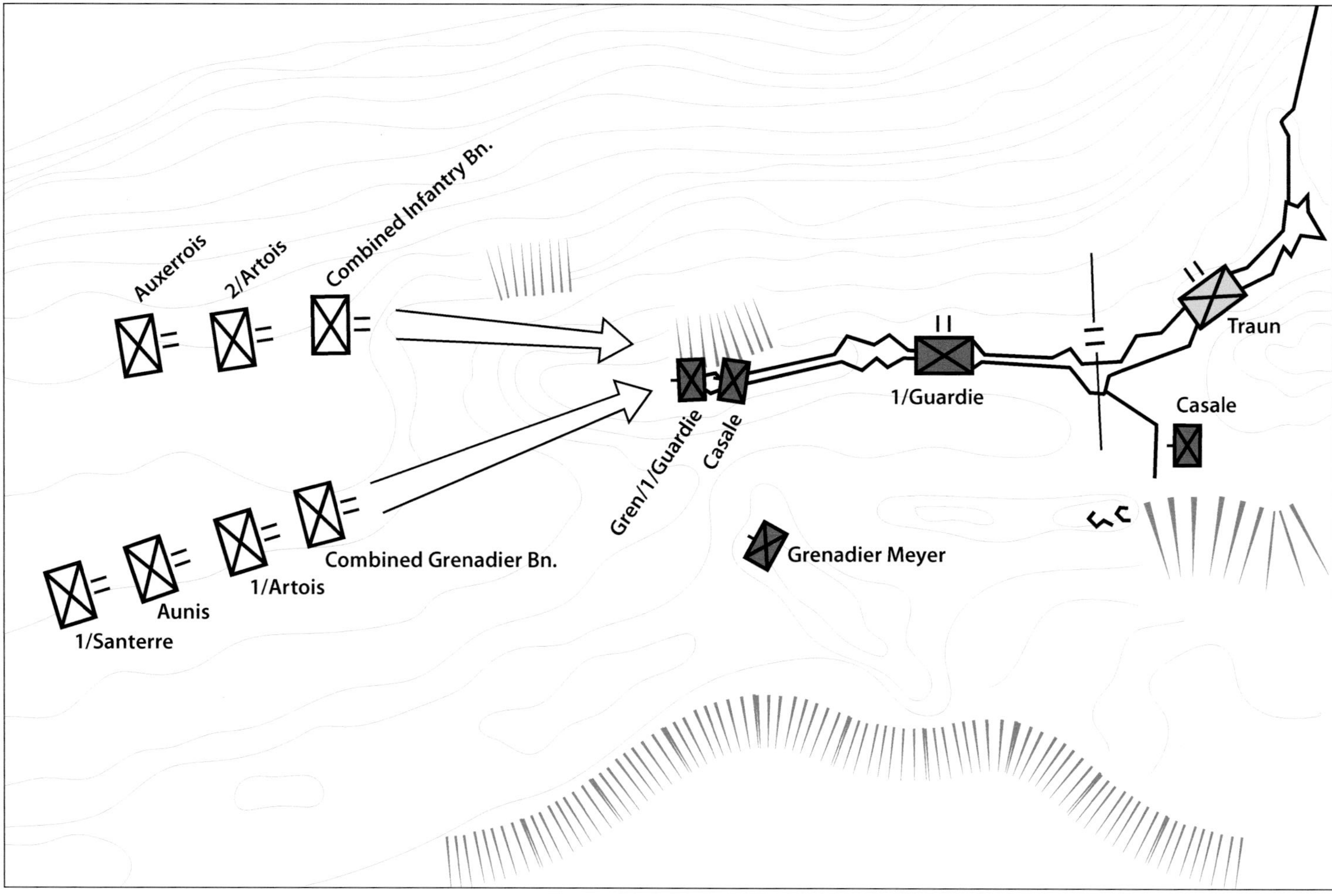

The attack of the French central column at 4:30 p.m. Despite the obvious numerical advantage, the attackers had to face the terrain, a steep rocky ridge, and field fortifications, a dry-stone wall two metres high. Two of the elite units, the grenadier companies of 1/Guardie and of Casale, defended this position.

engagement area as quickly as possible and occupy the fortification. But it was not that simple; the *à la Folard* attack was theoretically based on the ability of an infantry column to break through the enemy ranks. The bayonet assault, however, is based on a psychological factor, even before the predisposition of each soldier to fencing and hand-to-hand combat with his own bayonet is considered. Once in front of the enemy and eye contact has been established, one side is overcome by the fear of close combat, loses cohesion, panics, turns its back and flees in haste. This happened during a successful bayonet attack; well before physical contact. However, the enemy could refuse to give ground, especially if he was too tired to move, or if he had good cover, the so-called 'tactical foothold'. In spite of Folard's classicist ramblings, once an enemy was on the battlefield, equipped with functioning firearms, with a good supply of bullets and determined to defend itself strenuously, in a frontal attack the attacking columns, however massive and imposing, were bound to be stopped by the firepower of the defence. Or else the attackers had to resign themselves to the dangerous and time-consuming task of demolishing the entrenchments, relying on the ability to develop sufficient retaliatory fire.

At Assietta, the two companies deployed in the tenaille were protected by massive walls about five metres high, a field fortification within which it was possible to resist with some effectiveness even in situations of clear numerical inferiority. The two units chosen for the defence of the Testa dell'Assietta were grenadiers. These were the grenadier company of 1/Guardie, under the orders of *Capitano* Tommaso Caldora, and that of the Reggimento Casale, commanded by *Capitano* Giorgio Scozia. Both were composed of soldiers selected from among those who showed a marked aptitude for combat in general. Even before this, men who were imposing because of their physical appearance and height,[72] were sought after who could be identified as 'natural fighters' or 'veterans'; that is, the 20 percent of soldiers identified by S.L.A. Marshall as the only proportion who actually fight, overcoming the natural repulsion to kill that is typical of human beings.[73] Similar men were also sought after in the French army, and as in the Sardinian and Austrian armies, they were grouped together in grenadier companies. It was no coincidence that these 'natural fighters' were sought out and chosen by their battalion commanders for inclusion in the grenadier companies, which were almost always intended to form elite assault units. At Assietta the French always placed at the head of their attacking columns either a grenadier formation battalion – that is, an amalgam of several grenadier companies detached from individual ordinary infantry battalions – or a battalion composed of selected infantry. These units would lead the other units forward and break through the enemy lines. This type of troop was explicitly relied upon, since:

> [W]e have learned through experience that a grenadier, simply because he is called a grenadier, is more highly regarded, less likely to desert and fights better. I have often noticed that when soldiers are assigned from other companies to the

---

72   In the Sardinian army the expected height of a grenadier was 1.71 metres: Sterrantino, *Le armi da fuoco del Vecchio Piemonte*, p.119.

73   Grossman, *On Killing*, pp.18-37.

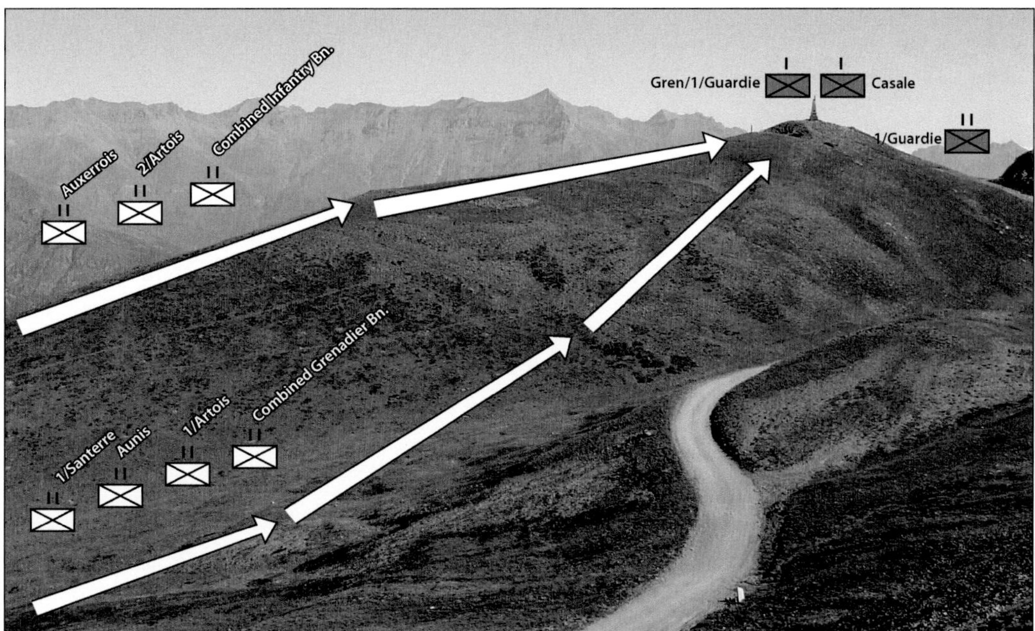

The Testa dell'Assietta seen from the tactical command post of the Chevalier de Belle-Isle. The French column advanced from left to right up the slope, only to be stopped by the field fortifications and the firepower of the adversary. (Author's photo, annotation by George Anderson)

grenadier company, they take on something of the grenadier spirit as soon as they put on their fur caps. Appearance and conduct are transformed.[74]

But these advantages were expensive. The missions were dangerous and the French grenadiers at Assietta paid far too high a price for their elite rank. Moreover, these companies were for the line regiments 'a constant trickle of tall, useful men'.[75]

D'Arnaud's column at the base of the Testa dell'Assietta rise divided into two bodies – one on the right and one on the left – which, taking advantage of the ridge leading to the summit, began to climb completely out of sight of the defenders. 'The centre column approached the redoubt, or tenaille of the Grenadiers, which ends there, and protected by a kind of shelter divided into two corps, which were now within range of a pistol shot from the tenaille, and both came running up to the two salient corners of the tenaille'.[76] D'Arnaud and his staff were at the head of the right-hand corps, while the left-hand column was under the orders of *Maréchal de Camp* d'Andlau, seconded from Belle-Isle's staff to act as second-in-command. The exposed position of the commanders and their staffs was confirmed by the tenaille defenders themselves: 'nothing was more brilliant than the valour of the enemy in this attack, their generals to animate the soldiers showed themselves in the

---

74   Cogniazzo, *Freymüthige Beytrag zur Geschichte*, p.106.
75   W. Dalrymple, *Tacticks* (Dublin: George Bonham, 1782), p.10.
76   Priocca Report I.

first ranks, those that followed were composed of officers of all ranks'.[77] 'The generals were at the head. Whole ranks of officers followed them and showed the soldiers the paths to victory or death'.[78] D'Arnaud, in doing so, was exposing himself, the commander of one of the attacking columns, to a very high risk of being wounded or killed in the early stages of the battle. He probably wanted to make sure that his column would impact at the point he had selected and advance along the axis he had chosen.

The front of the entrenchment was not particularly wide, probably no more than about 30 metres; it was manned by 107 officers, non-commissioned officers and grenadiers – 55 from 1/Guardie and 52 from Casale – of whom at least 80 were deployed in two ranks ready to open fire.

D'Arnaud had no intention of reducing himself to 'firing on the redoubt', not least because his tactical disposition 'made no provision for such an eventuality'.[79] As soon as he had crossed the ridge line, and was now about 100 metres away from the enemy line, he began to approach the walls of the fortification at a run, or an accelerated pace, aiming for the tops of the tenaille: 'We started off with incredible speed and were at the foot of the parapet in an instant'.[80] The distance was bridged in a short time, but not before the defenders were able to carry out a general discharge towards the battalion that was the first to emerge from the crest; it was the one that had climbed the slope facing the Val Chisone, the very one where d'Arnaud was. The management of the firing and the defence in general of the Testa dell'Assietta was entrusted to the lieutenant colonel of 1/Guardie, Paolo Federico Novarina, Conte di San Sebastiano. The target was the front of the battalion itself and was about 20 metres wide, so the hail of bullets that came from the tenaille left the French commander with no chance: 'Monsieur d'Arnaud decided to take his grenadiers to the foot of the entrenchment, which formed a sort of ditch at the back of the hill, and was killed as he emerged [from the crest]'[81]. More precisely, 'd'Arnaud [was killed] on our left on the Pragelato side'.[82] With him, a good part of his own staff was put out of action. The attack could not have had a worse start, and the management of the battle was now in the hands of the battalion commanders.

However, the burst of musketry was not enough to stop the momentum of the French. Transformed into a compact mass of running men, the two columns hit the imposing drystone wall. The two battalions of the first line, on the left the battalion of selected infantry companies and on the right the battalion of combined grenadiers, merged into a single crowd crowded in front of the narrow front of the Testa dell'Assietta redoubt. Some of the soldiers began to slide along the walls towards the north, where they did not advance much due to a rocky escarpment and the steep drop just beyond the northern salient. Along the

---

77   Minutoli, *Relation des campagnes faites par S.M.*, p.238.
78   Priocca Report I.
79   De Mailly, *Mémoire sur l'attaque.*
80   Blondel d'Azincourt, *Du champ de bataille vis-à-vis des retranchements d'Exilles*, p.411.
81   De Mailly, *Mémoire sur l'attaque.* All French sources confirm that d'Arnaud was killed at the first shot: 'M. Darnaud was killed by the first shots from a musket', SHD, A1, 3240, 36; 'M. d'Arnaud was killed at the first discharge', Blondel d'Azincourt, *Du champ de bataille vis-à-vis des retranchements d'Exilles*, p.411.
82   *Lettre écrit par M. Perron major des Milices et châtelain Royal de Val Cluson a Guigas Sécretaire de Guerre de S.M. de Fenestrelles le 19 Juin 1769*, BRT, Miscellanea 102.

southern front the slope was much more forgiving, and some of the grenadiers began to manoeuvre westwards in search of a gap in the trenches. The second row of the column, where 1/ and 2/Artois had been placed to the right and left respectively, remained slightly behind to provide some fire cover for the other two units engaged at the base of the redoubt. The remaining four battalions remained close to the ridge line, 120 metres from the redoubt, waiting to exploit the breakthrough that was expected any moment.

However, instead of a rapid breakthrough, a close-range battle began between elite French and Sardinian troops. Having failed to make a breakthrough along the tenailled front of the Testa dell'Assietta, the tactical position of the French soldiers quickly became very dangerous as they were targeted from the front by the Sardinian grenadiers, and also received fire on the flank and from the rear from the high ground parallel to the position, occupied by the grenadier company of Meyer and

Grenadiers of the Reggimento Guardie. The redoubt of the Testa dell'Assietta was garrisoned by two elite grenadier companies, of 1/Guardie and Casale. These two units not only held their ground against a massive French attack, but also inflicted appalling losses on the enemy. (Detail from The Surrender of Asti by H. de La Pegna, private collection)

Thomasset's volunteers. Alciati's plan was working like a charm: the Piedmontese general had calculated with great precision the distance between the high ground and the southern front of the fortifications, about 130 metres. This was an optimal distance for the use of the infantry's musket, and the reinforced company he had sent to that sector was extremely effective in hitting French soldiers who were carrying out demolition work at the base of the fortifications or trying to get around the dangerous enemy position from the south:

Despite the fire from the front, and from the flanks of the tenaille, and that of our volunteers, stationed on a mountain ridge parallel to the redoubt, where Signor Cavalier Alciati had Meyer's Grenadier Company pass, and despite an infinite number of dead, and wounded, the enemy generals, officers and soldiers did not slow down their ardour [in the assault].[83]

In reality, apart from firing muskets at any enemy protruding from the parapet of the fortification to kill them, or simply to force them to keep their heads down, the French could do no more than huddle together and try to make a practicable breach; that is, one that the infantry could penetrate with every tool at their disposal. The firing of hundreds of muskets in such a small area of the battlefield quickly reduced visibility, preventing the attackers from effectively hitting the defenders visible beyond the parapet of the redoubt. While the artillery resumed firing, concentrating on the great communication and against the line of maximum resistance,[84] the French soldiers 'advanced bravely on both sides up to the foot of the redoubt', getting within touching distance of fortifications and attempting to destroy the entrenchments' foundations with tools.[85] These operations were also observed by the Mayer grenadiers and Thomasset's volunteers, 'who reported that they were working at the foot of the entrenchment to demolish it'.[86] In particular, efforts were concentrated against the recessed corner of the trench.

Inside the trenches, however, no one was showing any signs of losing morale or willingness to continue fighting. This fact struck the Sardinian officers, who feared they would have to manage a difficult retreat under enemy fire and bayonets: 'Our grenadiers did marvellous things, and encouraged by the presence of Alciati, Colloredo and Martinengo, as well as by the example of their brave officers, they never stopped fighting, and made the enemy pay with a toll of blood and their lives for every inch of ground they gained at our expense'.[87] Not only did the Sardinian grenadiers not give ground, but they fought with the intention of shooting down all the French who tried to enter the redoubt. The assault had definitely lost momentum; by 5:00 p.m., 45 minutes into the attack, half of the battalions in the central column had taken part in the fight, but the friction of combat had literally ground them down. These were the best units at d'Arnaud's disposal: one battalion of selected infantry companies, one battalion of converged grenadiers and the two battalions of the Régiment d'Artois, approximately 2,000 men. The losses among the officers, who marched in the front ranks and exposed themselves dangerously in the course of the fight, were appalling; without command or an element of control, the companies of the first two battalions, targeted frontally and from behind, had straggled. The men, taking advantage of the smoke, disengaged independently, whether wounded or not. In the front lines only those few officers who were still unharmed remained, or those soldiers who were naturally combat ready and had decided not to give up. Even before opening a breach, however, they had to find a way to survive, immersed in the smoke of burning gunpowder, clinging to

---

83   Priocca Report I.
84   The resumption of artillery fire, suspended during the early stages of the assault to facilitate the approach of the attack column, is confirmed by Priocca Report I: 'despite the fire of their artillery and their muskets that continually fired on everything that appeared above the redoubt'.
85   Priocca Report I.
86   BRT, Manoscritto Militare n.5, *Relation des campagnes faites au service de S.M. le Roy de Sardaigne pendant le guerre d'Italie (1742-1747)*.
87   Priocca Report I

the dry-stone walls of the trenches just a few metres away from an enemy determined not to leave them any quarter. Those who were still in the vicinity of the fortifications tried to keep as far back as possible by flattening themselves on the surfaces of the entrenchment: 'A good part of the enemy were so attached against the redoubt that the musket shots could not reach them, the grenadiers fired with one hand from above the parapet, and threw large stones at them which did them a lot of damage, and even climbed up the parapet to sink their bayonets into [their] skulls'.[88]

The use of the bayonet, which forced the grenadier to expose his entire figure on the edge of the parapet, was possible thanks to the smoke produced by the gunpowder detonations, which reduced visibility to only 10 metres. The absence of wind prevented this veritable smoke screen around the Testa dell'Assietta from dissipating, and this was an important factor working in favour of the defenders; the artillery could not fire in that direction because they could no longer distinguish friend and foe, while the grenadiers could climb the parapets to hit the French who were trying to demolish the base of the entrenchment, or who were simply trying to take cover from the incoming fire. Not mentioned in the usual narrative of the battle, and barely hinted at in the iconography, the smoke that enveloped the entire battlefield of 19 July 1747 was undoubtedly one of the elements that most influenced its progress. The plateau was completely enveloped by the smokescreen created by the thousands of musket detonations, as could easily be observed from Val Chisone, where from the Fort of Fenestrelle it was possible to observe the fighting fronts from the position of the smoke.[89]

The management of the battle at that time was entrusted to the highest-ranking officer still alive, the commander of the Régiment d'Artois, Nicolas-Louis de Loménie, Comte de Brienne. He had already seen his two grenadier companies destroyed by the defenders' fire,[90] and, given that the situation was becoming desperate, he decided to try everything. He advanced decisively towards the breach that was forming in the receding corner of the tenaille, dragging his staff and the two battalions of his regiment behind him. He was seriously wounded by a musket shot: the close range – at that time the battle was being fought at between 1.5 and 3 metres – meant that the ball practically took his arm off. Despite the wound, he decided to return forward towards the breach. To those who tried to stop him, he

---

88   Priocca Report I. The throwing of stones and the wounding of French soldiers is confirmed by the service status of some of them at the Invalid Corps in Paris: the soldier – of an unspecified regiment – Jean Thedés, 'wounded behind the right thigh from a stone at Assietta in 1747'. SHD, 2Xy41; Pierre Joseph Betrand, also of an unidentified regiment, was recorded as suffering 'from poor eyesight after he received a stone blow to the head in the battle of the Assietta'. SHD, 2Xy55; Pierre Valâde, a soldier in the Grenadiers Royaux de Modêne, showed 'an old wound in his left arm from a stone blow received in the Assietta combat'. SHD, 2Xy57; *Capitaine* Charles François Hebrard Du Bousquet, of the Grenadiers Royaux de Modene, 'was wounded by a stone blow at the Assietta; he received on the same occasion to the leg and to the head two gunshots'. Stone throwing, as anachronistic as it may seem on a modern-era battlefield dominated by firepower, was also foreseen and described in tactical treatises of the period, as described in Le Cointe, *Le Science des Postes Militaire*, pp.151-154.

89   *Lettera del Sig. Intendente Baldoino di Santa Margarita. Nuove sulla disfatta de nemici all'attacco del Col de la Sieta*, AST, Corte Materie Militari, Imprese, Mazzo 7 da Inventariare.

90   One of the two company commanders of the grenadiers, *Capitaine* Antoine de Gévaudan, had been killed at the head of his men. M. Lainé, *Archives généalogiques et historiques de la Noblesse de France* (Paris: Lainé, 1825-1844), Vol.II, p.15.

replied: 'I have one more arm left to serve the king!'[91] A second shot in the chest left him no chance. By this time all the officers were either dead or wounded, or unable to control a mass of soldiers who had lost their reference points even among the troops. Soldiers form social groups linked by friendship and hinged, if possible, on someone identified as a 'natural fighter' or 'veteran' and in battle they fight more decisively and effectively if they are flanked by other men they know and trust, while their performance will be far less, or the fight even abandoned completely, when these elements are missing.[92] The grenadier and elite infantry companies had been decimated, and the massive losses had destroyed the cohesion of the units. In a very short time, the two battalions of the Régiment d'Artois had suffered devastating losses; 10 officers had fallen in combat, 23 had been wounded, while 101 non-commissioned officers and men had died and 338 had been wounded. For Artois the losses represented 40 percent of the regiment's personnel.[93] The survivors began to retreat, taking advantage of the shelter offered by the smoke screen surrounding the tongue and seeking cover where the ridge became steeper.

By this time it was 5:30 p.m., and de Mailly's column was also heavily engaged in combat.

4:45 p.m. Assietta ridge, Austro-Sardinian Right Flank

French: 10 infantry battalions, one squadron of dismounted dragoons, 5,140 men. Austro-Sardinians: three infantry battalions, 1,224 men.

Maréchal de Camp de Mailly had decided not to follow his commander's orders to the letter. If the Chevalier de Belle-Isle wanted to occupy the recessed corner at the junction between the main line of defence and the communication with the Testa dell'Assietta, then d'Arnaud's column would take care of this during its advance. For its part, it would have secured the advanced enemy works on the left and would have carried out the main attack further to its left, sufficiently far from the dangerous receding corner. To move further to the right was tantamount to outright suicide.

The point selected to force the adversary's entrenchments was at the first redan on the left, located in a dominating position with respect to the redoubt that closed the front towards the north. At the same time, it was necessary to secure the left flank by occupying the redoubts of the Riobacon Ruins. Having received the order to attack, de Mailly began the assault on the Assietta entrenched camp. It was then 4:15 p.m.

De Mailly's massive column began to advance towards the north-western front of the Sardinian entrenched camp. In all, the French troops had to cover a distance of 780 metres before reaching the left redan, their tactical objective. The journey time was fairly

---

91   The anecdote of the Comte de Brienne was transcribed in the diary of the Duc de Luynes in Versailles on 28 July 1747. *Mémoires du duc de Luynes*, p.272. Later it was also reported in R.A. Bouillevaux, *Les Moines du Der, avec pièces justificatives, notes historiques et notices sur le bourg et le canton de Montier-en-Der et la ville de Wassy* (Montier-en-Der: Jules Thiébaut, 1845), p.360; L.M. Chaudon, F.A. Delandine, *Noveau Dictionnaire Historique* (Lyon: Bruyset ainé, 1807), Vol.VII, p.260; M. Fillassier, *Dictionnaire historique d'Éducation* (Paris: Amable Costes, 1818), Vol.III, p.169.
92   Marshall, *Men Against Fire*, pp.145-149.
93   SHD, A1-3240-42, *État des officiers qui se sont le plus distingués la journée du 19.*

The advance of de Mailly's column seen from the positions of the Meyer and Forgách regiments. On the left is visible the Testa dell'Assietta, where the assault of d'Arnaud's column took place almost at the same time. (Author's photo, annotation by George Anderson)

short, and in just over 20 minutes the entire column was at the base of the escarpment to be attacked, less than 200 metres from the enemy defences. Now came the difficult part; the final section of the route below the entrenched line, just under 100 metres, was completely uphill with a gradient of 36 percent. The first unit, the converged battalion of grenadiers and a company of pioneers, began to climb towards the field works. In the first ranks, if one looked up, one could clearly make out the heads and tricorns of the opposing units. The commander of the column, *Maréchal de Camp* de Mailly, was at the head of the column, on horseback.

Maggior Generale Alciati, concentrating on the defence of the Testa dell'Assietta and its communication, had seconded *General-Feldwachtmeister* Colloredo to oversee the fighting on the right wing. He was to command three battalions, two of which – Forgách and Traun – were imperial and depended on him as an Austrian general. Moreover, and this is not to be overlooked, he knew German, a language spoken by the officers and the majority of the soldiers in the Reggimento Meyer, and the combat tactics were also perfectly similar; facts that made command and control much easier. Colloredo took his post between the Traun and Forgách battalions, at a point on the ridge from which he could have a complete view of the engagement area of the attacked front and evaluate the appropriate actions to be taken. However, the enemy seemed to cooperate with the general plan of defence; the French column marched straight towards the entrenchment, without implementing any

The attack by de Mailly's column at 4:45 p.m., seen from the Testa dell'Assietta. The decision to proceed with a column attack *à la Folard* made the French numerical advantage null and void, to the advantage of the two Austro-Sardinian battalions in charge of defending this sector of the field. (Author's photo, annotation by George Anderson)

The attack by de Mailly's column at 4:45 p.m, seen from the French rear. The decision to detach the two companies of 2/and 3/Bourbonnais to the sides of the assault column did not guarantee sufficient covering fire to allow the rest of the unit to reach the entrenchments. (Author's photo, annotation by George Anderson)

The sector of the entrenchments held by the battalions of Meyer and Forgách. In front of these defences the advance of de Mailly's column was stopped by the fire of the defenders. The volume of fire was such that the French could not even reach the foot of the trenches. (Author's photo, annotation by George Anderson)

outflanking manoeuvre towards the Susa Valley. In the meantime a reinforced battalion was entering the range of individual Sardinian and Austrian muskets.

Battalion commanders had to carefully consider the distance within which to make the first discharge: too early a volley would have no effect on the advancing enemy unit, but waiting too long would have meant allowing the adversary to get too close to the entrenchments. 'We must train the soldiers first of all to hold their own fire, and to withstand that of the enemy. Under normal circumstances a battalion is defeated as soon as it has opened fire, and the enemy still has his reserve fire'.[94]

The fire had to be general and hit the French battalion in front and behind, so it was up to Colloredo to judge time and distance. We do not know whether special signals were placed on the ground, such as piles of stones or coloured poles, to signal to the troops deployed in the trenches when the enemy had arrived within effective range of their guns, or whether the 'trigger' in this case was a relief, a particular rock. Whatever the Austrian general's point of reference, he certainly wanted to make sure that he got the maximum possible effect from the fire of the battalions at his disposal. 'We let them approach at close range'[95], he wrote,

94   J.S. Quincy, *Histoire militaire du regne de Louis le Grand* (Paris: Denis Mariette, Jean-Baptiste Delespine, Jean-Baptiste Coignard, 1726), Vol.VIII, p.67.
95   Priocca Report I. Literally the translation is: 'We let them come within the small range of the musket'.

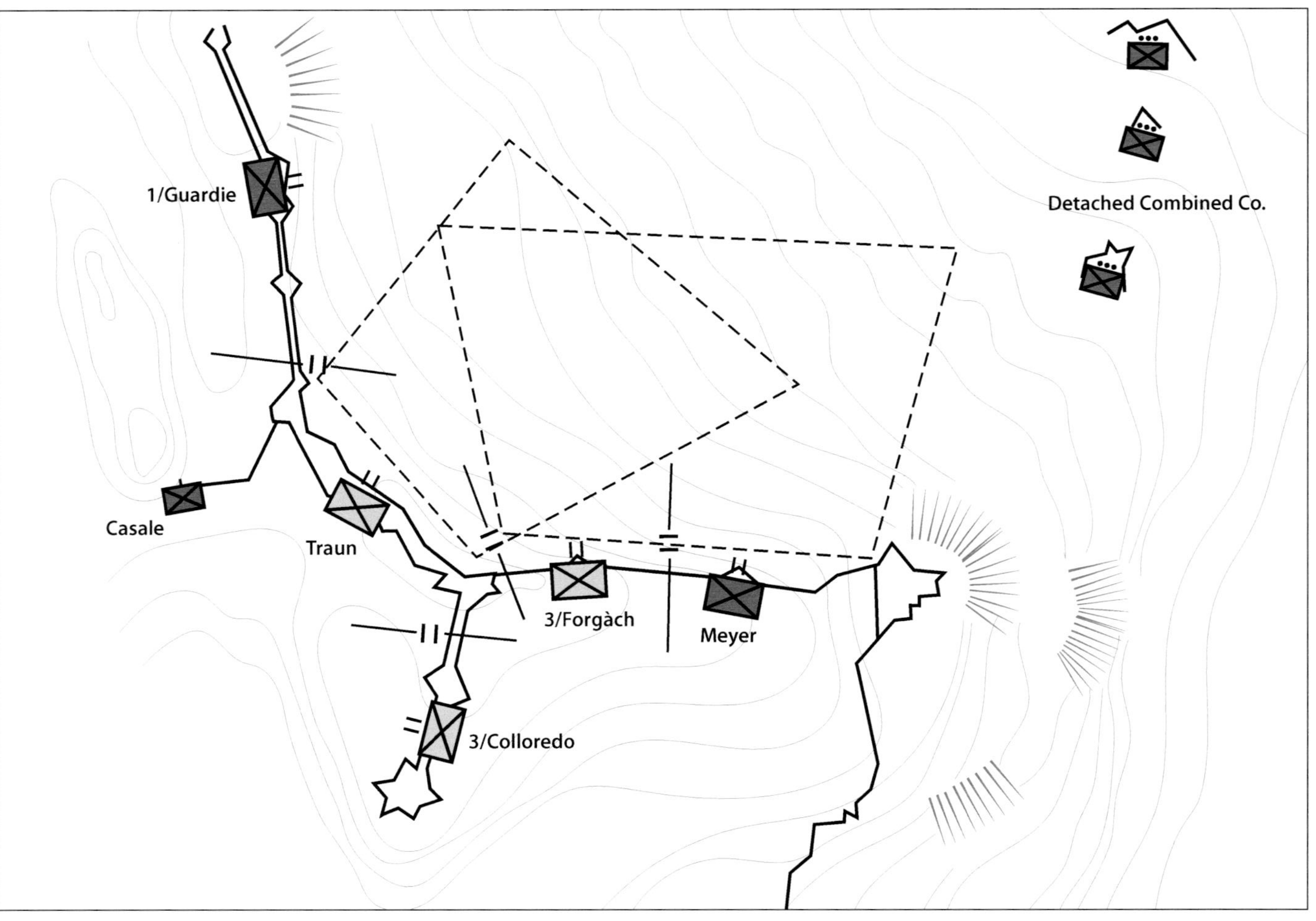

The tactical disposition of the western defences of the Assietta entrenched camp. The engagement areas of Austrian battalions of Traun and Forgàch and the Sardinian Swiss Reggimento Meyer were arranged to cover with infantry fire the re-entrant angle of the camp. This disposition was able to repel all the French attacks in this sector.

presumably around 70 metres. After that everyone, friend and foe alike, could hear the roll of drums beating out the sequence of orders:[96]

– *Schlacht an!*

In a few moments, 339 muskets were lowered towards the slowly advancing French. The battalion commander's orders were transmitted by the drums, which beat out a precise musical sequence known to all the men. Within the companies it was the turn of the captains and lieutenants to shout out the order that had been given, repeating it to each of the platoons. The Austrian and Sardinian soldiers of the Meyer and Forgách regiments had a relatively small target in front of them. The French battalion had a front about 20 metres wide, with a flank that extended about 90 metres. This gave the imperial soldiers of Traun, deployed less than 250 metres from the lily unit's right flank, a very inviting target, although the distance was particularly long for the weapons at their disposal. The individual soldier was not aiming at one particular enemy, but at the 'mass' of enemies. This aspect was underlined by the targeting orders, *Schlacht an!* (*en joue* in French, literally lowering the weapon) rather than *ziele/viser* (to aim). As the distance diminished, so did the soldiers' reference points for where to aim their weapons in relation to the advancing line of infantry. Having as a principle the idea of hitting the torso of the enemy soldier at a distance of 150 metres, the target was about 50 centimetres above the heads of the enemy. At 115 metres the target was the head; between 90 and 60 metres the target was the chest, and below 50 metres the target was the knees. Many, given the natural reluctance of human beings to kill, aimed at nothing: 'the closer you are to the enemy the more frightened you are, and a coward, who will shoot a brave soldier at a hundred paces, will not have the courage to do the same at a short distance'.[97]

– *Feuer!*

The effect of the first discharge was disruptive. According to de Mailly, 'the vanguard had advanced barely a hundred paces when it was hit by a discharge that completely annihilated it'.[98] In reality, this initial fire, carried out by 200 men of Meyer and 64 of Forgách, did not have the capacity to completely destroy a column of 12 grenadier companies, with a strength of 576 men, but it could certainly halt its advance. Given the firing tactics of the Sardinians and Austrians, with battalions deployed in two and four ranks respectively, a second and third volley was more than enough to inflict losses of such severity that the French grenadiers were routed. The head of the column was hit and knocked flat by the enemy's discharge, and within seconds the two front companies were annihilated. The fire developed by the battalion of Traun, given the distance, had a negligible effect, although it is quite possible that some of the shots actually hit the flank of the column. Although inaccurate, the heavy 18.3 millimetre lead balls fired from *Ordinäre Flinte* M1722 at a distance of 200 metres still had sufficient stopping power to kill a person, or at least inflict a disabling wound.[99] After all, the Austrians were carrying out a saturation fire, rather than targeting individuals.

---

96   The orders, extracted for the Austrians from the *Regulament und Ordnung des Gesammten Kaiserlich-Königlichen Fuß-Volks*, p.195 and for Sardinians from the *Recueil de ce qui se pratique dans le Régiment Suisse de Saconay* (Ivreé: Unknown Publisher, 1694), p.13, are identical.

97   J.A. Guibert, *Essai général de tactique* (Liege: C. Plomteux, 1773), Vol.I, p.216.

98   De Mailly, *Mémoire sur l'attaque.*

99   See the data reported in D-D. Scott, J. Bohy, N. Boor, C. Haecker, W. Rose, P. Severts, *Colonial Era Firearms Bullet Performance: a Live Fire Experimental Study for Archaeological Interpretation*, 2017, at

The Austro-Sardinian front line was soon enveloped in smoke produced by the detonation of thousands of muskets, which used black powder ammunition. A smoke screen enveloped the entrenchments, allowing the attackers to get as close as possible to the perimeter of the camp. However, the infantry defensive fire was such that the French battalions, sent on the assault one after the other, were quickly put out of action. (Detail the Battle of Casteldelfino by J.P. Verdussen, private collection)

The French soldiers soon had a rather confused idea of what was going on. Smoke soon made the view of the battlefield rather limited. Over 1,200 muskets, spread over just over 400 metres of trenches, were firing at the approaching enemy and a heavy blanket of smoke, resembling a thick fog, began to envelop the battalions engaged in firing. The infantrymen's individual weapons, loaded with black powder, emitted clouds of thick, greyish-white smoke, which hung low and which only a very strong wind – totally absent on 19 July 1747 – could disperse. This artificial fog represented a real obstacle to visibility on the battlefield, and the soldier engaged in the battle would not be able to see effectively beyond 50 metres ahead.

Volleys of musket balls streaked through the air and across the field, inflicting bruises, piercing uniforms and hats at long range, killing or seriously wounding at short range. The wounds could be tremendous; 'first of all an enemy bullet gave him a severe blow on his right knee. Then one hit him under the left arm and lodged near the spine, from which it had to be removed. Finally, the most tremendous and serious wound was caused by a deliberately

---

< http://modernheritage.net/research.html>, accessed 1 August 2022. This study is very important for understanding the effectiveness of eighteenth-century muzzle-loading weapons.

The French columns climbed up the side of the Assietta ridge only to be mowed down by the fire of their adversaries. The detail of de La Pegna's canvas illustrates in a schematic but effective manner the dramatic tactical situation in which de Mailly's column found itself. (Detail from The Battle of Assietta by H. de La Pegna, private collection)

engraved lead ball, which he received on his neck under the chin'.[100] When a musket ball struck at full force, it often travelled an eccentric trajectory as it passed through tissues of varying texture within the human body, causing severe damage in its path. The side most affected was the left, the one most exposed to enemy because of the posture to be assumed when firing the individual weapon. When a man was shot down, not only did the soldiers lose a comrade-in-arms, but the unit was deprived of an element of strength:

> One could receive the enemy with muskets loaded with large lead bullets, because this large lead bullet goes very far, hits those in the eyes, the face or the belly of those, frightens them by the nature of the wounds, which if they are smaller on the surface are no less deep, and the soldiers who received them will not fail to cause such confusion among their troop that their plans fail.[101]

---

100 C.F. Pauli, *Denkmale berühmter Feld-Herren* (Halle: Johann Gottfired Trampe, 1768), pp.283-284.
101 Le Cointe, *Le Science des Postes* Militaire, p.159. Regarding the variety of wounds one could face in an eighteenth- or nineteenth-century battle, a useful reference is M. Crumplin, G. Glover, *Waterloo after the Glory. Hospital Sketches and Reports on the Wounded After the Battle* (Warwick: Helion, 2019).

Sometimes a lifeless body could be the subject of macabre humour, although more often the screams of the wounded were a sound the soldiers did not like to hear, making them afraid for action and combat. It was standard procedure to forbid the troops from rescuing the wounded and carrying them off the battlefield. Without this precaution, four or five men would have left the ranks of the unit for every casualty incurred.

The grenadier battalion still had sufficient tactical 'weight' to continue the advance, but officers were needed who were able to manage the situation and the fight. These, however, were all dead or wounded at the time, hit by enemy fire as they were deployed almost entirely at the head of the column. *Capitaine* Joseph Teyssier de Tournier, of the Grenadiers Royaux de Modéne, received seven musket shots in various parts of his body. De Tournier was fortunate in that the blows he received did not damage any vital organ, and he was thus able to recover from his injuries. On 5 July 1759 he was accepted into the Corps of Invalids.[102] A colleague of his from the same unit, Charles François Hebrard du Busquet, was hit by two balls that struck him in the leg and head, and he also received a stone that put him out of action for good. Du Bousquet survived his injuries, and returned to service. On 14 July 1760 he became battalion commander, until his transfer to the Invalid Corps on 14 March 1765, where he could enjoy a pension of 400 livres per year.[103] De Mailly, having miraculously escaped the hail of bullets that was slaughtering his men, 'tried to regroup those who remained', to no avail.[104] 'What is it that destroys the courage of the troops in action, what makes them run for their lives? I'll tell you – it's the casualties they have to bear'.[105]

Losses incurred in an action affect a unit's strength in combat not so much by their absolute number, but by the rate at which they are incurred. A loss of 40 percent in two days is more detrimental than a loss of 70 percent of combat strength over two weeks of battle. This principle has direct application to the circumstances of eighteenth century combat, which was extremely compact in every respect, and losses in this percentage could be inflicted or sustained in a matter of minutes. The soldier could suffer physical and mental collapse as soon as his moral resources had been completely drained by the intensity of the action in progress:

> In a moment I was overcome by such fear that it robbed me of all my courage, and terror made my legs tremble. A child would have thrown me to the ground. About this 'cannon fever' I have often talked with officers of all ranks, as well as with gallant privates. They assured me on their word that anyone who claims to have been in battle, and has never experienced this terrible fear, must be considered a braggart and a liar. But they all spoke of one thing which I myself had noticed, namely, that this feeling is conveyed in this way in the early, middle, and late stages of a battle, that the stronger men support the weaker, and that a general flight

---

102 SHD/GR/2Yy58.
103 SHD/GR/2Yy58.
104 De Mailly, *Mémoire sur l'attaque.*
105 F.W. Zanthier, *Versuche über die Marsche der Armeen, die Lager, Schlachten un den Operations-Plan* (Dresden: Waltherischen Hofbuchhandlung, 1778), p.107.

occurs only when this fear grips the greater part of the army, and the weaker men drag the strong with them.[106]

Tried, frightened, exhausted from the continuous days of marching in the mountains, surrounded by corpses, once they had lost all control exercised by the officers, the soldiers strayed and fled. The first soldiers to abandon their units were those in the rear ranks. The men on the front could see their surviving officers, see the enemy, assess fairly accurately the danger they were in, decide what to do and how to deal with the enemy. The men in the rear ranks could see none of this, prevented from seeing by the bodies of the soldiers in front of them. Between them, and often below them, were the bodies of the wounded and the dead, while from the front only shouts and gunfire could be heard. Each unit was surrounded by a cordon of officers and non-commissioned officers; a first line of captains and lieutenants was positioned just in front of the first rank, or within it, with the main task of regulating the march and its direction. From this position they could command the diversionary manoeuvres to be put in place, the opening of fire, preventing a lack of fire discipline that could lead to the soldiers firing at will (*feu de billebaude*). It was a very exposed and dangerous fighting position, not only because of the shots that could come from the enemy, but also from their own men, from untrained or ill-intentioned soldiers. Another cordon of officers and non-commissioned officers stretched out at the rear of the battalion, employed in every useful circumstance to keep the troops cohesive in action, shouting orders, pushing the soldiers back into place with their hands, or putting them back in line with spontoons or partisans levelled at their kidneys, keeping the unit compact as best they could. Losses, however, increased with every enemy volley, and a killed or wounded graduating officer was one less element of control.

By this time the battalion was routed, out of control, as the officers, all leading the unit, had been wounded and killed. The battalion commander, *Colonel* de Gouy of the Régiment de La Reine, was seriously wounded when he was shot in the thigh.[107] At that point the unit turned from an orderly mass into a routed crowd:

> The flight crowd is created by a threat. Everyone flees; everyone is drawn along. The danger which threatens is the same for all... They feel the same excitement and the energy of some increases the energy of others... So long as they keep that the danger is equally distributed... No one is going to assume that he, out so many, will be the victim and, since the sole movement of the whole flight is towards salvation, each is convinced that he personally will attaint it... Everyone who falls by the way acts as a spur to others. Fate has overtaken him and exempted them. He is a sacrifice offered to danger. However important he may have been to some of them as companion in flight, by falling he becomes important to all of them... The natural end of the flight is the attainment of the goal; once this crowd is in safety it dissolves.[108]

---

106 C.D. Küster, *Bruchstück seines Campagnelebens im siebenjährigen Kriege* (Berlin: Karl Maßdorffs Buchhandl, 1791), pp.61-62.

107 *Extrait des état de service de M. le Comte de Mailly*, in Bourcet, *Principes de la Guerre de Montagne*, p.293.

108 Keegan, *The Face of Battle*, p.172.

De Mailly was unable to stop the grenadiers fleeing to the rear. As he tried to rally his panicked men he was hit by a musket bullet to the ankle; fortunately for him it was a spent ball and it was not necessary to evacuate him from the battlefield.[109] He marched alongside the second battalion that followed, 1/Bourbonnais. One of the *Petit Vieux* of the *Armée Royale*, the regiment saw its 1st Battalion advancing immediately after the grenadier battalion, and like them deployed in column 'like a vanguard'.[110] Intended to give depth to the assault units that preceded it, it now found itself acting as a vanguard for the forcing of entrenchments. The infantrymen of 1/Bourbonnais, thanks to the smoke from their muskets, were able to get even closer to the entrenchments. Suddenly they found themselves facing the mouths of 350 muskets, to which were added another 175 on the right flank at a distance of 200 metres. The men of Meyer and Forgách opened fire from about 50 metres away, and the effect was devastating. The French battalion advanced in column, presenting a narrow 20-metre front and 97.5 metre flank. The discharge from the entrenchment was able to stop the French battalion's advance immediately. Once stationary, 1/Bourbonnais became an optimal target for the Austro-Sardinian troops, who decimated it with a second volley. According to De Mailly, who was observing the fight from a few dozen metres away, the volley reached 'the head [of the battalion which] was hit hard, the Monsieur de Goas, colonel [commander of the regiment], up to the twelfth rank were knocked down'.[111] This meant that within seconds six out of 16 companies had been destroyed, and 288 men had been wounded and killed, 37.5 percent of the battalion's strength. This included the regimental commander, Louis de Biran d'Armagnac, Comte de Goas, and most of the officers in the unit. One of the company commanders, *Capitaine* Jean Baptiste De Lille de Penfenteyo, was immediately shot in the right arm, which was fractured, and received a second shot in the left foot. Unable to stand upright, he fell badly and sustained a series of bruises to his left thigh.[112] Decimated after a firefight lasting a few minutes, the men of 1/Bourbonnais were unable to continue to withstand the fire of the opposing battalions and began to retreat.

It is worth asking what kind of fire was put in place by the Austro-Sardinians. While the Austrians had in their de facto regulation a fire by ranks, the Sardinians, on the other hand, could fire individually. The discharges heard by de Mailly can be, in this case, only the Austrian ones of Forgách and Traun, while the Reggimento Meyer fired with much less regularity but with greater speed since the cadence of the shot was decided by the individual soldier. However, there is the possibility that Colloredo, the allied commander in charge of commanding the sector attacked by de Mailly, had decided to order a firing by ranks that also involved the Sardinian troops. After all, the enemy was 'collaborating', by launching a

---

109   Ledieu, *Le Maréchal de Mailly*, p.7.
110   De Mailly, *Mémoire sur l'attaque.*
111   De Mailly, *Mémoire sur l'attaque.* The colonel, Louis de Biran, born in August 1721, was killed in the fight. [F.A. Aubert de La Chenaye-Desbois], *Dictionnaire de la Noblesse, contenant les Généalogies, l'Histoire & la Chronologie des Familles Nobles de France* (Paris: Duchesne, 1770-1786).Vol.III, p.534
112   De Lille was one of the company commanders of 1/Bourbonnais, as confirmed by the rolls of April 10, 1748. SHD, 1Yc 192, *1er registre, Bourbonnais, 1e batallion.* On 12 April 1770 he became part of the Invalid Corps, with the rank of *capitaine premiere classe* and a pension of 400 livres. The injuries sustained 23 years earlier marked the body of the elderly officer: 'His right arm was crippled by a musket shot he received at Assietta in 1747, where he received at the same time a second blow to his left foot and numerous bruises to his left thigh'. SHD/GR/2Xy58.

single battalion after another to attack. Therefore, the psychological effect of a full discharge at close range could be the optimal tactical solution.

If we consider only the battalions of Forgách and Meyer, engaging at close range the head of 1/Bourbonnais, it means that of 528 shots, 288 – 54 percent – wounded or killed an enemy soldier. The figure is very high for eighteenth-century close-range combat. For example, in the famous close combat of Fontenoy, out of 7,105 French soldiers present, 1,266 (17.8 percent) were wounded or killed, while the survivors withdrew from the front.[113] The idea that emerges that on this specific front the French battalion was targeted by two close discharges by 3/Forgách, and by the less orderly but faster firing carried out by Meyer.

If de Mailly wanted to reach the trenches, he would have had to approach the enemy fortifications with a different tactic. Meanwhile, from his left flank came cries of victory.

5:15 p.m. Ruins of Riobacon, Austro-Sardinian Right Flank

French: one combined battalion, 500 men.
Sardinians: one company of Reggimento Meyer, 120 men.

Maggior Generale Alciati had decided to maintain the garrison of the redoubts on the right flank of the camp. His intention, as had been the case for the defence of the tenaille of the Testa dell'Assietta, was to have an advanced force capable of striking the enemy columns on the flank. In this case, a composite company of the Swiss Reggimento Meyer was detached, a total of 120 men deployed inside three small fortifications, known as the Ruins of Riobacon. These redoubts, open to the gorge, were more than 200 metres from the main perimeter of the camp and were also at a lower altitude than the route followed by the bulk of de Mailly's column, with the result that any resistance would have been in vain. Alciati's decision to maintain the garrison in the three redoubts was the biggest tactical error made by the Austro-Sardinians during the course of the day. Once outflanked they could no longer be effectively defended and had to be abandoned, and the French did not let the opportunity pass. De Mailly had prepared a combined battalion, 12 companies strong for a total of about 500 men, whose mission was precisely to conquer the redoubts and neutralise their garrison.

The French unit had assumed a peculiar formation compared to the other battalions; it marched with a front of three companies that marched parallel to the main column. On reaching the level of the redoubts to be attacked, the French commander, *Lieutenant Colonel* Antoine de Bordenave,[114] ordered a conversion to the left by company. The battalion thus found itself with a front of four companies, which were divided up as follows:[115]

---

113 The French losses are described in detail in Susane, *Histoire de l'Infanterie Française*; Vol.II, pp.87-88, 154-155; Vol.IV, p.162; Vol.V, p.54.
114 Antoine de Bordenave had been *lieutenant colonel* of the Régiment de Bourbonnais since 20 August 1746. J. de Courcelles, *Dictionnaire historique et biographique des Généraux Français, depuis le onzième siècle jusqu'en 1820* (Paris: De Courcelles, 1820-1823), Vol.II, p.436.
115 The tactical arrangement of de Bordenave's column is well described in Minutoli, *Des Campagnes Faites par S.M*, Vol.II, p.100, 'Piano dei trinceramenti della Sietta, stati attaccati dalle Truppe Francesi sotto gli ordini del Cav.re di Bell'Isle ai 19 Luglio 1747',

- A column of six companies to attack the rearmost redoubt.
- Two columns of three companies each to attack the two most advanced redoubts.

The French found themselves practically at the throat of the fortifications, in control of the altitude, and moreover outnumbered the defenders. The latter had just enough time to fire two volleys in disorder, after which Bordenave's column 'attacked them with bayonets fixed and jumped into the trenches, from which it drove them out without losing a single man'.[116]

The commander of the Sardinian detachment, once he sensed the French manoeuvre, hastened to disengage from the fight:

> [the French] detached a body, which descended through the woods, pushed forward, passing towards our right, in the interval that exists between the entrenchments of Assietta, and those of the Ruins of Riobacon. Since that ground was not at all entrenched, it was not difficult for them to advance, and as our pickets would have found themselves cut off by this movement, they wisely withdrew to the Argueil.[117]

At that moment only one cry was heard from the victorious French soldiers: '*Vive le Roi!*'.[118]

5:20 p.m., Assietta Ridge, Austro-Sardinian Right Flank

French: eight infantry battalions, one squadron of dismounted dragoons, 4,040 men. Austro-Sardinians: three infantry battalions, 1,104 men.

The capture of the Riobacon redoubts had suddenly improved the morale of the French troops and given de Mailly some hope. The men of 1/Bourbonnais, who were retreating after being fired upon by Austro-Sardinian regiments, saw, or were able to comprehend in some way, the victorious outcome of the French assault. They stopped and moved forward again in a disorderly fashion. The fire coming from the entrenchments was sufficient to stop this resumption of the offensive.

De Mailly ordered the Brigade Bourbonnais, at that time with *Capitaine* du Bourdet the most senior officer still alive, to attack the entrenchments. At that moment du Boudert had two tactical advantages that he could use to his advantage. The tactical layout of the Brigade Bourbonnais was still as expected for an attack *à la Folard,* but there were now four battalions, side by side, two by two. In the front line were 3/Bourbonnais on the left and 2/Bourbonnais Regiment on the right. On each side of the column two companies were deployed in line for the necessary fire support. In the second line were deployed the single-battalion regiments of Soissonais on the left and Des Landes on the right. The front of the column had six companies deployed on a 60 metre front, with no less than 280 men capable, at least theoretically, of engaging the enemy in bayonet combat before fire.

---

116 De Mailly, *Mémoire sur l'attaque.*
117 Priocca Report I.
118 De Mailly, *Mémoire sur l'attaque.*

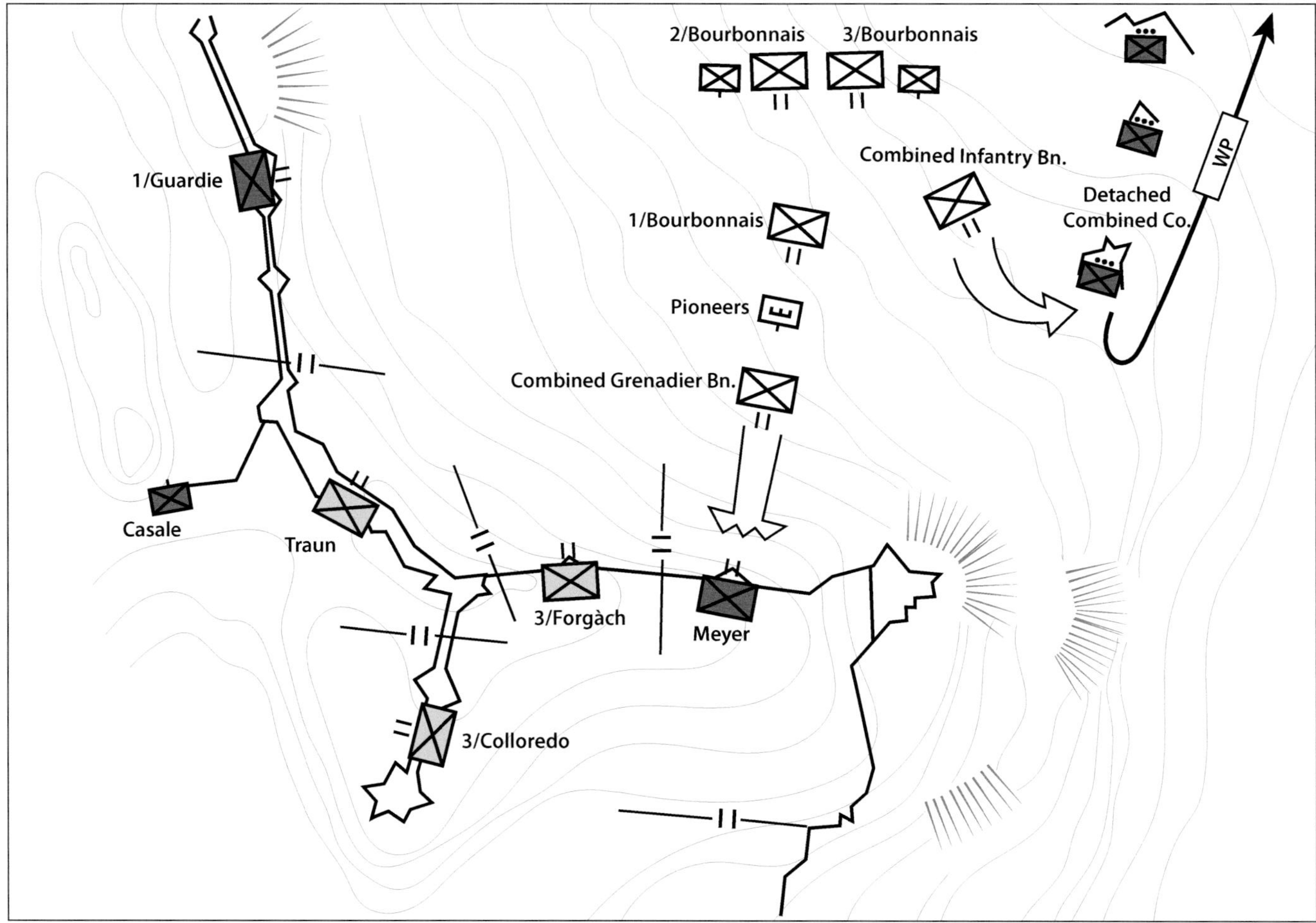

The attack of 5:20 p.m. against the sector held by 3/Forgàch and the single-battalion Reggimento Meyer. This kind of attack, called *à la Folard*, had very little chances of success. Only a combined infantry battalion on the left of the column could storm the Riobacon Redoubts, held by a single company of Meyer. This was the only part of the camp conquered by the French during the battle.

De Mailly had realized that attacking with edged weapons without adequate firepower was suicide. One had to get as close as possible to the entrenchment, hit the opponents with one's own fire, kill or wound them, force them to retreat or take cover as much as possible and then attack with the bayonet. Another advantage was the smoke from the gunfire. There was no wind blowing, so the smokescreen produced by the defenders' guns remained like a blanket of fog covering the defenders' view. The plan now was for the two leading battalions and the two supporting companies to breach the entrenchment, after which the two battalions in the second line would exploit their success and advance towards the Assietta pass. De Mailly briefly communicated his concept of action to the battalion commanders, indicated the direction of the attack, and let the Brigade Bourbonnais advance.

Graf Colloredo, on the other hand, was now convinced that what he faced was the bulk of the enemy column. Up until then he had managed the battle as best he could, but he was not at all at ease: he had no reserves to deploy, except to move the inactive companies of the Reggimento Mayer to the most exposed sector of the battle front, a solution that he put into practice during the battle. There was nothing else he could do but expose himself personally to combat:

> [I]f an officer stationed in a redoubt is attacked by the enemy, he should not enjoy firing himself and his men, but on the contrary he should be occupied only in verifying that all his soldiers do their duty well and that they do not shoot in the air. If he perceives that their ardour in the course of the enemy attack is slowing down, he will animate them with his voice. And if he sees that the enemy is making more progress on one side than the other, he will run to that place, to strengthen it. I know that this movement is sometimes dangerous, and that it would be better to have a small reserve to employ if necessary; but can an officer who has only a small detachment, whose parapet can scarcely be garrisoned by soldiers two ranks deep, be able to take away twelve or fifteen men to constitute a reserve?[119]

At that very moment there was fierce fighting at the Testa dell'Assietta, and the Conte di Bricherasio would never have sent one of the battalions of the Gran Serin to his assistance. If for any reason he managed to stop a French breakthrough, the Austrian general had no units to deploy to close the gap. He had to rely on the combat effectiveness *of* his men, wait for the French to advance and hope that they would persist with an attack *à la Folard*. They were able to approach up to 50 metres from the entrenchments, about the same distance as 1/Bourbonnais had come, and here the firefight began.

The Austro-Sardinians could see the head of the French column, larger than the previous one, in the middle of the smoke of the battle. The Austrians engaged the enemy with the usual regular volleys, the Swiss of Meyer began to fire much more rapidly, as expected from the Sardinian doctrine. Now, however, the French were also firing back. But against what? A line of heads and cocked hats, musket barrels rising for a few moments above the outline of the trenches, a few arms and little else. The smoke produced by the gunfire made it possible to decrease the distance to the enemy positions but the losses increased more and more as the

---

119 Le Cointe, *Le Science des Postes Militaire*, p.157.

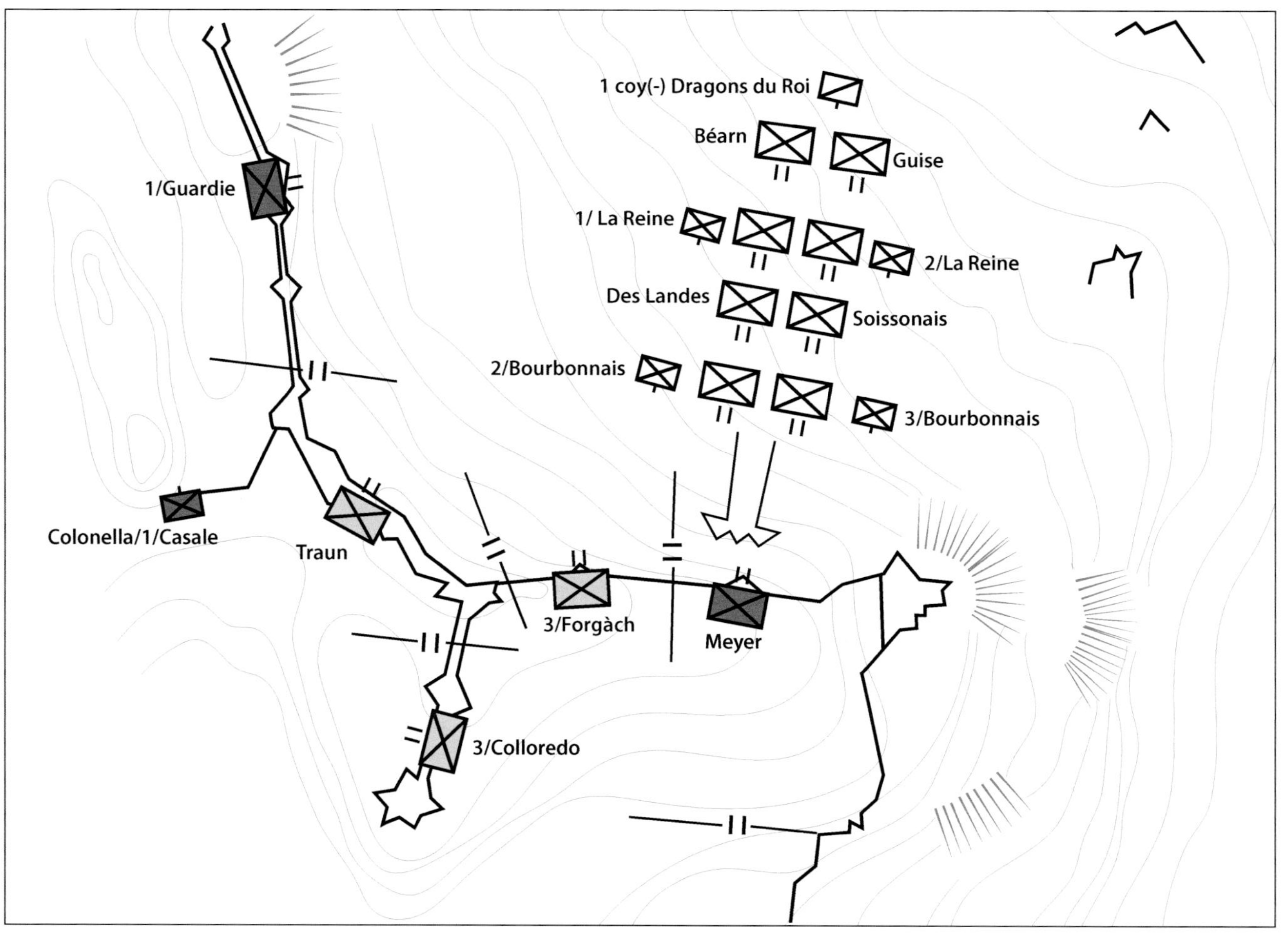

From 5:20 p.m. de Mailly's column tried to breach the fieldwork of the Sardinian camp, only ending the action at 6:30 p.m. after suffering appalling losses. Despite the numerical advantage, the tactical disposition *à la Folard* with no artillery support deprived the French of any possibility to storm the enemy fieldworks.

minutes passed. At about 5:45 p.m. 2/Bourbonnais was no longer able to continue the fight due to the losses suffered. Surrounded by smoke that was becoming thicker and thicker, the men had to march uphill towards an enemy that they could no longer see but who continued to fire and strike. The Austro-Sardinians were practically shooting blind, but this allowed them to maintain their rate of fire. The enemy was invisible or almost invisible, indistinct silhouettes shrouded in the 'fog of war'; any psychological qualms about firing at fellow men were removed by the physical absence of the adversary. Automatically, or according to a precise rhythm set by drums and regimental music, the Austrian or Sardinian soldier would load and fire, saturating the kill zone in front of the entrenchments with lead. The rain of bullets destroyed the cohesion of the two Bourbonnais battalions; the first to give way was the 2nd Battalion, which 'bent [backwards] like the previous one. Finally, de Mailly brought forward [towards the enemy] the third [3/Bourbonnais], which marched with unparalleled firmness. It was commanded by a certain Dubourdet'.[120]. In the end, even this battalion, left alone, could not do much and had to retreat in tatters. The three battalions of Bourbonnais had suffered the deaths of 19 officers and the wounding of 52 others – 67 percent of the officer corps – while among the troops the figures were 133 killed and 446 wounded respectively, making a total of 650 men knocked out of action, 40 percent of the present strength.[121]

At this point, only two battalions, those of Soissonais and Des Landes, advanced towards the ridgeline, with the result that they had to stop due to the intensity of the enemy fire. The two French units, without any supporting companies, approached the entrenchment which was now enveloped in the smoke of burning gunpowder. According to the brigade's tactical disposition, the two battalions should have exploited the breach opened by the leading battalions. The leading battalions had now withdrawn in tatters and the trenches were being fired at with increasing intensity. The battalions advanced without opening fire, tragically repeating the first attacks made by the two battalions of the vanguard. The commander of the Régiment de Soissonais, *Colonel* Guy-Marie de Lopriac de Coëtmadeuc, Comte de Donges, was shot dead, while the commander of the Régiment Des Landes, Pierre-Emé de Marcieu, was wounded. The situation, already serious, became completely untenable around 6:00 p.m., when the losses of officers and men became such that the two units had to retreat in disorder. Thrown into the trenches without any provision or order whatsoever to open fire on the enemy, Soissonais and Des Landes had suffered impressive losses. Soissonais suffered the loss of three officers killed, including the regimental commander, and the wounding of 11 others. Amongst the troops, 52 were killed and 176 wounded, making a total of 259 men, 45 percent of the total. Des Landes had three dead officers and 11 wounded; among the latter was the unit commander. Amongst the soldiers and non-commissioned officers there were 56 killed and 189 wounded, making a total of 259 men put out of action, 48 percent of the total.[122]

---

120 De Mailly, *Mémoire sur l'attaque. Capitaine* Dubourdet was one of the 3/Bourbonnais company commanders. He survived the battle, as he was present at the regimental review of 10 April 1748. SHD, 1Yc 192, *1er registre, Bourbonnais, 3e bataillon.*

121 *État des officiers qui se sont le plus distingués la journée du 19*, SHD, A1-3240-42. Some soldiers were also hit by stone throwing, as happened to Pierre Joseph Bertrand, soldier of Bourbonnais who in 1763 complained of 'weak eyesight after receiving a stone blow to the head in the battle of the Assietta'. SHD/GR/2Xy41.

122 *État des officiers qui se sont le plus distingués la journée du 19*, SHD, A1-3240-42; Report by Villemur. Also in this case some men were hit by stone blows, such as soldier Jean Thedés of Des Landes, 'long

It was 6:00 p.m.: the attack was not yet over, and more French battalions were approaching the trenches.

5:30 p.m. Testa dell'Assietta

French: three infantry battalions, 1,614 men.
Austro-Sardinians: one infantry battalion, two companies of grenadiers, one company of volunteers, 950 men.

The Chevalier de Belle-Isle could not believe his eyes. The first reports informed him of the death of d'Arnaud. Not only had the attack against the Testa dell'Assietta been repulsed, but the attack on the left was making no progress. The French commander at that moment knew that:

- D'Arnaud's column had three infantry battalions at its disposal, a force still sufficient to force the defences of the Testa dell'Assietta.
- De Mailly's column was still engaged in combat and could have broken through at any time into its assigned sector, also thanks to the action of the opposing column;.
- The main effort against the enemy position, the attack against the Gran Serin, had not yet begun.

Maréchal de Camp d'Andlau had assumed command of the central column,[123] but did not seem able to resume the attack immediately. However, it was necessary to maintain the effort against the Testa dell'Assietta in order to tie down as many enemy forces as possible as these, if not engaged, could reinforce the other threatened sectors. Since the commander of the central column had been killed, it was necessary for someone to replace him, an officer who was clear about the entire plan of action for the attack against the Sardinian camp. The Chevalier had no hesitation, mounted his horse and, with his aide-de-camp, rode towards the French troops' assembly point, which was located 120 metres away from the Tenaille. We do not know whether he was taking a calculated risk, consistent with the development of the French attacks in progress, or whether he was simply a desperate man who saw his plan of action – with his ambitions – crumble before the enemy entrenchments. The fact is that, as commander-in-chief, he lost sight of the overall vision of the battle and began to fight like a company commander, risking his own life.

Once off his horse, the situation he found was not the most encouraging. The first four battalions had been all but wiped out, and the other four did not seem to have much desire to come out into the open and attack the enemy fortifications. Nevertheless, he collected the battalion commanders and planned a new attack in an expeditious manner:

---

ago wounded in the right thigh by a stone'. SHD/GR/2Xy40.
123   *Affaire de l'Assiette pres d'Exiles,* SHD, A1, 3240, 39.

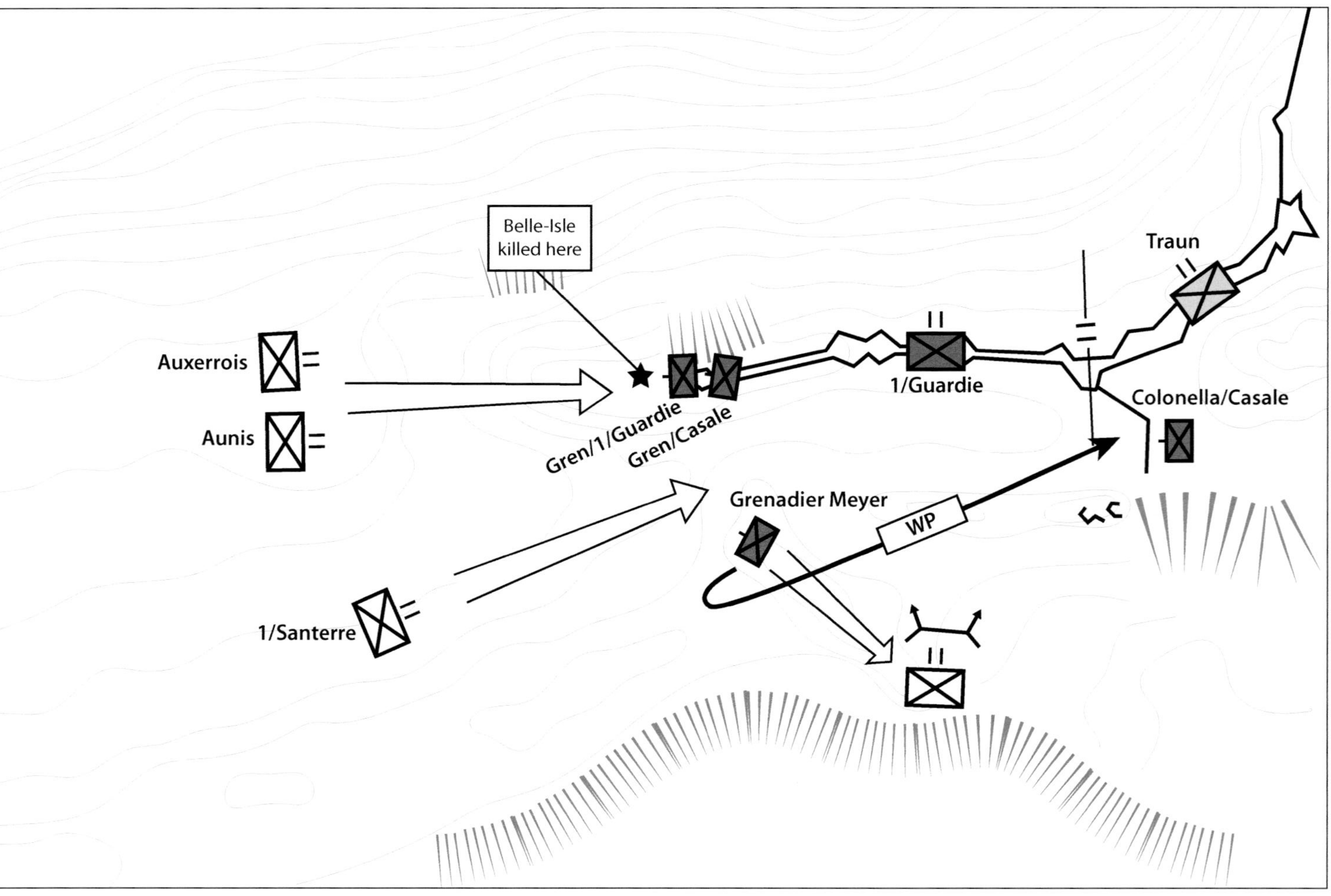

The attack at 5:30 p.m. against the Testa dell'Assietta redoubt. This action was a desperate measure against the Austro-Sardinian forces in the area. The presence of the French commander-in-chief was not sufficient to breach the defences and the commander himself, the Chevalier de Belle-Isle, was killed in action.

- The battalion of the Régiment de Santerre would attack on the right and dislodge the Sardinian troops stationed on the ridge south of the Tenaglia, in order to avoid a reverse firing.
- The battalions of the Régiments d'Auxerrois and Aunis would attack from the left and right respectively to widen the breach that was forming in the receding corner of the tenaille and occupy the Testa dell'Assietta. Once the breakthrough had been achieved, they would exploit their success and engage the enemy in the communication between the Tenaglia and the line of maximum resistance of the camp.

At least three opposing battalions could be counted on in this sector, and these units were not to reinforce other sectors but rather to confront the French forces stationed at the Testa dell'Assietta. Belle-Isle had greatly reduced the tactical tasks of the central column, but even so the situation was by no means simple.

In any case, the Régiment de Santerre, which until then had not been engaged in combat at all, moved along the southern slope of the Testa dell'Assietta, occupying the collar that joins the latter with the crest garrisoned by the grenadier company of the Reggimento Meyer and by Thomasset's volunteers, who were immediately engaged in combat. The French battalion commander's idea was, most likely, to fix the opposing force with fire from the ridge, to outflank their position from the left and force the small enemy unit to surrender or retreat. The 58 grenadiers and the 100 Sardinian volunteers realized the danger they were in, that is, of being cut off from the field, forcing them into an 'indispensable retreat'.[124] The disengagement was not easy, as the French continued to target the retreating enemy, and up to a distance of 250 metres they remained vulnerable to enemy fire until they were able to re-enter the camp. One grenadier from Meyer was killed, a second was seriously wounded, and two others were missing in action.[125] Once the area was secured, the men of Santerre remained to guard the area and to fire at the Testa dell'Assietta and its communications, in order to secure the enemy troops in their positions. During the attack, their fire continued to hit the communication between the Testa dell'Assietta and the camp proper, even managing to seriously wound one of the company commanders of 1/Guardie, the Marchese di Fassati.[126]

The Chevalier of Belle-Isle had secured his right flank, now it was time to attack the Tenaille again. He dismounted from his horse, sword in hand, and with his aide-de-camp, *Capitaine* Blondel d'Azincourt, at his side, began to advance. But at that moment the two battalions that were to attack, those of Auxerrois and Aunis, refused to move forward. If the grenadier battalion had failed, how could they succeed? 'Having commanded the fourth assault, the troops began to mutiny, seeing themselves exposed to a manifest massacre, and not being able to accept either the threats or the authority of the Commanding General, he took a flag from the hands of one of his standard bearers and had several officers follow him

---

124 Priocca Report I.
125 The two 'missing' grenadiers are very likely to be considered deserters. The wounded grenadier, Abram Adam, from Amsterdam, died on 21 July 1747 in Susa. AST, Sezioni Riunite, Ministero della Guerra, Ufficio Generale del Soldo, Ruolini di Rivista, Reggimento Meyer, Vol.8, 1747.
126 *Capitano* Francesco Ignazio Antonio Fassati, injured in action on 19 July, died on the 21st of the same month at the Susa Hospital from his injuries. AST, Sezioni Riunite, Ministero della Guerra, Ufficio Generale del Soldo, Ruolini di Rivista, Reggimento Guardie, Vol.89, 1747.

to animate the soldiers'.[127] Gathering together groups of grenadiers, survivors of the first attack, who had remained behind the tenaille, he advanced towards the Testa dell'Assietta: 'Belle-Isle gathered our soldiers under enemy fire and returned to the charge with the same vivacity, but with very little success'.[128] Again a thousand men rushed forward towards the tenailled walls of the Testa dell'Assietta and crashed into the fortifications.

The defenders took advantage of the moment of relative calm to supply the two companies stationed at Testa dell'Assietta with ammunition and evacuate the most seriously wounded. The smoke from the gunfire enveloped the fortifications, the adversaries were always just a few metres away, and the fighting was in full swing on the entire western front. *Maggior Generale* Alciati, for the moment, decided to leave the two grenadier companies of 1/Guardie and Casale stationary in their positions and not to relieve them. As long as the left flank was under attack it was better to keep the few reserves intact. Now, if nothing else, he could count on the Meyer grenadier company, which had just returned to the camp: its losses had been minimal and the unit could be immediately redeployed. The only problem was ammunition, which was becoming scarce everywhere. To make up for the lack of ammunition, stones began to be thrown, which had been specially piled up in the trenches at regular intervals or at key points. There is no specific doctrinal reference, among the materials made by the Sardinian army of the eighteenth century, which describes the use of stones in close combat. However, this use is confirmed by archival sources – just think of the reports of witnesses and French soldiers wounded in combat, and of archaeological ones. During the reconnaissance for the drafting of this volume, piles of stones were still visible in some sectors of the Assietta battlefield.

The French, few in number this time, found themselves once again enveloped in the smoke of gunfire, leaning against a virtually intact fortification and engaged in a deadly close combat. As Belle-Isle approached the tenaille, he was shot in the arm. The impact threw him against the tenaille, where he was 'stuck against the trenches'. He tried, as far as he could, to 'work with some grenadiers to bring down the clods, stones and tree trunks that made them up, and he also used his teeth'.[129] Blondel d'Azincourt retraced his steps and began to incite the soldiers of the three battalions who, at just over 100 metres, had not yet entered into the thick of the action. Anxious, worried about the fate of his commander and furious with the soldiers who would not advance, he decided to appeal to their sense of honour. 'I tried to revive our soldiers; I snatched a flag from the hand of a young ensign and carried it straight to the trenches. The column actually followed me, and I remained for an hour in that situation, without anyone being able to get up'.[130] The French officer retrieved

---

127   *Notizie delle guerre sostenute dalle Armi Austro-Sarde contro i Gallispani fino alla conclusione del Trattato d'Acquisgrana raccolte in un volume, e scritta da incognito autore nel quale si trova pure il giornale dell'assedio posto sotto Cuneo dai Gallispani li 13 7.bre e levato il dì 20. 8.bre 1744. Con due relazioni dei viaggi fatti, si crede dalla medesima persona in Piemonte nel 1747 e nel 1748*, AST, Corte, Materie Militari, Imprese, mazzo 8 d'addizione. The narration of the battle was delivered on 8 August 1747 by the anonymous writer directly to Carlo Emanuele III at the Royal Palace in Turin.

128   Blondel d'Azincourt, *Du champ de bataille vis-à-vis des retranchements d'Exilles*, p.411.

129   This was because he was evidently no longer able to use one of his arms. Blondel d'Azincourt, *Du champ de bataille vis-à-vis des retranchements d'Exilles*, p.411. This detail clarifies the reasons why splinters of wood were found in Belle-Isle's teeth. Pajol, *Les Guerres sous Louis XV*, Vol.III, p.260.

130   Blondel d'Azincourt, *Du champ de bataille vis-à-vis des retranchements d'Exilles*, p.411.

a flag and carried it to the side of the Chevalier de Belle-Isle. He knew that soldiers would never leave their insignia alone near the enemy. Eventually the battalions of Auxerrois and Aunis advanced and their thousand men impacted against the fortifications of the Testa dell'Assietta, but the fire of the defenders prevented any forward progress. In particular, it became necessary for the 1/Guardie and Casale grenadiers to saturate the area where a small breach had been created at the recessed corner of the tenaille with their fire.

The French tried everything: 'most of the grenadiers and soldiers [French] were wounded by blows from axes, bayonets and pickaxes, in the hands, arms and head, blows that they received while trying to climb the entrenchments of the enemies, who made a chilling slaughter'.[131]

> We cannot on this occasion refrain from mentioning the action of a grenadier who, having climbed on the shoulders of one of his comrades, attached himself to the faggots of the redoubt and reached the top by climbing, grabbed a [French] flag that had been planted on the redoubt and fought sabre in hand until he was riddled with bullets; someone else would follow him, when he was shot down.[132]

It is possible that this is the same episode, described by the Sardinian side as follows:

> Others did not fail to give ever new proof of valour and one of them climbed up the parapet of the redoubt. Unfortunately, he ended his life too gloriously, but too quickly, having fallen under the iron of a corporal of the grenadiers of the Reggimento Casale, who drove his bayonet into his belly.[133]

The fighting continued to rage and the two French battalions, huddled around the drystone walls of the trenches, were literally being ground down by the friction of the intense firefight. 'I remained for an hour in that situation, without anyone being able to climb. The grenadiers defending the damned redoubt were pelting us with large rocks, which they were throwing all the time, and killing an incredible number of men'.[134] The commander of the Régiment d'Auxerrois, Louis Joseph de Montcalm-Gozon, Marquis de Saint-Véran, was then shot and knocked unconscious to the ground.[135]

While his command action in New France are well known, Montcalm's command action of 19 July 1747 appears to be still to be investigated. Montcalm was commander of Auxerrois but held the rank of *brigadier*, and at that time he was also in command of the Brigade d'Artois, having delegated the management of his regiment to *Lieutenant Colonel*

---

131 Letter from the Comte de Marcieu, Lieutenant General of the Dauphiné, to the Duc de Belle-Isle, Grenoble, 26 July. SHD, A1, Vol.3240, 136.

132 De Mailly, *Mémoire sur l'attaque*. The anecdote became public and was also reported by other writers: Louis François Armand Du Plessis Duc de Richelieu, *Mémoires du Maréchal Duc de Richelieu* (Paris: Chez Buisson, 1793), Vol.VII, pp.221-222.

133 Priocca Report I. The Comte de Malines confuses this episode with the killing of the Chevalier of Belle-Isle, who in his story dies of a bayonet thrust in the chest. Robbone (ed.), 'Le "Memorie" del Conte Roberto Malines', pp.286-287.

134 Blondel d'Azincourt, *Du champ de bataille vis-à-vis des retranchements d'Exilles*, p.411.

135 Pinard, *Chronologie Historique-Militaire*, Vol.V, p.616.

Damour. The Brigade d'Artois in fact formed the central column, which was divided into various groups, under the command of two *maréchaux de camp*, Arnaud and d'Andlau. There are two possible hypotheses: firstly, Montcalm was with d'Arnaud at the head of the column and was immediately wounded in the initial stages of the battle; or, secondly, was placed in command of the battalions of the second echelon and was wounded during the second assault on the Testa dell'Assietta. This reconstruction favours the second hypothesis, taking into account that the two remaining battalions, Auxerrois and Aunis, would have remained without coordination and without a commander able to manage both. This instead Montcalm, with his rank of *brigadier*, could have easily done, giving the appropriate orders to his regiment and to the commander of Aunis, *Colonel* François-Emery de Durfort, Comte de Civrac.

After Montcalm fell, the surviving officers were unable to control their men and the two battalions of Auxerrois and Aunis began to disintegrate. By this time they had suffered 137 and 193 casualties, 25 and 36 percent respectively.[136] The soldiers took advantage of the fog produced by the gunfire and fled towards the line of departure. The Chevalier de Belle-Isle, his aide-de-camp and isolated groups of grenadiers persisted in maintaining their positions behind the tenaille. Unable to climb it, they tried, with great difficulty, to demolish it stone by stone, amidst continuous musket fire and stone throwing, the latter becoming more and more numerous. If the situation was untenable for the French, inside the redoubt 'the powder began to run out, and the weapons were out of order. The grenadiers fought practically only with stones'.[137]

At about 6.15 p.m. Belle-Isle abandoned his position and broke away from the wall where he had been leaning. He realized that the soldiers were retreating for a second time and, together with Blondel d'Azincourt, who was still following him clutching his flag, he went to the receding corner of the tenaille, where a small gap had formed, hoping to draw the soldiers' attention and thus bring them forward. It was, however, one of the most dangerous spots on the entire battlefield. He received a second musket shot, this time in the head, which killed him instantly. His aide-de-camp also became one of the French casualties at Assietta: 'Finally, what can I tell you that is more distressing. The poor Chevalier of Belle-Isle, or rather this hero, was killed, and I saw more than 1,500 men fall on my flanks. I left [my position] because of a hole in my head caused by a large stone'.[138]

The circumstances of the death of the Chevalier de Belle-Isle varies according to the source that one goes to read. The two most credible versions are the testimonies of the cca Report, since the writer was able to speak with the defenders of the Testa dell'Assietta and with French prisoners of war, and that of Blondel d'Azincourt, who accompanied the Chevalier of Belle-Isle on the assault as his aide. All other testimonies and reports written in the following days seem to be false embellishments that even from hour to hour were added to the meagre initial narrative. Without listing all the deviation elements, we can affirm with relative certainty that:

---

136   Auxerrois had suffered the loss of 30 men killed and 107 wounded. Aunis in turn reported 43 dead and 150 wounded in action. *État des officiers qui se sont le plus distingués la journée du 19*, SHD, A1-3240-42; Report of Villemur.

137   Priocca Report I.

138   Blondel d'Azincourt, *Du champ de bataille vis-à-vis des retranchements d'Exilles*, p.411.

At 6:15 p.m. the Chevalier de Belle-Isle was killed in combat. This detail in this painting is actually full of inaccuracies: the Sardinian units had no flags with them during the battle, the redoubt of the Testa dell'Assietta did not have a second order of fire and, finally, Belle-Isle had no flag in his hand. A first bullet, a 17.3 calibre lead ball, had caused a serious wound to his arm while a second shot, aimed at his head, killed him instantly. Both shots were fired by grenadiers, a detail that is correctly included in the canvas. (Detail from The Battle of Assietta by H. de La Pegna, private collection)

- The Chevalier received two musket shots, one in the arm and one in the head.
- He did not have a flag with him, which was instead carried on the field by his aide-de-camp. After all, he had been hit in the initial stages of the assault by a 17.3 calibre bullet in the arm, certainly a very serious injury that had probably involved the significant loss of organic tissues, if not the fracture or partial amputation of the arm.
- He uttered no encouragement cry before the fatal shot.[139]

---

139 The oldest version of a dying cry is the one described in in Chevrier, *La Vie politique et militaire de monsieur le Maréchal Duc de Bell'Isle*, p.220, where he cried '*à moi braves enfants!*', but, we should note, is said to have done so while dismounting from the horse. This detail makes this testimony at least doubtful. Subsequently, in the *Mémoires du Maréchal duc de Richelieu*, Vol.VII, p.221, his cry is given as '*à mon secours françois*'. The Italian officer and military historian Domenico Guerrini considered it right to quote a passage from a poem by poet Giuseppe Bartoli, *Battaglia del colle dell'Assietta*, in which Belle-Isle is imagined planting the flag on the entrenchments exclaiming '*Le voilà dans la terre du Roy!*' Guerrini, *La Brigata dei Granatieri di Sardegna*, p.514n. Since then, this detail has been uncritically accepted as valid by all those who have described the Battle of Assietta.

In the second half of the nineteenth century Vittorio Dabormida decided that the two soldiers who had killed Belle-Isle were Giovanni Battista Ellena, nom de guerre 'La Chiusa', private of Colonnello Company, and Giovanni Domenico Adami, from Cortanze di Cervere, war name 'Adam', private of the Second Colonnello Company, both of 1/Guardie.[140] Their participation in the well-known episode is to be considered doubtful, if not entirely an invention. The companies responsible for the defence of the Testa dell'Assietta during the attack in which the Chevalier of Belle-Isle participated were the grenadier companies of 1/Guardie and Casale. The grenadiers were perfectly recognized during the fight, due to their showy headgear, by Blondel d'Azincourt. Only later, during the last assault on the Testa dell'Assietta, were they reinforced: by the grenadier companies of Meyer and 3/Forgách, supported by the Second Colonnello Company under *Capitano* Carlo Emanuele Valesa di Montalto (per Priocca Report II), or by the Colonnello Company of *Capitano* Giuseppe

The aide-de-camp of the Chevalier de Belle-Isle, Barthélémy Augustin Blondel d'Azincourt (1719-1795). *Capitaine* of the Régiment de Normandie, in this portrait he bears the cross of the order of Saint Louis that he had earned in the field in 1745. It was he who on 19 July 1747 took up a flag and marched alongside the Chevalier towards the Testa dell'Assietta: 'The poor knight of Belle-Isle, or rather this hero, was killed, and I saw more than 1,500 men fall on my flanks'. The flag he held in his hands was not abandoned in the field, but was returned to the unit 'in a thousand pieces, because of the musket shots'. The longest piece was barely 60 centimetres long; a clear testimony to the ferocity of the fighting. (Portrait by Jean-Baptiste Perroneau, private collection)

Antonio Asinari di Clavesana (per Priocca Report I), both of 1/Guardie. The turnover of the companies is well described in the Priocca Report, in both its versions. One can easily guess where the legend was born; Ellena, like his other comrades, remained in service for a long time, remaining attached to the Reggimento Guardie until 1793, the year of his death. He was 74 years old and he was one of the last surviving veterans of the War of the Austrian Succession

---

140   Dabormida, *La Battaglia dell'Assietta*, p.130. Dabormida's main source was P. de Choulot, G. Ferrero, *Essai sur la Brigade des Gardes et la Brigade de Savoie* (Torino: Boca, 1845), p.56.

and, together with Louis Eugène de Courten (1715-1802) – in July 1747 commander of the Swiss battalions of the Reggimento Kalbermatten deployed at the Gran Serin – one of the last to have participated in the battle of Assietta. Even the children, six in all, followed the military career of their father, the last of whom died, with the rank of *luogotenente*, in 1823. We can imagine how the memories, handed down, modified, distorted, have transformed a veteran soldier into an undisputed protagonist of the battle itself.

After Belle-Isle fell, Blondel d'Azincourt emerged from the smoke enveloping the Testa dell'Assietta. Dirty from head to toe, partly his own blood flowing from the head wound, and partly that of the soldiers who had fallen on him throughout the fight, he staggered down the ridge leading to the base of the attack, which had become a gathering point for straggling regiments and the many wounded. He looked for the battalion to which the flag he was carrying belonged: 'my flag had been blown to smithereens by musket fire; as soon as I returned it to its battalion after the death of the Chevalier, the largest piece was two feet long'.[141] It was then 6.30 p.m.

6:00 p.m. Assietta Ridge, Austro-Sardinian Right Flank

French: 4 infantry battalions, 1 squadron of dismounted dragoons, 2,252 men.
Austro-Sardinians: 3 infantry battalions, 1,104 men.

De Mailly still had an entire brigade, La Reine, to try and break through the attack front assigned to him. The tactical layout of the brigade was, as with the Brigade Bourbonnais, suitable for an attack *à la Folard,* with the four battalions paired two by two. In the front row were 2/La Reine on the left and 1/La Reine on the right. On each side of the column two companies were deployed in line for the necessary fire support. In the second row the single-battalion regiments of Guise on the left and Béarn on the right were deployed. As in the previous attack, the front of the column had six companies deployed on a 60-metre front, with no less than 280 men capable, at least theoretically, of engaging the enemy with the bayonet, before opening fire.

However, the men of the Brigade La Reine had a tactical advantage over the two opposing battalions. The smoke from the gunfire now covered the attack front, and the French battalions were able to approach with relative impunity. For Colloredo this was the most critical moment; the enemy was approaching, but where? At what point would they attack the front held by the men of Meyer and Forgách?

The French appeared about ten metres from the base of the trenches, and immediately the Austro-Piedmontese fire resumed with maximum intensity. The attacking column suffered one or two general discharges, and the two battalions of La Reine were thrown back. Protected by the smoke screen created by the shooting, the battalions reorganized and de Mailly drove them back to the attack. The French commander, to mitigate the gunfire coming from the right flank, shifted the axis of advance to the left in the

---

141 Blondel d'Azincourt, *Du champ de bataille vis-à-vis des retranchements d'Exilles*, p.411. To understand the damage suffered by the flag, it should be useful to know that a flag of the French army of the War of the Succession of Austria was a square of cloth with a side of 162 centimetres.

direction of the 'Inferior Redoubt'. The French 'with shouts of rage moved up to the foot of the entrenchment',[142] and impacted along the section of the entrenchment between the 'Inferior Redoubt' and the first redan on the left, roughly in the centre of the Reggimento Meyer sector. This time De Mailly's men opened fire; two companies had been detached to the flanks of the column for this purpose. The situation was tactically similar to what d'Arnaud's column had suffered earlier at the Testa dell'Assietta. The walls of the entrenchments were lower here, however, and the Sardinian soldiers were perfectly recognizable; faces, hats, musket barrels and parts of the trunk could be seen a few metres away. The point of impact corresponded to that held by the Zürcher Company; *Capitano* Johann Ulrich Zürcher was shot in the head and died instantly. Five other soldiers were killed by enemy fire, and at least one other was seriously wounded.[143] The French battalions became disordered after the impact, crushing along the front of the entrenchment both to the right and to the left. In doing so they also activated other companies of the Sardinian regiment; the Colonnella and the Luogotenente Colonnella. In the course of the firefight, Meyer had 13 soldiers killed and four others seriously wounded.[144] The situation was no longer as fluid as it had been at the start of the battle, and the enemy was now close to the fortifications. Moreover, after almost two hours of almost continuous fire, some of the muskets were unserviceable and ammunition was becoming scarce. Rocks were thrown at the attackers and they suffered losses.[145] However, the Austro-Sardinian retaliatory fire was devastating; the two battalions of La Reine suffered 140 dead and 442 wounded, making a total of 583 casualties, 55 percent of their strength.[146] Among the losses was the regiment's commander, *Colonel* Louis de Biran d'Armagnac, Comte de Goas, who was wounded in action. The other two regiments that took part in the attack, and who deployed in the second line, also suffered losses serious enough to prevent them from continuing the attack; Béarn had 29 killed and 95 wounded, 23 percent of their strength, and Guise 39 killed – including the regimental commander, *Lieutenant Colonel* Alexandre de Beauregard – and 110 wounded, 28 percent of their strength[147]

The defenders were beginning to show signs of giving way, but the attack had been a bloodbath for the French: 'what remained of the column was almost entirely destroyed

---

142   De Mailly, *Mémoire sur l'attaque.*

143   AST, Sezioni Riunite, Ruolini di Rivista, Reggimento Meyer, Vol.8, 1747.

144   Transported to the hospital in Pinerolo, they died of wounds sustained in the weeks following the battle. AST, Sezioni Riunite, Ruolini di Rivista, Reggimento Meyer, Vol.8, 1747.

145   SHD, 2Xy40; Jean Pouderoux, drummer of Béarn, who 'complains of pains in his left thigh where he received a blow from a stone'; Antoine Nouveau, drummer of Béarn 'received a stone hit at the Assietta affair'; Mathieu Nonnat, *caporal* of Béarn, 'feels discomfort in his knee due to a patella broken by a stone blow in the fight of the Assietta'; Antoine Dominique Leclerc, soldier of Regiment Béarn, 'has pain in his head from a stone blow he received at the Assietta'. The soldiers in question were all transferred to the Invalids in 1763.

146   *État des officiers qui se sont le plus distingués la journée du 19*, SHD, A1-3240-42; Report of Villemur. Two flags were also lost during the attack: *Mercure Historique et Politique*, Tomo CXXIII, La Haye, Juillet 1747, p.181.

147   *État des officiers qui se sont le plus distingués la journée du 19*, SHD, A1-3240-42; Report of Villemur. The Régiment de Guise probably lost one of its flags which, later collected by Austrian soldiers, was mistaken for that of a Spanish battalion given the particular geometry of the banner's design. *Mercure Historique et Politique*, Tomo CXXIII, La Haye, Juillet 1747, p.181.

by the last of the enemy fire. Finally, only two or three hundred men remained of two brigades'.[148] The four French units had to be disengaged as quickly as possible before they were annihilated. Covered by the Dragons du Roi detachment and the less damaged companies of Béarn and Guise, de Mailly organized a rearguard of 350 men, half a battalion's strength. Deployed in two ranks, the unit held a front of about 110 metres, more than enough to protect the remnants of the brigades flowing back towards the line of departure, a task made easier by the enemy who seemed to have no intention of coming out of the trenches and counter-attacking. Upon arriving at the base of the crest of the Testa dell'Assietta the French commander received news 'from an officer in the column of the Chevalier de Belle-Isle',[149] that the Chevalier himself along with d'Arnauld had died in the fighting. In the meantime, relays from *Lieutenant Général* Villemur had also arrived, informing him that he would shortly be attacking the fortifications of the Gran Serin. It was necessary to secure the enemy on the western edge of the plateau. But with what?

Shouts of jubilation rang out from the entrenchments. On at least one sector of the perimeter, the attacks had all been repulsed and the enemy was in full retreat. Colloredo, once he was certain that the enemy had no intention of continuing their offensive action, went to make contact with Alciati to obtain fresh information on the general situation of the battle. It was 6:30 p.m. and the enemy's main attack had not yet developed.

6:30 p.m. Gran Serin, Austro-Sardinian Rear Flank

The first French troops had set foot on the summit of the Gran Serin at 3:30 pm. After three hours they were now all concentrated on the southern platform of the broad summit of the mountain, and were reorganizing to attack the summit redoubt.

De Villemur had decided to use the best troops at his disposal to force the Gran Serin defences. He knew he had a relatively small force in front of him, two battalions at most, so the two columns *à la Folard* could break through the entrenched front. No reliable documentation has yet been found of how the attack columns were composed, in particular that of de Villemur. The reconstruction proposed below takes into account the seniority of the units, which the commander had to evaluate during the planning and deployment phase of his units, and the losses suffered during the combat.

- The first column, under de Larnage, with 1,963 men, would attack on the right and would be the force in charge of making the main breakthrough on the Gran Serin to open the way for the second column. Spearheading the column were two combined battalions, made up of an amalgam of 13 companies from battalions at de Villemur's disposal and six companies detached from the Grenadiers Royaux du Modène. Two other battalions followed, 2/ and 1/Condé. Altogether the column had a narrow front of 40 metres and a length of 203 metres, which was too long for the size of the Gran Serin.

---

148 De Mailly, *Mémoire sur l'attaque.*
149 De Mailly, *Mémoire sur l'attaque.*

The battalions, for the time being, were massed on the eastern edge of the summit, awaiting orders to advance.

- The second column, under de Villemur, with 3,912 troops, was to exploit the success of de Larnage, penetrate through the gap opened by it, and head west to occupy the Grande Comunicazione, eventually the Colle dell 'Assietta. If he had arranged the battalion columns side by side, two by two, Villemur would have created a column with a front of 40 metres and a flank of about 400 metres. He then decided to deploy the battalions in two ranks, maintaining their column formation. The units were arranged as follows: in the first line, from left to right, 1/Royal Roussillon, 3/, 2/ and 1/Mailly; in the second line were, again from left to right, 1/Saintonge, 1/Périgord, 1/Boulonnais and 1/Guyenne.[150] The column was 80 metres wide and about 180 metres deep.

- The third column, under de Laval, with 1,467 men at its disposal, was the smallest of the three, and consisted of the units most exhausted by the approach march. It was made up of the following single-battalion regiments, listed from front to rear: Beauce, Beaujolais, and Agenois. The column's task was a simple covering one; starting from the Grange dell'Assietta it would control the roads coming up from Fenestrelle and would fix, with a forward march, the Austro-Sardinian battalions stationed in defence of the hill.

The French general could easily see that in the other sectors d'Arnaud and Mailly had not yet made the desired breakthrough. If anything, they were pinning a good number of the enemy's troops in the trenches, which for the moment were far from the decisive sector of the battlefield. Confident, he began to give the final orders for the attack to the column and battalion commanders:

- The first column would attack and occupy the Gran Serin redoubt with a bayonet attack *à la Folard*. The soldiers were clearly ordered to 'advance with bayonets on their muskets without firing'.[151]

- The second column would break through the entrenchment on the left of the redoubt itself, and would attack, taking advantage of the dominance of altitude, the Austro-Sardinian columns that were rushing towards the summit.

- The third column would fix, with a demonstrative attack towards the Assietta pass, the opposing forces that would have tried to reinforce the Gran Serin.

The Conte di Bricherasio, on the other hand, was living in excited moments. From his command post inside the Redoubt of the Great Serin he could see the French battalions

---

150   The layout of de Villemur's column is not easy to reconstruct. Certainly, the space of the Gran Serin crest, although very large, did not allow the usual tactical arrangement for an attack *à la Folard*. That the French commander has adapted his deployment to the narrowness of places can be deduced from the drawings in the *Carte Topographique en mesure d'une partie des Vallès d'Oulx et Pragelas, avec le Rétranchèmens de L'Assiette, les Campemens et mouvemens des François et les postes qu'ils attaquerent le 19 Juillet 1747*, AST, Corte, Carte Topografiche e Disegni, Carte Topografiche per A e B, Pragelato 1. References to the tactical arrangement described in the text can also be deduced from other topographic maps, such as *Plan des retranchements du Col de l'Assiette*, BRT, Assietta Dis.III, 38.

151   *Lettera del Sig. Intendente Baldoino di Santa Margarita. Nuove sulla disfatta de nemici all'attacco del Col de la Sieta*, AST, Corte Materie Militari, Imprese, Mazzo 7 da Inventariare.

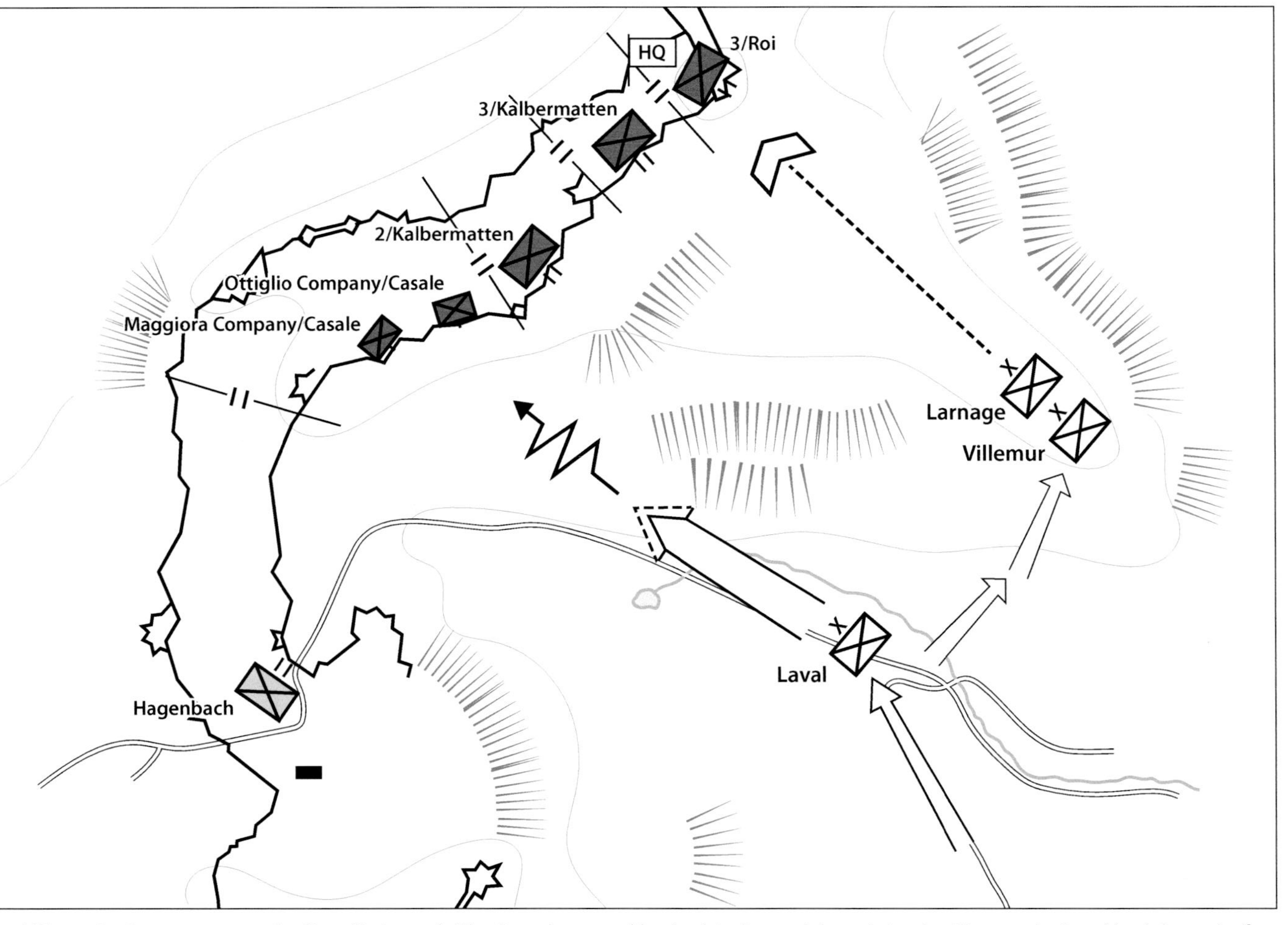

Villemur's plan to conquer the Gran Serin peak. The French general had at his disposal three brigades. That under Laval had the task of fixing as many enemy units as possible with a feint. The two other brigades, led by Larnage and by Villemur in person, had the task to storm and conquer the Gran Serin Redoubts. On paper, a quite simple operation…

amassing and attacking the most critical sector of the entrenched field, defended by only two battalions. Fortunately for him, by 6:00 p.m. 3/Roi had arrived at Gran Lago, situated on a plateau just east of Gran Serin. It would take about half an hour for the unit to march over and deploy within the summit redoubt. The Piedmontese commander had to quickly reorganize his defences; the Val di Susa militiamen were made to flow towards the Gran Lago and form a link with 1/Monfort. Inside the Gran Serin redoubt 3/Roi was placed; to follow on the right, along the entrenchments of the Great Communication the men of 3/Kalbermatten were deployed, alongside which the 2/Kalbermatten was placed. Bricherasio thus had at his disposal a small brigade consisting of three solid Swiss battalions, all of which were German-speaking. The linguistic homogeneity, which was certainly no accident – the Reggimento Chiablese, which spoke French, remained in the Argueil – would have favoured the understanding of orders. But there was no reserve, and the enemy attack would be conducted with a disparity of forces of almost one-to-four in favour of the attackers. There was little left to do: all available forces had to be called up from the other sectors of the camp and concentrated on the Gran Serin. Only in this way would it be possible to save the small allied army stationed at Assietta, for which the retreat routes were arranged.

The orders of the Piedmontese general were as follows:[152]

- *Luogotenente Colonnello* de Courten, in command of the three Swiss battalions, would defend the summit of the Gran Serin in order to keep the passage to the Vallette pass free.
- *Brigadiere Generale* Martinengo was to immediately take command of all the units present between the summit of the Gran Serin and the Gran Lago, specifically 1/Monfort Regiment and the Militia units present, in order to cover the retreat in case of necessity and set up new lines of resistance. In case of necessity, 1/Sicilia, stationed at Colle delle Vallette, was also available.
- *Maggior Generale* Alciati would send all the necessary reinforcements for the defence of the Gran Serin.

The commander was not sure he could hold the position. More soldiers were needed, and quickly. Messengers immediately left to look for Alciati.

6:45 p.m., Testa dell'Assietta, Alciati's Command Post

The tactical situation along the entire western sector was still unclear. Certainly the attacks on the Dora side had ended, but around the Testa dell'Assietta firing was still going on, as small groups of French soldiers kept in contact with the Sardinian troops. This gave *Maggior Generale* Alciati the impression that the fighting had only slowed down for a moment. In the meantime, the messengers from the Conte di Bricherasio arrived, describing how serious the situation on Gran Serin was, with the request to bring reinforcements towards the summit of Gran Serin as a matter of urgency. However, no one had bothered to give Alciati the fullest

---

152 Priocca Report I.

possible information about the strength of the attack and what troops Bricherasio had at his disposal to defend the Gran Serin. At that moment, Alciati was completely unaware of the arrival of 3/Roi and believed that the commander's situation was particularly critical.

Alciati decided it was time to disengage and retreat towards the Gran Serin. He immediately sent *Brigadiere Generale* Martinengo to Bricherasio's command post, as he had been ordered, and began to round up the freshest units to send to the commander's aid. The following units were immediately available to him:[153]

- One battalion Reggimento Meyer, without grenadier company.
- One battalion Regiment Hagenbach.
- Colonnella Company Reggimento Casale.
- About 800 militiamen, part of the Pragelato militia and part Waldensians.

The role of the militia in these phases of the fight is still not entirely clear. It is possible that they remained to garrison the retrenchments assigned to them even after the departure of the Colonnella company of the Reggimento Casale. Alciati at that time most likely concentrated on recalling the line infantry units to send to the Gran Serin. The militiamen would have guaranteed an excellent protective screen in the event of a general retreat.

Alciati then thought about organizing the disengagement from the French forces. The battalions of Forgách, Traun and Colloredo, under the command of Colloredo, would be deployed on the western ridge of Assietta and would protect the retreat of the grenadier companies from the Testa dell'Assietta, after which it would be the turn of 1/Guardie. In this way, the disengagement would take place in stages and as safely as possible. The retreat would begin as soon as Alciati deemed it necessary.

The first rearguard units, lined up in columns, began to march towards the threatened sector. Alciati would send the Colonnella company, commanded by *Capitano* Vittorio Sobrino, to re-join the other two companies of Casale, the Maggiora and Ottiglio, deployed on the left flank of the Kalbermatten battalions, while Meyer and Hagenbach would serve as reserves deployed on the northern edge of the Great Communication. For the Casale company, the route was very short, a maximum of 15 minutes' march; however, the other two battalions would take about 30 minutes to reach the Gran Serin, and about an hour to pass the entire column.

At that moment the much-feared attack on the Gran Serin began.

7:00 p.m. Gran Serin, Austro-Sardinian Rear

French: 10 infantry battalions, two combined battalions, 5,875 men.
Austro-Sardinians: three infantry battalions, 2,002 men.

Villemur, at his tactical command post on a small rise south of the Gran Serin peak, was feeling optimistic. The French attacks on the other sectors of the field continued, securing

---

153 Priocca Report I; Minutoli, *Relation des campagnes faites par S.M.*, pp.246-247.

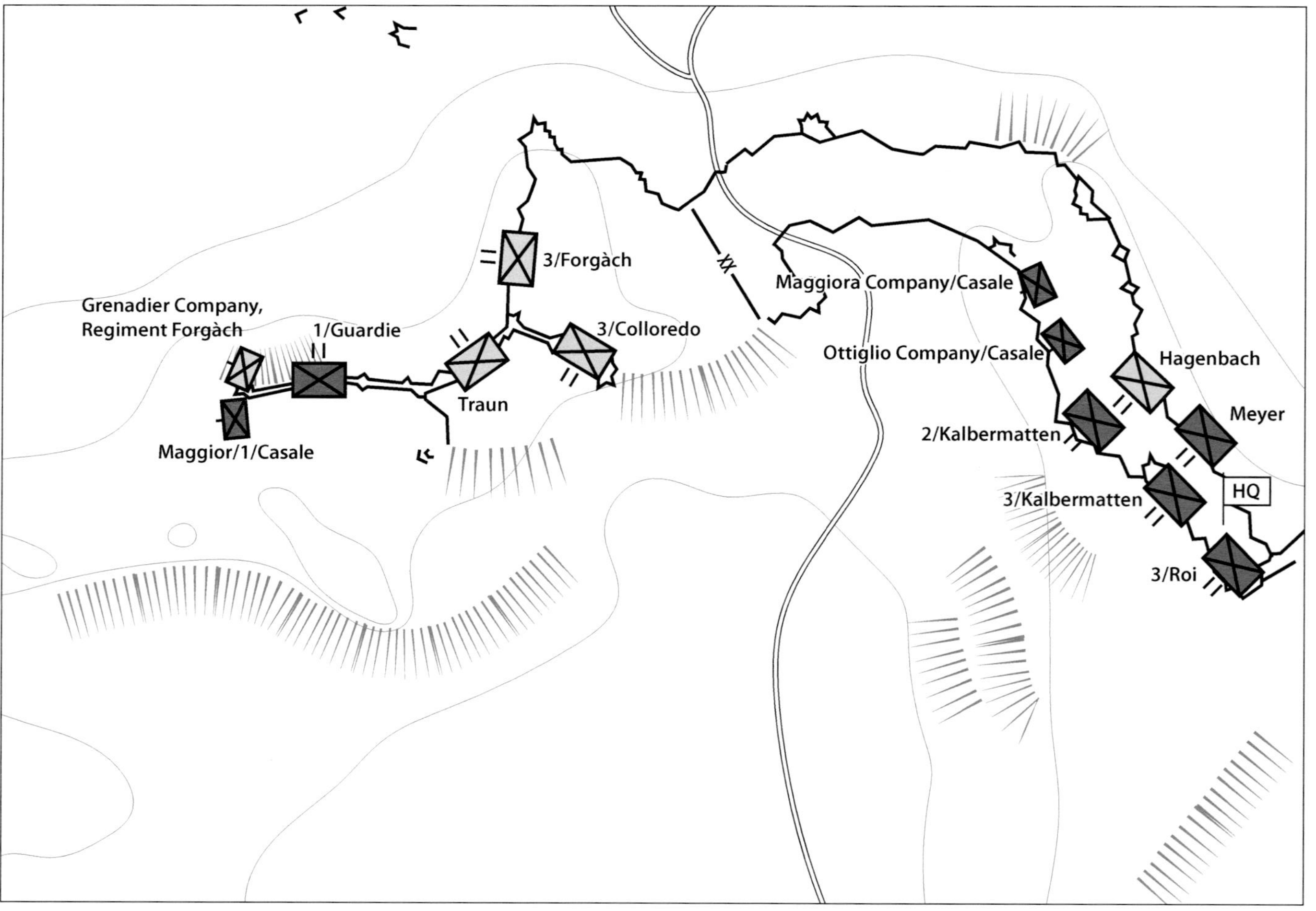

The Austro-Sardinian tactical disposition on 19 July 1747, at the end of the battle. The Austro-Sardinian commander, Bricherasio, saw the Gran Serin position under the threat of a massive enemy attack, which occurred late in the afternoon. So, he ordered the abandonment of the western side of the camp in order to have all the viable units en route to defend on the Gran Serin summit.

a number of enemy battalions in their positions. He now faced an estimated enemy force of no more than three infantry battalions, and the field fortifications the enemy had erected were far less complex than those de Mailly and d'Arnaud had faced in the afternoon. The Sardinian commanders themselves would later admit that the trench profiles were

> [I]nsufficient for good defence unless the troops are placed behind the parapet on several lines, that the redoubts are too small to provide any considerable footholds for this great expanse of entrenchment, that in many places they are tight against a wall, so that the troops can only make a palisade fire, and if the enemy assaults them by pushing them back from the parapet, they are obliged to uncover themselves entirely, and to climb in confusion on the curtain to save themselves.[154]

In short, the defenders were perfectly visible to the adversaries, and the soldiers remained uncovered from the chest upwards, enjoying far less protection than the grenadiers posted at the Testa dell'Assietta or the units on the right flank. These defences, according to the French commander, could be easily overcome. The main problem was that his men were tired. They had been marching for days, they were physically exhausted, and now they would have to make the decisive assault.

The Conte di Bricherasio had very few options. The only choice he had, given the passive defences at his disposal, was to slow down the enemy forces as much as possible by exploiting the firepower of the three available battalions, waiting to receive reinforcements and, if necessary, allowing the bulk of the forces involved to retreat. Luckily for him, the two regiments involved, Kalbermatten and Roi, were among the most solid and experienced units available in the entire army of His Majesty the King of Sardinia.[155] Moreover, the units at his disposal, with the exception of 1/Guardie and three Austrian battalions, were now all concentrated at Gran Serin. Another element that worried the allied commander was the lack of ammunition. Just then, around 7:00 p.m., Signor Giovanni Battista Guigas, the merchant from Fenestrelle who had been sent in a hurry by the governor of the Fenestrelle stronghold to check the situation on the field, appeared at his command post. Sardinian tactical doctrine favoured a defence based on firepower, but would the ammunition issued to the soldiers and in the high-altitude depots have been enough? Bricherasio was not entirely sure. Without mules for transport, the logistical resources in terms of ammunition and food were not great. Bricherasio decided to keep Guigas with him; if necessary, he would send him back to Fenestrelle to collect food and ammunition.[156]

The first French column advanced slowly, keeping to the right of the summit ridge; its objective, the summit of Gran Serin, at an altitude of 2,589 metres, was less than 300

---

154 Benedetto Maurizio, Duca del Chiablese, *Relation de mon voyage fait en 1766*; AST, Corte, Carte Topografiche e Disegni, *Carte Topografiche Segrete*, 2 F II. Subsequently, in fact, 'the insufficiency of these profiles was recognized by the Engineer himself who had designed them because first of all after the agreement of 19 July, he made them triple the thickness and height at the head of the Serran [Gran Serin]'.

155 On the Swiss regiments in Sardinian service, organization, tactics and their battle effectiveness see Cerino-Badone, "An Army inside the Army"', pp.171-198.

156 Gabotto, *La verità sulla battaglia dell'Assietta*, p.232n; Peyronel, Usseglio, *Di qui non si passa!... forse*, p.383.

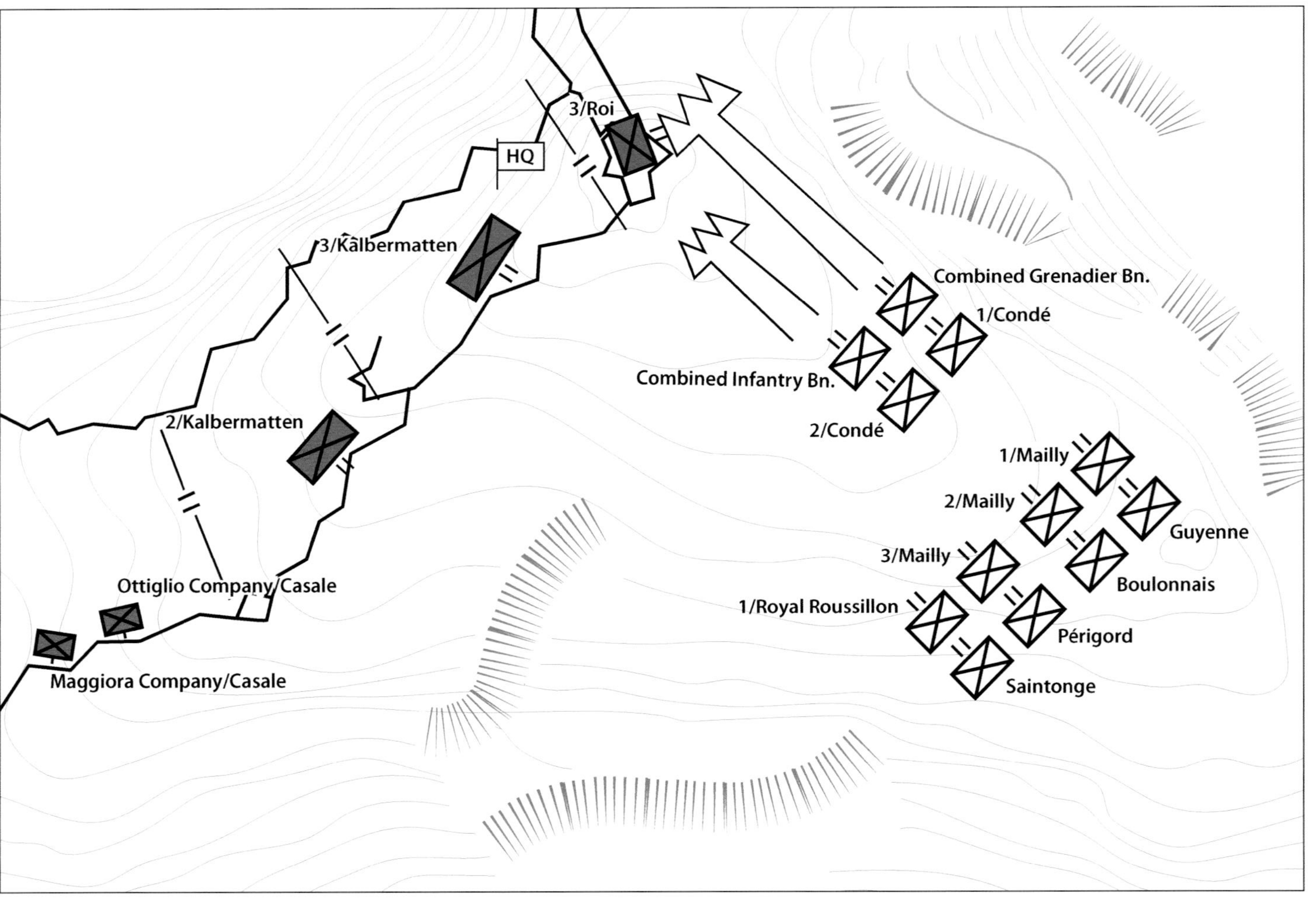

The first attack against the Gran Serin at 7:00 p.m. Four crack infantry battalions surrounded the redoubt on the top of the hill, but the firm defence of the Swiss 3/Roi, which reached the battlefield less than an hour before, defeated every French attempt to storm the Sardinian position.

metres away with a positive difference in height of about 90 metres. The French unit suffered at least four musket discharges from the Oschwald Company of 3/Kalbermatten and the Maggiora Roguin Company of 3/Roi. The French assaulted the enemy entrenched line, but were unable to get close to the enemy positions and engage in bayonet fighting. In order to be successful, a bayonet attack must be conducted against untrained troops in an unfortunate tactical situation, shaken by prolonged artillery bombardment, who are likely to flee due to previous combat situations. The Swiss of the Reggimento Roi had no intention of turning their backs on their adversary – they did not even have the physical space – while the supreme commander came within a few metres of them. The French therefore found themselves facing an adversary who not only did not give ground but was also determined to fight.

So, the column, whose head had already been hit hard by the fire coming from the redoubt and wounding and killing the officers in charge of the unit, stopped a few metres away and tried to return the fire it was receiving. The battalion deployed on the right tried to move along the eastern slopes of the Gran Serin, to look for a possible opening in the trenches. The result was to engage in combat against five other companies of 3/Roi, which began firing at the opposing forces at greatly reduced range. 3/Roi was made up of five companies to which a sixth was added, the grenadiers, formed by converging the grenadiers from each company. This organization was common to all the Swiss regiments in Sardinian pay. The Roi grenadiers were the ones who had the least number of casualties by far, only two wounded by gunshots. We can thus hypothesize that this unit was used as a reserve, and was deployed behind the battalion engaged in combat ready to move to close any leaks or support the line of combat in a crisis.

Deprived of their officers, who lay dead or wounded on the ground; tired, shocked by the adversary's resistance and exhausted by the continuous marches to which they had been subjected, the French soldiers began to abandon the fight and withdraw. Soon both battalions abandoned the fight and returned to the starting line of attack. Two more battalions, 2/ and 1/Condé, then advanced. The two battalions, side by side and in column, went straight towards the Gran Serin redoubt; as had happened in the first assault, 2/Condé also attacked the redoubt at the central tenaille, while 1/Condé moved along the eastern flank, in order to once again try to bypass the fortifications on the right, or at least find a less heavily guarded sector of the trenches.

This assault also had no hope of success; some 1,100 French soldiers were attacking 708, and numbers were turning against the attackers. The subtle formation adopted by the Swiss meant that local crises in some places were quickly averted by the presence of the reserve grenadier company. A battalion of two ranks could easily have been broken through and routed in the open field, but in this case entrenchment, training, continuous fire and the arrival of the reserves succeeded in halting the enemy's advance, at the cost of 22 dead and 12 wounded, 4.8 percent of the forces engaged.[157] The Régiment de Condé had suffered much greater losses. The decision to deploy officers at the head of the attacking columns resulted in the loss of 36 officers, two killed and 34 wounded, 50 percent of the total. Amongst the

---

157   AST, Sezioni Riunite, Ministero della Guerra, Ufficio Generale del Soldo, Ruolini di rivista, Reggimento Roy, Vol.30, 1747. One of the fallen was *Capitano* Sigismond Steiguer, Bernese and commander of the company of the same name, who was killed in combat.

soldiers, 84 were killed and 281 wounded, 38 percent of the total.[158] The regiment had been literally crushed by the fire of the Swiss soldiers, to the point that the unit's flag, worn down by the fire coming from the trenches, was abandoned among the corpses that were piling up. It was only when they retreated that it was recovered by *Capitaine* Jean-Bruno Frévol de Lacoste.[159] The battle lasted a total of about 50 minutes and resulted in a victory for the Swiss of 3/Roi.

7:30 p.m. Testa dell'Assietta

French: one reinforced infantry battalion, 700 men.
Austro-Sardinians: one infantry battalion, two companies of grenadiers, one company of volunteers, 950 men.

De Mailly and d'Andlau decided that it was necessary to fix the opposing forces present in the western sector of the camp, especially while Villemur's attack was in full swing. From Height 2,563 they could observe the first Austro-Sardinian units marching towards the Gran Serin. The French artillery opened a harassing fire in order to force the adversary to seek more circuitous routes, losing time and cohesion.[160]

D'Andlau resumed command of the central column and returned to attack the Testa dell'Assietta. He was no longer interested in pushing his offensive action to the limit, but rather in keeping the enemy occupied. He had at his disposal the battalion of the Régiment de Santerre, which had just reclaimed the right flank of the Testa dell'Assietta, and the survivors of the Grenadiers Royaux du Modène, a total of no more than 700 men. Given the type of attack he had in mind, d'Andlau arranged his forces in a column with two companies side by side, placing another two companies on the wings. The front thus had an extent of 40 metres and was able to fire more effectively than before. They advanced again on the ridge leading to the tenaille built on the Testa dell'Assietta and, at a distance of about 120 metres at the change of slope, began to fire at the enemy positions. The French battalion was at sufficient range not to suffer too much damage from the adversary's fire and had enough firepower to suggest that a new attack in grand style was underway.

The defenders 'collaborated' perfectly with d'Andlau's plan; *Luogotenente Colonnello* San Sebastiano, as soon as the gunfire resumed in his sector, informed Colloredo that the French had once again attacked the Testa dell'Assietta. He probably informed his direct superior that he did not feel able to hold the position because the companies assigned to defend the position, after five hours of fighting, had suffered serious losses and had to be replaced. The

---

158   *État des officiers qui se sont le plus distingués la journée du 19*, SHD, A1-3240-42; Report Villemur.
159   G. Touchard-Lafosse, *La Loire Historique, pittoresque et bibliographique, de la source de ce fleuve à son embouchure dans l'océan* (Tours: R. Pornin et Cie., 1851), Vol.II, p.382.
160   The fire of the French guns at this moment of the battle is confirmed by the *Carte Topographique en mesure d'une partie des Vallès d'Oulx et Pragelas, avec le Rétranchèmens de L'Assiette, les Campemens et mouvemens des François et les postes qu'ils attaquerent le 19 Juillet 1747*, AST, Corte, Carte Topografiche e Disegni, Carte Topografiche per A e B, Pragelato 1.

The bust of *Luogotenente Colonnello* Paolo Federico Novarina, Conte di San Sebastiano (1710-1765), commander of 1/Guardie. The French were skilful in securing his forces at the Testa dell'Assietta, while the decisive attack on the Gran Serin took place. Twice he refused to abandon the position and move his battalion to help Bricherasio and his three Swiss battalions. The victory made his insubordination go unnoticed, which was covered up with promotions, decorations and rich pensions. However, the king always denied him the coveted command of a national infantry regiment, giving him a disappointing position of colonel commander of the provincial Reggimento Aosta. (Original preserved in the Castle of San Sebastiano da Po, now lost).

grenadier company of 1/Guardie had five dead and 11 wounded,[161] and 17 muskets were unserviceable,[162] while the grenadiers of Casale had four dead and one seriously wounded with eight muskets out of service.[163] The ammunition was practically exhausted, and the two companies were no longer able to sustain combat. Colloredo could at that moment either begin the retreat, or replace the advanced companies. He decided to replace them, as the fighting had effectively begun and the French no longer seemed as aggressive as in the initial stages of their attacks. However, he knew the risks of exposing his flanks and rear to the enemy in the middle of a close fight.

---

161 This was 29 percent of the company's total. AST, Sezioni Riunite, Ministero della Guerra, Ufficio Generale del Soldo, Ruolini di rivista, Reggimento Guardie, Vol.89, 1747.

162 This was 30 percent of the company's individual armaments. Individually, this is almost the same percentage of personnel injured or killed in combat. *État des Pertes faites par le Premier Bataillon du Regiment des Gardes à l'Affaire du 19.e Juillet 1747 au Col de l'Assiette.* AST, Sezioni Riunite, Ministero della Guerra, Ufficio Generale del Soldo, Ordini Generali Misti, Mazzo 81, 1747-1748.

163 This is nine percent of the company's force, and 15 percent of individual armaments. The seriously injured grenadier Giovanni Antonio Berrino, would die in the following days at the Royal Hospital in Pinerolo. The rolls of Casale, unlike those of the Guardie, do not report the wounded, though they do report damaged or lost individual equipment. AST, Sezioni Riunite, Ministero della Guerra, Ufficio Generale del Soldo, Ruolini di rivista, Reggimento Casale, Vol.33, 1747.

Josip Kazimir Drašković von Trakošćan (1714-1765). One of the forgotten heroes of the Battle of Assietta, *Obristwachtmeister* Drašković, commander of 3/Forgách, replaced the exhausted grenadier companies of 1/Guardie and Casale with grenadiers from his unit and Reggimento Meyer in the final phase of the battle. In the course of the Seven Years War he reached the rank of *Generalfeldzeugmeister*. (Courtesy of the Croatian Historical Museum, Zagreb)

The Reggimento Meyer grenadier company, with a total of 51 men, a platoon of grenadiers from 3/Forgách, with a total of two officers and 20 grenadiers,[164] and the Colonnella company of 1/Guardie, commanded by *Capitano* Asinari di Clavesana, with 76 men, took up position at the Testa dell'Assietta. Given the arrangement of the Regiment, whose main front was facing south, the senior company, the Colonnella, found itself with its right flank close to the Testa dell'Assietta. It was so natural that San Sebastiano sent the closest company. The defenders of the Testa dell'Assietta totalled 148, led by Forgách's *Oberstleutnant* Josip Kazimír Drašković, Graf von Trakošćan. Drašković asked Colloredo directly if he could take part in the battle at the Testa dell'Assietta with a platoon of grenadiers:

> [A]fter the enemy had been pushed back from our side, he voluntarily jumped with a lieutenant and 20 men into the Piedmontese redoubt, where the grenadiers of the King's Guardie Regiment had run out of ammunition and could only drive back the French with their bayonets and stones. Our soldiers mentioned above helped them by defending the redoubt to the end.[165]

---

164 Colloredo Report, KA, Alten Feldakten, Krieg in Italien, VII, 1. The grenadier companies had a total strength of 100 men, divided into four platoons of 25 men each.

165 Colloredo Report, KA, Alten Feldakten, Krieg in Italien, VII, 1. Official Austrian report of GFZM Browne to Empress Maria Theresia, Lodi, 22 July 1747. KA, FA Krieg in Italien VII b.

The reinforcements 'threw themselves on the enemy to the battle cry of "Maria Theresia"'.[166] The French fire welcomed the new defenders, and *Fähnrich* Lobkowitz, who commanded the Austrian grenadiers, had the misfortune to be shot in the left arm.[167]

7:50 p.m. Austro-Sardinian Reserve Force Assembly Area at Gran Serin

Maggior Generale Alciati was at the head of the battalions of Meyer and Hagenbach, which were taking up position near the summit of the Gran Serin. He had been subjected to enemy artillery fire, which was not very accurate and in fact felt like a nuisance rather than a real danger; he had distinctly heard the beginning of the fighting on the Gran Serin and was perfectly aware of how much his commander needed the troops who were with him at that moment. He decided that the four battalions still stationed in the western sector of the camp should immediately join the three Swiss battalions in order to contend with the enemy for possession of the key terrain of Gran Serin. Alciati had partial information about the tactical situation on the Gran Serin; he had received orders from Bricherasio announcing a general retreat, he knew that only two battalions were guarding the decisive point of the camp, while the French attacks had been underway for more than 40 minutes. All the available troops were needed there, and immediately; he sent a relay with a written order to the San Sebastiano to 'think of nothing but retreating'. The Piedmontese commander, until then impeccable, was beginning to lose his cool: according to him it was necessary for the battalions deployed in the western sector to disengage from the battle and move on to Gran Serin. The first unit to move was to be that of San Sebastiano, then the others would follow; but 1/Guardie, despite a written order already given to its commander, was not moving.

The first Priocca Report clarifies very well the whole story of the final defence of the Testa dell'Assietta and the 'refusal' of the San Sebastiano. As Ferdinando Gabotto had guessed in 1906, the problem was not so much the fact that the commander of 1/Guardie had completely misrepresented his tactical situation, allowing himself to be fixed on his positions by a secondary enemy attack and refusing to abandon his positions, as for the lack of clarity of the orders and the loss of lucidity on the part of Alciati. The latter saw the Great Serin as lost, urgently directing all the troops towards the threatened peak to retreat westwards, presumably on Fenestrelle. This order, as far as we can deduce at the present state of research, did not explain the intentions of the commander, did not count the Austrian forces – three battalions of which one practically not yet used in action – but only the Sardinian element, a battalion short of ammunition and with its elite company now out of action. The orders for San Sebastiano were at least incomplete, and the exhortation to only think of the retreat leads us to assume that verbal indications had already been delivered in advance. Note too that all this took place without the knowledge of the commander in the field, the Conte di Bricherasio, who actually could have needed troops elsewhere, rather than at the

---

166 Arneth, *Maria Theresia's erste Regierungsjahre*, Vol.III, p.303. Drašković obtained promotion to *oberst* for this action. His conduct was still mentioned at the end of the nineteenth century in the *Tapferkeits-Auszeichnungen und besusione Denkwürdigkeiten*, the 'medals of valour and special awards', in the Roll of Honour of the KuK IR Nr.32, aka the old IR Forgách; see Thürheim, *Gedenkblätter*, Vol.I, p.212.

167 Colloredo Report, KA, Alten Feldakten, Krieg in Italien, VII, 1.

Gran Serin. It is no coincidence that this passage was removed from the final report. All the hagiography on the defence of the Testa dell'Assietta, accompanied by heroic and mocking phrases, seems at this point to be a historical license by Dabormida.[168]

7:50 p.m. Gran Serin, Austro-Sardinian Rear

French: eight infantry battalions, 3,912 men.
Austro-Sardinians: three infantry battalions, 2,002 men.

It was the decisive moment and both sides knew it. For the French it was the last potential opportunity to break through the opposing front, for the Austro-Sardinians it was necessary to defend the path of retreat at any cost. The units of de Larnage's column were retreating, and by now they had ceased to be cohesive units; reduced to tatters, they trickled downwards to repeat the path of the advance.

De Villemur was probably informed at this time of Belle-Isle's death and the secondary attack on the Testa dell'Assietta in order to fix the enemy forces in that sector. He was the highest-ranking officer and the entire French corps engaged in combat on the ridge came under his command. He decided to go along with d'Andlau and de Mailly's initiative and proceed with a second attack, but in order to do so he had to reshape his plan of operations; this time he decided to make the best use of the mass of his units and, although they were not arranged in a line, they formed a front of over 80 metres. The battalions remained in column, as a certain depth was needed to overcome enemy resistance if the action was to turn into close combat with the bayonet. The French commander issued verbal instructions to the unit commanders:

- The units would approach the enemy entrenchments and, with an attack *à la Folard,* break through the enemy perimeter with a bayonet charge.
- Once the perimeter of the adversary's camp had been broken through, the battalions of the first line would advance to set up a front with a north-south alignment to intercept any groups of reinforcements coming from the Assietta pass.
- The battalions of the second line would manoeuvre towards their right, bypassing the summit from the north and attacking the throat of the Gran Serin redoubt.
- In the meantime, de Laval's third column would continue to threaten the Assietta pass in order to secure as many enemy forces as possible in their positions.

The problem was figuring out where to strike effectively, and finding a segment of the entrenchments that was not particularly high, or even unfinished. The Gran Serin redoubt had proved too tough a nut to crack, and the manoeuvre on the right had found only other entrenchments and fierce defenders. On the left, descending towards the Assietta pass, the earth entrenchment seemed, however, to be easy to negotiate, and the Sardinian battalions could be clearly distinguished, a sign that the earthworks were low or incomplete. In

---

168 Dabormida, *La Battaglia dell'Assietta*, p.136.

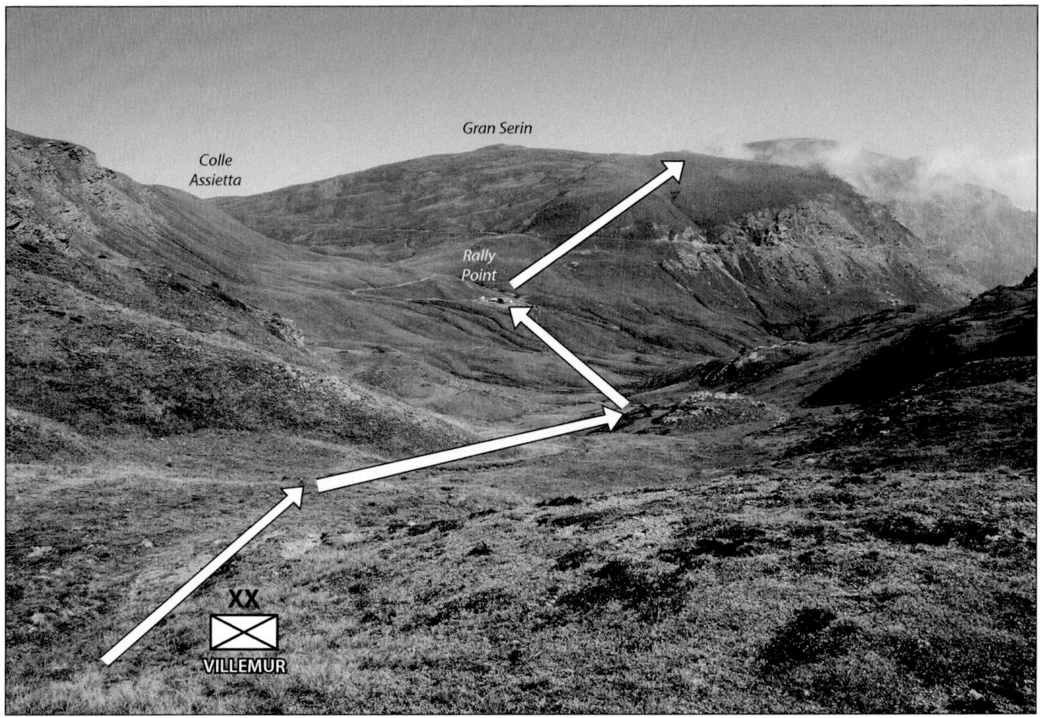

The Gran Serin seen from the path covered by Villemur's column. The relative slowness of the column is due to the tactical necessity of checking the route and taking precautions against possible Austro-Sardinian counterattacks. (Author's photo, annotation by George Anderson)

that sector the entrenchments could be easily overrun. De Villemur gave precise instructions to the commanders as to where to direct the attack manoeuvre; once he was satisfied that all had fully understood his orders, he returned to his command post and ordered the attack to begin.

Bricherasio, on the other hand, waited. The losses suffered in the first attack had been acceptable, and the balance of power was slowly shifting to his advantage. He was now almost certain that the retreat from the Assietta entrenched camp was no longer necessary – so long as the available ammunition was enough to repel the mass of incoming enemies. He decided that it would not be enough. Therefore, at about 8:00 p.m., he sent Signor Guigas back to Fort St Charles at Fenestrelle with the task of forming a convoy loaded with ammunition for the troops at high altitude and returning to camp as soon as possible.[169] It was now only a matter of minutes before the attack would begin.

---

169 Guigas returned to Fenestrelle, where he arrived at around 10:00 p.m., 'in the darkness of the night and along the disastrous paths of the Vallette, where he fell and suffered a strain of the kidneys which he still suffers from'. Quoted in Peyronel, Usseglio, *Di qui non si passa!*, p.383.

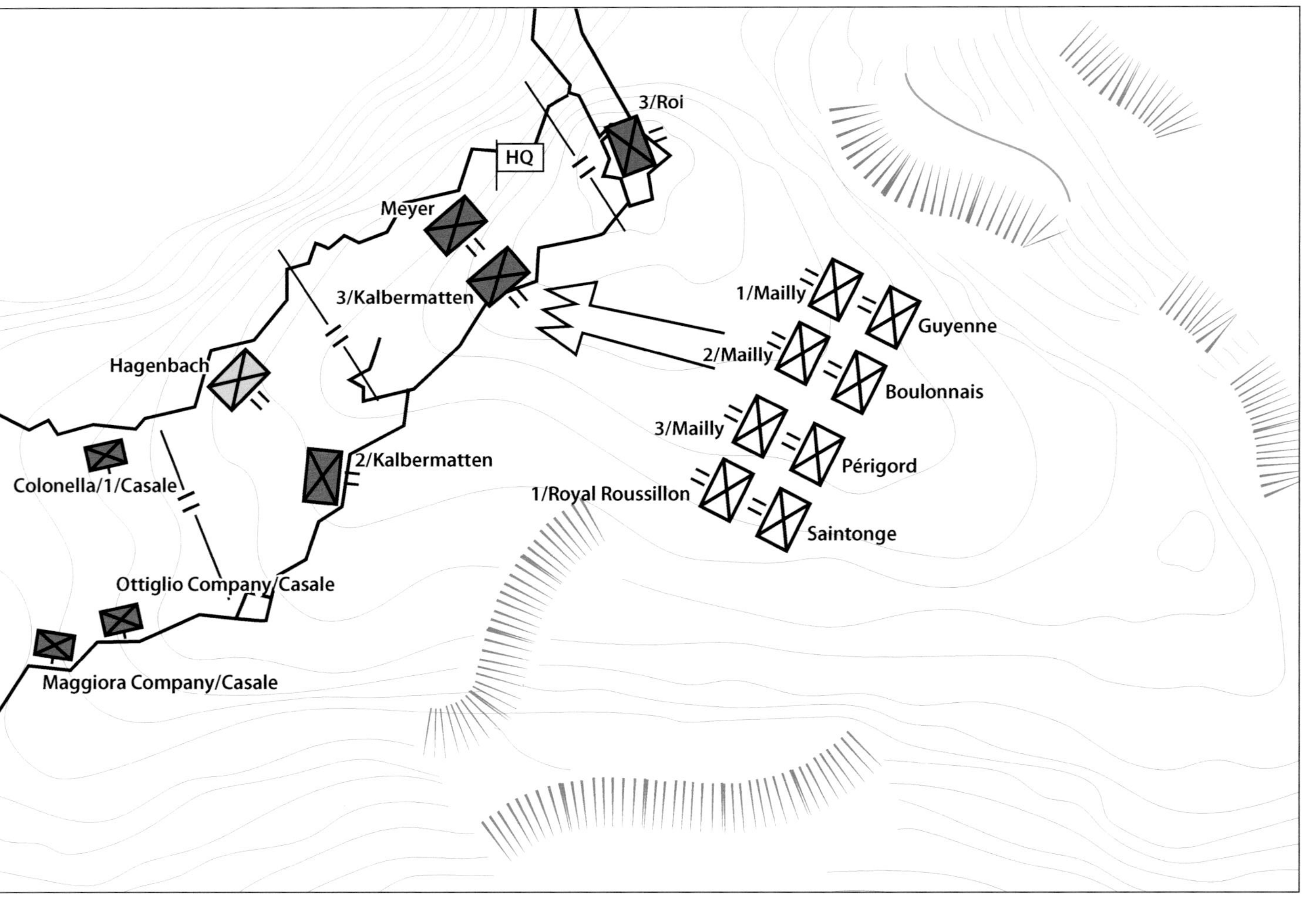

The last French attack against the Gran Serin. When this attack was launched at 7:50 p.m., a sufficient reserve force was gathered to face this threat. Despite every effort, even this attempt to force the defences also proved futile.

8:00 p.m. Testa dell'Assietta

French: one reinforced infantry battalion, 700 men.
Austro-Sardinians: one infantry battalion, two companies of grenadiers, one company of volunteers, 950 men.

Luogotenente Colonnello San Sebastiano felt that the French attack was growing in intensity. He had had to rotate grenadier the companies, and now had to hold the position with an amalgamation of Swiss, Austrian and Piedmontese units. He did not feel at all secure, plus his battalion was placed in a position that was becoming increasingly difficult as time went on. If the French had broken through to the Gran Serin, he would have found himself cut off. After all, his men had been holding the position for some three-and-a-half-hours, they had inflicted terrifying losses on the enemy and he could be sure that the French were eager to slaughter the tenaille defenders if the opportunity arose. This could materialize if he was forced to retreat. Once the defenders' backs were seen, the attackers would surely increase the intensity of their efforts.

Although he had only empirical knowledge of this, and was not even fully aware of it, the commander of 1/Guardie knew well that it was at the moment the bayonet charge forced the soldiers on either side of the fight to turn their backs and flee that the killing really began. Losing eye contact with the attacker allows him to advance towards the enemy to hit and kill him; it is a process whereby the victim's physical distance can be denied when his face cannot be seen. The essence of that physical distance may simply revolve around how the killer can, or cannot, see the victim's face. There seems to be some kind of intuitive understanding of this process in our cultural perception that sees shooting or stabbing in the back as a cowardly act, and it seems that soldiers intuitively understand that when they turn their backs they run a greater risk of being killed by the enemy. Not having to look at the victim's face provides a form of psychological distance that assists the soldier in his subsequent denial, rationalization and acceptance of killing another human being, the greatest fear of a man in uniform on a battlefield.[170]

On the strength of these considerations, San Sebastiano made his decisions after receiving an order from Alciati inviting him to clear the Testa dell'Assietta. Increasingly concerned by the intensity of the firing, he began to consider what to do. He felt that the attack he was experiencing was the main effort of the French to break through the defences, although the smoke prevented him from getting a clear idea of what was really going on. It was not possible to retreat, as

> [T]he enemies were too close, and he did not want to care about the safety of his troops who were fighting there, since the long retreat he would have to make in the presence of a much superior enemy was impossible. He then replied to his general that he would remain at his post, and that he considered that it was possible for him to defend himself, and impossible to retreat.[171]

---

170 For this problem see Grossman, *On Killing*.
171 Robbone (ed.), 'Le "Memorie" del Conte Roberto Malines', p.284.

D'Andlau had achieved his aim; the defenders of the Testa dell'Assietta, and the Austrian battalions supporting them, remained in place, and would not retreat to the Gran Serin.

8:00 p.m. Gran Serin, Austro-Sardinian Rear

French: eight infantry battalions, 3,912 men.
Austro-Sardinians: three infantry battalions, 2,002 men.

De Villemur's column had to advance along the ridge, bending slightly to the left with respect to the summit of Gran Serin. The distance to be covered was about 450 metres in all, with a minimum difference in height of between 10 and 20 metres. The decisive battle for the possession of the Gran Serin was more like a battle on the plains than in an alpine environment. However, this fact should not be misleading; the chances of breaking through such a front were rather low, especially if there was no artillery support. The most capable commanders in defence were looking for just such positions, in particular 'terrain that is nearly level but with enough of slope left to form a natural glacis on the side where the enemy can come. This is a wise method: it is the fruit of experience that shows sweeping fire to be more formidable than plunging fire. Moreover, the soldier on the crest of the glacis has every advantage that a hill can offer without any of its disadvantages'.[172] In addition, although the French attacked with almost a two-to-one advantage, this proportion of forces was completely insufficient to have any chance of forcing their opponent's fortified line.

The French advance was ordered; the first wave of attack saw in the front line, from left to right, 1/Royal Roussillon, 3/, 2/ and 1/Mailly. Villemur was correct in his assessment of the protection that the entrenchments could offer the defenders, but he had not taken into account the fact that by attacking in that sector he was driving into a recessed corner of the fortified front. 'In fact, the entrenchments flanking this redoubt are so well constructed that on the day of the action of 19 July, the Reggimento Kalbermatten defending those on the right, fired at a height of six degrees as if in an amphitheatre, and twice split the column commanded by Monsieur de Villemur in half'.[173] The French column, as per orders received, had bent slightly to the left, heading towards the sector of the entrenchment defended by 3/Kalbermatten Regiment, commanded by *Maggiore* Benoit de Vignes. Reaching a point 100 metres from the entrenchments, the French troops went into a sort of concave corner, where, with a minimal depression, the defenders had plenty of time to identify their targets and open fire. Instinctively, the soldiers of 3/Kalbermatten aimed at the centre of the enemy formation, which had to stop when the defenders' volleys reached it. As the volleys fell on the heads of the columns, they managed to regroup a little and tried to move away to the right and left, breaking their front. The two battalions that moved to the right, 1/ and 2/ Mailly, ended up in the engagement area of the Gran Serin redoubt, suffering fire from 3/

---

172   Frédérick II, *Réflexions sur la tactique et sur quelques parties de la guerre, ou, Réflexions sur quelques changements dans la façon de faire la guerre*, in *Œuvres de Frédérick le Grand* (Berlin: Rodolphe Decker, 1856), Vol.XXVIII, pp.155-156.

173   *Osservazioni sulla difesa delle valli Stura, Mayra, Varaita, di San Martino, di Pragelato, & di Exilles*, in AST, Carte Topografiche e Disegni, Carte Topografiche Segrete, 7 FII rosso.

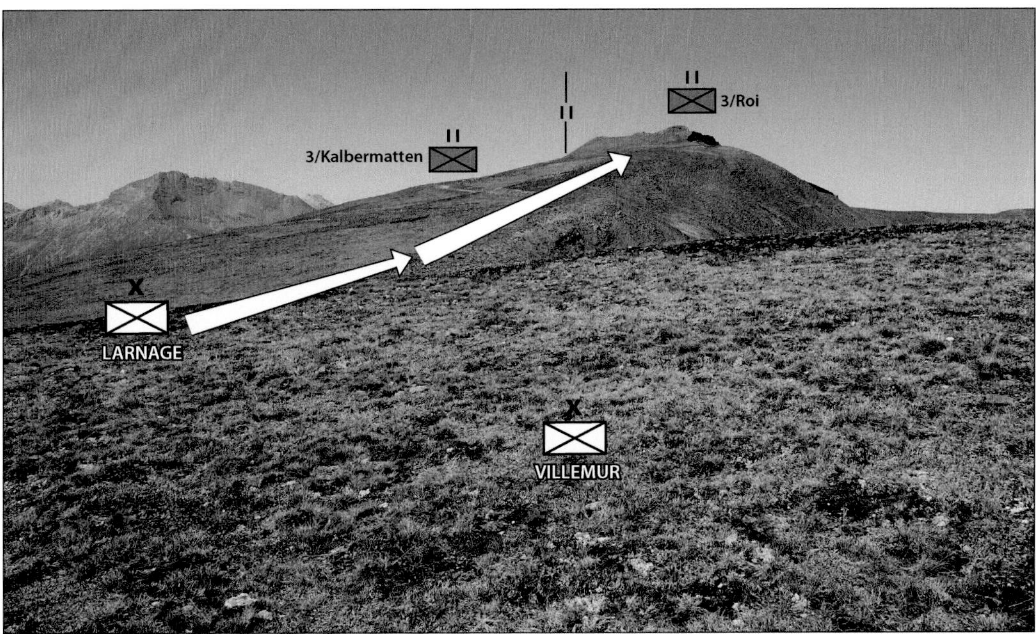

The summit of the Gran Serin along the line of attack of Villemur's column. Today, the hill is characterised by the construction of a large artillery battery, built at the end of the nineteenth century. However, in spite of the transformations, the wide manoeuvring spaces that an eventual assailant could have used are evident. On the other hand, the killing zone for the troops deployed in defence is perfectly unobstructed and ideal for developing a saturation fire that would prevent any approach to the entrenched field defences. (Author's photo, annotation by George Anderson)

Roi; the two battalions on the left, 3/Mailly and 1/Royal Roussillon, in their movement to the right, exposed their right flank to the Sardinian battalions, the 3/ and 2/Kalbermatten, which continued to fire on the masses of the opposing battalions for at least ten minutes. The officers of Royal Roussillon, in particular, in their attempt to reorder the ranks, ended up exposing themselves excessively and suffering serious losses. The French units, with no officers left, volley by volley began to disintegrate into a mob of men fleeing to the rear. The French had tried to fight back and return fire. Yet as had been the case with the battalions of de Mailly's column, the tactical layout of the column was ideal for manoeuvre and impact, but was not at all conducive to line fire: the attackers were stopped by the enemy's firepower, and were unable to inflict significant losses on the enemy.

At 8:30 p.m. the first attack made by Villemur's column had failed: Mailly had seven dead officers and 23 wounded, including the Marquis Louis-Victor de Mailly, commander of the regiment, who was abandoned on the battlefield,[174] 103 dead soldiers and non-commissioned officers, plus a further 344 wounded, 30 percent of the total. Royal Roussillon had it

---

174 Mailly was later recovered, cured and returned to the French. J. Gosselin, *Mailly et ses seigneurs, sires et haut-bers de Mailly-le-Franc* (Péronne: Trépant, 1876), pp.95-96.

The western slopes of the Gran Serin. While the western approaches are much gentler and allow the deployment and manoeuvring of thousands of men, the mountain on the eastern side is characterised by cliffs and overhangs. This fact prevented *Lieutenant Général* de Villemur from attacking the Gran Serin redoubt from multiple directions. Moreover, two other Sardinian battalions, 1/Monfort and a mixed battalion of militia, were present in the area. (Author's photo, annotation by George Anderson)

even worse: two officers were killed and 17 wounded, including the Comte de Haussonville and Sieur de Bourdeville, respectively commander and second-in-command of the regiment. Fifty percent of the officers were therefore casualties. The soldiers had 32 dead and 109 wounded, bringing the total losses to 160, 30 percent of the total.[175]

However, the attack by Villemur's column had not yet concluded. The French commander, at this point, would have preferred to disengage, but the attack and control procedures of the eighteenth century did not allow him to intervene effectively with timely orders consistent with the new tactical situation that had arisen on the battlefield. Thus, at 8:30 p.m. the second line, with Saintonge, Périgord, Boulonnais and Guyenne, advanced and overtook the remains of the first line and aimed towards the entrenchment, partially masked by the smoke of the gunfire; this had allowed them to come within 100 metres of the positions held by the Swiss of 3/Kalbermatten. The illusion of being able to get close enough to charge effectively with the bayonet was extinguished by the sound of hundreds of detonations and the arrival of a mass of musket balls from the Sardinian lines. The soldiers lined up

---

175   *État des officiers qui se sont le plus distingués la journée du 19*, SHD, A1-3240-42; *Relation de l'affaire de l'Assiette, 19 juillet, par M. de Villemur,* in Arvers and de Vault, *Guerre de la Succession* d'Autriche, Vol. II, pp.753-754.

The Sardinian killing zone on the summit of the Gran Serin, seen from the position of 3/Kalbermatten. Larnage's command attacked first to the left, directed against the Gran Serin redoubt, while Villemur himself attacked more to the right along the communication between the redoubt and the Assietta pass. Hundreds of French soldiers were killed and wounded here on the late evening of 19 July, decimated by the firepower of the Sardinian units. It is clear that it was possible to manoeuvre in this place with battalions in line formation, which could have used their firepower to approach the entrenchments and conquer them at gunpoint. The French decision to proceed with an attack *à la Folard* cost the French the conquest of Gran Serin and ultimately the battle. (Author's photo, annotation by George Anderson)

behind the fortifications again instinctively aimed at the centre of the line, and the battalions of Périgord and Boulonnais were hit by a storm of lead that immediately halted their advance. The French practice of placing regimental commanders, standard bearers, and most company commanders at the head of the units proved to be a complete failure. When the first volley fired by the Swiss impacted on 1/Périgord, five officers were immediately killed and five more seriously wounded. Three of them were *Lieutenant-Colonel* de Dungy, who was shot twice in the arm and leg, *Capitaine* de Maudet, who was shot in the stomach, and *Lieutenant* d'Auzac, who was shot in the hand.[176]

Complicating matters was the wounding of the regimental commander, *Colonel* Innocent-Marie de Vassignac, Marquis d'Imécourt, who was immediately put out of action. D'Imécourt,

---

176 The list of the wounded officers, and the type of their wounds, is transcribed in in Grémillet, *Un Régiment pendant deux siécles*, pp.88-89. Taking into account that the officers per battalion were 38 in all, fully staffed, the percentage of losses reached 26 percent of the total. *État des officiers qui se sont le plus distingués la journée du 19*, SHD, A1-3240-42; *Relation de l'affaire de l'Assiette, 19 juillet, par M. de Villemur*, in Arvers and de Vault, *Guerre de la Succession* d'Autriche, Vol.II, pp.753-754.

Innocent-Marie de Vassinhac, Marquis d'Imécourt. Colonel commander of the Régiment Périgord, he was one of those officers who put glory and honour before a more careful tactical approach. During the last French attack on the Assietta, d'Imécourt was seriously wounded by a bullet that 'passed through his body from side to side'. Transported to Briançon, he died on 6 September 1747, and he was buried in the Collegiate Church of Briançon. (Grémillet, *Un Régiment pendant deux siècles*, p.88)

seriously wounded by a bullet that 'went through his body from side to side', was taken to Briançon where he was treated, without success. Due to his injuries he died on 6 September 1747, and was buried in the Collegiate Church of Briançon.[177] Boulonnais had four officers killed, including the regimental second-in-command, de Morel, while the regimental commander, François-Joseph de Damas, Marquis de Ruffey, was one of 17 wounded. As had been the case with the first wave, the second wave opened up in the middle; the battalions of Guyenne and Boulonnais moved to the right, crashing into the redoubt of the Gran Serin, while Saintonge and Périgord massed on the left and entered the sector of responsibility of 2/ Kalbermatten. The smoke from the musketry, which in the absence of wind remained close to the trenches, allowed the French to reorganise and attack the positions held by the Swiss. The officers who had survived the first discharges wanted to open fire in turn, but 'our fire had very little effect'.[178] The two Kalbermatten battalions suffered losses, but their ability to hit the enemy was not affected. The position of the French battalions became more and more difficult

---

177 Grémillet, *Un Régiment pendant deux* siècles, pp.88, 389.
178 SHD, *Relation de l'affaire de l'Assiette*, A1-3227-196.

as the minutes went by; the attackers could not get close enough to the entrenchments to attempt to scale them, and their tactical disposition did not allow them to develop a sufficient volume of fire to force the defenders to retreat from the parapets. The officers continued to remain at the head of their units, and they paid dearly for this choice; Saintonge had six officers killed and 11 wounded, 45 percent of the total, while Guyenne was less damaged, counting only one officer killed and six wounded. Losses continued to mount until, at about 8:40 p.m., what remained of de Villemur's column began to retreat; with no officers capable of handling the fight, unable to carry out any form of evasive manoeuvre within the Piedmontese engaged area, the French soldiers, starting with those at the rear of the battalion columns, abandoned their positions and began to retreat. Saintonge had lost, with 35 dead and 108 wounded, 27 percent of its force; Périgord had 45 dead and 139 wounded, or 34 percent; Boulonnais had 40 dead and 132 wounded, 32 percent while Guyenne left 32 dead and 109 wounded on the field.[179] Amongst the ranks of the two Swiss battalions that opposed the French attack were 16 killed and 24 seriously wounded. 2/Kalbermatten had two dead and 16 wounded, while 3/Kalbermatten suffered greater casualties, 14 dead and eight wounded. The higher number of deaths than the wounded can be explained by the greater proximity of the French troops to the entrenchment and the exposure of the trunk and the head by the Swiss soldiers attested in defence of the field works of the Gran Serin.[180]

The three euphoric Swiss battalion commanders repeatedly asked for permission to attack the routed enemy column. *Luogotenente Colonnello* de Courten and *Maggiore* de Vignes at the head of 2/ and 3/Kalbermatten, and *Maggiore* Roguin of 3/Roi wanted to get out of the trenches and throw back the mass of French soldiers who were moving disorderly towards the Grange dell'Assietta. Bricherasio dryly ordered them to hold their positions. The objective of the fight was to keep communications open with Fenestrelle, not to destroy the enemy, and ammunition was dangerously scarce.

This was probably a mistake on the part of Bricherasio, as the opposing forces, already tested by the marches of the past few days and by all the victims, had suffered devastating losses and an impressive moral collapse. The three battalion commanders, all Swiss and veterans, had the tactical situation clearly before them. But the goal of the Sardinian commander at that moment was to save his forces and keep an open path towards Fenestrelle. Bricherasio's refusal is mentioned in both Priocca accounts, although it is absent in Minutoli's. In the first report drawn up by Priocca it is clear how much the relationship between Bricherasio and the three Swiss commanders was not particularly happy, given the strongly defensive approach desired precisely by the first:

> The three Swiss battalions behaved according to their custom [that is, they fought bravely] and the enemies were forced to retreat. That was a very dangerous movement for them, and their total defeat would have been the inevitable end, if the lack of ammunition had not forced the Conte di Bricherasio to constantly resist

---

179 *État des officiers qui se sont le plus distingués la journée du 19*, SHD, A1-3240-42; *Relation de l'affaire de l'Assiette, 19 juillet, par M. de Villemur*, in Arvers and de Vault, *Guerre de la Succession d'Autriche*, Vol. II, pp.753-754.

180 AST, Sezioni Riunite, Ministero della Guerra, Ufficio Generale del Soldo, Ruolini, Reggimento Kalbermatten, Vol.58, 1747.

the requests that the commanding officers of the corps made him, to allow them to leave the field, given the certainty they had of being able to throw them back, given the superiority we had over them.[181]

It was 9:00 p.m. and for the French the battle was definitely lost. de Villemur continued to secure part of the opposing line with de Laval's column, but with 1,803 men he had no chance against the opposing defences. He could only form a strong rearguard with the few companies that had not broken up during the attack, and thereby manage the retreat. With no discipline left to march, the confused mass of defeated battalions would reach the Testa del Mottas within two hours, three at the most. These were now the priorities for the French commander:

- To repel the probable opponent's counter-attack.
- To re-join the other French troops at the Testa del Mottas.
- To plan subsequent moves with the other column commanders.

De Villemur still had a relatively fresh force, the four battalions of the De Laval column, to deploy as a rearguard. This was already being deployed around the Grange dell'Assietta to counter any possible adversary sorties. For the moment, apart from a few small groups of soldiers, no unit seemed to be leaving the defensive perimeter of the Austro-Sardinian camp.

The Conte di Bricherasio breathed a sigh of relief; with just three battalions in the line he had faced and defeated four times the enemy force, and the camp defences had not been breached. Even better, communications with Fenestrelle had not been broken. However, the enemy was still in front of him; his columns were repositioning themselves along the line of attack, and for the moment showed no sign of moving away from Assietta. They had undoubtedly suffered very heavy losses, but it seemed clear that the balance of forces on the field still leaned in favour of the attackers. The situation of the Austro-Sardinian forces around 9:00 p.m. was as follows:

- 1/Guardie. Ammunition almost exhausted. Elite companies (Grenadier, Colonnello) out of action. Not employable in combat.
- Reggimento Casale. Three companies ready for combat, grenadier company out of action.
- 2/Kalbermatten. Ammunition depleted. Available for limited defensive actions.
- 3/Kalbermatten. Ammunition depleted. Available for limited defensive actions.
- 3/Roi. Ammunition depleted. Available for limited defensive actions.
- Reggimento Meyer. Ammunition depleted. Available for limited defensive actions.
- Battalion of Hagenbach. Ready for combat.
- Battalion of Traun. Ready for combat.
- 3/Colloredo. Ready for combat.
- 3/Forgách. Ammunition depleted. Available for limited defensive actions.

---

181   Priocca I. On the lack of pursuit see also the acquittal arguments by Alberti, *La Battaglia dell'Assietta*, pp.88-89.

In all, therefore, the three Austrian battalions of Colloredo, Hagenbach and Traun, and the three companies of Casale could be employed; the forces of a weak brigade. 1/Monfort and 1/Sicilia could be brought in from the Vallette Pass, thus assembling a total force of about six battalions, about 2,800 men. Although battered, the French still had a respectable force at their disposal, and at least 10,000 infantrymen were capable of facing the offensive actions of the Austro-Sardinians. In addition, they could return to the attack the next day, so it was better to save the little ammunition left and wait for the convoy of mules which, it was hoped, would reach the Assietta camp by morning. The Piedmontese commander sent for Alciati, Martinengo and Colloredo to establish the details of what to do.

The battle was over. The Austro-Sardinians had inflicted devastating losses on the French king's army and gained an impressive victory.

9

'The entrenchments were covered with dead and wounded…'

At 9:39 p.m. on 19 July 1747, the sun had definitely set. The moon, risen on a completely clear starry sky, would become full on the 21st; at that moment it illuminated the battlefield, which could not yet be defined as silent. The Austro-Sardinian units remained deployed in their posts, while the French columns were in motion to return to the starting line of the attack.

11:00 p.m. Monte Gran Costa, Link-up Area for the French Columns

The decision of the Conte di Bricherasio not attack de Villemur's retreating column allowed it to regain the plateau of Mount Gran Costa around 11.00 p.m. The French general already knew that Belle-Isle was dead, and had been informed by the messengers that reached him that all the attacks had failed. Once he had gained the main ridge he could find the elements of the other two columns that had gathered, re-forming line in battle order to face the enemy. He immediately called *Marechaux de Camp* de Mailly and d'Andlau to ask for information on the situation of the surviving forces. The situation was in fact dramatic; not only had the assaults failed, but an impressive number of officers had been injured or killed, with the practical result that entire units were left without an effective command and control system. To make matters worse was the result of the first count of losses, estimated at around 5,000 men missing, which meant that of the nearly 16,000 soldiers available in the morning, only about 11,000 remained at that time. If, as it seemed, 10 opposing battalions were arriving for the next day, it was necessary to disengage as soon as possible.

De Villemur gave his first instructions:[1]

- The battle was lost and the French forces would immediately leave the ridge line.
- D'Andlau's column was to withdrawn on Oulx by way of the Val di Susa.
- Villemur's own column would retreat towards the Val Chisone, aiming first for Traverses and then retreating towards the Passo di Sestriere. From there he would reach Cesana.

---

1   De Mailly, *Mémoire sur l'attaque.*

- The Brigade Poitou would remain in defence of the Sestriere Pass to protect the left flank of the retreating columns.
- The column of d'Escars, already recalled on the 18th by the Chevalier de Belle-Isle at the end of a tiring excursion at high altitude, was to leave its quarters of Salbertrand to go and deploy in Oulx.
- De Mailly was to command the rearguard, formed of those of his battalions still effective along with of all the surviving grenadiers capable of fighting, for a total of about 3,100 men, intended to protect the retreat of the other columns.
- The rearguard would remain deployed in line of battle on the Costapiana hill trying to collect all the wounded they could and round up the stragglers who wandered on the battlefield.
- The rearguard would remain in front of the entrenchments facing any enemy sorties until midnight 19/20 July, after which it would in turn begin to retreat towards the east, detaching a reinforced battalion, 700 men in all, at Col Bourget to cover from high Sauze d'Oulx.
- The six 4-pounder pieces would reach Montgenèvre by the 20th, while the seven 4-pounder pieces would remain in storage at Sauze d'Oulx until 22 July.

For de Villemur not only was the battle lost, but the whole campaign was now compromised. His intent by now was only to reach the valley floor and the Oulx logistics hub as soon as possible, clear out the warehouses and return to Briançon where he could set up the defence of the Montgenèvre pass. He wrote a letter to the Piedmontese commander, giving instructions for the body of the Chevalier de Belle-Isle to be recovered and returned to the French.[2] The Chevalier's valet with a drummer and four men destined to carry the body were sent to the Austro-Sardinian camp to carry out this task. After completing this task, the French commander took to the road himself, following his column that was descending towards Sestriere and leaving de Mailly to handle the rearguard.

De Mailly's seemed to be a relatively easy task, as the enemy showed no intention of leaving the entrenched camp. But a sore mass of wounded lay stretched out on the ground, carried in arms by their comrades who were now retreating. Others, mostly stranded or injured who had awakened in the cold of the night but still able to get up and walk, were approaching the French positions, whose white uniforms were perfectly distinguishable by the moonlight. All this aching humanity had to be evacuated in some way, if it was not to be left in the enemy's hands.

10:00 p.m. Gran Serin, Bricherasio's Command Post

Generals Alciati and Colloredo arrived at the command post of the Conte di Bricherasio ar Gran Serin at around 10:00 p.m. to plan the subsequent defence operations of the camp. The commander was immediately clear and, 'after consulting the general officers, gave

---

2 AST, Corte, Materie Militari, Imprese, Materie Militari, Mazzo 8 d'addizione; *Relazioni della vittoria riportata sui francesi dalle Truppe di S.M., ed Imperiali sotto il comando del Conte di Bricherasio al Colle dell'Assietta verso Exilles. Con copia di lettera dei generali francesi relative ai feriti.*

the necessary provisions to defend all the places, if by chance the enemies had the fantasy of restarting the attack the following day'.[3] The fact that the French formations were still deployed in the battle at the Testa del Mottas seemed to suggest the imminent arrival of reinforcements along the line of the ridge.

Bricherasio in effect confirmed the tactical planning of 18 July, by which he envisaged the following objectives:

- Resist the enemy attack by supporting the battalions on the fortifications of the entrenched camp.
- Delay the conquest of Colle dell'Assietta as much as possible.
- Withdraw when necessary towards the Gran Serin;
- In the event of an enemy withdrawal, all forces in the entrenched camp to remain in place until reinforcements and a specific order from the Secretariat of War arrived.

Although recognising that the enemy could have suffered very serious losses, the Sardinian commander decided not to exploit the success, but to remain fixed on his positions. The forces at his disposal were still inferior to those of the enemy, and the battalions involved in the battle needed rest. In addition, the small army at his disposal had sufficient strength to repel an attack, but was not large enough for offensive action, even with limited objectives. Bricherasio would not move on 20 July, nor even in the following days.

The entrenchments were practically intact, except in some sectors on the western edge of the plateau: in particular those of the Testa dell'Assietta had suffered damage that needed urgent repair. Two companies of grenadiers, the combined one of 2/ and 3/Kalbermatten at the Gran Serin and that of 3/Forgách at the Testa dell'Assietta, left the camp to check the state of the works and restore the dry stone walls, or escort the soldiers commanded to the works.[4] Partly still shrouded in the smoke of the gunshots, the environment was imbued with an acrid smell of human blood, urine and faeces, while the screams and moans of the wounded could be heard everywhere. A large number of corpses and dying were scattered around the fortifications, or along the approach roads. The soldiers of the eighteenth century did not have with them the necessary first aid kit with which to clean and bandage the wounds. Loss of blood, dehydration and fever during the night caused the death of all those wounded who could not be rescued, and surely others were killed in the following hours by Austro-Sardinian soldiers who were looking for loot to plunder. It was a situation that veterans recognized as familiar, especially at the end of a fight.[5] The ground behind the fortifications was literally covered with corpses and wounded. Grenadiers began to rummage among the bodies lying on the ground, looking for valuables, trophies, or

---

3   AST, Corte, Materie Politiche per Rapporto dall'Interno, Storie della Real Casa, Categoria III, Storie Particolari, Mazzo 24, Minutoli, *Report des campagnes faites par S.M.*, Vol.V, pp.247-248.
4   Minutoli, *Report des campagnes faites par S.M.*, Vol.V, p.246.
5   In the course of modern and contemporary firefighting, about 50 percent of soldiers lose bladder control, and 25 percent sphincters. The same also happens to injured personnel. This aspect, little or no neglected by war memorials, is effectively described in Grossman, *On Combat*, pp.33-36; Holmes, *Acts of War*, p.178; D. Malfoy-Noël, *L'épreuve de la bataille (1700–1714)* (Montpellier: Presses Universitaires de la Méditerranée PULM, 2007), p.111.

anything worth collecting. The Austrians recovered three flags, while the Swiss found a finial with a white taffeta cravat. Two of the flags certainly belonged to the Régiment de La Reine, of de Mailly's column, while a third banner, erroneously identified as belonging to a Spanish battalion, was probably one of the flags of the Régiment de Guise.[6]

During their reconnaissance, the grenadiers of 1/Guardie identified 'the Chevalier of Belle-Isle and the Monsieur de Arnaud, an infinity of other high-ranking people, whose corpses were at the tip of the redoubt. In the pockets of the first two were found the papers containing the plans of the campaign, and a list of the forces of their army, which the Conte di Bricherasio sent to the king'.[7] The fact that they brought such confidential materials with them is not surprising, as the French army was a moving army, without a camp and a fixed command post. We cannot exclude the fact that neither of them had deemed it necessary to deprive themselves of the precious papers, as they still contained the commands to follow also for the exploitation of success. *Luogotenente* Giuseppe Maria Balbis, or Balbi, deputy commander of the Grenadier Company of 1/Guardie,[8] 'accepted from a grenadier a snuffbox of the Chevalier de Belle-Isle in which a beautiful lady was depicted'.[9] Some seriously wounded French officers were recovered, 'among the most important', but once the most urgent restorations were completed, the grenadiers returned to the camp and 'waiting, all the troops spent the night lined up with weapons ready'.[10]

In the meantime, Bricherasio was able to dedicate himself to the much more pleasant task of announcing the victory to his sovereign. The first report was a short written note that was entrusted to *Maggiore* Panissera of the Reggimento Casale with the task of transmitting it directly to the King in Turin,[11] along with the papers found in the pockets of the Chevalier of Belle-Isle. Panissera left immediately, descending into Val di Susa in the direction of Exilles, followed shortly after by the *Maggiore* Perrone of the militia, who instead had to go to Fenestrelle to inform the governor of the incident and make sure that the convoy with ammunition was actually on the march.[12]

---

6   *Mercure Historique et Politique*, Tomo CXXIII, La Haye, Juillet 1747, p.181.
7   The originals of these papers are now preserved in the National Archive in Turin, Corte, Materie Militari, Mazzo 8 d'addizione. Other copies have been transcribed and bound in the volume Manoscritto Militare 7 alla Biblioteca Reale di Torino. It is not a particularly voluminous documentation, 45 small sheets at all, which were folded and stored in the capacious pockets of the uniform coats.
8   AST, Sezioni Riunite, Ministero della Guerra, Ufficio Generale del Soldo, Ruolini di Rivista, Reggimento Guardie, Vol.89, 1747; *Personale degli Ufficiali dell'esercito del re di Sardegna dal 1725 al tutto il 1747*, BRT, Manoscritto Militare 36.
9   Priocca Report I.
10 Priocca Report I.
11 The original report still exists; *Avis de l'affaire du 19 juillet 1747 arivée au col de l'Assiete sur Exilles porté au Roy par le Chevr de Panisera maïor du Regimnt de Casal le 20 juilt a 8 hes du mattin*, BRT, Ms Mil 154.
12 Situation was confirmed by Intendente Baldoino of Forte San Carlo di Fenestrelle. Letter from the Intendant Baldoino, Fenestrelle 19 July 1747; AST, Corte, Materie Militari, Imprese, Mazzo 7 da inventariare.

20 July 1747

De Mailly should have resumed the march towards Oulx around midnight, but was delayed by the need to deal with 'the evacuation of the wounded, who could only be transported to Sauze d'Oulx during the night'.[13] The French commander was forced to manage a mass of wounded who had to somehow be evacuated. The Field Hospital (*Hôpital ambulant*) had been set up by the French at Seu, and there during the night a mass of 600 wounded arrived who, summarily treated, were immediately directed towards the valley floor: all those who could walk were routed towards Oulx, and a total of three officers and about 100 soldiers were abandoned, whose conditions did not allow their transport.[14] In the early hours of the morning the valet and drummer were sent off to retrieve the bodies of the Chevalier de Belle-Isle and d'Arnaud. It had not been possible to send the two delegates into the night, given the risk of being killed by some overzealous or nervous enemy sentry. Having recovered the bodies of the two officers, the retrograde manoeuvres began; at 10:00 a.m. on 20 July, the rearguard began to withdraw, to move towards Sauze d'Oulx, where it stood in defence until noon. De Mailly, during the retrograde movement towards the valley floor, could only observe the disastrous situation of the Seu field hospital, clogged with seriously injured who could not be evacuated. He was thus forced to leave a logistics officer, *Commissaire de guerre* de Launay, and write a letter to the count of Bricherasio to entrust him with their care.[15]

On the morning of 20 July, the French troops were largely concentrated at Colle del Sestriere and Oulx. De Villemur had charged the orders of the Brigade Poitou and d'Escars' column, which had reached Salbertand on 19 July, to operate as rearguard forces to the army that was preparing to cross the Alps.[16] The French realized they were being followed by Austro-Sardinian patrols, with which they had some minor clashes in the following two days.[17] Until the 21st, the greatest concern was not so much that of resuming the retreat with maximum speed – the enemy was in fact fixed on his positions and gave no hint of moving – but that of evacuating all possible wounded and the contents of the warehouses already set up in Val di Susa. These tasks were entrusted to the *Commissaire de guerre* Brunet de l'Argentière. On the evening of the 19th he had already received the first information, sent by a servant who was charged with bringing provisions to *Maréchal de Camp* d'Arnaud; that the battle was by no means ending with a victory, but that on the contrary all the attacks

---

13   De Mailly, *Mémoire sur l'attaque.*

14   The number of the wounded abandoned by the French at the grange of Seu is reported in all the reports of the battle by the Piedmontese and the Austrian side, is taken up in the correspondence of Bricherasio with the Minister of War and it is possible that it refers to a first erroneous assessment made by the *Commissaire de guerre* de Launay. The actual figure of 100 non-transportable wounded is detailed in the letter from de Villemur to the Comte d'Argenson of 21 July 1747, in Arvers and de Vault, *Guerre de la Succession* d'Autriche, Vol.II, p.755.

15   AST, Corte, Materie Militari, Imprese, Materie Militari, Mazzo 8 d'addizione; *Relazioni della vittoria riportata sui francesi dalle Truppe di S.M., ed Imperiali sotto il comando del Conte di Bricherasio al Colle dell'Assietta verso Exilles. Con copia di lettera dei generali francesi relative ai feriti.* This convention between the belligerent forces is reported, as an example of humanity, in L. Gillot, *La révision de la Convention de Genève* (Paris: Université de Paris, 1901), p.23.

16   Arvers and de Vault, *Guerre de la Succession d'Autriche*, Vol.II, p.701.

17   Minutoli, *Report des campagnes faites par S.M.*, Vol.V, p.253.

had been repelled with heavy losses and with the death of the Chevalier de Belle-Isle and d'Arnaud himself.[18] Having organized a first council of war on how to manage the crisis that was announced to be imminent, around nine in the evening the first survivors from the battlefield began to arrive in Oulx, mainly stragglers, who 'not only confirmed our losses, but they extremely exaggerated them'.[19] The first wounded arrived at midnight, officers transported downstream with stretchers, and de Villemur's orders for *Colonel* Dormessant to send the available squadrons of the Dragons du Roi with all the equipment of the army headquarters to Montgenevre. The withdrawal order sparked panic. The dragoons dismantled the headquarters and set off at full speed for the frontier with France. Likewise, all the officers in charge of logistics and the various services behaved in a similar fashion, leaving the camp without caring about what they would have left in the hands of the enemy and, what is worse, without caring about what would become of the wounded who still had to descend from the mountain.

At six in the morning only de l'Argentière and his staff remained in Oulx; the officer quickly made a list of what remained in the village church, converted into a logistic store, and he gave the orders to evacuate all the materials present. He then got ready 'to give aid to the officers and wounded soldiers who began to arrive en masse on the morning of the 20th'.[20]

The triage, the system for selecting wounded soldiers according to classes of increasing urgency based on the severity of the injuries reported, was invented and put into practice only during the Napoleonic wars by the chief surgeon of the *Grande Armée*, Dominique-Jean Larrey.[21] De l'Argentière did something similar, having at his disposal few means and an increasing number of wounded: soldiers who did not show such wounds as to require transport on a mule or on a stretcher were urged to continue on foot towards Cesana, making them believe they risked being taken prisoner at any moment. Those injured in the legs, or otherwise unable to move, were temporarily treated in Oulx, where the good offices of the French officer allowed him to recover wine, brandy, and other kinds of comfort. The church was transformed into a field hospital, along with some agricultural structures nearby, while the officers found hospitality with the wealthy families of the village.

> On these occasions it is quite normal to look for warm houses, equipped with excellent fixtures, and for this reason to prefer the house of a farmer rather than his barns; but experience has convinced us that air is more necessary than heat. Consequently, not only the barns, and the stables, but above all the churches are the best hospitals starting from June until October.[22]

---

18   Brunet de l'Argentière, *Mémoire de la Guerre*, p.73.
19   Brunet de l'Argentière, *Mémoire de la Guerre*, p.73.
20   Brunet de l'Argentière, *Mémoire de la Guerre*, p.74.
21   D.J. Larrey, *Mémoires de Chirurgie Militaire, et Campagnes* (Paris: J. Smith, F. Buisson, 1812-1817), Vol.III, pp.3-4. P.N. Skandalakis, P.Lainas, J.E. Skandalakis, P.Mirilas, 'To afford the wounded speedy assistance: Dominique Jean Larrey and Napoleon', in *World Journal of Surgery*, 30 (8), August 2006, pp.1392-1399. The memoirs of the medical officer are collected in D.J. Larrey, *Mémoires de Chirurgie Militaire, et Campagnes* (Paris: J. Smith, F. Buisson, 1812-1817).
22   M. Pringle, *Observations sur le Maladies des Armées dans les camps et dans les garnisons* (Paris: Ganeau, 1755) Vol.I, pp.161-162.

These wounded had to be evacuated anyway, and de l'Argentière ordered them to be 'loaded onto mules destined for the transport of food and those of the flying hospital on some car in the town, to the point that on the morning of the 22nd there were only 130 [wounded] who could only be transported with stretchers'.[23] Stretchers were not part of the endowment of an eighteenth century army, but the ever-practical de l'Argentière managed to solve the problem with an expedient: 'I had two crossbars cut and fastened to two poles, and nailed on them a double layer of bags for food; in this way a light and comfortable stretcher was made in an instant'.[24]

On 20 July de Villemur also appeared at the Oulx camp, obliged to juggle a thousand difficulties in the midst of the chaos of a retreat and the drafting of the first reports on the battle just ended. He found, to his amazement, that only de l'Argentière had remained in his post, despite the orders specifying not to dismantle the camp, only the headquarters. After making sure that the necessary arrangements had been made for the evacuation of the wounded and materials from the camp, he set up his command at Sauze d'Oulx, taking over from de Mailly, and from there continued to manage the retreat of his forces.

Two days later, on 22 July, 'at 7 am there was neither a wounded nor an empty sack in Oulx',[25] and 'all the troops withdrew to Montgenèvre, where the *Maréchal* de Belle-Isle had sent the Marquis d'Argouges, *Lieutenant Général*, with orders for the destination of the troops and generals'.[26] For the French army, the Assietta campaign was over.

Dawn of Death

At 3:26 a.m. on 20 July it began to dawn, and by four in the morning the sun had already risen.[27] During the morning the drummer and valet sent by de Villemur reached the entrenchments to recover the body of the Chevalier de Belle-Isle and *Maréchal de Camp* d'Arnaud. Pleased to be able to collect information directly in the opposing camp, the Conte di Bricherasio gave his permission for the transport of the bodies, already recovered and identified, and the convoy 'left with a convenient escort'.[28] The information that reached the Sardinian commander was reassuring; the losses suffered had been such that, the French 'were far from thinking' of resuming the attack the same morning.[29]

The first lights of the sun flooded the meadows of Assietta, and the scene was chilling, with 'the area around the retrenchments covered with dead and wounded'.[30] But the French troops were still lined up for battle on the flat summit of Monte Costapiana, and for the moment Bricherasio had no intention of letting his guard down. In the morning the long-awaited convoy of mules arrived from Fenestrelle with ammunition that was distributed to

---

23   Brunet de l'Argentière, *Mémoire de la Guerre*, p.74.
24   Brunet de l'Argentière, *Mémoire de la Guerre*, pp.74-75.
25   Brunet de l'Argentière, *Mémoire de la Guerre*, p.75.
26   De Mailly, *Mémoire sur l'attaque*.
27   On 20 July 1747 the sun rose at 4:02 a.m. The precise calculation is possible thanks to the calculator present on the site <http://www.spectralcalc.com/solar_calculator/solar_position.php>.
28   Priocca Report I.
29   Priocca Report I.
30   Priocca Report I.

the Austro-Sardinian troops, then at 10:00 a.m. the French began to retire definitively from the battlefield.

Bricherasio had the intention of monitoring the retreat of the French which he had followed at a safe distance by the grenadiers of Kalbermatten and Forgách, and by a contingent of Waldensian militiamen,[31] while 'the imperial and Piedmontese generals allowed their troops to roam the battlefield, looking for all the booty they could find'.[32] The soldiers were at that moment exhausted by the tension and physical efforts of the previous day, to the point that they could not do anything other than throw themselves to the ground and sleep, even if many men devoted themselves to looting and collecting the weapons abandoned by the enemy. After the battle collection continued of all enemy weapons, swords and firearms intended for the exhausted Royal Arsenal depot in Turin. Whilst there are doubts about the actual number of individual firearms collected, we know that at least 170 infantry swords were collected and redistributed later to the troops, specifically among the ranks of the 1/Guardie.[33]

The dead lost stockings, shoes, shirts, uniforms, and they were abandoned on the ground completely naked. The raiders killed the most seriously injured soldiers they could find, robbing and stripping the bodies, whether they were friends or enemies. Gilbert Romane, of the Régiment Des Landes, was lying unconscious on the ground near the retrenchment attacked by de Mailly's column; an enemy soldier, probably thinking he was in agony and about to die, decided to finish him off with a bayonet thrust in the back. The pain of his wounds woke him up and made him scream, and at that point the soldiers patrolling the battlefield chose to rescue him rather than kill him.[34] Something very similar also happened to soldier Pierre Chicot, of the Régiment de Mailly. A musket shot had hit him in the left shoulder, leaving him agonizing on the ground near the Redoubt of the Great Serin. A grenadier from one of the Swiss regiments decided to finish him off with a sabre blow in the face. The blow disfigured the unfortunate Chicot but did not kill him; later he was collected and cared for.[35]

While patrols were leaving the camp, a part of the garrison of the entrenched camp continued to garrison the field works, cooked and mainly slept, while the rest of the soldiers 'worked all of the 20th and 21st to extract the wounded from the mass of the dead, and about 300 were recovered'.[36]

The Sardinian commander, in addition to monitoring the movements of the enemy, had logistical-health emergencies to fulfil:

---

31   Minutoli, *Report des campagnes faites par S.M.*, Vol.V, p.253; BRT, Manoscritto Militare 129, *Relazione della battaglia, ed attacco dato dai francesi ai trinceramenti del colle dell'Assietta, Exiles, e Fenestrelles, difesi dai Piemontesi, Tedeschi, e milizie valdesi l'anno 1747.*

32   *Journal Universel, ou Memorie, pour servir à l'Historie Civile, Politique, Ecclésiatique, & Littérarire du XVIII Siécle*, Tome XIII, Aout 1747, Amsterdam 1747, p.546.

33   AST, Sezioni Riunite, Camerale Piemonte, Articolo 170, Magazzino Merci; Conto 1751-1752, Caricamento, Cap.41, 42, 43, 44; Conto 1753-1754, Scaricamento, Cap.53, N.o 2.

34   Romane was saved from the bayonet thrust, and he returned to his regiment. On 20 January 1763 he joined the corps of the Invalids. SHD/GR/2Xy40.

35   Chicot was welcomed into the Invalid Corps on 10 March 1763, 'disfigured by the effect of a sabre blow, and suffering greatly in the left shoulder following a shot'. SHD/GR/2Xy40.

36   Priocca Report I.

- The corpses of soldiers killed in combat should be buried as soon as possible.
- The Austro-Sardinian wounded had to be evacuated to Fenestrelle and Susa.
- If necessary to take charge of the French wounded and evacuate them to the hospitals in Susa and Chisone Valley.

No less than 1,300 human bodies were piled around the retrenchments, mostly cadavers, but also wounded and dying. The bodies of the more disciplined soldiers lay in regular lines, piled up where they had massed for the attack, or isolated over a larger area where the units had retreated and left the most seriously wounded behind. The corpses of the Austro-Sardinian soldiers, 71 in all, were already collected at the end of the fight,[37] and were left for the time being inside the camp. The dead were to be buried as soon as possible. Beyond the ethical evaluations, if soldiers saw 'their comrades left without burial, they will rightly believe that they will be treated with the same contempt if they happen to die'.[38] The putrefaction of the corpses exposed to the open air, and piled up close to the tents, would have polluted the air and caused an epidemic among the soldiers. Human corpses decompose through various stages that are now known in the forensic field as ADD – Accumulated Degree Days – and which are based on average daily temperatures. An advanced state of putrefaction is reached around 400 ADDs, or 20 days of exposure with an average temperature of 20 degrees Centigrade, necessary to transform a human corpse of 68 kilograms into a skeleton. At Assietta, with cooler temperatures, the decomposition process would certainly have been slowed down, but certainly not eliminated. Fluids would have leaked from the corpses and saturated the soil with potassium, calcium, magnesium, phosphorus, ammonium, sulphates and other substances.[39] This soup, fetid with a sweet and cloying odour, something between that of fruit and rotten meat, impregnates shoes that tread the sodden ground around the corpse. It takes years for the stench that permeates the soil and air to disappear.[40] It is therefore not surprising that the soldiers preferred to avoid the dead and the corvée intended for their burial. In any case, the bodies were not dragged too far from the entrenchments, as the transports were all necessarily done by hand. One of the mass graves, the only one identified to date with relative certainty, was dug at the base of the ridge leading to Testa dell'Assietta, not far from the starting line of the attack of the French columns. The excavation, given the terrain, was not too deep and the bodies were covered with stones and clods of earth, making the burial similar to a large mound which, over 250 years later, is still easily recognizable.[41] Elsewhere the bodies were buried singly, or in groups

---

37   *Capitano* Fassati, who died in Susa on 21 July from wounds sustained in combat, is not included in this total. AST, Sezioni Riunite, Ministero della Guerra, Ufficio Generale del Soldo, Ruolini di Rivista, Reggimento Guardie, Vol.89, 1747.

38   A.N. Santa Cruz y Marcenado, *Réflexions militaires et politiques* (La Hague: Jacques van den Kieboom, 1735-1740), Vol.VI, p.182.

39   D.O. Carter, M. Tibbett, *Cadaver Decomposition and Soil: Processes*, in *Soil Analysis in Forensic Taphonomy: Chemical and Biological Effects of Buried Human Remains* (Boca Raton: Routledge, 2008), pp.29–52.

40   M. Roach, *Stiff: The Curious Lives of Human Cadavers* (New York & London: W.W. Norton & Co Inc., 2003, p.70.

41   The burial mound was identified during a survey carried out by the author in July 2008, together with Prof. Piero Garoglio and Dr Eugenio Garoglio.

The Austro-Sardinians buried a total of 1,032 corpses in mounds similar to the one shown in the photograph and existing near Testa dell'Assietta. About 20 metres long, this artificial relief is the cover of one of the many mass graves dug on the battlefield. Given the characteristics of the terrain, it was not possible to dig deep, but it was easier to cover the bodies with stones and clods of earth. The result was to create a kind of mound, one of which was identified during a reconnaissance carried out on the battlefield in 2007. (Author's photo)

of two or three at a time, as large mass graves were, as far as we know, completely out of place on the battlefields of the eighteenth century.[42] In all, the Austro-Sardinian soldiers collected and buried 1,032 corpses, a figure that they officially communicated to de Villemur.[43]

The bodies of the officers were interred together with those of the soldiers; only Belle-Isle's corpse had already been requested and taken from the battlefield on de Villemur's instructions. On the afternoon of 20 July, the body had reached Sauze Oulx, and the following morning the funeral of the Chevalier took place. The body was interred in the presbytery of the Parish Church, in the presence of de Villemur, de Mailly and d'Andlau. The ceremony was conducted by the local parish priest, who wrote a report of the funeral. On the tomb the phrase *Hic inter salices, pulchra insula iacet* was engraved. On the desire of the family, in particular thanks to the offices of the Archbishop of Embrun, Bernardin-François Fouquet, a relative of the Chevalier, the body was exhumed and transported to the crypt of

---

42   Duffy, *Military Experience in the Age of Reason*, p.193.

43   *Villemur au maréchal de Belle-Isle, Au Camp de Tournous le 3 Aoust 1747 a dix heures du soir*, SHD Série A1, Vol.3240.

the cathedral of Embun.[44] The body of d'Arnaud was also requested by the French during the same morning of the 20th; the request was accepted and d'Arnaud was buried in the parish church of Salbertrand.[45]

The wounded were far more complicated to deal with than the dead. The Austro-Sardinians had equipped hospitals in Susa and Pinerolo, called 'Royal Hospitals'. Another collection centre was located inside the Fortress of Fenestrelle, which was immediately mobilized to welcome the wounded arriving from the battlefield; in all, 101 Austro-Sardinian soldiers were evacuated from the battlefield.

The transfer of the French wounded was more laborious, if only for their greater number. Between 20 and 21 July about 300 wounded were recovered from the battlefield, in addition to which more than 100 were abandoned at the field hospital at Seu. Overall, the French soldiers collected and cared for by the Austro-Sardinians numbered 412, who were concentrated at Fenestrelle and in the village of Laux.[46] To transport the wounded collected on the battlefield and to the field hospital of Seu, Bricherasio requested 740 porters and 182 stretchers from the communities of the Susa Valley.[47]

Counting Losses

The two opposing armies soon began to count the losses they had suffered. The data for the Austro-Sardinian losses is very precise, as we have the rolls of the regiments that participated in the battle. In all, the allied army recorded 72 dead, 101 wounded or hospitalized due to illness, of whom 53 (52 percent) died by the end of the year, 25 deserters, three prisoners and one soldier executed. This was 3.37 percent of the total force.

Table 12. Losses Suffered by the Austro-Sardinian troops During the Battle of Assietta

Unit	Effective Strength	Dead	Injured or sick	Died of wounds	Deserters	Prisoners	Executed	Total losses
1/Guardie	745	12	36	7	–	–	–	48
Casale	316	4	1	1	3	2	–	11
2/Kalbermatten	595	2	18	16	5	–	–	25
3/Kalbermatten	699	14	8	8	9	1	1	33
3/Roi	708	22	17	12	5	–	–	44
Meyer	721	13	5	4	3	–	–	21

---

44   Peracca, *La Valle di Oulx e le Guerre di Successione d'Austria*, p.51. P. Guillaume, 'Les ossements du chevalier de Belle-Isle à Embrun', in *Bulletin de la Société d'Études des Hautes-Alpes*, 6, 1887, pp.219-220; Peracca, *La Valle di Oulx e le Guerre di Successione d'Austria*, pp.80-81. The request to be able to recover the bodies of commanding officers, or those of a certain rank, to be buried in their family graves, was a common practice in the eighteenth century although very often the first presentable corpse that could be recovered on the battlefield was instead delivered to the unfortunate relatives! See Duffy, *Military Experience in the Age of Reason*, p.193.

45   Priocca Report I.

46   Brunet de l'Argentière, *Mémoire de la Guerre*, p.73.

47   Peracca, *La Valle di Oulx e le Guerre di Successione d'Austria*, p.62.

Unit	Effective Strength	Dead	Injured or sick	Died of wounds	Deserters	Prisoners	Executed	Total losses
3/Colloredo	218							
3/Forgách	258	5	16	–	5	–	–	26
Hagenbach	297							
Traun	303							
Militia and Volunteer Units	1,300	–	–	–	–	–	–	–
Total	6,160	72	101	53	25	3	1	208

Sources: AST, Sezioni Riunite, Ministero della Guerra: Ufficio Generale del Soldo; Ruolini di Rivista; Reggimento Guardie, Vol.89, 1747; Reggimento Kalbermatten, Vol.58, 1747; Reggimento Roi, Vol 30, 1747; Reggimento Meyer, Vol.8, 1747; Reggimento Casale, Vol.33, 1747: Ordini Generali e Misti, 1747, Mazzo 48, *Stato de Battaglioni trovatisi presenti agli attacchi ed interventi alla difesa de Trinceramenti dell'Assietta li 19 scorso Luglio*. KA, Alten Feldakten I-VI, Krieg in Italien, 1747: Ständ und Dienst Tabella, 18 June 1747, Cartone 581; Colloredo to Browne, 20 July 1747, Cartone 582.

The total losses of the allied forces were extremely light, particularly taking into account the disproportion of the forces in the field. The unit that had the most soldiers knocked out in absolute terms, 1/Guardie, being also the strongest unit in the army, had a loss rate of 6.44 percent of the losses. Proportionally, the hardest-hit unit was the Reggimento Casale, which lost 12 percent. However, after a period of rest all of these battalions should in theory still have been able to sustain high intensity combat.

Even the Sardinian units that had remained unrelated to the fighting of 19 July had suffered the wear and tear of the campaign and the stay at high altitude. Some units, such as 1/Sicilia, paid a relatively high rate of losses for their presence at high altitude to guard the entrenchments. The following table illustrates their losses:

Table 13. Losses suffered During the Assietta Campaign by Sardinian Troops Present in the Operational Area but not Engaged in Combat on 19 July 1747

Unit	Effective	Dead	Deaths from injury or illness	Deserters	Total losses
2/Savoia	551	–	9	7	16
1/Sicilia	622	–	23	7	30
Chiablese	672	–	2	–	2
1/Monfort	623	–	6	–	6
Total	2,468	–	37	14	57

Sources. AST, Sezioni Riunite, Ministero della Guerra, Ufficio Generale del Soldo, Ruolini di Rivista; Reggimento Savoia, Vol. 82, 1747; Reggimento Sicilia, Vol. 55, 1747; Reggimento Chiablese, Vol. 20, 1747; Reggimento Monfort, Vol. 84, 1747.

Unlike Bricherasio, de Villemur on the contrary knew he had to justify to his superiors the loss of thousands of men. In the days immediately following the battle, the French commander wrote a first report in which he announced to the Minister of War, the Comte d'Argenson, that 'our losses, both dead and wounded, are about 5,000'.[48] He attached to this report a table with the list of losses divided by regiment, which all subsequent Italian and French military historians have always taken for granted.[49] In all, he lamented the death of 94 officers, the wounding of 337 others and the loss, including dead and wounded, of 4,553 non-commissioned officers and private soldiers, for a total of 4,984 casualties, 31.3 percent of the forces present. It was an unprecedented figure: at Fontenoy, on 11 May 1745, the French forces had suffered 7,137 losses, 14.5 percent of the total, but at least the day ended with a victory.[50] At Piacenza, on the other hand, the decisive battle for control of northern Italy during the War of the Austrian Succession, the losses had been immense, 9,000 for the Spaniards and 4,000 for the French, but even then it was a clash of such dimensions that this amounted to a loss of only 16 percent for defeated Franco-Spanish army.[51] The ministry of war, while taking the figures given by de Villemur for granted, began to insist upon more precise reports about the losses and, above all, about the officers killed and wounded in combat.[52] With some of the wounded left in Piedmont, the hospitals of the Dauphiné saturated, and the threat of an Austro-Sardinian invasion against the south-eastern borders of France, it was certainly not easy for de Villemur to be able to reconstruct in detail who was absent from the ranks and why. Fifteen days after the battle he gave up the ghost. Picking up the pen, he wrote to his commander that he was unable to give a precise number of the wounded, nor even their precise location. He complained that some regimental commanders had inflated their losses, and others, even knowing how many soldiers were actually missing, 'ignore who is dead and who is wounded'.[53] We can add that they also ignored those who had deserted, another voice typical of the losses of an eighteenth century battle. Every day, de Villemur wrote, 'I discover some people wounded who have been hospitalized', often far from the centre of Briançon.[54] Nonetheless, communications with the enemy allowed him to learn that 1,032 corpses had been buried on the battlefield. To these must be added the 250 injured who died between the various field hospitals in the days following the clash. In his letter, de Villemur concluded as follows: 'this makes only 1,300 men [dead], and according to the investigations I made after various battles in which I found myself, the wounded are roughly double [the number of dead], therefore between dead and wounded we should not have more than 4,000 men, or a little less'.[55]

---

48   *Report de l'affaire de l'Assiette, 19 juillet, par M. de Villemur*, Arvers and de Vault, *Guerre de la Succession d'Autriche*, Vol.II, p.753.

49   *État des officiers et soldats tués ou blessés à l'attaques des retranchementrs de l'Assiette, 19 juillet*, Arvers and de Vault, *Guerre de la Succession d'Autriche*, Vol.II, p.754.

50   J.P. Bois, *Fontenoy 1745. Louis XV, arbitre de l'Europe* (Paris: Economica, 1996), pp.101-106; D. Gandilhon, *Fontenoy. La France domine l'Europe* (Paris: Histoire & Collections, 2008), p.76.

51   G. Bodart, *Losses of Life in Modern Wars. Austria-Hungary; France* (Oxford: Clarendon Press, 1916), p.100. Assietta is also mentioned here as 'the bloodiest battle of the war', due to the enormous losses suffered by the French 'where they lost forty percent dead and wounded and four percent prisoners'; Browning, *War of the Austrian Succession*, p.276; Ilari, Boeri, Paoletti, *La Corona di Lombardia*, p.201.

52   D'Argenson to Villemur, 1 August 1747, Arvers and de Vault, *Guerre de la Succession d'Autriche*, Vol.II, p.761.

53   Villemur to Duc de Belle-Isle, 3 August 1747, SHD Série A1, Vol.3240.

54   The officer in charge of their management was the *Commissaire des Guerres* Pierre-Nicolas de Lasalle. C. Mahon, 'Un commissaire des guerre sous l'Ancien Regime. Pierre-Nicolas de Lasalle', in *Le Carnet de la Sabretache. Revue militaire rétrospective*, Vol.VIII, 1900. pp.343-353.

55   Villemur to Duc de Belle-Isle, 3 August 1747, SHD Série A1, Vol.3240.

By comparing various sources, we can assume that the overall French losses at Assietta were ultimately 1,174 dead and 3,929 wounded, as follows:

Table 14: Losses Suffered by the French Forces on 19 July 1747

Brigade	Regiment	Officers/ Soldiers	Officers				Soldiers		Total by Regiment			
			Killed	Wounded	Total	Losses as %	Killed	Wounded	Killed	Wounded	Total	Losses as %
Bourbonnais	Bourbonnais	106/1500	19	52	71	67%	133	446	152	498	650	40%
	Des Landes	38/500	3	11	14	37%	56	189	59	200	259	48%
	Soissonnais	38/500	3	11	14	37%	52	176	55	187	242	45%
	Total	**182/2,500**	**25**	**74**	**99**	–	**241**	**811**	**266**	**885**	**1,151**	–
La Reine	La Reine	72/1,000	16	25	41	57%	124	417	140	442	582	54%
	Béarn	38/500	3	8	11	29%	26	87	29	95	124	23%
	Guise	38/500	10	13	23	61%	29	97	39	110	149	28%
	Total	**148/2,000**	**29**	**46**	**75**	–	**179**	**601**	**208**	**647**	**855**	–
Artois	Artois	72/1,000	10	23	36	50%	101	338	111	361	472	44%
	Auxerrois	38/500	2	13	15	39%	28	94	30	107	137	25%
	Aunis	38/500	3	18	21	55%	40	132	43	150	193	36%
	Santerre	38/500	–	11	11	29%	23	76	23	87	110	20%
	Total	**186/2,500**	**15**	**65**	**83**	–	**192**	**640**	**207**	**705**	**912**	–
Mailly	Mailly	106/1,500	7	23	30	28%	103	344	110	367	477	30%
	Boulonnais	38/500	4	9	13	34%	36	123	40	132	172	32%
	Agenois	38/500	2	9	11	29%	18	62	20	71	91	17%
	Total	**186/2,500**	**13**	**41**	**54**	–	**157**	**529**	**170**	**570**	**740**	–
R. Roussillon	R. Roussillon	38/500	2	17	19	50%	32	109	34	126	160	30%
	Périgord	38/500	5	5	10	26%	40	134	45	139	184	34%
	Guyenne	38/500	1	6	7	18%	31	103	32	109	141	26%
	Beaujolais	38/500	1	16	17	45%	16	53	17	69	86	16%
	Total	**152/2,000**	**9**	**44**	**53**	–	**119**	**399**	**128**	**443**	**571**	–
Condé	Condé	72/1,000	2	34	36	50%	84	282	86	316	402	38%
	Saintonge	38/500	6	11	17	45%	29	97	35	108	143	27%
	Beauce	38/500	1	5	6	16%	21	72	22	77	99	18%
	Total	**148/2,000**	**9**	**50**	**59**	–	**134**	**451**	**143**	**501**	**644**	–
Grenadiers Royaux de Modène		68/1,200	6	24	30	50%	46	154	52	178	230	18%
Total (including senior officers)		**1,066/ 14,700**	**106**	**344**	**450**	**42%**	**1,068**	**3,585**	**1,174**	**3,929**	**5,103**	**32%**

Sources: SHD-T A1: 3227, 198, 199; 3240: 35, 36.

In fact, as probably de Villemur had guessed, battalion commanders often had no idea where their soldiers were, and simply they referred to a soldier who was absent at that moment as 'wounded'. In reality, it was not known for a man so-listed where he was, if really hit by the enemy and hospitalized in one of the countless hospitals that had sprung up in the Dauphiné, or if he had deserted, or had been absent for any reason. In the following weeks many of them re-joined the ranks, and some French commentators were able to say that the casualties were in the end '80 officers and 1,400 soldiers [killed], 750 men wounded'.[56]

Once healed, the soldiers who had been wounded in combat returned in dribs and drabs to their units. At least 137 of them applied over the years to be transferred to the Invalid Corps, certifying the injuries they had suffered in the course of the fight. The information obtained from the enrolment registers makes them a particularly interesting source, allowing us to have an even more precise vision of the nature of the infantry combat around the entrenched camp of Assietta. The main agents of destruction of the battle were individual firearms: 114 of these people, 83 percent, were hit by a musket shot, and of these 22 received multiple gunshot wounds. The left side, which was most exposed due to the marching and shooting posture, turned out to be the most affected part of the body; 44 soldiers were hit in left limbs or in that side of the body. The injuries could not only be incapacitating, but could even cause major mutilations. The large lead bullets used by the infantry of the time were capable of crushing bones, removing large parts of muscle mass, or severing body parts, as had happened to Pierre Joseph Le Fevre, known as La Motte, a grenadier of the Régiment de Mailly, who had 'the index finger of his left hand removed by a musket shot'.[57]

The stones thrown by the defenders hit eight soldiers, about six percent of the total, a sign that stones were actually one of the most used forms of 'ammunition' employed by Austro-Sardinian soldiers and that, despite appearances, they proved to be particularly effective. A stone thrown with enough power was able to put a man out of action immediately, if not to kill him. Mathieu Nonnat, known as Charlemagne, *caporal* of the Régiment de Béarn, had 'his kneecap split by a stone blow'.[58]

Medical treatment, despite the elaborate surgical treatments that existed, could do little, especially if the bullet had lodged in the skull. Remy Gaumont, called Gatinois, of the Régiment de Béarn was shot in the head. The bullet did not penetrate the cranial cavity, but 'he lost his left eye following the operation he suffered from the extraction of a ball he received in the head'.[59] Despite everything, Remy was lucky and he managed to heal; surgeon Hugues Ravaton, chief surgeon of the Landau military hospital during the War of the Austrian Succession, judged similar wounds as 'among the most dangerous' and almost always fatal.[60]

Only two men, Gilbert Romane of Des Landes and Pierre Chicot of Mailly, were wounded by an edged weapon, and both, as we have seen, in particular circumstances; found wounded and unconscious on the battlefield, an enemy attempted to give them a final blow. Soldiers

---

56 *L'Esprit des Journaux, par une Société de Gens de Lettres*, Tomo I, 1776 p.22. The comments and evaluations on the Battle of Assietta were part of a review of the work by de Pezay, *Histoire des Campagne de M. le Maréchal de Maillebois en Italie*.

57 Pierre Joseph La Fevre died in service at Aiguemort on 15 October 1758. SHD/GR/2Xy53.

58 Mathieu Nonnat, SHD/GR/2Xy40.

59 Remy Gaumont, despite his injury, served as a soldier of the Invalid Corps until 21 November 1774, the day of his death. SHD/GR/2Xy40.

60 H. Landau, *Chirurgie d'Armée, ou Traité del Plaies d'armes à feu, et d'armes blanches* (Paris: Didot le Jeune, 1768), pp.174-175.

also incurred serious injuries even far from the epicentre of the clash. Another man of the Régiment de Béarn, *Caporal* Laurent Rigault, known as La Jeunesse, was seriously injured, his left foot suffering a permanent disability 'having taken a sprain while he was on artillery duty' during the Assietta campaign.[61]

The end of the fighting did not mean the end of stress and fatigue, even for those who had been lucky enough not to be hit by a bullet or bayonet. Many soldiers still had noises in their ears, smells in their noses, and before their eyes all the horrors of war and fighting at close range; a similar experience does not simply go away with a good night's sleep or heavy drinking. At the current state of research we do not have much information about psychological disorders that afflicted veterans of eighteenth-century wars, although it is almost certain that these problems afflicted all soldiers of the modern era. As early as the seventeenth century the Spaniards in Flanders were able to recognize something very similar to Post Traumatic Stress Disorder, which was named *mal de corazon*, and the officers recommended the immediate dismissal of these soldiers no longer fit for service.[62] This could also happen to officers: the Marquis Louis-Victor de Mailly, grandson of the general and commander of the Régiment de Mailly, was just 24 years old in 1747. He was shot in the head during the fight under the summit of the Great Serin. Left for dead, he passed out and was abandoned on the battlefield for no less than five hours. Recovered, he was treated and returned in France but he never managed to recover completely from that experience which 'imprinted in the character of the Marquis a background of melancholy that remained in him for the rest of his life'.[63]. The mother later wrote to her cousin that 'my son is totally ruined'.[64] In short, post-traumatic stress disorder plagued his days until his death in 1774.

The News Spreads

Fenestrelle

The stronghold of Fenestrelle had been chosen as the logistical base of the small army of the Conte di Bricherasio. From the Piazza d'Armi of the San Carlo Fort and the batteries of the Forte delle Valli, the Assietta ridge is perfectly visible. On the afternoon of July 19, the entire garrison stood with their noses upwards to watch the unfolding of the fight. The noises of the shots could be perfectly distinct, 'it sounded like a drum roll, so much was the noise of the gunshots';[65] to everyone's relief it was possible to see from the smoke produced by the black powder ammunition that the front had not moved beyond the entrenchments, a sign that the enemy had not managed to break through: 'The fire continued very lively until half-past seven and eight o'clock at the entrenchments of the Sieta, and having at such a

---

61   Laurent Rigaud served in Paris until 16 December 1789, the date of his death. SHD/GR/2Xy40.

62   Hanlon, *Italy 1636*, p.150; Geoffrey Parker, *Global Crisis: War, Climate Change and Catastrophe in the 17th Century* (New Haven and London: Yale University Press, 2013), p.591.

63   Gosselin, *Mailly et ses seigneurs*, pp.95-96; Ledru, *Histoire de la maison de Mailly*, Vol.I, pp.228-229.

64   Ledru, *Histoire de la maison de Mailly*, p.229n.

65   The contemporary testimony comes from the parish priest of La Ruà, today the capital of the municipality of Pragelato (TO), in Susa. Peracca, *La Valle di Oulx e le Guerre di Successione d'Austria*, p.49.

time ceased without ever being seen through the smoke that the enemy was able to advance a step, nor gain anything on the entrenchments'.[66] However, hours passed before some more certain news reached the valley floor. Jean Baptiste Guigas arrived first with orders to prepare a convoy of ammunition supplies as soon as possible. Intendant Baldoino, in charge of gathering all possible information, managed to intercept two French deserters late in the evening, 'one grenadier of the Périgord Regiment, and the other of the Mailli Regiment, who were in action', who stated 'that their two aforementioned Regiments are defeated'.[67] A little later, *Maggiore* Perrone, commander of the militia of Pragelato, arrived at the fort accompanying the first wounded. He confirmed the words of the French deserters and ascertained the state of the convoy that was to leave with the long-awaited precious ammunition for Bricherasio. The battle had ended in a completely unexpected victory. Baldoino began writing a letter to inform Turin of what had happened.

From the battlefield, winners and losers sent reports, at first very meagre, later richer in detail about what had happened in the valleys of western Piedmont.

Turin

Maggiore Panissera of the Reggimento Casale, sent to Turin by the Conte di Bricherasio from the battlefield, passed through the door of the Royal Palace at eight in the morning of 20 July. He delivered a short and succinct report on the battle directly to the sovereign's secretariat.

> The Enemies attacked us on the 19th at 10 in the morning in several columns and came back to the charge up to four times so that the affair lasted until the onset of night[. T]he last assault was between 4 and 5 o'clock in the evening when they came with all their forces, which consisted of 48 Battalions, all Generals at the head of their divisions, sword in hand and protected by 9 pieces of 4-pounder cannon, but they were repulsed at this last assault as before. At nightfall they retreated towards the Sestriere pass. They had several officers of note killed and injured, among others, the Chevalier de Bellisle, his arm swept away, M. de Mailly *Maréchal de Camp*, de Villemure *Lieutenant Général* killed[,] M. de Ruffi Genl. wounded, M. de Beauregard Brigadier captured. We took 3 flags from them[,] the prisoners and deserters agree that their loss is about 5,000 [,] in all ours is only 120 between dead and killed including the officers who are 7 or 8 in number...[68]

The text contains obvious exaggerations, such as the number of opposing battalions, their artillery, inaccuracies regarding the pursuit of grenadiers and the beginning of the battle. However, the basic gist, that the enemy had withdrawn to the starting lines of its attack,

---

66   Letter from Intendente Baldoino, Fenestrelle 19 July 1747, AST, Corte, Materie Militari, Imprese, Mazzo 7 da inventariare.

67   Letter from Intendente Baldoino, Fenestrelle 19 July 1747, AST, Corte, Materie Militari, Imprese, Mazzo 7 da inventariare.

68   *Premier Avis de l'Affaire de 19 Juillet 1747 sur Exilles, arrivée du Col de l'Assiette au Roy par le chev.e de Panissera, Maior de Regim.nt de Casal, le 20.e Juillet a 8. heures du matin*, BRT, Manoscritto Militare 154.

after suffering impressive losses, was correct. At that moment, no one could yet predict what the French would do in the following hours, but for the moment the danger of a deep invasion and the investment of the Fort of Exilles seemed to fade.

Of capital importance for Austro-Sardinian intelligence was the correspondence and documents found in the pockets of the right body of the Chevalier de Belle-Isle, which Bricherasio sent to Turin together with the first report. The allied command found itself in possession of extremely important information, such as the battle order of the *Armée d'Italie*; the composition of the forces detached in the Dauphiné and destined for the invasion of western Piedmont; the plan of operations compiled on 13 July to Guillestre with Bourcet and Monteynard; the orders given to the column and brigade commanders; above all, the letters from the Duc de Belle-Isle dated 13, 14 and 15 July. Carlo Emanuele III had a real treasure in his hands; in addition to the state of the enemy forces, the king of Sardinia was able to understand in detail how his opponents planned at a strategic, operational and tactical level, as well as their immediate and future objectives and, above all, the existing differences between the Franco-Spanish allies.

On 22 July the king wanted to celebrate the victory in the capital 'with the solemn singing of a Te Deum'. There would not only be the sung mass, but also the entire garrison – the reserve company of the provincial Reggimento Aosta and part of the city militia – 'to accompany the tripled discharge of the musketry, which is also matched by that of the Artillery'.[69] On the 22nd the king decided to reward the troops who had obtained a victory as striking as it was unexpected: additional food rations arrived for the soldiers and 'a month's free pay'.[70] By November of that year, however, the extra pay month had not yet been paid to all units. In particular, the men of 2/ and 3/ Kalbermatten, whose combat action was decisive, did not receive their extra money. After complaints reached the Court, the Royal Decree of 12 November 1747 resolved, at least officially, the dispute.

Vienna

On 20 July the Austrians drew up their own report on the battle, very dry and devoid of excessive details, which Colloredo sent directly to the headquarters of *Feldzeugmeister* Browne, who was at that moment in transfer to Piedmont from the Ligurian front after the abandonment of the siege of Genoa. The officer in charge of relaying the report was to have been the *Obristwachtmeister* of the Regiment Hagenbach, the Irishman Francis O'Neillan, who 'with his courage and his usual activity, distinguished himself in this action in a very particular way'. Colloredo wanted to reward the officer by giving him the task of communicating the news of the victory to the commander in the field of the imperial troops.[71] Francis O'Neillan (1729-1757) was the son of Francis Patrick O'Neillan, a former general of the imperial armies. Friend of Giacomo Casanova, who claimed he had 'never known a boy as addicted to debauchery as O'Neilan', who 'had to necessarily fall victim to Mars or Venus'. In place of a nagging venereal disease he chose the lead of a bullet, and the young Irishman

---

69   AST, Sezioni Riunite, Ministero della Guerra, Ufficio Generale del Solso, Ordini Generali e Misti, 1747, Mazzo 48, Regio Viglietto del 22 luglio1747.

70   AST, Sezioni Riunite, Ministero della Guerra, Ufficio Generale del Soldo, Ordini Generali e Misti, 1747, Mazzo 48.

71   Colloredo's report, KA, FA Krieg in Italien 1747 VII 16a.

was killed in combat by the Prussians while he was breaking down the gates of Hirschwald in Saxony on 20 February 1757, during the Seven Years War.[72] However O'Neillan, injured or ill, was unable to move and *Hauptmann* Hoffer was chosen, who was also entrusted with the three flags collected on the battlefield.

Hoffer managed to intercept Browne at Lodi on 22 July, where he gave him Colloredo's report, the captured banners, and a verbal account of the facts of the action. On the same day, other reports were sent to the Court of Vienna.[73] In the meantime, Minister Bogino had come to Milan to urge the arrival of the imperial army in Piedmont. In order to overcome any resistance, it was necessary to guarantee every possible logistical support from the Sardinian side. The imperial doubters, in particular as regards the reimbursement of provisioning expenses in Sardinian territory, were won over at the end of a meeting marked by a rather tense atmosphere; on the one hand Bogino was keen to hurry the Imperialists on their way to the Alps, on the other hand the Imperialists did not want to bear the military expenses for the defence of Piedmont. In the end, with difficulty and with mutual distrust, an agreement was concluded.[74]

The war council of the empress met to comment on the incident on 7 August, in the presence of ministers von Königsegg and von Harrach.[75] The news of the great allied victory counterbalanced the failure of Genoa and was immediately made public; the report of the battle was disseminated to the German-speaking public through a series of gazettes and press notices.[76] By mid-August it was known in German countries that the armies of Empress Maria Theresia had achieved an important success against the arms of the kingdom of France.

Paris

De Villemur was certainly not in a good mood. He had escaped a bloody battle, and now he was in the position of having to account for the defeat that he had inherited. He decided to entrench himself behind superlatives, presenting to the Minister of War a brief, but unclear, report in which he declaimed 'immense losses [...], extremely serious [...], particularly affected troops [...]'.[77] The letter, written in the night of 19-20 July, probably

---

72   L. McInerney, 'The O'Neylons of Dysert and Austria', in *Shannon Archaeological & Historical Society*, "The Other Clare", Vol 42 (2018), pp.25-32.

73   The official Austrian report of Browne to the Empress Maria Theresia was drawn up in Lodi on 22 July 1747. KA, FA Krieg in Italien 1747 VII b.

74   AST, Corte, Sezioni Riunite, Ministero della Guerra, Ufficio Generale del Soldo, Ordini Generali e Misti, 1747, Mazzo 48, *Appuntamenti per la Sussistenza dell'Armata I.R. che deve marciare in Piemonte, presi dal Commissariato di S.M.I.R., con S.E. il Sig. Conte Bogino Primo Segretario di Guerra di S.M. Sarda, nella Conferenza de 20 Luglio 1747, coll'intervento de Soggetti medesimi nominati nella prima, sovra il Piano Militare*.

75   J.J. Khevenhüller-Metsch, *Aus der Zeit Maria Theresias* (Wien: Holzhausen, 1907), Vol.II 1745-1749, p.171.

76   Colloredo's report became the basis for the following printed texts rendered as an example: *Zuverlässig Nachricht von dem am 20. Juli 1747 vorgefallenen Treffen zwischen den Franzosichen, Spanischen, wie auch Kayserl. und Konigl. Sardinischen Wöltern in Col della Sietta, and der Seite von Exilles und Fenestrelles in ner Nachgrafschaft Saluzzo, in Fürstenthum Piedmont*, Leipzig 1747; *Di Neue Europäische Fama*, Vol.145, Leipzig 1747, pp.135-141.

77   Villemur to d'Argenson. SHD série A1, Vol.3227, pièce 181.

reflected the state of mind of the French commander; moreover, it is interesting to note that the officer informed the top of the army directly without preparing any report for his direct commander, the Duc de Belle-Isle, who still did not know what had happened in the Piedmontese valleys. The complete court of Louis XV, with the secretaries of state, war and foreign affairs, was in those days in Tongres near Maastricht to follow the evolution of war operations on the Dutch front. D'Argenson saw the letters of the Chevalier de Belle-Isle of 16 July and those of de Villemur of 19-20 July delivered simultaneously.[78]

It was one thing to confront the distant Minister of War, quite another to confront one's immediate superior and announce that not only was the battle lost, but that the immediate superior's younger brother had also fallen in the battle. Moreover, as the chief was a man of war, he could not be fooled with a simple report full of suggestions and catchphrases. De Villemur therefore wrote a second, more detailed report, which he sent in duplicate to the Comte d'Argenson and the Duc de Belle-Isle.[79] He decided, however, that to accompany his report would be *Capitaine* Blondel d'Azincourt, injured in the head while fighting alongside the Chevalier de Belle-Isle, and another officer linked to the Belle-Isle family, the Chevalier de Mortagne. The two messengers arrived in Nice in the evening of 23 July, four days after the end of the battle. They introduced themselves to the Duc de Belle-Isle, who was impatient to receive news from the Alpine front. D'Azincourt and Mortagne informed him of what had happened:

> The Marshal of Bell'isle, dejected by this terrible news, fell on the table where he was writing, with his head in his hands. After staying like this for two hours he stood up like an ancient Roman, and said to M. Patiot, commissioner of war and his first secretary, honouring his internal moral strength: 'I no longer have a brother, but I have a homeland, let's work to save it'. In fact he spent the night in dictating orders for the defence of Dauphiné, whose command fell, by right of seniority, to M. d'Argouges, *Lieutenant Général* of the Army.[80]

The following day, 25 July, Belle-Isle wrote to the Comte d'Argenson, exonerating his brother for the defeat he had suffered and bluntly accusing his Spanish ally:

> Only last night, sir, I was informed of that unfortunate affair of the 19 July afflicted with the most acute pain that the irreparable loss of my brother causes me. And they are also one of the most capable and skilled lieutenant generals, among those promoted by the king, in commanding his armies. I am also heartbroken by the task that was assigned to him, which would have been fulfilled in a different way if he had lived. Finally, I am heartbroken by the impossibility in which I find myself in replacing him, and by the lack of daily care that my health and my illnesses require. I am too overcome with anger to be able to attend to my needs; I have conferred with the Marquis de La Mina, about which I cannot rejoice in this circumstance.

---

78   D'Argenson to Villemur, SHD série A1, Vol.3228, pièce 11.
79   Villemur to d'Argenson, SHD, série A1, Vol.3227, pièce 195; Villemur to Belle-Isle, SHD, série A1, Vol.3240, pièce 67.
80   Chevrier, *Vie politique et militaire de M. le Maréchal Duc de Bell'Isle*, p.220.

I have never been free to act with the necessary speed; the order of the king that I received, to be precise four days after my brother's departure, forced me to send a courier to suspend his movements, until the Marquis de La Mina had made his decisions. They were two days of negotiation, and as I have already mentioned, these gave the king of Sardinia time to get twelve more battalions to the entrenchments in question, of which three were Austrians, who arrived in the night between the 18th and the 19th. Despite the precious time lost, the action could still succeed. My brother sent me in his last letter that he would not start anything without being absolutely sure of success. But he is gone, and I cannot add anything else.[81]

Distraught, angry, disappointed; the Duc de Belle-Isle remained for at least a day in such conditions that he could not make any decisions. 'I cannot do all this; I cannot reason or comment; you will do it better than me. I cry for the king, the state, the situation, the army, and I pity myself for being in charge and not being able to reason'.[82]

On Tuesday 25 July, the news that the army of the Chevalier of Belle-Isle had been defeated in the Alps, and its commander killed, came to the Court of Versailles.[83] In the presence of the king, the story of the battle became at least an unwelcome subject, to the point that one of the sovereign's pages wrote to his uncle that 'we don't want to talk about the adventure of Exilles, we are so rightly dismayed by it'.[84] In Paris the details of the battle had already spread over the course of Sunday 23 July.[85] In addition to the general consternation, criticism and ironic jokes began to circulate to mock the Chevalier de Belle-Isle and his vainglory. People said that 'the Chevalier de Belle-Isle behaved like a drunken musketeer'.[86] and that 'the facts justify the idea that people made of what happened, that is, that it was the biggest and most impudent gamble a general could make in war. Fortunately for him, death saved him from the shame that would have remained for such a reckless action'.[87]. Even Louis XV went so far as to comment that 'it was for ambition that the Chevalier de Belle-Isle crippled my army'.[88]

---

81   A. de Broglie, *Maurice de Saxe et le Marquis d'Argenson* (Paris: Calmann Lévy, 1891), Vol.II, pp.309-310.

82   Broglie, *Maurice de Saxe*, p.311.

83   L. Dussieux, E. Soulié (eds), *Mémoires du Duc de Luynes sur la Cour de Louis XV (1735-1758)* (Paris: Firmon Didot Frères, Fils et Cie., 1860-1865), p.271.

84   M. De Lordat, C. Charpentier (eds), *Un page de Louis XV. Lettres de Marie-Joseph de Lordat a son oncle Louis, Compte de Lordat, Baron de Bram, Brigadier des Armées du Roi (1740-1747)* (Paris: C. Charpentier, 1908), p.411

85   A first report on the battle was made public through a *Report et Plan des Attaques formées par M. le Chevalier de Belle-Isle contre les retranchemens des piemontois, sous Exiles*, Lille 1747. This pamphlet was not widely circulated, and to date we know only a copy kept in the archives of the French army: SHD, A1-3240-37, A1-3240-35 e 35bis. Much more popular were the *Suite de la Clef, ou Journal Historique surl le Matieres du Tems*, Tome LXII, Paris, Juillet 1747, pp.231-233; *Journal Universel, ou Mémoires pour servir à l'Historie Civile, Politique, Ecclésiastique, & Littéraire du XVIII Siécle*, Tome XIII, Amsterdam, Aout 1747, pp.534-538; *Mercure Historique et Politique*, Tomo CXXIII, La Haye, Juillet 1747, pp.170-182. Some of these gazettes, especially those printed in Holland, had a clear intent to negatively influence French public opinion.

86   Edmond-Jean-François Barbier, *Chronique de la Régence et du Règne de Louis XV (1718-1763) ou Journal de Barbier* (Paris: C. Charpentier, 1857-1866), Vol.IV, p.255.

87   Broglie, *Maurice de Saxe*, p.312.

88   Broglie, *Maurice de Saxe*, p.312.

London

On 21 July the Resident in Turin of the British Crown, Arthur Villettes, and its special envoy, Lieutenant General Thomas Wentworth, were promptly informed of what was coming in the Susa Valley.[89] The Marchese Giuseppe Solaro del Breglio, advisor of Carlo Emanuele III and tutor of the heir to the throne, the Prince of Piedmont Victor Amadeus, on the orders of the sovereign, directly delivered a note in the hands of the British resident that bore a brief report on the victorious battle.[90] The news, as also happened with the Austrian allies, was transmitted with extreme rapidity to Britain: it was excellent news for His Majesty's Prime Minister, Henry Pelham. The expenditure of £200,000 a year to finance the Sardinian Army had finally found valid justification on the battlefield. The news was immediately published in various gazettes in the United Kingdom.[91]

De Villemur Loses Courage

De Villemur's report painted a tragic picture of France's situation on the Western Alps front:

> I present a brief report of this event and the state of the officers who were killed and wounded. I have not yet been able to obtain a state of the exact number of soldiers, which I will have the honour to send as soon as they are communicated to me. I have estimated that we have had at least 4,000 men killed or wounded. I have given orders to M. Bailly to leave all siege ammunition where it is and not to advance anything on Briançon until further notice. It is no longer possible to think of the siege of Exilles and, consequently, the army cannot, in the situation in which it finds itself, leave these valleys too soon. According to the information I was able to gather, 16 Piedmontese and 3 Austrian battalions were present in the

89   F. Scoplis, *Delle Relazioni Politiche tra la Dinastia di Savoia ed il Governo Britannico (1240-1815)* (Torino: Stamperia Reale, 1853), p.88. Arthur Villette was a British diplomat by now an expert in the Piedmontese environment. From 1734 he was the secretary of the British resident in Turin, and later he became the official resident himself. Between 1750 and 1765 he became the English ambassador to the Swiss Federal Diet in Bern. C. Storrs, 'Savoyard diplomacy in the eighteenth century (1684-1798)', in D. Frigo (ed.), *Politics and diplomacy in Early Modern Italy. The structure of diplomatic practice, 1450-1800* (Cambridge: Cambridge University Press, 2000), p.218; R. Lodge, *Studies in Eighteenth Century Diplomacy 1740-1748* (London: John Murray, 1930), pp.201-202. For the diplomatic events between London and Turin in the years 1747-1748, see the interesting contribution E. Mazza, E. Piccoli, '"Disguised in scarlet". Hume and Turin in 1748', in *I Castelli di Yale*, XI (11), pp.71-108. On Wentworth (1693-1747), see the entry edited by Paula Watson for *The History of Parliament: the House of Commons 1715-1754*, at <http://www.historyofparliamentonline.org/volume/1715-1754/member/wentworth-thomas-1693-1747>, accessed 1 August 2022.

90   *Mercure Historique et Politique*, Tomo CXXIII, La Haye, Juillet 1747, pp.170-172.

91   The first newspaper to broadcast the news was the *London Gazette*, which published the news as early as 22 July, after which it was presented in other newspapers: *The Gentleman's Magazine*, London, July 1747, pp.327-328. Other gazettes, such as *Scots Magazine*, preferred instead to publish the Austrian report instead of the Sardinian one: *The Scots Magazine*, Edinburgh, July 1747, p.339-341. The printed reports were also issued in Holland, where the news was spread by the *Nederlandsch Gedenkboek of Europische Mercurius*, Amsterdam, July 1747, pp.28-32.

entrenchments on the day of the attack. According to what I have been told their losses have been few, while among ours there are some battalions that have suffered so much, that they are no longer able to serve the rest of the campaign.[92]

According to the indications provided by de Villemur, out of 20,000 men, 4,000 were killed or wounded. This was a figure comparable to that suffered at the Battle of Lauffeld, fought on the Flanders front by the *Armée Royale* on 2 July 1747; but in that case the number of French troops engaged in combat was at least four times higher.[93] To worsen the situation were the losses reported in the corps of officers: 106 dead and 344 wounded, or 42 percent of the officers present at the combat.[94] This was a very high percentage, especially when compared again with the losses of Lauffeld where the losses among the officers were 90 killed and 500 wounded. Regiments of de Mailly's and d'Arnaud's columns bemoaned the loss on average of 50 percent, while the units of the other brigades left the battlefield with 'only' 30, a third of their officers, as casualties.

Another key passage in De Villeur's reports was his belief that the whole campaign, and in particular the siege of Exilles, was now completely impossible to carry out. The decision to block all incoming artillery trains and retreat to the border to secure the passes led his superiors to believe that the battle had ended in an unprecedented rout and that an invasion of France from the southeast was now inevitable. In truth, given the total inactivity of the enemy, an intermediate solution was possible, pending more detailed orders from the Duc de Belle-Isle. The French forces, though defeated, were still able to immediately face a defensive fight, especially if deployed in force in Oulx and Salbertrand in the Val di Susa, at Colle del Sestrière at the end of Val Chisone, maintaining the crest of Col Burget.

With the retreat to the west of Montgenèvre, what is described in the report as an 'unsuccessful' episode became in effect a military catastrophe. Without too many surprises, the French commander underlined the tactical difficulties encountered during the fight; the roughness of the terrain, the entrenchments erected by the Piedmontese, the effectiveness of enemy fire, even if the enemy forces present on the battlefield on 19 July were greatly increased:

> The enemies defended their lines, which the formation of the terrain made practically unassailable, with their best troops, namely 16 battalions and 2000 Waldensians. The number of soldiers we assigned to this first attack was not considerable. [...] The Enemies made such strong and well directed musket volleys that the brigades were annihilated. In an instant the ground was covered with dead and wounded. Our fire had very little effect on the enemy, since the entrenchments were of considerable height. Not only did they dominate us at high altitude, but they were well equipped with palisades everywhere, and our troops were forced to retreat, after having attacked up to three times.[95]

---

92   Villemur to d'Argenson, *Au camp du Sause Doulx ce 21e juillet 1747*. SHD, série A1, Vol.3227, pièce 195. Villemur to *Maréchal* de Belle-Isle, SHD, série A1, Vol.3240, pièce 67.
93   Browning, *War of the Austrian Succession*, pp.313-317.
94   SHD, série A1, Vol.3227, pièce 199.
95   *Report de l'affaire de l'Assiete*, SHD, série A1, Vol.3227, pièce 196.

Obviously the 16 enemy battalions and the 2,000 Waldensians did not exist at all; they were a figure destined to justify a severe defeat. De Villemur probably knew very well, as he had been commissioned by the Chevalier de Belle-Isle to collect intelligence information about the enemy forces during the day of 16 July, identifying the presence of just seven enemy battalions.

The remains of de Villemur's army were concentrated in Tournoux, where the units initially placed around Barcellonette were also transferred. Teams of peasants were recruited and sent to build field fortifications on Montgenèvre. In turn, the French army moved the warehouses and almost all the Spanish contingent beyond the Varo, while the French army fortified itself in Nice near the village of La Turbie, to block the route from Saorgio along the Tenda valley and from Oneglia. In early August the two allied armies were therefore deployed in depth, with 20 battalions in Provence, 80 in Nice and 20 in the Dauphiné. The Franco-Spanish device had repositioned itself in anticipation of enemy moves. In fact, the system of 'Navettes' devised during the 1709 campaign by the Duc de Berwick had been put back into operation; three combat groups, arranged on three logistic hubs, could cover the entire Alpine front. Montmélian and Fort Barreaux on the left, Briançon-Château Queyras in the centre and Tournoux on the left were the pivots that would support the movements of the French forces. Thanks to the control of the Galibier, Izoard, Vars and Cayolle crossings, the Bourbon troops could guarantee mutual coverage and the rapid influx of reserves from one threatened sector to another.[96]

Everywhere in the Dauphiné one could see these movements of troops, while the news of the defeat spread like wildfire: the army of the Chevalier de Belle-Isle had been defeated and soon the Austro-Sardinian army would arrive.

Much Ado About Nothing

Yet the Austro-Sardinian army did not come at all. In 1742 or 1744, a similar victory on the Alpine front would have been the prelude to an offensive in the south of France and the investment of an opposing stronghold. Now these ambitious projects were completely sunk due to the lack of resources.

For Turin, the objective of the entire campaign of 1747 was not to recover the operational initiative and launch an offensive in French territory, but to block the opposing offensive attempts and contain any enemy progression towards the west. Likewise, the Empress Maria Theresia gave precise instructions to the commander of the imperial forces in Italy, Browne, to bring the troops back to Liguria and 'to take all necessary measures for the

---

96   For a description of this operative plan, still valid throughout the nineteenth century, see A. Petiot and Monmerqué (eds), *Mémoires du Maréchal de Berwick* (Paris Paris: Foucault, 1828), Vol.II, pp.146-150; P.H. Grimoard, *Tableau Historique de la Guerre de la Révolution de France, depuis con commencement en 1792, jusq'a la fin de 1794* (Paris: Treuttel et Würtz, 1808), Vol.I, pp.163-189; A. Marga, *Géographie Militaire* (Paris: Berger-Levrault et Cie., 1885), Vol.I, pp.344-352. This defensive arrangement implemented by the French was still the subject of study by the Italian military intelligence in the twentieth century: BSMT, N. Brancaccio, *Appunti su alcune operazioni militari nelle Alpi Cozie*, 1913

reconquest of Genoa'.[97] One could no longer hope to inflict a severe blow on France, but in Vienna they hoped to at least conquer the capital of a small Italian state. The capacity and willingness of the imperial war machine to support the warring forces on the Italian front were deteriorating as autumn approached. The Austrian forces, 70,000 men scattered between the Riviera di Ponente and the Duchies of Modena and Parma, suddenly became very difficult to manoeuvre with the speed of the previous years, and after the failure of the second siege of Genoa and the Battle of Assietta the Empress ordered Browne to spare his units as much as possible, while the Varadian light infantry units unilaterally considered their task completed and resumed their way home to Hungary.[98] Discipline, after five years of uninterrupted warfare, was deteriorating more and more day by day.

After the battle, the Austro-Sardinian front settled along the Exilles-Saorgio-Oneglia-Savona line, defended by a force of 70 battalions, to which were added the exhausted Austrian battalions returning from the siege of Genoa. In mid-August, one month after the Battle of Assietta, the Austro-Sardinian War Council decided on a counter-offensive to be launched along the Stura valley against the Dauphiné and the Nizzardo. It was, however, more of a demonstration in strength than a real offensive. Carlo Emanuele III decided anyway to take part; on 20 August the troops were centred in Borgo San Dalmazzo, while on the 21st the king of Sardinia left Turin for Cuneo.[99] The advance stalled at the Argentera Pass on 31 August; a second attempt, made on 30 September, was rejected. This last defensive victory, albeit limited, was obtained by *Lieutenant Général* de Villemur.[100]

The French no longer wanted to face the terrible Piedmontese front, and at the same time the Austrians were no longer able to effectively support their troops in the Italian theatre; the operations were limited to a series of incursions and minor fights on the Riviera di Ponente for the control of Ventimiglia. The end of these small operations, which gradually faded in the course of autumn and then ceased completely in winter, also marked the end of hostilities and the campaign of 1747, with the exception of Corsica where fighting would continue into 1748, ended in a standstill. The French had failed in their invasion of Piedmont, the allies had missed the occupation of Genoa and no one wanted to continue the fighting in a land 'where everything has been taken away, the doors, the windows, the windows, the jambs. Looking at the landscape, one might believe that he is in front of one of those wild lands that man has forgotten to colonize'.[101] It was known that diplomatic contacts were under way and that peace would pay dividends equal to the costs incurred.

So, they would continue killing each other at random, waiting for the new year and peace.

---

97   E. Guglia, *Maria Theresia. Ihr Leben und ihre Regierung* (München and Berlin: R, Oldenbourg, 1917), Vol.I, p.299; Arneth, *Maria Theresia's erste Regierungsjahre*, Vol.III, pp.305-306.

98   Browning, *War of the Austrian Succession*, p.313.

99   Minutoli, *Report des campagnes faites par S.M.*, Vol.V, pp.251-375; Atlas, Vol II, *Ordre de Battaille de l'Armée Austrosarde dand la Vallée de Sture en Septembre 1747*; Moris, *Opération Militaires dans Les Alpes et les Apennins*, pp.288-305; Arvers and de Vault, *Guerre de la Succession d'Autriche*, Vol.II, pp.775-802.

100   For the French side as usual Arvers and de Vault, *Guerre de la Succession d'Autriche*, Vol.II, pp.775-802.

101   Browning, *War of the Austrian Succession*, p.313.

10

Conclusions

Unlike the Battle of Turin in 1706, that of Assietta does not have any great monuments such as the Basilica of Superga. Carlo Emanuele III did, however, celebrate the victory with a painting by Hyacinth de La Peigne, a Flemish painter specialized in war scenes,[1] which was exhibited in the rooms of the Royal Palace of Turin, where it is still kept today. Certain of the importance of the subject, La Peigne also asked if he could reproduce a printed version; Carlo Emanuele III, aware of the propaganda effect of such an operation, gave his immediate consent. As early as 1747, the Venetian poet Giuseppe Bartoli dedicated a poem to the Austro-Sardinian victory, entitled *The Battle of the Assietta Pass*.[2] At that point, the battlefield became a place of interest and curiosity for monarchs,[3] soldiers and all the travellers passing through the Susa Valley. Assietta, in a short time, became the symbolic battle of the Kingdom of Sardinia, much more than that of Turin fought 41 years earlier.

Understanding The Battle Through Combat Functions

Battle is the ultimate goal of an army, and it can win and lose the battle it is fighting. The historian often finds himself having to close his narrative by describing the final state of the

---

1   A. Signorelli, 'Assietta: Iconografia di una battaglia', in *Bollettino della Società Piemontese di Archeologia e Belle Arti*, Nuova Serie – XLVI, 1994, pp.177-197. The painting was completed in 1751. A second painting, actually known as 'Passaggio notturno all'Assietta' (Night Passage to Assietta), painted by Jan Peter Verdussen, actually depicts the Battle of Casteldelfino in 1743, a battle at which Carlo Emanuele III was present in person.

2   Giuseppe Bartoli, *La Battaglia del Colle dell'Assietta, seguita ai XIX di Luglio dell'anno MDCCXLVII. Stanze di Giuseppe Bartoli* (Stamperia Reale: Torino, 1747).

3   Among the most famous personalities we mention the Emperor of Austria Joseph II. P.G. Corino, 'Ricognizioni e viaggiatori settecenteschi ai trinceramenti', in G. Amoretti, M.F. Roggero, M. Viglino (eds), *I Trinceramenti dell'Assietta 1747-1997*, Torino 1997, pp.61-72; G. Claretta, 'L'Imperatore Giuseppe II a Torino nel giugno 1769. Memorie aneddotiche', in *Archivio Storico Italiano, Quinta Serie*, Tomo VI, Firenze 1890, pp.387-425. The visit to the frontier of Prince Karl Wilhelm Ferdinand von Braunschweig-Wolfenbüttel, mortally wounded at the battle of Jena-Auerstedt while fighting against Napoleon's *Grande Armée*, is particularly interesting from the point of view of his military analysis. R. Sconfienza, 'I Progetti del Duca di Brunswick per la difesa del Regno di Sardegna', in *Annales Sabaudiae*, Anno II, n. 2, 2006, pp.63-118. Among travelers, we should certainly mention de Sade (ed. Maurice Lever), *Viaggio in Italia*.

battle, who won and who lost. At one time, the victorious army was the one that camped on the battlefield, but this parameter is not useful in making a final analysis of a battle and the forces that took part in it. On this occasion the concept of Combat Functions comes to the rescue of military history. Present in the NATO doctrinal publication AJP 3.2 Allied Joint Doctrine for Land Operation of March 2016, they are conceptual tools available to commanders and their staffs to understand, visualize and describe combat situations in a functional manner. The analysis using Combat Functions as a whole visualizes, and helps to better understand, how combat was planned and managed by the two armies.[4] According to NATO doctrine, there are six Combat Functions in total: command and control, manoeuvre, fire, intelligence, logistics, and protection.

Command and Control

This Combat Function encompasses all the related elements (information, activities, actions, processes, tasks, systems, people, organizations, units and capabilities) that make it possible for the commander to exercise command and control. The command and control system of eighteenth-century armies forced high commands to give their subordinates a great deal of freedom of action. Some subordinates were educated and prepared to act independently, others less so. The Sardinians, as well as to some extent the Austrians, lacked anything similar to the future German system of command, called *Auftragstaktik* or 'mission tactics', whereby:

> [T]he officer must be regarded more than a mere machine that works only when activated. He must often act without orders. There are occasions when an officer has to command or move a single platoon, or give particular instructions. Sometimes the orders he gives are inadequate, or he finds himself in new circumstances. In all these cases the officer will be able to help himself with greater ease if he has an understanding of the manoeuvre as a whole, its objective and his part in achieving it.[5]

Sardinian and Austrian officers, faithful to their war of position, the *Stellungskrieg*, received detailed written orders, from which they deviated little, failing to take advantage of advantageous tactical situations when they arose.

The French, for their part, were always more aggressive and dynamic than their adversaries. Courage, initiative and manoeuvring ability – see for example the approach march to the Assietta plateau, the events of d'Escars' column and de Villemur's manoeuvre on the Gran Serin – were certainly not lacking in the commanders of the *Armée Royal*.

---

4   For a new approach to an analysis of events in war, the reader is referred to R.G. Bowdish, *Campaign, Operation, and Battle Analysis* at <https://www.airuniversity.af.edu/Portals/10/ASPJ/journals/ Chronicles/bowdish.pdf>, or the excellent *Warfighter: Middle Earth* at <https://angrystaffofficer. com/2016/11/04/warfighter-middle-earth/>, both accessed 27 July 2022.

5   Rohr, *Turpin von Crissé*, Vol.I, p.XVI. Regarding the birth of *Auftragstaktik*, see Citino, *The German Way of War*.

Manoeuvre

This Combat Function encompasses all those elements that make possible the movement and employment of forces to reach positions of constant relative advantage over the adversary. The Austro-Sardinians, strengthened by a road network at high altitudes that had been prepared beforehand and constantly maintained, were able to bring to the Assietta camp the units necessary for its defence with perfect timing, without overloading the logistic arm and causing excessive fatigue to the units in transit. Once in the camp the manoeuvring of the units was minimal, and the greatest difficulty was in managing the meagre reserves available to the Conte di Bricherasio.

The French forces were able to manoeuvre effectively throughout the campaign, despite the difficult mountain environment and adverse weather conditions, and they were able to reach the Assietta ridge with good timing, and to attack the opposing camp in a coordinated manner. The alleged delays in de Villemur's march were dictated by the need to coordinate the movement of thousands of men in confined spaces and on rather steep slopes. If the plan had worked properly, the French would have attacked at the Gran Serin at a time when the Austro-Sardinian forces were in full retreat and pressed by two French corps, de Mailly's and d'Arnaud's.

Intelligence

This includes all the related elements that allow an understanding of the mission variables inherent in the terrain, weather conditions and the situation of the opposing forces. The Sardinians had carried out an accurate study of the terrain – the choice of building an entrenched camp at Assietta is proof of this – correctly assessing which were the key points on the battlefield itself. The Gran Serin was for the Conte di Bricherasio, throughout the battle, the key topographic point to be defended at all costs. In addition, the weather conditions of the period, in particular the need on the French side to close the campaign before the arrival of autumn, was another element that was positively exploited by the Austro-Sardinian side. For the rest, the French incursion into the upper Susa Valley, although foreseen, was initially a surprise for the Sardinian commanders, who were expecting an attack in force further south in the Stura di Demonte valley, also due to the deception plan implemented by the enemy.

Thanks to the planning work by *Colonel* de Bourcet, and the direct experience of a number of senior officers who were already familiar with the operational area, the French had a very good knowledge of the terrain, and in fact they never groped blindly. Relations with the local population, who voluntarily or involuntarily provided good information to the Chevalier de Belle-Isle and his men, allowed them to obtain a precise picture of the situation on the battlefield. It was known that the enemy was entrenched, and in fact the Chevalier wanted to have the heavy field artillery with him at all costs; the critical element, which played a fundamental part in the management of the battle, was the bad information regarding the timing of the arrival of reinforcements for the small Austro-Sardinian army stationed on the ridge. The reinforcements were due to arrive within days, but the French were now convinced that they were only a few hours' march away. Hence the decision to attack without waiting for the precious artillery delayed by the lack of sufficiently wide roads.

Protection

This includes all those functions related to safeguarding and maintaining the combat power of the forces. The Assietta entrenched camp worked to perfection that day. The unfortunate choice by the French to attack *à la Folard*, along with their lack of field artillery, allowed the defenders to contain any attack, allowing a small force to defend itself all round. This solution was particularly advantageous on the Western Alps front, along the watershed lines. Having to face an enemy capable of outflanking their positions and attempting an attack at the throat of their works, as happened at Pietralunga in 1744, this appeared to be the best possible solution.

The French did not forget the Assietta fortifications. The Treaty of Paris of 15 May 1796, which put an end to the War of the Alps between the Kingdom of Sardinia and the French Republic, provided in point 15 that:

> The fortifications of Exilles, Brunetta and Susa, as well as the entrenchments built above this town [that is, the Assietta entrenched camp], will be demolished at the expense of HM Sardinia, under the supervision of commissioners appointed for this purpose by the Executive Directorate. The King of Sardinia may not build or repair any fortifications on this part of the border.[6]

This is why today some section the fortifications of the entrenched camp, like the Testa dell'Assietta, are an incoherent mass of rubble.

Fire

This Combat Function encompasses all the elements involved in supporting indirect and, if included, inter-force fire. Indecision about the real intentions of the adversary meant that no artillery pieces were transported to the Assietta entrenched camp, although this action was in fact planned and even mountain pieces could be recovered in the Piedmont arsenals. The Sardinian firing tactics worked perfectly; designed for the close defence of the field fortifications, the Austro-Sardinian fire action blocked any attempt by the French to break through the defensive perimeter. The fire was so effective that the attackers, except in particular sectors such as the Testa dell'Assietta, could not even approach the entrenchments.

The French paid dearly for choosing an attack *à la Folard* to engage the enemy in a close combat. Without field artillery, which would undoubtedly have caused serious losses to the defenders and opened dangerous gaps in their fortifications, these assaults were destined to fail, regardless of the commanders' manoeuvring skills. With no possibility of retaliating to the enemy fire, channelled into the Austro-Sardinian kill zones, the French columns were ground down one after the other.

Support

This Combat Function encompasses all the related elements that generate and maintain the conditions for conducting operations until the mission is accomplished. The Assietta camp, and other nearby encampments, had a fair amount of supplies of food and water.

---

6   Clercq, *Recuil des Traitès de la France*, Vol.I, pp.271-275.

Ammunition, however, was not stocked in large quantities and some of the forces deployed ran out of ammunition in the course of the fight. Only a convoy organized during the day of 19 July from Fenestrelle allowed the Austro-Sardinians to supply their soldiers with ammunition and be ready to resume battle the following day. The collection of the wounded was the most critical aspect: unable to recover them within the camp, they had to be transported to collection centres in the valley bottom.

The French were setting up a large logistics centre at Sauze d'Oulx, and during the course of the battle they had no shortage of supplies. There was no plan to transport the most seriously wounded, who were left to the mercy of the enemy.

Lessons Learned

Put on a peace footing, the army of Carlo Emanuele III, though tried by the struggle, had in fact gained a considerable reputation among the Italian armies. The years following the conclusion of the conflict were of frenetic activity. The reforms of 1750-1751 took account of the experience gained: tactical formations, precise orders and regulations common to all units were established, and armaments and equipment were finally standardized. Only the artillery did not benefit. At the outbreak of the Seven Years War, the Sardinian army clearly outclassed that of France, and at least in terms of infantry and cavalry it could qualitatively hold its own against the forces of the Austrian Empire, but it was clearly inferior in terms of artillery equipment, which remained the same as in the first half of the eighteenth century.

The victories achieved during the War of the Austrian Succession, and the Assietta in particular, aroused curiosity and admiration throughout Europe, and some wanted to come and see the Sardinian military machine for themselves. The young Prussian historian Johann Wilhelm Daniel von Archenholz visited Piedmont during his trip to Italy in 1780. A veteran of the Seven Years War, he considered the fame earned by the Piedmontese to be out of all proportion to its real substance:

> I have not undervalued the army of the king of Sardinia, which however regular, is at present unaccustomed to war, and in many respects deficient in military accomplishments. Notwithstanding, this monarch is a considerable ally for any prince who is engaged in war in northern parts of Italy; in spite of the smallness of his army, he is not easy to be overcome, on account of the great number of fortresses in the country, which will often frustrate, to a conqueror, all the advantages he may have gained in the open field; it is these fortresses which render the king of Sardinia the most formidable prince in Italy, but this is nothing in the balance of political Europe.[7]

Von Archenholz may have been unsympathetic in his harsh judgment, but he had a point. The Battle of Assietta became the battle par excellence for the Sardinian army. The use of field fortifications to support static combat tactics and the geostrategic need to maintain

---

7   J.W. Archenholtz, *A Picture of Italy* (London: G.G.J. and J. Robinson, 1791), Vol.I, pp.115-116.

the concept of the army in being made the events of 19 July 1747 the ideal battle model for the Sardinian army. This approach to warfare remained in place throughout the eighteenth century and beyond, regardless of the theatres of operation involved. The tactical regulations of the Sardinian army therefore remained strongly tied to the annihilation of the adversary by direct musket and artillery fire and the construction of elaborate entrenched camps designed to protect the forces involved in combat. The result was that it was, from a tactical and operational point of view, an outdated army for the second half of the eighteenth century. In the 1770s, when a war against the Austrian Empire seemed likely, the war plans in eastern Piedmont and in south-western Lombardy also included this passive operational and tactical attitude.[8] Therefore, no new artillery pieces, similar to the lighter and more effective French Gribeauval and Austrian Liechtenstein systems, were introduced, the army instead remaining faithful to the use of the heavy Model 1760 pieces designed by Papacino d'Antonj and similar to the outdated pieces of the Vallière system. A new field artillery system was developed only in 1792. If the enemy decided to fight according to the old rules, that is, to attack the entrenched camps of the Sardinian army head on, then spectacular and unexpected victories could still be obtained, such as Authion in the Maritime Alps, fought between 8 and 12 June 1793 against the French Republic.[9]

With thousands killed in action, the French began to ask serious questions about the effectiveness of Folard's columns. While training soldiers to fight with such tactics provided significant savings in terms of time and gunpowder, merciless battlefield experience suggested that such columns needed at least a rethink. While the war was still going on, mindful of the clash at Fontenoy on 11 May 1745, Maurice de Saxe wrote to the Chevalier de Folard to abandon both the pikes and the tactics of the Roman legions altogether, and 'to leave there (on the fields of Fontenoy) Epaminondas' column and all the columns in the world'.[10] Twelve years later, during the Seven Years War at Rossbach on 5 November 1757, three regiments of the French army (Piémont, Poitou and Mailly) found themselves in the tactical situation of having to attack the Prussian line *à la Folard*. The result was disastrous: the four battalions of the Régiment de Piémont alone suffered over 1,000 men wounded or killed, 34.7 percent of the total strength.[11] In a report sent to the Viennese court it was written that 'if the Chevalier de Folard could know how things went, he would curse his sacred columns'.[12] At the same time, however, some of the surviving officers of the Battle of Assietta were able to put into practice the same tactics used by the Austro-Sardinians; in the distant colonies of *Nouvelle France*, today Canada, on 8 July 1757 *Maréchal de Camp* Louis-Joseph de Montcalm entrenched his 3,600 men on the heights of Fort Carillon and was able to repel a British force of 6,000 regular soldiers and 12,000 colonial auxiliaries.[13]

The alternative to Folard's doctrine, and this was the route taken towards the end of the century, was to ensure that the columns had sufficient firepower and a dense frontal

---

8   About the doctrinal and tactical problems of the Sardinian Army in the second half of the eighteenth century, see Cerino Badone, *Sulla Strada di Fiandra*, pp.136-149.

9   About this Battle. see Ilari, Crociani, Paoletti, *La Guerra delle Alpi*, pp.107-119.

10   Bois, *Fontenoy 1745*, p.136.

11   Susane, *Histoire de l'Infanterie Française*, Vol.II, pp.279-280.

12   C. Duffy, *Prussia's Glory. Rossbach and Leuthen 1757* (Chicago: Emperor's Press, 2003), p.80.

13   Pell, 'The Cradle of Carillon', pp.269-299.

coverage of light troops. The experience of the battlefield, the varying quality of the troops and the ideas of the commanders led to the creation of a new tactic called *Ordre Mixte* codified by 1796. Depending on the terrain, the quality of the opponent, the tactical needs of the moment and the mission to be accomplished, a unit could be deployed in open order and operate as light infantry, in line to make the best use of its firepower, or in column to move as fast as possible, exploit a gap in the enemy front or close a gap in its own lines. A *demibrigade*, the new French version of a regiment, consisting of three battalions, was theoretically capable of simultaneously providing a light infantry screen, a line front, and a column ready for a bayonet attack. The adversary was subjected to artillery fire, from batteries now equipped with the excellent pieces of the Gribeauval system, and assaulted by swarms of light infantry, able to absorb retaliatory fire in the best possible way. The combined firepower of the cannon and muskets would inflict such severe damage that a final assault in column would send the survivors fleeing and mark the collapse of the enemy front. Between 1804 and 1805, while the last veterans of the Assietta were dying off in the barracks of the *Hôtel des Invalides* in Paris,[14] under the eyes of Napoleon Bonaparte, at the Boulogne camp, these tactics were tried and tested until they were brought to perfection. The units were brought up to full strength with the arrival of conscripts who underwent an intense cycle of exercises, forming what was to become the *Grande Armée*.[15]

The Austrians had fought with valour at Assietta and had made an important contribution to the final victory on 19 July. The Austrian *Stellungtaktik*, however, developed differently from the Sardinian one. Whereas in Piedmont it was decided to rely on large entrenched camps, the Austrians did not always have this option. Their opponents, in particular the Prussians, were more mobile than the French. Therefore, although they themselves were very skilled at building entrenched camps, they preferred to rely on exploiting any tactical foothold the terrain could offer, such as a hill, a river, a forest. The steep hills of northern Bohemia during the War of the Bavarian Succession (1778-1779) provided Austrian commanders with excellent positions on which to entrench their men while waiting for the enemy. Friedrich II of Prussia examined these defences and noted that:

> [T]he Austrian army was arranged in three lines, surrounded and supported by its immense artillery. The first line is formed at the base of the hills, on low ground but with enough slope to form a natural glacis on the side where the enemy can reach. This is an intelligent method: it is the result of experience that shows that raging fire is better than shooting from above. Moreover, the soldiers on the crest of the glacis have all the advantages that a dominant position can offer, without any disadvantages.[16]

---

14   Jean Bournelle, known as *Laverdure*, soldier of the Régiment Soissonais, wounded by a musket shot in the knee during the Battle of Assietta, died at the Invalides on 4 May 1809, aged 79. Jean Bournelle, SHD/GR/2Xy40. Before him, on 23 April 1805, Mathieu Nichet, known as *Gonesse*, wounded in the head during the battle by a musket shot, died at the age of 84. Mathieu Nichet, SHD/GR/2Xy40.

15   Griffith, *The Art of War of Revolutionary France*; G. Nafziger, *Imperial Bayonets. Tactics of the Napoleonic Battery, Battalion and Brigade as found in Contemporary Regulations* (London: Greenhill Books, 1996).

16   Frédérick II, *Réflexions sur la tactique*, pp.155-156; J. Luvaas, *Frederick the Great on the Art of War* (New York: Hachette Books, 1966), pp.263-305.

An attempt was made to give the front a concave, amphitheatre-like shape, where every salient or rise was transformed into a fortified battery in order to best crossfire in the kill zone. The concentration of cannon was impressive and the enemy front was 'furnished with artillery like a citadel. The result was to storm a fortress'.[17]

The Army in Being, 1815-1915

The concept of the Army in Being, for the Kingdom of Sardinia, did not end with the close of the eighteenth century. The Sardinian state, restored during the Congress of Vienna as an Austrian client state on the border with Lombardy-Veneto, promptly recycled the concept in 1815. The army was to be spared major field combat, but this made the army an army in being. In its basics this strategy envisaged that if, despite military defeat, the army was still virtually intact, at least it was still a credible force to contend with. It would take a long and arduous campaign, if not two, and bloody and uncertain fighting against fortified positions, before finally annihilating the Sardinian army, which was backed by a screen of powerful fortresses and complex entrenched camps. Unable to destroy it, Turin's adversaries needed to have the Sardinian army allied or, at least, neutral, to guarantee themselves a decisive advantage in the Italian campaign. Thus, the Sardinian king's army always remained an important card to play in diplomatic negotiations. Leaving this order of ideas and inaugurating a strategy linked to great offensive operations, without having effectively prepared the army, risked having disastrous consequences, as in fact the war of 1848-1849 against Austria did. The war of 1859 was prepared in a defensive manner, with the Sardinian army deployed in a defensive position behind the entrenched camps of eastern Piedmont awaiting the arrival of the French forces, on whom the main part of the war effort fell. The highly idealized interpretation of the Battle of Solferino, and that of San Martino in particular, and the Mezzogiorno campaigns of 1860, deluded many into thinking that the new Italian armed forces were also ready to support an aggressive strategy for their country. The disasters of 1866, including Garibaldi's *empasse* in the Trentino, were a cold shower for many and the demonstration that an upgraded Italian Army was needed.[18] Once the Italian leadership had regained confidence in their own means, the Triple Alliance was concluded with the Austro-Hungarian and German empires, and the first colonial actions launched; in 1889 the Ethiopian empire came to be considered *de jure* an Italian protectorate, while in 1890 Eritrea was officially declared a colony. This situation let the Chief of Staff Enrico Cosenz (1820-1898) to plan offensive actions against the potential adversary of the moment, France, going so far as to draw up plans for landings in Provence and large-scale offensive actions between the Maritime Alps and the Ligurian coast.[19] The defeat at Adua in 1896 and the manifest lack of the

---

17   Frédérick II, *Réflexions sur la tactique et sur quelques parties de la guerre*, p.158.
18   To this end, the War School was founded in Turin in 1867 to train officers of the Royal Army. E. Ciancarini, *La Scuola di Guerra di Torino. La Formazione degli ufficiali nel Regio esercito (1867-1915)* (Civitavecchia: Prospettiva Editrice, 2013).
19   On Italy's war plans see M. Gabriele, *La frontiera nord-occidentale dall'Unità alla Grande Guerra. Piani e studi operativi italiani verso la Francia durante la Triplice Alleanza* (Roma: USSME, 2006).

armed forces' ability to mount a major offensive against their adversaries brought the army's leadership back down to earth.

In reality, the order of operations drawn up for the Battle of Adua envisaged an advance towards the enemy, reaching a tactically strong position and there waiting for the adversary's attack, which would be stopped by the superior firepower of the Italian units. It is worth noting that two of the four brigade commanders present at Adua, Vittorio Dabormida and Matteo Albertone, were professors at the Turin War School, respectively of military history and military art. Albertone's failure to follow orders and commander-in-chief Oreste Baratieri's woeful lack of command and control led to the day's tragic conclusion.[20] Dabormida, the author of the book *La Battaglia dell'Assietta*, was killed in action, while Albertone was taken prisoner. A third teacher, of tactics, *Colonnello* Cesare Airaghi, was also killed in combat.[21]

In the early years of the twentieth century the general staff leadership was no longer able to guarantee the success of an offensive against France: first the fear of possible French landings, then the exhaustion of the forces employed in Libya. These elements had led to an overall weakening of the army to such an extent that the then chief of staff, Alberto Pollio (1852-1914), had to renounce major offensives in enemy territory and return to a strategy of defending the Italian peninsula very similar to that planned in the 1870s. Plans for general or partial permanent fortification of the territory, functional to mobilization (planned for 23 days in 1914), occupied a considerable part of the armed forces' budget for at least 30 years, while elite mountain troops were created and strengthened, such as the *Alpini*, who had a decidedly defensive vocation since their foundation in 1872.

This choice of strategic direction would have worked with a certain effectiveness, despite the technical limitations of the permanent Italian fortifications of the period, had a defensive strategy been maintained regardless. However, the subsequent adoption of a plan of attack against the Austrians made it clear in retrospect how much better it would have been to direct expenditure towards strengthening the railway lines, the field and siege artillery, and the cavalry and the infantry companies themselves, chronically understrength and commanded by elderly captains. In 1913, Austrian 'inattention' to the Italian ally – see Conrad's plan for an attack to the south following the Messina earthquake – and the victorious conclusion of the Libyan conflict, prompted Pollio to change his war plans, which now included a conflict against Austria-Hungary. In December 1913 the chief of the general staff modified the mobilisation plan envisaged in 1904, and reconfirmed in 1909, moving forward astride the Tagliamento three army corps previously massed with 12 others on both sides of the middle and lower Piave. This was certainly not a return to Cosenz's offensive spirit, as in the end Pollio merely grafted a possible counter-offensive onto the defensive, for which the new deployment laid the necessary foundations.

The new chief of staff, Luigi Cadorna (1850-1928), was the commander who drew up the most aggressive plans after Cosenz. He immediately envisaged an offensive *brusquée* in August 1914, insisting on Italy's immediate entry into the war. This insistence was later tempered by the realization of the country's warlike unpreparedness or, if one prefers, its

---

20   O. Bovio, 'Adua', in *Studi storico militari*, 1997, pp.300-328.
21   Ciancarini, *La Scuola di Guerra*, pp.166-168.

purely defensive vocation. In the end he prepared plans for a great offensive with two armies that, having reached the Tagliamento a day before the end of the mobilization, would have crossed the Isonzo and aimed for Ljubljana and Krainburg, objectives that were to be reached within 45 days from the start of hostilities and after two battles of great proportions. Apart from the fact that the events of 1914 – the Marne for strategic planning and Tannenberg for the validity of Russian aid – should at least have suggested a less aggressive approach to enemy defences, the basic problem with Italian strategy on the eve of the First World War lay in the mentality of those who planned it. Trained in the writings of Jomini, with little or no knowledge of Clausewitz,[22] Cadorna gave priority to geographical objectives, rather than prioritizing the destruction of the enemy's will to fight. This approach definitely closed the door to other strategic actions that were probably more promising for Italy's 1915 deployment on the side of the Entente: an operation in the style of the Dardanelles along the Dalmatian coast, or in the Balkans. But the ghost of Assietta continued to haunt the Italian army, and the memory of that victory in 1915 was very much alive in everyone's mind, especially those who wore the uniform. On entering the Turin Military Academy, cadet officer Paolo Caccia Dominioni was immediately captivated by it:

> I had not imagined how grand that ancient tradition of the "vieux Piémont" was: sculpted bronze shafts, baroque architecture, the battle of Assietta, the Royal Armory, Emanuele Filiberto and Carlo Amedeo, Pietro Micca, genius like us and Camillo Benso Conte di Cavour already a cadet in the same building. Even though we were trainee officers, we immediately entered into that high style, so different from my previous military experience.[23]

Thus the long shadow of the Assietta stood out until 8 February 1934, when the concepts of 'war of rapid progress' began to be outlined, of which the chief of staff Alberto Pariani was the spokesman in Italy,[24] and it was decided that the XXVI Infantry Brigade would take the name of the Assietta Military Division, the 26th of the Royal Italian Army.

The Italian Way of War

In various lectures given at the Scuola di Applicazione in Turin, not far from the places frequented by the young Caccia Dominioni, the present author has often asked the following question: what are the victories par excellence of the Italian Army?

There are three examples of victories 'par excellence'. The first two can be taken for granted, and are Second Piave 'The Battle of the Solstice', and the Battle of Vittorio Veneto in 1918. Thanks to these two gigantic battles, Italy ended the First World War victoriously. The

---

22   V. Ilari, 'Clausewitz in Italy', in R. Pommerin (ed.), *Clausewitz Goes Global. Carl von Clausewitz in the 21st Century* (Berlin: Carola Hartmann Miles-Verlag, 2011), pp.173-202.
23   P. Caccia Dominioni, *1915-1919 Diario di guerra* (Milano: Mursia, 1993), pp.36-37. It should be remembered that until 1943 the current Military Academy had been split into two: infantry and cavalry were based in Modena, while artillery and engineers were based in Turin.
24   O. Bovio, *Storia dell'Esercito italiano* (Roma: USSME, 1996), p.313.

first was a battle that saw Italian forces lined up on the defensive along the Piave confront, contain, and then repel the last major Austrian offensive on the Italian front.[25] At Vittorio Veneto it was the Italian army that attacked, but as brilliant as they had been in planning and conducting defensive operations on the Piave, on this occasion they demonstrated all their tactical shortcomings. Fortunately for the Italians, the British contingent at Greve di Papadopoli, an island in the middle of the river, specifically the 7th and 23rd Divisions of the XIV British Corps under Lieutenant General James Babington, demonstrated their superior tactics and training to their allies and enemies, breaking through the front and creating a bridgehead that was promptly exploited in the following days.[26]

The third battle is that of Gazala, fought between 26 May and 21 June 1942, to all intents and purposes the greatest Italian victory of the Second World War, although the laurels must be shared with the German ally. At the end of the battle, hard-fought and uncertain until almost the final two phases, the Axis forces were able to inflict a stiff defeat on the British forces, a success that turned into the conquest of the port of Tobruk in Cyrenaica. The Italian units, in particular those belonging to the 132nd Armoured Division *Ariete*, were able first to contain the British attack, led by four brigades – three infantry and one armoured – to repel it and, in the end, to annihilate two of the adversary's great units with the German assistance.[27]

Second Piave, Vittorio Veneto and Gazala, although they belong to two different conflicts, and despite the fact that the first two were decisive for final Italian victory while the third was not, were battles that allow us to understand one fundamental thing: the Italian armed forces have *always* expressed the best fighting qualities during defensive operations. Every army has an original core, a 'father', who passes on its 'genes'; that is, traditions, doctrines, tactics, strengths and weaknesses. Often these elements have not been erased but, on the contrary, have survived and are still recognizable within each armed force today. British and American military historians became aware of this around the 1980s and began to investigate the phenomenon carefully. A number of monographs were published that had as their basic root the title *The [any country] Way of War*. This led to *The Russian Way of War* by Richard W. Harrison,[28] followed by *The German Way of War* by Robert Citino.[29] Lastly *The British Way of War in Northwest Europe 1944-5* by Louis Paul Devigne was added to the list.[30] But what about Italy?

Just take a look at the uniforms during important occasions such as parades and ceremonies, where the blue sash immediately gives us the answer we are looking for. The Army of

---

25   USSME, *L'Esercito Italiano Nella Grande Guerra (1915–1918). Le Operazioni del 1918*, (Roma: USSME, 1988), Vol.V, I,

26   USSME, *L'Esercito Italiano Nella Grande Guerra*, Vol.V, II, p.142.

27   About this battle see M. Montanari, USSME, *Le Operazioni in Africa Settentrionale. El Alamein*, (Roma: USSME, 1989), pp.157-292.

28   R.W. Harrison, *The Russian Way of War. Operational Art 1904-1940* (Lawrence: Kansas University Press, 2001). For the modern Russian forces L.W. Grau, C.K. Bartles, *The Russian Way of War. Force Structure, Tactics, and Modernization of the Russian Ground Forces* (Fort Leavenworth: Foreign Military Studies Office (FMSO), 2017).

29   Citino, *German Way of War*.

30   L.P. Devine, *The British Way of War in Northwest Europe 1944-5. A Study of two Infantry Divisions* (London: Blomsbury, 2015).

the Italian Republic is nothing more than the evolution or, if one prefers, the nationwide transposition of the 'Armata Sarda'. Yes, it is still the army of the War of Succession of Austria and the Assietta, the War of the Alps and Authion, the two Wars of the Risorgimento. For Italy, Assietta, like it or not, is what the Americans call Gettysburg and the Russians call Borodino.

This is the Italian Way of War.

Order of Battle of the Austro-Piedmontese Army 19 July 1747

Commander in Chief: *Luogotenente Generale* Conte di Bricherasio
Strength: circa 6,160 men

At Col de l'Assietta under *Maggior Generale* Alciati

Advanced Position at the Butte de l'Assietta and Left Wing, *Brigadiere Generale* Conte di Martinengo

    1/Reggimento Guardie
    Reggimento Casale (Two Companies)
    800 Militia

Right Wing, *General-Feldwachtmeister* Graf Colloredo

    Reggimento Meyer
    3/Infanterie-Regiment Forgách
    Infanterie-Regiment Traun (One Battalion)
    3/Infanterie-Regiment Colloredo

Reserve

    Infanterie-Regiment Hagenbach (One Battalion)

At Col de Gran Serin under *Luogotenente Generale* Conte di Bricherasio

    2/Reggimento Kalbermatten
    3/Reggimento Kalbermatten
    3/Reggimento Roi
    Reggimento Casale (Two Companies)
    Susa Valley Militia (500 Men)

Appendix II

Order of Battle of the French Army 19 July 1747

Commander-in-Chief: *Lieutenant Général* Chevalier de Belle-Isle✝
Staff Officers: de Corsac, *Adjudant Maréchal Général de Logis*◆
    de Domgermain, *Adjudant Maréchal Général de Logis*
    de Landivisiau, *Adjudant Maréchal Général de Logis*
    d'Agieu, *Adjutant-Major Général d'Infanterie*◆
    de Grille, *Adjutant-Major Général d'Infanterie*
    de La Taille, *Adjutant-Major Général d'Infanterie*✝

Total personnel approximately 17,500 men
    27 French line battalions (> 1,050 officers + 14,700 NCOs and men)
    Two battalions of grenadiers (theoretical staff of 67 officers + 1,270 NCOs and men)
    One corps of light troops (theoretical strength 30 officers + 500 horsemen and fusiliers)
    One dragoon regiment (20 officers + 400 dragoons)
    One pioneer company (2 officers + 48 pioneers)
    Artillery detachment (200 men)
    Mobile hospital (> 20 surgeons)
    Milice de Briançon (at least 2 companies ~ 200 men)
    Two Spanish battalions (maximum 700 men in total)

Organization

Battle Corps

Left Column	MdC Mailly d'Hautcourt	9 bns. (+)	~ 5,100 Men
Center Column	MdC d'Arnaud MdC d'Andlau	5 bns. (+)	~ 3,400 Men
Right Column	LG de Villemur MdC de Larnage	13 bns. (-)	~ 9,300 Men

Other Troops

Light troops in Val Chisone	Marquis de Gantès	Volontaires de Gantès	~ 200 cavalry ~ 300 fusiliers
Controlling the rear of the bulk of the army	Part of Dragons du Roi	2-3 sqns.	~ 250-300 dragoons
Reserve (Sestriere)	*Brig.* Comte de Revel	Régt. de Poitou (3 Bns.)	~ 1,600 Men
Corps of d'Escars	Marquis d'Escars	6 coys. grenadiers, 6 fusilier piquets	~ 900 Men

Left Column: *Maréchal de Camp* Comte de Mailly d'Haucourt♦

Nine battalions + reinforcements = ~ 5, 080-5,090 men (~ 280-290 officers + 4, 800 troops)

Brigade Bourbonnais

Regiment	Bns.	Colonel & Lieutenant-Colonel	Strength	Losses
Bourbonnais	3	*Col.* Louis de Biran d'Armagnac, Comte de Goas (*Brigadier*)✝ *Lt. Col.* Antoine de Bordenave	106 + 1,500	650/40%
Soissonais	1	*Col.* Guy-Marie de Lopriac de Coëtmadeuc, Comte de Donges✝ *Lt. Col.* de Maubeuge	38 + 500	259/46%
Des Landes	1	*Col.* Pierre-Emé, Marquis de Marcieu♦	38 + 500	242/45%

Brigade La Reine

Regiment	Bns.	Colonel & Lieutenant-Colonel	Strength	Losses
La Reine	2	*Col.* Charles de Gouy Marquis d'Arcy ♦ *Lt. Col.* François-Joseph Cayotte de la Cour	72 + 1,000	582/55%
Béarn	1	*Col.* Henri-Bernard de Thimbrune, Marquis de Valence (*Brigadier*) *Lt. Col.* François de Vatteville de la Fossé de la Motte	38 + 500	124/23%
Guise	1	Colonelcy vacant *Lt. Col.* Comte Alexandre de Beauregard✝	38 + 500	149/28%

Reinforcements

Regiment	Bns.	Colonel & Lieutenant-Colonel	Strength	Losses
Dragons du Roi	-	Detachment	100?	?
Grenadiers	- -	Three companies Grenadiers Royaux de Modène	150?	?
Pioneers	- -	One Company	50	?

Centre Column *Maréchaux de Camp* Comte d'Arnaud✝ and d'Andlau

5 battalions + Reinforcements = ~ 3,400 men (Officers ~ 180-190 + Troops ~ 3,200-3,220)

Brigade Artois

Regiment	Bns.	Colonel & Lieutenant-Colonel	Strength	Losses
Artois	2	*Col.* Nicolas-Louis de Loménie, Comte de Brienne✝ *Lt. Col.* François Sanglier de la Noblaye	72 + 1,000	472/45%
Aunis	1	*Col.* de Durfort, Comte de Civrac♦ *Lt. Col.* unknown	38 + 500	193/36%
Auxerrois	1	*Col.* Marquis de Montcalm (*Brigadier*)♦ *Lt. Col.* Damour	30 + 500	137/25%
Santerre	1	*Col.* François-Marie de Pérusse, Marquis d'Escars (*Brigadier*; detached) *Lt. Col.* de Viranelle	38 + 500	110/20%

Reinforcements

Regiment	Bns.	Colonel & Lieutenant-Colonel	Strength	Losses
12 Picquets	-	Detached from the Right Column	600	n/a
Grenadiers	-	Nine Companies Grenadiers Royaux de Modène	470?	n/a

Right Column: *Lieutenant Général* Marquis de Villemur and *Maréchal de Camp* Comte de Larnage✝

13 battalions ~ 6,900 men (~ 390 officers + 6,500 troops)

Brigade Mailly

Regiment	Bns.	Colonel & Lieutenant-Colonel	Strength	Losses
Mailly	3	*Col.* Louis-Victor, Marquis de Mailly, Comte de Rubempré♦ *Lt. Col.* Joseph de Bodin de Boisrenard	106 + 1,500	472/30%
Boulonnois	1	*Col.* François-Joseph de Damas, Marquis de Ruffey (*Brigadier*) *Lt. Col.* de Morel	38 + 500	172/32%
Agenois	1	*Col.* Marquis de Monteynard *Lt. Col.* de Preville (?)	38 + 500	91/17%

Brigade Royal Roussillon

Regiment	Bns.	Colonel & Lieutenant-Colonel	Strength	Losses
Royal Roussillon	1	*Col.* Charles de Cleron, Comte d'Haussonville (*Brigadier*)◆ *Lt. Col.* de Bourdeville	38 + 500	160/31%
Guyenne	1	*Col.* Joseph, Comte de Laval-Montmorency *Lt. Col.* Pierre-Louis Dumas de la Roque (?)	38 + 500	141/26%
Périgord	1	*Col.* Innocent-Marie de Vassignac, Marquis d'Imécourt *Lt. Col.* Charles-François de Danguy (or d'Angy?)◆	38 + 500	184/34%
Beaujolais	1	*Col.* Jacques-Gabriel Bazin, Marquis de Bezons◆ *Lt. Col.* de Séguy	30 + 500	86/16%

Brigade Condé

Regiment	Bns.	Colonel & Lieutenant-Colonel	Strength	Losses
Condé	2	*Col.* Charles-Claude, Marquis de Langeron (*Brigadier*) *Lt. Col.* Louis d'Arras d'Haudrecy	72 + 1,000	403/38%
Saintonge	1	*Col.* Louis-Joseph Bidé de la Grandville◆ *Lt. Col.* Chev. de Barain◆	38 + 500	142/27%
Beauce	1	Col. Louis-Marie de Mirepoix, Cte de Lévis-Léran *Lt. Col.* Etienne de la Coste	38 + 500	98/18%

Grenadiers

Regiment	Bns.	Colonel & Lieutenant-Colonel	Strength	Losses
Grenadiers Royaux de Modène	2	*Col.* Pierre de Raymond de Villeneuve, Chevalier de Modène◆ *Lt. Col.* Robert de Vernejoul (?)	68 + 1,202	230/18%
		• Six companies detached to d'Escars' Corps	~ 350?	
		• Three companies detached to the Left Column	~ 160?	
		• Nine companies assigned to the Centre Column	~ 470?	
		• Six companies, either in reserve or detached to the Right Column	~ 360?	

Other Formations

Dragons du Roi	• A dismounted detachment engaged in battle, assigned to the Left Column. • A detachment under cover near Pont-Ventoux
Volontaires de de Gantès	*Col.* Jean-François, Marquis de Gantès Two squadrons (200 hussars) and four companies (300 fusiliers), covering the Pragelato Valley
D'Escars' Corps	*Col.* François-Marie de Pérusse, Marquis d'Escars (*Brigadier*) • Six picquets drawn from the Brigade Artois (~300 men) • Six companies Grenadiers Royaux de Modène (~350 men)
Artillery	About 200 men • Six long 4-pounders • Seven mountain pieces
Milice de Briançon	At least two companies, deployed on the border, on the Bourget and Bousson hills.
Regimiento de Aragón, Dragones de Merida	Two Spanish battalions, not engaged in the battle; stationed near Sestriere or Traverses. They followed the Right Column.

Reserve – Brigade Poitou

Regiment	Bns.	Colonel	Strength
Poitou	3	François de Broglie, Comte de Revel (*Brigadier*)	106 + 1,500

First half at Pont de Cervières and Le Bourget between 15 and 16 July; second half in Sestriere on 18 July

Corps Deployed in Reserve in the Queyras

Regiment	Bns.	Colonel	Strength
Dauphiné	1	Comte de Vaubécourt	38 + 500
Luxembourg	1	Jacques-Charles, Marquis de Rochecourbon	38 + 500
Volontaires Royaux	2	Comte de Chabo-la Serre	40 + 800

Troops Remaining at the Tornoux Camp, *Maréchal de Camp* Comte d'Aultanne

Brigade La Roche-Aymon

Regiment	Bns.	Colonel
La Roche-Aymon	2	Marquis de la Roche-Aymon
Île-de-France	1	Marquis de Crussol (*Brigadier*)
La Tour d'Auvergne	1	de la Tour d'Auvergne

Brigade Bourgogne

Regiment	Bns.	Colonel
Bourgogne	1	Marquis d'Hérouville (?)
Béarn	1	–
Tournasis	1	Séraphin-Marie de Rioult de Douilly, Marquis de Cursay
Foix	1	Chevalier de Groslier (*Brigadier*)

Unbrigaded

Regiment	Bns.	Colonel
Salis-Mayenfeld	2	Baron Charles-Ulysse de Salis-Mayenfeld

Bibliography

Archival and Manuscript Sources

Archive Hadtörténeti Intézet és Múzeum, Budapest (AHI)
Maps Archive; H III e

Archivio di Stato di Torino (AST)
Corte
    Carte: Carte Topografiche e Disegni
    Materie Militari: Imprese; Ordini e Regolamenti; Levata Truppe Straniere
    Materie Politiche per il Rapporto all'interno: Storie della Real Casa
    Museo Storico
Sezioni Riunite
    Ministero della Guerra:
    Carte antiche d'Artiglieria
    Regia Segreteria di Guerra; Lettere ai Governatori; Regi Viglietti e Dispacci
    Ufficio Generale del Soldo: Ordini Generali e Misti; Raccolta Sovrane Determinazioni
    Ruolini di rivista
    Camerale di Piemonte

Biblioteca Reale di Torino (BRT)
Fondo Manoscritti Militari
Fondo Miscellanea
Fondo Disegni

Biblioteca Scuola Militare Teuliè, Milano (BSMT)
Fondo Manoscritti
    Geografia Militare. Considerazioni militari sui Teatri d'Operazioni Terrestri, Aerei, Marittimi e Coloniali, 1925.
    E. Bobbio, *La Valle Chisone.*
    N. Brancaccio, *Appunti su alcune operazioni militari nelle Alpi Cozie*, 1913.
    U. Stefanini, *Monografia della Valle della Dora Riparia*, 1913.
    Il Piemonte. Saggio e descrizione in scala topografica di una regione naturale, 1922.
    Teatro d'Operazioni Italo-Francese, 1930.

All these works are theses written by Italian officers to complete their staff training as lieutenants or captains. Of course, many old battlefields of the eighteenth century still had a strategic and operational value in the first half of the twentieth century

Service historique de la Defense, Armée de Terre, Vincennes (SHD)

Serie A1, 1M.
Serie 1Yc
Registre de réception des militaires invalides; vol.2Xy/40; vol.2Xy/41; vol.2Xy/53; vol.2Xy/55; vol.2Xy/57; vol.2Yy58

Wien Staat Archiv, Kriegsarchiv (KA)

Alten Feldakten, Österreichischer Erbfolgkrieg Italien (1747)
Musterlisten und Standestabelle der k.k. Armee (MLST)

Printed Primary Sources

1. General Histories of Eighteenth-Century Wars

Archenholz, J.W., *Geschichte des siebenjährigen Krieges in Deutschland* (Berlin: Haude und Spener, 1793).
D'Espié, F.F., *Mémoires de la Guerre d'Italie, depuis l'Année 1733, jusqu'en 1736, par un ancien Militaire qui s'est trouvé à toutes les Actions de ces trois fameuses Campagnes* (Paris: Duchesne, 1777).
Grimoard, P.H., *Tableau Historique de la Guerre de la Révolution de France, depuis con commencement en 1792, jusq'a la fin de 1794* (Paris : Treuttel et Würtz, 1808).
Quincy, J.S., *Histoire militaire du regne de Louis le Grand* (Paris: Denis Mariette, Jean-Baptiste Delespine, Jean-Baptiste Coignard, 1726).

2. Austrian Succession War

Campbell, J., *The Present State of Europe; Explaining the Interests, Connections, Political and Commercial Views of its Several Powers, Comprehending also, A clear and Concise History of each Country, so far as to show the Nature of their Present Constitutions* (London: Thomas Longman and Charles Hitch, 1753).
Voltaire, *Le siècle de Louis XV* (Unknown Publisher, 1769).

3. 1747 Campaign

Mauvillon, E., *Histoire de la dernière Guerre de Bohême* (Amsterdam: David Mortier, 1756).
Pezay, A. de, *Histoire des Campagnes de M. le M.al de Maillebois en Italie, pendant les années 1745 & 1746* (Paris: Imprimerie Royale, 1775).

4. Strategy and Tactics

Anon., *L'Esprit du Chevalier Folard tiré de ses commentaires sur l'Histoire de Polybe pour l'usage d'un officier* (Leipzig: Unknown Publisher, 1761).
Bourcet, P.J. de, *Principes de la Guerre de Montagne* (Paris: Imprimerie National, 1888).

Burtenbach, A.E. Schertel von, *Betrachtungen und Erfahrungen über Verschiedene Militärische Gegenstände* (Nuremberg: Felsecker, 1779).

Cogniazzo, J., *Freymüthige Beytrag zur Geschichte des östreichischen Militairdienstes* (Frankfurt: Unknown Publisher, 1779).

Dalrymple, W., *Tacticks* (Dublin: George Bonham, 1782).

De Savornin, *Sentimens d'un homme de guerre sur le nouveau systême du chevalier de Folard, par rapport à la colonne et au mélange des différentes armes d'une armée* (La Haye: Jean van Duren, 1732).

Fleming, H.F., *Der Vollkommene Teutsche Soldat* (Leipzig: Unknown Publisher, 1726).

Folard, Chevalier de, *Histoire de Polybe, nouvellement traduite du grec par Dom Vincent de Thuillier, Bénédictin de la Congregation de Saint Maur. Avec un commentaire ou un corps de science militaire enrichi de notes critiques et historiques, ou toutes les grandes parties de la Guerre, soit pour l'Offensive, soit pour la Défensive, sont expliquées, demontrées, & représentées en Figures. Ouvrage très-utile non seulement aux Officiers Généraus, mais même à tous ceux qui suivent le parti des armes. Par M. de Folard, Chevalier de l'Ordre de St Louis, Meistre de Camp d'Infanterie* (Paris: Pierre Ganduin, Julien-Michel Gandouin, Pierre-François Giffart, Nicolas-Pierre Armand, 1753-1754).

Frederick II, *Œuvres de Frédérick le Grand* (Berlin: Rodolphe Decker, 1846-1867).

Guibert, J.A.H., *Essai Général de la Tactique, précédé d'un discours sur l'état actuel de la Politique & de la Science Militaire en Europe* (Liege: C. Plomteux, 1773).

Küster, C.D., *Bruchstück seines Campagnelebens im siebenjährigen Kriege* (Berlin: Karl Maßdorffs Buchhandl, 1791).

Le Cointe, J.L., *Le Science des Postes Militaire, ou Traité des Fortifications de Campagne, à l'usage des Officiers particuliers d'Infanterie qui sont détachés à la Guerre* (Paris: Desaint & Saillant, 1759).

Naumann, G., *Sammlung ungedruckter Nachrichten, so die Geschichte der Feldzüge der Preußen von 1740 bis 1779* (Dresden: Waltherischen Hofbuchhandlung, 1782).

Pauli, C.F., *Denkmale berühmter Feld-Herren* (Halle: Johann Gottfired Trampe, 1768).

Porzio, L.A., *The Soldier's Vade Mecum* (London: R. Dodsley, 1747).

Rohr, F.M., *Des Herrn Grafen Turpin von Crissé. Versuche über die Kriegskunst* (Potsdam: Johann George Bauer, 1756).

Santa Cruz y Marcenado, A.N., *Réflexion militaires et politiques* (La Hague: Jacques van den Kieboom, 1735-1740).

Tielke, J.G., *Beiträge zur Geschichte des Krieges von 1756 bis 1763* (Freyberg: Bartheilischen Schriften, 1776).

Toulongeon, Hullin, *Une mission militaire en Prusse, en 1786* (Paris: Firmin Didot, 1881).

Turpin de Crissé, *Essai sur l'art de la guerre* (Paris: Prault, Jombert, 1754).

Warnery, C.E. von, *Anecdotes et Pensées historiques et militaire, ecrites vers l'année 1774* (Halle: Jean Jacques Court, 1781).

Zanthier, F.W., *Versuche über die Marsche der Armeen, die Lager, Schlachten un den Operations-Plan* (Dresden: Waltherischen Hofbuchhandlung, 1778).

5. Regulations and Tactical Instructions

a. Austrian Empire

Regulament und Ordnung, nach welchem sich gesambte unmittelbare Kayserliche Infanterie (Wien: Johann Paul Krauß, 1737).

Regulament und Ordnung des Gesammten Kaiserlich-Königlichen Fuß-Volks (Wien: Johann Peter van Gehlen, 1749).

b. Kingdom of France

Ordonnance du Roy, sur le Maniement des armes de l'Infanterie. Du premier Mars 1746 (Paris: Impremerie Royal, 1746).

Ordonnance du Roy, portant règlement pour l'habillemente de l'Infanterie françoise. Du 19 Janvier 1747 (Paris: Impremerie Royal, 1747).

Ordonnance du Roy, concernant le Corps des Volontaires de Gantés du 22 avril 1747 (Paris: Impremerie Royal, 1747).

Ordonnance du Roy, sur le Maniement des armes de l'Infanterie françoise & étrangère. Du 7 Mai 1750 (Paris: Impremerie Royal, 1750).

c. Kingdom of Sardinia

Recuil de ce qui se pratique dans le Régiment Suisse de Saconay, au service de Sa Majesté Britanique persentement dan les Armées de Son Altesse Roiale de Savoie, sous les Ordres de Mylord Galloway, à l'égard de la Justice & Police du Régiment: avec l'exercice Militaire, mis en François & en Allemand, pour l'intelligence des Officiers qui n'entendent que l'une de ces deus Langues (Ivreé: Unknown Publisher, 1694).

6. *Weapons and fortifications*

Papacino d'Antonj, V., *Dell'Artiglieria pratica per le Regie Scuole d'artiglieria e fortificazione* (Torino: Stamperia Reale, 1775).

Saint Remy, P. Surirey de, *Mémoires d'Artillerie* (Paris: Rollin, 1697).

Scharnhorst, G.J., *Über die Wirkung des Feuergewehrs* (Berlin: Nauck, 1813).

7. *Biographies and Memories*

Archenholtz, J.W., *A Picture of Italy* (London: G.G.J. and J. Robinson, 1791).

Bräker, U., *Lebensgeschichte und Natürliche Ebentheuer des Armen Mann im Tockenburg* (Zürich: Orell, Gessner, Füssli, 1789).

[Aubert de La Chenaye-Desbois, F.A.] *Dictionnaire de la Noblesse, contenant les Généalogies, l'Histoire & la Chronologie des Familles Nobles de France* (Paris: Duchesne, 1770-1786).

Chevrier, F.A. de, *La Vie politique et militaire de M. le Maréchal Duc de Bell'Isle* (La Haye: Van Duren, 1762).

Folard, Chevalier de, *Mémoires pour servir à l'Histoire de Monsieur le Chevalier de Folard* (Ratisbonne: Unknown Publisher, 1753).

[Lacombe de Prézel, H.], *Dictionnaire des Portraits Historiques, Anecdotes, et traits remarquables des Hommes Illustres* (Paris: Lacombe, 1758).

Pinard, M., *Chronologie Historique-Militaire* (Paris: Claude Herissant, 1760-1778).

Romainmoitier, May de, *Histoire militaire de la Suisse et celle des Suisses dans les différent services de l'Europe, composée et rédogée sur des ouvrages et pièces authentiques* (Lausanne: Heubach et Comp., 1788).

8. Economy

Beaumont, D. de, *Mémoire pour servir a l'Histoire Generale des Finances* (Amsterdam: Compagnie Néerlandaise des Indes Orientales, 1760).

9. Geography and climate

Marcus, J.R., *Curiöse und historiches Nachricht von dem im ietzigen 1740ten Jahre eingefallen ausserordentlichen strengen und langen Winter* (Leipzig: Johann Christoph Coernern, 1741).

Hamel, M. de, 'Observations botanico-météorologiques. Faites au château de Denainvilliers près Pliviers en Gâtinois, pour l'année 1747', in *Histoire de l'Academie Royale des Sciences*, Paris 1747, pp.500-530.

10. Medicine

Landau, H., *Chirurgie d'Armée, ou Traité del Plaies d'armes à feu, et d'armes blanches* (Paris: Didot le Jeune, 1768).

Larrey, D.J., *Mémoires de Chirurgie Militaire, et Campagnes* (Paris: J. Smith, F. Buisson, 1812-1817).

Pringle, M., *Observations sur le Maladies des Armées dans les camps et dans les garnisons* (Paris: Ganeau, 1755).

11. Gazettes and Printed Communications

a. Printed Communications

Discours du Duc de Boufflers au Senat de Genes (Paris: Couret de Villeneuve, 1747).

Report et Plan des Attaques formées par M. le Chevalier de Belle-Isle contre les retranchemens des piemontois, sous Exiles (Lille: P.S. Lalau, 1747).

Zuverlässig Nachricht von dem am 20. Juli 1747 vorgefallenen Treffen zwischen den Franzosichen, Spanischen, wie auch Kayserl. und Konigl. Sardinischen Wöltern in Col della Sietta, and der Seite von Exilles und Fenestrelles in ner Nachgrafschaft Saluzzo, in Fürstenthum Piedmont (Leipzig: Christian Chrenfried Fürsten, 1747).

b. Gazettes

Di Neue Europäische Fama, Vol.145, Leipzig 1747.

Journal Universel, ou Mémoires pour servir à l'Historie Civile, Politique, Ecclésiastique, & Littéraire du XVIII Siécle, Tome XIII, Amsterdam, Aout 1747.

London Gazette, No.8661, London, 25 July 1747.

Mercure Historique et Politique, Tome CXXIII, La Haye, Juillet 1747.

Nederlandsch Gedenkboek/Europische Mercurius, Amsterdam, July 1747.

Suite de la Clef, ou Journal Historique sur le Matieres du Tems, Tome LXII, Paris, Juillet 1747.

The Gentleman's Magazine, London, July 1747.

The Scots Magazine, Edinburgh, July 1747.

12. Poetry and literature

Anon., *L'Esprit des Journaux, par une Société de Gens de Lettres* (Paris: Imprimerie du Journal, 1776).

Bartoli, Giuseppe, *La Battaglia del Colle dell'Assietta, seguita ai XIX di Luglio dell'anno MDCCXLVII. Stanze di Giuseppe Bartoli* (Stamperia Reale: Torino, 1747).

Secondary Sources

Hanlon G., *Italy 1636. Cemetery of Armies* (Oxford: Oxford University Press, 2018). Basic text and model for the drafting of this volume. The book written by Gregory Hanlon represents, in my opinion, the comparison text for future monographs dedicated to the battles of the modern era.

1. General
Carutti, D., *Storia del Regno di Carlo Emanuele III* (Torino: Gianini e Fiore, 1859).
Costa de Beauregard, J.H., *Mémoires Historiques sur la Maison Royale de Savoie* (Turin: Pierre Joseph Pic, 1816).
Ilari, V., Paoletti, C., Crociani, P., *Bella Italia Militar. Eserciti e Marine nell'Italia pre-napoleonica (1748-1792)* (Roma: USSME, 2000).
Merlin, P., Rosso, C., Symcox, G., Ricuperati, G. (eds), *Il Piemonte Sabaudo. Stato e Territori in Età Moderna* (Torino: UTET, 1994).
Venturi F., *Settecento riformatore. Da Muratori e Beccaria 1730-1764* (Torino: Einaudi, 1969).

2. Eighteenth Century Warfare
Archenholtz, J.W., *Gemälde der preussischen Armee von und in dem siebenjährigen Kriege* (Osnabrück: Biblio Verlag, 1974).
Black, J., *European Warfare, 1660-1815* (London: Routledge & Kegan Paul, 1994).
Becker, C., *Relire Principes de la Guerre de montagnes du lieutenant général Pierre-Joseph de Bourcet* (Paris: Economica, 2008).
Becker, C., *Aux origines de l'Alpinisme Militaire. Fondation des Chasseurs Alpins et rôle du Général Arvers* (Villers-sur-Mer: Editions Pierre de Taillac, 2018).
Bourcet, P.J. de, *Principes de la Guerre de Montagnes* (Paris: Impremerie Nationale, 1888).
Bodart, G., *Losses of Life in Modern Wars. Austria-Hungary; France* (Oxford: Clarendon Press, 1916).
Cerino Badone, G., *Le Aquile e i Gigli. Una Storia mai scritta* (Torino: Omega, 2007).
Chartrand, R., Courcelle, P., *Gibraltar 1779-1783. The Great Siege* (Oxford: Osprey, 2003).
Chandler, D., *The Art of Warfare in the Age of Marlborough* (New York: Hippocrene Books, 1976).
Corvisier, A., *La Bataille de Malplaquet 1709. L'effondrement de la France évité* (Paris: Economica, 1997).
Delbrück, H., *Historische und politische Aufsätze* (Berlin: G. Stilke, 1907).
Duffy, C., *The Military Experience in the Age of Reasons* (London: Routledge & Kegan Paul, 1998).
Duffy, C., *Prussia's Glory. Rossbach and Leuthen 1757* (Chicago: Emperor's Press, 2003).
Gandilhon, D., *Fontenoy. La France domine l'Europe* (Paris: Histoire & Collections, 2008).
Gariglio, G., *Battaglie alpine del Piemonte sabaudo. Tre secoli di guerre sulle Alpi Occidentali* (Collegno; Chiaramonte Editore, 1999).

Ilari, V., Boeri, G., Paoletti, C., *Tra i Borbone e gli Asburgo* (Ancona: Nuove Ricerche, 1996).

Ilari, V., Crociani, P., Paoletti, C., *La Guerra delle Alpi* (Roma: USSME, 2000).

Jähns, M., *Geschichte der Kriegswissenschaften vornehmlich in Deutschland* (Leipzig: K. Oldenbourg, 1890).

Lynn, J.A., *The Bayonets of the Republic. Motivation and Tactics in the Army of Revolutionary France* (Chicago: University of Illinois Press, 1984).

Luvaas, J., *Frederick the Great on the Art of War* (New York: Hachette Books, 1966).

Malfoy-Noël, D., *L'épreuve de la bataille (1700–1714)* (Montpellier: Presses Universitaires de la Méditerranée PULM, 2007).

Nosworthy, B., *The Anatomy of Victory. Battle Tactics 1689-1763* (New York: Hippocrene Books, 1992).

Picaud-Monnerat, S., *La petite guerre au XVIIIe siècle* (Paris: Economica, 2010).

Reid, S., *British Redcoat vs French Fusilier* (Oxford: Osprey, 2016).

Showalter, D.E., *The Wars of Frederick the Great* (London: Longman, 1996).

Starkey, A., *War in the Age of Enlightenment 1700-1789* (Westport: Praeger, 2003).

Telp, C., *The Evolution of Operational Art 1740-1813. From Frederick the Great to Napoleon* (Abingdon: Routledge, 2003).

Watteville, O. de, *Le Cri de Guerre chez les differérents Peuples* (Paris: É. Lechevalier, 1889).

Wilkinson, S., *The Brain of the Army. A Popular Account of the German General Staff* (Westminster: Archibald Constable & Co, 1895).

Zane, M., *Notte di Pentecoste. La battaglia di Bolina. 1 giugno 1705* (Brescia: Liberedizioni, 2008).

3. Austrian Succession War

Arneth, A. von, *Maria Theresia's erste Regierungsjahre* (Wien: Wilhelm Braumüller, 1863-1865).

Bois, J.P., *Fontenoy 1745. Louis XV, arbitre de l'Europe* (Paris: Economica, 1996).

Browning, R., *The War of the Austrian Succession* (Stroud: Sutton Publishing, 1995).

Buffa di Perrero, C., *Carlo Emanuele III di Savoia a difesa delle Alpi nella campagna del 1744* (Torino: Fratelli Bocca, 1887).

Capaccio, R., Durante, B., *Marciando per le Alpi. Il ponente italiano durante la guerra di successione austriaca (1742-1748)* (Marene: Gribaudo, 1993).

El Hage, F., *La guerre de la Succession d'Autriche (1741-1748). Louis XV et le déclin de la France* (Paris: Economica, 2017).

Giuliano, B., *La campagna militare del 1744 nelle Alpi Occidentali e l'assedio di Cuneo* (Cuneo: Società per gli studi storici, archeologici ed artistici della Provincia de Cuneo, 1967).

Harding, R., *The Emergence of Britain's Global Naval Supremacy. The War of 1739-1748* (Woodbridge: Boydell, 2010).

K.k. Generalstab, *Kriege unter der Regierung der Kaiserin-Königin Maria Theresia. Oesterreichischer Erbfolge-krieg 1740-1748* (Wien: L.W. Seidel & Sohn, 1896-1905).

Ilari, V., Boeri, G., Paoletti, C., *La Corona di Lombardia. Guerre ed eserciti nell'Italia del medio settecento* (Ancona: Nuove Eidizioni, 1997).

Moris, H., *Opérations militaires dans les Alpes et les Apennins pendant la guerre de succession d'Autriche (1742-1748)* (Paris-Turin: L. Baudoin et Cie, Fratelli Bocca, 1886).

Pajol, P.C., *Les Guerres sous Louis XV* (Paris: Librairie de Formin-Didot et Cie, 1881-1891).

Rossi, E. de, *La diversione di Exilles. Episodio della Guerra della Prammatica Sanzione* (Roma: Rivista Militare Italiana, 1897).

Saluces, A. de, *Histoire Militaire du Piémont* (Torino: Pierre Joseph Pic, 1818).

Savio, P., *Asti occupata e liberata (1745-1746)* (Asti: Michele Varesio, 1927).

Vault, F.-E. de, Arvers, P., *Guerre de la Succession d'Autriche (1742-1748)* (Paris-Nancy: Librairie Militaire Berger-Levrault et Cie., 1892).

Weil, J., *La guerre de succession d'Autriche* (Paris: L. Baudoin, 1897).

Wilkinson, S., *The Defence of Piedmont 1742-1748. A Prelude to the Study of Napoleon* (Oxford: Clarendon Press, 1927).

4. 1747 Campaign

Alberti, A., *La battaglia dell'Assietta (19 di luglio del 1747). Note e documenti* (Torino: Enrico Voghera, 1902).

Amoretti, G., Roggero, M.F., Viglino, M. (eds), *I Trinceramenti dell'Assietta 1747-1997* (Torino: Omega, 1997).

Anderson, M.S., *The War of the Austrian Succession 1740-1748* (New York: Routledge, 2013).

Dabormida, V.E., *La Battaglia dell'Assietta. Studio Storico* (Roma: Carlo Voghera, 1877).

Rocchi, E., *Guerra di Montagna. La campagna del 1747 sulle Alpi* (Roma: Carlo Voghera, 1893).

Rothkirch, L. von, *Der Feldzug 1747 in Italien*, in *Österreichische militärische Zeitschrift* (Wien: V. Strauß's fel. Witwe & Sommer, 1842).

5. French Army

Bacquet, LH, *l'Infanterie au XVIIIe siècle. L'Organisation* (Paris-Nancy: Berger-Lavrault, 1907).

Belhomme, V.L.J.F., *Histoire de l'Infanterie en France* (Paris-Limoges: Henri Charles-Lavauzelle, 1893-1902).

Colin, J., *l'Infanterie au XVIIIe siècle. La Tactique* (Paris-Nancy: Berger-Levrault & Cie., 1907).

Lynn, J.A., *Giant of the Grand Siècle. The French Army 1610-1715* (Cambridge: Cambridge University Press, 1997).

Tuetey, L., *Les Officiers sous l'ancien régime. Nobles roturiers* (Paris: Plon-Nourrit, 1908).

6. Sardinian Army

Barberis, W., *Le armi del Principe. La tradizione militare sabauda* (Torino: Einaudi, 1988).

Bianchi, P., *Onore e Mestiere. Le riforme militari nel Piemonte del Settecento* (Torino: Zamorani, 2002).

Bianchi, P., *Sotto diverse bandiere. L'internazionale militare nello Stato sabaudo d'antico regime* (Milano: Franco Angeli, 2012).

Brancaccio, N., *L'esercito del Vecchio Piemonte. Gli Ordinamenti, Parte I – Da 1560 al 1814* (Roma: Stabilimento Poligrafico per l'amministrazione della Guerra, 1923).

Choulot, P. de, Ferrero, G., *Histoire de l'Armée Sarde* (Torino: Bocca, 1845-1846).

Loriga, S., *Soldati. L'istituzione militare nel Piemonte del Settecento* (Venezia: Marsilio, 1992).

Minola, M., *Assietta. Tutta la storia dal XVI secolo ad oggi* (Sant'Ambrogio di Torino: Susalibri, 2006).

Paoletti, C., *Capitani di Casa Savoia* (Roma: USSME, 2007).

Paoletti, C., *Dal Ducato all'Unità, Tre secoli e mezzo di storia militare piedmontese* (Roma: USSME, 2011).

Pinelli, F., *Storia Militare del Piemonte in continuazione di quella del Saluzzo cioè della Pace di Acquisgrana fino ai dì nostri* (Torino: Degiorgis, 1854).

Troubetzkoi, L. (ed), *Un Ambassadeur Russe à Turin (1792-1793). Dépêches e S.E. le Prince Alexandre Bélosselsky de Bélozersk* (Paris: Ernst Leroux, 1901).

7. Austrian Army

Duffy, C., *The Army of Maria Theresa. The Armed Forces of Imperial Austria, 1740-1780* (London: David & Charles, 1977).

Duffy, C., *Instrument of War* (Rosemont: Emperor's Press, 2000).

Duffy, C., *By Force of Arms* (Chicago: Emperor's Press, 2008).

Khevenhüller-Metsch, J.J., *Aus der Zeit Maria Theresias* (Wien: Holzhausen, 1907).

Leitnertreu, L. von, *Geschichte der Wiener-Neustädter Militärakademie* (Hermannstadt: Theodor Steinhaussen, 1852).

Thürheim, A., *Gedenkblätter aus der Kriegsgeschichte der K.K. oesterreichischen Armee* (Wien und Teschen: Buchhandlung für Militär-Literatur, 1880).

Wess, Mitchell W., *The Grand Strategy of the Habsburg Empire* (Princeton: Princeton University Press, 2018).

8. Spanish Army

Bragado Echavarrìa, J., *Los regimentos suizos al servicio de España en el siglo XVIII. Diplomacia, guerra y sociedad militar (1700-1755)* (Madrid: Ministeiro de Defensa, 2019).

Martínez Ruiz, E., *El ejército del Rey los soldados de la Ilustratión* (Madrid: Editorial Actas, 2018).

9. Regimental Histories

a. Austrian Empire

Czernczitz, G. Hubka von, *Geschichte des k. und k. Infanterie-Regiments Graf von Lacy Nr. 22, von seiner Errichtung bis zur Gegenwart* (Zara: Verlag des Regiments, 1902).

Treuenfest, G. Amon von, *Geschichte des k.k. Infanterie-Regiments Nr. 20 Friedrich Wilhelm, Kronprinz des Deutschen Reiches und Kronprinz von Preussen* (Wien: Verlag des Regiments, 1878).

Seeliger, E., *Geschichte des kaiserlichen und königlichen Infanterie-Regiments N° 32* (Budapest: Pester Buchdruckerei-Actien-Gesellschaft, 1900).

Wrede, A., *Geschichte der k.u.k. Wehrmacht. Die Regimenter, Corps, Branchen und Anstalten von 1618 bis Ende des XIX Jahrhunderts. Hrsg. von der Direktion des k.u.k. Kriegsarchivs* (Wien: L.W. Seidel & Sohn, 1898-1905).

b. Kingdom of France

Gebelin, J., *Histoire des Milices Provinciales (1688-1791)* (Paris: Librairie Hachette et Cie., 1882).

Grémillet, P., *Un Régiment pendant deux siècles (1684-1899). Historique du 81e de Ligne, ancien 6e Léger "l'Intrépide", cy-devant Périgord, La Marche, Conti, l'un des régimentes des princes* (Paris: Unknown Publisher, 1899).

Hennet, L., *Les Milices et les Troupes Provinciales* (Paris: Librairie Militaire de L. Baudoin et Cie., 1834).

Pommelles, Chevalier Des, *Tableau de la population de toutes les provinces de France, Mémoire sur les Milices* (Paris: Unknown Publisher, 1789).

Susane, L, *Histoire de la Cavalerie Française* (Paris: J. Hetzel 1874)

Susane, L., *Histoire de l'infanterie Française* (Paris: Terana, 1985).

c. Kingdom of Sardinia

Choulot, P. de, Ferrero, G., *Historie de l'Armée Sarde. Essai sur le Brigades des Gardes et de Savoie* (Turin: Bocca, 1845).

Guerrini, D., *La Brigata dei Granatieri di Sardegna* (Torino: Roux e Viarengo, 1902).

Rivoire, E.A., *Appunti cronologici sulle Milizie Valdesi* (Teramo: B. Cioschi, 1932).

10. Logistics

Lambert, R., *Ricordi Logistici e Tattici* (Firenze: Barbera, 1930).

Van Creveld, M., *Supplying War. Logistic from Wallenstein to Patton* (Cambridge: Cambridge University Press, 2004).

11. Weapons and Fortifications

Amoretti, G., Petitti, P. (eds), *Dal forte di Exilles alle Alpi. Storia e architettura delle fortificazioni di montagna* (Torino: Omega, 2003).

Amoretti, G., Petitti, P. (eds), *Il Forte di Exilles di Ignazio Bertola 1729-1745* (Torino: Omega, 2003).

Burk, W.H., *Historical and Topographical Guide to Valley Forge* (Philadelphia: John C. Winston 1912).

Barrera, F., *I sette forti di Exilles. Metamorfosi architettonica di un complesso fortificato* (Torino: Museo Nazionale della Montagna, 2002).

Boudriot, J., *Armes a feu francaises. Modeles reglementaires 1717-1836* (La Tour du Pin Cédex: Jean Boudriot, 1997).

Cerino Badone, G., *Potenza di Fuoco. Eserciti, tattica e tecnologia nella guerre europee (1500-1800)* (Milano: Edizioni Libreria Militare, 2013).

Cerino Badone, G., *Sulla Strada di Fiandra. Storia della Cittadella di Alessandria 1559-1859* (Alessandria: FAI, 2014).

Dawson, A.L., Dawson, P.L., Summerfield, S., *Napoleonic Artillery* (Ramsbury: Crowood Press, 2007).

Duffy, C., *The Fortress in the Age of Vauban and Frederick the Great, 1660-1789* (London: Routledge & Kegan Paul, 1989).

Gabriel, E., *Die Hand-Faustfeuerwaffen der habsburgischen Heere* (Wien: ÖBV, 1990).

Garoglio, E., Zannoni, F., *La difesa nascosta del Piemonte sabaudo. I sistemi fortificati alpini (secolo XVI-XVIII)* (Torino: Centro Studi e Ricerche storiche sull'Architettura Militare del Piemonte, 2011).

Hughes, B.P., *Firepower. Weapons Effectiveness on the Battlefield, 1630-1850* (London: Da Capo Press, 1974).

Müller, H., *Das Heerwesen in Brandenburg und Preussen von 1640 bis 1806. Die Bewaffnung* (Berlin: Brandenburgisches Verl.-Haus, 1991).

Naulet, F., *L'Artillerie Française (1665-1765). Naissance d'une Arme* (Paris: Economica, 2002).

Peyronel, E., Usseglio B., *Di qui non si passa! … forse. Forti, fortificazioni minori e fatti d'arme nella valli Pragelato, Perosa, Pellice e San Martino fra XVI e XVIII secolo* (Pinerolo: Alzani, 2015).

Petard, M., *Equipements Militaires de 1600 à 1870* (Olonne sur Mer: Sitol-Guibert, 1984).

Scott, D-D., Bohy, J., Boor, N., Haecker, C., Rose, W., Severts P., *Colonial Era Firearms Bullet Performance: a Live Fire Experimental Study for Archaeological Interpretation*, 2017, at <https://www.academia.edu/32411984/Colonial_Era_Firearm_Bullet_Performance_A_Live_Fire_Experimental_Study_for_Archaeological_Interpretation>

Sterrantino, F., *Le armi da fuoco del Vecchio Piemonte 1683-1799* (Torino: Accademia di San Marciano, 2002)

Vuillemin, H., *Du silex au piston. La grande aventure des fusils réglementaires français 1717-1865* (Paris: Tradition, 1997).

12. Economics

Fèlix, J., *Économie et finances sous l'Ancien Régime. Guide du chercheur 1523-1789* (Vincennes: Comité pour l'histoire économique et financière de la France, 1994).

Bailly, M.A., *Histoire Financière de la France, depuis l'origine de la monarchie jusq'a la fin de 1786* (Paris: Moutardier, 1830).

Dickson, P.G.M., *Finance and Government under Maria Theresia 1740-1780* (Oxford: Oxford University Press, 1987).

Marion, M., *Histoire Financière de la France depuis 1715* (Paris: Librairie Armand Colin, 1914-1931).

Norsa, P., *La Finanza Sabauda dal 1700 all'Unità d'Italia* (Unpublished Ms., 1957).

Prato, G., *Il costo della Guerra di Successione Spagnola e le spese pubbliche del Piemonte dal 1700 al 1713* (Torino: Bocca, 1907).

Prato, G., *La Vita economica in Piemonte a mezzo il Secolo XVIII* (Torino: Officine Grafiche della Società Tipografico-Editrice Nazionale, 1908).

C. Storrs (ed.), *The Fiscal-Military State in Eighteenth-Century Europe. Essays in honour of P.G.M. Dickson* (Farnham: Ashgate, 2009).

Quazza, G., *Le riforme in Piemonte nella prima metà del Settecento* (Modena: Società editrice modenese, 1957).

13. Diplomacy

Cesa, M., *Alleati ma rivali. Teoria delle alleanze e politica estera settecentesca* (Bologna: Il Mulino, 2007).

Clercq, M. de, *Recueil des Traitès de la France* (Paris: A. Durand et Pedone-Lauriel, 1865-1917).

Flassan, J.C.D. de, *Histoire Générale et raisonnée de la Diplomatie Française, opi de la politique de la France depuis la fondation de la Monarchie, jusqu'à la fin du règne de Louis XVI* (Paris: Treuttel et Würtz, 1811).

Frigo, D. (ed.), *Politics and diplomacy in Early Modern Italy. The structure of diplomatic practice, 1450-1800* (Cambridge: Cambridge University Press, 2000).

Gillot, L., *La révision de la Convention de Genève* (Paris: Université de Paris, 1901).

Lodge, R., *Studies in Eighteenth Century Diplomacy 1740-1748* (London: John Murray, 1930).

Scoplis, F., *Delle Relazioni Politiche tra la Dinastia di Savoia ed il Governo Britannico (1240-1815)* (Torino: Stamperia Reale, 1853).

14. Biographies

Barea Amorena, E., *Jaime de Guzmán y Spinola, Capitán General de Cataluña, II Marqués de la Mina* (San Vincente – Alicante: Editorial Club Universitario, 2016).

Bouillevaux, R.A., *Les Moines du Der, avec pièces justificatives, notes historiques et notices sur le bourg et le canton de Montier-en-Der et la ville de Wassy* (Montier-en-Der: Jules Thiébaut, 1845).

Broglie, A. de, *Maurice de Saxe et le Marquis d'Argenson* (Paris: Calmann Lévy, 1891).

Chagniot, J., *Le chevalier de Folard: la stratégie de l'incertitude* (Paris and Monaco: Du Rocher, 1997).

Chaudon, L.M., Delandine F.A., *Nouveau Dictionnaire Historique* (Lyon: Bruyset ainé, 1807).

Chevrier, F.A. de, *La Vie politique et militaire de M. le Maréchal Duc de Bell'Isle* (La Haye: Unknown Publisher, 1762).

Courcelles, J. de, *Dictionnaire historique et biographique des Généraux Français, depuis le onzième siècle jusqu'en 1820* (Paris: De Courcelles, 1820-1823).

Crollalanza, G.B. di, *Memorie Storico-genealogiche della Stirpe Waldsee-Mels, e più particolarmente dei Conti di Colloredo. Con documenti* (Pisa: Direzione del Giornale Araldico, 1875).

Duval, J.Y., *Le prix du sang bleu. Joseph-Augustin de Mailly 1708-1794* (Paris: Editions Le Sémaphore, 2000).

Gosselin, J., *Mailly et ses seigneurs, sires et haut-bers de Mailly-le-Franc* (Péronne: Trépant, 1876).

Guglia, E., *Maria Theresia. Ihr Leben und ihre Regierung* (München and Berlin: R, Oldenbourg, 1917).

Lacroix, J., *Eloge de le M. le Maréchal de Mailly, précédé d'un coup d'oeil historique sur le principaux évenemens militaires du régne de Louis XV* (Perpignan: P. Tastu, 1819).

Lainé, M., *Archives généalogiques et historiques de la Noblesse de France* (Paris: Lainé, 1825-1844).

Fillassier, M., *Dictionnaire historique d'Éducation* (Paris: Amable Costes, 1818).

Ledieu, A., *Le Maréchal de Mailly. Dernier Commandant pour le Roi à Abbeville* (Paris: Alphonse Picard et Fils, 1895).

Lendru, A., *Histoire de la Maison de Mailly* (Paris: Emilie Lechevalier, 1893).

Mazas, A., *Histoire de l'Ordre Royal et Militaire de Saint-Louis* (Paris: Firmin Didot Frères, Fils et Cie., E Dentu, 1851).

Surreaux, S., *Les Maréchaux de France des Lumières, Histoire et Dictionnaire d'une élite militaire dans la société d'Ancien Régime* (Paris: SPM, 2013).

Semeria, G.B., *Storia del Re di Sardegna Carlo Emanuele il Grande* (Torino: Reale Tipografia, 1831).

Wurzbach, C. von, *Biographisches Lexicon des Kaiserthums Oesterreich* (Wien: L.C. Zamarski, 1856-1891).

15. Memoirs

Berwick, Duc de (ed. A. Petiot, and Monmerqué), *Mémoires du Maréchal de Berwick* (Paris: Foucault, 1828).

Brunet de l'Argentière, *Mémoire de la Guerre sur le frontières du Dauphiné et de Savoie de 1742 à 1747* (Paris: A la Direction du Spectateur Militaire, 1887).

Choiseul, H., *Mémoires du duc de Choiseul* (Paris: F. Calmettes, 1904).

Barbier, E.J.F., *Chronique de la Régence et du Règne de Louis XV (1718-1763) ou Journal de Barbier* (Paris: C. Charpentier, 1857-1866).

Dussieux, L., Soulié, E. (eds), *Mémoires du duc de Luynes sur la cour de Louis XV (1735-1758)* (Paris: Firmon Didot Frères, Fils et Cie., 1860-1865).

Galleani d'Agliano, G., *Memorie Storiche sulla Guerra del Piemonte dal 1741 al 1747* (Torino: Stamperia Reale, 1840).

Gorani, G. (ed. A. Casati), *Memorie di giovinezza e di Guerra* (Milano: Mondadori, 1936).

Lordat, Comte de, *Un page de Louis XV. Lettres de Marie-Joseph de Lordat a son oncle Louis, Compte de Lordat, Baron de Bram, Brigadier des Armées du Roi (1740-1747)* (Paris: C. Charpentier, 1908).

Robbone, P. (ed.), 'Le "Memorie" del Conte Roberto Malines', *Annali dell'Istituto Superiore di Magistero del Piemonte*, Vol.VI, 1932.

Richelieu, Louis François Armand Du Plessis Duc de, *Mémoires du Maréchal Duc de Richelieu* (Paris: Chez Buisson, 1793).

Sade, D.-A.-F. de (ed. Maurice Lever), *Viaggio in Italia* (Torino: Bollati Boringhieri, 1996).

Garellis, E. (ed.), *L'alta valle Varaita a età Settecento. Don Bernard Tholosan e le sue "Memorie storiche sui fatti d'arme occorsi nella valle di Vraita nella guerra del 1742"* (Cuneo: Società per gli studi storici, archeologici ed artistici della Provincia di Cuneo, 2001).

16. Modern Tactical/Operational Studies

a. Tactical Manuals

Ministero della Guerra. Ispettorato dell'Arma del Genio, *Istruzione sui lavori da zappatore* (Roma: SMRE, 1937).

b. Studies

Adkin, M., *The Waterloo Companion. The Complete Guide to History's Most Famous Land Battle* (Mechanicsburg: Aurum, 2001).

Adkin, M., *Gettysburg Companion. A Guide to the Most Famous Battle of the Civil War* (Mechanicsburg: Aurum, 2001).

Bovio, O., *Storia dell'Esercito italiano* (Roma: USSME, 1996).

Bowden, S., *Glory Years. Napoleon at Austerlitz 1805-1807* (Chicago: Emperor's Press, 1997).

Caccia Dominioni, P., *1915-1919 Diario di guerra* (Milano: Mursia, 1993).

Ciancarini, E., *La Scuola di Guerra di Torino.La Formazione degli ufficiali nel Regio esercito (1867-1915)* (Civitavecchia: Prospettiva Editrice, 2013).

Citino, R.M., *The German Way of War. From the Thirty Years' War to the Third Reich* (Lawrence: Kansas University Press, 2005).

Coombe, J.D., *Derailing the Tokyo Express. The Naval Battles for the Solomon Islands that Sealed Japan's Fate* (Harrisburg: Stackpole Books, 1991).

Engen, R.C., *Canadians under Fire: Infantry Effectiveness in The Second World War* (Montreal and Quebec: McGill-Queen's University Press, 2009).

Griffith, P., *Battle Tactics of the American Civil War* (Ramsbury: The Crowood Press, 1987).

Griffith, P., *The Art of War of Revolutionary France 1789-1802* (London: Greenhill Books, 1998).

Gabriele, M., *La frontiera nord-occidentale dall'Unità alla Grande Guerra. Piani e studi operativi italiani verso la Francia durante la Triplice Alleanza* (Roma: USSME, 2006).

Grau, L.W., Bartles, C.K., *The Russian Way of War. Force Structure, Tactics, and Modernization of the Russian Ground Forces* (Fort Leavenworth: Foreign Military Studies Office (FMSO), 2017).

Harrison, R.W., *The Russian Way of War. Operational Art 1904-1940* (Lawrence: Kansas University Press, 2001).

Hittle, J.D., *The Military Staff. Its History and Development* (Harrisburg: Military Service Division, The Stackpole Company, 1961).

McGuigan, R., *"Into Battle!" British Orders of Battle for the Crimean War*, 1854-56 (Bowdon: Withycut House, 2001).

Montanari, M., *Le Operazioni in Africa Settentrionale. El Alamein* (Roma: USSME, 1989).

Nafziger, G., *Imperial Bayonets. Tactics of the Napoleonic Battery, Battalion and Brigade as found in Contemporary Regulations* (London: Greenhill Books, 1996).

Ufficio Storico Stato Maggiore Esercito, *L'Esercito Italiano Nella Grande Guerra (1915–1918). Le Operazioni del 1918* (Roma: USSME, 1988).

17. Medicine and psychology
a. Military medicine

Crumplin, M., Glover, G., *Waterloo after the Glory. Hospital Sketches and Reports on the Wounded After the Battle* (Warwick: Helion & Company, 2019).

Lenihan, P., *Fluxes, Fevers, and Fighting Men. War and Disease in Ancien Régime Europe 1648-1789* (Warwick: Helion & Company, 2019).

b. Psychology

Dixon, M., *On the Psychology of Military Incompetence* (London: Basic Books, 1976).

Du Picq, A., *Études sur le Combat* (Paris: Hachette-Dumaine, 1880) [Translated as *Battle Studies. Ancient and Modern Battle* (New York: Macmillan, 1921)].

Gabriel, R.A., *Military Psychiatry: A Comparative Perspective* (New York: Praeger, 1986).

Gabriel, R.A, *No More Heroes: Madness and Psychiatry in War* (New York: Hill & Wang, 1987).

Grossman, D., *On Killing. The Psychological Cost of Learning to Kill in War and Society* (New York: Back Bay Books, 1996).

Grossman, D., *On Combat. Psychology and Physiology of Deadly Conflict in War and in Peace* (New York: PPCT Research Publications, 1999).

Holmes, R., *Acts of War* (London: Weidenfeld & Nicolson, 2003).

Marshall, S.L.A., *Men Against Fire. The Problem of Battle Command* (New York; Infantry Journal, 1947).

Shalit, B., *The Psychology of Conflict and Combat* (New York: Praeger, 1988).

c. Veterinary

Bottani, T., *Delle Epizoozie, ossia delle epidemie contagiose e non contagiose che influirono negli animali domestici, utili principalmente all'agricoltura del veneto dominio in Italia* (Venezia: Tipografia Picotti, 1819).

d. Forensic Sciences

Roach, M., *Stiff: The Curious Lives of Human Cadavers* (New York & London: W.W. Norton & Co Inc., 2003).

18. Conflict Archaeology

Fox, R.A., *Archaeology, History, and Custer's Last Battle* (Norman: University of Oklahoma Press, 2003).

Harrington, P., *English Civil War Archaeology* (London: Batsford, 2004).

Scott, D., Babits, L., Haecker, C., *Fields of Conflict. Battlefield Archaeology from the Roman Empire to the Korean War* (Westport: Praeger, 2007).

19. Geography, Climate, and Local Studies

Behringer, W., *Kulturgeschichte des Klimas. Von der Eiszeit bis zur globalen Erwärmung* (München: Beck C.H., 2010).

Cappelli, A., *Cronologia, Cronografia e Calendario Perpetuo* (Milano: Hoepli, 1988).

Marga, A., *Géographie Militaire* (Paris: Berger-Levrault et Cie., 1885).

Nicolas, J., Nicolas, R., *La vie quotidienne en Savoie aux XVIIe et XVIIIe siècles* (Montmélian Cedex: La Fontaine de Siloé, 2005).

Parker, G., *Global Crisis: War, Climate Change and Catastrophe in the 17th Century* (New Haven and London: Yale University Press, 2013).

Peracca, L.F., *La Valle di Oulx e le Guerre di Successione d'Austria (1740-1750)* (Torino: Tipografia M. Massaro, 1909).

Touchard-Lafosse, G., *La Loire Historique, pittoresque et biographique, de la source de ce fleuve à son embouchure dans l'océan* (Tours: R. Pornin et Cie., 1851).

20. Methodology and Other Studies

Buono, A., Civale, G. (eds), *Battaglie. L'evento, l'individuo, la memoria* (Palermo: Mediterranea, 2014).

Förster, S., *The Battlefield: Towards a Modern History of War* (London: German Historical Institute London, 2008).

Keegan, J., *The Face of Battle* (London: Jonathan Cape, 1976).

Kühne, T., Ziemann, B., *Was ist Militärgeschichte?* (Paderborn: Ferdinand Schöningh Verlag, 2000).

Nowosadtko, J., *Krieg, Gewalt und Ordnung. Einführung in die Militärgeschichte* (Tübingen: Kimmerle, 2002).

21. Laws and Codes

Raccolta per ordine di Materie delle Leggi cioè Editti, Patenti, manifesti, Ecc. emanate negli stati di terraferma sino all'8 dicembre 1798 dai Sovrani della Real Casa di Savoia dai loro Ministri, Magistrati, Ecc. compilata dagli Avvocati Felice Amato e Camillo Duboin proseguita dall'Avvocato Alessandro Muzio colla direzione dell'intendente Giacinto Cottin (Torino: Davico e Picco, 1863).

Articles and Book Chapters

Alberti, A., 'Bourcet', in *Memorie Storico Militari*, Fascicolo III, December 1909, pp.263-279.

Bianchi, P., 'I documenti sui governatori nel Piemonte del Settecento', in L. Antonielli and C. Donati (eds), *Al di là della storia militare: una ricognizione sulle fonti* (Soveria Mannelli: Rubbettino, 2004), pp.77-98.

Bragado Echavarrìa. J., 'Los regimientos suizos al servicio de España en las guerras de Italia (1717-1748)', in *Cuadernos de Historia Moderna* 41 (2), 2016 pp.295-312.

Brathwaite, K-J.H., 'Effective in battle: conceptualizing soldiers' combat effectiveness', in *Defence Studies*, vol.18, no.1, 2018, pp.1–18.

Broad, J., 'Cattle Plague in Eighteenth-Century England', in *The Agricultural History Review*, Vol.31, No.2 (1983), pp.104-115.

Cadet, S., 'Proposta dell'Etiope minerale o Solfuro nero di Mercurio contro le Epizoozie di morbi acuti, ossia di corso rapido degli animali domestici', in *Atti della Reale Accademia dei Lincei*, Tomo XXIV – Anno XXIV, Roma 1870.

Calcagno, P., 'Occupare una città in Antico Regime', in *Mediterranea*, No.24, Anno IX, 2012, pp.81-110.

Carter, D.O., Tibbett, M., 'Cadaver Decomposition and Soil: Processes', in Soil Analysis in Carter, D.O., Tibbett, M. (eds), *Forensic Taphonomy: Chemical and Biological Effects of Buried Human Remains* (Boca Raton: Routledge, 2008), pp.29-51.

Cerino Badone, G., 'Il Cannone Disgiunto di Ignazio Bertola', in *Armi Antiche*, 2003, Torino 2006, pp.35-83.

Cerino-Badone, G., '"An Army inside the Army". The Swiss regiments of the Sabaudian army 1741-1750', in Jaun, R., Streit, P., Weck, H.D. (eds), *Schweizer Solddienst. Neue Arbeiten – Neue Aspekte. Service étranger Suisse. Nouvelles études – nouveaux aspects* (Porrentruy: Schweizerische Vereinigung für Militärgeschichte und Militärwissenschaft, 2010), pp.171-198.

Cerino Badone, G., 'Gli eserciti sabaudo e francese durante la Guerra di Successione Austriaca. L'impiego in campo', in Sconfienza, R. ed.), *La campagna gallispana del 1744. Storia e Archeologia Militare in un anno di guerra fra Piemonte e Delfinato* (Oxford: Archaeopress, 2012).

Chomon Ruiz, P., 'Battaglie in Val Varaita', in *Armi Antiche. Bollettino dell'Accademia di san Marciano*, Torino 1968, pp.73-112.

Claretta, G., 'L'Imperatore Giuseppe II a Torino nel giugno 1769. Memorie aneddotiche', in *Archivio Storico Italiano*, Quinta Serie, Tomo VI, Firenze, 1890, pp.387-425.

Corvisier, A., 'La mort du soldat depuis la fin du Moyen Age', in *Revue Historique*, T. 254, Fasc.1 (515) (luglio-settembre 1975), pp.3-30.

Fann, W., 'Peacetime Attrition in the Army of Frederick William I 1713-1740', in *Central European History*, XI (1978), pp.323-334.

Gabotto, F., 'La Verità sulla Battaglia dell'Assietta secondo la minuta della Relazione Priocca', in *Bollettino Storico-Bibliografico Subalpino*, Anno XI, N. III, Torino 1906, pp.227-234.

Garoglio E., I Valdesi in armi, da banditi religionari e miliziani del Re di Sardegna, in Tourn Boncoeur, S., Garoglio, E. (eds), *Le collezioni di armi del Museo valdese di Torre Pellice* (Torre Pellice: Museo valdese, 2015), pp.41-52.

E. Garoglio, 'Fortezza Piemonte. Geopolitica, tecnologia e uso tattico-strategico delle fortezze del Regno di Sardegna tra Antico Regime e Restaurazione, 1713-1831', in Chiara Devoti (ed.), 'Gli Spazi dei militari e l'urbanistica della città. L'Italia del Nord-Ovest (1815-1918)', *Storia dell'Urbanistica*, October 2018, pp.30-101.

Gasperini, D., 'Mortalità de' bovini seguita nel territorio trivigiano nell'anno MDCCXI', in Perco, D., *Malgari e pascoli. L'alpeggio nella provincia di Belluno* (Feltre: Pilotto, 1991), pp.171-204.

Genre, A., Tron D.E., 'Una canzona dell'Assietta in patois?', in *La Beidana. Cultura e storia nelle valli valdesi*, n. 30, luglio 1990, pp.71-78.

Ghisi, F., 'Complaites e canzoni storiche (XII-XIX sec.)', in *BSSV*, n. 134, Torre Pellice 1973, pp.122-134.

Guillaume, P., 'Les ossements du chevalier de Belle-Isle à Embrun', in *Bulletin de la Société d'Études des Hautes-Alpes*, An 6, Gap 1887, pp.219-220.

Sumner, P., 'General Hawley's Chaos', in *Journal of the Society for Army Historical Research*, XXVI, No.111 (Autumn 1949), pp.91-94.

Ilari, V., 'Clausewitz in Italy', in Pommerin, R. (ed), *Clausewitz Goes Global. Carl von Clausewitz in the 21st Century* (Berlin: Carola Hartmann Miles-Verlag, 2011), pp.173-202.

Knutsen, T.L., 'Old, Unhappy, Far-Off Things: The New Military History of Europe', in *Journal of Peace Research*, Vol.24, n.1, pp.87-98.

Kroener, B.R., 'Stato, società, «militare». Prospettive di una rinnovata storia militare della prima età moderna', in Donati, C., Kroener, B.R (eds), *Militari e società civile dell'età moderna (secoli XVI-XVIII)* (Bologna: Il Mulino, 2007), pp.11-21.

Manno, A., 'Breve nota sulla Battaglia dell'Assietta a proposito di una pubblicazione del Commendatore Carlo Negroni', in *Atti della R. Accademia delle Scienze di Torino*, Volume 17, Torino 1881, pp.799-811.

Mazza, E., Piccoli, E., '"Disguised in scarlet". Hume and Turin in 1748', in *I Castelli di Yale*, XI (11), pp.71-108.

Mahon, C., 'Un commissaire des guerre sous l'Ancien Regime. Pierre-Nicolas de Lasalle', in *Le Carnet de la Sabretache. Revue militaire rétrospective*, Vol.VIII, Paris 1900. pp.343-353.

McInerney, L., 'The O'Neylons of Dysert and Austria', in *Shannon Archaeological & Historical Society*, "The Other Clare", Vol 42 (2018), pp.25-32.

Mola di Nomaglio G., 'La Marchesa di Spigno, l'Assietta, le società segrete. I Novarina, tra enigmi e intrighi, nella Storia del Piemonte', in *Studi Piemontesi*, dicembre 2002, Vol. XXXI, fasc. 2, pp.407-427.

Negroni, C., 'Lettere di Gian Lorenzo Bogino di Prospero Balbo e del conte di Perrone', in *Miscellanea di Storia Italiana, edita per cura della Regia Deputazione di Storia Patria*, Tomo XXI, Torino 1883, pp.49-128.

Parker, G., review article on D.C. Baxter, J. Childs and A. Corvisier, in *The Journal of Modern History*, Vol.50, No.1 (Mar. 1978), pp.146-148.

Patria, E., 'Due ricerche storiche sull'Assietta', in *Armi antiche. Bollettino dell'Accademia di San Marciano*, Torino 1973, pp.275-358.

Pell, R.T., 'The Cradle of Carillon: Assietta', in *The Bulletin of the Fort Ticonderoga Museum*, Volume VIII, Number 7, 1951, pp.269-299.

Picaud-Monnerat, S., 'De la petite guerre «à la hongroise» a la petite guerre «à la française»: le rôle moteur de la guerre de succession d'Autriche (1740-1748)', in Gábor, H. (ed.), *Az értelem bátorsága tanulmányok perjés géza emlékére* (Budapest: Argumentum 2005), pp.519-538.

Potem, B. von, 'Ferdinand Ludwig Graf von Oeynhausen', in *Allgemeine deutsche Biographie*, (Leipzig: Duncker & Humblot, 1887), Vol.XXV, pp.28-30.

Rothkirch, L. von, 'Der Feldzug 1747 in Italien', in *Österreichische militärische Zeitschrift*, Tomo XI, Wien 1842, pp.120-135.

Sconfienza, R., 'I Progetti del Duca di Brunswick per la difesa del Regno di Sardegna', in *Annales Sabaudiae*, Anno II, n. 2, 2006, pp.63- 118.

Shils, E., Janowitz, M., 'Cohesion and Disintegration in the Wehrmacht in World War II', in Janowitz, M. (ed.), *Military Conflict: Essays in the Institutional Analysis of War and Peace* (Beverly Hills: Sage, 1975), pp.177-220.

Skandalakis, P.N., Lainas, P., Skandalakis, J.E., Mirilas, P., 'To afford the wounded speedy assistance: Dominique Jean Larrey and Napoleon', in *World Journal of Surgery*, 30(8), August 2006, pp.1392-1399.

Signorelli, A., 'Assietta: Iconografia di una battaglia', in *Bollettino della Società Piemontese di Archeologia e Belle Arti*, Nuova Serie – XLVI, 1994, pp.177-197.

Spiegel, H.X., 'Psychiatry with an infantry battalion in North Africa', in Mullens, W.S., Glass, A. J. (eds), *Neuropsychiatry in World War II* (Washington, D.C.: US Government Printing Office, 1973), Vol.2, Overseas Theaters, pp.111-126.

Spiller, R.J., 'S.L.A. Marshall and the Ratio of Fire', in *The RUSI Journal*, Winter 1988, pp.63-71,

Tron, E., 'Alcune precisazioni sul "Reggimento Valdese"', in *Bollettino della Società di Studi Valdesi*, Vol.72 (1951, n. 92), 75 (1954, n. 95), pp.41-65, 37-68.

Welvert, E., 'Jean-Baptiste Massieu', in *Revue d'Histoire de l'Eglise de France*, Année 1921, 36, pp.241-251.

Index

From Reason to Revolution – Warfare 1721-1815

http://www.helion.co.uk/series/from-reason-to-revolution-1721-1815.php

The 'From Reason to Revolution' series covers the period of military history 1721–1815, an era in which fortress-based strategy and linear battles gave way to the nation-in-arms and the beginnings of total war.

This era saw the evolution and growth of light troops of all arms, and of increasingly flexible command systems to cope with the growing armies fielded by nations able to mobilise far greater proportions of their manpower than ever before. Many of these developments were fired by the great political upheavals of the era, with revolutions in America and France bringing about social change which in turn fed back into the military sphere as whole nations readied themselves for war. Only in the closing years of the period, as the reactionary powers began to regain the upper hand, did a military synthesis of the best of the old and the new become possible.

The series examines the military and naval history of the period in a greater degree of detail than has hitherto been attempted, and has a very wide brief, with the intention of covering all aspects from the battles, campaigns, logistics, and tactics, to the personalities, armies, uniforms, and equipment.

Submissions

The publishers would be pleased to receive submissions for this series. Please email reasontorevolution@helion.co.uk, or write to Helion & Company Limited, Unit 8 Amherst Business Centre, Budbrooke Road, Warwick, CV34 5WE

You may also be interested in:

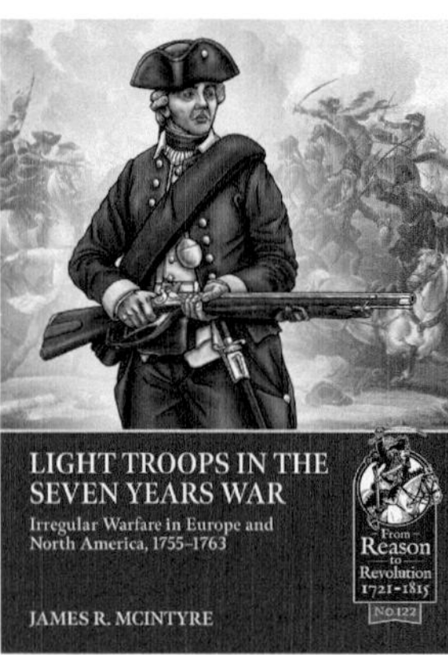

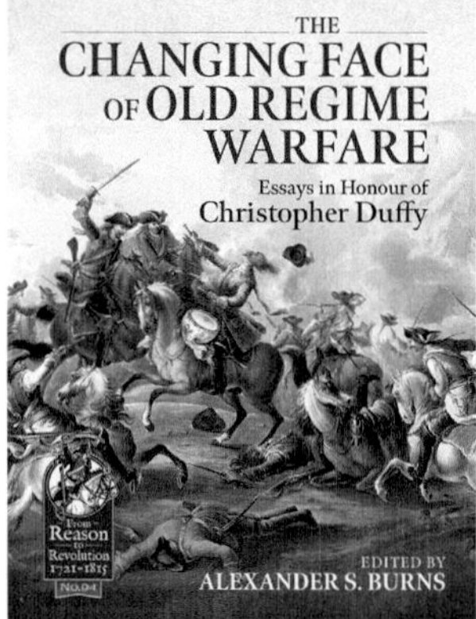

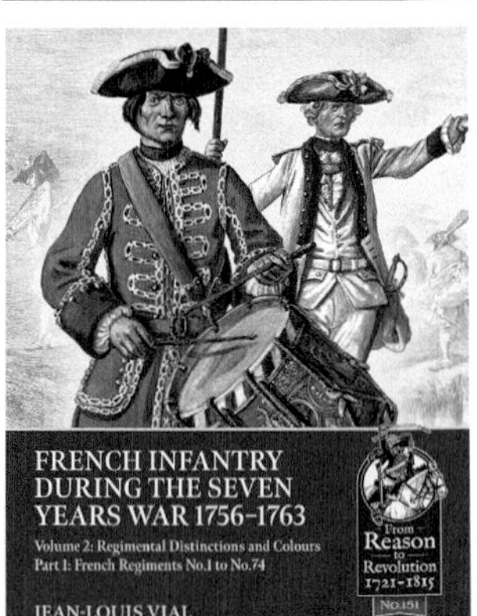